READINGS IN **WESTERN RELIGIOUS THOUGHT**
II. THE MIDDLE AGES THROUGH THE REFORMATION

WESTERN RELIGIOUS THOUGHT

II.
The Middle Ages Through The Reformation

Patrick V. Reid

PAULIST PRESS
New York/Mahwah NJ

Library of Congress Cataloging-in-Publication Data

(Revised for vol. 2)

Reid, Patrick V., 1944-
    Readings in Western religious thought.

    Includes bibliographies.
    Contents: v. 1. The ancient world—v. 2. The Middle Ages through the Reformation.
    1. Bible—Textbooks. 2. Judaism—History—To 70 A.D. 3. Church history—Primitive and early church, ca. 30-600. 4. Mediterranean Region—Religion. I. Title.
BL687.R45   1987   291.8   86-25152
ISBN 0-8091-2850-0 (pbk. : v. 1)
ISBN 0-8091-3533-7 (pbk. : v. 2)

Published by Paulist Press
997 Macarthur Boulevard
Mahwah, N.J. 07430

Printed and bound in the United States of America

CONTENTS

v

Acknowledgments are due to the following for permission to reproduce copyrighted translations.

George Braziller, Inc., New York © 1961. Rabbinical Writings in Arthur Hertzberg, *Judaism.*

The Catholic University of America Press, Washington, D.C. © 1950. Augustine, *The City of God,* translated by Demetrius B. Zema, et al., *Writings of Saint Augustine* (The Fathers of the Church Series).

Harvard University Press. Cambridge, Ma., © 1918. Boethius, *Consolation of Philosophy,* translated by H.F. Stewart, D.D., *Boethius: The Consolation of Philosophy.*

SCM Press, © 1958. *The Rule St. Benedict,* translated by Owen Chadwick, *Western Asceticism,* Library of Christian Classics, Vol. XII, pp. 291–337.

Paulist Press, © 1950. Gregory the Great, *Pastoral Care,* translated by Henry Davis, S.J., *St. Gregory the Great, Pastoral Care* in *Ancient Christian Writers,* Vol. 11.

Catholic University of America Press, © 1959. Gregory the Great, *Dialogues,* translated by Odo John Zimmerman, O.S.B., *St. Gregory the Great, Dialogues* in *Fathers of the Church* Vol. 39. I, I 1, 2, 3, 32, 36, IV, 41.

Catholic University of America Press, John of Damascus, *An Exact Exposition of the Orthodox Faith,* translated by Frederic H. Chase, Jr., *Saint John of Damascus Writings* in *The Fathers of the Church* Vol. 37.

Harper Collins, UK, Mohammed Marmaduke Pickthall, *The Meaning of the Glorious Koran.*

Hodder and Stoughton, London, © 1896, Martin Luther, *Address to the Christian Nobility of the German Nation* from *Luther's Primary Works,* ed. Henry Wace and C.A. Buchheim.

Oxford © 1911. *The Confessions of Augsburg* from B.J. Kidd, *Documents Illustrative of the Continental Reformation.* Public domain.

The Schleitheim Confession of Faith, translated by John C. Wegner, "The Schleitheim Confession," *Mennoite Quarterly Review,* 19 © 1945, 243ff.

John Calvin, *The Institutes of the Christian Religion,* translated by John Allen © 1813. Public domain.

Anglican Articles of Religion. Public domain.

Dolman, London © 1847. Ignatius Loyola, *The Spiritual Exercises,* translation adapted from Charles Seager, *The Spiritual Exercises of St. Ignatius Loyola.* Public domain.

B. Herder Book Co. St. Louis, © 1941, *Canons and Decrees of the Council of Trent* translated by H. J. Schroeder. Permission granted by TAN Books and Publishers, Inc.

John Murray Ltd., London, © 1951. Ibn Sina (Avicenna), *The Book of Deliverance,* translated by A. J. Arberry in *Avicenna on Theology.*

George Allen & Unwin Ltd, © 1953 and Humanities Press, Inc., New York, al-Ghazali, *That Which Delivers From Error,* translated by W. Montgomery Watt, *The Faith and Practice of al-Ghazali,* 19–30, 52–63, 68–85.

Luzac & Company, © 1954, 1961 and by Simon van den Bergh, Ibn Rushd (Averroes), *The Decisive Treatise, Unveiling of the Programs of Proof, Incoherence of the Incoherence,* translated by G. F. Hourani, *Averroes on the Harmony of Religion and Philosophy.* All permissions granted without a fee by Roy Yates Books distributors of Luzac & Co.

Paulist Press, New York, © 1980. Ibn Al-'Arabi, *The Bezels of Wisdom,* translated by R.W. J. Austin, *Ibn Al-'Arabi: The Bezels of Wisdom.*

SCM Press Ltd, London, Anselm, *Proslogium* and *Cur Deus Homo,* translated by Eugene R. Fairweather, *A Scholastic Miscellany: Anselm to Ockham,* Library of Christian Classics.

SCM Press, Abelard, © 1956. *Exposition of the Epistle to the Romans,* translated by Gerald E. Moffatt, *A Scholastic Miscellany: Anselm to Ockham,* Library of Christian Classics Vol X, pp 282–284.

PREFACE

This anthology is a sequel to *Readings in Western Religious Thought: The Ancient World*. Like the first volume, it was written with the conviction that the best introduction for the college student to the Western religious heritage is to read the primary texts which have shaped the Western religious consciousness. My first volume provided selections from the religious writings of the ancient Western world from the beginnings of civilization in Mesopotamia and Egypt (c. 3000 B.C.E.) to the collapse of the Roman Empire in the West (c. 450 C.E.). This volume continues the story of the Western religious heritage by tracing the history of the three great Western monothesims (Judaism, Christianity and Islam) from the fall of Rome through the Christian Reformation of the sixteenth century.

In contrast to the religions of ancient Greece and Rome, these three monotheisms, which emerged in the wake of the fall of Rome, continue to be living religious traditions in the West. They share basic beliefs rooted in the traditions of ancient Israel. All three believe in a Creator who has revealed a moral path of salvation to a chosen people, and will complete history with a judgment by which Divine justice will triumph, and individuals who have followed the path of salvation on earth will ultimately attain eternal life with God. We will discover that during this period all three struggled with common problems within their respective traditions: the interpretation of their sacred books, the basis for teaching authority within the community of faith, the relationship between faith and good works, the authority of philosophical reason in relation to faith, and the place of mysticism within the community.

Despite these common beliefs and problems, the interaction of these faiths, especially on the part of Christianity and Islam, has tragically often been one of rivalry for converts and political control, war fought in the name of the one true God, and hate-filled and uninformed persecution. An unbiased and sympathetic study of the basic writings of these great faiths of the West may contribute to the mutual respect which is necessary if humanity is to survive on this planet.

In the selection of texts I have tried to choose those documents which best reflect the basic religious values of the tradition and their adaptation in the course of history. I have attempted to make the selections long enough to give the flavor of the work and, at the

1

same time, varied enough to give the instructor an opportunity to introduce the student to a wide variety of religious texts. My introductory essays are designed to give a continuous narrative of the development of each tradition and a comparative analysis of the primary texts.

I am pleased to acknowledge the help I have received in preparing this collection: Providence College for granting me a half-year sabbatical to complete work on this volume, the Development of Western Civilization faculty at Providence College for their inspiration and shared insights during fifteen years of teaching in the program, and Sylvia White, secretary of the Development of Western Civilization Program for typing large portions of the text. A special thanks is due to Dr. Rodney Delasanta, the Director of the Liberal Arts Honors Program at Providence College, who read my essays and gave invaluable assistance in matters of style. Finally, I owe a debt of gratitude to my wife, Linda, and my two children, Rebekah and Timothy, who have been extremely supportive of my academic career.

1

RABBINIC JUDAISM

After the fall of Jerusalem and the Temple to the Romans in 70 C.E., the Jews began their long pilgrimage as a landless people who have been sustained for over nineteen hundred years by their efforts to be faithful to the Torah and their belief that they are God's chosen people. By 70 C.E. Jewish communities were found in Babylon, Egypt, Asia Minor, Greece, Macedonia, Dalmatia, Italy, Gaul, Spain and North Africa. In the Diaspora (dispersion) the central Jewish institution was the synagogue (assembly place) led by laymen called rabbis ("masters" of Torah). When the Temple, with its sacrifices and pilgrimage festivals conducted by priests, was destroyed, the local synagogue had to develop a form of Judaism with a non-sacrificial system of worship, study and social service.

The father of rabbinic Judaism was Johanan ben Zakkai, a Pharisee who escaped the destruction of Jerusalem and received permission from the Romans to establish an academy for teachers of Torah at Yabneh, a small coastal village in Judea (c. 71 C.E.). By focusing on the study and living of the Torah, the Pharisees at Yabneh were able to reformulate the whole system of Jewish faith and practice so that it could survive without a state, Temple, and land. They fixed the canon of the Hebrew Bible and established a new Sanhedrin, called Bet Din (House of Judgment), which functioned as an official body for expounding the terms of God's covenant. The rabbis also began the process of codifying the oral law of "the fathers" which had flourished for several centuries as a tradition of applying the written Torah to the changing circumstances of Jewish life. The Romans even gave the rabbis at Yabneh the authority to rule over all the Jews of the Roman Empire through their head rabbi who was given the title *Nasi* ("Prince" or "Patriarch").

The assembly at Yabneh continued teaching and transmitting oral Torah which had developed in Pharisaic circles. They believed that this tradition of oral Torah was like a "hedge" around the written Torah which had been handed down in a chain of tradition from Moses, to Joshua, the elders, the prophets and then to the men of the great synagogue. One tradition was called *midrash* (literally "teaching" or "investigation") which taught oral Torah in the form of an exposition of a biblical text. When the midrash yielded a legal teaching, it was called *halakah* (literally "walking") from the text in Exodus 18:20 which speaks of the way in which the people of Israel are "to walk." When the midrash produced non-legal teaching which explored the nature and meaning of the covenant, it was called *haggadah* (literally "narration"). Haggadah has a multitude of forms: biographical vignettes from the lives of the rabbis as models of piety, imaginative dialogues between God and biblical Israel, allegories, parables, and free flights of religious imagination. A second method for teaching was *Mishnah* (literally "repetition") which taught oral law independent of a scriptural basis by simply repeating and fixing in the memory an oral teaching of "the fathers" who had taught Torah from the time of Ezra to the present.

By 70 C.E. this tradition of oral Torah was a huge body of material which could no longer be easily retained in the memory. There were also conflicts in interpretation. Two basic schools had developed in connection with two great sages: Hillel (flourished 30 B.C.E.–10 C.E.) and Shammai (c. 50 B.C.E.–30 A.D.). Hillel had the gentle temperament of a saint and tended toward a more lenient interpretation of the Torah. He taught that Israel would bring other nations to God by loving peace, serving others and living humbly.

> Hillel and Shammai received the tradition from them. Hillel said: Be of the disciples of Aaron. Love peace and pursue peace; love your fellow creatures and bring them near to Torah. He also said: He who strives to exalt his name will in the end destroy his name; he who does not increase his knowledge decreases it; he who does not study has undermined his right to life; and he who makes unworthy use of the crown of the Torah will perish. He also said: If I am not for myself who will be? But if I am for myself only, what am I? And if not now, when? (Avot 1:12–14)

Shammai was of a sterner, more rigorist disposition. He emphasized the duty of Israel to study and do the Torah while also treating others with respect.

> Shammai said: Set a fixed time for the study of the Torah; say little and do much; and greet every person with a cheerful countenance. (Avot 1:15)

To bring order to this huge body of tradition, the Yabneh Sanhedrin began a process of defining the Jewish tradition in a way which was somewhat analogous to the function of the creeds and councils of the contemporary early Christian churches. The difference is that Judaism's dogma tended to be basically simple and beyond dispute: belief in the one Creator God and his revelation in the Torah, Prophets and Writings. Differences of opinion arose in matters of practice in observing Torah in the changed conditions of life in the Diaspora. The rabbis at Yabneh met these problems with a truly democratic spirit. They collected the various teachings and attempted to resolve outstanding differences in opinion by testing them against scripture, traditional use, and logical reasoning. Problems and disputes were settled by a majority vote. The traditions were collected and redacted in a mishnaic form by the pupils of Johanan ben Zakkai. A leading figure of this period was Rabbi Akiba (c. 50–135 C.E.) who began to arrange the halakahic material by subjects.

During the reign of Emperor Hadrian (117–138 C.E.), this work was interrupted by a Jewish revolt (132–135 C.E.) which led to repression of the Jews in Judea. When Hadrian attempted to rebuild Jerusalem with a temple dedicated to Jupiter on the site of the Jewish temple, the Jews rebelled under the leadership of Bar Kozibah who was hailed by Akiba and others as the messiah and therefore called Bar Kokhba ("Son of the Star"). After three years of brutal war, the Romans crushed the rebellion and took punitive measures against Jews. Teaching Torah, circumcision and sabbath observance were punishable by death. Jerusalem was renamed Aelia Capitolina, and Jews were allowed in the city only once a year to visit the "wailing wall." Several sages, including Akiba, died as martyrs for refusing to discontinue teaching Torah. A notable decision by the rabbis during Hadrian's persecutions was to allow a Jew to disobey any command of the Torah to escape death—except for murder, sexual immorality and idolatry.

THE MISHNAH

After Hadrian's persecution many Jews left the Holy Land; some went to Babylon where there was a thriving Jewish community which enjoyed relative peace under the Parthians. Others went to various communities in the Jewish Diaspora. The center of Jewish life in the Holy Land moved to an academy at Usha in northern Galilee where the leading teachers were Rabbi Meir and Rabbi Judah The Prince (135–220 C.E.). The latter was concerned about the continuation of the academy as a leader in Judaism and therefore devised a written instrument for the preservation of authoritative teaching to replace the academy. This was the Mishnah ("teaching"), a written codification of Jewish oral law which was designed to facilitate learning and discussion in the Torah academies. It contains the teachings of one hundred and forty-eight scholars in sixty-three books, or tractates, arranged in six major sections. The Mishnah gave both stability and flexibility to Judaism because it is both a code of fixed laws as well as a digest of divergent opinions. In this respect it differs from the creeds of the early Christian church which anathematized heretics with divergent opinions about the nature of Christ and other theological issues.

The teachings of the Jewish fathers are refreshingly pragmatic. They are not attempting to reconcile their faith with the principles of Greek and Roman philosophy like Philo (c. 20 B.C.E.–50 C.E.) or the early Christian fathers. Rather, they are preserving the traditions of the Law, the Prophets and the sacred Writings by emphasizing the importance of study and the living of the Torah, not for earthly reward or human honor, but for its own sake and reward in the world to come.

Many of the teachings of the fathers are similar to the wisdom and parabolic teachings of Jesus in the gospel traditions. Like Jesus, the fathers emphasize the primacy of deeds over words in the observance of the Torah. Although at times they are blatantly patriarchal in their attitude toward women, the rabbis insist on the dignity and respect due to each person who is created in the image of God. They also stress the virtue of humility, and the avoidance of greed, gluttony, lust and anxiety produced by excessive wealth. Although the sayings of the fathers are not speculative in a philosophical sense, they continue the biblical wisdom tradition of making insightful observations about wise and foolish people, proper attitudes toward property, various dispositions of character, types of students, and donors. All is done in a spirit of exhorting the person to recognize the wisdom of a life based on Torah.

THE TALMUDS

The Mishnah became the chief subject of study in the academies in both Palestine and Babylon. Both communities developed their own Talmuds or massive commentaries on the Mishnah. The *Palestinean Talmud* is the product of the mid-fourth century C.E. It is somewhat incomplete and only one-third the size of the *Babylonian Talmud* because of the difficult conditions for Jews in Palestine once Christianity became the official religion of the Roman Empire in the late fourth century C.E. Under Christian Roman emperors, Judaism became a political and religious heresy and the academies in Palestine rapidly declined. They gave up their previous authority to fix the Jewish lunar calendar and feasts each year, and by about 425 C.E. Emperor Theodosius II closed the Palestinean academies.

The Babylonian Jewish community continued to thrive and, although periodically persecuted by the Sassanids, had enough peace and security to develop a rich intellectual tradition. The *Babylonian Talmud* is the product of the early sixth century C.E. It is a massive work of thirty-six major divisions and contains an estimated two and half million words recording the teachings of two thousand sages over the course of eight hundred years. The large body of rabbinic literature also includes *midrashim* or haggadic comments, reflections and homilies on biblical texts like the Torah, and the texts for reading on various sabbaths and festivals.

Despite the fact that the Jews were now living as an exiled people, the rabbis never lost faith in the idea that God's covenant with them was irrevocable. As the midrash on the book of Hosea illustrates, The Holy One can no more break covenant with the descendants of the patriarchs than could Hosea dismiss his wife Gomer who had borne him three children. This covenant is manifest in the great gift of the Torah which Israel is privileged to live in the world. God's choice of the Israelites is not rooted in its greatness, but in love which chose them because they were the fewest and humblest of all peoples. Their greatness will continue to consist in their humility before God. The rabbis do not, however, naively assume that Israel is perfect as God's covenant people. As the allegory on the fruits for the harvest feast of Sukkoth illustrates, Israel is made up of all types: those who have learning and good deeds, those who have learning and no good deeds, those who have good deeds and no learning, and those who have neither learning nor good deeds. They are left together in this world by God so that they may atone for one another.

The burden of Israel's covenant is described beautifully in the allegory of the image of the dove from the Song of Songs. Like the dove, Israel is to be *faithful* to all the commandments given at Sinai and *distinguished* from other nations by its deeds of righteousness. It continues to visit the Temple site, as the dove always returns to its nest, even when its brood is taken. It is to attract the other nations to God, just as others are attracted to the dove. And, most profoundly, Israel's suffering because of its fidelity to God is understood as atoning for the sins of the nations. This belief is comparable to the Christian understanding of the atoning power of Christ's death and resurrection. What Christ is for the world in Christian theology, the faithful and suffering Jewish community is in the tradition of the rabbis.

According to the rabbis, and in contrast to medieval Christian theology, the other peoples of the world do not have to become Jews in order to find salvation. God made a covenant with all humanity through Noah after the flood (Gen 9), and the Talmudic teachers derive from the biblical texts seven precepts of this covenant with Noah: prohibitions of idolatry, adultery, bloodshed, profaning God's name, injustice, robbery, and cutting the flesh or a limb from a living animal. Each person who is faithful to these stipulations is righteous. Because of this belief, rabbinic Judaism lacked the missionary zeal of Christianity and Islam. Judaism did accept converts, however, but only when the proselyte showed a willingness to undertake the duty of promoting divine righteousness on earth by being thoroughly obedient to the whole Torah, both oral and written, and sharing in the sufferings of the Jewish people.

The rabbinical understanding of God is not derived from philosophical speculation but is rooted in the story of God's revelation in the scriptures. God is the one God who created the universe and revealed his saving will to Israel in the Torah. Just as the scriptures used anthropomorphic language to describe God, the rabbis daringly describe God in a human manner as dividing his day between study of Torah, judgment of sin, sustaining the universe by his mercy, playing with Leviathan and teaching schoolchildren.

Rabbinical writings do, however, have ways of speaking about God which are the equivalent of certain more philosophical concepts. The clever dialogue between Emperor Hadrian, who wants to see Israel's God, and Rabbi Joshua ben Hanaya illustrates that the presence of God is invisible and transcendent, beyond human comprehension. The concept of *Shekhinah* ("Indwelling presence") is the rabbis' way of speaking about God's immanence or presence to creation and history. Sin, as exemplified in the biblical stories of Adam, Cain, the flood, Babel, and Sodom, drives the Shekhinah away from the world, but God's revelation to the patriarchs and Moses through the Torah returns the Shekhinah to the world.

The rabbis find the various attributes of God reflected in the variety of divine names given to God in the scriptures. In the midrash on the revelation of the sacred name of God to Moses at the burning bush, God tells Moses:

"You want to know My name. I am called according to My deeds. At various times I am called Almighty, Lord of hosts, God, and Lord. When I judge My creatures, I am called God. When I wage war against the wicked, I am called Lord of hosts. When I suspend the punishment of man's sins, I am called Almighty. And when I have compassion upon My world, I am called Lord. . . ."

Although the rabbis take seriously the obligation to keep in some way the six hundred and thirteen precepts of the Torah, their approach to the Torah is not ultimately legalistic. They recognize, as Jesus did, that the most important obligations are summarized in shorter lists by the psalms and prophets, and that the intention with which one fulfills the Torah is all-important. Throughout the rabbinic literature the Torah is understood as a gift of life-giving wisdom to Israel, enabling those who follow it to overcome the impulse to evil which all humans have. The Torah functions in rabbinic literature in the same way faith in Jesus' life-giving death and resurrection does for the early Christian fathers.

The Talmuds not only provided an enlightened ethical code for the life of the Jews, but they also developed from the Bible, by means of reinterpretation and adaptation, a series of religious observances that were able to sustain Judaism after the cessation of the sacrificial cult in Jerusalem. My selections only give a sample of some of the more important religious observances of Talmudic Judaism.

Circumcision of the boy on the eighth day is the most ancient of Jewish rituals; it goes back to the time of Abraham (Gen 17) as a token of covenant between God and Israel and symbolizes the idea of a national consecration of Abraham's seed to the service of God.

In contrast to medieval Christianity, in which the celibate monks played a crucial role in preserving Christian ideals and learning in the early Middle Ages, Judaism had no tradition of celibacy. The family home was the center of Jewish life where the ideals of living Torah were inculcated, and the foundation of the home is the sacred bond of marriage. According to the rabbis, a major purpose of marriage is to procreate in fulfillment of the divine command "to be fruitful and multiply" (Gen 1:28) and in continuation of the role assigned to Israel to be a source of blessing for the nations of the world. Marriage is also understood as necessary for the joy, blessing and good which God intends for humanity. Rabbi Eliezer said: "A man who has no wife is not even a man, as it is stated: 'Male and female He created them and He named *them* man'" (Gen 5:2). Within the family husband and wife have obligations toward one another and for the instruction of children in the duties of the Torah. The children, likewise, have a sacred obligation to love and honor their parents.

Although the dietary regulations of Judaism may seem excessively scrupulous to outsiders, these are all designed to give to the animal process of eating an element of spirituality and to consecrate even this most human of activities to God.

The whole of Jewish life is consecrated by the "appointed Seasons," feasts and fasts which mark the Jewish calendar. The foremost of these is the weekly observance of the sabbath. As God labored and rested in creation (Gen 1:1–2:4a), so humans, as the image of God, labor in creative tasks for six days and rest on the seventh in order to attain the spiritual state necessary for the enjoyment of God's creation.

Jews also celebrate annually three great holidays which are days of rest. Originally associated with the harvest of the Holy Land, these festivals commemorate formative historical events in the history of Israel. Passover, celebrated in the spring, lasts eight days, and remembers the birth of the nation in the Exodus from Egypt. Shavuoth, the Feast of Weeks, comes seven weeks after Passover. It originally was the spring wheat harvest festival and now celebrates the revelation of the Ten Commandments on Mount Sinai. Sukkoth (booths) is the fall vintage harvest festival which also recalls the loving care of the Lord who protected the Israelites during their journey through the wilderness.

Rosh Hashanah (literally, "head of the year") occurs in September and begins a ten-day period of repentance, culminating with Yom Kippur ("Day of Atonement"). These are extremely solemn days because, according to tradition, this is the time in which all the world is judged before God's heavenly throne. It is a solemn and serious period in which the Jew turns from sin in the faith that God accepts and forgives a contrite heart.

Although the Talmuds were written for Jews in the Diaspora, the rabbis never give up their belief in the promise of the land. In their view, the Holy Land is the navel of the world, a land fashioned by God for service to him. Initially the rabbis understood the Second Exile of 70 C.E. as the result of sin in the same way that prophets like Jeremiah had interpreted the original Babylonian Exile. However, as time wore on, the doctrine of Israel as a "suffering servant" was used to explain the idea that the people of Israel were not suffering for their own sins but for the sins of others. The Exile was also understood as a time of testing, comparable to the trial of Abraham. The duty of the people was to remain faithful and never to forget Zion.

Although the Talmuds are not in any way systematic works of theology like the dogmatic works of Augustine, basic doctrines can be drawn from their traditions. According to the Talmud, the human person is created in the image of God and, because God acts in justice and mercy, humans must imitate God by practicing these virtues. Humans are partners with God in ruling the world and are to carry forward God's work by creating a just order in this world. This is not done by a withdrawal from society, as in Christian monasticism, but by an active life within society.

Although humans do have an "evil impulse" and the capacity to descend to the depths of depravity, Judaism does not have a doctrine of original sin. Sin is a personal rebellion against God which debases human nature. Punishment is not retribution, but chastisement by a loving Father to remind humans of their proper dignity and character. Rabbinic Judaism does not speak of grace in the traditional Christian sense; God's answer to sin is the gift of repentance and the Torah which is a path to righteousness.

Within the Hebrew Bible there is no doctrine of heaven and hell. God's blessings are meant to be enjoyed in this world. In the late biblical period, the book of Daniel, written during the persecutions of Antiochus IV (160s B.C.E.) expressed a belief in the ultimate resurrection of the just at the end of days. The doctrine of resurrection was debated in post-biblical times, and the Pharisees' view that there would be a resurrection of the dead eventually became normative. The rabbis developed various ingenious arguments for finding evidence of this belief in the Torah and Prophets. Concurrently the idea of a judgment of the individual in the afterlife also arose.

There are two conflicting tendencies in the rabbis' beliefs about the messiah; both are rooted in the Hebrew Bible. The prophecies of First Isaiah (8th century B.C.E.) describe a final age in which a Davidic king who will be endowed with God's spirit, rule wisely and justly, bring salvation to Judah and Israel, and restore a peaceable kingdom upon earth (see Isaiah 9 and 11). Second Isaiah (c. 540 B.C.E.) denationalized these expectations and identified the messiah with the Persian king Cyrus the Great who restored the Jews from Babylonian exile. Both tendencies are continued in the rabbis. As previously noted, Rabbi Akiba in the second century C.E. believed that Bar Kochba, the leader of the revolt against Rome, was the messiah. Other rabbis continued to await a distant messianic figure who would bring God's kingdom.

The translations are taken from Arthur Hertzberg, *Judaism* (New York: George Braziller, Inc., 1961) 24–25, 29, 34–36, 49, 57, 72–73, 89–91, 150–151, 155–156, 180–181, 186–189, 196–198, 207–211, 217.

THE RABBINICAL WRITINGS

The Nature of the Covenant

The Holy One, praised be He, said to Hosea "Your children have sinned." Hosea should have said "They are Your children, children of Your dear ones, children of Abraham, Isaac and Jacob; show them Your mercy." However, not only did he not say this, but he said "Lord of the universe! The entire world belongs to You. Displace them with another people." The Holy One, praised be He, thought: What shall I do with this old man? I shall tell him to marry a harlot and to beget children of harlotry and then I shall tell him to send her away. If he will be able to send her away, I will send Israel away. And it is written "The Lord said to Hosea: Go, take to yourself a wife of harlotry and have children of harlotry. . . . So he went and took Gomer the daughter of Dibla'im . . ." [Hosea 1:2–3]. When two sons and a daughter had been born to him, the Holy One, praised be He, said to Hosea "Could you not have learned from Moses, your teacher? Whenever I spoke with him he separated from his wife. You must do likewise." Hosea answered "Lord

of the universe! I have children from her, I cannot put her away or divorce her." The Holy One said to him, "Your wife is a harlot and your children are children of harlotry; you do not even know if they are really yours. Yet you refuse to divorce her. How, then, should I act toward Israel? They are the children of those whom I have tested, the children of Abraham, Isaac and Jacob, and one of the four possessions which I have acquired in My world: The Torah, heaven and earth, the Temple and Israel. And yet you tell Me to supersede them with another people!"

When he realized that he had sinned, Hosea rose to ask mercy for himself. The Holy One, praised be He, said to him "Before you ask mercy for yourself, ask mercy for Israel" (*Pesahim* 87 a–b).

The Nature of the Covenant People

The people of Israel are dear to God, for they are called His children. They are especially dear in that they were made aware of this, as it is written, "You are the children of the Lord your God . . ." [Deut 14:1]. The people of Israel are dear to God, for to them was given the beloved instrument [the Torah]. They are especially dear in that they were made aware that to them was given the precious instrument by which the world was created, as it is written, "For I have given you good doctrine; do not forsake My Torah" [Prov.4:2]. (*Mishnah Avot* 3:16)

"You have declared this day concerning the Lord that He is your God and that you will walk in His ways . . . and the Lord has declared this day that you are a people for His own possession . . ." [Deut 26:17–18]. The Holy One, praised be He, said to Israel: You have made Me unique in the world and I shall make you unique in the world. You have made Me unique, as it is written "Hear, O Israel, the Lord is our God, the Lord is *One*" [Deut 6:4], and I will make you unique, as it is written "Who is like Your people Israel, a nation that is *one* in the earth . . ." [I Chron 17:21] (*Berakhot* 6a).

"Your eyes are doves" [Song of Songs 1:15]. The dove is faithful; Israel was likewise faithful to the Holy One, praised be He, at Sinai. For they did not say that ten commandments, or twenty or thirty, were enough for them, but they said, "All that the Lord has spoken we will do and we will obey" [Ex 24:7]. The dove is distinguishable among all other birds; Israel is likewise distinguished, by deeds. The dove is modest; Israel is likewise modest. . . . The dove does not leave its nest even if someone has taken its brood; Israel likewise continues to visit the Temple site even though the Temple has been destroyed. The dove journeys, and returns to its nest; Israel likewise "shall come eagerly like birds from Egypt and like doves from Assyria" [Hos. 11:11]. Others are attracted to the dove; likewise, converts are attracted to Israel. The dove, unlike other birds, offers its neck for slaughter without struggling; children of Israel likewise give their lives for the Holy One praised be He. The dove does not leave its mate; Israel likewise does not leave the Holy One, praised be He. The dove atones for sins; Israel likewise

atones for the nations of the world (*Song of Songs Rabbah,* 1).

"It was not because you were more in number than any other people that the Lord set His love upon you and chose you, for you were the fewest of all peoples" [Deut 7:7]. The Holy One praised be He said to Israel: I set My love upon you because even when I grant you greatness you make yourselves small [i.e., humble] before Me. I gave greatness to Abraham, and he said "Behold, I am dust and ashes" [Gen 18:27]; to Moses and Aaron, and they said "But what are we?" [Ex 16:7]; to David, and he said "I am a worm, not a man" [Ps 22:7]. But the other nations of the world are not like you. I gave greatness to Nimrod, and he said "Let us build for ourselves a city, and a tower with its top in the heavens . . ." [Gen 11:4]; to Pharaoh and he said "Who is the Lord?" [Ex 5:2]. . . to Nebuchadnezzar and he said "I will ascend above the heights of the clouds; I will make myself like the Most High" [Isa 14:14] (*Hullin* 89a).

"And you shall take on the first day [of Sukkot] the fruit of goodly trees, branches of palm trees and boughs of leafy trees, and willows of the brook; and you shall rejoice before the Lord your God seven days" [Lev 23:40]. ". . . the fruit of goodly trees . . ." refers to Israel. Just as the *etrog* [citron] has both taste and fragrance, so Israel has men who have both learning and good deeds. ". . . branches of palm trees . . ." refer to Israel. Just as the fig has a taste but has no fragrance, so Israel has men who have learning but have no good deeds. ". . . boughs of leafy trees . . ." refer to Israel. Just as the myrtle has fragrance but has no taste, so Israel has men who have good deeds but have no learning ". . . willows of the brook . . ." refer to Israel. Just as the willow has neither taste nor fragrance, so Israel has men who have neither learning nor good deeds. What does the Holy One, praised be He, do with them? . . .He stated, "Let them be interrelated, united in one group, and they will be able to atone for one another. When Israel does so, I will be exalted. . . ." (*Leviticus Rabbah* 30:12).

The Covenant with All Men

The sons of Noah were given seven commandments, forbidding idolatry, adultery, bloodshed, profaning God's name, injustice, robbery, and cutting the flesh or a limb from a living animal (*Genesis Rabbah* 34:8).

I call heaven and earth as witnesses: The spirit of holiness rests upon each person according to the deed that each does, whether that person be non-Jew or Jew, man or woman, manservant or maidservant (*Seder Eliahu Rabbah,* Chap. 9).

The Holy One, praised be He, does not disqualify any creature; He accepts everyone. The gates are always open, and whoever wants to enter may enter (*Exodus Rabbah* 19:4).

Rabbi Jeremiah used to say: How do we know that even a non-Jew who fulfills the Torah is to be considered as the High Priest? Scripture states, "You shall therefore keep My statutes and My ordinances which, if a *man* do, he shall live by them" [Lev 18:5]. . . . And he said: Scripture does not state "This is the Law of the Priests, Levites and Israelites" but "This is the Law of man, O Lord God" [2 Sam 7:19]. And he said: Scripture does not state "Open the gates, that the Priests, Levites and Israelites may enter" but "Open the gates, that the righteous nation that keeps faithfulness may enter" [Isa 26:2]. And he said: Scripture does not state "This is the gate of the Lord; the Priests, Levites and Israelites shall enter therein" but "This is the gate of the Lord; the righteous shall enter therein" [Ps 118:20] (*Sifra, Aharei Mot* 86a).

"You shall have one ordinance both for the stranger and for the native" [Num 9:14]. [For the rabbis, "stranger" means proselyte.] Thus, this verse teaches that Scripture makes the proselyte equal to the native-born Jew as regards all the commandments of the Torah (*Sifre, Num.* 71).

A proselyte who has come of his accord is dearer to God than all the Israelites who stood before Him at Mount Sinai. Had the Israelites not witnessed the thunders, lightnings, quaking mountains and sound of trumpets, they would not have accepted the Torah. The proselyte, who saw not one of these things, came and surrendered himself to the Holy One, praised be He, and took the yoke of Heaven upon himself. Can anyone be dearer to God than such a person? (*Tanhuma, Lekh Lekha,* 6).

If anyone desires to be a convert during these times [*probably a period of persecution*], they should say to him, "Why do you want to convert? Do you not know that Israelites today are harried, and oppressed, persecuted and harassed, and that they suffer?" If he says, "I know and I am not worthy," he is accepted at once, and they explain some of the lighter and some of the more stringent commandments to him. . . . And as they tell him of the punishments for transgressing commandments, so they tell him of the rewards for observing them. . . However, they do not speak with him at great length nor do they go into great detail. If he agrees to accept everything, he is circumcised at once. . . . After he is healed, he must undergo ritual immersion and two scholars stand by, telling him some of the lighter and some of the more stringent commandments. After the ritual immersion he is an Israelite in every respect (*Yebamot* 47a–b).

Why was Abraham circumcised at the age of ninety-nine? To teach that if a man wants to convert he should not say, "I am too old; how can I convert?" This is the reason why Abraham was not circumcised until the age of ninety nine (*Tahuma, Likh Lekha*).

God

There is nothing on earth which is apart from the *Shekhinah* [God's presence] (*Numbers Rabbah* 13).

God fills the universe just as the soul fills the body of man (*Berakhot* 10a).

An emperor said to Rabbi Joshua ben Hananya: "I want to see your God." He replied, "You cannot see Him." "Nevertheless," the emperor said, "I want to see Him!" Rabbi Joshua stood him in the summer sun, and said "Look at the sun." "I cannot," answered the emperor. Rabbi Joshua said, "The sun is but one of the servants who stand in the presence of the Holy One, praised be He, and you cannot look at the sun. Is it not truer still that you cannot see God's Presence?" (*Hullin* 60a).

Originally, the *Shekhinah* [Presence of God] was on earth. When Adam sinned, it rose to the nearest firmament. When Cain sinned, it rose to the second. When the generation of Enosh sinned [in idolatry], it rose to the third. When the generation of the Flood sinned, it rose to the fourth. When the generation of the dispersal of nations [who tried to erect the Tower of Babel] sinned, it rose to the fifth firmament. When the men of Sodom sinned, it rose to the sixth. The wickedness of the Egyptians in the time of Abraham caused the *Shekhinah* to retreat to the seventh and most remote firmament.

The righteous counteracted the above effect. Abraham brought the *Shekhinah* down to the sixth firmament, Isaac brought it to the fifth, Jacob brought it to the fourth, Levi to the third, Kehat to the second and Amram to the first firmament. Moses brought it back from the heavens to earth (*Genesis Rabbah* 1:10).

Rabbi Judah said, quoting Rav: The day consists of twelve hours. During the first three hours, the Holy One, praised be He, is engaged in the study of Torah. During the second three He sits in judgment over His entire world. When He realizes that the world is deserving of destruction, He rises from the Throne of Justice, to sit in the throne of Mercy. During the third group of three hours,

He provides sustenance for the entire world, from huge beasts to lice. During the fourth, He sports with the Leviathan, as it is written, "Leviathan, which You did form to sport with" [Ps 104:26]. . . . During the fourth group of three hours (according to others) He teaches schoolchildren (*Avodad Zerah* 3b).

Torah: Teaching and Commandment

Rabbi Simlai expounded: Six hundred and thirteen commandments were transmitted to Moses on Mount Sinai. Three hundred sixty-five of them are negative commandments [i.e. prohibitions], corresponding to the number of days in the solar year. The remaining two hundred forty-eight are positive commandments [i.e., injunctions], corresponding to the number of limbs in the human body (*Makkot* 23b).

After Moses, David came and reduced the six hundred thirteen commandments to eleven, as it is written: "Lord, who shall sojourn in Your tabernacle? Who shall dwell on Your holy mountain? He who walks blamelessly, and does what is right, and speaks truth in his heart, who does not slander with his tongue, and does no evil to his friend, nor takes up a reproach against his neighbor, in whose eyes a reprobate is despised, but honors those who fear the Lord, who swears to his own hurt and does not change, who does not put out his money at interest, and does not take a bribe against the innocent" [Ps 15:1–5]. . . .

Then Isaiah came and reduced the commandments to six, as it is written, "He who walks righteously and speaks uprightly, he who despises the gain of oppressions, who shakes his hands lest they hold a bribe, who stops his ears from hearing of bloodshed, and shuts his eyes from looking upon evil" [Isa 33:15]. . . . Then Micah came and reduced them to three, as it is written, "It has been told you, O man what is good, and what the Lord requires of you: To do justice, to love mercy, and to walk humbly with your God [Mic 6:8]. . . . Then Isaiah came again and reduced them to two. "Thus says the Lord: Keep justice and do righteousness" [Isa 56:1]. Amos came and reduced them to one, as it is written, "Thus says the Lord to the house of Israel: Seek Me and live" [Amos 5:4]. . . . Habakuk came and also reduced them to one, as it is written, "The righteous shall live by his faith" [Hab 2:4] (*Makkot* 24a).

Rabbi Huna and Rabbi Jeremiah said in the name of Rabbi Hiyya bar Abba: It is written, "They have forsaken Me and have not kept My law" [Jer 16:11]. This is to say: "If only they *had* forsaken Me but kept My law! Since they then would have been occupied with it, the light which is in it would have restored them to the right path" (*Lamentations Rabbah,* Proem II).

Marriage

A wife must do the following for her husband: grind flour, bake bread, wash clothes, cook food, give suck to her child, make ready his bed and work in wool. If she brought him one maidservant [from her father's house], she need not grind or bake or wash. If she brought two maidservants, she need not cook or give her child suck. If she brought three maidservants, she need not make ready his bed or work in wool. If four, she may sit all day and do nothing. Rabbi Eliezer says: Even if she brought one hundred maidservants he should force her to work in wool, for idleness leads to unchastity (*Mishnah Ketubot* 5:5).

If a man has vowed to have no intercourse with his wife, the School of Shamai says that she may consent for two weeks; the School of Hillel says, for one week. Disciples of the sages, for purposes of study of the Torah, may stay away from their wives for thirty days without their consent. Laborers [whose work takes them to another city] may stay away for one week without their wives' consent. The marital duty enjoined upon husbands by the

Torah [. . . he shall not diminish her marital rights . . . Ex 21:10] is as follows: every day for those that are unemployed, twice a week for laborers, once a week for donkey-drivers [who lead caravans for short distances], once every thirty days for camel drivers, [who lead caravans for longer distances], and once every six months for sailors. So Rabbi Eliezer (*Mishnah Ketubot* 5:6).

No man may abstain from fulfilling the commandment "Be fruitful and multiply" [Gen 1:28], unless he already has children. According to the School of Shamai, "children" here means two sons, while the School of Hillel states that it means a son and a daughter, for it is written, "Male and female created He them" [Gen 5:2]. If he married a woman and lived with her for ten years and she bore no child, he is not permitted to abstain from fulfilling the commandment. If he divorced her she may marry another, and the second husband may live with her for ten years. If she had a miscarriage, the period of ten years is reckoned from the time of the miscarriage. The duty to be fruitful and multiply is incumbent upon the man but not upon the woman. Rabbi Johanan ben Baroka says: Concerning them both it is written: "God blessed them and God said to them: Be fruitful and multiply" [Gen 1:28]" (*Mishnah Yebamot* 6:6).

Rabbi Eliezer said: Whoever does not fulfill the duty of procreation is compared to a murderer, as it is said: "Whoever sheds the blood of man, by a man shall his blood be shed" [Gen 9:6], and immediately following it is written, "Be fruitful and multiply" [Gen 9:7]. Rabbi Akiva said: Such a man is compared to one who diminishes the divine image, as it is said "for God made man in His image" [Gen 9:6] and immediately following it is written "Be fruitful and multiply" [Gen 9:7]. Ben Azzai said: It is as though he did both (*Yebamot* 63b).

"I will establish My covenant between Me and you and your descendants after you . . . to be God to you and to your descendants after you" [Gen 17:7]. If you have no descendants, upon whom will the *Shekhinah* rest? Upon trees and stones?! (*Yebamot* 64a).

Rabbi Hanilai said: A man who has no wife lives without joy, without blessing, without good. Without joy, for it is written, "you and your household shall rejoice" [Deut 14:26]. Without blessing, for it is written "that a blessing may rest on your house" [Ezek 44:30]. Without good, as it is written, "It is not good for man to be alone" [Gen 2:18]. . . . Rabbi bar Ulla said: He lives without peace. . . Rabbi Joshua ben Levi said: A man who knows that his wife fears heaven and does not fulfill his marital duty of cohabitation is to be called a sinner. . . . Rabbi Eleazar said: A man who has no wife is not even a man, as it is stated: "Male and female He created them and He named *them* 'man'" [Gen 5:2]. "I will make man a helper to set over against him" [Gen 2:18]. If he proves deserving, she will be a helper, if not, she will be against him (*Yebamot* 62b–63a).

In Palestine, when a man marries, they ask him: "Finds or Found?" "Finds," as it is said "He who finds a wife finds something good" [Prov 18:22]. "Found," as it is said "I have found the woman whose heart is snares and nets and whose hands are fetters more bitter than death" [Eccles 7:26] (*Yebamot* 63b).

If a man and wife prove deserving, the *Shekhinah* dwells among them; if not, a fire consumes them (*Sotah* 17a).

The Holiness of the Land

Just as the navel is found at the center of a human being, so the Land of Israel is found at the center of the world, as it is stated: "Who dwell at the center of the earth" [Ezek 38:12], and it is the foundation of the world. Jerusalem is at the center of the Land of Israel, the Temple is at the center of Jerusalem, the Holy of Holies is at the center

of the Temple, the Ark is at the center of the Holy of Holies and the Foundation Stone is in front of the Ark, which point is the foundation of the world (*Tanhuma, Kedoshim*).

One may compel his entire household to go up with him to the Land of Israel, but none may be compelled to leave it. All of one's household may be compelled to go up to Jerusalem [from any other place in the Land of Israel], but none may be compelled to leave it (*Mishnah Ketubot* 13:11).

One should live in the Land of Israel, even in a city the majority of whose people are not Jews, rather than live outside of the Land, even in a city the majority of whose people are Jews. Whoever lives in the Land of Israel is considered to be a believer in God. . . . Whoever lives outside of the Land is considered to be in the category of one who worships idols. . . . Whoever lives in the Land of Israel lives a sinless life, as it is written, "The people who dwell there will be forgiven their iniquity" [Isa 33:24]. . . . Whoever is buried in the Land of Israel is considered as though he were buried beneath the Altar. . . . Whoever walks a distance of four cubits in the Land of Israel is assured of a place in the world to come (*Ketubot* 110b–111a).

Living in the Land of Israel equals in import the performance of all the commandments of the Torah (*Sifre, R'eh*).

Rabbi Zeira said: Even the conversation of those who live in the Land of Israel is Torah (*Leviticus Rabbah,* 34).

Ten measures of wisdom came into the world. The Land of Israel took nine, and the rest of the world took one (*Kiddushin* 49).

The Land of Israel is holier than all other lands (*Mishnah Kelim* 1:6).

The atmosphere of the Land of Israel makes men wise (*Baba Batra* 158b).

Galuth (Exile)

The wicked emperor, Hadrian, who conquered Jerusalem, boasted, "I have conquered

Jerusalem with great power." Rabbi Johanan ben Zakkai said to him, "Do not boast. Had it not been the will of Heaven, you would not have conquered it." Rabbi Johanan then took Hadrian into a cave and showed him the bodies of Amorites who were buried there. One of them measured eighteen cubits [approximately thirty feet] in height. He said, "When we were deserving, such men were defeated by us, but now, because of our sins, you have defeated us" (*Tanhuma* (Buber), *Devarim* 7).

Whenever Israel is enslaved, the *Shekhinah,* as it were, is enslaved with them. . . . For it says, "In all their affliction, He was afflicted" [Isa 63:10]. This teaches that He shares in the affliction of the group, but what of the affliction of the individual? Scripture states, "He will call upon Me and I will answer him; I will be with him in trouble" [Ps 91:15]. . . . It is written, "From before Your people, whom You did redeem to Yourself out of Egypt, the nation and its God" [after 2 Sam 7:23]. . . . Rabbi Akiva said: Were it not written in Scripture, it would be impossible to say such a thing. Israel said to God: You have redeemed Yourself, as it were. Likewise, you find that whenever Israel was exiled, the *Shekhinah,* as it were, went into exile with them, as it is written, "I exiled Myself to the house of your fathers when they were in Egypt" [after 1 Sam 2:27]. When they were exiled to Babylon, the *Shekhinah* went into exile with them as it is written, "For your sake I was sent to Babylon" [after Isa 43:14]. When they were exiled to Elam, the *Shekhinah* went into exile with them, as it is written, "I will set My throne in Elam" [Jer 49:30]. . . . And when they return in the future, the *Shekhinah,* as it were, will return with them, as it is written, "Then the Lord your God will return with your captivity" [Deut 30:3]. This verse does not state "The Lord will bring back" [Hebrew: *v'heshiv],* but "He will return" [Hebrew: *v'shav] (Mekhilta, Pisha* 14).

Man: His dignity and Possibilities

Let all your deeds be for the sake of heaven. They once asked Hillel where he was going. He answered, "I am going to perform a religious act (*mitzvah*)." "Which one?" "I am going to the bath house." "Is that a religious act?" "Yes. . . . Those who are in charge of the images of kings which are erected in theaters and circuses scour them and wash them and are rewarded and honored for it. How much more should I take care of my body, for I have been created in the image of God, as it is written, 'In the image of God He created man'" [Gen 5:1] (*Avot of Rabbi; Nathan Version* b, Chap. 38a).

Why was man created on the sixth day [after the creation of all other creatures]? So that, should he become overbearing, he can be told, "The gnat was created before you were" (*Sanhedrin* 38a).

"Consider the work of God; who can make straight what He has made crooked?" [Eccles 7:13]. When the Holy One, praised be He, created Adam, he showed him all of the trees in the Garden of Eden, telling him, "Behold, My works are beautiful and glorious; yet everything which I have created is for your sake. Take care that you do not corrupt or destroy My world" (*Ecclesiastes Rabbah* 7:13).

Rabbi Simon said: When the Holy One, praised be He, was about to create Adam, the angels were divided into two different groups. Some said, "Let him not be created," while others said, "Let him be created." "Love and Truth met together; Righteousness and Peace kissed each other" [Ps 85:10]. Love said, "Let him be created, for he will do loving deeds" but Truth said, "Let him not be created, for he will be all lies." Righteousness said, "Let him be created, for he will do righteous deeds," but Peace said, "Let him not be created, for he will be all argument and discord." What did the Holy One, praised be He, do? He seized Truth and cast it to the ground, as it is written, "Truth was cast down to the ground" [Dan 8:12]. Then the angels said to the Holy One:

Lord of the Universe! How can You despise Your angel Truth? Let Truth rise from the ground, as it is written, "Truth will spring up from the ground" [Ps 85:11] (*Genesis Rabbah* 8:5).

One day Elijah the prophet appeared to Rabbi Baruka in the market of Lapet. Rabbi Baruka asked him, "Is there any one among the people of this market who is destined to share in the world to come? . . . Two men appeared on the scene and Elijah said, "These two will share in the world to come." Rabbi Baruka asked them, "What is your occupation?" They said, "We are merry-makers. When we see a man who is downcast, we cheer him up. When we see two people quarreling with one another, we endeavor to make peace between them" (*Ta'anit* 22a).

When the Holy One, praised be He, was about to create men, the angels said, "'What is man, that You are mindful of him?' [Ps 8:5.] Why do You need man?" The Holy One, praised be He, answered, "Who, then, shall fulfill My Torah and commandments?" The angels said, "We shall." God answered, "You cannot, for in it is written 'This is the law when a man dies in a tent . . .' [Num 19:14], but none of you die. In it is written 'If a woman conceives, and bears a male child . . .' [Lev 12:2], but none of you give birth. It is written 'This you may eat . . .' [Lev 11:21], but none of you eat" (*Tanhuma Buber, B'hukotai* 6).

Rules of Conduct

Rabbi Hama ben Rabbi Hanina said: What does this verse mean?—"You shall walk after the Lord your God" [Deut 13:5]. Is it possible for man to walk after the *Shekhinah*? Is it not written, "The Lord your God is a consuming fire" [Deut 4:24]?—It means that we should walk after the attributes of the Holy One, praised be He.

He clothes the naked, as it is written, "The Lord God made for Adam and for his wife gar-ments of skins and clothed them" [Gen 3:21]. Thus you should clothe the naked.

The Holy One, praised be He, visited the sick, as it is written, "The Lord appeared to him [Abraham] by the oaks of Mamre" [Gen 18:1]. [According to rabbinic tradition, the elderly Abraham was recuperating from his circumcision, narrated in the seventeenth chapter.] Thus you should visit the sick.

The Holy One, praised be He, comforted mourners, as it is written, "After the death of Abraham, God blessed Isaac his son" [Gen 25:11]. Thus you should comfort mourners.

The Holy One, praised be He, buried the dead, as it is written, "He buried him [Moses] in the valley in the land of Moab" [Deut 34:6]. Thus you should bury the dead. . . .

Rabbi Simlai expounded: The Torah begins with an act of lovingkindness and it ends with an act of lovingkindness. It begins with an act of lovingkindness, as it is written, "The Lord God made for Adam and for his wife garments of skin and clothed them" [Gen 3:21]. It ends with an act of lovingkindness, as it is written, "He buried him [Moses] in the valley in the land of Moab" [Deut 34:6] (*Sotah* 14a).

This was a favorite saying of the rabbis of Javneh: I am a creature of God and my neighbor is also His creature; my work is in the city and his in the field; I rise early to my work and he rises early to his. As he cannot excel in my work, so I cannot excel in his. You might say that I do great things while he does small things. However, we have learned that it matters not whether a man does much or little, if only he directs his heart toward Heaven (*Berakot* 17a).

The Holy One, praised be He, daily proclaims the virtues of a bachelor who lives in a large city and does not sin, a poor man who restores a lost object to its owners and a rich man who gives a tithe of his profits in secret (*Peshahim* 113a).

The Holy One, praised be He, loves three: Whoever does not become angry, whoever does not become drunk, and whoever does not stand on his rights. The Holy One, praised be He, hates three: Whoever says one thing with his mouth and another thing in his heart, whoever knows of evidence in favor of someone but does not testify, and whoever sees a disgraceful thing in someone and testifies against him alone [since a minimum of two witnesses is needed to bring about a formal conviction, one witness merely gives the defendant a bad reputation] (*Peshahim* 113b).

Rav said: At judgment day every man will have to give account for every good thing which he might have enjoyed and did not (*Jerusalem Kiddushin* 66d).

He who refrains from wine is called a sinner [the Nazirite was required to bring a sin offering]. All the more, then, is he who painfully refrains from everything to be called a sinner. Also it was derived that he who habitually fasts is called a sinner (*Nedarim* 10a).

Sin and Repentance

The righteous descendants of Adam upon whom death has been decreed . . . approach Adam and say, "You are the cause of our death." Adam replies: "I was guilty of one sin, but there is not a single one among you who is not guilty of many sins" (*Tanhuma* (Buber), *Hukkat* 39).

The First Temple was destroyed because of the sins of idolatry, adultery and murder. . . . But during the time of the Second Temple, the people were engaged in the study of Torah, and the performance of commandments and the deeds of lovingkindness. Why, then, was the Second Temple destroyed? Because the people were guilty of groundless hatred. And this teaches that the sin of groundless hatred is considered to be as grave as the sins of idolatry, adultery and murder (*Yoma* 9b).

Rav Immi said, "There is no death without sin, and there is no suffering without transgression. There is no death without sin, as it

is written, 'The soul that sins, it shall die. The son shall not bear the iniquities of the father, nor shall the father bear the iniquities of the son. The righteousness of the righteous shall be upon him and the wickedness of the wicked shall be upon him'" [Ezek 18:20]. And there is no suffering without transgression, as it is written, 'I will punish their transgressions with the rod and their iniquity with scourges [i.e., suffering]'" [Ps 89:33].

The angels said to the Holy One, praised be He, "Lord of the universe! Why did You punish Adam with death?" He answered them: "I gave him one simple commandment to observe, and he transgressed it." The angels said, "But Moses and Aaron fulfilled the entire Torah and they died!" He said to them, "One fate comes to all, to the righteous and to the wicked . . . as is the good man so is the sinner" [Eccles 9:2]. . . .

Rabbi Simeon ben Eleazar said: "Moses and Aaron also died because of their sin, as it is written 'because you did not believe in Me, to sanctify Me in the eyes of the people of Israel' [Num 20:12.] Had you believed in Me, you would still be alive." . . .

On the other hand, there is death without sin, and there is suffering without transgression (*Shabbat* 55a–55b).

"There was a small city with few men in it, and a great king came against it and besieged it, building great siegeworks against it. But there was found in it a poor wise man, and he by his wisdom saved the city" [Eccles 9:14–15]. Rabbi Ammi bar Abba explained these verses in the following way: "There was a small city"—this is the body. "With few men in it"—these are the parts of the body. "And a great king came against it and besieged it"—this is the evil impulse. "He built great siegeworks against it"—these are sins. "But there was found in it a poor wise man"—this is the good impulse. "And he by his wisdom saved the city"—this refers to repentance and good deeds (*Nedarim* 32b).

May it be Your will, O Lord my God and God of my fathers, to shatter and bring to an end the yoke of the evil impulse from our heart; for You have created us to do Your will and we are under obligation to do Your will. You desire it and we desire it. What, then, hinders? The leaven in the dough [i.e., the evil impulse]. It is well-known to You that there is in us no power to resist it; but may it be Your will, my God and God of my fathers, to cause it to cease from ruling over us and to subject it. Then we shall do Your will as our own will, with a perfect heart (*Jerusalem Berakhot* 7d).

"Open to me, my sister, my love, my dove" (Song of Songs 5:2). Rabbi Issi said: The Holy One, praised be He, said to the Israelites, "Open to Me the gate of repentance as much as the eye of a needle, and I will open for you gates wide enough for carriages and wagons to pass through them" (*Song of Songs Rabbah* to 5:2).

Repentance is greater than prayer, for Moses' prayer to enter the land of Canaan was not accepted while the repentance of Rahab the harlot was accepted (*Seder Eliahu Zuta,* Chap. 4).

"Teach us to number our days" [Ps 90:12]. Rabbi Joshua said: If we knew the exact number of our days, we would repent before we die. Rabbi Eleazar said: Repent one day before your death. His disciples asked him, "Who knows when he will die?" Rabbi Eleazar answered, "All the more then should a man repent today, for he might die tomorrow. The result of this will be that all his life will be spent in repentance" (*Midrash Jehillim* 90:16).

Scripture states, "Let the wicked man forsake his way and the bad man his plans, and let him return to the Lord [i.e., repent] and He will have mercy upon him" [Isa 55:7]. God desires repentance, He does not desire to put any creature to death, as it is said, "I do not desire the death of the wicked man, but that the wicked man turn from his evil way and live" [Ezek 33:11] (*Pesikta Rabbati,* Chap. 44).

How do we know that he who repents is regarded as if he had gone up to Jerusalem, built the Temple and the altar and offered upon it all the sacrifices mentioned in the Torah? It is written, "The sacrifice acceptable to God is a broken spirit, a broken and contrite heart" [Ps 51:17] (*Leviticus Rabbah* 7:2).

Death and the World to Come

All of Israel has a share in the world to come, for it is written, "Your people shall all be righteous; they shall possess the land [interpreted here as referring to the world to come] forever, the shoot of My planting, the work of My hands, that I might be glorified" [Isa 60:21]. The following have no share in the world to come: He that says resurrection of the dead is not derived from the Torah, he that says that the Torah is not from Heaven and an Epicurean (*Mishnah Sanhedrin* 10:1).

How do I know that the resurrection of the dead is derived from the Torah? It is written, "The Lord said to Moses, you shall say to the Levites 'When you take the tithe from the people of Israel . . you shall give the Lord's offering to Aaron the priest. . . .'" [Num 18:25–28]. Did Aaron live forever? He did not even enter the land of Israel; how then could this verse apply? Therefore, we must infer that this verse teaches that Aaron will live in the future and Israel will then give him the offering. This teaches that the resurrection of the dead is derived from the Torah. . . . Rabbi Simlai said: How do we know that the resurrection of the dead is derived from the Torah? It is written, "I established My covenant with them [the patriarchs], to give them the land of Canaan . . ." [Ex 6:4]. The verse states not "to give you" but "to give them" [the patriarchs themselves]. This teaches that the resurrection of the dead is derived from the Torah.

The Sadducees asked Rabban Gamaliel: What evidence do you have that the Holy One, praised be He, revives the dead? He answered: I have proof from the Torah, the

Prophets and the Writings; but they did not accept his proof. In the Torah it is written, "Then the Lord said to Moses: You will sleep with your fathers, and will rise . . ." [Deut 31:16]. The Sadducees objected: It may mean that this people will rise up and go whoring after the strange gods of the land. In the Prophets it is written, "Your dead shall live, your [my] dead bodies shall rise. Awake and sing, you that sleep in the dust, for your dew is a dew of light, and on the land of the shades you will let it fall" [Isa 26:19]. But the Sadducees replied that this may refer to the dead that Ezekiel revived [Ezek 37]. In the Writings it is written, "Your palate is like finest wine that glides down smoothly for my beloved, moving gently the lips of those that are asleep [i.e., in the tomb]" [Song of Songs 7:10]. The Sadducees replied that this may refer to an ordinary movement of the lips while one sleeps. . . . Finally, Rabban Gamaliel quoted the verse ". . . the land which the Lord swore to give to your fathers, to give to them . . ." [Deut 11:9]. It is not said "to you" but "to them." This proves the resurrection of the dead [for since the patriarchs died before the occupation of the land, God's promise could be fulfilled only by raising them from the dead]. Others say that he cited the verse, "You who hold fast to the Lord your God are all alive this day" [Deut 4:4] (*Sanhedrin* 90b).

Rabbi Eliezer said: The nations [i.e., non-Jews] will have no share in the world to come, as it is written, "The wicked shall depart to Sheol, and all the nations that forget God" [Ps 9:17]. The first part of the verse refers to the wicked among Israel. However, Rabbi Joshua said to him: If the verse had stated, "The wicked shall depart to Sheol, and all the nations," I would agree with you. But the verse goes on to say "that forget God." Therefore it means to say that there are righteous men among the other nations in the world to come (*Tosefta Sanhedrin* 13:2).

When Rabbi Johanan ben Zakai was ill, his disciples visited him. When he saw them, he began to weep. They said to him, "Lamp of Israel, right hand pillar, mighty hammer! Why do you weep?" He answered them, "If I were being led before a king of flesh and blood, I would weep, even though his anger, if he were angry with me, would not be ever-lasting, though his prison, if he imprison me, would not hold me for eternity, though he could not sentence me to eternal death and though I could appease him with words and bribe him with money. And now I am being led before the Kings of kings, the Holy One, praised be He, who lives and endures to all eternity. If He is angry with me, His anger is eternal. If He imprisons me, His prison will hold me eternally. He could sentence me to eternal death. And I cannot appease Him with words nor bribe Him with money. And furthermore, two paths lie before me, one to the Garden of Eden, and one to Gehinnom, and I know not in which I will be led. Should I then not weep?"

We have learned that the judgment of the wicked in Gehinom lasts twelve months. Rabbi Eliezer asked Rabbi Joshua, "What should a man do to escape the judgment of Gehinnom?" He replied, "Let him occupy himself with good deeds." . . . "Better is a poor man who walks in integrity . . ." [Prov 19:1]. Whoever walks in blamelessness before his Creator in this world will escape the judgment of Gehinnom in the world to come (*Midrash Misle* 17:1).

Everything which the Holy One, praised be He, caused to be injured in this world will be healed in the world to come. The blind will be healed, as it is written, "Then the eyes of the blind shall be opened" [Isa 35:5]. The lame shall be healed, as it is written "Then shall the lame man leap as the hart" [Isa 35:6]. The dumb shall be healed, as it is written, "The tongue of the dumb shall sing" [Isa 35:6]. Everyone shall be healed. However, each man shall rise with the defects he had in life. The blind shall rise blind, the deaf shall rise deaf, the lame shall rise lame and the dumb shall rise dumb. They shall rise clothed as they were in life. . . . Why shall each man rise with those defects which he had in life? That the wicked of the world might not say, "After they died God healed them and then brought them here," implying that these were actually others. The Holy One, praised be He, said "let them rise with the defects they had in life, and then I shall heal them, as it is written, 'That you may know and believe Me and understand that I am He. Before Me there was no God formed, neither shall any be after Me'" [Isa 43:10]. Later, even the animals shall be healed, as it is written, "The wolf and the lamb shall feed together, and the lion shall eat straw like the ox" [Isa 65:25]. However, the one that brought injury to everyone shall not be healed, as it is written "And dust shall be the serpent's food" [ibid.]. Why? Because he brought everything to dust (*Tanhuma* (Buber), *Vayigash* a).

Rav used to say: In the world to come, there is neither eating nor drinking nor procreation, nor business dealings nor jealousy nor hate nor competition. But righteous men sit with their crowns on their heads and enjoy the splendor of the *Shekhinah* (*Berakot* 17a).

Rabbi Hiyya bar Abba said, quoting Rabbi Johanan: All of the prophecies of consolation and of good things to come delivered by the prophets apply only to the days of the Messiah, but as for the world to come, "no eye has even seen, O God, only You have seen" [*after* Isa 64:3] (*Berakot* 34b).

"You shall keep My statutes and ordinances, by doing which a man shall live; I am the Lord" [Lev 18:5]. This implies that man shall live in the world to come. In this world, man's end is death. How, then, can it be said "by doing

which a man shall live"? This "living" must refer to the world to come. "I am the Lord"; faithful to reward (*Sifra* 85d).

The Messiah

Rabbi Joshua bon Levi came upon Elijah the prophet while he was standing at the entrance of Rabbi Simeon ben Yohai's cave. . . . He asked Elijah, "When will the Messiah come?"

Elijah replied, "Go and ask him yourself."

"Where is he?"

"Sitting at the gates of the city."

"How shall I know him?"

"He is sitting among the poor covered with wounds. The others unbind all their wounds at the same time and then bind them up again. But he unbinds one at a time and binds it up again, saying to himself, 'Perhaps I shall be needed; if so I must always be ready so as not to delay for a moment.'"

Rabbi Joshua ben Levi went to the Messiah and said to him, "Peace unto you, my master and teacher."

The Messiah answered, "Peace unto you, son of Levi."

He asked, "When is the master coming?"

"Today," he answered.

Rabbi Joshua returned to Elijah, who asked, "What did he tell you?"

"He indeed has deceived me, for he said 'Today I am coming,' and he has not come."

Elijah said, "This is what he told you: 'Today—if you would hearken to His voice'" [Ps 95:7] (*Sanherdrin* 98a).

Rabbi Johanan ben Zakai said: If you should have a sapling in your hand when they tell you that the Messiah has arrived, first plant the sapling and then go to greet the Messiah (*Avot of Rabbi Nathan*, Version b, chap. 31).

2

WESTERN CHRISTIANITY IN
THE EARLY MIDDLE AGES

The primary focus of this volume will be on Western Christianity, the religion which shaped the worldview of Europe through the Reformation in the sixteenth century C.E. During the early medieval period, Christianity was gradually divided into two main branches: Roman Catholicism, in the lands of the Western Roman Empire which fell into the hands of the various Germanic tribes, and Eastern Orthodox or Byzantine Christianity, in the Eastern Roman Empire. Both shared a belief in the creeds of the early church councils. They confessed belief in the oneness of God, the centrality of Christ who, as the savior of the world had both a divine and human nature, in the Holy Spirit as the third person of the Trinity, in the Christian church as the community of salvation, and the future judgment of the world by Christ at his second coming. Despite these common beliefs, an increasing estrangement developed between Eastern Christianity and its patriarch at Constantinople, and the West which recognized Rome and its bishop, the pope, as the leader of Christendom. Gradually a series of differences in liturgical language and practice, theological emphases, and church discipline led to a schism between the two churches in 1054 C.E.

Western Christendom faced the dual challenge of both maintaining civilization in the wake of the collapse of Roman authority in the West, and converting to orthodox Roman Christianity the various Teutonic tribes who fell heir to the Roman territories. Next to the Bible itself, Augustine of Hippo (354–430 C.E.) had the most lasting influence on the vision of Western Christianity during the Middle Ages and beyond. As a product of the late Roman world, who converted to Christianity and became a great bishop and theologian, Augustine preserved in his voluminous writings, and especially in his *City of God*, a view of the church as existing for the kingdom of God, the true "eternal city" which will survive beyond the rise and fall of all empires and civilizations. Membership in this church was the unifying factor for Western Christians throughout the Middle Ages. Civil government, even that of the powerful Roman empire, had the positive function of preserving the temporal peace and liberty but could not claim ultimate allegiance. Augustine's life's work was completed just as the barbarians were attacking the empire. As Augustine lay dying of a fever, the Vandals were literally at the gates of Hippo.

AUGUSTINE, *CITY OF GOD*

My first volume concluded with Augustine's *Confessions,* an autobiography which recounts his personal spiritual odyssey through the religious and philosophical options of the late classical world to faith in the Christian God. The Christian section of the second volume begins with Augustine's *City of God,* which is his treatment of the communal journey of the human family throughout history. A measure of the importance of this work is that its images of God, the human condition, history and eschatology (the final outcome of history) prevailed throughout the Christian Middle Ages in the West.

The occasion for Augustine's writing the *City of God* was the sack of Rome in 410 C.E. by Alaric the Visigoth. This event sent shock waves through the Western empire. In a matter of a few days the glorious ancient city, which had ruled the civilized world for centuries, collapsed. Learned pagans charged that the recent rejection of the ancient Roman gods by Christian emperors was the cause of the city's fall. Augustine's friend, Marcellinus, a Christian imperial commissioner in North Africa, urged him to write a refutation of the charges against Christianity. Augustine began the *City of God* in 412, but did not complete it until 426, just four years before his death. In the course of fourteen years, it grew into a monumental Christian theology of history in twenty-two books containing a number of digressions on a variety of subjects.

As an heir of Roman civilization who had taught its literature and studied its philosophers and historians, Augustine was no doubt personally saddened by the collapse of Rome. Yet, in the midst of this apparent tragedy, he had reason for hope. His Christian faith convinced him that history is not controlled by the all too fickle "gods" of ancient Rome, nor is it the result of capricious chance or an uncaring, impersonal fate. Augustine believed that the same providential God who had guided *his* life, as described in the *Confessions*, was directing *all* human history. Rome, for all its former political grandeur, represented in Augustine's Christian-Platonic outlook the temporal, earthly, and ultimately unsatisfying city of man which was destined for destruction in God's providential plan. Christian believers were to live in this world as pilgrims on their way to an eternal, heavenly, and fulfilling destiny in the City of God.

In Books 1–10 Augustine responds to the charges that the abandonment of the old Roman gods and the acceptance of the Christian God led to the fall of Rome. Throughout these books he uses Roman literary, philosophical and religious sources, such as Cicero and Virgil.

His argument in Books 1–5 is that the Roman gods are not to be worshiped for physical and moral advantages in this life. If the Roman gods could not save Troy, the city of their origin according to Virgil, then they could not save Rome. Following Roman philosophers like Varro, Augustine goes on to show that Rome's gods did not contribute to its moral welfare and in fact promoted vice. The list of troubles in Roman history, long before the coming of Christ, is evidence that the old gods also did not prevent physical evils. Augustine concludes this section by arguing that neither the old Roman gods nor fate was responsible for the growth of the empire, but that the Christian God gave temporary power to Rome for its earlier natural virtues.

In this context Augustine treats the problems of evil and God's providence. He is aware that apparently "God's gifts and man's brutalities oftentimes fall indifferently and indiscriminately to the lot of both the good and the bad." Augustine's solution to the problem is a paradoxical one. On the one hand, he insists on the freedom of humans in choosing good or evil; otherwise laws, punishment, praise and blame would be meaningless. But as a Christian believer, Augustine also insists that God's providential control of creation extends to his foreknowledge of history and its outcome. This foreknowledge, however, does not take away human freedom. God foreknows human actions as free choices:

> For no one sins because God foreknew that he would sin. In fact, the very reason why a man is undoubtedly responsible for his own sin, when he sins, is because he whose foreknowledge cannot be deceived foresaw, not the man's fate or fortune or what not, but that the man himself would be responsible for his own sin. No man sins unless it is his choice to sin; and his choice not to sin, that, too, God foresaw. (Book V.10)

For Augustine, then, the cause of evil is not, as it was for the Manichaeans, a power at war with the good God for control of the universe and human's lives. Rather, Augustine, as a Christian-Platonist, understands evil as an absence of a good which arises when creatures choose to sin by rebelling against the goodness of the Creator. Therefore, the atrocities of the barbarian sack, in which, for example, innocent Christian women were raped, are not due to their personal guilt, nor are they evidence that Christians should be blamed for the fall of the city. The real evil in the fall of Rome was not the physical sack of the city, but the interior collapse in the lives of the decadent Romans whose wills were given over to passion.

In Books 6–10 Augustine is dialoguing with pagan philosophers like Varro and the Neoplatonists, who themselves had been critical of the traditional mythology and political theology of the old Roman religion. His argument is that if the Roman gods could not give earthly happiness, then they are surely worthless for granting immortality. Of the pagan philosophers, Augustine has the greatest respect for Plato who, according to Augustine, had taught to know, love, and imitate God. However, he is very critical of the Platonists' proud refusal to acknowledge the incarnate Christ, who became a "slave" and died on a cross in order to become the universal mediator of salvation, and of their system of "demons," lesser divine beings who were intermediate between gods and humans. These "demons" were, according to Augustine, responsible for the immorality in pagan religion.

Our selections are taken from Books 11–22 where Augustine sets forth his own theology of history, and here his sources are primarily the Old and New Testaments. The second half of the the *City of God* is divided into three sections: the origins of the two cities (Books 11–14), their histories (Books 15–18), and their final ends (Books 19–22).

Throughout the second half Augustine uses scripture, the divine word of God, as a source of a higher revealed truth which transcends mere philosophical truth arrived at by human reason. This understanding of the superiority of the revelation in scripture to human reason will be standard in Christian medieval theology. Following earlier Christian fathers, Augustine also interprets the scriptures typologically; i.e., the stories and images of the Old and New Testaments are taken as symbols or archetypes for Augustine's Christian Neoplatonism.

Augustine uses the term "city" (*civitas*) to mean an assemblage of people bound together by an agreement in the object of their love. For him, all humanity—past, present and future—belongs to one of two cities. The earthly city, or the city of man, is the community of those who love the peace and happiness of this world and show contempt for God. The City of God is that community which loves God to the point where it can transcend the things of this world. Augustine's image of the two societies is heavily influenced by Platonic thought which distinguishes between the ephemeral and ultimately unreal physical world of shadows, and the eternal and real world of the forms.

In Books 11–12 Augustine locates the origin of the two cities and of evil in the power of the creature's will to choose evil over the goodness of the Creator. Like other early Christian theologians, Augustine believed that all angelic natures were initially made good, but some, including Satan, fell by a choice of their own liberty over a continued sharing in God's good nature. This explanation of evil as a lack of the perfection of God's goodness is more optimistic than the pessimism of the Manichaeans, who held that evil was a near equal and eternal power which God has been forced to struggle against from the beginning.

For the origin of the two cities on earth (Book 13), Augustine, of course, turns to the story of the fall of Adam in Genesis 2–3. By his sin of disobedience to God's command, Adam incurred both physical and spiritual death which he would not have suffered if he had remained obedient. According to Augustine, the consequences of Adam's original sin are not limited to him but affect all his descendants who are born with a flawed human nature which is subject to physical death, ignorance of God's will, and concupiscence, a tendency to turn from God to the inferior and transitory realities of the earth. For Augustine, who had to struggle to master his sexual drive, the primary manifestation of concupiscence was in the sexual appetite. He does not say that human nature is evil in itself; it is good because it was created by the all-good God. However, in its present fallen condition, human nature revolts against itself and the will of God. Using Platonic terms, Augustine describes this condition as the soul's being deprived of its original mastery over the body. Augustine identifies this duality in the human person with Paul's concept of the flesh lusting against the spirit (Gal 5:17).

In the conclusion of his treatment of the origin of the two cities Augustine discusses their respective natures. The City of God lives in obedience to God's will and is based on the love of God (*caritas*); the city of man makes man its own standard and ultimately worships power; it sets itself up as god and is based on love of the creature over the

Creator (*cupiditas*). Consequently, the City of God is destined for eternity, whereas the earthly city approaches nothingness.

The history of the two cities is traced in Books 15–18 by using a typological reading of the Old Testament. The founder of the earthly city was Cain, a fratricide who murdered his brother Abel out of jealousy and subsequently built the first earthly city (Gen 4). Cain is the type of all citizens of the city of man and of all humans who begin in the flesh as sinners. Abel, his younger brother, is the type of citizens of the City of God. He lived on earth as a pilgrim and built no city here; he was a citizen of the everlasting heavenly city. Correspondingly, Rome, the representative of the earthly city in Augustine's time, was also founded by the fratricide, Romulus, who murdered his brother Remus out of a desire to have the glory of founding the Roman Republic.

Augustine follows Paul in insisting that membership in the City of God, or salvation, is not because of any human merit, but is the result of God's gratuitous saving grace in Christ. For Augustine, this Pauline doctrine had been confirmed in his own experience, and he applies it to all individuals. All begin like Cain as members of the earthly city, but some, like Abel, are chosen to be members of the City of God.

> We all experience as individuals what the Apostle says: "It is not the spiritual that comes first, but the physical, and then the spiritual" (1 Cor 15:46). The fact is that every individual springs from a condemned stock and, because of Adam, must be first cankered and carnal, only later to become sound and spiritual by the process of rebirth in Christ (Book XV. 1).

Augustine's understanding of the process of salvation steers a careful middle course between the pessimistic outlook of his former Manichaeism and the optimism of Pelagianism, a heresy which he fought against throughout his career as a Christian bishop. The Manichaeans saw humans as victims of a primeval struggle between the coequal forces of good and evil. Augustine insisted that God's providential love could move the human will to reject evil. Pelagius, a British monk, opposed Augustine's doctrine of original sin by saying that humans were able to save themselves through simply doing the demands of God's law by an unaided act of the will. For Augustine, the Pelagian view was naively optimistic; once sin enters the world, humanity is powerless to overcome it. Following Paul, he believed that only through the unmerited gift of God's grace in Christ can humanity be saved from sin. In responding to that grace, however, humans are free. Augustine's doctrine of salvation paradoxically attempts to hold together two seemingly incompatible concepts: the predestining love of God for certain elect, and human freedom in responding to or rejecting the unmerited gift of God's grace.

According to Augustine, the two cities intermingle in the course of history. He traces their histories to the time of Christ and the founding of the church. The symbols for the city of man are Babylon and Rome, and for the City of God are Israel and the church, but in both cases these communities are not simply identified with the realities they symbolize. They are like the shadows in Plato's cave which point to the higher realities.

The true members of the two cities are known to God alone and will be revealed only at the judgment.

> With so many sinners mingled with the saints, all caught in the single fishing net the gospel mentions, this life on earth is like a sea in which good and bad fishes caught in a net swim about indistinguishably until the net is beached, and the bad ones are separated from the good. Only then does God so reign in the good, as in his temple, that He may be all in all (1 Cor 15:28). (Book XVIII. 49)

In the course of their interlocking histories, both cities must relate to the material goods of the world. The difference between the two cities is in their understandings of ultimate peace and happiness. The aim of the city of man is to strive by human strength alone for health, security, human fellowship and an ordered life for the individual and the state. These are relative goods for Augustine, but they do not bring ultimate happiness. The citizens of the earthly city make them the highest ends and worship them as if they were gods. This is a disordered love, according to Augustine, and can only lead to nothingness and frustration. The citizens of the City of God, by contrast, live by faith and hope as pilgrims in this world. They use the things of this world and keep step with the civil law insofar as it pertains to life here below, but they do not make this earthly life their ultimate end. In the Middle Ages this view of the relative importance of this world and the next world become integral to Christian consciousness.

Augustine's eschatology in Books 19–22 is an interesting combination of biblical and classical Greek and Roman ideas. In many ways Augustine's vision of the end of the City of God captures the spiritual aspirations of the ancient world. Following the New Testament tradition, he believes that history will end with a bodily resurrection and judgment which will punish and reward individuals on the basis of their deeds. His actual descriptions of the punishments of hell and the joys of heaven, however, are admittedly speculative and heavily influenced by classical Greek and Roman ideas. The end of the city of man will be what Augustine calls "a second death" because the soul will be separated from God, its life. Instead of eternal peace, the wicked will experience eternal warfare in their very persons so that the various parts of the soul, as Plato described them, will be continuously at war with one another without any of them winning victory. Augustine describes the end of the City of God as a perfect and fulfilling union with God and other humans in a justly ordered society. His vision of heaven is influenced by Plato's concept of justice as well as the Christian apocalyptic traditions and belief in a resurrection of the body. All the elect will be joined in the praise of God and "there shall be the enjoyment of beauty which appeals to reason." The resurrected bodies will be seemly in appearance and will be perfectly submissive to the will of the spirit. The person will find true peace in God. Even the Homeric values of love of honor and glory will be satisfied because all will be rewarded according to their just merits. Justice will be established because all will accept the fairness of God's judgment. The soul will be free in that it will be liberated from the enslaving power of sin.

Suffice it to say that this 'seventh day' will be our Sabbath and that it will end in no evening, but only in the Lord's day—that eighth and eternal day which dawned when Christ's resurrection heralded an eternal rest both for the spirit and for the body. On that day we shall rest and see, see and love, love and praise—for this is to be the end without the end of all our living, that Kingdom without end, the real goal of our present life. (Book XXII. 30)

The translation is by Demetrius B. Zema, *et al.* in *Writings of Saint Augustine* (The Fathers of the Church series: Washington: The Catholic University of America Press, 1950), Vol. 7, 99–101, 169–170, 187–188, 288–289, 410–411, 413–415, 420–422, Vol. 8, 226–229, 248, 505–507.

BOOK XI.1: SCRIPTURE TELLS US THAT THERE IS A CITY OF GOD

The expression, "City of God," which I have been using is justified by that Scripture whose divine authority puts it above the literature of all other people and brings under its sway every type of human genius—and that, not by some casual intellectual reaction, but by a disposition of Divine Providence. For, in this Scripture, we read: "Glorious things are said of the, O city of God" (Ps 86:3); and in another psalm: "Great is the Lord, and exceedingly to be praised in the city of our God, in His holy mountain, increasing the joy of the whole earth"; and, a little later in the same psalm: "As we have heard, so have we seen, in the city of the Lord of hosts, in the city of our God: God hath founded it for ever" (Ps 47:1,2,9); and in another text: "The stream of the river maketh the City of God joyful: the most high hath sanctified his own tabernacle. God is in the midst thereof, it shall not be moved" (Ps 45:5,6).

Through these and similar passages too numerous to quote, we learn of the existence of a City of God whose Founder has inspired us with a love and longing to become its citizens. The inhabitants of the earthly city who prefer their own gods to the Founder of the holy City do not realize that He is the God of gods—though not, of course, of those false, wicked and proud gods who, because they have been deprived of that unchangeable

light which was meant for all, are reduced to a pitiful power and, therefore, are eager for some sort of influence and demand divine honors from their deluded subjects. He is the God of those reverent and holy gods who prefer to obey and worship the God rather than to have many others obeying and worshiping them.

In the ten preceding Books, I have done my best, with the help of our Lord and King, to refute the enemies of this City. Now, however, realizing what is expected of me and recalling what I promised, I shall begin to discuss, as well as I can, the origin, history, and destiny of the respective cities, earthly and heavenly, which, as I have said, are at present inextricably intermingled, one with the other. First, I shall explain how these two cities originated when the angels took opposing sides.

BOOK XII.22: GOD CREATED ONE MAN AS THE ORIGIN OF THE HUMAN RACE AND MADE MAN'S ETERNITY DEPEND UPON HIS OBEDIENCE HERE

. . . He (God) created man with a nature midway between angels and beasts, so that man, provided he should remain subject to his true Lord and Creator and dutifully obey His commandments, might pass into the company of the angels, without the intervention of death, thus to attain a blessed and eternal immortality. But, should he offend his Lord and God by a proud and disobedient use of his free will, then, subject to death and a slave to his appetites, he would have to live like a beast and be destined to eternal punishment and death. Therefore, God created one sole individual, not that he was meant to remain alone deprived of human companionship, but in order that the unity of society and the bond of harmony might mean more to man, since men were to be united not only by the likeness of nature but also by the affection of kinship. God did not even wish to create the woman who was to be mated with man in the same way that He created man but, rather, out of him, in order that the whole human race might be derived entirely from one single individual.

BOOK XIII.13: THE SIN OF ADAM AND ITS CONSEQUENCES

As soon as our first parents had disobeyed God's commandment, they were immediately deprived of divine grace, and were ashamed of their nakedness. They covered themselves with fig leaves (Gen 3:7,10), which, perhaps, were the first thing noticed by the troubled pair. The parts covered remained unchanged except that, previously, they occasioned no shame. They felt for the first time a movement of disobedience in their flesh, as though the punishment were meant to fit the crime of their own disobedience to God.

The fact is that the soul, which had taken perverse delight in its own liberty and disdained the service of God, was now deprived of its original mastery over the body; because it had deliberately deserted the Lord who was over it, it no longer bent to its will the servant below it, being unable to hold the flesh completely in subjection as would always have been the case, if only the soul had remained subject to God. From this moment, then, the flesh began to lust against the spirit (Gal 5:17). With this rebellion we are born, just as

we are doomed to die and, because of the first sin, to bear, in our members and vitiated nature, either the battle with or defeat by the flesh.

BOOK XIV. 28: THE NATURE OF THE TWO CITIES

What we see, then, is that two societies have issued from two kinds of love. Worldly society has flowered from a selfish love which dared to despise even God, whereas the communion of saints is rooted in a love of God that is ready to trample on the self. In a word, this latter relies on the Lord, whereas the other boasts that it can get along by itself. The city of man seeks the praise of men, whereas the height of glory for the other is to hear God in the witness of conscience. The one lifts up its head in its own boasting; the other says to God: "Thou art my glory, thou liftest up my head."

In the city of the world both the rulers themselves and the people they dominate are dominated by the lust for domination; whereas in the City of God all citizens serve one another in charity, whether they serve by the responsibilities of office or by duties of obedience. The one city loves its leaders as symbols of its own strength; the other says to its God, "I love thee, O Lord, my strength" (Ps 17:2). Hence, even the wise men in the city of man live according to man, and their only goal has been the goods of their bodies or of the mind or of both; though some of them have reached a knowledge of God, "they did not glorify him as God or give thanks but became vain in their reasonings, and their senseless minds have been darkened. For while professing to be wise" (that is to say, while glorying in their own wisdom, under the domination of pride), "they have become fools, and they have changed the glory of the incorruptible God for an image made like to corruptible man and to birds and four-footed beasts and creeping things" (meaning that they either led their people, or imitate them, in adoring idols shaped like these things), "and they worshiped and served the creatures rather than the Creator who is blessed forever" (Rom 1:21–25). In the City of God, on the contrary, there is no merely human wisdom, but there is a piety which worships the true God as He should be worshiped and has as its goal that reward of all holiness whether in the society of saints on earth or in that of angels of heaven, which is "that God may be all" (1 Cor 15:28).

BOOK XV.1: THE FOUNDER OF THE EARTHLY
CITY WAS CAIN, A MURDERER

Now, the first man born of the two parents of the human race was Cain. He belonged to the city of man. The next born was Abel, and he was of the City of God. Notice here a parallel between the individual man and the whole race. We all experience as individuals what the Apostle says: "It is not the spiritual that comes first, but the physical, and then the spiritual" (1 Cor 15:46). The fact is that every individual springs from a condemned stock, and because of Adam, must be first cankered and carnal, only later to become sound and spiritual by the process of rebirth in Christ. So, too, with the human race as a whole, as soon as human birth and death began the historical course of the two cities, the first to be born was a citizen of this world and only later came the one who was an alien in the city of men but at home in the City of God, a man predestined by grace and elected by grace. By grace an alien on earth, by grace he was a citizen of heaven. In and of himself, he springs from the common clay, all of which was under condemnation from the beginning, but which God held in His hands like a potter, to borrow the metaphor which the Apostle so wisely and deliberately uses. For, God could make "from the same mass one vessel for hon-

orable, another for ignoble use" (Rom 9:21). The first vessel to be made was "for ignoble use." Only later was there a vessel for honorable use. And as with the race, so, as I have said, with the individual. First comes the clay that is only fit to be thrown away, with which we must begin, but in which we need not remain. Afterwards comes what is fit for use, that into which we can be gradually molded and in which, when molded, we may remain. This does not mean that every one who is wicked is to become good, but that no one becomes good who was not once wicked. What is true is that the sooner a man makes a change in himself for the better the sooner he has a right to be called what he has become. The second name hides the first.

Now, it is recorded of Cain that he built a city, while Abel, as though he were merely a pilgrim on earth, built none. For, the true City of the saints is in heaven, though here on earth it produces citizens in whom it wanders as on a pilgrimage through time looking for the Kingdom of eternity. When that day comes it will gather together all those who, rising in their bodies, shall have that kingdom given to them in which, along with their Prince, the King of Eternity, they shall reign for ever and ever.

BOOK XV.5: THE FRATRICIDAL ACT OF THE
FOUNDER OF THE EARTHLY CITY AND THE
CORRESPONDING CRIME OF THE
FOUNDER OF ROME

Now, the city of man was first founded by a fratricide who was moved by envy to kill his brother, a man who, in his pilgrimage on earth, was a citizen of the City of God. It need not surprise us, then, that long afterwards, in the founding of that city which was to dominate so many peoples and become the capital of that earthly city with which I am dealing, the copy, so to speak, corresponded to the original—to what the Greeks call the archetype.

For, in both cases, we have the same crime. As one of the poets puts it: "With brother's blood the earliest walls were wet" (Lucan, *Pharsalia* 1.95). For Rome began, as Roman history records, when Remus was killed by Romulus, his brother. However, in this case, both men were citizens of the earthly city. It was the ambition of both of them to have the honor of founding the Roman republic, but that was an honor that could not be shared; it had to belong to one or the other. For, no one who had a passion to glory in domination could be fully the master if his power were diminished by a living co-regent. One of the two wanted to have the whole of the sovereignty; therefore, his associate was removed. Without the crime, his position would have had less power, but more prestige. However, the crime made everything worse than before.

In the case of the brothers Cain and Abel, there was no rivalry in any cupidity for the things of earth, nor was there any envy or temptation to murder arising from a fear of losing the sovereignty if both were ruling together. In this case, Abel had no ambition for domination in the city that his brother was building. The root of the trouble was that diabolical envy which moves evil men to hate those who are good for no other reason than that they are good. Unlike material possessions, goodness is not diminished when it is shared, either momentarily or permanently, with others, but expands and, in fact the more heartily each of the lovers of goodness enjoys the possession the more does goodness grow. What is more, goodness is not merely a possession that no one can maintain who is unwilling to share it, but it is one that increases the more its possessor loves to share it.

What, then, is revealed in the quarrel between Remus and Romulus is the way in which the city of man is divided against itself, whereas, in the case of Cain and Abel, what we see is the enmity between the two cities, the city of man and the City of God. Thus, we have two wars, that of the wicked at war with the wicked and that of the wicked at war with the good. For, of course, once the good are perfectly good, there can be no war between them. This much is true, however, that while a good man is still on the way to perfection one part of him can be at war with another of his parts; because of this rebellious element, two good men can be at war with each other. The fact is that in every one "the flesh lusts against the spirit, and the spirit against the flesh" (Gal 5:17).

The spiritual longing of one good man can be at war with the fleshly passion of another just as fleshly passion in one man can resist spiritual tendencies in another. And the war here is much like that between good and wicked men. So, too, a good deal like the war of the wicked against the wicked is the rivalry of fleshly desires in two good men, and this will continue until grace wins the ultimate victory of soundness over sickness in both of them.

BOOK XIX.17: WHAT PRODUCES PEACE AND DISCORD BETWEEN THE HEAVENLY AND EARTHLY CITIES

While the homes of unbelieving men are intent upon acquiring temporal peace out of the possessions and comforts of this temporal life, the families which live according to faith look ahead to the good things of heaven promised as imperishable, and use material and temporal goods in the spirit of pilgrims, not as snares or obstructions to block their way to God, but simply as helps to ease and never to increase the burdens of this corruptible body which weighs down the soul. Both types of homes and their masters have this in common, that they must use things essential to this mortal life. But the respective purposes to which they put them are characteristic and very different.

So, too, the earthly city which does not live by faith seeks only an earthly peace, and limits the goal of its peace, of its harmony, of authority and obedience among its citizens, to the voluntary and collective attainment of objectives necessary to mortal existence. The heavenly City, meanwhile—or, rather,—that part that is on pilgrimage in immortal life and lives by faith—must use this earthly peace until such time as our mortality which needs such peace has passed away. As a consequence, so long as her life in the earthly city is that of a captive and an alien (although she has the promise of ultimate delivery and the gift of the Spirit as a pledge), she has no hesitation about keeping step with the civil law which governs matters pertaining to our existence here below. For, as mortal life is the same for all, there ought to be common cause between the two cities in what concerns our purely human living.

Now comes the difficulty. The city of this world, to begin with, has had certain "wise men" of its own mold, whom true religion must reject, because either out of their own day-dreaming or out of demonic deception these wise men came to believe that a multiplicity of divinities was allied with human life, with different duties, in some strange arrangement, and different assignments: this one over the body, that one over the mind; in the body itself, one over the head, another over the neck, still others, one for each bodily part; in the mind, one over the intelligence, another over learning, another over temper, another over desire; in the realities, related to life, that lie about us, one over flocks and one over wheat, one over wine, one over oil, and another over forests, one over currency, another over navigation, and still another over warfare and victory, one over marriage, a different one over fecundity and childbirth, so on and so on.

The heavenly City, on the contrary, knows and, by religious faith, believes that it must adore one God alone and serve Him with that complete dedication which the Greeks call *latreia* and which belongs to Him alone. As a result, she has been unable to share with the earthly city a common religious legislation, and has had no choice but to dissent on this score and so to become a nuisance to those who think otherwise. Hence, she has had to feel the weight of their anger, hatred, and violence, save in those instances when, by sheer numbers and God's help, which never fails, she has been able to scare off her opponents.

So long, then, as the heavenly City is wayfaring on earth, she invites citizens from all nations and all tongues, and unites them into a single pilgrim band. She takes no issue with that diversity of customs, laws, and traditions whereby human peace is sought and maintained. Instead of nullifying or tearing down, she preserves and appropriates whatever in the diversities of divers races is aimed at one and the same objective of human peace, provided only that they do not stand in the way of the faith and worship of the one supreme and true God.

BOOK XIX.28: THE END OF THE WICKED

On the other hand, the doom in store for those who are not of the City of God is an unending wretchedness that is called "the second death," because neither in the soul, cut off from the life of God, nor in the body, pounded by perpetual pain, can there be said to be life at all. And what will make that second death so hard to bear is that there will be no death to end it.

Now, since unhappiness is the reverse of happiness, death of life, and war of peace, one may reasonably ask: If peace is praised and proclaimed as the highest good, what kind of warfare are we to think of as the highest evil? If this inquirer will reflect, he will realize that what is hurtful and destructive in warfare is mutual clash and conflict, and, hence, that no one can imagine a war more unbearably bitter than one in which the will and passions are at such odds that neither can ever win the victory, and in which violent pain and the body's very nature will so clash that neither will ever yield. When this conflict occurs on earth, either pain wins and death puts an end to all feeling, or nature wins and health removes the pain. But, in hell, pain permanently afflicts and nature continues to feel it, for neither ever comes to term, since the punishment must never end.

BOOK XXII.30: THE ETERNAL HAPPINESS OF THE CITY OF GOD

Who can measure the happiness of heaven, where no evil at all can touch us, no good will be out of reach; where life is to be one long laud extolling God, who will be all in all; where there will be no weariness to call for rest, no need to call for toil, no place for any energy but praise. Of this I am assured whenever I read or hear the sacred song: "Blessed are they that dwell in thy house, O Lord: they shall praise thee forever and ever" (Ps 83:5). Every fiber and organ of our imperishable body will play its part in the praising of God. On earth these varied organs have each a special function, but, in heaven, function will be swallowed up in felicity, in the perfect certainty of an untroubled everlastingness of joy. Even those muted notes in the diapason of the human organ, which I mentioned earlier, will swell into a great hymn of praise to the supreme Artist who has fashioned us, within

and without, in every fiber, and who, by this and every other element of magnificent and marvelous Order, will ravish our minds with spiritual beauty.

These movements of our bodies will be of such unimaginable beauty that I dare not say more than this: There will be such poise, such grace, such beauty as become a place where nothing unbecoming can be found. Wherever the spirit wills, there, in a flash, will the body be. Nor will the spirit ever will anything unbecoming either to itself or to the body.

In heaven, all glory will be true glory, since no one could err in praising too little or too much. True honor will never be denied where due, never be given where undeserved, and, since none but the worthy are permitted there, no one will unworthily ambition glory. Perfect peace will reign, since nothing in ourselves or in any others could disturb this peace. The promised reward of virtue will be the best and greatest of all possible prizes— the very Giver of virtue Himself, for that is what the Prophet meant: "I will be your God and you shall be my people" (Lev 26:12). God will be the source of every satisfaction, more than any heart can rightly crave, more than life and health, food and wealth, glory and honor, peace and every good—so that God, as St. Paul said, "may be all in all" (1 Cor 15:28). He will be the consummation of all our desiring—the object of our unending praise. And in this gift of vision, this response of love, the paean of praise, all alike will share, as all will share in everlasting life. . . .

BOETHIUS, *CONSOLATION OF PHILOSOPHY*

Like Augustine of Hippo, Boethius (c. 480–524 C.E.) is a key transitional figure in the thought of Western civilization. He is appropriately called the "last of the Romans and first of the scholastics" because he was dedicated to preserving dying Roman political order and the philosophical wisdom of the Greeks for the Latin West. His writings gave the medieval world much of what it was to know of classical philosophy for the next six hundred years.

During Boethius' life the last remnants of the old Roman order were dying. Born into a noble Roman family which had been Christian since the time of Constantine, Boethius himself had the benefit of a fine classical training in Greek thought, but within a few years the Byzantine emperor, Justinian, would close the Academy in Athens because it represented purely "pagan" learning. By the sixth century Roman political control in the West had collapsed and was being replaced by a series of Germanic successor states. Although Boethius would have preferred a life of scholarship, he served as a trusted political adviser to the barbarian king, Theodoric the Ostrogoth. In 523, however, he was accused of treason against the king, arrested, and cruelly tortured to death without trial.

Before his premature death, Boethius only partially succeeded in realizing his ambitious goal of translating from Greek into Latin all of Plato and Aristotle with commentaries in order to reconcile them on those points where they differed. He did finish translations of Porphyry's *Introduction to the Categories of Aristotle* and Aristotle's works on logic, and it was only through these translations that Aristotle's thought survived in the West until the twelfth century when Islamic and Jewish scholars in Spain reintroduced his thought. Boethius' works also included commentaries on Cicero, textbooks on arithmetic and music, and theological works on the Trinity and the Catholic faith.

Boethius' most important work was his *Consolation of Philosophy,* which he wrote while under arrest for charges of treason against Theodoric. In contrast to Augustine who turns to his Christian faith when dealing with the catastrophe of Rome's fall in the *City of God,* Boethius, although a Christian, chooses to find his consolation in a philosophical meditation on the problem of evil in a universe supposedly created and ruled by a just and good God. Boethius skillfully fuses several classical literary forms including the dialogue, the *consolatio* (a kind of moral meditation), the dream vision (see for example, Cicero's *Dream of Scipio*), and what is called Menippean Satire—a form of composition in which sections of prose alternate with verse. His philosophical ideas are a typically Roman eclectic combination of Plato, Aristotle, the Stoics, the Cynics, and probably Augustine. He never explicitly quotes scripture, the Christian fathers, nor the unique doctrines of the Christian faith.

Borrowing from Parmenides and Plato, as well as Roman authors, the *Consolation* takes the form of a dialogue between a disheartened Boethius and Philosophy who appears to him in the form of a lovely woman. Her appearance is allegorical. The transcendent power of philosophical reason is indicated in Lady Philosophy's majestic countenance and gleaming eyes which "surpassed in power of insight those of ordinary mortals." Her practical applicability, yet theoretical foundation are symbolized by her varying height and the two Greek letters, *pi* and *theta,* and the ladder connecting them which are woven on the border of her garment. Philosophy's ageless, yet perennial, character is aptly noted in that her "color was full of life" and her "strength was still intact though she was so full of years that by no means would it be believed that she was of our times." Lady Philosophy's beautiful garment, "woven with her own hand," illustrates her capacity to come to conclusions solely by the powers of reason. Finally, the dimmed and smoke-grimed color of her garments shows the long neglect of philosophical reasoning in Boethius' own time.

In Book 1 Lady Philosophy responds to Boethius' lament by diagnosing his illness like a physician treating a patient. Her tactics are drawn from both Platonic and Stoical philosophy. She first of all banishes the passionate Muses who inspired his opening lament; their poisonous passions have fostered his sorrows which can only be cured by reason. When Boethius finally has the power to ask Philosophy the reason for her descent to him in his "lonely place of banishment," she reminds him that philosophers have always suffered at the hands of the uninitiated herd. Boethius goes on to complain that he is suffering unjustly because his actions while in office were blameless, and he passionately demands to know why his innocence has received the punishment for vice, while criminals are "encouraged by impunity to dare any crime." Using the Platonic principles of dialectical reasoning and remembrance, Philosophy begins the long process of curing Boethius by reminding him that his external circumstances are not the cause of his problems. He has allowed himself to wander from that recollected inner state in which Lady Philosophy had placed a store of truths in his mind. She begins to restore this state by asking probing questions which force him to remember his convictions that the world is not governed by chance, but by a reasonable Creator who is the origin and goal to which all Nature tends. When Lady Philosophy goes on to ask Boethius to explain what a man is, he formulates an only partially correct definition that man is "an animal, rational and mortal." This interrogation leads Lady Philosophy to conclude that Boethius' sickness is caused by his forgetting the answers to certain basic questions: who he is as a man? what is the end of all things? and what is the means by which the world is governed? The fact that Boethius believes that the world is governed by divine reason, and not by chance, will be the tiny spark by which his vital fire will be rekindled.

In Book 2 Lady Philosophy explains the fickle nature of Fortune and the reasons happiness does not consist in the possession of her false goods. She begins by explaining that Boethius' sickness is caused by his longing for his former fortune. Because he thinks Fortune has changed toward him, he has lost his peace of mind. Lady Philosophy then speaks for Fortune in her own voice and explains that her very nature is like a turning wheel. At times she gives external gifts like wealth and honors, but at other times she may take them back. In any case, none of her gifts really belong to man by his nature. If Boethius wants happiness, which is possession of the highest Good, he must seek something beyond the unstable and external gifts of Fortune. Riches, power, high office, and fame are all false goods because the pursuit of them can demean and corrupt man, and none of them can bring lasting happiness.

In Book 3, which will not be included in this volume, Philosophy leads Boethius to see the nature of true happiness. She recalls for him that all men know that the true good is happiness, and all seek it, but, for the most part, by the wrong routes. Even the false paths, such as wealth, glory or fame, show that men have some idea of the truth; for the true good has features of each of these. Eventually she leads Boethius to the position that the whole and perfect Good is God, of which other goods are merely fragments or shadows. Humans then become happy by becoming God-like, that is by sharing or participating in the divine virtues of wisdom and justice. In the course of this proof, Lady Philosophy states as axiomatic the Platonic principle that all perfect things are prior to all imperfect things, a principle that will later form the basis for St. Anselm's ontological argument for God's existence.

In Book 4, which will not be included in this volume, Boethius complains that the doctrine of Divine Providence only aggravates the problem. Why, he asks, is justice so apparently lacking in the course of events? Philosophy's answer is twofold. First of all, she argues that virtue and vice are their own rewards. The good are always rewarded and the evil always punished by simply being what they are: good or evil. And, this reward or punishment will extend into eternity, because the soul is immortal. Secondly, Lady Philosophy makes an important distinction between Providence and Fate. Providence is the divine reason itself which arranges all things and dwells in God the supreme Director, who, as in Neoplatonism, is imaged as the center of a circle. Fate, on the other hand, is the disposition inherent in mutable things through which Providence binds everything to its decrees. The evolution of the temporal order unified in the divine mind is Providence. These same developments when considered from the perspective of the material world are a part of Fate. Humans live in the temporal order and they think that the wicked flourish and the innocent suffer. But they do not know who are the wicked and who are the innocent, still less what either needs. All fortune, seen from the divine center, is good and healing. The type we call "bad" drives good men and curbs bad ones—if they will cooperate with Providence. Thus, if humans participate in Providence more and suffer Fate less, it lies within their power to make of their fortune what they please.

The conclusion of Book 4 leaves Boethius with another difficulty. If God's Providence foresees all my actions, how am I free to act other than he has foreseen? To answer this formidable question, in Book 5 Lady Philosophy first observes that the character of knowledge depends, not on the object known, but on the capacity of the knower. Humans can only see things from the perspective of existence in time; they do not embrace this life as a simultaneous whole, and they do not grasp the future which is yet to be lived through. God, by contrast, has an ever-present eternal state in which he sees all (past, present, and future) in a single eternal now. God's seeing in an eternal present all that will unfold does not impose necessity on events from the perspective of those acting in time. One and the same act is necessary from the perspective of God's foreknowledge, but free when it is examined in its own nature. God is the ever prescient spectator of all things. To reiterate the importance of human freedom, Lady Philosophy ends with an exhortation that hope and prayers are not vain and calls upon Boethius to turn from vice to cultivate virtue because he lives under the eyes of a Judge who discerns all.

The immense importance of Boethius' reasoned approach to the problem of theodicy (a rational attempt to explain how an all-good and all-powerful God can permit evil and innocent suffering) is probably best seen in its popularity in the Middle Ages and beyond. Until the recovery of the works of Aristotle in the High Middle Ages, *The Consolation of Philosophy* was one of the few sources of information about the Greek tradition. Phrases and ideas from it are found in almost all the important works of medieval literature, and it was frequently translated into vernacular languages, most notably by King Alfred (c. 890) Chaucer (c. 1380) and by Queen Elizabeth I.

The translation is by H.F. Stewart, D.D., *Boethius: The Consolation of Philosophy* in *The Loeb Classical Library* (Cambridge, Massachusetts: Harvard University Press, 1918).

THE FIRST BOOK OF
BOETHIUS
CONTAINING HIS COMPLAINT AND MISERIES

I

I that with youthful heat did verses write,
Must now my woes in doleful tunes indite.
My work is framed by Muses torn and rude,
And my sad cheeks are with true tears
    bedewed:
For these alone no terror could affray
From being partners of my weary way.
The art that was my young life's joy and glory
Becomes my solace now I'm old and sorry;
Sorrow has filched my youth from me, the
    thief!
My days are numbers not by time but Grief.
Untimely hoary hairs cover my head,
And my loose skin quakes on my flesh half
    dead.
O happy death, that spareth sweetest years,
And comes in sorrow often called with tears.
Alas, how deaf is he to wretch's cries;
And loath he is to close up weeping eyes;
While trustless chance me with vain favours
    crowned,
that saddest hour my life had almost drowned:
Now she hath clouded her deceitful face,
My spiteful days prolong their weary race.
My friends, why did you count me fortunate?
He that is fallen, ne'er stood in settled state.

I

(Philosophy's appearance)
While I ruminated these things with myself, and determined to set forth my woeful complaint in writing, methought I saw a woman stand above my head, having a grave countenance, glistening clear eye, and of quicker sight than commonly Nature doth afford; her colour fresh and bespeaking unabated vigour, and yet discovering so many years, that she could not at all be thought to belong to our times; her stature uncertain and doubtful, for sometime she exceeded not the common height of men, and sometime she seemed to touch the heavens with her head, and if she lifted it up to the highest, she pierced the very heavens, so that she could not be seen by the beholders; her garments were made of most fine threads with cunning workmanship into an ever-during stuff, which (as I knew afterward by her own report) she had woven with her own hands. A certain duskishness caused by negligence and time had darkened their colour, as it is wont to happen when pictures stand in a smokey room. In the lower part of them was placed the Greek letter Π, and in the upper θ, and betwixt the two letters, in the manner of stairs, there were certain degrees made, by which there was a passage from the lower to the higher letter: this her garment had been cut by the violence of some, who had taken away such pieces as they could get. In her right hand she had certain books, and in her left hand she held a sceptre.

This woman, seeing the poetical Muses standing about my bed, and suggesting words to my tears, being moved for a little space, and inflamed with angry looks: "Who," saith she, "hath permitted these tragical harlots to have access to this sick man, which will not only not comfort his grief with wholesome remedies, but also nourish them with sugared poison? For these be they which with the fruitless thorns of affections do kill the fruitful crop of reason, and do accustom men's minds to sickness, instead of curing them. But if your flattery did deprive us of some profane fellow, as commonly it happeneth, I should think that it were not so grievously to be taken, for in him our labours should receive no harm. But now have you laid hold of him who hath been brought up in Eleatical and Academical studies? Rather get you gone, you Sirens pleasant even to destruction, and leave him to my Muses to be cured and healed."

That company being thus checked, overcome with grief, casting their eyes upon the ground, and bewraying their bashfulness with blushing, went sadly away. But I, whose sight was dimmed with tears, so that I could not discern what this woman might be, so imperious, and of such authority, was astonished, and, fixing my countenance upon the earth, began to expect with silence what she would do afterward. Then she coming nigher, sat down at my bed's feet, and beholding my countenance sad with mourning, and cast upon the ground with grief, complained of the perturbation of my mind with these verses.

II

Alas, how thy dull mind is headlong cast
In depths of woe, where, all the light once lost,
She doth to walk in utter darkness haste,
While cares grow great with earthly tempests tost.
He that through the opened heavens did freely run,
And used to travel the celestial ways,
Marking the rosy splendour of the sun,
And noting Cynthia's cold and watery rays;
He that did bravely comprehend in verse
the different spheres and wandering course of stars,
He that was wont the causes to rehearse

Why sounding winds do with the seas make wars,
What spirit moves the world's well-settled frame,
And why the sun, whom forth the east doth bring,
In western waves doth hide his falling flame,
Searching what power tempers the passing Spring
Which makes the earth her rosy flowers to bear,
Whose gift it is that Autumn's fruitful season
Should with full grapes flow in a plenteous year,
Telling of secret Nature every reason,
Now having lost the beauty of his mind
Lies with his neck compassed in ponderous chains;
His countenance with heavy weight declined,
Him to behold the sullen earth constrains.

II

"But it is rather time," saith she, "to apply remedies, than to make complaints." And then looking wistfully upon me: "Art thou he," saith she, "which, being long since nursed with our milk, and brought up with our nourishments, wert come to man's estate? But we had given thee such weapons as, if thou hadst not cast them away, would have made thee invincible. Dost thou not know me? Why dost thou not speak? Is it shamefastness or insensibleness that makes thee silent? I had rather it were shamefastness, but I perceive thou art become insensible." And seeing me not only silent but altogether mute and dumb, fair and easily she laid her hand upon my breast saying: "There is no danger; he is in a lethargy, the common disease of deceived minds; he hath a little forgot himself, but he will easily remember himself again, if he be brought to know us first. To which end, let us a little wipe his eyes, dimmed with the cloud of mortal things." And having thus said, with a corner of her garment she dried my eyes which were wet with tears.

III

Then fled the night and darkness did me
    leave,
Mine eyes their wonted strength receive,
As when swift Corus spreads the stars with
    clouds
And the clear sky a veil of tempest shrouds
The sun doth lurk, the earth receiveth night,
Lacking the boon of starry light;
But if fierce Boreas, sent from Thrace, make
    way
For the restoring of the day,
Phoebus with fresh and sudden beams doth
    rise,
Striking with light our wondering eyes.

III

(Boethius gains the power to address
Philosophy)

In like manner, the mists of sadness dissolved, I came to myself and recovered my judgment, so that I knew my Physician's face; wherefore casting mine eyes upon her somewhat steadfastly, I beheld my nurse Philosophy, in whose house I had remained from my youth, and I said: "O Mistress of all virtues, for what cause art thou come from heaven into this our solitary banishment? Art thou come to bear me company in being falsely accused?"

"Should I," saith she, "forsake thee, my disciple, and not divide the burden, which thou bearest through hatred of my name, by partaking of thy labour? But Philosophy never thought it lawful to forsake the innocent in his trouble. Should I fear any accusations, as though this were any new matter? For dost thou think that this is the first time that Wisdom hath been exposed to danger by wicked men? Have we not in ancient times before our Plato's age had oftentimes great

conflicts with the rashness of folly? And while he lived, had not his master Socrates the victory of an unjust death in my presence, whose inheritance, when afterward the mob of Epicures, Stoics, and others (every one for his own sect) endeavoured to usurp, and as it were in part of their prey, sought to draw me to them, exclaiming and striving against them; they tore the garment which I had woven with my own hands, and having gotten some little pieces of it, thinking me to be wholly in their possession, departed. Some of whom, because certain signs of my apparel appeared upon them, were rashly supposed to be my familiar friends, and condemned accordingly through the error of the profane multitude.

But if thou hast not heard of the flight of Anaxagoras, the poison of Socrates, nor the torments of Zeno, because they are foreign examples; yet thou mayst have heard of Canius, of Seneca, of Soranus, whose memory is both fresh and famous, whom nothing else brought to their overthrow but that they had been instructed in our school and were altogether disliking to the humours of wicked men; wherefore thou hast no cause to marvel, if in the sea of this life we be tossed with boisterous storms, whose chiefest purpose is to displease the wicked; of which though there be an huge army, yet it is to be despised, because it is not governed by any captain, but is carried up and down by fantastical error without any order at all. And if at any time they assail us with great force, our captain retireth her band into a castle, leaving them occupied in sacking unprofitable baggage. And from above we laugh them to scorn for seeking so greedily after most vile things, being safe from all their furious assault, and fortified with that defence which aspiring folly cannot prevail against.

IV

"Understandest thou these things," saith she, "and do they make impression in thy mind? Art thou 'like the ass, deaf to the lyre'? Why weepest thou? Why sheddest thou so many tears? Speak out; hide not thy thoughts. If thou expectest to be cured, thou must discover thy wound."

(Boethius complains to Philosophy.)

Then I, collecting the forces of my mind together, made her answer in these words: "Doth the cruelty of fortune's rage need further declaration, or doth it not sufficiently appear of itself? Doth not the very countenance of this place move thee? Is this the library which thou thyself hadst chosen to sit in at my house, in which thou hast oftentimes discoursed with me of the knowledge of divine and human things? Had I this attire or countenance when I searched the secrets of nature with thee, when thou describedst unto me the course of the stars with thy geometrical rod, when thou didst frame my conversation and the manner of my whole life according to the pattern of the celestial order? Are these the rewards which thy obedient servants have? But thou didst decree that sentence by the mouth of Plato: That commonwealths should be happy, if either the students of wisdom did govern them, or those which were appointed to govern them would give themselves to the study of wisdom. Thou by the same philosopher didst admonish us that it is a sufficient cause for wise men to take upon themselves the government of the commonwealth, lest, if the rule of cities were left in the hands of lewd and wicked citizens, they should work the subversion and overthrow of the good.

Wherefore, following this authority, I desired to practise that by public administration which I had learnt of thee in private conference. Thou and God Himself who had inserted thee in the minds of the wise, are my witnesses that nothing but the common desire of all good men brought me to be a magistrate. This hath been the cause of my grievous and irreconcilable disagreements with wicked men, and that which freedom of conscience carrieth with it, of ever condemning the indignation of potentates for the defence of justice.

V

(Philosophy reassures him and asks questions.)

When I had uttered these speeches with continued grief, she, with an amiable countenance and nothing moved with my complaints, said: "When I first saw thee sad and weeping, I forthwith knew thee to be in misery and banishment. But I had not known how far off thou wert banished, if thy speech had not betrayed it. O how far art thou gone from thy country, not being driven away, but wandering of thine own accord! Or if thou hadst rather be thought to have been driven out, it hath been only by thyself; for never could any other but thyself have done it; for if thou rememberest of what country thou art, it is not governed as Athens was wont to be, by the multitude, but 'one is its ruler, one its king,' who desires to have abundance or citizens, and not to have them driven away. To be governed by whose authority, and to be subject to her laws, is the greatest freedom that can be. Art thou ignorant of that most ancient law of thy city, by which it is decreed that he may not be banished that hath made choice of it for his dwelling-place; for he that is within her fort or hold need not fear lest he deserve to be banished? But whosoever ceaseth to desire to dwell in it, ceaseth likewise to deserve so great a benefit. Wherefore the countenance of this place moveth me not so much as thy countenance doth. Neither do I much require thy library adorned with ivory adornments, and its crystal walls, as the seat of thy mind, in which I have not placed books, but that which makes books to be esteemed of, I mean the sentences of my books, which were written long since. And that which thou hast said of thy deserts to the common good, is true indeed, but little in respect of the many things which thou hast done.

VI

First, therefore, wilt thou let me touch and try the state of thy mind by asking thee a few questions, that I may understand how thou art to be cured?" To which I answered: "Ask me what questions thou wilt, and I will answer thee." And then she said: "Thinkest thou that this world is governed by haphazard and chance? Or rather dost thou believe that it is ruled by reason?" "I can," quoth I, "in no manner imagine that such certain motions are caused by rash chance. And I know that God the Creator doth govern His work, nor shall the day ever come to draw me from the truth of that judgment."

"It is so," saith she, "for so thou saidst in thy verse a little before, and bewailedst that only men were void of God's care; for as for the rest, thou didst not doubt but that they were governed by reason. And surely I cannot choose but exceedingly admire how thou canst be ill affected, holding so wholesome an opinion. But let us search further; I guess thou wantest something, but I know not what.

Tell me, since thou doubtest not that the world is governed by God, canst thou tell me also by what means it is governed?" "I do scarcely," quoth I, "understand what thou askest, and much less am I able to make thee a sufficient answer." "Wast I," quoth she, "deceived in thinking that thou wantedst something by which, as by the breach of a fortress, the sickness of perturbations hath entered into thy mind? But tell me, dost thou remember what is the end of things? Or to what the whole intention of nature tendeth?" "I have heard it," quoth I, "but grief hath dulled my memory." "But knowest thou from whence all things had their beginning?" "I know," quoth I, and answered, that from God. "And how can it be that, knowing the beginning, thou canst be ignorant of the end? But this is the condition and force of perturbations, that they may alter a man, but wholly

destroy, and as it were root him out of himself, they cannot.

But I would have thee answer me to this also; dost thou remember that thou art a man?" "Why should I not remember it?" quoth I. "Well then, canst thou explicate what man is?" "Dost thou ask me if I know that I am a reasonable and mortal living creature? I know and confess myself to be so." To which she replied: "Dost thou not know thyself to be anything else?" "Not anything."

"Now I know," quoth she, "another, and that perhaps the greatest, cause of thy sickness: thou hast forgotten what thou art. Wherefore I have fully found out both the manner of thy disease and the means of thy recovery; for the confusion which thou art in, by the forgetfulness of thyself, is the cause why thou art so much grieved at thy exile and the loss of thy goods. And because thou art ignorant what is the end of things, thou thinkest that lewd and wicked men be powerful and happy; likewise, because thou hast forgotten by what means the world is governed, thou imaginest that these alternations of fortune do fall out without any guide, sufficient causes not only of sickness, but also of death itself. But thanks be to the author of thy health, that Nature hath not altogether forsaken thee. We have the greatest nourisher of thy health, the true opinion of the government of the world, in that thou believest that it is not subject to the events of chance, but to divine reason. Wherefore fear nothing; out of this little sparkle will be enkindled thy vital heat. But because it is not yet time to use more solid remedies, and it is manifest that the nature of minds is such that as often as they cast away true opinions they are possessed with false, out of which the darkness of perturbations arising doth make them that they cannot discern things aright, I will endeavour to dissolve this cloud with gentle and moderate fomentations; that having removed the obscurity of deceitful affections, thou mayest behold the splendour of true light."

THE SECOND BOOK OF BOETHIUS

I

(Philosophy proves that Boethius' grief is not justified in one of her followers.)

After this she remained silent for a while; and, having by that her modesty made me attentive, began in this wise: "If I be rightly informed of the causes and condition of thy disease, thou languishest with the affection of thy former fortune, and the change of that alone, as thou imaginest, hath over-thrown so much of thy mind. . . .

If thou thinkest that fortune hath altered her manner of proceeding toward thee, thou art in an error. This was always her fashion; this is her nature. She hath kept that constancy in thy affairs which is proper to her, in being mutable; such was her condition when she fawned upon thee and allured thee with enticements of feigned happiness. Thou hast discovered the doubtful looks of this blind goddess. She, which concealeth herself from others, is wholly known to thee. If thou likest her, frame thyself to her conditions, and make no complaint. If thou detestest her treachery, despise and cast her off, with her pernicious flattery. For that which hath caused thee so much sorrow should have brought thee to great tranquility. For she hath forsaken thee, of whom no man can be secure. Dost thou esteem that happiness precious which thou art to lose? And is the present fortune dear unto thee, of whose stay thou art not sure, and whose departure will breed thy grief? And if she can neither be kept at our will, and maketh them miserable whom she at last leaveth, what else is fickle fortune but a token of future calamity? For it is not sufficient to behold that which we have before our eyes; wisdom pondereth the event of things, and

this mutability on both sides maketh the threats of fortune not to be feared, nor her flatterings to be desired. Finally, thou must take in good part whatsoever happeneth unto thee within the reach of fortune, when once thou has submitted thy neck to her yoke. And if to her whom, of thine own accord, thou hast chosen for thy mistress, thou wouldst prescribe a law how long she were to stay, and when to depart, shouldst thou not do her mighty wrong, and with thy impatience make thy estate more intolerable, which thou canst not better? If thou settest up thy sails to the wind, thou shalt be carried not whither thy will desirest, but whither the gale driveth. If thou sowest thy seed, thou considerest that there are as well barren as fertile years. Thou hast yielded thyself to fortune's sway; thou must be content with the conditions of thy mistress. Endeavourest thou to stay the force of the turning wheel? But thou foolishest man that ever was, if it beginneth to stay, it ceasest to be fortune."

II

(Philosophy speaks for Fortune.)

"But I would urge thee a little with Fortune's own speeches. Wherefore consider thou if she asketh not reason. 'For what cause, O man, chargest thou me with daily complaints? What injury have I done thee? What goods of thine have I taken from thee? Contend with me before any judge about the possession of riches and dignities; and if thou canst show that the propriety of any of these things belong to any mortal wight, I will forthwith willingly grant that those things which thou demandest were thine. When Nature produced thee out of thy mother's womb, I received thee naked and poor in all respects, cherished thee with my wealth, and (which maketh thee now to fall out with me) being forward to favour thee, I had most tender care for thy education, and adorned thee with the abundance and splendour of all things which are in my power. Now it pleaseth me to withdraw my hand, yield thanks, as one that hath had the use of that which was not his own. Thou hast no just cause to complain, as though thou hadst lost that which was fully thine own. Wherefore lamentest thou? I have offered thee no violence. Riches, honours, and the rest of that sort belong to me. They acknowledge me for their mistress, and themselves for my servants, they come with me, and when I go away they likewise depart. I may boldly affirm, if those things which thou complainest to be taken from thee had been thine own, thou shouldst never have lost them. Must I only be forbidden to use my right? It is lawful for the heaven to bring forth fair days, and to hide them again in darksome nights. It is lawful for the year sometime to compass the face of the earth with flowers and fruits, and sometime to cover it with clouds and cold. The sea hath right sometime to fawn with calms, and sometime to frown with storms and waves. And shall the insatiable desire of men tie me to constancy, so contrary to my custom? This is my force, this is the sport which I continually use. I turn about my wheel with speed, and take a pleasure to turn things upside down. Ascend, if thou wilt, but with this condition, that thou thinkest it not an injury to descend when the course of my sport so requireth. Didst thou not know my fashion?

II

'If Plenty as much wealth should give, ne'er
    holding back her hand,
As the swift winds in troubled seas do toss up
    heaps of sand,
Or as the stars in lightsome nights shine forth
    on heaven's face,
Yet wretched men would still accuse their
    miserable case.
Should God, too liberal of His gold, their
    greedy wishes hear,

Since ravenous minds, devouring all, for more
    are ready still.
What bridle can contain in bounds this their
    contentless will,
When filled with riches they retain the thirst
    of having more?
He is not rich that fears and grieves, and
    counts himself but poor.'

III

Wherefore if fortune should plead with thee thus in her own defence, doubtless thou wouldst not have a word to answer her. But if there be anything which thou canst allege in thy own defence, thou must utter it. We will give thee full liberty to speak." Then I said: "These things make a fair show and being set out with pleasant rhetoric and music, delight only so long as they are heard. But those which are miserable have a deeper feeling of their miseries. Therefore, when the sound of these things is past, hidden sorrow oppresseth the mind."

IV

"Wherefore, O mortal men, why seek you for your felicity abroad, which is placed within yourselves? Error and ignorance do confound you. I will briefly show thee the centre of thy chiefest happiness. Is there anything more precious to thee than thyself? I am sure thou wilt say, nothing. Wherefore, if thou enjoyest thyself, thou shalt possess that which neither thou wilt ever wish to lose nor fortune can take away. And that thou mayst acknowledge that blessedness cannot consist in these casual things, gather it thus. If blessedness be the chiefest good of nature endued with reason, and that is not the chiefest good which may by any means be taken away, because that which cannot be taken away is better, it is manifest that the instability of fortune cannot aspire to the obtaining of blessedness. Moreover, he that now enjoyeth this brittle felicity, either knoweth it to be mutable or no. If not, what estate can be blessed by ignorant blindness? And if he knoweth it, he must needs fear lest he lose that which he doubteth not may be lost, wherefore continual fear permitteth him not to be happy. Or though he should lose it, doth he think that a thing of no moment? But so it were a very small good which he would be content to lose. And because thou art one whom I know to be fully persuaded and convinced by innumerable demonstrations that the souls of men are in no wise mortal, and since it is clear that casual felicity is ended by the body's death, there is no doubt, if this can cause blessedness, but that all mankind falleth into misery by death. But if we know many who have sought to reap the fruit of blessedness, not only by death, but also by affliction and torments, how can present happiness make men happy, the loss of which cause causeth not misery?"

V

(Philosophy examines the things prized
by men.)

"But since the soothing of my reasons begins to sink into thee, I will use those which are somewhat more forcible. Go to then, if the gifts of fortune were not brittle and momentary, what is there in them which can either ever be made your own, or, well weighed and considered, seemeth not vile and of no account? Are riches precious in virtue either of their own nature or of yours? What part of them can be so esteemed of? The gold or the heaps of money? But these make a fairer show when they are spent than when they are kept. For covetousness always maketh men odious, as liberality famous. And if a man cannot have that which is given to another, then money is precious when, bestowed upon others, by the use of liberality it is not possessed any longer. But if all the money in the whole world were gathered into one man's custody,

all other men should be poor. The voice at the same time wholly filleth the ears of many, but your riches cannot pass to many, except they be diminished, which being done, they must needs make them poor whom they leave. O scant and poor riches, which neither can be wholly possessed of many, and come to none without the impoverishment of others! Doth the glittering of jewels draw thy eyes after them? But if there be any great matter in this show, not men but the jewels shine, which I exceedingly marvel that men admire. For what is there wanting life and members endued with life but also with reason? Which, though by their maker's workmanship and their own variety they have some part of basest beauty, yet it is so far inferior to your excellency that it did in no sort deserve your admiration. Doth the pleasant prospect of the fields delight you? Why not? For it is a fair portion of a most fair work. So we are delighted with a calm sea, so we admire the sky, the stars, the sun, and the moon. Do any of these belong to thee? Darest thou boast of the beauty which any of them have? Art thou thyself adorned with May flowers? Or doth thy fertility teem with the fruits of summer? Why rejoicest thou vainly? Why embracest thou outward goods as if they were thine own? Fortune will make those things thine which by the appointment of Nature belong not to thee. The fruits of the earth are doubtless appointed for the sustenance of living creatures. But if thou wilt only satisfy want, which sufficeth Nature, there is no cause to require the superfluities of fortune. For Nature is contented with little and with the smallest things, and, if, being satisfied, thou will overlay it with more than needs, that which thou addest will either become unpleasant or hurtful. But perhaps thou thinkest it a fine thing to go decked in gay apparel, which, if they make a fair show, I will admire either the goodness of the stuff or the invention of the workman. Or doth the multitude of servants make thee happy? Who, if they be vicious, they are a pernicious burden to thy house, and exceedingly troublesome to their master; and if they be honest, how shall other men's honesty be counted amongst thy treasures? By all which is manifestly proved that none of these goods which thou accountest thine, are thine indeed. And if there is nothing in these worthy to be desired, why art thou either glad when thou hast them or sorry when thou losest them? Or what is it to thee, if they be precious by nature? For in this respect they would have pleased thee, though they had belonged to others. For they are not precious because they are come to be thine, but because they seemed precious thou wert desirous to have them. Now what desire you with such loud praise of fortune? Perhaps you seek to drive away penury with plenty. But this falleth out quite contrary, for you stand in need of many supplies, to protect all this variety of precious ornaments. And it is true that they which have much, need much; and contrariwise, that they need little which measure not their wealth by the superfluity of ambition, but by the necessity of nature. Have you no proper and inward good, that you seek your goods in those things which are outward and separated from you? Is the condition of things so changed that a living creature, deservedly accounted divine for the gift of reason, seemeth to have no other excellency than the possession of a little household stuff without life? All other creatures are content with that they have of their own; and you, who in your mind carry the likeness of God, are content to take the ornaments of your excellent nature from the most base and vile things, neither understand you what injury you do your Creator. He would have mankind to excel all earthly things; you debase your dignity under every meanest creature. For if it be manifest that the good of everything is more precious than that whose good it is, since you judge the vilest things that can be to be your

goods, you deject yourselves under them in your own estimation, which questionless cometh not unreservedly to pass; for this is the condition of man's nature, that then only it surpasseth other things when it knoweth itself, and it is worse than beasts when it is without that knowledge. For in other living creatures the ignorance of themselves is nature, but in men it is vice. . . .

THE FIFTH BOOK OF BOETHIUS

VI

(Philosophy explains the character of God's knowledge.)

"Seeing, therefore, as hath been showed, all that is known is not comprehended by its own nature but by the power of him which comprehendeth it, let us see now, as much as may, what is the state of the divine substance that we may also know what His knowledge is. Wherefore it is the common judgment of all that live by reason that God is everlasting, and therefore let us consider what eternity is. For this declareth unto us both the divine nature and knowledge. Eternity therefore is a perfect possession altogether of an endless life, which is more manifest by the comparison of temporal things, for whatsoever liveth in time, that being present proceedeth from times past to times to come, and there is nothing placed in time which can embrace all the space of its life at once. But it hath not yet attained tomorrow and hath lost yesterday. And you live no more in this day's life than in that movable and transitory moment. Wherefore, whatsoever suffereth the condition of time, although, as Aristotle thought of the world, it never began nor were ever to end, and its life did endure with infinite time, yet it is not such that it ought to be called everlasting. For it doth not comprehend and embrace all the space of its life together, though that life be infinite, but it hath not the future time which is yet to come. That then which comprehendeth and possesseth the whole fulness of an endless life together, to which neither any part to come is absent, nor of that which is past hath escaped, is worthy to be accounted everlasting, and this is necessary, that being no possession in itself, it may always be present to itself, and have an infinity of movable time present to it. Wherefore they are deceived who, hearing that Plato thought that his world had neither beginning of time nor should ever have any end, think that by this means the created world should be coeternal with the Creator. For it is one thing to be carried through an endless life, which Plato attributed to the world, another thing to embrace the whole presence of an endless life together, which is manifestly proper to the divine mind. Neither ought God to seem more ancient than the things created, by the quantity of time, but rather by the simplicity of His divine nature. For that infinite motion of temporal things imitateth the present state of the unmovable life, and since it cannot express nor equal it, it falleth from immobility to motion, and from the simplicity of presence, it decreaseth to an infinite quantity of future and past, and since it cannot possess together all the fulness of its life, by never leaving to be in some sort, it seemeth to emulate in part that which it cannot fully obtain and express, tying itself to this small presence of this short and swift moment, which because it carrieth a certain image of that abiding presence, whosoever hath it, seemeth to be. But because it could not stay it undertook an infinite journey of time, and so it came to pass that it continued that life by going whose plenitude it could not comprehend by staying. Wherefore, if we will give things their right names, following Plato, let us say that God is everlasting and the world perpetual. Wherefore, since every judgment comprehendeth those things which are subject unto it, according to its own nature, and

God hath always an everlasting and present state, His knowledge also surpassing all motions of time, remaineth in the simplicity of His presence, and comprehending the infinite spaces of that which is past and to come, considereth all things in His simple knowledge as though they were now in doing. So that, if thou wilt weigh His foreknowledge with which He discerneth all things, thou wilt more rightly esteem it to be the knowledge of a never fading instant than a foreknowledge as of a thing to come. For which cause it is not called providence or foresight, but rather providence, because, placed far from inferior things, it overlooketh all things, as it were, from the highest top of things. Why, therefore, wilt thou have those things necessary which are illustrated by the divine light, since that not even men make not those things necessary which they see? For doth thy sight impose any necessity upon those things which thou seest present?" "No." "But the present instant of men may well be compared to that of God in this: that as you see some things in your temporal instant, so He beholdeth all things in His eternal present. Wherefore this divine foreknowledge doth not change the nature and propriety of things, and it beholdeth them such in His presence as they will after come to be, neither doth He confound the judgment of things, and with one sight of His mind He discerneth as well those things which shall happen necessarily as otherwise. As you, when at one time you see a man walking upon the earth and the sun rising in heaven, although they be both seen at once, yet you discern and judge that the one is voluntary, and the other necessary, so likewise the divine sight beholding all things disturbeth not the quality of things which to Him are present, but in respect of time are yet to come. And so this is not an opinion but rather a knowledge grounded upon truth, when He knoweth that such a thing shall be, which likewise He is not ignorant that it hath no necessity of being. Here if thou sayest that cannot choose but happen which God seeth shall happen, and that which cannot choose but happen, must be of necessity, and so tiest me to this name of necessity, I will grant that it is a most solid truth, but whereof scarce any but a contemplator of divinity is capable. For I will answer that the same thing is necessary when it is referred to the Divine knowledge; but when it is weighed in its own nature that it seemeth altogether free and absolute. For there be two necessities: the one simple, as that it is necessary for all men to be mortal; the other conditional, as if thou knowest that any man walketh, he must needs walk. For what a man knoweth cannot be otherwise than it is known. But this conditional draweth not with it that simple or absolute necessity. For this is not caused by the nature of the thing, but by the adding a condition. For no necessity maketh him to go that goeth of his own accord, although it be necessary that he goeth while he goeth. In like manner, if providence seeth anything present, that must needs be, although it hath no necessity of nature. But God beholdeth those future things, which proceed from free-will, present. These things, therefore, being referred to the divine sight are necessary by the condition of the divine knowledge, and, considered by themselves, they lose not absolute freedom of their own nature. Wherefore doubtless all those things come to pass which God foreknoweth shall come, but some of them proceed from free-will, which though they come to pass, yet do not, by coming into being, lose, since before they came to pass, they might also not have happened. But what importeth it that they are not necessary, since that by reason of the condition of the divine knowledge they come to pass in all respects as if they were necessary? It hath the same import as those things which I proposed a little before—the sun rising and the man going. While they are in doing, they cannot choose

but be in doing; yet one of them was necessarily to be before it was, and the other not. Likewise those things which God hath present, will have doubtless a being, but some of them proceed from the necessity of things, other from the power of the doers. And therefore we said not without cause that these, if they be referred to God's knowledge, are necessary; and if they be considered by themselves, they are free from the bonds of necessity. As whatsoever is manifest to senses, if thou referrest it to reason, is universal; if thou considerest the things themselves, it is singular or particular. But thou wilt say, 'If it is in my power to change my purpose, shall I frustrate providence if I chance to alter those things which she foreknoweth?' I answer that thou mayest indeed change thy purpose, but because the truth of providence, being present, seeth that thou canst do so, and whether thou wilt do so or no, and what thou purposest anew, thou canst not avoid the divine foreknowledge, even as thou canst not avoid the sight of an eye which is present, although thou turnest thyself to divers actions by thy free-will.

But yet thou wilt inquire whether God's knowledge shall be changed by thy disposition, so that when thou wilt now one thing, and now another, it should also seem to have divers knowledge. No. For God's sight preventeth all that is to come and recalleth and draweth it to the presence of His own knowledge; neither doth He vary, as thou imaginest, now knowing one thing and now another, but in one instant without moving preventeth and comprehendeth thy mutations. Which presence of comprehending and seeing all things, God hath not by the event of future things but by His own simplicity. By which that doubt is also resolved which thou didst put a little before, that it is an unworthy thing that our future actions should be said to cause the knowledge of God. For this force of the divine knowledge comprehending all things with a present notion appointeth to everything its measure and receiveth nothing from ensuing accidents. All which being so, the free-will of mortal men remaineth unviolated, neither are the laws unjust which propose punishments and rewards to our wills, which are free from all necessity. There remaineth also a beholder of all things which is God, who foreseeth all things, and the eternity of His vision, which is always present, concurreth with the future quality of our actions, distrib-uting rewards to the good and punishments to the evil. Neither do we in vain put our hope in God or pray to Him; for if we do this well and as we ought, we shall not lose our labour or be without effect. Wherefore fly vices, embrace virtues, possess your minds with worthy hopes, offer up humble prayers to your highest Prince. There is, if you will not dissemble, a great necessity of doing well imposed upon you, since you live in the sight of your Judge, who beholdeth all things."

THE RULE OF SAINT BENEDICT

As we saw in volume 1, Christian monasticism had its beginnings in Egypt in the late third and early fourth centuries C.E. when the official toleration of Christianity by the Roman state removed the threat of martyrdom. The new "spiritual" martyrdom took the form of withdrawal by heroic individual ascetics like St. Antony of Egypt (c. 251–356 C.E.) to a hermetical life in the desert. As described in St. Athanasius' influential *Life of Antony,* Antony was motivated by a desire to follow in a literal manner the teachings of Jesus in the gospels, especially the injunction to the rich young man: "If thou wouldst be perfect, go and sell what thou hast and give to the poor; and come follow me and thou shalt have treasure in heaven" (Matt 12:21).

At approximately the same time, communal or cenobitical monasticism was also beginning in Egypt under the leadership of men like St. Pachomius (d.c. 346 C.E.), who is credited with writing the first rule establishing a common discipline for monks who wished to live, pray, and work together. The rule which eventually gained widest acceptance in Eastern Christianity was that of St. Basil the Great of Caesarea (c. 329–379 C.E.). Although he had briefly visited the hermits in Egypt, Basil did not advocate the hermetical life as the highest form of monasticism. His rule mandated a communal life of regular prayer, retirement from the world, distinctive dress, obedience to an abbot, and common rules for food, fasting and other ascetical practices. Although the monks had withdrawn from the regular congregation, they were to serve the community by establishing hospitals, visiting the sick, educating children, and distributing food and clothing.

Monasticism came to the West in a bewildering variety of forms. In Italy, southern Gaul, North Africa, and Ireland various monastic communities were formed under the influence of Eastern monastic traditions. While in exile in the West, Athanasius had introduced the hermetical ideals of Antony which were spread by Latin translations of his *Life of Antony.* This work influenced Ambrose, Jerome and Augustine—each of whom was associated with monasticism and wrote on the subject: In Gaul, Martin of Tours (d. c. 397), a convert and former Roman soldier from what is now modern Hungary, built a monastery at Liguge and practiced a form of monasticism influenced by the Egyptian hermetical models. He wrote no rule; but after he became Bishop of Tours, he engaged the monks in the missionary work of converting the peoples in the rural areas beyond the urban core of the old Roman *civitates*. John Cassian (c. 360–435), who had spent time with monastic communities at Bethlehem and Egypt, was the main source of Egyptian influence on Western monasticism. He founded a community of monks and another of nuns at Marseilles. In his *Institutes* and *Conferences* he makes the contemplation of God the final goal of monasticism. Beginners needed the routine of a cenobitical form of life, but the goal of the monastic vocation was to live as a silent, secluded hermit in contemplation of God.

The monastic tradition which eventually became dominant in the West is associated with Benedict of Nursia (c. 480–547 C.E.). By the sixth century Western monasticism was suffering from a lack of discipline because of the breakup of Western society in the wake of the collapse of Roman order and the establishment of the barbarian kingdoms. Benedict describes some of these problems in chapter one of the Rule. Some monks, called "Sarabaites" by Benedict, were living in small communities without the discipline of a rule and without the direction of an abbot. Others, the "Gyrovagi," or "Wanderers" rambled from place to place in search of an easy life, rather than the discipline of gospel living.

Our main source of information about Benedict is in Book 2 of the *Dialogues* of Pope Gregory the Great, who wrote a highly legendary life of Benedict. He was born in Nursia in Umbria and as a young man studied in Rome. The degenerate life of the city caused him to withdraw to a hermetical life in a cave at Mt. Subiaco. After an unsuccessful stay in a monastery, he returned to Subiaco where he established twelve small monastic communities. Eventually he was pressured to leave and with a small band of men moved to Monte Cassino, halfway between Rome and Naples, where he established another monastery in which he remained for the rest of his life.

Benedict's impact on Western monasticism came after his death through the Rule, which he wrote for his monks at Monte Cassino. It is not, nor does it pretend to be, completely original. Recent scholarship has shown that Benedict made use of a document known as *The Rule of the Master,* and he himself refers to the *Conferences* and *Institutes* of John Cassian and the Rule of Basil as "instruments to help the monk, who follows them, to lead a good life." His own Rule he humbly describes as a "little Rule for beginners" which is designed "with the object of showing that monks who keep it have at least something of virtuous character, and must have begun to live a truly good life."

In keeping with this purpose, Benedict produced a moderate and balanced Rule which avoided the extremes of hermetical asceticism, while at the same time carefully establishing the discipline and order necessary in a community of men at various levels of spiritual commitment. Benedict's Rule is not only within the spiritual means of men committed to the monastic vocation, but is also filled with the idealism of pursuing a life of following the Christ of the gospels. Testimony to its success is the fact that it is still being practiced today and has been the source of monastic and church renewal throughout the Western Church's history.

As is evident in the Prologue, the Rule is addressed to the layman who has experienced the call of God to "possess true and everlasting life." The monk was not ordinarily a priest and did not enter the monastery to save the world or to renew society, but to save his own soul. The guide for the monk's life is in Benedict's own words, "the gospel" whose teachings should lead to union with God. Although the Rule is filled with exhortation and words like "merit" and "deserve," Benedict also constantly reminds the monk of the gift of God's grace which enables him to follow the monastic vocation. In his own words, the one fit to dwell in the Lord's tabernacle is "He who fears the Lord without growing proud of his virtue and humbly acknowledges that what is good in him does not proceed from himself."

In a chaotic time when much of the barbarian West was only nominally Christian, Benedict's Rule kept alive the spirit of pursuing a life of gospel perfection. Wherever possible Benedict roots the monastic observances in the teachings of the gospel and the scriptures. For example, the instruments of good works in chapter 4 are drawn from the traditional commandments of the Old Testament and the ethical exhortations of the gospels and other New Testament writings. The vow of obedience to the abbot is based on quotations from the psalms which emphasize prompt obedience to God and Jesus' own words, "I came not to do mine own will, but the will of him that sent me" (John 6:38). The twelve degrees of humility are introduced with the quotation, "everyone that exalteth himself shall be humbled, and he that humbleth himself shall be exalted" (Lk 14:11). The schedule of seven hours for prayer throughout the monastic day is based on the phrase in Psalm 119, "Seven times a day have I praised thee." The practice of poverty in which the monk gives up personal property and shares all in common with his fellow monks is rooted in a desire to imitate the early Christian community described in Acts where the members held "everything in common" (Acts 4:32–35).

The center of the monk's day is the *Opus Dei,* "the work of God," or "the divine office." The monk sanctifies the entire day by a life of communal prayer rooted in the psalms of the Old Testament. Each of the liturgical hours has its particular character which is related to the rhythm of the day. Lauds, or morning prayer, is marked by a spirit of praise to God for the gift of creation and life and the beginning of a new day. Vespers, or evening prayer, is a time of thanksgiving for the blessings of life and the day just completed. Compline, or night prayer, has the tone of a request for protection from the evils of life and the approaching night. Benedict provides careful instruction mandating the number of psalms and prayers to be sung at each hour, and especially the manner in which they are to be sung: "Let us then reflect what behavior is proper for appearing in the presence of God and the angels, and so sing our psalms that the mind may echo in harmony with the voice."

Despite the gospel-based perfection found in the Rule, it is also filled with a spirit of sensible moderation in comparison to the extreme rigors of other monastic traditions of the early medieval period. In regulating such matters as food and drink, clothing, the flexibility of the daily schedule for various seasons, the number of psalms to be recited at various liturgical hours, the keeping of silence—Benedict shows the old Roman gift for practicality and order. The monk's day was a sensible blend of prayer, work and rest. Approximately three and a half hours were spent in reverently chanting the divine office; four and a half hours in reading and meditation; an hour for meals; eight and a half hours for sleep; and six and a half hours for work in the fields.

Benedict's gift for combining the spirit of gospel living and the Roman skill for stable government is most evident in his legislation for the organization of the community. At the head of the monastery is the abbot, the superior, who is to take the place of Christ in the monastery. The souls of the monks are committed to his care, and he has final authority in all matters. The monks are to give him total obedience as to Christ himself. However, he is not to be an arbitrary tyrant. His title reflects the very Fatherhood of God whom Jesus addressed as "Abba," and therefore he is "not to teach, establish, or command anything contrary to the law of the Lord." He is to teach primarily by example and is not to show partiality in his treatment of the monks based on their previous status as freeborn or slave. In his teaching of the monks he is to "mix gentleness with sternness: at one time to show the severity of a master, at another the tenderness of a father." In making decisions for the life of the monastery, the abbot is to assemble the whole community and listen to their opinions before resolving the matter in the way he judges most profitable. Once the brothers have humbly expressed their opinions, however, they are to abide by the decision of the abbot.

Another example of Benedict's prudence and administrative wisdom is his manner of dealing with the problems of the undisciplined and wandering monks. For Benedict the monastic vocation is a dual one. The monks must both live the discipline of the Rule and also remain in a particular monastery for life. Before a man is received into the monastery, he is put through a trial period, called a novitiate, in which he learns from a novice master the hardships and difficulties of the monastic life. During the course of the novitiate the Rule is read to him three times: at the end of the second, sixth and tenth months. If after mature deliberation the would-be monk wishes to observe the whole Rule and remain within the monastery, he makes a public profession in the oratory "of his stability, amendment of life and obedience." This solemn promise is written in his own hand in the form of a petition in the name of the abbot and the saints whose relics are contained in the oratory. It is then placed by the man's own hand upon the altar while he says, "Receive me, O Lord, according to thy word, and I shall live: and let me not be disappointed in my hope" (Ps 119:116).

Although the monks of the Middle Ages had an enormous impact on Western civilization because of their work in converting the Germanic tribes to orthodox Christianity, this activity is not envisioned by Benedict. He does give instructions for the reception of guests as Christ himself, but he does not command the monks to engage in missionary activity.

Benedict also did not understand the monastery as a center for scholarly activity and the preservation of the Christian and pagan classics. His provisions for "sacred reading" during the day were intended for the spiritual enrichment of the monk. Cassiodorus, a contemporary of Benedict and a former Roman senator, is the man who began the association of monasticism with scholarship and learning. When he retired from government service, he turned his estate into a center for education and the copying of sacred and secular manuscripts.

Benedict's Rule did not win immediate acceptance. Other monastic traditions under Eastern influence were older and more challenging and influenced the important Irish monastic traditions represented by the Rule of St. Columbanus (d.c. 615) which spread from Ireland to England and eventually to the continent. The political chaos in Italy in the sixth century also impeded the spread of Benedict's Rule. In the second quarter of the sixth century Italy was ravaged by Justinian's attempts to reconquer the West and, beginning in 568 C.E., the Lombards reinvaded Italy with catastrophic results for civilized life. Monte Cassino itself was destroyed sometime before 590 C.E. and was not rebuilt until the eighth century. Only during the Carolingian renaissance in the early ninth century, when a second Benedict, St. Benedict of Aniane, reconstituted the Rule, did it become obligatory in the monasteries of the Frankish Empire.

The translation is by Owen Chadwick, *Western Asceticism,* Vol. XII in The Library of Christian Classics, 291–337.

Prologue

Son, listen to the precepts of your master; take them to your heart willingly. If you follow the advice of a tender father and travel the hard road of obedience, you will return to God from whom by disobedience you have gone astray.

I address my discourse to all of you who will renounce your own will, enter the lists under the banner of obedience, and fight under the lead of your lawful sovereign, Christ the Lord.

First, I advise that you should implore the help of God to accomplish every good work you undertake; that he, who has now vouchsafed to rank us in the number of his children, may be more grieved at our doing amiss. For we ought always to use his grace so faithfully in his service, as to give him no occasion to disinherit his children like an angry parent, or to punish for eternity his servants, like a master incensed at their crimes—servants who have refused to follow him in the way to glory.

Let us then exert ourselves now. The Scripture awakens us, saying: "Now it is the hour to arise from sleep" (Rom 13:11); and with eyes wide open to the light of heaven, and ears receptive to the word of God, let us hear what his voice repeats to us every day. "Today if you will hear his voice, harden not your hearts" (Ps 95:8). And again, "He who hath ears to hear, let him hear what the Spirit saith unto the churches" (Matt 11:15; Rev 2:7). What does he say? "Come, my children, hearken unto me and I will teach you the fear of the Lord" (Ps 34:11). "Run while ye have the light of life, that the darkness of death overtake you not" (Jn 12:35).

The Lord, seeking to draw from the crowd one faithful servant, asks: "What man is he that desireth life and would fain see good days" (Ps 34:12–15)? If you reply: "It is I," God answers: "If you will possess the true and everlasting life, keep your tongue from evil and your lips from speaking guile. Depart from evil and do good: seek peace and pursue it. And when you have done this, then my eyes shall be open upon you, and my ears shall listen to your prayers, and even before you call upon me I will say: 'Behold, I am here.'" Dearest brethren, can we imagine anything more tender than this invitation of our Lord? See, in his goodness, he points out to us the way of life.

Let us then gird up our loins; let us walk by faith and try to serve him with good works; and thereby let us advance in his ways with the Gospel as our guide, that we may deserve to behold him who has called us to his kingdom. If we want to fix our dwelling there, we cannot arrive thereto without running in the ways of virtue. But let us inquire of the Lord with the prophet: "Lord, who shall dwell in thy tabernacle, or who shall rest upon thy holy hill?" Brethren, let us hear the Lord's answer to the question, an answer which shows the way to the heavenly tabernacle: "He that walketh without blame and does right; he that speaketh truth in his heart; he that hath kept his tongue from guilt, hath done no evil to his neighbor, and hath not believed slander of his neighbor" (Ps 15:1–3). He who drives the tempter and his temptations far from his heart, defeats his malice, and dashes his rising thoughts against the Rock Christ. He who fears the Lord without growing proud of his virtue and humbly acknowledges that what is good in him does not proceed from himself. He who gives God his due, and with the prophet blesses the work of God in himself: "Not unto us, O Lord, not unto us, but unto thy name give the glory" (Ps 115:1). The apostle Paul found nothing of his own to boast of in his preaching: "By the grace of God (says he) I am what I am" (1 Cor 15:10), and again, "He that glories, let him glory in the Lord" (2 Cor 10:17). On this account our Lord in the Gospel tells us: "He that heareth these words of mine and doeth them, I will make him like the wise man who hath built his house upon a rock. The floods came and the winds blew, and they beat upon that house, and it fell not, for it was founded upon a rock" (Matt 7:24–25).

. . . To conclude: I am to erect a school for beginners in the service of the Lord: which I hope to establish on laws not too difficult or grievous. But if, for reasonable cause, for the retrenchment of vice or preservation of charity, I require some things which may seem too austere, you are not thereupon to be frightened from the ways of salvation. Those ways are always strait and narrow at the beginning. But as we advance in the practices of religion and in faith, the heart insensibly opens and enlarges through the wonderful sweetness of his love, and we run in the way of God's commandments. If then we keep close to our school and the doctrine we learn in it, and persevere in the monastery till death, we shall here share by patience in the passion of Christ and hereafter deserve to be united with him in his kingdom. Amen.

2. What qualifications are required for an abbot?

An abbot qualified to govern a monastery, ought always to remember the name he bears, and to maintain by his good life the title of superior: for he is esteemed to supply the place of Christ in the monastery, being called by his name; according to the apostle: "Ye have received the spirit of the adoption of sons, whereby we cry Abba, Father" (Rom 8:15); and therefore the abbot ought not to teach, establish, or command anything contrary to the law of the Lord, but so to deliver his ordinances and teaching that they may work on the minds of his disciple like a leaven or seasoning of divine justice.

Let the abbot always remember that at the dreadful day of judgement he is accountable for the obedience of his disciples as for his own teaching. He is to remember that whatever the Father of the family finds ill in the flock, shall lie at the shepherd's door. He shall not be declared guiltless in the Lord's judgement unless he has taken all the pains he can for a disobedient and turbulent flock. If he has used his utmost care to cut out their sins, he may say to the Lord with the prophet: "I have not hid thy justice within my heart: I have declared thy truth and thy salvation: but they have despised and rejected me" (Ps 40:10; Isa 1:2). And eternal death shall be the punishment of them that have been disobedient to his care.

When anyone takes upon him the office of abbot, he is to instruct his disciples in two ways. That is: he is to lay before them what is good and holy, more by example than by words: to teach the law of the Lord by word of mouth to such as are of a quicker comprehension, and by example to those of harder hearts and meaner capacities. He ought to create by his conduct an aversion from the thing which he condemns in his discourse; then he will not himself prove a castaway while he preaches to others, and will avoid God's reproach: "Wherefore dost thou declare my righteousness and take my testament into thy mouth? For thou hatest discipline, yea and hast rejected my exhortation" (Ps 50:16–17), and, "thou hast seen a mote in thy brother's eye, and hast not seen the beam in thine own" (Matt 7:3).

He is not to be partial, or to love one more than another, unless upon consideration of greater virtue or obedience. He is not to prefer the freeborn monk above the slave, except some other reasonable cause intervene. In such case it is allowable that the abbot should dispose of persons as he judges expedient and fair. Otherwise everyone is to keep his proper place; because, whether slaves or freeborn, we are all one in Christ, and we have all enlisted in the same service under one common Lord who is no respecter of persons. The only reason why God puts one man above another is because the one lives a better life and is humble. Therefore the abbot's charity must extend equally to all and his discipline be impartial, to each according to his merits.

In his teaching the abbot is ever to observe this rule of the apostle: "Reprove, beseech, correct" (2 Tim 4:2): which consists in a judicious timing: to mix gentleness with sternness: at one time to show the severity of a master, at another the tenderness of a father: to use rigor with the irregular and the turbulent, but win to better things the obedient, mild, and patient. I warn him to reprove and chastise the careless or contemptuous.

Nor is he to dissemble the faults of those that go amiss, but to do his utmost to root them out as they begin to grow; always mindful of the danger of Eli the priest of Shiloh. Those who are of nobler character and are more capable of understanding he is to admonish twice. But mere profligates, stubborn, proud, or disobedient, the moment they begin to do amiss, must be reclaimed by the rod. The abbot must know what is written: "The fool is not corrected by words" (Prov 18:2): and, "strike thy son with the rod, and thou shalt deliver his soul from death" (Prov 23:13–14).

The abbot ought ever to remember what he is and what is meant by the name he bears, and to know that more is required of him to whose charge more is committed. Let him reflect how difficult and perplexing a business he undertakes, at once to govern many souls and to be subject to as many honors: to suit himself to everyone with regard to their capacity and condition; to win some by fair means, others by reprimands, others by dint of reason: that he may not suffer damage to his flock, but rather rejoice at the increase and improvement of it.

Above all, he is not to dissemble or undervalue the care of souls committed to his charge, for the sake of temporal concerns, which are earthly, transitory, and fleeting; but ever to reflect that the government of souls is his business, and that he is accountable for them. And if perhaps the monastery have too little money, he is not to be disturbed thereat; but to remember how it is written: "Seek ye first the kingdom of God and his righteousness, and all these things shall be added unto you" (Matt 6:33); and again, "Nothing is wanting to them that fear him" (Ps 34:10).

Let him further reflect that he has undertaken the care of souls, and is to prepare his accounts: let him be sure that at the day of judgement he will be answerable for as many souls as he has brothers, as well as for his own. If he is ever in dread of the severe examination which he is to undergo for the sheep committed to him, he will be as careful about himself as he is about his charges: and so he will together cure the sins of others by his government, and amend the faults in his own life.

4. Of the instruments of good works

First, to love the Lord God with all the heart, with all the soul, and with all the strength.

Next, to love the neighbor as oneself.

Next, not to kill.

Not to commit adultery.

Not to steal.

Not to covet.

Not to bear false witness.

To honour all men.

Not to do to another what we would not want done to ourselves.

To renounce oneself, in order to follow Christ.

To chastise the body.

Not to seek after pleasure.

To love fasting.

To relieve the poor.

To clothe the naked.

To visit the sick.

To bury the dead.

To help those that are in trouble.

To comfort the afflicted.

To eschew the ways of the world.

To prefer nothing before the love of Christ.

. . .

To love chastity.

To hate nobody.

Not to be addicted to jealousy.

Not to be envious.

Not to love contention.

To avoid ambition.

To venerate elders.

To love the younger.

To pray for our enemies, for the love of Christ.

To be reconciled to those who have quarreled with us, before the sun go down.

And never to despair of God's mercy.

These are the instruments of spiritual progress. If day and night we employ them, and at the day of judgement commend them into the hands of God, we shall be crowned with the reward he has promised "which neither eye hath seen nor ear hath heard, nor hath it entered into the heart of man what things God hath prepared for them that love him" (1 Cor 2:9).

The best place to practice these things is the monastery with its seclusion—provided that we remain steadily in the community and do not leave it.

5. Of obedience

The first degree of humility is a prompt and ready obedience. This is fitting for them who love Christ above all else. By reason of the holy duty they have undertaken, or for fear of hell, or for eternal glory, they make no more delay to comply, the very instant anything is a appointed them, than if God himself had given the command. Of these the Lord said: "At the very sound of my voice he hath obeyed me" (Ps 18:44). And again he declared to them that teach: "He that heareth you, heareth me" (Lk 10:16).

They who are of this temper abandon all, even to their very will; instantly clear their hands and leave unfinished what they had begun; so that the command is carried out in the moment it is uttered. Master and disciple are lent wings by the fear of God and the longing for eternal life, and so the command is obeyed in a flash.

It is for the sake of obedience that they enter into the narrow way of which the Lord said: "Narrow is the way that leadeth unto life" (Matt 7:14). The "narrowness" of the way is the opposite of the broad way suggested by self-will and desire and pleasure: and they follow it by delighting to dwell in a community, to be subject to their abbot, and to follow the judgement of another. Such men live up to the practice of our Lord, who tells us: "I came not to do mine own will, but the will of him that sent me" (Jn 6:38).

This obedience will be pleasing to God and man, when it is performed with no fear, no delay, no coldness, no complaint, no reply. The obedience we pay to superiors is paid to God: for he tells us: "He that heareth you, heareth me." And it is to be done with willing heart, "because God loveth the cheerful giver" (2 Cor 9:7). When the disciple obeys unwillingly, with a grudge in heart or mouth, though he does the thing, yet he is so far from being pleasing to God, who sees reluctance in the heart, that he acquires no merit, but only incurs the penalty of those that murmur, till he has made a due atonement.

7. Humility

Brethren, the Scripture asserts that "everyone that exalteth himself shall be humbled, and he that humbleth himself shall be exalted" (Luke 14:11). It shows us thereby that all exaltation is in some measure the pride which the prophet tells us he took care to shun: "O Lord, my heart is not exalted, nor mine eyes lifted up: I have not aspired to great things, nor wonders above myself" (Ps 131:1). And his reason for it is because (says he): "If I had not thought humbly of myself but had exalted my soul, thou wouldst have driven away my soul like an infant weaned from the breast of its mother" (Ps 131:2).

Therefore, brethren, if we want to attain true humility, and come quickly to the top of that heavenly ascent to which we can only mount by lowliness in this present life, we must ascend by good works, and erect the mystical ladder of Jacob, where angels ascending and descending appeared to him. That ascent and descent means that we go downward when we exalt ourselves, and rise when we are humbled. The ladder represents our life in this world, which our Lord erects to heaven when our heart is humbled. And the sides of the ladder represent our soul and body, sides between which God has placed several rungs of humility and discipline, whereby we are to ascend if we would answer his call.

The first degree, then, of humility is, to have the fear of God ever before our eyes: never to forget what is his due, and always to remember his commands: to revolve in the mind how hell burns those who have contemned God, and how God has prepared eternal life for them that fear him: to preserve ourselves from the sins and vices of thought, of the tongue, the eyes, hands, feet, self-will and fleshly desires. Man ought to think that God always looks down from heaven upon him, and that all he does lies open to his sight, is daily told him by the angels. The prophet shows this truth, when he describes God as present in our thoughts, "searching the heart and veins" (Ps 7:9); and, "Our Lord knows the thoughts of men" (Ps 94:11); and again, "Thou has understood my thoughts a great way off" (Ps 139:1); and, "The thought of man shall confess to thee" (Ps 76:10). That he may ever watch the perverseness of his thoughts, let the right-minded brother continually repeat in the language of his heart: "Then I shall be without blemish before him, if I keep myself from mine iniquity" (Ps 18:23). . . .

The twelfth degree of humility is, when the monk's inward humility appears outwardly in his comportment. And wherever he be, in the divine office, in the oratory, in the monastery, in the garden, on a journey, in the fields—wherever he is sitting, walking or standing, he is to look down with bowed head conscious of his guilt, imagining himself ready to be called to give account at the dread judgement: repeating in his heart what the publican in the Gospel said with eyes downcast: "Lord, I am not worthy, sinner that I am, to lift up my eyes to heaven" (Lk 18:13); and with the prophet "I am bowed down and humbled on every side" (Ps 119:107).

After he has climbed all these degrees of humility, the monk will quickly arrive at the top, the charity that is perfect and casts out all fear. And then, the virtues which first he practiced with anxiety, shall begin to be easy for him, almost natural, being grown habitual. He will no more be afraid of hell, but will advance by the love of Christ, by good habits, and by taking pleasure in goodness. Our Lord, by the Holy Spirit, will deign to show this in the servant who has been cleansed from sin.

16. How the divine office is to be performed through the day

"Seven times a day have I praised thee" (Ps 119:164), said the prophet. We shall perform this consecrated number of seven if we offer prayer (the duty of our profession) at the hours of Lauds, Prime, Terce, Sext, None, Vespers, and Compline. It was of these day hours that he said: "Seven times a day have I praised thee." Elsewhere the same prophet makes mention of the night office, "at midnight I rose to confess to thee" (Ps 119:62).

At these times, therefore, let us render praise to our creator "for the judgments of his justice" (Ps 119:62)—that is, Lauds, Prime, Terce, Sext, None, Vespers, Compline: and let us rise at night to confess to him.

19. How we ought to sing

We believe God is everywhere, and his eye beholds the good and wicked wherever they are: so we ought to be particularly assured of his special presence when we assist at the divine office. Therefore we must always remember the advice of the prophet, "To serve God in fear" (Prov 15:3): "to sing wisely" (Ps 2:11; 47:7): and that "the angels are witnesses of what we sing" (Ps 138:1). Let us then reflect what behavior is proper for appearing in the presence of God and the angels, and so sing our psalms that the mind may echo in harmony with the voice.

20. What reverence is needed for prayer?

If we want to ask a favor of any person of power, we presume not to approach but with humility and respect. How much more ought we to address ourselves to the Lord and God of all things with a humble and entire devotion? We are not to imagine that our prayers shall be heard because we use many words, but because the heart is pure and the spirit penitent. Therefore prayer must be short and pure, unless it be prolonged by a feeling of divine inspiration. Prayer in common ought always to be short, and when the sign is given by the superior, all should rise together.

33. Whether monks ought to have any property?

The vice of possessing property is particularly to be banished from the monastery. No one may presume to give or receive anything without the abbot's leave, or to possess anything whatever, not even book or tablets or pen. The monks' bodies and their wills are not at their own disposal. They must look to all their needs to be supplied by the common father of the monastery. No one may have anything which the abbot does not give or permit. "Everything shall be in common" (Acts 4:32) as the Scripture says: "Nor shall they presume to call anything their own" (Acts 4:35). And if anyone be found inclined to this especial vice, he shall be told of it once and twice: and if he do not make amends he shall be liable to punishment.

34. *Whether everyone ought to have the same?*

The Scripture tells us: "It was divided to every man severally, as he had need" (Acts 4:35). We distinguish partiality (which may God forbid) from a consideration of infirmities. He that needs less, should give God thanks and not be vexed. He that needs more, has an occasion to humble himself for his own infirmity and no reason to grow proud for being an object of pity. And by this means every member may live in peace. Above all there must be no grumbling, for any reason, by word or sign. The grumbler is to be severely punished.

39. *Of the quantity of food*

I am of the opinion that for normal nourishment, whether they are eating at noon or 3 o'clock, two dishes will be sufficient at each meal. This is to provide for the weakness of different people, so that the brother who cannot eat one dish may perhaps be able to eat the other. All the brethren are to be content with these two hot dishes: and if fruit or young vegetables can conveniently be had, they may be allowed a third.

A full pound of bread shall suffice for a whole day, whether they dine and sup, or have only one meal. If they sup as well as dine, the cellarer shall keep a third part of the bread for the evening.

Notwithstanding, it shall be in the abbot's power to increase the allowance, if he thinks fit, for those with heavier work. Yet he must take care to avoid excess or sudden temptation to gluttony. For nothing is so contrary to the life of a Christian as overeating: as our Lord said: "Take heed lest at any time your hearts be charged with surfeiting" (Lk 21:34).

The same quantity is not to be given to the younger children: they should be given less than the others, and always be frugal. Except the very weak, no one shall eat meat at any time.

40. *Of the quantity of drink*

"Every man hath his proper gift from God, the one after this manner, and another after that" (1 Cor 7:7). So it is a nice point to prescribe a certain measure of food and drink for others. Notwithstanding, having regard to the weakness of the sick, I am of the opinion that a hemina (probably between a pint and half a pint) of wine every day will suffice. Yet be it known to those whom God has granted the gift of abstinence, that they shall have an especial reward.

If the necessity of the place, or the hard work, or the heat of the summer, makes them need more, it shall be in the power of the superior to add to the allowance: yet always with caution, that they may not fall to the temptations of satiety and drunkenness. Although we read that wine is never for monks, it is hard to persuade modern monks of this. At least we must all agree that we are not to drink to satiety, but with moderation. "For wine makes even wise men to fall into apostasy" (Ecclus 19:2).

Where the poverty of the place prevents this measure being available, but much less, or even none at all; the monks there are to bless God, and not complain.

I give this especial instruction, that no one shall complain.

42. *Of silence after Compline*

Monks at all times ought to study silence, but most of all during the night. Throughout the year, whether they are having supper or fasting, a similar rule shall apply. In the time of year when they are having suppers, as soon as they rise from the table, they shall assemble in one place, and one of them shall read the *Conferences* or *The Lives of the Fathers;* or at least some book which will edify the listeners. They are not to read the first seven books of the Bible or the book of Kings, because that part of Scripture is not profitable to weak understandings at such a time: these books are to be read at other times.

If it is a time of year when they are fasting, they are to leave a short interval after Vespers, and assemble as before for the reading of the *Conferences*. The reader shall read four or five pages, or as much as time allows. During the interval, anyone who has been occupied on special duties has time to join the assembled brothers.

When they are all present, they shall say Compline. And after Compline, no one shall be allowed to speak. If any be discovered to break this rule of silence, he shall be gravely punished: unless it be on account of guests and their needs; and even then it must be done with composure and moderation and gentleness.

48. Of daily labor

Idleness is the enemy of the soul. Therefore the brothers must spend a fixed part of their time in sacred reading, and another fixed part in manual labor.

From Easter to September 14th they shall go out and work, at any necessary task, from 7 a.m. until 10 a.m. or thereabouts. From 10 a.m. until about noon, they shall employ their time in reading.

After dinner at noon, they may rest on their beds in silence. If anyone would rather read a book, he may, provided he does not disturb others.

The hour of None is to be advanced, and said about 2:30 p.m. and afterwards they shall return to their work until Vespers. If the circumstances or the poverty of the place require that the monks cut their corn themselves, they must not look upon it as a grievance. For they are truly monks if they live by the work of their hands, as our forefathers and the apostles have done before them. Yet all is to be done with moderation, by reason of weak constitutions.

From September 14th to the beginning of Lent they are to read quietly until 8 o'clock: then Terce shall be said: and from Terce to None they shall work at their appointed tasks. As soon as the first bell for None goes, they are to stop work and get themselves ready in time for the second bell. After the meal they are to apply themselves to reading and learning the psalms.

In Lent, they are to read from break of day until 9 a.m., and then work at their different tasks until 4 p.m. During Lent they are each to take one book of the Bible, and read the whole of it from beginning to end: these books are to be distributed at the beginning of Lent. Particular care should be taken that one or two of the elders be deputed to go round the monastery, and oversee the monks at the times appointed for reading, to discover if any of them be bored, or idle, or trifling away his time with frivolous talk instead of serious reading, unprofitable to himself and an interruption to others. If (though God forbid) any such person be found, let him be rebuked, twice if necessary; and if he then does not amend, he shall be punished in accordance with the Rule, severely enough to make the others afraid. No one shall converse with another brother at improper times.

On Sundays all shall employ their time in reading, except those who have been given special duties. If there be anyone so negligent and slothful that he neither can nor will meditate or read, he must be employed about some other work which he can do, and must not be idle. Those brothers who are sick or of tender constitutions must receive consideration from the abbot, and be employed in a craft or work suitable to their strength, that they may not be altogether idle, nor burdened with labor beyond their powers and so driven away from the monastery.

53. The manner of entertaining guests

All guests coming to the monastery shall be received as Christ himself: for he will one day say: "I was a stranger, and you took me in" (Matt 25:35). And everyone shall receive due honour, especially clerics and pilgrims.

As soon as he hears that a guest has arrived, the superior, or some of the brothers, shall meet him with all the kindness that charity suggests. They shall pray together, and then salute each other with the kiss of peace. They shall not give the kiss of peace until they have prayed, to make sure that the visitor is not one of the devil's devices.

The salutation shall be given with deep humility, whether the guests are arriving or departing. It shall be with a bow or with a prostration on the ground, for Christ is to be adored in them and is being received as the guest.

After their welcome, the guests are to be led to the oratory. Then the superior, or a monk appointed by him, shall sit with them. He shall cause the Scripture to be read before the guest, for the sake of edification, and afterwards shall entertain them kindly.

The superior shall be dispensed from fasting out of regard to the guest, unless it be a particularly important fast which cannot be broken. But the brothers shall continue to fast as usual.

The abbot shall pour the water over the guest's hands; and he, and the community, wash the feet of all the guests. After they have washed them they shall say the verse: "Lord, we have received thy mercy, in the midst of thy temple" (Ps 48:9).

They shall take particular care to entertain the poor and the pilgrims with more than common kindness, because Christ is most of all received in their persons. The awe which we have of the rich makes it natural for us to honour them. . . .

55. Of the clothes and shoes of the brethren

The brothers shall be furnished with clothes suitable to the situation and climate of the place where they live. More is required in

cold countries and less in hot. This is left to the abbot's discretion.

For temperate climates we are of the opinion that it is enough for each monk to have a cowl (the cowl for winter shall be of thicker stuff, that for the summer thin and worn), a tunic, a belt for their work, shoes and stockings.

The monks are not be be disturbed at the color or coarseness of these clothes, but to be content with what the country produces and can be had cheaply.

The abbot shall take care that their habits be not too short, but of the right size. . . .

For bedding, this shall be enough: a mattress, blanket, coverlet and pillow. The beds shall be frequently inspected by the abbot, to see that they contain no private property. If he finds anything for which he has not given leave, the culprit shall be subject to severe punishment.

To root this vice of private property entirely out of the monastery, the abbot shall allow everything that is necessary: cowl, tunic, stockings, shoes, belt, knife, pen, needle, handkerchief, tablets. Thus there will be no pretense of need. Yet the abbot is always to remember what is said in the Acts of the Apostles: "distribution was made to everyone according as he had need" (Acts 4:35). And in the same way he is to consider the infirmities of the needy, without having regard to the ill-will or the envy of others. But he must be mindful that God will deal with him according to his works.

58. Of the manner of receiving men into the monastery

When anyone presents himself to be admitted as a monk they shall not easily give him entrance; but, as the apostle advises: "Make trial of the spirits, to see if they are of God" (1 Jn 4:1). If he is importunate and goes on knocking at the door, for four or five days, and patiently bears insults and rebuffs and still persists, he shall be allowed to enter. He shall stay in the guest-room for a few days. Thence he shall go to the cell where the novices study and eat and sleep.

An elder, who has the address of winning souls to God, shall be appointed as the director of the novices. He is to watch over them carefully, and thoroughly examine whether they truly seek God, whether they are sincere in the worship of God, in obedience, in bearing trials. The novice shall be warned of all the hardships and difficulties on the road which leads to God.

If he promises to persevere in his resolution, at the end of two months they shall read this Rule to him, from beginning to end, and say to him: "Here is the Law under which you wish to be Christ's soldier. If you can observe it, enter: if you cannot, freely depart." If he remains firm, he shall be led back to the novice's cell, and his patience shall be further tried.

At the end of six months, the Rule shall be read to him that he may know what he is undertaking. And if he persists, after four months the Rule shall be read a third time. And if, upon mature deliberation, he promises to observe the whole Rule and to obey whatever commands he is given, he shall be admitted as a member of the community, and he shall know that by the Law of the Rule it shall not thenceforth be in his power to quit the monastery, nor to shake off the yoke of the Rule, which he might have accepted or refused during so long a time for deliberation.

The person to be received shall make public profession in the oratory, of his stability, amendment of life, and obedience. The promise is to be made before God and his saints, so that if at any time he break his promise he may know that he will surely be damned by God whom he is mocking.

He shall write down this promise in the form of a petition in the name of the saints whose relics are there, and of his own abbot. He shall write it with his own hand: or, if he cannot write, another shall do it at his instance, and he shall add his mark and with his own hand lay it upon the altar. As he places it on the altar, he shall say this verse: "Receive me, O Lord, according to thy word, and I shall live: and let me not be disappointed of my hope" (Ps 119:116). The whole community shall repeat this three times, and end with the Gloria. Then the novice shall throw himself at the feet of all, to ask their prayers; and afterwards he shall be looked upon as a member of the community.

If he has property, he shall first distribute it to the poor, or make it over to the monastery by a formal donation, without any reservation for himself. He knows that for the future he is not even master of his own body.

While he is still in the oratory, his own clothes shall be removed, and he shall be clad in the clothes of the monastery. But his clothes shall be kept in the wardrobe; so that if ever (God forbid) he should be enticed by the devil and consent to leave the monastery, he can be stripped of his habit and turned out.

His petition, which the abbot took from off the altar, is not to be returned to him, but preserved in the monastery.

73. That this Rule does not contain the whole law of righteousness

I have written this Rule with the object of showing that monks who keep it have at least something of virtuous character, and must have begun to live a truly good life. But men aspire to the perfect life; and for them there are the teachings of the holy fathers, which will lead those who follow them to true perfection. What page—even sentence—of the inspired Old and New Testaments is there that is not an excellent rule of life? What book of the holy Catholic fathers is there that does not point out the nearest way to come to our Creator? The *Conferences* of the fathers, their

Institutes and *Lives;* the Rule of our father, Saint Basil—these are instruments to help the monk, who follows them, to lead a good life; to us, idle and neglectful sinners, they are a reproach and shame.

Whoever you are, who desire to advance apace to the heavenly country, practice first, through Christ's help, this little Rule for beginners. And in the end, under God's protection, you will climb those greater heights of knowledge and virtue to which the holy fathers beckon you.

GREGORY THE GREAT, *PASTORAL CARE* AND *DIALOGUES*

By universal agreement the outstanding pope of the early medieval period was St. Gregory I the Great who was bishop of Rome from 590–604 C.E. He is also ranked as the last of the four Latin doctors of the church along with St. Jerome, St. Ambrose and St. Augustine. His life and writings demonstrate the Roman Catholic Church's response to the challenge of maintaining political stability and Christian values in an age when Roman order was disappearing in the West.

Gregory is an excellent example of the way in which the Roman church attracted men who in an earlier age may have served the Roman state. In fact, Gregory had embarked on a political career and had risen to the position of prefect of Rome, when in mid-life he turned his own home into a monastery and donated his family's estates in Sicily for the founding of six other monasteries. He was not, however, allowed to remain in the solitude of the monastery. By 579 the pope sent Gregory as nuncio to the emperor at Constantinople where he learned firsthand that Rome could no longer count on the East for protection from the Germanic tribes. When he returned to Rome six years later, Gregory was made abbot of the monastery of St. Andrew's, and in 590, when the pope died, the people and clergy of Rome made a reluctant Gregory the bishop of their city.

Gregory became pope at a time when Italy was suffering from both war and natural disaster. In the mid-sixth century, the Ostrogothic kingdom collapsed when Justinian's armies temporarily reconquered the West. The Byzantine emperor's wars left much of Italy a wilderness and made it easy prey for the Lombards who came into Italy in 568 C.E. and continued to ravage the peninsula throughout the seventh century. Flood, plague and famine followed in the wake of continual warfare, and as a result many believed that the end of the world was at hand.

In the midst of this chaos Gregory provided the church with farsighted leadership and spiritual guidance. He was forced by the absence of effective imperial authority in the West and the threat of the Lombard armies to take an active role in political affairs. In an effort to protect the city of Rome, he used revenues from the large papal land holdings to defend the city, to care for the poor in the city and to ransom captives. In 598, Gregory, not the emperor or his exarch, negotiated a truce with the Lombards. By taking on the duties of the imperial government, Gregory took an important step in making the papacy a temporal as well as a spiritual power.

Gregory also had the foresight to begin to direct the evangelization of the pagan Germanic tribes. Prior to this time, most Christian missionary efforts were initiated on a local level by individual bishops and monks, and many of the barbarian kingdoms were Arian, rather than orthodox or Nicene Christians. Gregory's efforts began to create a more united, orthodox Christendom in Europe. In 597 C.E. he sent a Roman monk by the name of Augustine to England to begin the work of converting the Anglo-Saxons and, when the Visigoths of Spain converted to orthodox Christianity in 587 C.E., he placed the Spanish church in the care of his friend Bishop Leander of Seville.

Gregory also had the wisdom to allow Christian missionaries to creatively adapt the gospel message to the worldview of Germanic culture without compromising its essentials. In a letter preserved by Bede in his *History of the English Church and Peoples,* Gregory gives a theoretical basis for accommodating the gospel to an illiterate and pagan culture.

(We) have come to the conclusion that the temples of idols among that people should on no account be destroyed. The idols are to be destroyed, but the temples themselves are to be aspersed with holy water, altars set up in them, and relics deposited there. For if these temples are well-built, they must be purified from the worship of demons and dedicated to the service of the true God. In this way, we hope that the people, seeing that their temples are not destroyed, may abandon their error and, flocking more readily to their accustomed resorts, may come to know and adore the true God. And since they have a custom of sacrificing many oxen to demons, let some other solemnity be substituted in its place, such as a day of Dedication or the Festivals of the holy martyrs whose relics are enshrined there. On such occasions they might well construct shelters of boughs for themselves around the churches that were once temples, and celebrate the solemnity with devout feasting. They are no longer to sacrifice beasts to the Devil, but they may kill them for food to praise God, and give thanks to the Giver of all gifts for the plenty they enjoy. If the people are allowed some worldly pleasures in this way, they will more readily come to desire the joys of the spirit.

Gregory's writings are not on the high theological level of Augustine, but they meet the pastoral needs of a church in an age when civilization was collapsing and authentic Christian spirituality was in danger of being lost. I have included selections from two of his works: *Pastoral Care,* a guide to Christian bishops in the care of their flocks, and the *Dialogues,* an account of the lives of Italian saints designed to inspire and edify ordinary Christian lay people in their pursuit of a life of Christian virtue.

Pastoral Care is addressed to a fellow bishop, John of Ravenna; it is a treatise on what sort of man the ideal pastor should be and how he should conduct himself. The tone throughout is hortatory. Gregory is not fighting heresy nor breaking new theological ground; he is attempting to insure the preservation of the Christian life by giving advice to the Christian bishop.

Part One treats the difficulties and requirements of the pastor's office. In the prologue and chapter one, Gregory explains his own reluctance to become bishop because of the fearful responsibility that the office of caring for souls entails. Such a task should be undertaken only with the greatest humility and integrity. Throughout chapter one Gregory attacks the hypocrisy of those who would assume such an office lightly or out of worldly ambition. He uses the diatribes of the prophets and of Jesus himself in the gospels against hypocrisy and irresponsible leadership to threaten anyone who would rashly assume the pastoral office.

Part Two is on the life of the pastor, and it treats the balance and spiritual wisdom that the shepherd of souls needs. In this section Gregory, the would-be contemplative, is trying to strike a balance between the life of prayer and service. Purity of thought should be combined with exemplary action which is discreet, compassionate and humble. Although necessarily occupied with external matters, the pastor should not neglect the inner life. He should also be prudent in his judgment of human character—a prudence rooted in meditation on the sacred Law.

Part Three illustrates Gregory's prudence as a pastor. Following Gregory of Nazianzus (c. 329–89 C.E.), he gives an elaborate and detailed treatment of how the teacher should adapt his discourse to the character of the hearers. Like a skilled physician or harpist, the pastor of souls is to lead his hearers to health or the harmony of a life of charity by distinguishing the kind of exhortation needed for each type of soul.

Finally, Part Four warns the pastor who has preached to others of the danger of pride and reliance upon his own virtues. To illustrate the need for a humility which recognizes one's humanity, Gregory uses several biblical texts. The prophet Ezekiel's elaborate allegory of the city of Jerusalem which trusted in its own beauty (Ezek 16), as well as David who believed himself strong but then fell into sin, warn the proud pastor of the danger of lusting for the praise and honor of others. The proper balance between humility and advancement in the life of virtue and contemplation in the pastor's life is again best illustrated by the prophet Ezekiel, who before he was led into contemplation of heavenly things was always addressed as "son of man" to remind him of his humanity and weakness. Fittingly, Gregory ends his portrait of the "ideal" pastor with a humble request for John of Ravenna's prayers.

> See, my good friend, compelled by the urgency of your remonstrances with me, I have tried to show what a pastor should be like. I, miserable painter that I am, have painted the portrait of an ideal man; and here I have been directing others to the shore of perfection, I, who am still tossed about on the waves of sin. But in the shipwreck of this life, sustain me, I beseech you, with the plank of your prayers, so that, as my weight is sinking me down, you may uplift me with your meritorious hand.

During the Middle Ages the *Pastoral Care* functioned like an ideal rule of life, ever reminding the secular clergy of their calling. During Gregory's own lifetime it was widely distributed in Spain, Ireland, England and even in a Greek translation in Antioch. In the Carolingian period a series of synods made its study obligatory for bishops, and at the close of the ninth century King Alfred the Great in England had it translated into West Saxon.

Our second selection is taken from Gregory's *Dialogues* which is a splendid example of hagiography, or the "lives of the saints." This was a most popular genre in the Middle

Ages because it provided ordinary Christians heroic models of Christian virtue and an assurance that the miraculous power of God was still active in their midst despite the often barbaric and chaotic circumstances of life.

The literary form of the work is a dialogue between Gregory and a young deacon of the papal household named Peter. This has, of course, classical and early Christian antecedents, and is particularly effective because Peter voices the concerns and anxieties of the ordinary Christian of the age, while Gregory provides examples of saints who exemplify Christian virtues and have thereby been the instrument for God's wondrous presence in Italy in recent times.

The *Dialogues* is a popular and practical version of Augustine's *City of God,* in that it provides Christians who find themselves distracted with the cares of maintaining life in the "city of man" with examples of people who have lived for heaven or "the City of God." In the opening to Book One Gregory sets the stage for the dialogue by describing an incident in which he chanced to meet with Peter when he himself was depressed and distracted because of the "worldly" burdens of his pastoral office and his longing for the spiritual repose of his earlier days in the monastery. Gregory describes his situation as being "tossed about on the waves of a heavy sea" and his soul as "a helpless ship buffeted by raging winds." When he expresses his regret that others have been able to totally abandon this world and live in seclusion to please their Creator, Peter is astonished that there have been such persons in Italy. He then asks Gregory to say something about these persons and in the process states the purpose of "the lives of the saints." They are meant to supplement the study of scripture which teaches how to attain virtue and persevere in it by "showing how this acquired virtue reveals itself in those who persevere in it." Living examples are always more effective than instruction because "as we compare ourselves with those who have gone before, we are filled with a longing for the future life" and "if we have too high an opinion of our own worth, it makes us humble to find that others have done better."

In Gregory's mind, his method in composing these "lives of the saints" is comparable to the evangelists Mark and Luke who were not eyewitnesses to the events of the gospel and therefore were dependent on the words of others. Gregory always states the authority upon which each account is based, but he also indicates that he has often retained only the substance of the narrative because the "crude language used by some would have been ill suited to my style of writing."

Book Two of the *Dialogues* is Gregory's "Life and Miracles of St. Benedict," and although it has a miracle in every chapter, its real purpose is to present Benedict as a person of Christian virtue who in Gregory's words, "While still living in the world, free to enjoy its earthly advantages . . . saw how barren it was with its attractions and turned from it without regret." In the opening chapter, for example, Gregory explains Benedict's decision to abandon his liberal studies in Rome and begin his life as a hermit as an effort to escape the life of vice of his fellow students in order to please God alone. The first miracle, the mending of his nurse's broken tray, illustrates Benedict's devotion and thoughtfulness, but more importantly, his unwillingness to receive the honors of this world.

When the miracle becomes known and the people display the tray over the door of the church, Benedict flees to the wilderness of Subiaco some thirty-five miles from Rome because "he wanted to spend himself laboring for God, not to be honored by the applause of men."

Gregory's description of how others became aware of Benedict's hermetical life illustrates how God revealed Benedict's virtuous life to provide the world with spiritual nourishment. He uses a contrast between the physical food necessary to sustain the body and the spiritual food that Benedict's wisdom offers to souls. When a priest is sent to visit Benedict with food on Easter, they exchange gifts; the priest brings food and Benedict enriches him with "talk about the spiritual life." Likewise, when the local shepherds discover Benedict's retreat, they supply him with the food he needs "and receive from his lips in return spiritual food for their souls."

As is standard in many lives of the saints, Gregory describes Benedict's triumph in a Christ-like manner over a temptation by Satan in the wilderness at the beginning of his religious life. In Benedict's case, the temptation, as Gregory describes it, is to abandon the lonely life with God in the wilderness for a life of lust. It comes in the form of the memory of "a woman he had once seen." He is able to overcome this temptation of the flesh "when suddenly with the help of God's grace he came to himself," Gregory's expression, based on the phrase in Luke's parable of the prodigal son (15:17) for searching into the soul and beholding oneself in the presence of the Creator. By violently flinging himself into a patch of nettles and briars, the saint puts "out the fires of evil in his heart" forever. This victory prepares Benedict "to instruct others" who wanted to forsake the world "in the practice of virtue."

The story of how Benedict shattered a pitcher by the sign of the cross illustrates the biblical theme found in Wisdom 2–3: that the just person's life is a threat to the wicked, but God does not allow their evil designs to triumph over his just ones. When the wayward monks of a certain monastery attempt to poison Benedict because of his strict discipline, the pitcher is shattered as he made the sign of the cross over it for the customary blessing during the meal.

Gregory's establishment of the monastery at Monte Cassino on the site of a temple to Apollo is a perfect illustration of the principles of adapting pagan sites to Christian uses which Gregory advocated in his letter to the missionaries to Anglo-Saxon England. Benedict destroys the idol to Apollo, overturns the altar and cuts down the tree in the sacred groves, but he then dedicates the site to Christian saints. He turns the temple of Apollo into a chapel under the patronage of Martin of Tours, an early Christian monk, and builds a chapel in honor of St. John the Baptist. This prepares the people of the countryside to receive his preaching of the true faith.

The final excerpt from the *Dialogues* is Gregory's explication of the doctrine of purgatory which became so crucial in medieval thought and the source of abuses later protested against by Martin Luther. Although Gregory can find no direct scriptural quotation to justify a belief in a period of purification after death for sinners who have not totally rejected God, he does attempt to argue on the basis of certain New Testament texts for his hypothesis that such a doctrine is necessary.

The translation of *Pastoral Care* is by Henry Davis, S.J. *St. Gregory the Great, Pastoral Care* in *Ancient Christian Writers,* Vol 11 (Westminster, Maryland, 1950) 20–23, 45, 89–90, 234–237. The translation of *Dialogues* is by Odo John Zimmerman, O.S.B. in *Saint Gregory The Great, Dialogues* in *Fathers of the Church* (New York: Fathers of the Church, Inc. 1959)

PASTORAL CARE

Salutation and Prologue

Gregory to his most reverend and most holy brother, John, fellow bishop.

Most dear brother, you reprove me with kind and humble regard for having wished to escape by concealment from the burdens of the pastoral care. Now, lest these burdens might appear light to some, I am explaining, by writing this book, how onerous I regard them, and he who has been so imprudent as to seek them may feel apprehension in having them.

The book is divided into four separate treatises, that it may bring its message to the mind of the reader in an orderly manner—as it were step by step.

The nature of the case requires that one should carefully consider the way in which the position of supreme rule ought to be approached, and when it is duly reached, how life should be spent in it; how, in a life of rectitude, one should teach others; and, in the proper performance of his teaching office, with what vigilance one should realize each day one's weakness. All this must be ensued lest humility be wanting when office is assumed, the way of life be at variance with the office accepted, teaching divest life of rectitude, and presumption overrate teaching.

Wherefore, before all else, fear must moderate the desire of compassing authority, and when this is attained by one who did not seek it, let his way of life recommend it. Then, too, it is necessary that the rectitude which is dis-

played in the pastor's way of life should be propagated by the spoken word. And, finally, I have only to add that consideration of our own weakness should abase every work accomplished, lest proud conceit empty it of its worth in the eyes of the hidden Judge.

I. The difficulties and requirements of the pastoral office

I.1 No one ventures to teach any art unless he has learned it after deep thought. With what rashness, then, would the pastoral office be undertaken by the unfit, seeing that the government of souls is the art of arts (cf. Gregory of Nazianzus, *Orat* 2.16). For who does not realize that the wounds of the mind are more hidden than the internal wounds of the body? Yet, although those who have no knowledge of the powers of drugs shrink from giving themselves out as physicians of the flesh (cf. Gregory of Nazianzus, *Orat* 2.16–34), people who are utterly ignorant of spiritual precepts are often not afraid of professing themselves to be physicians of the heart, and though, by divine ordinance, those now in the highest positions are disposed to show a regard for religion, some there are who aspire to glory and esteem by an outward show of authority within the holy church. They crave to appear as teachers and covet ascendancy over others, and, as the Truth attests: "They seek the first salutations in the market place, the first places at feasts, and the first chairs in the synagogues" (Matt 23:6 f.).

These persons are all the more unfitted to administer worthily what they have undertaken, the office of pastoral care, in that they have attained to the tutorship of humility by vanity alone; for, obviously, in this tutorship the tongue purveys mere jargon when one thing is learned and its contrary taught. Against such as these the Lord complains by the mouth of the Prophet: "They have reigned . . . not by me; they have been princes and I knew not" (Hos 8:4). These reign by their own conceit, not by the will of the Supreme Ruler; they are sustained by no virtues, are not divinely called, but being inflamed by their cupidity, they seize rather than attain supreme rule.

Yet the Judge within both advances and ignores them, because those whom He tolerates on sufferance, He actually ignores by the sentence of His reprobation. There, even to some who come to Him after having worked miracles, He says: "Depart from me, ye workers of iniquity, I know you not" (Lk 13:27; Matt 7:23). This unfitness of pastors is rebuked by the voice of the Truth, through the Prophet, when it is said: "The shepherds themselves knew no understanding" (Isa 56:11). Again, the Lord denounces them, saying: "And they that held the law knew me not" (Jer 2:8). Therefore the Truth complains of not being known by them, and protests that it does not know the high office of leaders who know Him not, because they who do not know the things that are the Lord's, are ignored by the Lord, as Paul says: "But if any man know not, he shall not be known" (1 Cor 14:38).

This unfitness of the pastors does, in truth, often accord with the deserts of their subjects, because, even if the former have not the light of knowledge through their own fault, it is due to a severe judgment that through their ignorance they, too, who follow, should stumble.

It is, therefore, for this reason that the Truth in person says in the Gospel: "If the blind lead the blind, both fall into the pit" (Matt 15:14; Lk 6:39). . . .

II. The life of the pastor

II.1 The conduct of a prelate should so far surpass the conduct of the people, as the life of a pastor sets him apart from his flock. For one who is so regarded that the people are called his flock, must carefully consider how necessary it is for him to maintain a life of rectitude. It is necessary, therefore, that he should be pure in thought, exemplary in conduct, discreet in keeping silence, profitable in speech, in sympathy a near neighbor to everyone, in contemplation exalted above all others, a humble companion to those who lead good lives, erect in his zeal for righteousness against the vices of sinners. He must not be remiss in his care for the inner life by preoccupation with the external; nor must he in his solicitude for what is internal fail to give attention to the external.

III. How the ruler should teach and admonish his subjects by his holy life

PROLOGUE

We have shown, then, what the character of the pastor should be: let us now set forth his manner of teaching. Well, as long before us Gregory of Nazianzus of revered memory has taught (*Orat* 2.16–34), one and the same exhortation is not suited to all, because they are not compassed by the same quality of character. Often, for instance, what is profitable to some, harms others. Thus, too, herbs which nourish some animals, kill others; gentle hissing that calms horses, excites young puppies; medicine that alleviates one disease, aggravates another; and bread such as strengthens the life of robust men, destroys that of little children.

Wherefore, the discourse of a teacher should be adapted to the character of the hearers, so as to be suited to the individual in his respective needs, and yet never deviate from the art of general edification. For what else are the minds of attentive hearers but, if I may say so, the taut strings of a harp, which the skillful harpist plays with a variety of strokes, that he may not produce a discordant melody? And it is for this reason that the strings give forth a harmonious melody, because they are not plucked with the same kind of stroke, though plucked with the one plectrum. Hence, too, every teacher, in order to edify all in one virtue of charity, must touch the hearts of his hearers by using one and the same doctrine, but not by giving to all one and the same exhortation.

. . .

IV. How the preacher when he has done everything as required, should return to himself, to prevent his life or preaching from making him proud

Now, seeing that often when a sermon is delivered with due propriety and with a fruitful message, the mind of the speaker is exalted by joy all his own over his performance, he must needs take care to torment himself with painful misgivings: in restoring others to health by healing their wounds, he must not disregard his own health and develop tumors of pride. Let him not, while helping his neighbors, neglect himself, let him not, while lifting up others, fall himself. In many instances, indeed, the greatness of certain men's virtues has been an occasion of their perdition, in that they have felt inordinately secure in the assurance of their strength, and they died suddenly because of their negligence. For as virtue struggles against vice, the mind, as it were exhilarated by this virtue, flatters itself; and it comes to pass that the soul of one actually engaged upon doing good casts aside all anxiety and circumspection, and rests secure in its self-confidence. In this its state of inertia the cunning Seducer enumerates all the man has done well, and aggrandizes him with conceited thoughts about his pre-eminence over all others.

Whence it happens that in the eyes of the just Judge the consciousness of virtue is a pitfall for the soul. In calling to mind what it has done, in exalting itself before itself, it falls in the presence of the Author of humility. Wherefore, it is said to the soul that is proud: "Whom dost thou excel in beauty? Go down and sleep with the uncircumcised" (Ezek 32:19); which means in plain words: "Since you exalt yourself because of the beauty of your virtues, it is this your beauty that is hurrying you on to your ruin." Hence, under the figure of Jerusalem, the soul which vaunts its virtue is reproved, when it is said: "Thou wast perfect through my beauty, which I had put upon thee, saith the Lord, but trusting in thy beauty, thou playedst the harlot because of thy renown" (Ezek 16:14). The mind is lifted up in confidence of its beauty, when with blithe self-assurance it glories over its virtues. But through this same confidence it is led on to play the harlot: that is, when by its thoughts the mind robs and deceives itself, evil spirits seduce and corrupt it with numerous vices. Note, too, that it is said: "Thou playedst the harlot because of thy renown"— meaning that when the soul has no regard for the Supernal Ruler, it at once seeks its own praise and begins to arrogate to itself all the good it has received for its mission as a herald of the Giver. Its desire is to spread the glory of its esteem, and its one concern is to impress all with its admirable qualities. Therefore, it plays the harlot because of its renown, when, forsaking the wedlock of its lawful bed, it prostitutes itself to the corrupting spirit in its lust for praise. Hence David says: "He delivered their strength into captivity, and their beauty into the hands of the enemy" (Ps 78:61). Virtue is, indeed, delivered into captivity, and beauty into the hands of the foe, when the ancient Enemy lords it over the deceived soul for its elation in well-doing.

Often this elation in virtue in a measure tempts the minds even of the elect, though it does not quite overcome them. In this case when the mind is lifted up, it is deserted, and deserted, it is recalled to fear. It is for this reason that David says again: "In my abundance I said I shall never be moved." But because in the assurance of his virtue he became conceited, he presently added what he had endured: "Thou turnedst away Thy face from me, and I became troubled" (Ps 30:7f.); which is as if he were saying plainly: "I believed myself strong in my virtues, but when I was deserted, I came to realise how great my weakness was." Wherefore, he says again: "I have sworn and am determined to keep the judgments of Thy justice." But because it was beyond his power to continue to observe his oath, he at once, on being troubled, discovered his weakness. Therefore, he betook himself at once to the help of prayer, saying: "I have been humbled, O Lord, exceedingly. Quicken thou me according to Thy word" (Ps 119:107).

Sometimes, too, divine guidance recalls to the mind the recollection of its infirmity before advancing it by gifts, lest it pride itself on the virtues it has received. Wherefore, the Prophet Ezekiel, as often as he is led to the contemplation of heavenly things, is first called "son of man" (Ezek 2:1,3,6,8; 3:1,3,4,6; etc.), as though the Lord plainly admonished him saying: "That you may not proudly lift up your heart because of what you are to see, consider carefully what you are. When you penetrate the sublimest things, remember that you are a man; for when you are enraptured above yourself, you will be recalled in anxiety to yourself by the curb of your infirmity." . . .

See, my good friend, compelled by the urgency of your remonstrances with me, I have tried to show what a pastor should be like. I, miserable painter that I am, have painted the portrait of an ideal man; and here I have been directing others to the shore of perfection, I, who am still tossed about on the waves of sin. But in the shipwreck of this life,

sustain me, I beseech you, with the plank of your prayers, so that, as my weight is sinking me down, you may uplift me with your meritorious hand.

DIALOGUES

I. Some men of the world had left me feeling quite depressed one day with all their noisy wrangling. In their business dealings they try, as a rule, to make us pay what we obviously do not owe them. In my grief I retired to a quiet spot congenial to my mood, where I could consider every unpleasant detail of my daily work and review all the causes of my sorrow as they crowded unhindered before my eyes.

I sat there for a long time in silence and was deeply dejected when my dear son, the deacon Peter, came in. He had been a very dear friend to me from his early youth and was my companion in the study of sacred Scripture. Seeing me so sick at heart he asked, "Have you met with some new misfortune? You seem unusually sad."

"Peter," I replied, "This daily sadness of mine is always old and always new: old by its constant presence, new by its continual increase. With my unhappy soul languishing under a burden of distraction, I recall those earlier days in the monastery where all the fleeting things of time were in a world below me, and I could rise far above the vanities of life. Heavenly thoughts would fill my mind, and while still held within the body I passed beyond its narrow confines in contemplation. Even death, which nearly everyone regards as evil, I cherished as the entrance into life and the reward for labor. . . .

"Such, in fact, is generally the way our mind declines. First we lose a prized possession but remain aware of the loss; then as we go along even the remembrance of it fades, and so at the end we are unable any longer to recall what was once actually in our possession. That is why, as I have said, when we sail too far from shore, we can no longer see the peaceful harbor we have left. At times I find myself reflecting with even greater regret on the life that others lead who have totally abandoned the present world. Seeing the heights these men have reached only makes me realize the lowly state of my own soul. It was by spending their days in seclusion that most of them pleased their Creator. And to keep them from dulling their spiritual fervor with human activities, God chose to leave them free from worldly occupations."

And now I think it will be best if I present the conversation that took place between us by simply putting our names before the questions and the answers we exchanged.

Peter: I do not know any persons in Italy whose lives give evidence of extraordinary spiritual powers, and therefore I cannot imagine with whom you are comparing yourself so regretfully. This land of ours has undoubtedly produced virtuous men, but to my knowledge no signs or miracles have been performed by any of them; or, if they have been, they were till now kept in such secrecy that we cannot even tell if they occurred.

Gregory: On the contrary, Peter, the day would not be long enough for me to tell you about those saints whose holiness has been well established and whose lives are known to me either from my own observations or from the reports of good, reliable witnesses.

Peter: Would you do me the favor, then, of saying at least something about them? Interrupting the study and explanation of the Scriptures for such a purpose should not cause grave concern, for the amount of edification to be gained from a description of miracles is just as great. An explanation of holy Scripture teaches us how to attain virtue and persevere in it, whereas a description of mir-

acles shows us how the acquired virtue reveals itself in those who persevere in it. Then, too, the lives of the saints are often more effective than mere instruction for inspiring us to love heaven as our home. Hearing about their example will generally be helpful in two ways. In the first place, as we compare ourselves with those who have gone before, we are filled with a longing for the future life; secondly, if we have too high an opinion of our own worth, it makes us humble to find others have done better.

Gregory: I shall not hesitate to narrate what I have learned from worthy men. In this I am only following the consecrated practice of the Scriptures, where it is perfectly clear that Mark and Luke composed their Gospels, not as eyewitnesses but on the word of others. Nevertheless, to remove any grounds for doubt on the part of my readers, I am going to indicate on whose authority each account is based. You should bear in mind, however, that in some instances I retain only the substance of the original narrative; in others, the words as well. For if I had always kept to the exact wording, the crude language used by some would have been ill suited to my style of writing. . . .

II. The life and miracles of St. Benedict: founder and abbot of the monastery which is know as the citadel of Campania

There was a man of saintly life; blessed Benedict was his name, and he was blessed also with God's grace. Even in boyhood he showed mature understanding, for he kept his heart detached from every pleasure with a strength of character far beyond his years. While still living in the world, free to enjoy its earthly advantages, he saw how barren it was with its attractions and turned from it without regret.

He was born in the district of Norcia of distinguished parents, who sent him to Rome for a liberal education. But when he saw many of his fellow students falling headlong into vice, he stepped back from the threshold of the world in which he had just set foot. For he was afraid that if he acquired any of its learning he, too, would later plunge, body and soul, into the dread abyss. In his desire to please God alone, he turned his back on further studies, gave up home and inheritance and resolved to embrace the religious life. He took this step, well aware of his ignorance, yet wise, uneducated though he was.

I was unable to learn about all his miraculous deeds. But the few I am going to relate I know from the lips of four of his own disciples: Constantine, the holy man who succeeded him as abbot; Valentinian, for many years superior of the monastery at the Lateran; Simplicius, Benedict's second successor; and Honoratus, who is still abbot of the monastery where the man of God first lived.

1. *The mending of a broken tray*

When Benedict abandoned his studies to go into solitude, he was accompanied only by his nurse, who loved him dearly. As they were passing through Affile, a number of devout men invited them to stay there and provided them with lodging near the Church of St. Peter. One day, after asking her neighbors to lend her a tray for cleaning wheat, the nurse happened to leave it on the edge of the table and when she came back found it had slipped off and broken in two. The poor woman burst into tears; she had only borrowed this tray and now it was ruined. Benedict, who had always been a devout and thoughtful boy, felt sorry for his nurse when he saw her weeping. Quietly picking up both the pieces, he knelt down by himself and prayed earnestly to God, even to the point of tears. No sooner had he finished his prayer than he noticed that the two pieces were joined together again, without even a mark to show where the tray had been broken. Hurrying back at once, he cheer-

fully reassured his nurse and handed her the tray in perfect condition.

News of the miracle spread to all the country around Affile and stirred up so much admiration among the people that they hung the tray at the entrance of their church. Ever since then it has been a reminder to all of the great holiness Benedict had acquired at the very outset of his monastic life. The tray remained there many years for everyone to see, and it is still hanging over the doorway of the church in these days of Lombard rule. Benedict, however, preferred to suffer ill-treatment from the world rather than enjoy its praises. He wanted to spend himself laboring for God, not to be honored by the applause of men. So he stole away secretly from his nurse and fled to a lonely wilderness about thirty-five miles from Rome called Subiaco. A stream of cold, clear water running through the region broadens out at this point to form a lake, then flows off and continues on its course. On his way there Benedict met a monk named Romanus, who asked him where he was going. After discovering the young man's purpose, Romanus kept it secret and even helped him carry it out by clothing him with the monastic habit and supplying his needs as well as he could.

At Subiaco, Benedict made his home in a narrow cave and for three years remained concealed there, unknown to anyone except the monk Romanus, who lived in a monastery close by under the rule of Abbot Deodatus. With fatherly concern this monk regularly set aside as much bread as he could from his own portion; then from time to time, unnoticed by his abbot, he left the monastery long enough to take the bread to Benedict. There was no path leading from the monastery down to his cave because of a cliff that rose directly over it. To reach him Romanus had to tie the bread to the end of a long rope and lower it over the cliff. A little bell attached to the rope let Benedict know when the bread was there, and he would come out to get it. The ancient Enemy of mankind grew envious of the kindness shown by the older monk in supplying Benedict with food, and one day, as the bread was being lowered, he threw a stone at the bell and broke it. In spite of this, Romanus kept on with his faithful service.

At length the time came when almighty God wished to grant him rest from his toil and reveal Benedict's virtuous life to others. Like a shining lamp his example was to be set on a lampstand to give light to everyone in God's house (cf. Matt 5:15). The Lord therefore appeared in a vision to a priest some distance away, who had just prepared his Easter dinner. "How can you prepare these delicacies for yourself," He asked, "while my servant is out there in the wilds suffering from hunger?"

Rising at once, the priest wrapped up the food and set out to find the man of God that very day. He searched for him along the rough mountainsides, in the valleys, and through the caverns, until he found him hidden in the cave. They said a prayer of thanksgiving together and then sat down to talk about the spiritual life. After a while the priest suggested that they take their meal. "Today is the great feast of Easter," he added.

"It must be a great feast to have brought me this kind visit," the man of God replied, not realizing after his long separation from men that it was Easter Sunday.

"Today is really Easter," the priest insisted, "the feast of our Lord's Resurrection. On such a solemn occasion you should not be fasting. Besides, I was sent here by almighty God so that both of us could share in His gifts."

After that they said grace and began their meal. When it was over they conversed some more and then the priest went back to his church (cf. Acts 9:10–19).

At about the same time some shepherds also discovered Benedict's hiding place. When they first looked through the thickets and caught sight of him clothed in rough skins, they mistook him for some wild animal. Soon, however, they recognized in him a servant of God, and many of them gave up their sinful ways for a life of holiness. As a result, his name became known to all the people in that locality and great numbers visited his cave, supplying him with the food he needed and receiving from his lips in return spiritual food for their souls.

2. *The saint overcomes a temptation of the flesh*

One day, while the saint was alone, the Tempter came in the form of a little blackbird, which began to flutter in front of his face. It kept so close that he could easily have caught it in his hand. Instead, he made the sign of the cross and the bird flew away. The moment it left, he was seized with an unusually violent temptation. The evil spirit recalled to his mind a woman he had once seen, and before he realized it his emotions were carrying him away. Almost overcome in the struggle, he was on the point of abandoning the lonely wilderness, when suddenly with the help of God's grace he came to himself.

He then noticed a thick patch of nettles and briers next to him. Throwing his garment aside he flung himself into the sharp thorns and stinging nettles. There he rolled and tossed until his whole body was in pain and covered with blood. Yet, once he had conquered pleasure through suffering, his torn and bleeding skin served to drain the poison of temptation from his body. Before long, the pain that was burning his whole body had put out the fires of evil in his heart. It was by exchanging these two fires that he gained the victory over sin. So complete was his triumph that from then on, as he later told his disciples, he never experienced another temptation of this kind.

Soon after, many forsook the world to place themselves under his guidance, for now that he was free from these temptations he was ready to instruct others in the practice of virtue. That is why Moses commanded the Levites to begin their service when they were twenty-five years old or more and to become guardians of the sacred vessels only at the age of fifty (cf. Num 8:24–28).

Peter: The meaning of the passage you quote is becoming a little clearer to me now. Still, I wish you would explain it more fully.

Gregory: It is a well-known fact, Peter, that temptations of the flesh are violent during youth, whereas after the age of fifty concupiscence dies down. Now, the sacred vessels are the souls of the faithful. God's chosen servants must therefore obey and serve and tire themselves out with strenuous work as long as they are still subject to temptations. Only when full maturity has left them undisturbed by evil thoughts are they put in charge of the sacred vessels, for then they become teachers of souls.

Peter: I like the way you interpreted that passage. Now that you have explained what it means, I hope you will continue with your account of the holy man's life.

3. *A glass pitcher is shattered by the sign of the cross*

Gregory: With the passing of this temptation, Benedict's soul, like a field cleared of briers, soon yielded a rich harvest of virtues. As word spread of his saintly life, the renown of his name increased. One day the entire community from a nearby monastery came to see him. Their abbot had recently died, and they wanted the man of God to be their new superior. For some time he tried to discourage them by refusing their request, warning them that his way of life would never harmonize with theirs. But they kept insisting, until in the end he gave his consent.

At the monastery he watched carefully over the religious spirit of his monks and would not tolerate any of their previous disobedience. No one was allowed to turn from the straight path of monastic discipline either to the right or to the left. Their waywardness, however, clashed with the standards he upheld, and in their resentment they started to reproach themselves for choosing him as abbot. It only made them the more sullen to find him curbing every fault and evil habit. They could not see why they should have to force their settled minds into new ways of thinking.

At length, proving once again that the very life of the just is a burden to the wicked (cf. Wis 2:12–20), they tried to find a means of doing away with him and decided to poison his wine. A glass pitcher containing this poisoned drink was presented to the man of God during his meal for the customary blessing. As he made the sign of the cross over it with his hand, the pitcher was shattered, even though it was well beyond his reach at the time. It broke at his blessing as if he had struck it with stone.

Then he realized it had contained a deadly drink which could not bear the sign of life. Still calm and undisturbed, he rose at once and, after gathering the community together, addressed them. "May almighty God have mercy on you," he said. "Why did you conspire to do this? Did I not tell you at the outset that my way of life would never harmonize with yours? Go and find yourselves an abbot to your liking. It is impossible for me to stay here any longer." Then he went back to the wilderness he loved, to live alone with himself in the presence of his heavenly Father.

Peter: I am not quite sure I understand what you mean by saying "to live with himself."

Gregory: These monks had an outlook on religious life entirely unlike his own and were all conspiring against him. Now, if he had tried to force them to remain under his rule, he might have forfeited his own fervor and peace of soul and even turned his eyes from the light of contemplation. Their persistent daily faults would have left him almost too weary to look to his own needs, and he would perhaps have forsaken himself without finding them. For, whenever anxieties carry us out of ourselves unduly, we are no longer with ourselves even though we still remain what we are. We are too distracted with other matters to give any attention whatever to ourselves.

Surely we cannot describe as "with himself" the young man who traveled to a distant country where he wasted his inheritance and then, after hiring himself out to one of its citizens to feed swine, had to watch them eat their fill of pods while he went hungry. Do we not read in Scripture that, as he was considering all he had lost, "he came to himself and said, 'how many hired servants there are in my father's house who have more bread than they can eat'" (Lk 15:17)? If he was already "with himself," how could he have come "to himself?"

Blessed Benedict, on the contrary, can be said to have lived "with himself" because at all times he kept such close watch over his life and actions. By searching continually into his own soul he always beheld himself in the presence of his Creator. And this kept his mind from straying off to the world outside.

. . .

Gregory: As Benedict's influence spread over the surrounding countryside because of his signs and wonders, a great number of men gathered round him to devote themselves to God's service. Christ blessed his work and before long he had established twelve monasteries there, with an abbot and twelve monks in each of them. There were a few other monks whom he kept with him, since he felt that they still needed his personal guidance.

The destruction of the altar of Apollo on Monte Cassino

Gregory: Although he moved to a different place, Peter, his enemy remained the same. In fact, the assaults he had to endure after this were all the more violent, because the very Master of evil was fighting against him in open battle.

The fortified town of Cassino lies at the foot of a towering mountain that shelters it within its slope and stretches upward over a distance of nearly three miles. On its summit stood a very old temple, in which the ignorant country people still worshiped Apollo as their pagan ancestors had done, and went on offering superstitious and idolatrous sacrifices in groves dedicated to various demons.

When the man of God arrived at this spot, he destroyed the idol, overturned the altar and cut down the trees in the sacred groves. Then he turned the temple of Apollo into a chapel dedicated to St. Martin (Martin of Tours), and where Apollo's altar had stood, he built a chapel in honor of St. John the Baptist. Gradually, the people of the countryside were won over to the true faith by his zealous preaching.

Such losses the Enemy could not bear in silence. This time he did not appear to the saint in a dream or under a disguise, but met him face-to-face and objected fiercely to the outrages he had to endure. His shouts were so loud that the brethren heard him, too, although they were unable to see him. According to the saint's own description, the Devil had an appearance utterly revolting to human eyes. He was enveloped in fire and, when he raged against the man of God, flames darted from his eyes and mouth. Everyone could hear what he was saying. First he called Benedict by name. Then, finding that the saint would not answer, he broke out in abusive language. "Benedict, Benedict, blessed Benedict!" he would begin, and then add, "You cursed Benedict! Cursed, not blessed! What do you want with me? Why are you tormenting me like this?"

From now on, Peter, as you can well imagine, the Devil fought against the man of God with renewed violence. But, contrary to his plans, all these attacks only supplied the saint with further opportunities for victory.

32. A dead boy is raised to life

And now, here is a remarkable miracle that was the result of his prayer. One day, when he was out working in the fields with his monks, a farmer came to the monastery carrying in his arms the lifeless body of his son. Brokenhearted at his loss, he begged to see the saintly abbot and on learning that he was at work in the fields, left the dead body at the entrance of the monastery and hurried off to find him. By then the abbot was already returning from his work. The moment the farmer caught sight of him he cried out, "Give me back my son! Give me back my son!"

Benedict stopped when he heard this. "But I have not taken your son from you, have I?" he asked.

The boy's father only replied, "He is dead. Come! Bring him back to life."

Deeply grieved at his words, the man of God turned to his disciples. "Stand back, brethren!" he said. "Stand back! Such a miracle is beyond our power. The holy Apostles are the only ones who can raise the dead (cf. Acts 9:36–41; 20:9.10). Why are you so eager to accept what is impossible for us?"

But overwhelming sorrow compelled the man to keep on pleading. He even declared with an oath that he would not leave until Benedict restored his son to life. The saint then asked him where the body was. "At the entrance to the monastery," he answered.

When Benedict arrived there with his monks, he knelt down beside the child's body

and bent over it. Then, rising, he lifted his hands to heaven in prayer. "O Lord," he said, "do not consider my sins but the faith of this man who is asking to see his son alive again, and restore to this body the soul You have taken from it."

His prayer was hardly over when the child's whole body began once more to throb with life. No one present there could doubt that this sudden stirring was due to a heavenly intervention. Benedict then took the little boy by the hand and gave him back to his father alive and well.

Obviously, Peter, he did not have the power to work this miracle himself. Otherwise he would not have begged for it prostrate in prayer.

36. The monastic rule he wrote

Gregory: I should like to tell you much more about this saintly abbot, but I am purposely passing over some of his miraculous deeds in my eagerness to take up those of others. There is one more point, however, I want to call to your attention. With all the renown he gained by his numerous miracles, the holy man was no less outstanding for the wisdom of his teaching. He wrote a *Rule for Monks* that is remarkable for its discretion and its clarity of language. Anyone who wishes to know more about his life and character can discover in his *Rule* exactly what he was like as abbot, for his life could not have differed from his teaching.

IV. 41 After death, purgatory

Peter: I should like to know if we have to believe in a cleansing fire after death.

Gregory: In the Gospel our Lord says, "Finish your journey while you still have the light" (Jn 12:35). And in the words of the Prophet He declares, "In an acceptable time I have heard thee, and in the day of salvation I have helped thee" (Isa 49:8). St Paul's comment on this is: "And here is the time of pardon; the day of salvation has come already" (2 Cor 6:2). Solomon, too, says, "Anything you can turn your hand to, do with what power you have; for there will be no work, nor reason, nor knowledge, nor wisdom in the nether world where you are going" (Eccl 9:10). And David adds, "For his mercy endures forever" (Ps 118:1). From these quotations it is clear that each one will be presented to the Judge exactly as he was when he departed this life. Yet, there must be a cleansing fire before judgment, because of some minor faults that may remain to be purged away. Does not Christ, the Truth, say that if anyone blasphemes against the Holy Spirit he shall not be forgiven "either in this world or in the world to come" (Matt 12:32)? From this statement we learn that some sins can be forgiven in this world and some in the world to come. For, if forgiveness is refused for a particular sin, we conclude logically that it is granted for others. This must apply, as I said, to slight transgressions, such as persistent idle talking, immoderate laughter, or blame in the care of property, which can scarcely be administered without fault even by those who know the faults to be avoided, or errors due to ignorance in matters of no great importance. All these faults are troublesome for the soul after death if they are not forgiven while one is still alive. For, when St. Paul says that Christ is the foundation, he adds: "But on this foundation different men will build in gold, silver, precious stones, wood, grass, or straw . . . and fire will test the quality of each man's workmanship. He will receive a reward, if the building he had added on stands firm! If it is burnt up, he will be the loser; and yet he himself will be saved, though only as men are saved by passing through fire" (1 Cor 3:12–15).

Although this may be taken to signify the fire of suffering we experience in this life, it may also refer to the cleansing fire of the world to come, and, if one accepts it in this sense, one must weigh St. Paul's words carefully. When he says that men are saved by passing through fire, he is not referring to men who build on this foundation in iron, bronze, or in lead, that is, in mortal sins which are indestructible by fire. He specifies those who build on this foundation in wood, grass, and straw, that is, in venial or trivial sins which fire consumes easily. In this connection we should also remember that in the world to come no one will be cleansed even of the slightest faults, unless he has merited such a cleansing through good works performed in this life.

3

BYZANTINE CHRISTIANITY

Although this text is primarily a reader in the development of Western Christian thought, it is appropriate to give a sample of Eastern Christian theology by way of comparison with theological developments in the West, and also because of its impact on Western theology and the eventual division of Christendom between East and West.

Constantine's decisions to support the Christian church and to move the capital of the Roman empire to the East had a lasting impact on the history of Christianity. When the emperor made the ancient town of Byzantium into a new Christian Rome and the Eastern capital of the empire, he was creating an inevitable rival to Rome as the leading see in Christendom. From the fourth century C.E. onwards, an increasing estrangement developed between the Greek-speaking Eastern part of the church whose primary see became this new "city of Constantine," Constantinople, and the Latin-speaking West which recognized Rome as the primary see of Christendom. Gradually a series of differences in such matters as the role of the emperor in the church, the jurisdiction of the various patriarchal sees, liturgical language and practice, theological emphasis, disciplinary matters like priestly celibacy and the date for the celebration of Easter, as well as dogmatic disputes led to a permanent schism in 1054 C.E. between the Roman church and the Byzantine or Eastern Orthodox church.

The theology of the Byzantine churches is based on scripture and the definitions of the Seven Ecumenical Councils of the early church which were all held in the East in the fourth through eighth centuries C.E. and defined the paradoxical Christian mysteries of the Trinity and the full divinity and humanity of Christ. The spirit of Byzantine theology is a kind of Christian Platonism in which the physical world is seen as an epiphany of a superior spiritual world. God as Father, Son and Spirit is mystery, best symbolized by ineffable light, but the divine mystery has been revealed through material creation and in history in the Law, the Prophets, and finally in Christ the incarnate Word of God. History is understood as a dynamic saving process which begins with the life of the Trinity, is most fully revealed in the incarnation of Christ, and will end with the divinization of the material world.

JOHN OF DAMASCUS, *AN EXACT EXPOSITION OF THE ORTHODOX FAITH* FROM *FOUNT OF KNOWLEDGE*

The last and greatest of the early medieval Eastern theologians who had a comparable significance to Augustine in the West was John of Damascus or John Damascene (d.c. 749 C.E.). He was born as a Christian in Damascus, Syria. As a young man, he apparently succeeded his father as a tax collector for the Muslim Omayyad califs. Sometime around 715 C.E. he entered the St. Sabas Monastery near Jerusalem, and he lived and wrote there until his death.

Our selections are taken from *The Fount of Knowledge* which is John Damescene's greatest contribution to the history of Christian theology. It was composed at the request of his good friend and former fellow monk, Coasmas, the bishop of Maiuma. The book is divided into three sections. In the first, John gives an exposition of the philosophy of Aristotle as a rational tool for the explication of the Christian faith. In the second, he lists and describes one hundred heresies of various kinds. The third and most important section, entitled *An Exact Exposition of the Orthodox Faith,* is divided into four books. Book 1 treats of God in unity and trinity. The second considers God's creation, both invisible and visible, with special attention given to man and his faculties; it concludes with an account of the Fall. Book 3 is Damascene's treatment of Christology in the context of God's concern for human salvation in light of the Fall; it gives a lucid and thorough explication of the orthodox Christian faith in the union of the two natures, divine and human, in the one person, *hypostasis,* of Christ. Book 4 continues the treatment of Christology and goes on to consider faith, baptism, the eucharist, the genealogy of Jesus and Mary, the veneration of saints and their relics, the cult of icons (holy images), and a number of other disparate subjects. The book concludes with a chapter on the resurrection. Both the outline and the theological positions of John Damascene's *Fount of Knowledge* had an important influence on the great Dominican medieval theologian, St. Thomas Aquinas.

The opening selection from Book 1 illustrates the Eastern theologians' sense of the mystery of the ineffable God who has revealed himself in the harmony of creation, through the Law and the Prophets, and finally in his only-begotten Son. In this section John reflects the character of orthodox theology which is rooted in scripture and the decisions of the ecumenical councils of the early church. He also uses the "negative theology" of Pseudo-Dionysius, a fifth-century Syrian mystical writer who was influenced by Neoplatonic philosophy, and insisted on the inadequacy of our human language to express the mystery of God beyond the metaphorical language revealed in the scriptures. Damascene's proofs for the existence of God from the necessity for an uncreated and unchangeable being and from the harmony and design of the universe are typical of Eastern theology, which emphasizes at one and the same time the otherness of God and yet sees the physical world as an epiphany of God. Both arguments will later be used by Thomas Aquinas in his famous five proofs for the existence of God at the beginning of his *Summa Theologica.*

John's discussion of the reason why the Son, rather than the Father or Holy Spirit, became man illustrates the Eastern approach to Christology. Like the great Athanasius before him, Damascene believes the reason for the incarnation is soteriological, i.e., the Son acted to restore the possibility of salvation for humanity once it had fallen into sin and the power of Satan. The Son, who has the property of filiation (sonship) in the eternal life of the Trinity and was the agent of the original creation in which humanity was created in God's image and likeness, acts out of love for his creation to restore the divine image that was lost by sin by taking to himself our nature. John ends this section by praising Christ for the paradoxical power of his action in restoring humanity through the apparent weakness of the cross, suffering and death. His contrast between God's powerful action in liberating the Israelites from Egypt and his gentle action in Christ stresses the interior change within the believer that is accomplished through the persuading power of God's love.

> It was not by force that He led sinners to virtue, not by having them swallowed up by the earth, nor by having them burnt by fire, nor by ordering them stoned to death; it was with gentleness and forbearance that He persuaded men to choose virtue and for virtue's sake to undergo sufferings with rejoicing. Sinners were formerly tormented, yet they clung to their sin, and sin was accounted a god by them; but now, for piety and virtue's sake, they choose torments, tortures, and death.

This understanding of the reason for the incarnation stands in sharp contrast to the juridical and "feudal" approach which will be taken in the Western tradition by St. Anselm in his *Cur Deus Homo* (c. 1033–1109 C.E.) who begins with the idea that humankind's sin has offended the justice of God the Father and then reasons to the necessity of a God-man to rectify that offended justice.

John's brief justification for the use of icons in the Christian church reflects the famous iconoclastic controversy which ravaged the Eastern church during his life. When the Byzantine emperor, Leo III, the Isaurian (c. 675–741 C.E.), enforced his edicts against the use of icons in the Christian church, John Damascene wrote three *Apologies* which defended the use of icons and argued against the principle of the emperor's interference in ecclesiastical matters. In the second *Apology* he states:

> It does not belong to kings to legislate for the Church . . . to kings belongs the maintenance of civil order, but the administration of the church belongs to the shepherds and teachers.

This is a perfect statement of the Byzantine principle of *symphonia,* a harmony between church and state based on a division of function, as opposed to the evils of Caesaropapism.

John's primary argument for the use of icons is from the mystery of the incarnation. In Christ the invisible and limitless spiritual God has become visible and taken on the limits of human flesh. He is the primary *icon* or image of the living God. The fact of the incarnation supersedes the former commandment given to Moses prohibiting image-making because ancient Israel was prone to idolatry. Now Christians may depict the likeness of Christ, Mary and the saints because the material order has been redeemed by Christ. John also distinguishes between the true worship (*latreia*) due the infinite God, who became flesh in Christ, and the veneration or honor (*time*) due to the icons which merely represent in matter the mysteries of salvation. He is insistent upon the educational value of the images which function as a book for the illiterate to raise their minds and hearts to the mysteries which are symbolized in them.

The Seventh Ecumenical Council, which met at Nicea in 787 C.E., restored the use of icons with the qualification that they be paintings or sculptures in low relief. A second iconoclastic controversy began in 814 C.E. under Emperor Leo V, the Armenian. Persecution of those devoted to the icons ended with the death of Emperor Theophilus in 842 C.E. His widow, Theodora, succeeded in having Methodius, a supporter of the icons, elected patriarch of Constantinope, and on the first Sunday of Lent a feast was celebrated in honor of the icons. This feast is still kept in Eastern Orthodox churches as the "Feast of Orthodoxy."

The translation is by Frederic H. Chase, Jr. in *Saint John of Damascus Writings* in *The Fathers of the Church* Series (New York: Fathers of the Church, Inc., 1958) 165–170, 337–339, 370–373.

I.1 Our Knowledge of God and the Divine Nature

"No man hath seen God at any time: the only-begotten Son who is in the bosom of the Father, he hath declared him" (Jn 1:18). The Godhead, then is ineffable and incomprehensible. For "no one knoweth the Father, but the Son: neither doth any one know the Son, but the Father" (Matt 11:27). Furthermore, the Holy Spirit knows the things of God, just as the spirit of man knows what is in man (cf. 1 Cor 2:11). After the first blessed state of nature, no one has ever known God unless God Himself revealed it to him—not only no man, but not even any supramundane powers: the very Cherubim and Seraphim, I mean.

Nevertheless, God has not gone so far as to leave us in ignorance, for through nature the knowledge of the existence of God has been revealed by Him to all men. The very creation of its harmony and ordering proclaims the majesty of the divine nature (cf. Wis 13:5;

Rom 1:20). Indeed, He has given us knowledge of Himself in accordance with our capacity, at first through the Law and the Prophets and then afterwards through His only-begotten Son, our Lord and God and Saviour, Jesus Christ. Accordingly, we accept all those things that have been handed down by the Law and the Prophets and the Apostles and the Evangelists, and we know and revere them, and over and above these things we seek nothing else. For, since God is good, He is the author of all good and is not subject to malice or to any affection. For malice is far removed from the divine nature, which is unaffected and only good. Since, therefore, He knows all things and provides for each in accordance with his needs, He has revealed to us what it was expedient for us to know, whereas that which we were unable to bear He has withheld. With these things let us be content and in them let us abide and let us not step over the ancient bounds (cf. Prov 22:28) or pass beyond the divine tradition.

I.2

Now, one who would speak or hear about God should know beyond any doubt that in what concerns theology and the Dispensation (term for incarnation) not all things are inexpressible and not all are capable of expression, and neither are all things unknowable nor are they all knowable. That which can be known is one thing, whereas that which can be said is another, just as it is one thing to speak and another to know. Furthermore, many of those things about God which are not clearly perceived cannot be fittingly described, so that we are obliged to express in human terms things which transcend the human order. Thus, for example, in speaking about God we attributed to Him sleep, anger, indifference, hands and feet, and the like.

Now, we both know and confess that God is without beginning and without end, everlasting and eternal, uncreated, unchangeable, inalterable, simple, uncompounded, incorporeal, invisible, impalpable, uncircumscribed, unlimited, incomprehensible, uncontained, unfathomable, good, just, the maker of all created things, all-powerful, all-ruling, all-seeing, the provider, the sovereign, and the judge of all. We furthermore know and confess that God is one, that is to say, one substance, and that He is both understood to be and is in three Persons—I mean the Father and the Son and the Holy Ghost—and that the Father and the Son and the Holy Ghost are one in all things save in the being unbegotten, the being begotten, and the procession. We also know and confess that for our salvation the Word of God through the bowels of His mercy, by the good pleasure of the Father and with the cooperation of the All-Holy Spirit, was conceived without seed and chastely begotten of the holy Virgin and Mother of God, Mary, by the Holy Ghost and of her became perfect man; and that He is perfect God and at the same time perfect man, being of two natures, the divinity and the humanity, and in two

intellectual natures endowed with will and operation and liberty—or, to put it simply, perfect in accordance with the definition and principle befitting each, the divinity, I mean, and the humanity, but with one compound hypostasis. And we know and confess that he hungered and thirsted and was weary, and that He was crucified, and that for three days He suffered death and the tomb, and that He returned into heaven whence He had come to us and whence He will come back to us at a later time. To all this holy scripture and all the company of the saints bear witness.

But what the substance of God is, or how it is in all things, or how the only-begotten Son, who was God, emptied Himself out and became man from a virgin's blood, being formed by another law that transcended nature, or how He walked dry-shod upon the waters, we neither understand nor can say (cf. Pseudo-Dionysius, *The Divine Names* 2.9). And so it is impossible either to say or fully to understand about God beyond what has been divinely proclaimed to us, whether told or revealed, by the sacred declarations of the Old and New Testaments.

I.3

Now, the fact that God exists is not doubted by those who accept the sacred scriptures—both the Old and New Testaments, I mean—nor by the majority of the Greeks, for, as we have said, the knowledge of God's existence has been revealed to us through nature. However, since the wickedness of the Evil One has so prevailed over men's nature as even to drag some of them down to the most unspeakable and extremely wicked abyss of perdition and to make them say that there is no God (of whose folly the Prophet David said: "the fool hath said in his heart: There is no God [Ps 13:1]), then the Lord's disciples and Apostles, made wise by the All-Holy Spirit, did by His power and grace show signs from God and draw up those people alive in the net of their miracles from the depths of ignorance of God to the light of his knowledge. Similarly, the shepherds and teacher who succeeded to their grace of the Spirit and by the power of their miracles and the word of their grace enlightened those who were in darkness and converted those who were in error. Now, let us who have not received the gifts of miracles and teaching, because by our being given to material pleasures we have made ourselves unworthy, let us invoke the aid of the Father and of the Son and of the Holy Ghost, and discuss some few of the things which the expounders of grace have handed down to us.

All things are either created or uncreated. Now, if they are created, then they are also definitely changeable, for things whose being originated with change are definitely subject to change, whether it be by corruption or by voluntary alteration. If, on the other hand, they are uncreated, then it logically follows that they are definitely unchangeable. For, of those things whose being is contrary, the manner of being, which is to say, properties, is also contrary. Who, then, will not agree that all beings that fall within our experience, including even the angels, are subject to change and alteration and to being moved in various ways? The intellectual beings—by which I mean angels and souls and demons— change by free choice, progressing in good or receding, exerting themselves or slackening; whereas the rest change by generation or corruption, increase or decrease, change in quality or change in position. Consequently, things which are changeable must definitely be created. Created beings have certainly been created by something. But the Creator must be uncreated, for, if He has been created, then He has certainly been created by some one else—and so on until we arrive at something which has not been created. Therefore, the Creator is an uncreated and entirely unchangeable being. And what else would that be but God?

What is more, the very harmony of creation, its preservation and governing, teach us that there is a God who has put all this together and keeps it together, ever maintaining it and providing for it. For how could such contrary natures as fire and water, earth and air, combine with one another to form one world and remain undissolved, unless there were some all-powerful force to bring them together and always keep them that way (cf. Athanasius, *Against the Pagans,* 35–36)?

What is it that has ordered the things of heaven and those of earth, the things which move through the air and those which move in the water—nay, rather, the things which preceded them: heaven and earth and the nature of fire and water? What is it that combined and arranged them? What is it that set them in motion and put them on their unceasing and unhindered courses? Or is it that they had no architect to set a principle in them all by which the whole universe be moved and controlled? But who is the architect of these things? Or did not he who made them also bring them into being? We shall certainly not attribute such power to spontaneity. Even grant that they came into being spontaneously; then, whence came their arrangement? Let us grant this, also, if you wish. Then, what maintains and keeps the principles by which they subsisted in the first place? It is most certainly some other thing than mere chance. What else is this, if it is not God (cf. Gregory Nazianzen, *Sermon* 28.16)?

IV.4. Why it was the Son of God that became man, and not the Father or the Holy Ghost; and what He accomplished, when He became man

The Father is the Father and not Son (cf. Gregory Nazianzen, *Sermon* 39.12). The Son is Son and not Father. The Holy Ghost is Spirit and neither Father nor Son. This is so because that which is a property is unalterable; else, how would it be a property were it to be altered and changed? For this reason the Son of God becomes Son of Man, namely, that His peculiar property may remain unaltered. For, while He was Son of God, He was incarnate of the holy Virgin and became Son of Man without giving up His property of filiation.

The Son of God became man in order that He might again grace man as He had when He made him. For He had made him to His own image, understanding and free, and to His own likeness, that is to say, as perfect in virtues as it was possible for human nature to be, for these virtues are, as it were, characteristics of the divine nature—freedom from care and annoyance, integrity, goodness, wisdom, justice, freedom from all vice. Thus, He put man in communion with Himself and through this communion with Himself raised him to incorruptibility, "for he created man incorruptible" (Wisd 2:23). But, since by transgressing the commandment we obscured and canceled out the characteristics of the divine image, we were given over to evil and stripped of the divine communion. "For what fellowship hath light with darkness" (2 Cor 6:14)? Then, since we had been removed from life, we fell subject to the destruction of death. But, since He had shared with us what was better and we had not kept it, He now takes His share of what is worse, of our nature I mean to say, that through Himself and in Himself He may restore what was to His image and what to His likeness, while also teaching us the virtuous way of life which He has made easy of ascent for us through Him, and that, having become the first fruits of our resurrection, He may by the communication of life free us from death and restore the useless and worn-out vessel, and so that, having called us to the knowledge of God, He may redeem us from the tyranny of the Devil and by patience and humility teach us to overthrow the tyrant.

Indeed, the worship of demons has ceased. Creation has been sanctified with the divine blood. Altars and temples of idols have been overthrown. Knowledge of God has been implanted. The consubstantial Trinity, the uncreated Godhead is worshiped, one true God, Creator and Lord of all. Virtue is practiced. Hope of the resurrection has been granted through the resurrection of Christ. The demons tremble at the men who were formerly in their power. Yes, and most wonderful of all is that all these things were successfully brought about through a cross and suffering and death. The Gospel of the knowledge of God has been preached to the whole world and has put the adversaries to flight not by war and arms and camps. Rather, it was a few unarmed, poor, unlettered, persecuted, tormented, done-to-death men, who, by preaching One who had died crucified in the flesh, prevailed over the wise and powerful, because the almighty power of the Crucified was with them. That death which was once so terrible has been defeated and He who was once despised and hated is now preferred before life. These are the successes consequent upon the advent of the Christ; these are the signs of His power. For it was not as when through Moses He divided the sea and brought one people safely through out of Egypt and the bondage of Pharaoh. Rather, He delivered all humanity from death's destruction and the tyrant that was sin. It was not by force that He led sinners to virtue, not by having them swallowed up by the earth, nor by having them burnt up by fire, nor by ordering them stoned to death (cf. Num 16:31–33,35; Lev 20:2); it was with gentleness and forbearance that He persuaded men to choose virtue and for virtue's sake to undergo sufferings with rejoicing. Sinners were formerly tormented, yet they clung to their sin, and sin was accounted a god by them; but now for piety and virtue's sake, they choose torments, tortures, and death.

Well done, O Christ, O Wisdom and Power and Word of God, and God almighty! What should we resourceless people give Thee in return for all things? For all things are Thine and Thou asketh nothing of us but that we be saved. Even this Thou hast given us, and by Thy ineffable goodness Thou art grateful to those who accept it. Thanks be to Thee who has given being and grace of well-being and who by the ineffable condescension hast brought back to this state those who fell from it.

IV.16 The defense of icons

Since there are certain people who find great fault with us for adoring and honoring both the image of the Saviour and that of our Lady, as well as those of the rest of the saints and servants of Christ, let them hear how from the beginning God made man to His own image (Rom 8:29). For what reason, then, do we adore one another, except because we have been made to the image of God. As the inspired Basil who is deeply learned in theology, says: "the honor paid to the image redounds to the original (Basil, *On the Holy Ghost* 18.45), and the original is the thing imaged from which the copy is made. For what reason did the people of Moses adore from round about the tabernacle which bore an image and pattern of heavenly things, or rather, of all creation (cf. Exod 33:10). Indeed, God had said to Moses: "See that thou make all things according so the pattern which was shown thee on the mount" (cf. Heb 8:5). And the Cherubim, too, that overshadowed the propitiatory, were they not the handiwork of men (cf. Exod 25:40,20)? And what was the celebrated temple in Jerusalem? Was it not built and furnished by human hands and skill (cf. 1 Kgs 6)?

Now, sacred scripture condemns those who adore graven things, and also those who sacrifice to the demons. The Greeks used to sacrifice and the Jews also used to sacrifice; but the Greeks sacrificed to the demons, whereas the Jews sacrificed to God. And the sacrifice of the Greeks was rejected and condemned, while the sacrifice of the just was acceptable to God. Thus, Noe sacrificed "and the Lord smelled a sweet savor" (Gen 8:21) of the good intention and accepted the fragrance of the gift offered to Him. And thus the statues of the Greeks happen to be rejected and condemned, because they were representations of demons.

But, furthermore, who can make a copy of the invisible, incorporeal, uncircumscribed, and unportrayable God? It is, then, highly insane and impious to give form to the Godhead. For this reason it was not the practice in the Old Testament to use images. However, through the bowels of His mercy God for our salvation was made man in truth, not in the appearance of man, as he was seen by Abraham or the Prophets, but really made man in substance. Then He abode on earth, conversed with men, worked miracles, suffered, was crucified, rose again, and was taken up; and all these things really happened and were seen by men and, indeed, written down to remind and instruct us, who were not present then, so that, although we have not seen, yet yearning and believing we may attain to the blessedness of the Lord. Since, however, not all know letters nor do all have leisure to read, the Fathers deemed it fit that these events should be depicted as a sort of memorial and terse reminder. It certainly happens frequently that at times when we do not have the Lord's Passion in mind we may see the image of His crucifixion and, being thus reminded of His saving Passion, fall down and adore. But it is not the material which we adore, but that which is represented; just as we do not adore the material of the Gospel or that of the cross, but that which they typify. For what is the difference between a cross which does not typify the Lord and one which does? It is the same way with the Mother of God, too, for the honor paid her is referred to Him who was incarnate of her. And similarly, also, we are stirred up by the exploits of the holy men to manliness, zeal, imitation of their virtues, and the glory of God. For, as we have said, the honor shown the more sensible of one's fellow servants gives proof of one's love for the common Master, and the honor paid to the image redounds to the original. This is the written tradition, just as is worshiping toward the east, adoring the cross and so many other similar things (cf. Basil, *On the Holy Ghost* 27.66).

Furthermore, there is a story told (cf. Eusebius, *Eccles. Hist.* 1.13) about how, when Abgar was lord of the city of Edessenes, he sent an artist to make a portrait of the Lord, and how, when the artist was unable to do

this because of the radiance of His face, the Lord Himself pressed a bit of cloth to His own sacred and life-giving face and left His own image on the cloth and so sent this to Abgar who had so earnestly desired it.

And Paul, the Apostle of the Gentiles, writes that the Apostles handed down a great many things unwritten: "Therefore, brethren, stand fast: and hold the traditions which you have learned, whether by word or by our epistle" (2 Thess 2:14); and to the Corinthians: "Now I praise you, brethren, that in all things you are mindful of me and keep my ordinances as I have delivered them to you" (1 Cor 11:2).

4

MUHAMMAD AND ISLAM

Early in the seventh century C.E. (c. 610 C.E.) in the interior of Arabia, unnoticed by the rest of the world, an illiterate prophet named Muhammad began preaching an ethical monotheism to his fellow Arabs. Muhammad called the new religion Islam which in Arabic means "submission" or "surrender" to Allah, the one true God. His followers were called Muslims, those who do Islam by committing themselves totally into the hands of Allah, the sovereign divine ruler, whose will they follow in every aspect of life. By the time of the prophet's death in 632 C.E., Islam controlled most of the Arabian peninsula. Within a century Syria, Palestine, Egypt, North Africa, Spain and part of France were in Muslim control. By the ninth century Islam had produced a brilliant and creative culture much superior to Christian medieval Europe which was still in a Dark Age.

Before Muhammad the Arab peoples had been culturally and religiously inferior to the other peoples of the Near East. The desolate Arabian peninsula with its forbidding deserts, arid steppes and barren mountains had largely been insulated from attack, and none of the great Near Eastern empires had conquered it. Only in a few oases and the southwestern coastal area was there enough water sufficient for agriculture. In this region, called the Hejaz, a few cultured cities like Mecca had developed as centers of the caravan trade and religious pilgrimage. The interior was inhabited by hearty bedouin who lived a nomadic and tribal life with their camels, flocks and herds. These Arab tribes were not united among themselves and often fought with one another. They recognized no authority beyond the tribe with its *shaykh* (leader) and traditional oral customs (*sunnah*). The highest values within the tribe were hospitality, generosity, fidelity to one's word, and military prowess.

Muhammad was born into the Quraysh tribe which, about four generations earlier, had taken control of the barren valley of Mecca, with its shrines and wells. They soon built a thriving community that flourished on commerce and caravan trade, and rapidly rose to become one of most powerful tribal groups in peninsula. Although now an urban tribe, the Quraysh maintained contacts with the desert. It was customary to send children to live for a time with a nomad group. Muhammad spent part of his childhood with such a group. Although Islam had its origins in the city of Mecca, it blended elements of an individualistic urban religion with some of the austere and militant values of the nomadic life in the desert.

Religiously, the bedouin Arabs were still animists and polytheists; they believed in a number of spiritual and demonic powers (*jinns*) whom they propitiated. Spirits associated with rocks and springs and trees were of particular importance. They were also influenced by the astral religion of ancient Semitic peoples. At the shrines near Mecca, the Arabs honored al-Lat, the goddess of the sun; al-Uzzah, the morning star; and al-Manat, the goddess of destiny. They also recognized a superior deity called Allah (The God), but his function was vague and did not figure strongly in their thinking or practice.

Pilgrimages to shrines at different places in the peninsula also played an important role in the life of the Arabs. The most important center was Mecca with its Ka'bah, a rectangular stone building, containing a black stone believed to have fallen from heaven. The Meccans had a tradition that they were descendants of Abraham through his son Ishmael; some also believed that the temple at Mecca had been established by Abraham and Ishmael for the worship of the one true God. But by Muhammad's time each clan of the Quraysh had erected its own deity in the sacred precincts of the shrine. Muhammad incorporated the pilgrimage to the Ka'bah at Mecca into Islam, but his first act upon conquering the city was to purify the shrine of its idols to restore the exclusive worship of Allah.

The career of Muhammad has its closest parallels in the lives of Moses and the Hebrew prophets in that he experienced a call in mid-life to reform the religious life of his people. Orphaned at an early age, Muhammad was raised first by his maternal grandfather and then by a paternal uncle, Abu Talib, the head of the Hashim clan of the Quraysh tribe. As a young man, Muhammad travelled with his uncle's caravans as far as Syria and was deemed so responsible that he was given the epithet, *Al-Amin*, "the trustworthy." At the age of twenty-five he married Khadijah, a wealthy widow for whom he worked in the caravan trade. His marriage gave him the economic security to pursue his religious interests; he was accustomed to withdraw into the desert near Mecca for prayer during the month of Ramadan. Throughout his youth and early adulthood, Muhammad was troubled by the decadent polytheism of his fellow Arabs and was a *hanif*, "one who turns away" from the idols. In his travels Muhammad had also come into contact with the teachings of the "peoples of the Book," the traditions of Judaism and Christianity which had penetrated the Arabian peninsula. Muhammad was convinced that his people stood under the terrible judgment of the one true God for their idolatry and immorality.

Muhammad first began receiving revelations at age forty in the year 610 C.E. while at prayer in a cave on Mt. Hira near Mecca. His initial response was one of reluctance, much like Moses and many of the Hebrew prophets (see Exodus 3–4, Isaiah 6, Jeremiah 1, Ezekiel 1–3). According to Muhammad's earliest biography by Ibn Ishaq (d. c. 768), while asleep or in a trance he heard a voice say: "Read!" He responded: "I cannot read."

The voice insisted two more times: "Read!" Finally Muhammad answered: "What can I read?" Then the voice said:

> Read: In the name of thy Lord Who createth
> Createth man from a clot.
> Read: And it is thy Lord the Most Bountiful
> Who teacheth by the pen,
> Teacheth man that which he knew not (Sur. 96:1–5).

When he awoke, the words remained "as if inscribed upon his heart." He went out of the cave on to the hillside and heard the same awe-inspiring voice say: "O Muhammad! Thou art Allah's messenger, and I am Gabriel." When he raised his eyes, he saw the angel standing in the sky above the horizon and heard him repeat the message. Muhammad stood still, turning his face away from the brightness of vision, but wherever he stood the angel confronted him. Eventually the apparition left. Understandably, Muhammad was disturbed by the vision and for a long time uncertain of its significance. Khadijah continually reassured him and expressed the hope that he was to be the Prophet to the Arab people. Several times in the Qur'an there are reassurances to Muhammad that the revelations do not come from an evil spirit, but from a divine source. There were also gaps between revelations, but eventually they resumed and Muhammad gained a clear conception of his mission as agent of a divine message to his generation. By 613 C.E. he had begun his career as preacher, reformer and prophet.

The content of Muhammad's initial preaching centered around the proclamation of Allah as the one sovereign deity who created the universe, controls the destiny of humankind, and will judge the world in his kindness, mercy and justice. These beliefs are beautifully expressed in the opening of the Qur'an:

> Praise be to Allah, Lord of the Worlds,
> The Beneficent, the Merciful.
> Owner of the Day of Judgment,
> Thee (alone) we worship; Thee (alone) we ask for help.
> Show us the straight path,
> The path of those whom Thou hast favored;
> Not (the path) of those who earn Thine anger nor of those who go astray.

Initially, many Meccans were indifferent to Muhammad's preaching, but when he began to gain a following among members of his own family and the lower classes, the leaders of the Quraysh became hostile because he was undermining the established authority of tribal tradition and leadership, as well as threatening the trade connected with the religious rites associated with the tribal idols and pilgrimages. At first the Quraysh ridiculed Muhammad's religious credentials; when this failed they attempted to bribe the prophet with the offer of a position of leadership in the community. When

Muhammad refused, they resorted to persecuting him and his followers. Muhammad was protected by his clan, but some of his followers were forced to migrate to Ethiopia.

During this time Muhammad continued to receive revelations. One of the most important stories associated with this period is Muhammad's miraculous night journey from the Ka'bah in Mecca to the future sight of the Dome of the Rock in Jerusalem. The tradition has similarities to the account of Moses' transfiguration in the book of Exodus (see Exod 34). According to the tradition, Muhammad was carried by Buraq, a winged horse with a peacock's tail and the face of a woman. In Jerusalem Muhammad was ascended into heaven where he entered the presence of Allah himself.

When Khadijah and his uncle Abu Talib died in 619, Muhammad no longer had the protection of his clan. Because of the increased threat of persecution for his followers and assassination for himself, Muhammad began negotiations with Yathrib, an agricultural city two hundred miles to the north of Mecca. The citizens of Yathrib were looking for an outside leader to settle long-standing tribal disputes and were prepared for Muhammad's monotheistic teachings by a Jewish group which had spoken of an Arabian prophet who would introduce the worship of the one true God. In 621 C.E., at pilgrimage time, Muhammad entered into negotiations with the citizens of Yathrib and was able to secure an agreement that he and his followers would be accepted and given protection. Gradually his followers drifted away from Mecca to Yathrib, and on September 24, 622 C.E., the prophet joined them. Muhammad's flight to Yathrib is called the *hijrah* in Arabic and subsequently came to mark the beginning of the Islamic calendar. Yathrib later became known as Medina from the Arabic expression *Madinat al-Nabi,* "city of the prophet."

In the period from 622 C.E. to his death in 632 C.E., Muhammad successfully united the contending factions in Medina and by war and treaty conquered the Arabian peninsula for Islam. The Muslims' two greatest victories were against the Meccans in the Battle of Badr (624 C.E.) and the Battle of the Ditch (625 C.E.). By all accounts Muhammad was a brave warrior and a brilliant strategist. It is estimated that he fought in twenty-seven campaigns, nine with hard fighting, and planned a total of thirty-eight. By January, 630 C.E., he was strong enough to return to Mecca in triumph. Muhammad was a magnanimous victor; he offered a general amnesty to his enemies under the condition that they accept Islam. According to tradition, the prophet himself directed the cleansing of the sanctuary at Mecca of all elements of polytheism, including the three hundred and sixty idols.

During this time, Muhammad became not just a prophet, but a political leader, warrior chieftain, military strategist and judge. Correspondingly, the revelations during the Medinan period were concerned with governing issues: the conduct of war, marriage, women's rights, property, orphans' rights, business, and ethics in general.

When Muhammad died in 632 C.E., most of the Arabian peninsula was Muslim. His religious and moral accomplishments were impressive. He had destroyed idolatry in Arabia, united once warring tribes in a monotheistic faith, eliminated infanticide, protected the rights of orphans, raised women from the status of chattels, effectively limited drunkenness, adultery, and made the Arabs more sincere and honest in their business dealings. Muhammad had also given them a sense of mission as Allah's chosen people to bring a message of universal human brotherhood to the world.

THE QUR'AN

Our selections are taken from the Qur'an (literally "recitations"), the sacred scriptures of Islam, which are understood by the Muslim as the very words of Allah given in direct revelation to Muhammad while he was in a trance-like state. The revelations contained in the Qur'an were spoken over a period of approximately twenty years. During the Meccan period Muhammad's prophetic utterances were preserved orally by his followers, but in the Medinan period, many of his speeches were recorded in writing on stones or palm leaves at or immediately after their utterance. Nonetheless, no authoritative, organized edition of revelations had been made at Muhammad's death.

The official Arabic text of the Qur'an was compiled under the Caliph 'Uthman (644–56), and its present arrangement of 114 surahs is neither chronological, nor thematic. Rather, the longer surahs are placed at the beginning and the shorter ones at the end. According to scholars, this often reverses the chronological order, as many of the shorter, more poetic surahs at the end of the Qur'an are dated to the early period of Muhammad's initial preaching in Mecca. The title for each surah is taken from a word which occurs with the surah.

The language and style of the Qur'an is poetic and sonorous in Arabic. It is meant to be recited and heard in Arabic, not read silently in translation. To the English reader much of this is lost, and the text often appears to be repetitious, to make abrupt changes in subject matter, and to even be contradictory.

The content of the Qur'an is extremely varied. Each surah begins with the phrase: "In the name of Allah, the Beneficent, the Merciful." Alongside the many praises to Allah for his oneness, greatness, mercy and compassion are impressive portrayals of the final resurrection, the last judgment, the beauties of paradise, and the torments of hell. In many places Jewish and Christian stories are recounted, although they are usually rendered differently from the versions found in the Hebrew scriptures and the Christian New Testament. Much of the Qur'an is devoted to regulations concerning objects of the cult, ethical and social life and to events in the prophet's life.

According to the Qur'an, Islam, the one true monotheistic religion, began with Abraham and has been revealed to various prophets in the traditions of the peoples of the Book, including Moses and Jesus. Moses taught the Torah and Jesus the gospel, but their followers subsequently distorted their authentic preaching. The Jews repeatedly fell into idolatry, and Christians have distorted Jesus' message by making him into a God along with Allah. Muhammad is the last of the prophets who has been called to restore authentic Islam, submission to the one true God.

The Qur'an holds Jesus in very high esteem. Along with Abraham, Moses, and Muhammad, Jesus is one of the great prophets. Many Christian beliefs are reiterated:

the virgin birth, the titles of Jesus as "Messiah" and "Word of God," his miracle working, his preaching of the gospel and the Torah to the Jews. But the central Christian beliefs in the crucifixion and the resurrection from the dead are denied. Although the Jews thought they had crucified Jesus, God rescued him and took him to himself in a kind of ascension. And, of course, Christian beliefs in the divinity of Jesus and the Trinity are rejected as incompatible with Muslim monotheism.

> They surely disbelieve who say: Lo! Allah is the Messiah, son of Mary. The Messiah (himself) said: O Children of Israel, worship Allah, My Lord and your Lord. Lo! whoso ascribeth part-ners unto Allah, for him Allah hath forbidden Paradise. His abode is Fire. For evil-doers there will be no helpers (Surah V:72).

Allah is understood as the absolute sovereign over creation and history. Although he will subject humans to a terrifying Day of Judgment at the resurrection, his nature is com-passionate and merciful as well as just. The terrors of hell and rewards of paradise are pictured in graphic terms which reflect life in the Arabian peninsula.

Humans were created by God, but are not wounded by original sin, as in Christian theology. They are always free to respond to the call of Allah to surrender to his will. The ethical code of Islam is quite similar to that of biblical Judaism. Allah forbids murder, adultery, theft, and enjoins his people to care for parents, orphans and the needy. Holy war in Allah's name is allowed when the people are subjected to persecution, and those who die as martyrs are promised the rewards of paradise.

The cult of Islam has its basis in the Qur'an and is quite simple in comparison to Christianity. This no doubt contributed to its rapid spread. There is no priestly caste or sacramental system as in Christianity. Each Muslim approaches Allah directly from the so-called "Five Pillars" of Islam. The first of these is public profession of faith in the for-mula: "There is no God but Allah and Muhammad is His messenger." To utter this for-mula in front of Muslim witnesses is to gain entrance into the Muslim community. The second obligation is ritual prayer (*salah*); the Qur'an mentions prayer twice a day, but subsequently the tradition developed, on the basis of Muhammad's example, of prayer five times a day. The prayers involve specific words and rituals, including ablutions and prostrations in the direction of Mecca. The mosque, "place of prostration," is the prefer-able place of prayer in community with other believers. A special effort is made by all Muslims to go to the mosque for the noon prayer on Friday, the Day of Gathering. The third observance is the monthly fast during Ramadan, the month in which Muhammad received the first of the Qur'an's revelations. The fast involves refraining from food, drink, tobacco, and sexual activity from dawn to dusk. It is a time for restricting the car-nal appetites which can dominate the human person. The fourth pillar is almsgiving. The Qur'an frequently exhorts Muslims to give part of their wealth to help the needy, particularly orphans. The last and most elaborate of the five pillars is the pilgrimage to Mecca at least once during one's lifetime.

The translation is taken from Mohammed Marmaduke Pickthall, *The Meaning of the*

Glorious Koran (New York: George Allen and Unwin, Ltd.) 31, 44–45, 48–52, 64–67, 77–81, 93, 97–98, 100–101, 103, 133, 189–190, 204–206, 234, 384–385, 445.

SURAH I: THE OPENING

1. In the name of Allah, the Beneficent, the Merciful.
2. Praise be to Allah, Lord of the Worlds:
3. The Beneficent, the Merciful:
4. Owner of the Day of Judgement.
5. You alone we worship; You alone we ask for help.
6. Show us the straight path:
7. The path of those whom you have favored; not the path of those who earn Your anger nor of those who go astray.

SURAH II: THE COW

125. And when we made the house at Mecca a resort for mankind and a sanctuary, saying: Take as your place of worship the place where Abraham stood to pray. And we impose a duty upon Abraham and Ishmael, saying: Purify My House for those who go around and those who meditate therein and those who bow down and prostrate themselves in worship.

126. And when Abraham prayed: My Lord! Make this a region of security and bestow upon its people fruits, such of these as believe in Allah and the Last Day, He answered: As for him who disbelieveth, I shall leave him in contentment for a while, then I shall compel him to the doom of fire—a hapless journey's end.

127. And when Abraham and Ishmael were raising the foundations of the house, Abraham prayed: Our Lord! Accept from us this duty. Lo! You, only You are the hearer, the Knower.

128. Our Lord! And make us submissive unto Thee and of our seed a nation submissive unto Thee, and show us our ways of worship and relent toward us. Lo! Thou, only Thou, art the Relenting, the Merciful.

129. Our Lord! And raise up in their midst a messenger from among them who shall recite unto them Thy revelations, and shall instruct them in the Scripture and in wisdom and shall make them grow. Lo! Thou, only Thou, art the Mighty, Wise.

130. And who forsaketh the religion of Abraham save him who befooleth himself? Verily we chose him in the world, and lo! in the hereafter he is among the righteous.

131. When his Lord said unto him: Surrender! he said: I surrender to the Lord of the Worlds.

132. The same did Abraham enjoin upon his sons, and also Jacob, (saying): O my sons! Lo! Allah hath chosen for you the (true) religion; therefore die not save as men who have surrendered (unto Him).

135. And they say: Be Jews or Christians, then ye will be rightly guided. Say (unto them, O Muhammad): Nay, but (we follow) the religion of Abraham, the upright, and he was not of the idolaters.

136. Say (O Muslims): We believe in Allah and that which is revealed unto us and that which was revealed unto Abraham, and Ishmael, and Isaac, and Jacob, and the tribes, and that which Moses and Jesus received, and that which the Prophets received from their Lord. We make no distinction between any of them, and unto Him we have surrendered.

137. And if they believe in the like of that which ye believe, then are they rightly guided. But if they turn awry, then are they in schism, and Allah will suffice thee (for defense) against them. He is the Hearer, the Knower.

139. Say (unto the People of the Scripture): Dispute ye with us concerning Allah when He is our Lord and your Lord? Ours are our works and yours your works. We look to Him alone.

140. Or say ye that Abraham, and Ishmael, and Isaac, and Jacob, and the tribes were

Jews or Christians? Say: Do ye know best, or doth Allah? And who is more unjust than he who hideth a testimony which he hath received from Allah? Allah is not unaware of what ye do.

177. It is not righteousness that you turn your faces to the East and the West; but righteous is he who believes in Allah and the last Day and the angels and the Scripture and the Prophets; and give his wealth, for love of Him to kinsfolk and to orphans and the needy and the wayfarer and those who ask, and to set slaves free; and observes proper worship and pays the poor-due.

185. The month of Ramadan in which was revealed the Qur'an, a guidance for mankind, and clear proof of the guidance, and the criterion (of right and wrong). And whosoever of you is present, let him fast the month, and whosoever of you is sick or on a journey, (let him fast the same) number of other days. Allah desireth for you ease; he desireth not hardship for you; and (He desireth) that ye should complete the period, and that ye should magnify Allah for having guided you, and that peradventure ye may be thankful.

187. It is made lawful for you to go unto your wives on the night of the fast. They are raiment for you and ye are raiment for them. Allah is aware that ye were deceiving yourselves in this respect and He hath turned in mercy toward you and relieved you. So hold intercourse with them and seek that which Allah hath ordained for you, and eat and drink until the white thread become distinct to you from the black thread of the dawn. Then strictly observe the fast till nightfall and touch them not, but be at your devotions in the mosques. These are the limits imposed by Allah, so approach them not. Thus Allah expoundeth His revelations to mankind that they may ward off (evil).

190. Fight in the way of Allah against those who fight against you, but begin not hostilities. Lo! Allah loveth not aggressors.

191. And slay them where ye find them, and drive them out of the places whence they drove you out, for persecution is worse than slaughter. And fight not with them at the Inviolable Place of Worship until they first attack you there, but if they attack you (there) then slay them. Such is the reward of disbelievers.

192. But if they desist, then lo! Allah is forgiving, Merciful.

193. And fight them until persecution is no more, and religion is for Allah. But if they desist, then let there be no hostility except against wrongdoers.

194. The forbidden month for the forbidden month, and forbidden things in retaliation. And who attacketh you, attack him in like manner as he attacked you. Observe your duty to Allah, and know that Allah is with those who ward off (evil).

195. Spend your wealth for the cause of Allah, and be not cast by your own hands to ruin; and do good. Lo! Allah loveth the beneficent.

196. Perform the pilgrimage and the visit (to Mecca) for Allah. And if ye are prevented, then send such gifts as can be obtained with ease, and shave not your heads until the gifts have reached their destination. And whoever among you is sick or hath an ailment of the head must pay a ransom of fasting or almsgiving or offering. And if ye are in safety, then whosoever contenteth himself with the Visit for the Pilgrimage (shall give) such gifts as can be had with ease. And whosoever cannot find (such gifts), then a fast of three days while on the pilgrimage, and of seven when ye have returned; that is, ten in all. That is for him whose folk are not present at the Inviolable Place of Worship. Observe your duty to Allah, and know that Allah is severe in punishment.

197. The pilgrimage is (in) the well-known months, and whoever is minded to perform the pilgrimage therein (let him remember that) there is (to be) no lewdness nor abuse

nor angry conversation on the pilgrimage. And whatsoever good ye do Allah knoweth it. 211. Ask the Children of Israel how many a clear revelation We gave them! He who altereth the grace of Allah after it hath come unto him (for him), lo! Allah is severe in punishment.

213. Mankind were one community, and Allah sent (unto them) Prophets as bearers of good tidings and as warners, and revealed therewith the Scripture with the truth that it might judge between mankind concerning that wherein they differed. And only those unto whom (the Scripture) was given differed concerning it, after clear proofs had come unto them, through hatred one of another. And Allah by His will guided those who believe unto the truth of that concerning which they differed. Allah guideth whom He will unto a straight path.

SURAH III: THE FAMILY OF ʿIMRAN

19. Lo! Religion with Allah is The Surrender (Al-Islam) to his will and guidance. Those who formerly received the Scripture differed only after knowledge came to them. . . .

23. Have you not seen how those who have received the Scripture invoke the Scripture of Allah in their disputes that it may judge between them: then a faction of them turn away, being opposed to it?

31. Say, (O Muhammad, to mankind): If ye love Allah, follow me; Allah will love you and forgive you your sins. Allah is Forgiving, Merciful.

32. Say: Obey Allah and the messenger. But if they turn away, lo! Allah loveth not the disbelievers (in His guidance).

33. Lo! Allah preferred Adam and Noah and the Family of Abraham and the Family of ʿImran (the father of Moses) above (all His) creatures.

34. There were descendants one of another. Allah is Hearer, Knower.

35. (Remember) when the wife of ʿImran (the mother of Mary) said: My Lord! I have vowed unto Thee that which is in my belly as a consecrated (offering). Accept it from me. Lo! Thou, only Thou, art the Hearer, the Knower!

36. And when she was delivered she said: My Lord! Lo! I am delivered of a female—Allah knew best of what she was delivered—the male is not as the female; and lo! I have named her Mary, and lo! I crave Thy protection for her and for her offspring from Satan the outcast.

37. And her Lord accepted her with full acceptance and vouchsafed to her a goodly growth; and made Zachariah her guardian. Whenever Zachariah went into the sanctuary where she was, he found that she had food. He said: O Mary! Whence cometh unto thee this (food)? She answered: It is from Allah. Allah giveth without stint to whom He will.

38. Then Zachariah prayed unto his Lord and said: My Lord! Bestow upon me of Thy bounty goodly offspring. Lo! Thou art the hearer of prayer.

39. And the angels called to him as he stood praying in the sanctuary: Allah giveth thee glad tidings of (a son whose name is) John, (who cometh) to confirm a word from Allah, lordly, chaste, a Prophet of the righteous.

40. He said: My Lord! How can I have a son when age hath overtaken me already and my wife is barren? (The angel) answered: So (it will be). Allah doeth what He will.

41. He said: My Lord! Appoint a token for me. (The angel) said: The token unto thee (shall be) that thou shalt not speak unto mankind three days except by signs. Remember thy Lord much, and praise (Him) in the early hours of night and morning.

42. And when the angels said: O Mary! Lo! Allah hath chosen thee and made thee pure, and hath preferred thee above (all) the women of creation.

43. O Mary! Be obedient to thy Lord, prostrate thyself and bow with those who bow (in worship).

44. This is of the tidings of things hidden. We reveal it unto thee (Muhammad). Thou wast not present with them when they threw their pens (to know) which of them should be the guardian of Mary, nor wast thou present with them when they quarreled (thereupon).

45. (And remember) when the angels said: O Mary! Lo! Allah giveth thee glad tidings of a word from Him whose name is the Messiah, Jesus, son of Mary, illustrious in the world and the Hereafter, and one of those brought near (unto Allah).

46. He will speak unto mankind in his cradle and in his manhood, and he is of the righteous.

47. She said: My Lord! how can I have a child when no mortal hath touched me? He said: So (it will be). Allah createth what He will. If He decreeth a thing, He saith unto it only: Be! and it is.

48. And He will teach him the Scripture and wisdom, and the Torah and the Gospel.

49. And will make him a messenger unto the children of Israel, (saying): Lo! I come unto you with a sign from your Lord. Lo! I fashion for you out of clay the likeness of a bird, and I breathe into it and it is a bird, by Allah's leave. I heal him who was born blind, and the leper, and I raise the dead, by Allah's leave. And I announce unto you what ye eat and what ye store up in your houses. Lo! herein verily is a portent for you, if ye are to be believers.

50. And (I come) confirming that which was before me of the Torah, and to make lawful some of that which was forbidden unto you. I come unto you with a sign from your Lord so keep your duty to Allah and obey me.

51. Lo! Allah is my Lord and your Lord, so worship Him. That is a straight path.

52. But when Jesus became conscious of their disbelief, he cried: Who will be my helpers in the cause of Allah? The disciples said: We will be Allah's helpers. We believe in Allah and bear thou witness that we have surrendered (unto Him).

53. Our Lord! we believe in that which Thou hast revealed and we follow him whom Thou hast sent. Enroll us among those who witness (to the truth).

54. And they (the disbelievers) schemed, and Allah schemed (against them): and Allah is the best of schemers.

55. (And remember) when Allah said: O Jesus! Lo! I am gathering thee and causing thee to ascend unto Me, and am cleansing thee of those who disbelieve and am setting those who follow thee above those who disbelieve until the Day of Resurrection. Then unto Me ye will (all) return, and I shall judge between you as to what wherein ye used to differ.

56. As for those who disbelieve I shall chastise them with a heavy chastisement in the world and the Hereafter; and they will have no helpers.

57. And as for those who believe and do good works, He will pay them their wages in full. Allah loveth not wrongdoers.

58. This (which) We recite unto thee is a revelation and a wise reminder.

59. Lo! the likeness of Jesus with Allah is as the likeness of Adam. He created him of dust, then He said unto him: Be! and he is.

60. (This is) the truth from thy Lord (O Muhammad), so be not thou of those who waver.

61. And whoso disputeth with thee concerning him, after the knowledge which hath come unto thee, say (unto him): Come! We will summon our sons and your sons, and our women and your women, and ourselves and yourselves, then we will pray humbly (to our Lord) and (solemnly) invoke the curse of Allah upon those who lie.

62. Lo! This verily is the true narrative. There is no God save Allah, and lo! Allah is the Mighty, the Wise.

63. And if they turn away, then lo! Allah is aware of (who are) the corrupters.

64. Say: O People of the Scripture (Jews and Christians)! Come to an agreement between us and you: that we shall worship none but Allah, and that we shall ascribe no partner unto Him, and that none of us shall take others for lords beside Allah. And if they turn away then say: Bear witness that we are they who have surrendered (unto Him).

65. O People of the Scripture! Why will ye argue about Abraham, when the Torah and the Gospel were not revealed till after him? Have ye then no sense?

66. Lo! ye are those who argue about that whereof ye have some knowledge: Why then argue ye concerning that whereof ye have no knowledge? Allah knoweth. Ye know not.

67. Abraham was not a Jew, nor yet a Christian; but he was an upright man who surrendered (to Allah), and he was not of the idolaters.

68. Lo! those of mankind who have the best claim to Abraham are those who followed him, and this prophet and those who believe (with him); and Allah is the Protecting Friend of the believers.

185. Every soul will taste death. And ye will be paid on the Day of Resurrection only that which ye have fairly earned. Whoso is removed from the Fire and is made to enter Paradise, he indeed is triumphant. The life of this world is but comfort of illusion.

186. Assuredly ye will be tried in your property and in your persons, and ye will hear much wrong from those who were given the Scripture before you, and from the idolaters. But if ye persevere and ward off (evil), then that is of the steadfast heart of things.

195. And their Lord hath heard them (and He saith): Lo! I suffer not the work of any worker, male or female, to be lost. Ye proceed one from another. So those who fled and were driven forth from their homes and suffered damage for My cause, and fought and were slain, verily I shall remit their evil deeds from them and verily I shall bring them into Gardens underneath which rivers flow—a reward from Allah. And with Allah is the fairest of rewards.

SURAH IV: WOMEN

1. O mankind! Be careful of your duty to your Lord Who created you from a single soul and from it created its mate and from them twain hath spread abroad a multitude of men and women. Be careful of your duty toward Allah in Whom ye claim (your rights) of one another, and toward the wombs (that bare you). Lo! Allah hath been a Watcher over you.

2. Give unto orphans their wealth. Exchange not the good for the bad (in your management thereof) nor absorb their wealth into your own wealth. Lo! that would be a great sin.

3. And if ye fear that ye will not deal fairly by the orphans, marry of the women, who seem good to you, two or three or four; and if ye fear that ye cannot do justice (to so many) then one (only) or (the captives) that your right hands possess. Thus it is more likely that ye will not do injustice.

4. And give unto the women (whom ye marry), free gift of their marriage portions; but if they of their own accord remit unto you a part thereof, then ye are welcome to absorb it (in your wealth).

5. Give not unto the foolish (what is in) your (keeping of their) wealth, which Allah hath given you to maintain; but feed and clothe them from it, and speak kindly unto them.

6. Prove orphans till they reach marriageable age; then, if ye find them of sound judgement, deliver over unto them their fortune; and devour it not by squandering and in haste lest they should grow up. Whoso (of the guardians) is rich, let him abstain generously (from taking of the property of orphans); and whoso is poor let him take thereof in reason (for his guardianship). And when ye deliver up their fortune unto orphans, have (the

transaction) witnessed in their presence. Allah sufficeth as a Reckoner.

15. As for those of your women who are guilty of lewdness, call to witness four of you against them. And if they testify (to the truth of the allegation) then confine them to the house until death take them or (until) Allah appoint for them a way (through new legislation).

16. And as for the two of you who are guilty thereof, punish them both. And if they repent and improve, then let them be. Lo! Allah is Relenting, Merciful.

79. Whatever of good befalleth thee (O man) it is from Allah, and whatever of ill befalleth thee is from thyself. We have seen thee (Muhammad) as a messenger unto mankind and Allah is sufficient as witness.

152. But those who believe in Allah and His messengers and make no distinction between any of them, unto them Allah will give their wages; and Allah was ever Forgiving, Merciful.

156. And because of their disbelief and of speaking against Mary a tremendous calumny;

157. And because of their saying: we slew the Messiah Jesus son of Mary, Allah's messenger—They slew him not nor crucified, but it appeared so unto them; and lo! those who disagree concerning it are in doubt thereof; they have no knowledge thereof save pursuit of a conjecture; they slew him not for certain,

158. But Allah took him up unto Himself. Allah was ever Mighty, Wise.

159. There is not one of the People of the Scripture but will believe in him before his death, and on the Day of Resurrection he will be a witness against them—

160. Because of the wrongdoing of the Jews We forbade them good things which were (before) made lawful unto them, and because of their hindering Allah's way.

161. And of their taking usury when they were forbidden it, and of their devouring people's wealth by false pretenses. We have pre-

pared for those of them who disbelieve a painful doom.

SURAH V: THE TABLE SPREAD

5. This day are (all) good things made lawful for you. The food of those who have received the Scripture is lawful for you, and your food is lawful for them. And so are the virtuous women of the believers and the virtuous women of those who received the Scripture before you (lawful for you) when ye give them their marriage portions and live with them in honour, not in fornication, nor taking them as secret concubines. Whoso denieth the faith, his work is vain and he will be among the losers in the Hereafter.

6. O ye who believe! When ye rise up for prayer, wash your faces, and your hands up to the elbows, and light rub your heads and (wash) your feet up to the ankles. And if ye are unclean, purify yourselves. And if ye are sick or on a journey, or one of you cometh from the closet, or ye have had contact with women, and ye find not water, then go to clean, high ground and rub your faces and your hands with some of it. Allah would not place a burden on you, but He would purify you and would perfect His grace upon you, that ye may give thanks.

14. And with those who say: "Lo! we are Christians," We made a covenant, but they forgot a part of that whereof they were admonished. Therefore We have stirred up enmity and hatred among them till the Day of Resurrection, when Allah will inform them of their handiwork.

15. O people of the Scripture! Now hath Our messenger come unto you, expounding unto you much of that which ye used to hide in the Scripture, and forgiving much. Now hath come unto you light from Allah and a plain Scripture.

16. Whereby Allah guideth him who seeketh His good-pleasure unto paths of peace. He bringeth them out of darkness unto light by

His decree, and guideth them unto a straight path.

17. They indeed have disbelieved who say: Lo! Allah is the Messiah, son of Mary. Say: Who then can do aught against Allah, if he had willed to destroy the Messiah son of Mary and his mother and everyone on earth? Allah's is the Sovereignty of the heavens and the earth and all that is between them He createth what He will. And Allah is Able to do all things.

18. The Jews and Christians say: We are sons of Allah and His loved ones. Say: Why then doth He chastise you for your sins? Nay, ye are but mortals of His creating. He forgiveth whom He will, and chastieth whom He will. Allah's is the Sovereignty of the heavens and the earth and all that is between them, and unto Him is journeying.

19. O people of the Scripture! Now hath Our messenger come unto you to make things plain after an interval (of cessation) of the messengers, lest ye should say: There came not unto us a messenger of cheer nor any warner. Now hath a messenger of cheer and a warner come unto you. Allah is Able to do all things.

44. Lo! We did reveal the Torah, wherein is guidance and light, by which the Prophets who surrendered (unto Allah) judged the Jews, and the rabbis and the priests (judge) by such of Allah's Scripture as they were bidden to observe, and thereunto were they witnesses. So fear not mankind, but fear Me. And barter not My revelations for a little gain. Whoso judgeth not by that which Allah hath revealed: such are disbelievers.

45. And we prescribed for them therein: The life for the life, and the eye for the eye, and the nose for the nose, and the ear for the ear, and the tooth for the tooth, and for wounds retaliation. But whoso forgoeth it (in the way of charity) it shall be expiation for him. Whoso judgeth not by that which Allah hath revealed: such are wrong-doers.

46. And We caused Jesus, son of Mary to follow in their footsteps, confirming that which was (revealed) before him, and We bestowed on him the Gospel wherein is guidance and a light, confirming that which was (revealed) before it in the Torah—a guidance and an admonition unto those who ward off (evil).

72. They surely disbelieve who say: Lo! Allah is the Messiah, son of Mary. The Messiah (himself) said: O Children of Israel, worship Allah, My Lord and your Lord. Lo! whoso ascribeth partners unto Allah, for him Allah hath forbidden Paradise. His abode is the Fire. For evil-doers there will be no helpers.

73. They surely disbelieve who say: Lo! Allah is the third of three; when there is no God save the One God. If they desist not from so saying a painful doom will fall on those of them who disbelieve.

75. The Messiah, son of Mary, was no other than a messenger, messengers (the like of whom) had passed away before him. And his mother was a saintly woman. And they both used to eat (earthly) food. See how we make the revelations clear for them, and see how they are turned away!

SURAH VII: THE HEIGHTS

158. Say (O Muhammad): O mankind! Lo! I am the messenger of All to you all—(the messenger of) Him unto whom belongeth the Sovereignty of the heavens and the earth. There is no God save Him. He quickeneth and He giveth death. So believe in Allah and His messenger, the Prophet who can neither read nor write, who believeth in Allah and in His words and follow him that haply ye may be led aright.

SURAH XIV: ABRAHAM

35. And when Abraham said: My Lord! Make safe this territory, and preserve me and my sons from serving idols.

36. My Lord! Lo! they have led many of

mankind astray. But whoso followeth me, he verily is of me. And whoso disobeyeth me—Still Thou art Forgiving, Merciful.

37. Our Lord! Lo! I have settled some of my posterity in an uncultivatable valley near unto Thy holy House (the valley of Mecca), our Lord! that they may establish proper worship; so incline some hearts of men that they may yearn toward them, and provide Thou them with fruits in order that they may be thankful.

38. Our Lord! Lo! thou knowest that which we hide and that which we proclaim. Nothing in the earth or in the heaven is hidden from Allah.

39. Praise be to Allah Who hath given me, in my old age, Ishmael and Isaac! Lo! my Lord is indeed the Hearer of Prayer.

40. My Lord! Make me to establish proper worship, and some of my posterity (also); our Lord! and accept the prayer.

41. Our Lord! Forgive me and my parents and believers on the day when the account is cast.

47. So think not that Allah will fail to keep His promise to His messengers. Allah is Mighty, Able to Requite (the wrong).

48. On the day when the earth will be changed to other than the earth, and the heavens (also will be changed) and they will come forth unto Allah, the One, the Almighty,

49. Thou wilt see the guilty on that day linked together in chains,

50. Their raiment of pitch, and the Fire covering their faces,

51. That Allah may repay each soul what it hath earned. Lo! Allah is swift at reckoning.

52. This is a clear message for mankind in order that they may be warned thereby, and that they may know that he is only One God, and that men of understanding may take heed.

SURAH XVII: THE CHILDREN OF ISRAEL

1. Glorified be He Who carried His servant by night from the Inviolable Place of Worship (Mecca) to the Far Distant Place of Worship (Jerusalem) the neighbourhood whereof We have blessed, that We might show him of Our tokens! Lo! He, only He is the Hearer, the Seer.

2. We gave unto Moses the Scripture, and We appointed it a guidance for the Children of Israel, saying: Choose no guardian beside Me.

22. Set not up with Allah any other god (O man) lest thou sit down reproved, forsaken.

23. Thy Lord hath decreed, that ye worship none save Him, and (that ye show) kindness to parents. If one of them or both of them to attain old age with thee, say not "Fie" unto them nor repulse them, but speak unto them a gracious word.

24. And lower unto them the wing of submission through mercy, and say: My Lord! Have mercy on them both as they did care for me when I was little.

25. Your Lord is best aware of what is in your minds. If ye are righteous, then lo! He was ever Forgiving unto those who turn (unto Him).

26. Give the kinsman his due, and the needy, and the wayfarer, and squander not (thy wealth) in wantonness.

27. Lo! the squanderers were ever brothers of the devils, and the devil was ever an ingrate to his Lord.

28. But if thou turn away from them, seeking mercy from thy Lord, for which thou hopest, then speak unto them a reasonable word.

31. Slay not your children, fearing a fall to poverty. We shall provide for them and for you. Lo! the slaying of them is great sin.

32. And come not near unto adultery. Lo! it is an abomination and an evil way.

33. And slay not the life which Allah hath forbidden save with right. Whoso is slain wrongfully, We have given power unto his heir, but let him not commit excess in slaying. Lo! he will be helped.

34. Come not near the wealth of the orphan save with that which is better till he come to

strength; and keep the covenant. Lo! of the covenant it will be asked.

35. Fill the measure when ye measure, and weigh with a right balance; that is meet, and better in the end.

SURAH XX: TA HA

130. Therefore (O Muhammad), bear with what they say, and celebrate the praises of thy Lord ere the rising of the sun and ere the going down thereof. And glorify Him some hours of the night and at the two ends of the day, that thou mayst find acceptance.

SURAH LVI: THE EVENT

1. When the event befalleth—
2. There is no denying that it will befall—
3. Abasing (some), exalting (others);
4. When the earth is shaken with a shock
5. And the hills are ground to powder
6. So that they become a scattered dust,
7. And ye will be three kinds:
8. (First) those on the right hand; what of those on the right hand?
9. And (then) those on the left hand; what of those on the left hand?
10. And the foremost in the race, the foremost in the race:
11. Those are they who will be brought nigh
12. In gardens of delight;
13. A multitude of those of old
14. And a few of those of later time,
15. On lined couches,
16. Reclining therein face to face.
17. There wait on them immortal youths
18. With bowls and ewers and a cup from a pure spring
19. Wherefrom they get no aching of the head nor any madness,
20. And fruit that they prefer
21. And flesh of fowls that they desire.
22. And (there) fair ones with wide, lovely eyes,
23. Like unto hidden pearls,
24. Reward for what they used to do.
25. There hear they no vain speaking nor recrimination
26. (Naught) but the saying: Peace, (and again) peace.
27. And those on the right hand; what of those on the right hand?
28. Among thornless lote-trees
29. And clustered plantains,
30. And spreading shade,
31. And water gushing,
32. And fruit in plenty
33. Neither out of reach nor yet forbidden,
34. and raised couches;
35. Lo! We have created them a (new) creation
36. And made them virgins,
37. Lovers, friends,
38. For those on the right hand;
39. A multitude of those of old
40. And a multitude of those of later time.
41. And those on the left hand: What of those on the left hand?
42. In scorching wind and scalding water
43. And shadow of black smoke,
44. Neither cool nor refreshing.
45. Lo! heretofore they were effete with luxury
46. And used to persist in the awful sin.
47. And they used to say: When we are dead and have become dust and bones, shall we then, forsooth, be raised again,
48. And also our forefathers?
49. Say (unto them, O Muhammad): Lo! those of old and those of later time
50. Will all be brought together to the tryst of an appointed day.

SURAH XCVI: THE CLOT

In the name of Allah, the Beneficent, the Merciful

1. Read: In the name of thy Lord who createth,
2. Createth man from a clot.

3. Read: And thy Lord is the Most Bounteous,

4. Who teacheth by the pen,

5. Teacheth man that which he knew not.

6. Nay, but verily man is rebellious

7. That he thinketh himself independent!

8. Lo! unto thy Lord is the return.

9. Hast thou seen him who dissuadeth

10. A slave when he prayeth?

11. Hast thou seen if he (relieth) on the guidance (of Allah)

12. Or enjoineth piety?

13. Hast thou seen if he denieth (Allah's guidance) and is forward?

14. Is he then unaware that Allah seeth?

15. Nay, but if he cease not. We will seize him by the forelock

16. The lying, sinful forelock—

17. Then let him call upon his henchmen!

18. We will call the guards of hell.

19. Nay! Obey not thou him. But prostrate thyself, and draw near (unto Allah).

5

JEWISH THEOLOGY AND MYSTICISM
FROM 750–1400 C.E.

GAON SAADIA BEN JOSEPH

During the Middle Ages, Judaism continued as a minority religion in regions ruled by both Muslims and Christians. While living under Muslim rule in the Middle East in the eighth through tenth centuries C.E., the Jews produced new forms of rabbinic literature and also began to creatively struggle with two perennial problems for religious traditions in the West. The first was the relation between the original scriptural revelation and the ongoing voice of authority in the community. This question was raised by Jews who advocated the written Hebrew scriptures as the sole basis for Jewish doctrine and practice and questioned the validity of a revealed oral law which was the basis for the rabbinical interpretation of the scriptures in the Talmud. This is essentially the same problem that the Christian tradition would face during the Protestant Reformation of the sixteenth century C.E. The second problem was the relation between the revealed tradition of the scriptures and the Talmud and the truth claimed by Greek philosophy which relies solely upon the powers of human reason. This problem will also occupy both Muslim and Christian thinkers throughout the High Middle Ages.

Because Jews were considered a "people of the Book," the Abbasid caliphs at Baghdad allowed them to continue their traditions and, as a result, the Babylonian academies flourished as major centers of Jewish life. The leader of the academy was given the title *Gaon* or "Excellency," and the Jews of North Africa and Europe submitted questions of doctrine and observance to these rabbinic leaders (*geonim*) of Babylon. Their answers became a new form of authoritative rabbinic literature. The Talmud was still regarded as the standard of covenant fidelity, but the rabbinic authorities were accepted as the spiritual heirs of the sages who had created it.

In the eighth century C.E., partly in rebellion against this rabbinic authority and partly as a reflection of fundamentalist trends in the Muslim community, some Jews, largely Arabic speaking, formed a group of dissidents known as *Karaites* ("devotees of scripture"). Like the Sadducees of old, they challenged the oral traditions of the rabbis as being the work of men rather than God. This of course undermined the authority of the *Talmud* which was based on an oral tradition traced back to Moses. To define the terms of God's covenant with Israel, the Karaites insisted, Jews must simply read scripture literally rather than rely on rabbinic exegesis. When the practices of rabbinic Judaism were submitted to this fundamentalist test, many were found to have no scriptural warrant. The Karaites began to live a rigorous and simplified form of Judaism. For example, no lights or fires were allowed on sabbath; phylacteries (*tefillim*) were eliminated; the feast of Hanukkah was dropped, and some Karaites moved to Jerusalem to await the arrival of the Messianic Age. The Karaite movement had several causes: a criticism of the opulence of the distant Babylonian community, the language barrier between the Aramaic of the Talmud and the Arab tongue of Karaites, and an emphasis on reason over established religious authority.

The scholar who led a vigorous and sophisticated response to Karaism was Saadia ben Joseph (882–942 C.E.) who was also the pioneer of Jewish philosophy in the Middle Ages. Born in obscurity in Egypt, he became the leading scholar and rabbi of his age. He was the first non-Babylonian to be appointed to the exalted position of Gaon of the renowned Talmudic academy of Sura in Babylon. In order to make the Hebrew Bible accessible to Arabic-speaking Jews, Saadia translated it into Arabic and added a popular commentary in Arabic to explain the train of thought in the rabbinic interpretations.

In his greatest work entitled *Book of Doctrines and Beliefs* Saadia, again writing in Arabic, gives reasonable arguments for the necessity of an authoritative tradition to hand on the scriptural revelation. First of all, in a very rationalistic way he asserts that the scriptures, for all their variety, contain only three essential elements: (1) commandments and prohibitions, (2) rewards and punishments which are the fruits of the former, and (3) edifying stories about those who prospered by good service or who perished because of corruption. He then argues that for these lessons to be passed on to posterity people of authority were required to hand them down. For Saadia these authorities were the rabbinical academies. Without a trustworthy tradition of what Saadia calls "true reports in this world," all respect for commands and prohibitions will break down and the management of human affairs will become impossible.

In defense of the communal rabbinic tradition that produced the Talmud, Saadia argues that traditions can be distorted in two ways: either by a wrong idea or through willful distortion. He believes that these can remain unnoticed only if they emanate from an individual because in a large collective group, like the rabbinical academies, if its members willfully decide to invent a story, some will relate how they came to agree upon the story.

Saadia was also the first Jewish thinker since Philo to master the prevailing philosophical tradition of his age and effectively harmonize it with the Jewish faith. By the ninth century a revival of Greek rationalism (made available in Arabic translations of Plato and Aristotle) had provoked learned Muslims and Jews to question the claims of revealed scripture. Saadia, as a thoroughgoing rationalist, believed that God was the source of all truth, and therefore the truth discovered by reason could not contradict that given by God in revelation. There was no possibility of a conflict between reason and revelation. Whenever biblical texts appeared to contradict human reason, as when the Torah ascribed physical attributes to God, such statements were to be taken allegorically and not literally.

In his *The Book of Beliefs and Opinions,* Saadia identifies four sources of knowledge: sensation, intuition, reason, and authentic tradition which included scriptural revelation. The first three correspond to the methods of Greek philosophy. The fourth, of course, is the divinely revealed truth that God has given to Judaism. The truth in revelation does not contradict what humans can know by reason. Saadia believed that God had empowered humans to derive both metaphysical truth and moral laws by means of unaided reason. What then was the purpose of revelation? One was that certain ritual laws of the Torah were not derivable from reason. A second was that revelation yielded truth in incorruptible form, while human reason was liable to error. Finally, the detailed application of God's moral law would gain no consensus without the authority of revelation. In short, revelation demonstrated truth about God's existence and his moral law more rapidly and persuasively than reason alone. In the thirteenth century C.E., Thomas Aquinas, the great Dominican scholastic, will come to essentially the same conclusions about the relationship between faith and reason and the necessity for the Christian revelation.

JUDAH HALEVI, *THE BOOK OF THE KHAZARS*

By the time of Saadia's death, Babylonia was already on the wane as the leading center for Jewish intellectual life. Six years later, the academy at Sura closed. Jews in search of economic opportunity and intellectual and spiritual freedom began to turn westward to the Jewish community in Muslim Spain which was to produce in the ninth through the twelfth centuries a golden age of Jewish culture and the two greatest Jewish writers of the Middle Ages: the poet and polemicist, Judah HaLevi, and the great Talmudist and philosopher, Moses Maimonides.

Jews had been living in Spain since Roman times, but they had suffered persecution under Christian Visigothic rulers in the seventh and early eighth centuries. With the Muslim conquest of Spain in 711 C.E., the Jewish communities had new opportunities for religious freedom and cultural creativity. Their Muslim rulers allowed them to observe their faith and gave them a vital role in what was the most sophisticated and learned culture in Europe during the period from 800–1100 C.E.

As the center of Muslim power gravitated to the Ummayad dynasty of Cordoba, the pendulum of Jewish authority also swung west. Aramaic, the language of the Talmud, was native to Babylonia, but in Spain, where Jews spoke Arabic, it was a foreign language. By the tenth century the Spanish community had assumed a commanding place in the inner life of world Jewry.

The emergence of Muslim philosophical schools also spurred Jewish intellectual and scholarly life. Particularly, the translation and commentaries on the philosophical works of Aristotle raised the important questions of how to reconcile reason and revelation, human freedom and divine foreknowledge, and the scriptural doctrine of creation with Aristotle's concept of an eternal world.

Rabbi Judah HaLevi (1085–1142 C.E.) was born in Toledo, Spain, at the end of this period, just as Christians were beginning the *Reconquista* of Spain. Like Maimonides, he was the kind of universal genius which Christian Europe would not produce until the time of the Renaissance in Italy in the fourteenth and fifteenth centuries. Not only was he a rabbi with a thorough knowledge of the scriptures and the Talmuds, but he was also a physician and the greatest Jewish poet of the Middle Ages.

Initially, Judah HaLevi was attracted to Neo-Aristotelian philosophy, but in time he came to reject it in favor of a romantic and almost mystical defense of the Jewish faith as the only complete source of truth. His greatest work is written in Arabic and entitled *Book of Arguments in Behalf of the Defense of the Faith,* but it is more commonly known by the title *The Book of the Khazars.* It is a dramatic dialogue based on an earlier romantic episode in Jewish history. In 740 C.E. the Khazars, a Tartar people living on the west bank of the Caspian Sea, converted to Judaism. The correspondence between a Spanish Jew, Hasdai ibn Shaprut (915–970 C.E.) and Joseph, the last Khazar king, documents that this conversion took place after an Aristotelian philosopher, a Christian, a Muslim, and a Jewish rabbi presented their beliefs to the Khazar king. Judah HaLevi reconstructs this episode and makes his *The Book of the Khazars* a dialogue between the Khazar king and a Jewish rabbi who is a spokesman for his ideas.

It is both a polemic in behalf of Judaism and a critique of those Jews who would reduce Jewish faith to an Aristotelian rationalism. According to Judah HaLevi, the Khazar king rejected the philosopher because his doctrine left him cold, and when the Muslim and Christian presented their faiths, both appealed to the Jewish scriptures as proof of the truth of their claims. The king had not first consulted a Jew because he had inferred from their degraded state that their doctrines could not be true. But now he summons a Jewish rabbi who proceeds to engage the king in a lengthy dialogue about the truth of Jewish tradition.

The rabbi begins by asserting Jews believe in the God who has revealed himself to them in the course of their history: in the promises to the patriarchs Abraham, Isaac, and Jacob; in the Exodus in which he freed them from slavery in Egypt, in the giving of his Torah at Sinai; in the journey through the wilderness and in the gift of the promised land of Canaan; and in the teachings of the prophets. Judah's rabbi places particular emphasis on the reality of the revelation of the Torah at Sinai. After the lightnings, thunder and earthquake, God's voice was actually heard by the over six hundred thousand Israelites who made the journey out of Egypt. God himself engraved the Ten Commandments on the tablets that were given to Moses. According to Judah's rabbi, the validity of the Jewish tradition rests on the testimony of those witnesses and their successors who stood at Mount Sinai. It is not dependent upon the rational proofs of philosophers who can disagree about such things as the eternity of the physical world.

The Book of the Khazars takes a very enlightened attitude toward Christianity and Islam. Both faiths are stages in the spiritual growth of humanity. But, even in rejecting

Judaism, they reflected its rise, as both draw upon the traditions in the Hebrew scriptures. In their present forms, both have remnants of idolatry, according to Judah's rabbinical spokesman. For example, Christians venerate images like the cross and the Muslims honor the Kaaba by their pilgrimages.

When questioned about why Israel's faith has not been accepted by the world and why Jews have suffered rejection throughout their history, the rabbi answers that Israel is the heart of humanity which assimilates the vices of its neighbors and suffers for them. Its sufferings are not a sign of God's rejection. They are meant to cleanse and purify Israel from all taint of evil.

The Book of the Khazars does not take a completely negative attitude toward human reason and rational law, but it places a special emphasis on Jewish ceremonial law. Rational laws are indispensable for the successful running of any society and are necessary for Israel's special divine law to be perfected. However, in contrast to what we will see in Maimonides, Judah HaLevi has a much more positive view of Israel's unique ritual laws. For him, Israel's ethical laws are preliminary to the ceremonial law which in its fullness brings God's presence, the *Shekhinah,* down to humankind. But for this to occur there must be a land, a Temple, sacrificial cult, and ceremonial law. For Judah HaLevi, Palestine is literally a holy land, the only place which possesses the spiritual qualities for full revelation and a union between God and man. As long as Israel, the heart of humanity, is in exile and the Temple in ruins, no prophet is available and the *Shekhinah* has withdrawn from the world.

Interestingly, at the end of *The Book of the Khazars* the rabbi announces his intention to leave the land of the Khazars for Jerusalem. There alone, says the rabbi, can the life of the Jew be complete. Not content to await the coming of the messianic age, Judah HaLevi himself believed that a Jew's love of the Torah was not complete unless living and dying in the Holy Land was the goal of one's life. His incomparable Hebrew poetry expresses this longing, and toward the end of his life he journeyed to Zion, although he apparently died, possibly as a martyr, before reaching his destination.

The translation of *The Book of the Khazars* is by H. Hirshfeld in Judah HaLevi, *The Kuzari: An Argument for the Faith of Israel* (1905). The poems are from Nina Salaman *Poetry of Judah HaLevi* (Philadelphia: Jewish Publication Society, 1928).

THE BOOK OF THE KHAZARS

(The philosopher is setting forth his creed, with particular emphasis on what sets him apart from the Christian and the Muslim faiths.)

There is no favor or dislike in the nature of God because He is above desire and intention, since a desire intimates a want in the person who feels it, and not until it is satisfied does he become, so to speak, complete; if it remains unfulfilled, he lacks completion. In the same way God is, in the opinion of the philosophers, above the knowledge of individuals, because the latter change with the times, while there is no change in God's knowledge. He, then, does not know you, much less your thoughts or actions, nor does He listen to your prayers or see your movements. If philosophers say that He created you, they only use a metaphor, because He is the Cause of causes in the creation of all creatures, but not because this (specific act) was His intention from the beginning. He never created man. For the world is without beginning, and there never arose a man except through one who came into existence before him, in whom are united forms, gifts, characteristics inherited from father, mother and other relations, besides the influences of climate, countries, food and water, spheres, stars and constellations. Everything is reduced to a Prime Cause, not to a Will proceeding from this, but an Emanation from which emanated a second, a third, and a fourth cause. . . .

(The rabbi responds.)

There is an excuse for the philosophers. Being Greeks, science and religion did not come to them as inheritances. They belong to the descendants of Japheth, who inhabited the north, while that knowledge coming from Adam, and supported by the divine influence, is only to be found among the progeny of Shem, who represent the successors of Noah and constituted, so to speak, his essence. This knowledge has always been connected with this essence, and will always remain so. The Greeks only received it, when they became powerful, from Persia. The Persians had it from the Chaldeans (or Babylonians). It was only then that the famous Greek philosophers arose, but as soon as Rome assumed political leadership, they produced no philosopher worthy of the name.

The Khazar king: Does this mean that Aristotle's philosophy is not deserving of credence?

The Rabbi: Certainly. He exerted his mind, because he had no tradition from any reliable source at his disposal. He meditated on the beginning and end of the world, but found as much difficulty in the theory of the beginning as in that of the eternity of the world. Finally, these abstract speculations which made for

the eternity of the world prevailed, and he found no reason to inquire into the chronology or derivation of those who lived before him. Had he lived among a people with well-authenticated and generally acknowledged traditions, he would have applied his deductions and arguments to establish a theory of creation, however difficult, instead of the eternity of the world, which is even more difficult to accept.

The Khazar king: Is there any decisive proof?

The Rabbi: Where could we find one for such a question? Heaven forbid that there should be anything in the Bible to contradict that which is manifest or proved! On the other hand, it tells of miracles and changes of ordinary things, newly arising, or changing one into the other. This proves that the Creator of the world is able to accomplish what He wills, and whenever He wills. The question of eternity and creation is obscure, while the (rational) arguments on either side are evenly balanced. But the theory of creation derives greater weight from the prophetic tradition of Adam, Noah and Moses, which is more deserving of credence than mere speculation. If, after all, a believer in the Law finds himself compelled to admit an eternal matter and the existence of many worlds prior to this one, this would not impair his belief that this world was created at a certain epoch, and that Adam and Noah were the first human beings. . . .

(The weakness of dialectical theology.)

The Rabbi: . . . This theology has no value, save as an exercise in dialectics. . . . A simple, wise man, such as a prophet, can impart to others little by way of formal instruction, nor can he solve a problem by dialectical methods, while the master of dialectical theology possesses such an aura of learning that those who hear him consider him as superior to the simple pious man whose learning consists of beliefs which no one can induce him to abandon. Yet the supreme achievement of the master of dialectical theology, in all that he learns and teaches, would be that there should come into his own soul and the souls of his students those very same beliefs which are present by nature in the soul of the simple man.

It happens that the science of dialectical theology destroys many true beliefs in a man's heart by leading him into doubts and conflicting opinions. The masters of dialectical theology are like experts on poetic meters who investigate scansion. Such experts make a great fuss and use a lot of formidable terms to describe a skill which comes easily to someone naturally gifted in poetry, who sense the meter and so never breaks in any way the rules of scansion. . . . The same may be said about those who possess a natural aptitude for living according to the divine law and for drawing near to God: through the words of the pious sparks kindled in their souls, which become rays of illumination in their hearts. A man not endowed with such a natural gift has necessarily to resort to dialectical theology, which may not bring him any benefit, and indeed may conceivably cause him positive harm. . . .

(The literal reality of the Divine Voice at Sinai)

The Rabbi: Heaven forbid that I should assume what is against sense and reason. The first of the Ten Commandments enjoins the belief in divine providence. The second command contains the prohibition of the worship of other gods, or the association of any being with Him, the prohibition to represent Him in statues, forms or images, or any personification of Him. How should we not deem Him above personification, since we do so with many of His creations, e.g., the human soul, which represents man's true essence. . . . We must not, however, endeavor to reject the conclusions to be drawn from revelation. We say,

then that we do not know how the intention became corporealized and the speech evolved which struck our ear (on Sinai), nor what new thing God created from nothing, nor what existing thing He employed. He does not lack the power. We say that He created the two tablets and engraved a text on them, in the same way that He created the heavens and the stars by His will alone. God desired it and they became concrete as He wished it, engraved with the text of the Ten Words. We also say that He divided the Red Sea and formed it into two walls, which He caused to stand to the right and the left of the people (on their way out of Egypt), for whom He made easy wide roads and smooth ground for them to walk on without fear and trouble. This rendering, constructing and arranging are attributed to God, who required no tool or intermediary, as would be necessary for human toil. As the water stood at His command, shaped itself at His will, so the air which touched the prophet's ear assumed the form of sounds, which conveyed the matters to be communicated by God to the prophet and the people. . . .

I do not maintain that this is exactly how things occurred; the problem is no doubt too deep for me to fathom. But the result was that everyone who was present at the time became convinced that the matter proceeded from God directly. It is to be compared to the first act of creation. The belief in the Law connected with those scenes (on Sinai) is as firmly established in the mind as the belief in the creation of the world, and that He created it in the same manner in which He—as is known—created the two tablets, the manna, other things. Thus disappear from the soul of the believer the doubts of the philosophers and the materialists.

(How can lowly Israel be the chosen people?)

The Khazar king: . . . The perfection of his (Moses') work was marred by the fact that his

book was written in Hebrew, which made it
unintelligible to the people of Sind, India and
Khazar. They would, therefore, be unable to
practice all his laws until some centuries had
elapsed, or they had been prepared for it by
changes of conquest or alliance, but not
through the revelation of the prophet himself,
or another who would stand up for him and
testify to his law.

The Rabbi: Moses invited only his people
and those of his own tongue to accept the law,
while God promised that at all times there
should be prophets to expound His law. This
He did as long as they found favor in his sight
and His presence was with them.

The Khazar king: Would it not have been
better or more commensurate with divine wisdom if all mankind had been guided on the
true path?

The Rabbi: Or would it not have been best
for all animals to have been reasonable
beings? You have apparently forgotten what
we said previously concerning Adam's progeny, and how the spirit of divine prophecy rested on one person (in each generation), who
was chosen from his brethren and was the
essence of his father. It was he on whom this
divine light was concentrated. He was the ker-
nel, while the others were as husks which had
no share in it. (All) the sons of Jacob were,
however, distinguished from other people by
godly qualities, which made them, so to speak,
an angelic caste. . . . We do not deny that the
good actions of any man, to whichever people
he may belong, will be rewarded by God. But
the priority belongs to people who are near
God during their life, and we estimate the
rank they occupy after death accordingly. . . .

(Now the Khazar king asks whether we
should expect that God's chosen people would
be singled out by their position in the world.)

The Rabbi: I see you reproaching us with
our degradation and poverty, while the best of
other religions boast of both (high station in

this world and the next). Do they not glorify
him (that is, Jesus) who said: "He who strikes
you on the right cheek, turn to him the left
also; and he who takes your coat, let him have
your shirt as well" (Matt. 5:39–40)? He and
his friends and followers, after hundreds of
years of contumely, flogging and slaying,
attained their well-known success, and in the
very things they glorify. This is also the history of the founder of Islam (that is,
Muhammad) and his friends, who eventually
prevailed and became powerful. The nations
boast of these, but not of those kings whose
power and might are great, whose walls are
strong and whose chariots are terrible. Yet
our relation to God is a closer one than if we
had reached greatness already on earth.

The Khazar king: This might be so, if your
humility were voluntary, but it is involuntary,
and if you had power you would slay.

The Rabbi: You have touched our weak
spot, O King of the Khazars. If the majority of
us, as you say, would learn humility toward
God and His Law from our low station,
Providence would not have forced us to bear it
for such a long period. Only the smallest portion (of us) thinks this; the majority may
expect reward, because they bear their degradation, partly from necessity, partly from
their own free will. . . . If we bear our exile
and degradation for God's sake, as is meet, we
shall be the pride of the generation which will
come with the Messiah, and accelerate the
day of deliverance we hope for.

Now we do not allow anyone who embraces
our religion theoretically by means of word
alone to take equal rank with ourselves, but
demand actual self-sacrifice, purity, knowledge, circumcision and numerous religious
ceremonies. The convert must adopt our way
of life entirely. . . . Those, however, who
become Jews do not take equal rank with
born Israelites, who are specially privileged to
attain to prophecy, while the former can only
achieve something by learning from them,

and become pious and learned, but never prophets. . . .

(Israel the heart of the nations)

The Rabbi: Israel is to peoples as the heart is to the limbs. It is greater in sicknesses than all, and it is greater than all in health.

The Khazar king: Make this clearer to me.

The Rabbi: The heart is constantly attacked by sickness—by care, worry, fright, anger, hatred, love and dangers. Its nature suffers perpetual flux and change through too much and too little. And beside this, bad food and bad drink, motion, the efforts of labor, sleeping and waking, all act upon the heart while the limbs are at rest.

The Khazar king: Now I clearly see in what way it is greater in sickness than all the limbs, but make it clear to me in what way it is greater than all in health. . . .

The Rabbi: The relation of the divine to us is as the relation of soul to heart. And therefore it is said: "You only have I known of all the families of the earth, therefore I will visit upon you all your iniquities." Those are the sicknesses. But what our masters said of health is this: "He forgives the iniquities of his people, of Israel, by always obliterating the former." Thus he does not allow iniquities to accumulate within us, and so cause utter destruction, as he did in the case of the Amorite of whom it is said: "For the iniquity of the Amorite is not yet full." God let him go his ways until the sickness of his iniquities was so great that it resulted in death. And just as the heart, in its very root and nature, is of such harmony in its blending that the power of life is bound up with it, thus is it also with Israel, with its root and its nature. And as the heart is attacked by sickness by way of the other parts of the body, by way of the greeds of the liver and of the stomach, as a result of the poor mixing of juices—so Israel is attacked by sickness because of its mingling with other peoples, as it is said: "But mingled

themselves with the nations and learned their works." And so it must not seem strange to you that it is written: "Surely diseases he did bear and our pains he carried." Thus we are in distress, the world is at peace. But the distress that strikes us is meant to keep our faith firm, to cleanse us completely, and to cast out the dross from our midst. Through what we have that is clear and upright, the divine is connected with the world. You know that the elements originated so that minerals could originate from them, and then plants, and then animals, and then men, and finally the elect among men. All that was created was for the sake of these elect, so that the divine might inhabit them. But these elect originated for the sake of the most elect, of the prophets and the devout.

(Jewish asceticism)

The Rabbi: The divine law imposes no asceticism on us. It rather desires that we should keep the equilibrium and grant to every mental and physical faculty its due, as much as it can bear, without overburdening one faculty at the expense of another. If a person gives way to licentiousness, he blunts his mental faculty; he who is inclined to violence injures some other faculty. Prolonged fasting is no act of piety for a weak person who, having succeeded in desires, is not greedy. For him feasting is a burden and self-denial. Neither is diminution of wealth an act of piety, if it is gained in a lawful way, and if its acquisition does not interfere with study and good works, especially for him who has a household and children. He may spend part of it in almsgiving, which would not be displeasing to God; but to increase it would be better for himself.

Our Law, as a whole, is divided between fear, love and joy, by each of which one can approach God. Your contribution on a fast day does nothing nearer to God than your joy on the Sabbath and the holy days, if it is the outcome of a devout heart. . . . The observance of the Sabbath is itself an acknowledgment of His omnipotence (in its recollection of the Exodus), and at the same time an acknowledgment of the creation by the divine Word. . . . The observance of the Sabbath is therefore nearer to God than monastic retirement and asceticism.

(The nature of ritual acts)

The Rabbi: All these ceremonies, the remission of sins on the Day of Atonement, the cleansing of the sanctuary from impurities by means of the he-goat of Azazel, with all the accompanying ceremonies; the blessing of Israel through Aaron's uplifted hands, and the reciting of the verse "The Lord bless you"; upon every one of these ceremonies the Divine Influence rested. . . . Who, then, can calculate actions upon which the Divine Influence rests, save God alone? . . . .

. . . You slaughter a lamb and smear yourself with its blood in skinning it, cleaning its entrails, washing, dismembering it and sprinkling its blood. Then you arrange the wood, kindle the fire, place the body upon it. If this were not done in consequence of a divine command, you would think little of all these actions and think that they estranged you from God rather than bringing you nearer to Him. But as soon as the whole is properly accomplished, and you see the divine fire, or notice in yourself a new spirit, unknown before, or see true visions and great apparitions, you are aware that this is the fruit of the preceding acts, as well as of the great influence with which you have come in contact. . . .

(The journey to Jerusalem)

The rabbi was then anxious to leave the land of Khazar and betake himself to Jerusalem. The king was reluctant to have him go and expressed his feeling in these words: What is it that you seek in Jerusalem and the land of Canaan, now that the Divine Presence is no longer there? If one's desire is great and one's mind pure, it is possible to approach God in any place. Why face dangers on land and water and among various peoples?

The Rabbi: The visible Presence has, indeed, disappeared, because it does not reveal itself save to a prophet, or in a favored community, or in a place set apart. This is what we look for in the passage, "For they shall see, eye to eye, the Lord returning to Zion," and what we say in our prayers: "Let our eyes behold when Thou returnest to Zion." As regards the invisible and spiritual Presence, it is with every born Israelite who leads a virtuous life, who has a pure heart and an upright mind before the God of Israel. The land of Canaan is in special favor with the God of Israel, and no function can be perfect except there. Heart and soul are wholly pure and immaculate only in the place believed to be specially selected by God. If this is true in a figurative sense, how much more so in reality! So the longing for this springs from disinterested motives, particularly for him who wishes to live there and atone for past transgressions, since he has had no opportunity to offer the sacrifices ordained by God for intentional and unintentional sins. He is supported by the saying of the sages, "Wandering atones for sins," especially if his wandering brings him to the place of God's choice. The dangers he runs on land and on sea do not belong to the category of "You shall not tempt the Lord," for this verse refers to risks one takes when traveling with merchandise in the hope of gain. He who incurs even greater dangers because of his ardent desire to obtain forgiveness, is free from reproach if he has balanced the account of his years, expressed gratitude for his past life, and exults in spending the remainder of his days in seeking the favor of the Lord. He braves danger and gives fervent praise to God if he escapes. But should he perish through his sins, he has obtained the divine favor, and may be confident of having atoned for most of his sins by his death. In my opinion this is better than to seek the dangers of war in order to win fame and gain spoils through courage and endurance. This kind of danger is inferior even to that of men who go to war for hire.

The Khazar king: I thought you loved freedom, yet now you seem willing to assume new religious duties, which you will be obliged to fulfill in the Land of Israel but which are in abeyance here.

The Rabbi: I seek freedom only from serving the many people whose favor means nothing to me, and which I should never gain though I worked for it all my life. And even if I could obtain it, serving men and courting their favor still would not profit me. I prefer to seek the service of One whose favor is gained by even a small effort, and yet helps in this world and in the coming world. This is the favor of God. To serve him is true freedom; to be humble before him true honor. . . . It is written: "Thou wilt arise, and have compassion upon Zion; for it is time to be gracious unto her, for the appointed time is come. For Thy servants take pleasure in her stones, and love her dust." This means that Jerusalem can be rebuilt only when Israel will yearn for this so deeply that they love her stones and her dust.

The Khazar king: If this is so, it would be a sin to hinder you. Rather is it a merit to assist you. May God grant you his help and be your protector and friend. May he favor you in his mercy.

SELECTED POEMS

My Heart is in the East

My heart is in the east, and I in the uttermost west.

How can I savour food? How shall it be sweet to me?

How shall I render my vows and my bonds, while yet

Zion lies beneath the fetters of Edom, and I in Arab chains?

A light thing would it seem to me to leave all the good things of Spain—

Seeing how precious in mine eyes it is to behold the dust of the desolate sanctuary.

To Jerusalem

Beautiful height! O Joy! the whole world's gladness!

O great King's city, mountain blest!

My soul is yearning unto thee—is yearning

From limits of the west.

The torrents heave from depths of mine heart's passion

At memory of thine olden state,

The glory of thee borne away to exile,

Thy dwelling desolate.

And who shall grant me, on the wings of eagles,

To rise and seek thee through the years,

Until I mingle with thy dust beloved

The waters of my tears?

MOSES MAIMONIDES, *MISHNEH TORAH, THE GUIDE OF THE PERPLEXED HELEK: SANHEDRIN,* CHAPTER TEN

By the eleventh and twelfth centuries C.E., Spanish Jews were being caught in the cross fire of the Christian *Reconquista* and Muslim efforts to hold on to Spain. The zeal of the Christian crusaders was matched by Muslim fanaticism which compelled non-Muslims to convert, leave the country, or lose their lives.

When Maimonides, or Moses ben Maimon, was only thirteen, the Almohads (a puritanical Muslim group from N. Africa) conquered Cordoba and closed the synagogues. Faced with the demand to convert to Islam, Maimonides' family remained for a while as secret Jews but then migrated to Morocco, then to Palestine (which was then under Christian rule), and eventually to Egypt.

A brilliant Talmudist and physician to Saladin's court, Maimonides was recognized as the unofficial leader of Egyptian Jewry. His *Mishneh Torah* (second Torah) is a fourteen-volume codification of Talmudic and Gaonic law. Written in readable Hebrew, it is intended to be a comprehensive survey of the demands of Jewish piety and includes everything from the norms of sexual behavior and business ethics to the details of the Temple service, once Zion had been restored and the Temple rebuilt. I have included Maimonides' discussion of the degrees of charity which is found in the section of the *Mishneh Torah* entitled "Laws of Giving to the Poor." It illustrates both the Jewish conception of God as being especially concerned for the poor and the experience of persecution which was so much a part of Maimonides' family experience, as well as that of his fellow Jews throughout Europe and the Near East. His analysis of the types of charity emphasizes the need for sensitivity, tact, and graciousness in the giving of alms, as well as the importance of the interior dispositions of kindness and sympathy.

In his most famous philosophical work, *The Guide of the Perplexed,* Maimonides attempts to reconcile traditional Jewish faith and philosophical reason, particularly Aristotelianism. As he states in the Introduction, his audience is not "the vulgar" or the "beginners in speculation" but scholarly believers who have mastered the Law and have studied philosophy. These intellectuals are "perplexed" by the apparent conflicts between the literal meaning of the Bible stories and the truths of philosophy. Maimonides proposes to resolve these difficulties by teaching "the science of the Law in its true sense." A second and related purpose is to explain "very obscure parables occurring in the books of the prophets" by going beyond their "external" sense to the "internal one."

His method for achieving these is largely an allegorical and rationalistic interpretation of the scripture in the tradition of Philo and Saadia. He insists that reason and faith do not conflict if properly interpreted, although their range and content may differ. Like Philo and the Muslim philosophers who interpreted the Qur'an, Maimonides argues that the Hebrew Bible cannot be interpreted literally; the scholar must be aware that its language is metaphorical and must be interpreted rationally. For example, by an analysis of the use of the terms "image" and "likeness" in the Hebrew Bible he argues that the statement in Genesis that man is created "in the image and likeness of God" does not mean that God actually has a physical body like man. Rather, as a good Aristotelian, Maimonides argues that the terms "image" and "likeness" refer to "the specific form of a thing," and for man that is his capacity for intellectual apprehension. Therefore, man's being in the image of God consists in his rational capacities which set him apart from the rest of creation. This, according to Maimonides, is a purely spiritual capacity and does not require a body. Therefore, if properly understood, the statement, "Let us make man in our image and likeness," does not require that God be corporeal, but rather implies that man in his rational capacity somehow shares in God's purely spiritual divine intellect.

Because God is purely spiritual and the language of the Bible is so anthropomorphic, Maimonides has difficulty establishing the possibility of any positive knowledge of God. In a passage in which he discusses Moses' dialogues with God after the golden calf incident (Exod 33–34), Maimonides argues that Moses, "the master of those who know" requested to know God's "essence and true reality." In the course of the dialogue Moses learns that God's "essence cannot be grasped as it really is." Rather, God reveals his "ways" to Moses which are his attributes or characteristics that are known through his actions in the world: his goodness revealed through creation, his mercy, justice, etc. However, although we speak of these as proceeding from God as if he were a person, "the meaning is not that He . . . possesses aptitudes of the soul." Even the attributes like "First" and "Last" or "One" are metaphorical when applied to God. Because we are bodily creatures in time and space, while God is eternal and spiritual, our knowledge of God is severely limited.

> . . . all men, those of the past and those of the future, affirm clearly that God, may he be exalted, cannot be apprehended by the intellect, and that none but He Himself can apprehend what He is, and that apprehension of Him consists in the inability to attain the ultimate term in apprehending Him.

In a complicated section at the beginning of Part II of *The Guide of the Perplexed,* Maimonides offers proofs for the existence of God, who is neither a body, nor a force in a body, and who is one, as opposed to many. The bases for these proofs are twenty-six premises drawn from Aristotelian philosophy. His arguments are primarily three: the fact of motion implies an Unmoved Mover who is pure act; the existence of contingent beings implies a Necessary Being; the existence of causality implies a First Cause. Variations of these arguments will also be used by Thomas Aquinas in his *Summa Theologica,* the great synthesis of Christian theology and Aristotelian thought.

Although Maimonides is heavily influenced by Aristotle's philosophy, he rejects Aristotle's thought when he thinks it endangers the truths of revelation. In contrast to Avicenna (c. 980–1037 C.E.), the great Muslim philosopher from Persia, whose Aristotelianism led him to posit an eternal world which has always co-existed with God, Maimonides argues in favor of a created world which had a beginning in time. He recognizes that by reason alone one cannot definitively prove either position, but he argues that Aristotle's necessary and eternal world makes it impossible for there to be a revelation of the Law, human freedom in response to that Law, and the miracles of the biblical tradition. Only if God freely created can there also be the possibility of intervention in history to reveal his will and to save his people.

As a Jew, Maimonides was very interested in the nature of prophecy, which is the very foundation of biblical revelation. Using Aristotelian categories, he interpreted biblical prophecy in rather rationalistic terms as a continuous flow of reason and inspiration from God to the human mind, a flow that was in proportion to the person's disciplined preparation. However, in contrast to those who are pure rationalists, Maimonides did add that God could refuse inspiration even to those who prepared themselves. He identifies the prophecy of Moses as different in kind from all others. It is a perfect expression of the divine will, and no further revelation is needed to complete it.

In his interpretation of the Jewish law Maimonides, in the tradition of Saadia, distinguishes several functions. One is to give true opinion about the existence and nature of God to ordinary people who are not capable of philosophical reflection. Accordingly, the law commanding sabbath observance teaches that God is the creator of the world because the motive given for its observance according to Exodus 20:11 is that "In six days the Lord made the heavens and the earth . . ." But Maimonides also points out that in the second version of the Decalogue in Deuteronomy 5, the sabbath also serves the more practical function of giving the body a day of rest. The motive for the commandment in this case is that at one time the Israelites were slaves in Egypt, when they were not allowed to have a day of rest (Deut 5:15). According to Maimonides, the biblical laws prescribing animal sacrifice were a kind of divine ruse to wean Israel from homage to pagan deities who commanded their animal sacrifices. Under the influence of Aristotelian philosophy, Maimonides, in contrast to Judah HaLevi, looked for rational reasons for the unique observances of Jewish law. For example, he interpreted some of the dietary laws as antidotes to gluttony, and circumcision as a way of keeping man's sexual drive under control.

Judaism's uniqueness, Maimonides insists, is grounded in the Torah revealed by Moses to the children of Israel. As such it is superior to Christianity and Islam, even though these religions were divinely ordained ways of leading other peoples to monotheism.

Our final selections are taken from Maimonides' commentary on the Mishnah text *Sanhedrin* 10:1, which concerns those who have a share in the world to come. In typical scholastic fashion, Maimonides describes five views found among Jews concerning the nature of the world to come. He then goes on to argue that, although many, like children, observe the Torah simply out of a desire for a reward or a fear of punishment, the only proper motive is a disinterested love of God and his commandments which are desirable for their own sake. In his discussion of the nature of the world to come, Maimonides first distinguishes three ways of interpreting the sayings of the sages (the rabbis). He rejects both fundamentalism and the kind of rationalism which ridicules the sayings of the fathers as folly. In their place he advocates an allegorical interpretation which aims at the rational truth hidden in the rabbis' riddles and parables.

In his interpretation of the nature of the world to come, Maimonides sees a harmony between Aristotle's understanding of human perfection and that found in the Bible. There are four grades of human perfection in ascending order: possessions, bodily constitution, moral virtues, and intellectual virtues, the highest of which is the understanding of the ethical activity of God. For Maimonides, the observance of the Torah is a way of cultivating the virtues that make a decent society possible and of acquiring those beliefs that qualify a person for immortality. He looks forward to a messianic age when the prevailing conditions of justice and peace will enable human beings to devote themselves to observance of the Torah and the acquisition of the philosophical virtues, thereby drawing closer to the knowledge of God. In the world to come our happiness will consist in an angelic-like existence in which "our souls will become wise out of the knowledge of God the Creator. . . . " Maimonides' more traditional Jewish opponents maintained that his teachings were more Greek than Jewish and that his system of salvation was intellectually elitist.

Although Judaism has always been primarily a religion which emphasized correct observance, or orthopraxis, rather than correct doctrine, or orthodoxy, Maimonides concludes his treatise with a list of Thirteen Principles upon which Judaism is based. His explanations of each are quite philosophical, but they are always rooted in a specific biblical text or texts. Although they are included in the Jewish Prayer Book, these never became an official creed within Judaism. They did lead other scholars to write on Jewish dogma and began a long and often bitter debate on the role of dogma within Judaism.

Maimonides' *Guide of the Perplexed* was originally written in Arabic, but it was translated into Hebrew and then into Latin at the court of colorful and controversial Frederick II, Holy Roman Emperor and King of Sicily. In its Latin translation Maimonides' project of reconciling faith and reason, the Bible and Aristotle, was to have an important impact on Christian theologians like Thomas Aquinas.

The translation of the *Mishneh Torah* is by Moses Hyamson, (Boys Town Publishers, 1962). The translation of *The Guide of the Perplexed* is by Shlomo Pines, *The Guide of the Perplexed* (University of Chicago Press, 1963). The translation of *Helek: Sanhedrin, Chapter Ten* is by Arnold J. Wolf, "Maimonides on Immortality and the Principles of Judaism" (*Helek: Sanhedrin, Chapter Ten*) (American Jewish Congress, 1966).

MISHNEH TORAH

BOOK SEVEN: SEEDS

Gifts to the Poor   Chapter 10

7. There are eight degrees of charity, one higher than the other. The highest degree, exceeded by none, is that of the person who assists a poor Jew by providing him with a gift or loan or by accepting him into a business partnership or by helping him find employment—in a word, by putting him where he can dispense with other people's aid. With reference to such aid, it is said, "You shall strengthen him, be he a stranger or a settler, he shall live with you" (Lev 25:35), which means strengthen him in such manner that his falling into want is prevented.

8. A step below this stands the one who gives alms to the needy in such manner that the giver knows not to whom he gives and the recipient knows not from whom it is that he takes. Such exemplifies performing the meritorious act for its own sake. An illustration would be the Hall of Secrecy in the ancient sanctuary where the righteous would place their gift clandestinely and where poor people of high lineage would come and secretly help themselves to succor.

The rank next to this is of him who drops money in the charity box. One should not drop money in the charity box unless one is sure that the person in charge is trustworthy, wise, and competent to handle the funds properly, as was Rabbi Hananya ben Teradyon.

9. One step lower is that in which the giver knows to whom he gives but the poor person knows not from whom he receives. Examples of this were the great sages who would go forth and throw coins covertly into poor people's doorways. This method becomes fitting and exalted, should it happen that those in charge of the charity fund do not conduct its affairs properly.

10. A step lower is that in which the poor person knows from whom he is taking but the giver knows not to whom he is giving. Examples of this were the great sages who would tie their coins in their scarves which they would fling over their shoulders so that the poor might help themselves without suffering shame.

11. The next degree lower is that of him who, with his own hand, bestows a gift before the poor persons asks.

12. The next degree lower is that of him who gives only after the poor person asks.

13. The next degree lower is that of him who gives less than is fitting but gives with a gracious mien.

14. The next degree lower is that of him who gives morosely.

15. There have been great sages who, before praying, would give a coin to the needy, because it is said, "I will behold your face in righteousness" (Ps 17:15).

16. A species of charity is the maintenance of one's minor sons and daughters who have passed the age at which the father is obligated to support them, provided the purpose of such maintenance be that of educating the sons in sacred lore and of keeping the daughter in the right path, removed from shame. Similarly to be classed as charity is the maintenance of one's father and mother.

In giving charity, precedence should be accorded to one's own relatives. . . .

18. A man should always exert himself and should sooner endure hardship than throw himself, as a dependent, upon the community.

The sages admonished, "Make your Sabbath a weekday, sooner than become dependent." Even one who is learned and honored should, if impoverished, work at various trades, yes, despicable trades, in order to avoid dependency. Better to strip the hides of beasts that have sickened and died than to tell people, "I am a great sage, my class is that of a priest, support me. . . . "

Outstanding scholars worked as hewers of wood, as carriers of beams, as drawers of garden water, as iron workers, as blacksmiths, rather than ask anything of the community and rather than accept any preferred gratuity.

THE GUIDE OF THE PERPLEXED

INTRODUCTION TO PART 1

The first purpose of this treatise is to explain the meanings of certain terms occurring in the books of prophecy. . . . It is not the purpose of this treatise to make its totality understandable to the vulgar or to beginners in speculation, nor to teach those who have not engaged in any study other than the science of the Law—I mean the legalistic study of the Law. For the purpose of this treatise and of all those like it is the science of the Law in its true sense. Or rather its purpose is to give indications to a religious man for whom the validity of our Law has become established in his soul and has become actual in his belief—such a man being perfect in his religion and character, and having studied the sciences of the philosophers and come to know what they signify. The human intellect having drawn him on and led him to dwell within its province, he must have felt distressed by the externals of the Law and by the meanings of the above-mentioned equivocal, derivative, or amphibolous terms, as he continued to understand them by himself or was made to understand them by others. Hence he would remain in a state of perplexity and confusion as to whether he should follow his intellect, renounce what he knew concerning the terms in question, and consequently consider that he has renounced the foundation of the Law. Or he should hold fast to his understanding of these terms and not let himself be drawn on together with his intellect, rather turning his back on it and moving away from it, while at the same time perceiving that he had brought loss to himself and harm to his religion. He would be left with those imaginary beliefs to which he owes his fear and difficulty and would not cease to suffer from heartache and great perplexity.

This treatise also has a second purpose: namely, the explanation of very obscure parables occurring in the books of the prophets, but not explicitly identified there as such. Hence an ignorant or heedless individual might think that they possess only an external sense, but no internal one. However, even when one who truly possesses knowledge considers these parables and interprets them according to their external meaning, he too is overtaken by great perplexity. But if we explain these parables to him or if we draw his attention to their being parables, he will take the right road and be delivered from this perplexity. That is why I have called this treatise the *Guide of the Perplexed*. . . . My speech in the present treatise is directed, as I have mentioned, to one who has philosophized and has knowledge of the true sciences, but believes at the same time in the matters pertaining to the Law and is perplexed as to their meaning because of the uncertain terms and the parables. . . .

INSTRUCTION WITH RESPECT TO THIS TREATISE

. . . To sum up: I am the man who when the concern pressed him and his way was straitened and he could find no other device by which to teach a demonstrated truth other than by giving satisfaction to a single virtu-

ous man while displeasing ten thousand ignoramuses—I am he who prefers to address that single man by himself, and I do not heed the blame of those many creatures. For I claim to liberate that virtuous one from that into which he has sunk, and I shall guide him in his perplexity until he becomes perfect and he finds rest.

INTRODUCTION

One of seven causes should account for the contradictory or contrary statements to be found in any book or compilation.

The first cause: The author has collected the remarks of various people with differing opinions, but has omitted citing his authorities and has not attributed each remark to the one who said it. Contradictory or contrary statements can be found in such compilations because one of the two propositions is the opinion of one individual while the other proposition is the opinion of another individual.

The second cause: The author of a particular book has adopted a certain opinion that he later rejects; both his original and later statements are retained in the book.

The third cause: Not all the statements in question are to be taken in their external sense; some are to be taken in their external sense while some others are parables and hence have an inner content. Alternatively, two apparently contradictory propositions may both be parables and when taken in their external sense may contradict, or be contrary to, one another.

CHAPTER 1
(THE INCORPOREALITY OF GOD AND MAN AS GOD'S IMAGE.)

"Image" (*tzelem*) and "likeness" (*demut*). People have thought that in the Hebrew language "image" denotes the shape and configuration of a thing. This supposition led them to the pure doctrine of the corporeality of God, on account of His saying: "Let us make man in our image, after our likeness" (Gen 1:26). For they thought that God has a man's form, I mean his shape and configuration. The pure doctrine of the corporeality of God was a necessary consequence to be accepted by them. They accordingly believed in it and deemed that if they abandoned this belief, they would give the lie to the biblical text; that they would even make the Deity to be nothing at all unless they thought that God was a body provided with a face and a hand, like them in shape and configuration. However, He is, in their view, bigger and more resplendent than they themselves, and the matter of which He is composed is not flesh and blood. As they see it, this is as far as one can go in establishing the separateness of God from other things. . . .

Now I say that in the Hebrew language the proper term designating the form that is well-known among the multitude, namely, that form which is the shape and configuration of a thing, is *toar*. . . . Those terms are never applied to the Deity, may He be exalted; far and remote may this thought be from us. The term "image," on the other hand, is applied to the natural form, I mean to the notion in virtue of which a thing is constituted as a substance and becomes what it is. . . . In man that notion is that from which human apprehension derives. It is on account of this intellectual apprehension that it is said of man: "In the image of God created He him" (Gen 1:27). . . . That which was meant in the Scriptural dictum, "Let us make man in our image" (Gen 1:26), was the specific form, which is intellectual apprehension, not the shape and configuration. We have explained to you the difference between "image" and "form," and have explained the meaning of "image."

As for the term "likeness" (*demut*), it is a noun derived from the verb *damah* (to be like), and it too signifies likeness in respect of a notion. . . . Now man possesses as his proprium something in him that is very strange

as it is not found in anything else that exists under the sphere of the moon, namely, intellectual apprehension. In the exercise of this, no sense, no part of the body, none of the extremities are used; and therefore this apprehension was likened to the apprehension of the Deity, which does not require an instrument, although in reality it is not like the latter apprehension, but only appears so to the first stirring of opinion. It was because of this something, I mean because of the divine intellect conjoined with man, that it is said of the latter that he is "in the image of God and in His likeness" (Gen 1:26–27), not that God, may He be exalted, is a body and possesses a shape.

CHAPTER 54
(MOSES' KNOWLEDGE OF GOD AND THE LIMITS OF HUMAN KNOWLEDGE OF GOD.)

Know that the master of those who know, Moses our Teacher, peace be on him, made two requests and received an answer to both of them. One request consisted in his asking Him, may He be exalted, to let him know His essence and true reality. The second request, which he put first, was that He should let him know His attributes. The answer to the two requests that He, may He be exalted, gave him consisted in His promising him to let him know all His attributes, making it known to him that they are His actions, and teaching him that His essence cannot be grasped as it really is. Yet He drew his attention to a subject of speculation through which he can apprehend to the furthest extent that is possible for man. For what has been apprehended by (Moses), peace be on him, has not been apprehended by anyone before him nor will it be apprehended by anyone after him.

His request regarding the knowledge of (God's) attributes is conveyed in his saying "Show me now Your ways, that I may know You" (Exod 33:13), and so on. Consider the wondrous notions contained in this dictum. For his saying, "Show me now Your ways, that I may know You," indicates that God, may He be exalted, is known through his Attributive qualifications; for when he would know the "ways," he would know Him. . . .

When (Moses) asked for knowledge of the attributes and asked for forgiveness for the nation, he was given a (favorable) answer with regard to their being forgiven. Then he asked for the apprehension of His essence, may He be exalted. This is what he means when he says, "Show me, I pray You, Your glory" (Exod 33:18), whereupon he received a (favorable) answer with regard to what he had asked for at first—namely, "Show me Your ways." For he was told: "I will make all My goodness pass before you" (Exod 33:19). In answer to his second demand, he was told: "You can not see My face" (Exod 33:20), and so on. This dictum—"all my goodness"—alludes to the display to him of all existing things of which it is said: "And God saw every thing that He had made, and, behold, it was very good" (Gen 1:31). By their display, I mean that he will apprehend their nature and the way they are mutually connected so that he will know how He governs them in general and in detail. . . . Accordingly, the apprehension of these actions is an apprehension of His attributes, may He be exalted, with respect to which He is known. The proof of the assertion that the thing, the apprehension of which was promised to him, was the actions of God, may He be exalted, is the fact that what was made known to him were simply pure attributes of action: "merciful and gracious, long-suffering . . ." (Exod 34:6–7). It is then clear that the "ways"—for a knowledge of which he had asked and which, in consequence, were made known to him—are the actions proceeding from God, may He be exalted. The sages call them "characteristics" and speak of the "thirteen characteristics." This term, as they use it is applied to moral qualities. Thus: "There are

four characteristics among people who give charity . . . ; there are four characteristics among people who go to the house of learning . . ." ("Ethics of the Fathers" 5:13–14). This expression occurs frequently. The meaning here is not that He possesses moral qualities, but that He performs actions resembling the actions that in us proceed from moral qualities—I mean from aptitudes of the soul; the meaning is not that He, may He be exalted, possesses aptitudes of the soul. Scripture has restricted itself to mentioning only those "thirteen characteristics," although Moses apprehended "all His goodness"—I mean to say all His actions—because these are the actions proceeding from Him, may He be exalted, in respect of giving existence to men and governing them. This was Moses' ultimate object in his demand, the conclusion of what he says being: "That I may know You, to the end that I may find grace in Your sight and consider that this nation is Your people" (Ex 33:13)—that is, a people for the government of which I need to perform actions that I must seek to make similar to Your actions in governing them.

CHAPTER 59

As everyone is aware that it is not possible, except through negation, to achieve an apprehension of that which is in our power to apprehend and that, on the other hand, negation does not give knowledge in any respect of the true reality of the thing with regard to which the particular matter in question has been negated—all men, those of the past and those of the future, affirm clearly that God, may He be exalted, cannot be apprehended by the intellects, and that none but He Himself can apprehend what He is, and that apprehension of Him consists in the inability to attain the ultimate term in apprehending Him. Thus all the philosophers say: We are dazzled by His beauty, and He is hidden from us because of the intensity with which He becomes manifest, just as the sun is hidden to eyes that are too weak to apprehend it. This has been expatiated upon in words that it would serve no useful purpose to repeat here. The most apt phrase concerning this subject is the dictum occurring in the Psalms, "Silence is praise to You" (Ps 65:2), which interpreted signifies: silence with regard to You is praise. This is a most perfectly put phrase regarding this matter. For of whatever we say intending to magnify and exalt, on the one hand we find that it can have some application to Him, may He be exalted, and on the other we perceive in it some deficiency. Accordingly, silence and limiting oneself to the apprehensions of the intellects are more appropriate—just as the perfect ones have enjoined when they said: "Commune with your own heart upon your bed, and be still" (Ps 4:4).

PART 2
CHAPTER 13
(THE ETERNITY OF THE WORLD OR CREATION IN TIME.)

There are three opinions of human beings, namely, of all those who believe that there is an existent Deity, with regard to the eternity of the world or its production in time.

The first opinion, which is the opinion of all who believe in the Law of Moses our Teacher, is that the world as a whole—I mean to say, every existent other than God, may He be exalted—was brought into existence by God after having been purely and absolutely nonexistent, and that God, may He be exalted, had existed alone, and nothing else—neither an angel nor a sphere nor what subsists within the sphere. Afterward, through His will and His volition, He brought into existence out of nothing all the beings as they are, time itself being one of the created things. . . .

The second opinion is that of all philosophers of whom we have heard reports and whose discourses we have seen. They say that

it is absurd that God would bring a thing into existence out of nothing. Furthermore, according to them, it is likewise not possible that a thing should pass away into nothing; I mean to say that it is not possible that a certain being, endowed with matter and form, should be generated out of the absolute nonexistence of that matter, or that it should pass away into absolute nonexistence of that matter. To predicate of God that He is able to do this is, according to them, like predicating of Him that He is able to bring together two contraries in one instant of time, or that He is able to create something that is like Himself, may He be exalted, or to make Himself corporeal, or to create a square whose diagonal is equal to its side, and similar impossibilities. . . .

The third opinion is that of Aristotle, his followers, and the commentators of his books. He asserts what also is asserted by the people belonging to the sect that has just been mentioned, namely that something endowed with matter can by no means be brought into existence out of that which has no matter. He goes beyond this by saying that the heaven is in no way subject to generation and passing-away. His opinion on this point may be summed up as follows. He thinks that this being as a whole, such as it is, has never ceased to be and will never do so; that the permanent thing not subject to generation and passing-away, namely, the heaven, likewise does not cease to be; that time and motion are perpetual and everlasting and not subject to generation and passing-away; and also that the thing subject to generation and passing-away, namely, that which is beneath the sphere of the moon, does not cease to be. . . .

CHAPTER 25

On the other hand, the belief in eternity the way Aristotle sees it—that is, the belief according to which the world exists in virtue of necessity, that no nature changes at all, and that the customary course of events cannot be modified with regard to anything—destroys the Law in its principle, necessarily gives the lie to every miracle, and reduces to inanity all the hopes and threats that the Law has held out, unless—by God—one interprets the miracles figuratively also, as was done by the Islamic internalists (allegorists); this however, would result in some sort of crazy imaginings. . . .

Know that with a belief in the creation of the world in time, all the miracles become possible and the Law becomes possible, and all questions that may be asked on this subject, vanish. Thus it might be said: Why did God give prophetic revelation to this one and not to that? Why did God give this Law to this particular nation, and why did He not legislate to the others? Why did He legislate at this particular time, and why did He not legislate before it or after? Why did He impose these commandments and these prohibitions? Why did He privilege the prophet with the miracles mentioned in relation to him and not with some others? What was God's aim in giving this Law? Why did He not, if such was His purpose, put the accomplishment of the commandments and the nontransgression of the prohibitions into our nature? If this were said, the answer to all these questions would be that it would be said: He wanted it this way; or His wisdom required it this way. And just as He brought the world into existence, having the form it has, when He wanted to, without our wisdom in His particularizing the forms of the world and the time of its creation—in the same way we do not know His will or the exigency of His wisdom that caused all the matters, about which questions have been posed above, to be particularized. If, however, someone says that the world is as it is in virtue of necessity, it would be a necessary obligation to ask all those questions; and there would be no way out of them except through a recourse to unseemly answers in which there would be combined the giving the

lie to, and the annulment of, all the external meanings of the Law with regard to which no intelligent man has any doubt that they are to be taken in their external meanings. It is then because of this that this opinion is shunned and that the lives of virtuous men have been and will be spent in investigating this question.

CHAPTER 31

(SABBATH OBSERVANCE.)

Perhaps it has already become clear to you what is the cause of the Law's establishing the Sabbath so firmly and ordaining "death by stoning" for breaking it. The master of the prophets has put people to death because of it. It comes third after the existence of the Deity and the denial of dualism. For the prohibition of the worship of anything except Him only aims at the affirmation of the belief in His unity. You know from what I have said that opinions do not last unless they are accompanied by actions that strengthen them, make them generally known, and perpetuate them among the multitude. For this reason we are ordered by the Law to exalt this day, in order that the principle of the creation of the world in time be established and universally known in the world through the fact that all people refrain from working on one and the same day. If it is asked: What is the cause of this? the answer is: "For in six days the Lord made" (Exod 20:11).

For this commandment two different causes are given, corresponding to two different effects. In the first Decalogue, the cause for exalting the sabbath is stated as follows: "For in six days the Lord made," and so on. In Deuteronomy (5:15), on the other hand, it is said: "And you shall remember that you were a slave in Egypt. Therefore the Lord your God commanded you to keep the sabbath day." This is correct. For the effect, according to the first statement, is to regard that day as noble and exalted. As it says: "Wherefore the Lord blessed the sabbath day, and hallowed it" (Exod 20:11). This is the effect consequent upon the cause stated in the words: "For in six days," and so on. However, the order given us by the Law with regard to it and the commandment ordaining us in particular to keep it are an effect consequent upon the cause that we had been "slaves in Egypt" where we did not work according to our free choice and when we wished and where we had not the power to refrain from working. Therefore we have been commanded inactivity and rest so that we should conjoin the two things: the belief in a true opinion—namely, the creation of the world in time, which, at once and with the slightest speculations, shows that the Deity exists—and the memory of the benefit God bestowed upon us by giving us rest "from under the burdens of the Egyptians" (Ex 6:7). Accordingly, the sabbath is, as it were, of universal benefit, both with reference to a true speculative opinion and to the well-being of the state of the body.

CHAPTER 32
(PROPHECY.)

The opinions of people concerning prophecy are like their opinions concerning the eternity of the world or its creation in time. I mean by this that just as the people to whose mind the existence of the Deity is firmly established, have, as we have set forth, three opinions concerning the eternity of the world or its creation in time, so there are three opinions concerning prophecy. . . .

The first opinion—that of the multitude of those among the pagans who considered prophecy as true and also believed by some of the common people professing our Law—is that God, may He be exalted, chooses whom He wishes among men, turns him into a prophet, and sends him with a mission. According to them it makes no difference

whether this individual is a man of knowledge or ignorant, aged or young. However, they also posit as a condition his having a certain goodness and sound morality. For up to now people have not gone so far as to say that God sometimes turns a wicked man into a prophet unless He has first, according to this opinion, turned him into a good man.

The second opinion is that of the philosophers. It affirms that prophecy is a certain perfection in the nature of man. This perfection is not achieved in any individual from among men except after a training that makes that which exists in the potentiality of the species pass into actuality. . . . According to this opinion, it is not possible that an ignoramus should turn into a prophet; nor can a man not be a prophet on a certain evening and be a prophet on the following morning, as though he had made some discovery. Things are rather as follows: When, in the case of a superior individual who is perfect with respect to his rational and moral qualities, his imaginative faculty is in its most perfect state and when he has been prepared in the way that you will hear, he will necessarily become a prophet, inasmuch as this is a perfection that belongs to us by nature. According to this opinion, it is not possible that an individual should be fit for prophecy and prepared for it and not become a prophet, no more than it is possible that an individual having a healthy temperament should be nourished with excellent food without sound blood and similar things being generated from that food.

The third opinion is the opinion of our Law and the foundation of our doctrine. It is identical with the philosophic opinion except for one thing. For we believe that it may happen that one who is fit for prophecy and prepared for it should not become a prophet, namely on account of the divine will. To my mind this is like all the miracles and takes the same course as they. For it is a natural thing that everyone who according to his natural disposition is fit for prophecy and who has been trained in his education and study would become a prophet. But he who is prevented from it is like him who has been prevented, like Jeroboam (1 Kgs 13:4), from moving his hand or, like the King of Aram's army going out to seek Elisha (2 Kgs 6:18), from seeing. As for its being fundamental with us that the prophet must possess preparation and perfection in the moral and rational qualities, it is indubitably the opinion expressed in their dictum: "Prophecy only rests upon a wise, strong, and rich man" (BT. Shabbath 92a). . . . As for the fact that someone who prepares is sometimes prevented from becoming a prophet, you may know from the history of Baruch, son of Neriah. For he followed Jeremiah, who taught, trained and prepared him. And he set himself the goal of becoming a prophet, but was prevented, as he says: "I am weary with my groaning and find no rest" (Jer 45:3). Thereupon he was told through Jeremiah: "Thus shall you say to him: Thus says the Lord, etc. . . . And do you seek great things for yourself? Seek them not" (Jer 45:2,5). It is possible to say that this is a clear statement that prophecy was too great a thing for Baruch. Similarly, it may be said, as we shall explain, that in the passage, "Yes, her prophets find no vision from the Lord" (Lam 2:9), this was the case because they were in exile.

CHAPTER 35
(MOSES IS UNIQUE AMONG THE PROPHETS.)

To my mind the term "prophet" used with reference to Moses and to the others is amphibolous. The same applies, in my opinion, to his miracles and to the miracles of others, for his miracles do not belong to the class of the miracles of other prophets. The proof taken from the Law as to his prophecy being different from that of all who came before him is constituted by His saying: "And I appeared to Abraham, etc., but by My name, the Lord, I made not known to them" (Exod 6:3). Thus it informs us that his (Moses') apprehension was not like the Patriarchs', but greater—nor, all the more, like that of others who came before. As for the difference between his prophecy and that of all those who came after, it is stated by way of communicating information in the dictum: "And there has not arisen a prophet since in Israel like Moses, whom the Lord knew face to face" (Deut 34:10). Thus is has been made clear that his apprehension is different from that of all men who came after him in Israel, which is "a kingdom of priests and a holy nation" (Exod 19:6) and "in whose midst is the Lord" (Num 16:3) and, all the more, from the apprehension of those who came in other religious communities.

As for the difference between his miracles in general and those of every prophet in general, it should be said that all the miracles worked by the prophets or for them were made known to very few people only. Thus, for example, the signs of Elijah and Elisha. . . . The same holds good for the signs of all the prophets except Moses our Master. For this reason scripture makes it clear, likewise by way of information with reference to him, that no prophet will ever arise who will work signs both before those who are favorably and those who are unfavorably disposed toward him as was done by Moses.

CHAPTER 39
(ONLY ONE LAW, THAT REVEALED TO MOSES.)

Hence, according to our opinion, there never has been a Law and there never will be a Law except the one that is the Law of Moses our Teacher. The explanation of this, according to what is literally stated in the prophetic books and is found in the tradition, is as follows. Not one of the prophets—such as the patriarchs, Shem, Eber, Noah, Methuselah, and Enoch—who came before Moses our Teacher, has ever said to a class of people: God has sent me to you and has commanded me to say to you such and such things; He has forbidden you to do such and such things. This is a thing that is not attested to by any text of the Torah and that does not figure in any true tradition. These men only received prophetic revelation from God according to what we have set forth. He who received a great overflow, as for instance Abraham, assembled the people and called them by the way of teaching and instruction to adhere to the truth that he had grasped. Thus Abraham taught the people and explained to them by means of speculative proofs that the world has but one Deity, that He has created all things that are other than Himself, and that none of the forms and no created thing in general ought to be worshiped. This is what he instructed the people in, attracting them by means of eloquent speeches and by means of the benefits he conferred upon them. But he never said: God has sent me to you and has given me commandments and prohibitions. Even when the commandment of circumcision was laid upon him, his sons, and those who belonged to him, he circumcised them alone and did not use the form of a prophetic call to exhort the people to do this. . . .

As for the prophets from among us who came after Moses our Teacher, you know the text of all their stories and the fact that their function was that of preachers who called upon the people to obey the Law of Moses, threatened those who rejected it, and held out promises to those who were firm in observing it. We likewise believe that things will always be this way. As it says: "It is not heaven" (Deut 30:12), and so on; "for us and for our children for ever" (Deut 29:28). And that is as it ought to be; for when a thing is as perfect as it is possible to be within its species, it is impossible that within that species there should be found another thing that does not fall short of that perfection either because of excess or deficiency. Thus in comparison with

a temperament whose composition is of the greatest equibalance possible in the species in question, all other temperaments are not composed in accordance with this equibalance because of either deficiency or excess. Things are similar with regard to this Law, as is clear from its equibalance. For it says: "Just statues and judgments" (Deut 4:8); now you know the meaning of "just" is equibalanced. For these are manner of worship in which there is no burden and excess—such as monastic life and pilgrimage and similar things— nor a deficiency necessarily leading to greed and being engrossed in the indulgence of appetites, so that in consequence the perfection of man is diminished with respect to his moral habits and to his speculation—this being the case with regard to all the other nomoi of the religious communities of the past. When we shall speak in this treatise about the reason accounting for the commandments, their equibalance and wisdom will be made clear to you insofar as this is necessary. For this reason it is said with reference to them: "The Law of the Lord is perfect" (Ps 19:8). As for those who deem that its burdens are grievous, heavy, and difficult to bear—all of this is due to an error in considering them. I shall explain later on how easy they are in true reality according to the opinion of the perfect. For this reason it says: "What does the Lord your God require of you" (Deut 10:12), and so on. And it says: "Have I been a wilderness to Israel?" (Jer 2:31), and so on. However, all this refers to the virtuous, whereas in the opinion of those who are unjust, violent, and tyrannical, the existence of a judge who renders tyranny impossible is a most harmful and grievous thing. As for the greedy and the vile, the most grievous thing in their opinion is that which hinders their abandoning themselves to debauchery and punishes those who indulge in it. Similarly everyone who is deficient in any respect considers that a hindrance in the way of the vice that he prefers because of his moral corruption is a great burden. Accordingly, the facility or difficulty of the Law should not be estimated with reference to the passions of all the wicked, vile, morally corrupt men, but should be considered with reference to the man who is perfect among the people. For it is the aim of this Law that everyone should be such a man. Only that Law is called by us divine Law, whereas the other political regimens—such as the *nomoi* of the Greeks and the raving of the Sabians and of others—are due, as I have explained several times, to the action of groups of rulers who were not prophets.

HELEK: SANHEDRIN

CHAPTER 10
(LIFE IN THE WORLD TO COME.)

The Mishnah

Now I can begin to discuss the matter with which I am really concerned. Know that just as the blind man cannot image color, as the deaf person cannot experience sounds, and as the eunuch cannot feel sexual desire, so bodies cannot attain spiritual delights. Like fish, who do not know what the element of fire is, because they live upon its opposite, the element of water, so are the delights of the spiritual world unknown in this material world. Spiritual delight does not come within our experience at all. We enjoy only bodily pleasure of eating, drinking, and sexual intercourse. Other levels of delight are not present to our experience. We neither recognize nor grasp them at first thought. They come to us only after great searching.

It could hardly be otherwise, since we live in a material world and are, therefore, able to achieve only inferior and discontinuous delights. Spiritual delights are eternal. They last forever; they never break off. Between these two kinds of delight there is no similarity of any sort. It is, therefore, inappropriate

for us who are masters of Torah or theologians to say that angels, stars, and spheres experience no delight. On the contrary, they really experience great delight in that they know by experience the true being of God the Creator. With this knowledge they enjoy delight which is both perpetual and uninterrupted. They have no bodily delight, nor could they, since they have so physical senses, as we do, through which they could get our kind of gratification.

We will be like them after death. Those men who choose to purify themselves will reach this spiritual height. They will neither experience bodily pleasures, nor will they want them. They will resemble a powerful king. He would hardly want to go back to playing ball with children as he did before he became king. Such games attracted him when he was a child and was unable to understand the real difference between ball playing and royal power. Like children we now praise and glorify the delights of the body and do not understand the delights of the soul.

If you consider carefully the nature of these two kinds of delight, you will perceive the inferiority of the first and the superiority of the second, even in this world. Thus, you find that most men will exert extraordinary amounts of intellectual and physical energy laboring at ordinary tasks in order to acquire honor and be exalted by their fellowmen. The pleasure which honor brings is not of the same sort as the pleasure derived from eating and drinking. Similarly, many men pursue vengeance over their enemies more intensely than they pursue any bodily pleasures. Many others deny themselves the keenest of bodily delights because they fear shame and public disgrace or because they seek to acquire a reputation for virtue. If this is the case even in this material world, how much more must it be so in the spiritual world! That world is the world to come.

In the world to come our souls will become

wise out of the knowledge of God the Creator, as the higher physical bodies do, or even wiser. This spiritual delight is not divisible into parts, nor can it be described, nor can any analogy explain it. It is as the prophet said when he was awe-stricken at the lofty magnificence of that good: "How great is Your goodness which You have hidden away for them that fear You" (Ps 31:30). Our sages also wrote: "In the world to come there is no eating, drinking, washing, anointing, or sexual intercourse; but the righteous sit with their crowns on their heads and enjoy the radiance of the Divine Presence" (Berakhot 17a). In this passage the expression "with crowns on their heads" signifies the immortality of the soul being in firm possession of the Idea which is God the Creator. The "crown" is precisely the Idea which great philosophers have explicated at length. The expression, "they delight in the radiance of the Divine Presence" means that souls enjoy blissful delight in their attainment of knowledge of the truly essential nature of God the Creator, a delight which is like that experienced by the holy angels who know His existence first-hand.

The ultimate good, the final end is to achieve this supernal fellowship, to participate in this high glory in which the soul is forever involved with the existence of God the Creator, who is the cause and source of its existence and its goal. This has already been explained by the earlier philosophers.

This is incomparably good, for how could that which is eternal and endless be compared with anything transient and terminable? That is the meaning of the biblical statement: "That it may be well with you, and that you may prolong your days" (Deut 22:7)—in the world that is infinitely long, add the rabbis (Kiddushin 39b, Hullin 142a).

Utterly evil punishment consists in the cutting off of the soul so that it perishes and does not live eternally. This is the penalty of *karet* to which the Torah refers, as in the phrase: "That soul shall utterly be cut off" (Num 15:31). Interpreting this phrase, our sages said: "The word *hikkaret* (utterly cut off) refers to the world to come" (Sanhedrin 64b, 90a). On the other hand, scripture also says: "The soul of my master shall be bound in the bundle of life with the Lord your God" (1 Sam 25:29).

It follows that if a person has deliberately and regularly chosen physical delights, has despised the truth and loved falsehood, he will be cut off from that high level of being and remain disconnected matter. The prophet has already explained that the world to come cannot be apprehended by the bodily sense, in the verse: "The eye has not seen it, O Lord, except You" (Isa 64:3). The sages taught emphatically that the prophets prophesied only about the days of the Messiah, but that concerning the world to come, "eye has not seen it, O Lord, only You" (Berakhot 34b, Shabba 63a, Sanhedrin 99a).

Now let me explain the meaning of the promises of good and threats of evil punishment which are contained in the Torah. What these promises and punishments mean is that God says to you, "If you do these commandments, I will help you in your effort to do them and to achieve perfection in them. I will remove all the obstacles and difficulties which stand in your way." . . .

If you consider these things carefully and fully, you will understand that it is as though He were saying to you, "If you do some of these commandments out of love and with genuine effort, I will help you to do all of them, and I will remove the oppressive obstacles that prevent you from doing them. But if you refuse to perform any of them out of disdain for the commandment, then I will bring upon you the very obstacles that prevent you from doing all of them, so that you cannot achieve perfect existence in the world to come." This is the meaning of the statement of the sages: "The reward of a commandment is the commandment itself, and the reward of a sin is sin" (*Ethics of the Fathers* 4:2).

The Garden of Eden is a fertile place containing the choicest of the earth's resources, numerous rivers, and fruit-bearing trees. God will disclose it to man some day. He will teach man the way to it, and men will be happy there. It is possible that many exceedingly wonderful plants will be found there, plants which are far pleasanter and sweeter than those which we now know. None of this is impossible or improbable. On the contrary, paradise would be possible even if it were not written of in the Torah. How much more sure then is it since the Torah specifically promises it!

Gehenna is a name for the pain and the punishment which will come upon the wicked. No specific description of this punishment is contained in the Talmud. One teacher says that the sun will come so close to the wicked that it will burn them. He finds proof for this belief in the verse: "For behold, the day comes, it burns as a furnace; the day that comes shall set them ablaze, says the Lord of hosts, that it shall leave them neither root nor branch" (Mal 3:19). Others say that a strange heat will be produced within their own bodies to incinerate them. They find support for this position in the Scriptural words: "Your own spirit is a fire which will consume you (Isa 33:11).

The resurrection of the dead is one of the cardinal principles established by Moses our Teacher. A person who does not believe in this principle has no real religion, certainly not Judaism. However, resurrection is only for the righteous. This is the meaning of the statement in *Bereshit Rabbah* (ch. 13) which declares: "The creative power of rain is for both the righteous and the wicked, but the resurrection of the dead is only for the righteous." How, after all, could the wicked come back to life, since they are dead even in their lifetimes? Our sages taught: "The wicked are called dead even while they are still alive; the righteous are alive even when they are dead" (*Berakot* 18b). All men must die and their bodies decompose.

The "days of the Messiah" refers to a time in which sovereignty will revert to Israel and the Jewish people will return to the land of Israel. Their king will be a very great one, with his royal palace in Zion. His name and his reputation will extend throughout all the nations in even greater measure than did King Solomon's. All nations will make peace with him, and all countries will serve him out of respect for his great righteousness and the wonders which occur through him. All those who rise against him will be destroyed and delivered into his hands by God. All the verses of the Bible testify to his triumph and our triumph with him. However, except for the fact that sovereignty will revert to Israel, nothing will be essentially different from what it is now. This is what the sages taught: "The only difference between this world and the days of the Messiah is that oppression by other kingdoms will be abolished" (*Berakhot* 34b; *Shabbat* 63a, 151b; *Pesahim* 68a; *Sanhedrin* 91b, 99a). . . .

The great benefits which will occur in those days include our release from oppression by other kingdoms which prevents us from fulfilling all the commandments—a widespread increase of wisdom, in accordance with the Scriptural promise: "For the earth shall be full of the knowledge of the Lord, as waters cover the sea (Isa 11:9)—and the end of the wars, again in accordance with the Scriptural statement: "Nation shall not lift up sword against nation, neither shall they learn war any more" (Mic 4:3). In those days perfection will be widespread, with the result that men will merit the life of the world to come.

But the Messiah will die, and his son and his grandson will reign in his stead. The prophet has already predicted his death in the verse: "He shall not fail nor be crushed till he has set the right in the earth" (Is 42:2).

However, his reign will be a very long one. All human life will be longer, for when worries and troubles are removed men live longer. There is no reason for surprise that the Messiah's reign will extend for thousands of years. As our sages have put it: "When good is gathered together it cannot speedily be dissipated."

We do not long and hope for the days of the Messiah because of an increase of productivity and wealth which may occur then, or that we may ride on horses and drink wine to the accompaniment of song, as some confused people think. The prophets and the saints looked forward to the days of the Messiah and yearned for them because then the righteous will be gathered together in fellowship, and because goodness and wisdom will prevail. They desired it also because of the righteousness and abundant justice of the Messianic king, because of the salutary influence of his unprecedented wisdom, and because of his nearness to God, as described: "The Lord said to me: 'You are My son: this day I have begotten you'" (Ps 2:7). They also anticipate the performance of all the commandments of the Torah of Moses our Teacher, with neither inertia on the one hand nor compulsion on the other, in fulfillment of the Scriptural promise: "And they shall teach no more every man his neighbor and every man his brother, saying: 'Know the Lord': for they shall all know Me, from the least of them to the greatest of them, says the Lord: for I will forgive their iniquity and their sin I will remember no more" (Jer 31:34). Similarly, it is written: "I will put My Torah in their inward parts, and I will write it in their heart" (Jer 31:33). Scripture also says: "And I will take away the stony heart of your flesh, and I will give you a heart of flesh" (Ezek 36:26). There are many other verses with the same promise.

Thus, men will achieve the world to come. The world to come is the ultimate end toward which all our effort ought to be devoted. Therefore, the sage who firmly grasped the knowledge of the truth and who envisioned the final end, forsaking everything else, taught: "All Jews have a share in the world to come" (*Sanhedrin* 10:1).

Nevertheless, even though this is the end we seek, he who wishes to serve God out of love should not serve Him to attain the world to come. He should rather believe that wisdom exists, that this wisdom is the Torah; that the Torah was given the prophets by God the Creator; that in the Torah He taught us virtues which are the commandments and vices that are sins. As a decent man, one must cultivate the virtues and avoid the sins. In so doing, he will perfect the specifically human which resides in him and will be genuinely different from the animals. When one becomes fully human, he acquires the nature of the perfect human being; there is no external power to deny his soul eternal life. His soul thus attains the eternal life it has come to know which is the world to come, as we have explained. This is the meaning of the verse: "Be not as the horse or as the mule, which have no understanding; whose mouth must be held in with bit and bridle" (Ps 32:9). Restraints which prevent animals from acting in accordance with their nature are external ones, like the bit and the bridle. With man, the influences which restrain him are his control of self. When a man achieves human perfection, it restrains him from doing those things which are called vices and which withhold perfection from him; it urges and impels him toward those things which are called virtues and which bring him to full perfection. This is what all the teaching of the sages have made clear to me about this most important matter. . . . We must remember in connection with this subject, and indeed with all others, that our religion is based on the following thirteen principles:

The First Fundamental Principle: To believe in the existence of the Creator; that this is an Existent complete in all the senses of the word "existence." . . .

The Second Fundamental Principle: We are told to believe that God is one, the cause of all oneness. . . .

The Third Fundamental Principle: We are to believe that He is incorporeal, that His unity is physical neither potentially nor actually. . . .

The Fourth Fundamental Principle: We are to believe that the One is absolutely eternal; no thing existed before Him, as many Scriptural verses prove. . . .

The Fifth Fundamental Principle: Only He, blessed be He, is rightfully worshiped, magnified, and obeyed. . . .

The Sixth Fundamental Principle is Prophecy. One should know that among men are found certain people so gifted and perfected that they can receive pure intellectual form. . . .

The Seventh Fundamental Principle is the prophecy of Moses our Teacher. We are to believe that he was the chief of all other prophets before and after him, all of whom were his inferiors. . . .

The Eighth Fundamental Principle is that the Torah came from God. We are to believe that the whole Torah was given us through Moses our Teacher entirely from God. . . .

The Ninth Fundamental Principle is the authenticity of the Torah, i.e., that this Torah was precisely transcribed from God and no one else. . . .

The Tenth Fundamental Principle is that God knows all that men do and never turns His eyes away from them, as those who say "The Lord has abandoned this earth" (Ezek 8:12; 9:9) claim. . . .

The Eleventh Fundamental Principle is that God rewards those who perform the commandments of the Torah and punishes those who transgress its admonitions. . . .

The Twelfth Fundamental Principle refers to the Messianic Era. We are to believe as fact that the Messiah will come and not consider him late. . . .

The Thirteenth Fundamental Principle is the Resurrection of the Dead, which we have already explicated.

When a man believes in all these fundamental principles, and his faith is thus clarified, he is then part of that "Israel" whom we are to love, pity, and treat, as God commanded, with love and fellowship. Even if a Jew should commit every possible sin, out of lust or mastered by his lower nature, he will be punished for his sins but will still have a share in the world to come. He is one of the "sinners of Israel." But if a man gives up any one of these fundamental principles, he has removed himself from the Jewish community. He is an atheist, a heretic, an unbeliever who "cuts among the plantings." We are commanded to hate him and to destroy him. Of him it is said: "Shall I not hate those who hate You, O Lord?" (Ps 139:21).

MOSES DE LEON, *ZOHAR: THE BOOK OF ENLIGHTENMENT* (JEWISH KABBALAH)

In the end, Maimonides' rationalism proved inadequate to the spiritual needs of Jews in Spain during the centuries of the Christian *Reconquista*. Although Jews and Muslims were not officially expelled until 1492, throughout the thirteenth and fourteenth centuries European Jews were subjected to systematic persecution from both the church and various national monarchies. In these times of suffering, they turned increasingly to mysticism, known in Judaism as Kabbalah.

The biblical roots of Jewish mysticism are found in the visionary experiences of Moses and the prophets like Isaiah and Ezekiel, as well as the personal piety of the psalms and the apocalyptic visions of Daniel. In the Talmud also, the rabbis often spoke of God's chariot throne and the mysteries of creation, but the term Kabbalah, or "receiving" the esoteric traditions of Judaism, was first used at the beginning of the eleventh century C.E.

Like all mysticism, the Kabbalistic literature is based on a profound inner experience of God which is ultimately incommunicable. In a manner similar to Muslim and Christian mystics of the Middle Ages, the Kabbalists express their mystical experiences through an allegorical and mystical reading of scripture. In contrast to philosophers who, through disciplined mental exertion seek a higher rational truth in scripture, the Kabbalists humbly accept scripture as the source of a higher truth and await a divine illumination from it. Words, ideas, and practices found in the scriptures are neither challenged nor questioned. The Kabbalist assumes that they contain profound mysteries which are waiting to be revealed.

The climax of the Kabbalistic movement in Spain was the appearance in the thirteenth century C.E. of the *Zohar* or *The Book of Enlightenment*. It takes the form of a long midrash on the Torah, with shorter sections on Ruth and the Song of Songs. Ostensibly, the *Zohar* is a series of discussions between Rabbi Shim'on ben Yohai and his disciples, set in the second century C.E. The historical Rabbi Shim'on was a mystic and visionary who had to spend several years hiding in a cave from the Romans. Many Kabbalists believed him to be the actual author of the *Zohar,* and they honored his tomb in Galilee as a sacred site. According to critical scholarship, however, the true author is Moses de Leon (1250–1305 C.E.), a Spanish Kabbalist. He claimed to have "discovered" the *Zohar,* but according to other accounts, including those of his wife, he wrote the book himself during moments of ecstasy in which he believed he was writing under divine guidance. His claim that the book comes from Rabbi Shim'on is comparable to that of the Jewish apocalyptic writings of the last centuries B.C.E. and the first two centuries C.E. These visionary writings were also often attributed to ancient worthies like Daniel, Enoch, Moses, or the Patriarchs.

In the *Zohar,* God is conceived of as *Ein Sof,* "Infinite." Our dull human intellects can know nothing of God who is eternal darkness. Yet from God emanates a series of spiritual powers or beings through which the world came into existence. These powers are the Ten Sefirots, or "aspects" of God which continue to make God manifest in the world. They are given a variety of names such as Crown, Understanding, Wisdom, Judgment, Love, Compassion, Majesty, Endurance, Righteousness, and *Shekhinah* ("Divine Presence"). The Kabbalists discuss their function and relation to one another, often dividing them into male and female aspects of God. These emanations might be understood as the moral values inherent in God's nature which are made available to the world. They should not be understood as "persons" as in Christian trinitarian thought, but as channels of God's self-revelation. Through mystical encounter, these sefirot are also the way of return to God.

Our first selection from the *Zohar* entitled "How to Look at Torah" illustrates the many-layered allegory of Kabbalistic interpretation. Rabbi Shim'on begins by warning that the Torah does not present "mere stories and ordinary words." Rather, "all the words of Torah are sublime words, sublime secrets!" Just as the angels had to put on material garments to descend into this world so, too, the Torah, who is personified like Lady Wisdom in Proverbs, put on the "garment" of a story in descending to this world. Fools who are content with the simple stories of the Torah look only at its garment. Beneath the garment are the body and soul of the Torah. Those who go farther in their penetration of the Torah's secrets look at its body, the commandments of the Torah. Finally, "the wise ones" (the mystics) "look only at the soul, root of all, real Torah!" In the days to come, the Kabbalists will "look at the soul of the soul of the Torah" which is the Holy Ancient One. In an even more cosmic and sexual series of allegorical images, the Zohar connects the physical cosmos, the community of Israel, and the presence of God with Israel through the Torah. It understands "the heavens and their hosts," as the garment, "the Communion of Israel" as "the body," which is the feminine element "who receives the soul, the Beauty of Israel," the masculine aspect of God, which is the real Torah. The soul of the soul of the Torah is the Holy Ancient One whom the mystics will contemplate "in the time to come."

Our second selection, entitled "The Old Man and the Beautiful Maiden," contains a charming parable which uses erotic images from the Bible, but also possibly from the courtly love traditions of the Middle Ages, for both the Torah's love for the mystic and the mystic's devotion to finding the deeper meaning of the Torah. The allegory is very reminiscent of Bernard of Clairvaux's famous sermons on The Song of Songs. In the parable the Torah is personified as a lovely princess who is beautiful, yet "hidden deep within her palace." The mystic is her secret lover; all others are completely unaware of their relationship. Out of devotion to the Torah, "this lover passes by her gate constantly, lifting his eyes to every side." Torah invites further devotion by opening "a little window in her hidden palace" and revealing "her face to her lover." Full revelation of Torah's secrets is not immediate, as the princess "then swiftly withdraws, concealing herself." By revealing and concealing herself, Torah "with love . . . approaches her lover to arouse love with him."

The allegory also reflects the various stages of insight into the Torah. Like a medieval princess, Torah sends her messenger with a "hint" to her prospective lover. Like Lady Wisdom in Proverbs, she says, "Who is the fool without a heart? / Have him turn in here" (Prov 9:4). The first stage of insight into Torah is *derasha,* "seeking" the Torah's meaning through midrashic exegesis, which is like the princess speaking with her lover "behind a curtain which was drawn." Then she converses through a veil which is the *haggadah* or "telling" the story of Torah through allegory. The final stage of the gift of insight into Torah is the princess' revelation of "herself face to face" in which she "tells him (her lover) all her hidden secrets. . . ." The mystic's new state is that of "a perfect human being, / husband of Torah, master of the house." The Torah has now revealed to him "all her secrets . . . withholding nothing, concealing nothing."

The final selection from "God, Israel, and *Shekhinah*" reflects the Jewish experience in the Middle Ages of suffering persecution in exile from the land of Israel. It also illustrates God's special love for Israel, even to the point of being dependent upon her fate in history. In this parable God's relation to Israel is like that of a king to "a single son who kept misbehaving." Rather than banish his son alone from the land and the kingdom so that he will be prey to "wild beasts and wolves or robbers," the king decides that "I and you together (will) leave the land/ and both of us go into exile." The Queen Mother in the allegory is the *Shekhinah*, the Divine Presence with Israel through the Torah. Because of Israel's sins she, too, "was sent away" from the palace, the land of Israel. Because "neither the son nor the queen is present" and "the palace is totally desolate," God announces "I Myself will be with you" in exile. In the last parable of "the tanner's market," Israel is God's lover, whose exilic condition is like living in the smelly "tanner's market." But "since she is there, it appears to him (God her lover) as a market of spice-peddlers/ with all the world's finest aromas."

In the *Zohar* not only are humans dependent upon God, but God is dependent upon them. The spiritual forces of the divine world are conserved and enhanced by our righteousness and devotion, and they are dissipated by our sin. Human actions affect self, society, and even the cosmos.

The translation is by Daniel Chanan Matt in *Zohar: The Book of Enlightenment* (New York: Paulist Press, 1983) 43–45, 121–126, 159–162.

ZOHAR

"HOW TO LOOK AT TORAH"

Rabbi Shim'on said
"Woe to the human being who says
that Torah presents mere stories and
    ordinary words!
If so, we could compose a Torah right now
    with ordinary words
and better than all of them!
To present matters of the world?
Even rulers of the world possess words more
    sublime.
If so, let us follow them and make a Torah
    out of them!
Ah, but all the words of Torah are sublime
    words, sublime secrets!

Come and see:
The world above and the world below are
    perfectly balanced:
Israel below, the angels above.
Of the angels it is written:

'He makes His angels spirits'
(Psalms 104:4).
But when they descend, they put on the
    garment of this world.
If they did not put on a garment befitting
    this world
they could not endure in this world
and the world could not endure them.

If this is so with the angels, how much more
    so with Torah
who created them and all the worlds
and for whose sake they all exist!
In descending to this world,
if she did not put on the garments of this
    world
the world could not endure.

So this story of Torah is the garment of Torah.
Whoever thinks that the garment is the real
    Torah
and not something else—
may his spirit deflate!

He will have no portion in the world that is
    coming.
That is why David said:
'Open my eyes
so that I can wee wonders out of Your Torah!'
(Psalms 119:18), what is under the garment
    of Torah!

Come and see
There is a garment visible to all.
When those fools see someone in a good-
    looking garment
they look no further.
But the essence of the garment is the body;
the essence of the body is the soul!

So it is with Torah.
She has a body:
the commandments of the Torah,
called 'the embodiment of Torah.'

This body is clothed in garments:
the stories of this world.
Fools of the world look only at that garment,
    the story of Torah;
they know nothing more.
They do not look at what is under that
    garment.
Those who know more do not look at the
    garment
but rather at the body under that garment.
The wise ones, servants of the King on high,
those who stood at Mt. Sinai,
look only at the soul, root of all, real Torah!

Come and see:
So it is above.
There is garment and body and soul and soul
    of soul.
The heavens and their host are the garment.
The Communion of Israel is the body
who receives the soul, the Beauty of Israel.
So She is the body of the soul.
The soul we have mentioned is the Beauty of
    Israel

who is real Torah.
The soul of the soul is the Holy Ancient One.
All is connected, this one to that one.

Woe to the wicked who say that Torah is
    merely a story!
They look at this garment and no further.
Happy are the righteous
who look at Torah properly!
As wine must sit in a jar,
so Torah must sit in this garment.
So look only at what is under the garment!
So all those words and all those stories—
they are garments!"

"THE OLD MAN AND THE
BEAUTIFUL MAIDEN"

Rabbi Hiyya and Rabbi Yose met one night
    at the Tower of Tyre.
They stayed there as guests, delighting in
    each other.
Rabbi Yose said, "I am so glad to see the face
    of *Shekhinah*.
For just now, the whole way here, I was
    pestered by an old man,
a donkey driver, who kept asking me riddles
    the whole way: . . .

'What is a beautiful maiden who has no
    eyes
and a body concealed and revealed?
She comes out in the morning and is
    hidden all day.
She adorns herself with adornments that
    are not.'

All this he asked on the way; I was annoyed.
Now I can relax!
If we had been together, we would have
    engaged in words of Torah
instead of strange words of chaos."
Rabbi Hiyya said, "That old man, the donkey
    driver,
do you know anything about him?"

He answered, "I know that there is nothing
    in his words.
If he knew anything, he should have opened
    with Torah;
then the way would not have been empty!"

Rabbi Hiyya said, "That donkey driver, is he
    here?
For sometimes in those empty fools, you
    discover bells of gold!"

He said to him, "Here he is fixing up his
    donkey with food."

They called to him; he came before them.
He said to them, "Now two are three, and
    three are like one."

Rabbi Yose said,
"Didn't I tell you that all his words are
    empty nonsense?" . . .

Rabbi Yose said, "Of all the words I heard
    you say,
there was one that really amazed me.
Either you said it out of folly, or they are
    empty words."

The Old Man said, "And which one is that?"

He said, "The one about the beautiful
    maiden. . . . "

The Old Man covered himself. . . .
The Old Man opened and said
"'Moses went inside the cloud and ascended
    the mountain . . .'
(Exodus 24:18).
What is this cloud?
The one of which it is written: 'I have placed
    My bow in the cloud'
(Gen 9:13).
We have learned that the Rainbow took off
    Her garments
and gave them to Moses.

Wearing that garment, Moses went up the
    mountain;
from inside it he saw what he saw,
delighting in the All, up to that place."

The Comrades approached and threw
    themselves down
in front of the Old Man.
They cried, and said, "If we have come into
    the world
    only to
hear these words from your mouth,
it is enough for us!"

The Old Man said,
"Friends, Comrades, not for this alone did I
    begin the word.
An old man like me doesn't rattle with just a
    single word.
Human beings are so confused in their minds!
They do not see the way of truth in Torah.
Torah calls out to them every day, in love,
but they do not want to turn their heads.
Even though I have said that Torah removes
    a word from her sheath,
is seen for a moment, then quickly hides
    away—
that is certainly true—
but when she reveals herself from her sheath
and hides herself right away,
she does so only for those who know her
    intimately.

A parable.
To what can this be compared?
To a lovely princess,
beautiful in every way and hidden deep
    within her palace.
She has one lover, unknown to anyone; he is
    hidden too.
Out of his love for her, this lover passes by
    her gate constantly.
What does she do?
She opens a little window in her hidden
    palace

and reveals her face to her lover,
then swiftly withdraws, concealing
    herself.
No one near the lover sees or reflects,
only the lover,
and his heart and his soul and everything
    within him
flow out to her.
And he knows that out of love for him
she revealed herself for that one moment
to awaken love in him.

So it is with a word of Torah:
She reveals herself to no one but her
    lover.
Torah knows that he who is wise of heart
hovers about her gate every day.
What does she do?
She reveals her face to him from the palace
and beckons him with a hint,
then swiftly withdraws to her hiding place.
No one who is there knows or reflects;
he alone does,
and his heart and his soul and everything
    within him
flows out to her.
That is why Torah reveals and conceals
    herself.
With love she approaches her lover
to arouse love with him.

Come and see!
This is the way of Torah:
At first, when she begins to reveal herself to
    a human
she beckons him with a hint.
If he knows, good,
if not, she sends him a message, calling him
    a fool.
Torah says to her messenger:
'Tell that fool to come closer, so I can talk
    with him!'
as it is written:
'Who is the fool without a heart?
Have him turn in here!' (Prv 9:4)

He approaches.
She begins to speak with him from behind a
    curtain she has drawn,
words he can follow, until he reflects a little
    at a time.
This is *derasha* ("search").
Then she converses with him through a
    veil,
words riddled with allegory.
This is *haggadah* ("telling" or "expounding").

Once he has grown accustomed to her,
she reveals herself face to face
and tells him all her hidden secrets,
all the hidden ways,
since primordial days secreted in her heart.

Now he is a perfect human being,
husband of Torah, master of the house.
All her secrets she has revealed to him,
withholding nothing, concealing nothing.

She says to him, 'Do you see that word,
that hint with which I beckoned you at
    first?
So many secrets there! This one and that
    one!'

Now he sees that nothing should be added to
    those words
and nothing taken away.
Now the *peshat* ("plain meaning") of the
    verse, just like it is!
Not even a single letter should be added or
    deleted.

Human beings must become aware!
They must pursue Torah to become her
    lovers! . . ."

He was silent for a moment.
The Comrades were amazed;
they did not know if it was day or night,
if they were really there or not. . . .
"Enough, Comrades!

From now on, you know that the Evil Side
    has no power over you.
I Yeiva Sava, have stood before you
to awaken your awareness of these words."

They rose like one who is awakened from his
    sleep
and threw themselves down in front of him,
unable to utter a word.
After a while they began to cry.
Rabbi Hiyya opened and said
"'Set me as a seal upon your heart,
as a seal upon your arm' (Song of Songs
    8:6). . . .
Love and sparks from the flame of our heart
    will escort you!
May it be the Will
that your image be engraved in your heart
as your image is engraved in ours!"

He kissed them and blessed them, and they
    left.

When they rejoined Rabbi Shim'on
and told him everything that happened,
he was delighted and amazed.
He said, "You are so fortunate to have
    attained all this!
Here you were with a heavenly lion,
a powerful hero compared with whom many
    heroes are nothing,
and you did not know how to recognize him
    right away!
I am amazed that you escaped his punish-
    ment!
The Blessed Holy One must have wanted to
    save you!"

He called out these verses for them:
"The path of the righteous is like the light of
    dawn,
growing brighter and brighter until the day
    is full.
When you walk, your stride will be free;
if you run, you will not stumble.

Your people, all of them righteous, will
    inherit the land forever;
a sprout of My planting, the work of My
    hands, making Me glorious!"

"God, Israel and *Shekhinah*"
Rabbi Abba said,
"'I will discipline you Myself, seven for your
    sins.'
I disciplined you through other deputies,
as has been established.
'Myself'
Now I will confront you!
Seven will be aroused against you!
Come and see the pure love of the Blessed
    Holy One for Israel.
A parable:
There was a king who had a single son who
    kept misbehaving.
One day he offended the king.
The king said, 'I have punished you so many
    times
and you have not received.
Now look, what should I do with you?
If I banish you from the land and expel you
    from the kingdom,
perhaps wild beasts or wolves or robbers will
    attack you
and you will be no more.
What can I do?
The only solution is that I and you together
    leave the land!'"

So, 'Myself': I and you together will leave the
    land!
The Blessed Holy One said as follows:
'Israel, what should I do with you?
I have already punished you, and you have
    not heeded Me.
I have brought fearsome warriors and flam-
    ing forces to strike at you and you have
    not obeyed.
If I expel you from the land alone,
I fear that packs of wolves and bears will
    attack you

and you will be no more.
But what can I do with You?
The only solution is that I and you together
     leave the land
and both of us go into exile.
As it is written:
"I will discipline you,"
forcing you into exile;
but if you think that I will abandon you—
"Myself" too, along with you!'

'Seven for your sins'
This means Seven, who will be banished
     along with you.
Why? 'For your sins,'
as it is written:
'For your crimes, your Mother was sent
     away' (Isaiah 50:1)
The Blessed Holy One said
'You have made Me homeless as well as
     yourselves,
for the Queen has left the palace along with
     you.

Everything is ruined, My palace and yours!
For a palace is worthless to a king unless he
     can enter with his queen.
A king is only happy when he enters the
     queen's palace
and finds her with her son;
they all rejoice as one.
Now neither the son nor the queen is pre-
     sent;
the palace is totally desolate.
What can I do?
I Myself will be with you!'

So now, even though Israel is in exile,
the Blessed Holy One is with them and has
     not abandoned them.
And when Israel comes out of exile
the Blessed Holy One will return with them,
as it is written:
'YHVH your God will return' (Deut 30:3)
He Himself will return!
This has already been said."

6

ISLAMIC THEOLOGY AND MYSTICISM
FROM 750–1400

THE SHIITE-SUNNI SPLIT

With the death of Muhammad, the Muslim community lost its living voice of guidance, and consequently its earliest crises were over leadership and establishing an authentic legal authority for the ongoing governance of the community. The conflict over who should succeed Muhammad resulted in the Shiite-Sunni split which persists in Islam to this day.

The Sunnis believe that Muhammad left no instructions for choosing a successor, and therefore the community itself had to resolve the problem of succession. They recognize the validity of the election of the first four caliphs—Abu Bakr (r. 632–634 C.E.), Umar (r. 634–644 C.E.), Uthman (r. 644–656 C.E.), and Ali (r. 656–661 C.E.)—all of whom were early converts to Islam and trusted companions of the prophet. The Sunnis also attempt to trace the practices and doctrines of Islam back to the Qur'an and the public *sunnah* (tradition) of the prophet, Muhammad.

The Shiah Ali (the party of Ali), on the other hand, do not recognize the first three caliphs and the principle of electing Muhammad's successor. They claim that Ali ibn Abi Talib, who was the cousin and son-in-law of Muhammad, was, as the prophet's closest male relative, his only legitimate heir. The Shiites have many traditions in which Muhammad is reported to have designated Ali as his chosen successor and also point to passages in the Qur'an which, in their view, have the same purpose. All this material, they allege, was suppressed by the Sunnis to aid the unjust cause of Ali's detractors. In the Shiite tradition it is customary to pronounce curses on the first three caliphs for their usurpation of this high office.

When Ali finally became caliph, he achieved only partial recognition as leader of the Muslim community (*ummah*). Instead, he became involved in a complicated power struggle with, among others, Muawiyah, the governor of Syria, and a member of the powerful Umayyad family. When Ali was assassinated by a member of the fanatical Khawarij sect, Muawiyah consolidated his power and became the founder of the Arab kingdom of Damascus and the Umayyad dynasty which endured until it fell to the

Abbasids in 750 C.E. The hopes of the Shiah fell upon Ali's two sons: Hasan and Husayn. The first renounced any claim to the caliphate, and Husayn fell in battle with the Umayyads at Karbala in Iraq in 680 C.E.

Having failed to attain power in the political sphere, the Shiah turned to the religious exaltation of Ali's family. They developed a gnostic type theology which asserted that Muhammad chose Ali to be the recipient of esoteric Islamic teaching that no one else was capable of understanding. According to the Shiah, this profound lore has been passed from father to son in the family of Ali, and all who would find salvation must learn from it. In its extreme form, the Shiites developed a kind of doctrine of incarnation in which the divine light was fully incarnate in Ali and transferred upon his death to a new locus among his descendants. Ali came to be revered even above the prophet Muhammad. In its more moderate form, Ali and his descendants were seen as mortal, but a divine spark was transmitted from one to the other by a transmigration so that there was always a source of divine guidance for the community. In Shiite theology, Ali and his line of descendants are called *imams* or leaders who bear divine wisdom and guidance. Legitimate rule belongs to the *imam*, and he alone in each age is the source of divine guidance and truth. There is no hope for proper life and reward hereafter except through devotion to the *imam*.

In contrast to the gnostic tendencies of the Shiites, the Sunnis, who represented the majority of Muslims, developed a more publicly accessible legal tradition and theology to meet the changing needs of the Muslim community as it conquered more sophisticated cultures in the Near Eastern and Mediterranean worlds. Although in some sections the Qur'an provides quite detailed legislation for such things as property inheritance, it was not adequate for guiding Muslims in all new situations. Almost immediately, jurists felt the need to supplement the Qur'an with other authorities, and they turned to a time honored Arabic custom of using the sunnah or tradition of the ancestors. In the case of Sunni Muslims, this became the sunnah of the prophet and his early companions found in tales of the early community, called *hadith*. Of course, this solution to the problem of guidance was not without its problems. Even the traditions of the prophet did not cover all situations, and as a result some traditions were fabricated much as in the Christian apocryphal gospels. Also, there is the difficulty of establishing what is authentic tradition. Whose sunnah does one honor and how is its authenticity to be determined? This was especially important for jurists who required precise statements of obligations and prohibitions for the Islamic life.

In a work entitled *The Treatise* Muhammad ibn-Idris al Shafi`i (c. 787–820 C.E.), a famous jurist, developed a solution to these problems which became standard for the Sunnis. In *The Treatise* he distinguishes four sources for sacred law: 1) the Qur'an itself, 2) Muhammad's divinely inspired practice, 3) the consensus of the Muslim community, and 4) personal reasoning by analogy to the Qur'an, the sunnah, and the consensus of the community.

Each of these sources is rooted in the revelation found in the Qur'an. For example, the Qur'an itself states the obligation to "perform the prayer, pay the *zakat* (alms tax), perform the pilgrimage, and observe the fast," as well as the prohibition of certain disgraceful acts like adultery, drinking of wine, etc. For the mode of performing these obligations established in the Qur'an, the Muslim turns to the second source of *fiqh* or right conduct, the words of the Prophet, to learn such things as the number of prayers (each day) and the (amount of) zakat. The third category are those actions performed in imitation of the prophet's example. This is based on the Qur'anic teaching that one is to obey God's apostle and have recourse to his decision. Finally, the fourth category of using personal reasoning is based in the sayings in the Qur'an which speak of God putting believers to the test to see if they will strive and endure.

THE BEGINNINGS OF MUSLIM THEOLOGY

The Qur'an itself seems to discourage rational speculation about the nature of God and other theological issues. But political developments and questions raised by contact with both the philosophical traditions of the Greeks and more developed religious traditions like Judaism and Christianity led Muslim thinkers into rational theology or *kalam*.

Part of the impetus toward thinking about theological issues came from political developments which raised the questions of God's control over human events and human free will, the very questions debated by Augustine and Pelagius in the Christian tradition in the fifth century C.E. and later by Luther and Erasmus in the sixteenth century C.E. Since the Umayyad rise to power involved warfare against Muhammad's companions and respected family, they were severely criticized by other factions within Islam. The Umayyads in turn found it necessary to use religious propaganda to legitimize their rule and undercut religious arguments against their usurpation of power. One of the most useful religious ideas in this connection was predestination which is found in many sections of the Qur'an. If all happens as Allah wills, then Umayyad rule from Damascus, rather than Mecca or Medina, was the result of divine intervention and cannot be opposed. Their party was called the Jabariyah, from the Arabic *jabr*, "force."

Their opponents, like the Pelagians in the Christian tradition, insisted that human beings have free will and the power to choose their course of action. Opposition to the Umayyads is not only not sinful, it is a duty incumbent upon any right-thinking Muslim. The opposition party was called Qadariyah, from the Arabic *qadr*, "power" or "free will." The dispute between these parties, as so often in theology, was political as well as theological.

The Umayyads also adopted a large number of institutions and practices from foreign sources in governing their kingdom. Although this was probably necessary, it earned the scorn of religious conservatives because it opposed the sunnah of the prophet. The most radical opposition came from the Khawarij, a fanatical group which held that the innovations of the Umayyads made them sinners and apostates from Islam. Disobedience to such rulers, not only was permissable, it was necessary.

According to the Khawarij, the Umayyads are to be subject to the death penalty that the Qur'an mandates for apostasy.

Considerations of the issues raised by the Khawarij produced earnest discussion of the role of faith (*imam*) and good works (*islams*) in determining who is a true member of the Muslim community and who ultimately will be saved. Some held that there is no faith without works and that the latter are proof of the former. Others argued that faith alone makes a true Muslim. A third compromise position made a distinction between serious sins and lesser ones. Serious sin excludes one from Islam. Less serious sins are forgivable and do not affect membership in the community. All of these disputes are similar to those between the reformers and the Roman Catholic Church during the Reformation.

Another major stimulus toward theological thinking, which began as early as the eighth century C.E., came from contact with the traditions of conquered peoples. Muslims sincerely believed that they were the bearers of a new dispensation superior to former religions, but they found it hard to convince Jews and Christians who had older and more sophisticated religious traditions. In Damascus debates between Muslims and Christians over the merits of their respective faiths were regularly sponsored by the court. In the course of their conquests, Muslims also encountered other religions: Zoroastrianism, Manichaeanism, and Buddhism. In this pluralistic context, Muslim thinkers were forced to sharpen their grasp of the essentials of their own faith and develop more effective tools of expression. The development of a full scale theology (*kalam*) was the product of a small, but important group called Mu`tazilah.

The Mu`tazilites were founded by Wasil ibn-`Ata (d. 748) at Basra. In the dispute between the Kharijites and the mainline Sunnis over the question of the role of faith and good works in determining who is a true Muslim, the Mu`tazilites took a middle position, hence their name which means "withdrawers." The Kharijites argued that a Muslim guilty of a grave sin was no better than an unbeliever. In contrast, the mainline Sunnis took the position that faith alone was enough for salvation on the basis of the following *hadith*:

> The Prophet said: "The people of Paradise will enter Paradise and people of Hell will enter Hell; then God will say, "Take out (of the Fire) those in whose hearts there was the weight of a mustard seed of faith." And they will be taken out of the Fire (of Hell), already black, and thrown into the river of life. There they will sprout, just as seeds sprout beside the torrent . . . (from the collection of hadith by Muhammad ibn Isma`il al-Bukhari).

The Mu`tazilites position was that persons guilty of "grave sin" were neither believers, nor unbelievers, but occupy a middle position.

The focus of the Mu`tazilites' theological effort was on what they considered the two main themes of Islam: God's absolute unity and God's justice in judging the world. They attempted to develop the logical implications of these ideas and in the process prove the superiority of Muslim faith to other religions on the basis of texts and rational argument.

In addressing the question of God's unity, the Mu`tazilites had to consider the nature of language about Allah in the Qu'ran. Their solution to the problem of its anthropological language about God was to point to passages which describe Allah as immeasurably higher than all creatures and utterly unlike creation.

> Allah! There is no God save Him, the Alive, the Eternal. Neither slumber nor sleep overtaketh Him. Unto Him belongeth whatsoever is in the heavens and whatsoever is in the earth. . . . He knoweth that which is in front of them and that which is behind them, while they encompass nothing of His knowledge save what He will. His throne includeth the heavens and the earth, and He is never weary of preserving them. He is the Sublime, the Tremendous (Surah II:255ff).

Such statements of divine transcendence were to be taken seriously, but anthropological statements, which refer to God as having bodily parts, were to be understood as metaphors for which a rational theological meaning could be supplied. For example, references to Allah's hands were interpreted as statements about his power or solicitude.

They also went on to attack the general belief that all humans would literally see Allah with their own eyes at judgment. According to the Mu`tazilites, the human senses cannot grasp God, who is beyond material definition. Terms which describe Allah as an eternal, living, knowing, willing, and seeing Being are not real entities existing within God. This would lead to doctrines like the Christian belief in the Trinity. Rather, such attributes are indisguishable from one another in God's essence which is absolute unity (*tawhid*).

In a dispute reminiscent of the Arian controversy over the nature of Christ in the early Christian church, the Mu`tazilites rejected the general Muslim view that the Qur'an is the eternal word of God. Instead, they insisted that the Qur'an was created in time as the revealed guidance from God to humanity. To make the Qur'an eternal would be equivalent to making it equal to God, the worse blasphemy according to Islam. During the early part of the ninth century C.E., this Mu`tazilite position became official doctrine under the Abbasid dynasty, and those who held for the eternity of the Qur'an were subject to persecution. But with the accession of Al-Mutawakkil (r. 847–861 C.E.) as caliph, the traditional doctrine that the Qur'an is eternal became the official position, and those believing in the Qur'an as created were subject to official persecution. The fact that theological positions came into favor depending upon the attitude of the ruling power is quite similar to the nearly contemporaneous disputes over iconoclasm in the Byzantine church.

In their discussion of God's justice and the related question of divine determinism the Mu`tazilites rejected the idea of predestination in favor of human freedom to choose between good and evil. They did not embrace this idea out of a humanism which exalts human dignity. Rather, they argued that without human freedom the moral quality of justice attributed to God in the Qur'an is undermined.

ASH`ARI

The orthodox Sunni reaction to the Mu`tazilites is best exemplified by the thinking of Ali ibn Isma`il al-Ash`ari (873–935 C.E.). In his younger days al-Ash`ari was attracted to the thinking of the Mu`tazilites, but at the age of forty he rejected theology for the strict school of interpretation founded by Ahmad ibn Hanbal (780–855 C.E.). This school held that the revelation in the Qur'an was the limit and guide of human reason. If the prophetic deposit of revelation did not yield to rational explanation, then it had to be accepted on authority. Ash`ari's *The Elucidation of Islam's Foundations* begins with Sunni profession of faith in the form of a praise of God, in the traditional language of the Qur'an, as Creator who is all-powerful, all-knowing, the just judge, yet forgiving and merciful. This is followed by a statement of faith that Muhammad is God's Chosen Servant, Apostle, and Prophet who labored strenuously for God's Word. Muhammad brought revelation in the form of the Qur'an, "a glorious Book" which "is a missive sent down from the Wise and Praiseworthy."

This is followed by an exposition of the belief "of the deviators and innovators," primarily the Mu`tazilites. All of their errors are attributed to personal opinion in interpretation of the Qur'an which goes against the traditions of the Prophet and the Companions. Among the errors listed are the createdness of the Qur'an, attributing to humans the power to create evil and control one's eternal destiny for good or evil, the concomitant denial of God's sovereign will in determining all things, and the denial of the anthropomorphic language about God in the Qur'an.

In his exposition of Sunni belief Ash`ari accepts the literal truth of the anthropomorphic language about God in the Qur'an but makes the qualification that the modality with which God possesses these features is beyond human understanding. The standard formula is *bila kayfa*, "without asking how and without likening (to human features)." He also argues that divine qualities like knowledge exist eternally in the reality of God and have no existence apart from that reality except in the abstractions of human reason. This does not diminish the unity of God any more than it does for one human person who has many qualities. Ash`ari defends the eternity of the Qur'an as God's word or Speech by distinguishing between the eternal speech of God which is his message of guidance to humanity and the created sounds of a reciter or the pages on which the Qur'an is written.

In his discussion of God's sovereignty and human freedom, Ash`ari, like all Sunnis, tended toward a determinism much like that of the voluntarist Christian philosophers of the fourteenth century C.E. To say that God did not will and create everything seems to them to impugn God's power and providence. Ash`ari was even willing to accept the idea that God wills and creates evil, but without God himself being evil. The commandments of God fixed the value limits for human beings. Humans can be said to be good or evil in reference to these norms, but God is above these limits.

> The proof that He is free to do whatever He does is that He is the Supreme Monarch, subject to no one, with no superior over Him who can permit or command, or decide, or forbid, or prescribe what He shall do and fix a bound for Him. This being so, nothing can be evil on the part of God. For a thing is evil on our part only because we transgress the limits set for us and do what we have no right to do. But since the creator is subject to no one and bound by no command, nothing can be evil on His part. (Abu al-Hasan al Ash`ari, *The Theology of al-Ash`ari,* trans. Richard J. McCarthy [Beirut: Imprimerie Catholique, 1953], p. 99.)

Ash`ari also used reason to prove certain truths of the Muslim faith. For example, he argued for God's existence as a Necessary Being from the fact that this finite world is only possible or contingent. He also believed it was possible to prove God's unity, knowledge, power, life, etc. by rational argument.

IBN-SINA (AVICENNA), *BOOK OF DELIVERANCE*

None of the earlier theological disputes within Islam involved the kind of philosophical thinking that challenged the Muslim community in the ninth through twelfth centuries C.E. By 850 C.E. Muslims were in control of Syria, Egypt, and Persia, which had all been in contact with the world of Greek philosophy and science. Under the Abbasids in the ninth century C.E., Persia and the capital city of Baghdad became the center of the Muslim world, and in 832 C.E. the Abbasid caliph al-Ma'mun founded there the famous House of Wisdom which was designed to both encourage and bring some order into the development of Greek influence on Islamic philosophy and science in his realm. It had an observatory, a large library, and a team of translators who were commissioned to translate Greek scientific and philosophical texts into Arabic.

Greek philosophy came to the Muslim world largely through Christian mediation. Since the days of the Christian apologists in the second century C.E., Christian thinkers had been using Neoplatonism and Stoicism to express the Christian faith in response to the threats of various heretical movements. In the Byzantine East, as we saw in the work of John Damascene, there was also a large body of the works of Aristotle available in Syriac translations, and Christian scholars had even produced more or less reliable translations of an eclectic range of philosophical texts into Arabic. In the period from 750–1000 C.E. much of Plato, Aristotle, and the Neoplatonic tradition were translated into Arabic. In this process Muslim philosophers like Al-Farabi (c. 870–c. 950 C.E.) also wrote commentaries on works like Aristotle's *Organon*.

One of the most striking features of these early Muslim philosophers is that they shared the conviction of the Neoplatonic philosophers like Porphyry that all the various philosophical schools represent different aspects of one philosophy. In fact, mistakes were made in attributing certain Neoplatonic works to Aristotle. For example, Books IV–VI of Plotinus' *Enneads* were thought to be *The Theology of Aristotle*.

This unique blend of Neoplatonic and Aristotelian philosophy was seen as a challenge to traditional Islamic theology and threatened those who were expert in these forms of knowledge. There were several reasons for this reaction. First of all, these Muslim philosophers were undeniably arrogant in their claims that philosophy gave a comprehensive and more rational account of the same realities as theology without reference to the revelation in the Qur'an, which was treated as largely parabolic and allegorical. What the Qur'an taught the masses in imaginative language, the philosopher could discover for himself by the use of reason. To traditionalists, philosophy was therefore seen as an proud interloper in a space already occupied by theology. Secondly, Neoplatonic and Aristotelian philosophy seemed to contradict some of the most important beliefs of Islam. For example, Aristotle had taught that the material world is eternal, whereas traditional Muslim theology was based on the belief, found in the Qur'an, that the world was created by God and had a beginning in time. Some philosophers also held the Aristotelian position that the soul is the form of the body and ceases to exist at death. This of course contradicted the central Islamic belief in a bodily resurrection and rewards and punishments in an afterlife. Finally, these Muslim philosophers all shared the Neoplatonic belief in God as a necessary Being by whose self-thought dependent being is caused or emanated. Each level of dependent being is the necessary and automatic effect of the one above and in turn causes the one below. This chain produces a hierarchy of ten celestial intelligences; nine are identified with the souls of the celestial spheres in Ptolemy's astronomy and the tenth is the Agent Intellect which directs the changing sublunary world which we occupy. According to traditional Muslim theologians, this Neoplatonic worldview threatened the idea of God's direct knowledge of and providential guidance of the world.

Possibly the greatest of the Muslim philosophers of Persia was Abu `Ali b. `abd Allah ibn Sina, known in the West as Avicenna (980–1037 C.E.). Ibn Sina, like so many of the great Muslim and Jewish philosophers of the Middle Ages, was a universal scholar. He wrote at least one hundred and sixty books on a wide variety of topics: philosophy, medicine, science, mathematics, and mysticism. He was also heavily involved in Persian politics and led an active life marked by great changes of fortune. He frequently served as an advisor to a number of Persian rulers and even ended up in prison at one point. His last thirteen years were spent in relative stability in Isfahan where he died in 1037 C.E.

Ibn Sina's philosophical studies led him to adopt a series of positions which were the source of continual controversy in both the medieval Muslim world and later in the Christian universities of thirteenth century Europe. For our purposes, these positions can be grouped around four topics: God and creation, psychology, revelation, and the afterlife.

Ibn Sina's understanding of God and creation seems to deny the view found in the Qur'an where God creates by an act of the will and at a point in time. Using assumptions from Aristotelian and Neoplatonic philosophy, Ibn Sina begins by arguing that all beings must either have a reason (cause) for their existence or not. Those that have a reason for their existence are contingent or possible beings; they need not exist because the cause for their existence is outside themselves. A being which has no cause for existence outside itself is a necessary being. He then rules out the possibility of an infinite chain of contingent beings as an absurdity and argues that to explain the existence of any contingent beings one must posit a Necessary Being. This argument is tantalizingly similar to the ontological argument of his near contemporary St. Anselm of Canterbury (1033–1109 C.E.). The following quotation illustrates the closely reasoned way in which Ibn Sina comes to these conclusions about the nature of God as a Necessary Being without any reference to the revelation found in the Qur'an.

> Whatever has being must either have a reason for its being or have no reason for it. If it has a reason, then it is contingent, equally before it comes into being (if we make this mental hypothesis) and when it is in the state of being—for in the case of a thing whose being is contingent the mere fact of its entering upon being does not remove from it the contingent nature of its being. If on the other hand it has no reason for its being in any way whatsoever, then it is necessary in its being. This rule having been confirmed, I shall now proceed to prove that there is in being a being which has no reason for its being.
>
> Such a being is either contingent or necessary. If it is necessary, then the point we sought to prove is established. If on the other hand it is contingent, that which is contingent cannot enter upon being except for some reason which sways the scales in favor of its being and against its non-being. If the reason is also contingent, there is then a chain of contingents linked one to the other, and there is no being at all; for this being which is the subject of our hypothesis cannot enter into being so long as it is not preceded by an infinite succession of beings, which is absurd. Therefore contingent beings end in a Necessary Being. (Avicenna, *On Theology,* trans. by A.J. Arberry [John Murray Ltd., Publishers, 1951]).

Although all other beings are contingent in that they do not have the reason or cause for their existence within themselves, Ibn Sina argued that their very existence as possible beings logically implies that they are necessary from the perspective of God, the necessary Being who is their cause.

> Thus it is now clear that everything necessary of existence by another thing is possible of existence by itself. And this is reversible, so that everything possible of existence by itself, if its existence has happened, is necessary of existence by another thing; because inevitably it must either truly have an actual existence or not truly have an actual existence—but it cannot not truly have an actual existence, for in that case it would be impossible of existence. . . . It remains then that that thing, regarded with respect to its essence, is possible, but regarded with respect to its actual relation to its cause, it is necessary. If we think of that connection no longer holding, then it is impossible. But when one considers the essence of the thing itself, unrelated to anything else, the thing itself is possible in itself. (*Book of Deliverance,* trans. by G. Hourani, "Ibn Sina on necessary and possible existence," *Philosophical Forum,* 6, 74–86.)

It is this view of creation as both necessary and eternal that caused the most problems for traditional thinkers in the Muslim, Jewish, and Christian traditions. It seems to contradict the plain sense of the creation stories in the Bible and the Qur'an which imply that God freely chose to create in time.

Ibn Sina's psychology is heavily influenced by Neoplatonic thought and was often subsequently misinterpreted as denying the discrete individuality of each human soul. For Ibn Sina the Agent Intellect is the direct agent of creation; it creates the four elements of the world and gives physical bodies their substantial forms. It is also responsible for giving to humans their capacity to know the forms by abstraction. All humans have possible intellects, the capacity to know the forms of things. But it is the Agent Intellect that "radiates the forms" to our created minds in a kind of divine illumination. This idea was understood by some as endangering the belief in the discrete individuality of each soul. This, however, is not really fair to Ibn Sina, for his psychology was more Platonic than Aristotelian. He believed that the soul and the body were separate substances and that the soul both pre-existed the body and will continue in existence after death. As a philosopher, he understood the afterlife as being largely dependent upon one's capacity for knowledge. Ibn Sina's essentially Platonic view of the soul is quite evident in his famous Ode on the Soul.

> It descended upon thee from out of the regions above,
> That exalted, ineffable, glorious, heavenly Dove.
> 'Twas concealed from the eyes of all those who its nature would ken,
> Yet it wears not a veil, and is ever apparent to men.
> Unwilling it sought thee and joined thee, and yet, though it grieve,
> It is like to be still more unwilling thy body to leave.
> It resisted and struggled, and would not be tamed in haste,
> Yet it joined thee, and slowly grew used to this desolate waste,
> Till, forgotten at length, as I ween, were its haunts and its troth
> In the heavenly gardens and groves, which to leave it was loath.
> Until, when it entered the D of its downward Descent,
> And to earth, to the C of its center, unwillingly went,
> The eye(I) of Infirmity smote it, and lo, it was hurled
> Midst the sign-posts and ruined abodes of this desolate world.
> It weeps, when it thinks of its home and the peace it possessed,
> With tears welling forth from its eyes without pausing or rest,
> And with plaintive mourning it broodeth like one bereft
> O'er such trace of its home as the fourfold winds have left.
> Thick nets detain it, and strong is the cage whereby
> It is held from seeking the lofty and spacious sky.
> Until, when the hour of its homeward flight draws near,
> And 'tis time for it to return to its ampler sphere,
> It carols with joy, for the veil is raised, and it spies
> Such things as cannot be witnessed by waking eyes.
> On a lofty height doth it warble its songs of praise.

(For even the lowliest being doth knowledge raise.)
And so it returneth, aware of all hidden things
In the universe, while no stain to its garment clings.
Now why from its perch on high was it cast like this
To the lowest Nadir's gloomy and drear abyss?
Was it God who cast it forth for some purpose wise,
Concealed from the keenest seeker's inquiring eyes?
Then is its descent a discipline wise but stern,
That the things that it hath not heard it thus may learn,
So 'tis she whom Fate doth plunder, until her star
Setteth at length in a place from its rising far,
Like a gleam of lightning which over the meadows shone,
And, as though it ne'er had been, in a moment is gone.
(trans. by E.G. Browne in *Lit. Hist. of Persia,* Vol 2, 110–11.)

Our selections from Ibn Sina's main work, *Book of Deliverance,* concentrate on his attitudes toward the revelation found in the Qur'an. In general, Ibn Sina, like many philosophers in the three great religious traditions, is a kind of rational elitist. In the section on the need for a prophet as a lawgiver, he begins with the premise that the masses are not capable of reasoning to God's existence and that most, if left on their own, would pursue lives of self-interest with the understanding that justice is that which favors them. Therefore, in order to assure the survival and complete realization of the human race, it is necessary for God to reveal a law code to a lawgiver (the prophet Muhammad) who is set apart from others by his power to work miracles. The fundamental principle of this law code is that there is One God who is Creator, Almighty and Omniscient, and whose commands must be obeyed. The masses are won over to this view largely through fear of punishment and desire for reward, for the prophet teaches them that this Creator God has prepared a life of bliss for those who obey and a life of wretchedness for those who disobey.

Ibn Sina is convinced that the masses can only understand parables and symbols of the truth but not the "higher" truths of metaphysics and theology. They can be taught that God is mighty and majestic by reference to parables and symbols of what they consider is mighty and majestic. But they are not capable of understanding such abstract philosophical concepts as the idea that God cannot be defined spatially and is neither outside nor within the world. Even if the prophet knows these metaphysical truths, he is not to let on and instead should confine himself to images that ordinary folk can understand. Likewise, his pictures of the afterlife should appeal to the imagination of the masses. Happiness and misery should be pictured in the concrete physical terms found in the Qur'an which appeal to the desire for sensual gratification. But scattered throughout the revelation (the Qur'an) there should be phrases like "eye has not seen nor ear heard," which hint at a higher level of meaning for those who are more philosophically minded so that they will be encouraged to go further in their speculations.

Even Ibn Sina's treatment of prayer and the Muslim acts of worship is highly rationalistic. They are understood as "means of securing the survival of his (the prophet's) code and laws in all spheres of human welfare," rather than as ways to commune with God. The Muslim tradition of praying five times a day is a way of repeatedly calling to mind God and the afterlife. Men are to be motivated to do this as a means of winning God's favor and qualifying for a great reward. Some of the prescribed acts, like holy war and pilgrimage, are even materially advantageous. The noblest observance is prayer in which the performer "assumes he is addressing God in private converse." Rather than looking for a higher spiritual meaning in the rituals which precede and accompany prayer, Ibn Sina analyzes them as comparable to the attitudes one assumes in coming before a great king.

In his discussion of the afterlife, Ibn Sina distinguishes between the physical pleasures and punishments spoken of in the Qur'an and the spiritual pleasure sought by those who are philosophers. He suggests that even if the philosophers were offered physical pleasures they would disdain them out of their spiritual desire to approach ever nearer to the First Truth. In the last section it is clear that Ibn Sina does not believe in the literal truth of bodily resurrection after death. Rather, he suggests that some of the souls who are still attached to the earth and a literal understanding of the Qur'an may "imagine" that they are experiencing the physical pleasures described there.

The translation is by A.J. Arberry, *Avicenna on Theology* (London: John Murray, 1951) 42–44, 44–45, 45–47, 64, 74–75.

IBN-SINA (AVICENNA), *BOOK OF DELIVERANCE*

(The Prophet as lawgiver.)

Now it is not feasible that men should be left to their own opinions in this matter (the need for a code of law) so that they will differ each from the other, every man considering as justice that which favors him, and as injustice that which works against his advantage. The survival and complete self-realization of the human race requires the existence of such a lawgiver. . . .

It follows therefore that there should exist a prophet, and that he should be a man; it also follows that he should have some distinguishing feature which does not belong to other men, so that his fellows may recognize him as possessing something which is not theirs, and so that he stand out apart from them. This distinguishing feature is the power to work miracles.

Such a man, if and when he exists, must prescribe laws for mankind governing all their affairs, in accordance with God's ordinance and authority, God inspiring him and sending down the Holy Spirit upon him. The fundamental principle upon which his (that is, the prophet's) code rests will be to teach them that they have One Creator, Almighty and Omniscient, whose commandments must of right be obeyed; that the Command must belong to Him who possesses the power to create and that He has prepared for those who obey Him a future life of bliss but wretchedness for such as disobey Him. So the masses will receive prescriptions, sent down upon his tongue from God and the Angels, with heedful obedience.

(The inability of the masses to understand any more than symbols of the truth.)

It is not necessary for the prophet to trouble their minds with any part of the knowledge of God, save that He is One, True and has no like; as for going beyond this doctrine, so as to charge them to believe in God's existence as not to be defined spatially or verbally divisible, as being neither outside the world nor within it, or anything of that sort—to do this would impose a great strain upon them and would confuse the religious system which they already follow. . . . Not every man is ready to understand metaphysics (or theology), and in any case it would not be proper for any man to disclose that he is in possession of a truth which he conceals from the masses; indeed, he must not allow himself to hint at any such thing.

The prophet's duty is to teach men to know the majesty and might of God by means of symbols and parables drawn from things which they regard as mighty and majestic, imparting to them simply this much, that God has no equal, no like and no partner. Similarly he must establish in them a belief in an afterlife in a manner that comes within the range of their imagination and will be satisfying to their souls; he will liken the happiness and misery to be experienced there in terms which they can understand and conceive. As for the truth of these matters, he will only adumbrate it to them very briefly, saying that it is something which "eye has not seen nor ear heard." . . . God certainly knows the beneficent aspect of all this, and it is always right to take what God knows exactly for what it implies. There is therefore no harm in his discourse being interspersed with sundry hints and allusions, to attract those naturally qualified for speculation to undertake philosophical research into the nature of religious observances and their utility in terms of this world and the next.

(The uses of prayer and acts of worship.)

Now this person, the prophet, is not the kind that often comes into this world, or in every age: the gross (human) matter able to receive his sort of perfection occurs in but few temperments. It follows from this that the prophet must devise means of securing the survival of his code and laws in all the spheres of human welfare. . . . He must therefore prescribe certain acts which men should repeat at close intervals, so that if the time for the performance of one is missed, there may soon be an opportunity for performing the next like act while the memory is still fresh and has not yet been obliterated. These acts must of course be linked up with some means of calling God and the afterlife to mind, else they will be useless: this mnemonic can only consist of set words to be uttered, or set resolves to be intended in the imagination. Men must be told that these acts are means of winning God's favor and of qualifying for great and generous reward. . . .In a word, these acts should be reminders; and these reminders must be either certain motions, or the denial of certain motions resulting in other motions. The former category may be illustrated by the instance of formal prayers, the latter by fasting. . . .

He should also if possible mix in with these observances other interests, in order to strengthen and extend the code, and to make their practice generally advantageous in a material sense also. Examples of this are Holy War and pilgrimage. He should specify certain places in the world as the most suitable for worship, stating that they belong exclusively to God; certain obligatory acts must also be specified as being done for God's sake only—as for instance the offering of sacrifices, which are a great help in this connection. The place which is advantageous in this context, if it be the town where the lawgiver took refuge and dwelt, will also serve the purpose of bringing him to mind, an advantage second only to that of remembering God and the Angels. . . .

The noblest of these observances from a certain point of view is that one in which the performer assumes that he is addressing God in private converse, that he is turning to God and standing before Him. This observance is prayer. Certain steps preparatory to prayer must also be prescribed, similar to those which a man customarily undertakes of his own accord before entering the presence of a human ruler; namely, purification and cleansing. The regulations laid down for these should be effective and impressive. The act of prayer should further be accompanied by those attitudes and rules of conduct usually observed in the presence of kings: humility, quietness, lowering the eyes, keeping the hands and feet withdrawn, not turning about and fidgeting. For every moment of the act of worship appropriate and seemly rules should be prescribed. All these conditions of religious observance serve the useful purpose of keeping people's thoughts fixed firmly upon the recollection of God, and in this way they will continue in their close attachment to the laws and ordinances of the Faith.

(The afterlife.)

The afterlife is a notion received from religious teaching; there is no way of establishing its truth save by way of religious dogma and acceptance of the prophets' reports as true; these refer to what will befall the body at the resurrection, and those corporeal delights or torments which are too well known to require restating here. The true religion brought into this world by our Prophet Muhammad has described in detail the state of happiness or misery awaiting us hereafter so far as the body is concerned. Some further support for the idea of the hereafter is attainable through reason and logical demonstration—this is confirmed by prophetic teaching—namely, that happiness or misery posited by spiritual appraisement, though it is true that our conjecture falls short of realizing the full picture of them now, for reasons which we shall explain. Metaphysicians have a greater desire to achieve this spiritual happiness than the happiness which is purely physical; indeed, they scarcely heed the latter, and were they granted it would not consider it of great moment in comparison to the former kind, which is proximity to the First Truth, in a matter to be described presently. Let us therefore consider this (spiritual) state of happiness, and of contrasting misery; the physical sort is fully dealt with in the teachings of religion.

(The problem of a literal resurrection of the body.)

It may be true, as some theologians state, that when souls, supposing they are pure, leave the body, having firmly fixed within them some such beliefs concerning the future life as are appropriate to them, being the sort of picture that can properly be presented to the ordinary man, when souls such as these leave the body, lacking both the force to draw them upward to complete perfection . . . but all their spiritual dispositions are turned toward the lower world and drawn to the corporeal . . . these souls may well imagine all those afterlife circumstances in which they believed as actually taking place before them, the instrument reinforcing their imagination being some kind of celestial body.

In this way the pure souls will really be spectators of the events of the grave and the resurrection about which they were told in this world, and all the good things of the afterlife; while the wicked souls will similarly behold, and suffer, the punishment which was portrayed to them here below. Certainly the imaginative picture is not weaker that the sensual image; rather it is the stronger and clearer of the two. This may be observed in dreams: the vision seen in sleep is often of greater moment in its kind that the impression of the senses. . . . As you know, the image seen in dreams and that sensed in waking are alike simply impressed upon the soul; they

differ only in this, that the former kind originates from within and descends into the soul,
while the latter sort originates from without
and mounts up to the soul. It is when the
image has already been impressed that the
act of contemplation is consummated. It is
this impression, then, that in reality pleases
or pains the soul, not any external object.

ABU HAMID MUHAMMAD AL-GHAZALI,
THAT WHICH DELIVERS FROM ERROR

The Muslim theologian and mystic who responded to the challenge of the philosophers
was Abu Hamid Muhammad al-Ghazali (1058–1111 C.E.). He began his academic career
as a brilliant young scholar in an official school (*madrasas*) of Islamic theology in
Baghdad. Despite great success as a renowned theologian, in mid-life he began to have
spiritual and intellectual doubts about the truths of the Muslim faith which he attempted to resolve by a study of philosophy. This led to a period of skepticism when he doubted everything except necessary rational truths. Eventually Ghazali had a psychological
and physical breakdown. He abandoned his position as a theologian and embraced the
life of a Sufi mystic. After eleven years of living as a Sufi, Ghazali was persuaded to
return to the teaching of theology, but as a Sufi who went beyond traditional theology in
advocating a spirituality which leads to a mystic encounter with God in love.

Our selections are taken from his autobiography, *That Which Delivers from Error*
which he wrote just as he was returning to teaching in 1106 C.E. In it he recounts his
spiritual journey from what he calls "the plain of naive and second-hand belief to the
peak of direct vision" which he found in Sufi mysticism.

Ghazali's spiritual odyssey is somewhat comparable to Augustine's in *The Confessions*.
Like Augustine, Ghazali goes through various stages in his search for Truth (God) which
he finally finds in the mystical ways of the Sufis. Ultimately, Ghazali's response to philosophy's rationalism is that there is a higher truth and reality which transcends reason.
This truth is contained in the revelations given to the prophet Muhammad in the Qur'an,
and the way to encounter the reality of the God revealed there is through the Sufi path
of mystical experience. Like Augustine, Ghazali believed that humans were meant for
love of God and that reason only had a limited role in this task.

> I saw that man was constituted of body and heart; by "heart" I mean the real nature of his
> spirit which is the seat of his knowledge of God, and not the flesh and blood which he shares
> with the corpse and the brute beast. I saw that just as there is health and disease in the
> body, respectively causing it to prosper and to perish, so also there is in the heart, on the one
> hand, health and soundness—and "only he who comes to God with a sound heart" (Qur'an
> 26,86) is saved—and, on the other hand, disease, in which is eternal and other worldly
> destruction—as God most high says, "in their hearts is disease"(Qur'an 2,9). (*That Which
> Delivers from Error*)

Unlike Augustine who resisted embracing Christian faith until his mid-thirties,

Ghazali began as a traditional believer and theologian. Both, however, had problems with a simple, naive understanding of traditional faith and turned to a study of philosophy in their search for truth. As a young man Augustine was inspired by Cicero's exhortation to a philosophical life in his *Hortensius,* but he found the Christian scriptures by comparison "to be unworthy to be compared with the majesty of Cicero." His independent intellectual search led him to investigate all the spiritual and philosophical options of late Roman antiquity: Manicheanism, skepticism, the Academics, Neoplatonic philosophy, and finally Christianity. Likewise, Ghazali tells us that from his "early youth" he was curious about all types of sects within Islam as well as the teachings of various philosophers, theologians, and mystics. The cosmopolitan environment in Persian Baghdad made him realize that most people follow the beliefs of their parents, be they Christian, Jewish, or Muslim. At this stage he tells us that he rejected "the bonds of mere authority" and "his inherited beliefs" and began to search for our "original nature" apart from the belief derived from parents and teachers. In this rational period he decided to accept as true only "certain knowledge in which the object is disclosed in such a fashion that no doubt remains along with it." On the basis of this criteria, he initially accepted as true only "sense perception and necessary truths," like the law of contradiction. However, upon reflection he realized that sense perceptions are often deceiving, as in the case of a shadow of a stick or the gnomon of a sundial which appears to be motionless but upon experiment and observation is shown to be moving "gradually and steadily by infinitely small distances in such a way that it is never in a state of rest." Even at this stage he considered the possibility that there may be a supraintellectual apprehension which would make the intellectual judgments we make in waking consciousness appear "like dreaming." This is the state that the Sufis claim as their special "state" or ecstasy. But during this early period, Ghazali did not embrace Sufism, and instead lapsed into a period of skepticism until he says, "God cured me of my malady" and "the necessary truths of the intellect became once more accepted, as I regained confidence in their certain and trustworthy character." Like Augustine, Ghazali believes that this transformation was not due to "systematic demonstration or marshalled argument," but by a divine illumination which he describes as "a light which God most high cast into my breast."

In the course of his autobiography, Ghazali examines the truth claims of four major groups within Islam: the theologians, who claim they are "exponents of thought and intellectual speculation"; those who, like the Shiites, rely upon "authoritative instruction" from an infallible imam; the philosophers, who use logic and demonstration; and finally the Sufis or Mystics, who claim to have entered the "presence" of God "and possess vision and intuitive understanding." Ghazali finally rejects the first three as either inadequate or in error and becomes a wandering Sufi mystic.

Although Ghazali spent the early part of his academic career as a theologian, he came to see the weaknesses of traditional Islamic theology (*kalam*). Its purpose "was merely to preserve the creed of orthodoxy and to defend it against the deviations of heretics." This apologetic purpose did not satisfy Ghazali's own spiritual hunger. The writings of the theologians were not really creative for they were simply defending "naive belief" in the

Qur'an and the Traditions "by making explicit the contradictions of their opponents and criticizing them in respect to the logical consequences of what they admitted." Theology was completely incapable of entering into real dialogue with those who, like Ghazali himself, had philosophical questions. The theologians did not have a thorough understanding of the methods of philosophy and consequently could not "dispel universally the darkness of confusion" that arose from the study of various philosophical systems.

In order to understand philosophy for himself, Ghazali spent two years in private study of the philosophers' books, while still teaching traditional theology. After he had mastered "a complete understanding of the sciences of the philosophers," he spent an additional year reflecting on "how far it (philosophy) was deceitful and confusing and how far true and a representation of reality." He was able to classify the philosophers into three groups: materialists, naturalists, and theists; and to conclude that each of them denied important truths of Muslim faith. The materialists claim that the world is eternal and deny the need for a Creator. The naturalists believe in a Creator, but deny the resurrection and the last day. Finally, the theists, including their Muslim interpreters like Farabi and Ibn Sina, "argue against the truth of religion." According to Ghazali, there are three points in which philosophers like Ibn Sina differ from the faith of Muslims.

> a. They say that for bodies there is no resurrection; it is bare spirits which are rewarded or punished, and the rewards and punishments are spiritual, not bodily. . . . These exist, as well, but they speak falsely in denying the bodily punishments and in their pronouncements disbelieve the Divine Law. b. They believe that God knows universals but not particulars. This too is plain unbelief. The truth is that "There does not escape Him the weight of an atom in the heavens or in the earth" (Sura 34:3). c. They say that the (cosmos) is everlasting, without beginning or end. But no Muslim has adopted any such view on this question. (Quoted in Montgomery Watt, *The Faith and Practice of Ghazali,* 35, 38).

In sum, for Ghazali, the philosophers' error lies in taking "men as the criterion of the truth and not the truth (as revealed in the the Qur'an) as the criterion of men."

Ghazali's argument against those who rely on the authoritative instruction of an imam is very reminiscent of Augustine's experience of disappointment when he finally met Faustus, a Manichean bishop who was supposed to clarify Augustine's questions about esoteric and confusing points in Manichean doctrine. In the following passage, Ghazali recounts his experience in questioning those who followed a particular imam.

> Yet when we asked them what knowledge they had gained from this infallible person, and raised objections against them, they did not understand these, far less answer them, and in their perplexity had recourse to the "hidden Imam" and said one must journey to see him.

Ghazali goes on to express astonishment over people squandering their lives in search of such an instructor and boasting over finding him, "yet without learning anything at all from him." He concludes that for Muslims Muhammad is the infallible instructor and not some secret imam.

Ghazali's account of the ways of mysticism is not simply that of an outside observer but the story of his own spiritual conversion. He knew that Sufism included "both intellectual belief and practical activity," and by private reading he was able to acquaint himself with "the intellectual side" of mysticism. But at this stage he also realized that what is "most distinctive of mysticism is something which cannot be apprehended by study, but only by immediate experience, by ecstasy and by moral change." It is the difference between "knowing" and "being" as, for example, in the difference between a physician's knowing the definition of health and actually being healthy.

Ghazali's decision to embrace the mystical life was tortured and difficult in a way quite reminiscent of Augustine's decision to become a Christian and give up his life of lust and his teaching of rhetoric. Although Ghazali does not describe himself as a terrible sinner in the way Augustine does, he came to realize that the theological sciences he was teaching "were unimportant and contributed nothing to the attainment of eternal life." Upon reflection, he also discovered that his motive in teaching "was the desire for an influential position and public recognition." Like Augustine, Ghazali experienced a long period of hesitation about the resolve to quit his teaching and then abandon his resolution because of a desire for "safety and security." Finally, the failure of his mental and bodily health forced a decision upon Ghazali. Like Augustine, Ghazali understood these events as God's actions in his life.

> God caused my tongue to dry up so that I was prevented from lecturing. . . . This impediment in my speech produced grief in my heart, and at the same time my power to digest and assimilate food and drink was impaired. . . . My powers became so weakened that doctors gave up hope of successful treatment. "This trouble arises from the heart," they said, "and from there it has spread through the constitution; the only method of treatment is that the anxiety which has come over the heart should be allayed."

Ghazali concludes the account of his conversion experience in the following way:

> Thereupon, perceiving my impotence and having altogether lost my power of choice, I sought refuge with God most high as one who is driven to Him, because he is without further resources of his own. He answered me, He who "answers him who is driven (to Him by affliction) when he calls upon Him" (Qur'an 27,63). He made it easy for my heart to turn away from position and wealth, from children and friends.

Ghazali's experience throughout this process is remarkably similar to Augustine's famous experience of God's grace in the garden at Milan and his subsequent decision to give up teaching rhetoric. The psychosomatic symptoms both men experience when they try to continue teaching after realizing that they are called to a converted life are remarkably similar. Both lose their voices when they attempt to teach what they now understand as empty wisdom and are grateful that this malady gives them the opportunity to leave their professional positions for a life of spiritual reflection and retirement. Augustine's account bears an uncanny resemblance to Ghazali's.

Furthermore that very summer, under the too heavy labor of teaching, my lungs had begun to give way and I breathed with great difficulty, the pain in my breast showed that they were affected and they no longer let me talk with any strength for too long at a time. At first this had disturbed me, because it made it practically a matter of necessity that I should lay down the burden of teaching, or a least give it up for the time if I was to be cured and grow well again. But when the full purpose of giving myself leisure to meditate on how You are the Lord arose in me and because a settled resolve—as you know, O my God—I actually found myself glad to have this perfectly truthful excuse to offer parents who might be offended . . . . So I was full of joy, and I put up with the space of time that still had to run—I fancy it was about twenty days. But to bear the time took considerable fortitude. Desire for money, which formerly had helped me to bear the heavy labor of teaching, was quite gone; so that I should have . . . found it altogether crushing if patience had not taken the place of covetousness. Some of your servants, my brethren, might think that I sinned in this, since having enrolled with all my heart in Your service, I allowed myself to sit for so much as an hour in the chair of untruthfulness. It may be so. But, most merciful Lord, have You not pardoned and remitted this sin, along with others most horrible and deadly, in the holy water of baptism? (*Confessions* Book IX)

During the eleven years he lived as a wandering Sufi, Ghazali experienced the stages of the mystic way which make a striking contrast to the philosophers' understanding of the purpose of religion. In contrast to Ibn Sina who thought of religion as a lower path to God reserved for the masses who were not capable of true philosophical insight, Ghazali discovered in Sufi mysticism a path which led to an "immediate experience" of God and a healing for the human heart. The ritual practices of Islam do not have some rational purpose as the philosophers taught; rather they are spiritual medicine for the heart which comes from the suprarational revelation granted to the prophets, especially Muhammad.

I came of necessity to realize that in the case of the medicines of formal worship, which have been fixed and determined by the prophets, the manner of their effectiveness is not apprehended by the intellectual explanation of the intellectuals; one must rather accept the statements of the prophets who apprehended those properties by the light of prophecy, not by intellectual explanation. . . .
In general, the prophets are the physicians of the diseases of hearts. The only advantage of the intellect is that it informed us of that, bearing witness to prophetic revelation by believing and to itself by being unable to apprehend what is apprehended by the eye of prophecy; then it took us by the hand and entrusted us to prophetic revelation, as the blind are entrusted to their guides and anxious patients to sympathetic doctors. Thus far may the intellect proceed. In what lies beyond it has no part, save in the understanding of what the physician communicates to it.

In the Christian tradition, this is the relationship between reason and faith that will become a cornerstone in Thomas Aquinas' great theological system, and it is also the relationship that Dante so brilliantly dramatizes through the roles of Virgil (reason), Beatrice (faith), and Bernard of Clairvaux (contemplation) in his incomparable *Commedia.*

In the concluding sections of *That Which Delivers from Error,* Ghazali explains his reasons for returning to the teaching of theology. The laxity of leaders, mystics, and philosophers in their observance of the law of the Qur'an had led the masses into laxity "in conduct according to the norms elucidated by prophecy." Ghazali's return to teaching was spiritually motivated. Because of the orders of the Seljuk sultan Muhammad and on the advice of a number of Sufis, he left the monastic retreat and returned to the public office of teaching. His motive for teaching, however, had been radically changed.

> I had been disseminating the knowledge by which worldly success is attained; by word and deed I called men to it; and that had been my aim and intention. But now I am calling men to the knowledge whereby worldly success is given up and its low position in the scale of real worth is recognized.

Ghazali's work is generally recognized as reviving a spirit of true religion in Islam. A popular Muslim belief held that at the beginning of each Muslim century God would raise up a reviver of true Islam. Ghazali believed that he was this man chosen by God, and indeed Islam attained a new vibrancy in the following centuries because of the influence of Sufi mysticism on those who endeavored to be faithful to the legal system of Muslim law. And, although in the next generation Ibn Rushd (Averroes) (1126–1198), the great Spanish Muslim philosopher, would defend philosophy against the attacks of Ghazali, the latter's mystical understanding of the Muslim faith would prevail over Rushd's rationalism.

The translation is by W. Montgomery Watt, *The Faith and Practice of al-Ghazali* (London: George Allen & Unwin Ltd & Humanities Press, Inc., New York, 1953) 19–30, 52–63, 68–85.

THAT WHICH DELIVERS FROM ERROR

(Ghazali's search for religious truth from his youth.)

From my early youth, since I attained the age of puberty before I was twenty, until the present time when I am over fifty, I have ever recklessly launched out into the midst of these ocean depths, I have ever bravely embarked on this open sea, throwing aside all craven caution; I have poked into every dark recess, I have made an assault on every problem, I have plunged into every abyss, I have scrutinized the creed of every sect, I have tried to lay bare the inmost doctrines of every community. All this I have done that I might distinguish between true and false, between sound tradition and heretical innovation. Whenever I meet one of the Batiniyah (those who look for hidden meaning in religious rituals), I like to study his creed; whenever I meet one of the Zahiriyah (those who study the externals), I want to know the essentials of his belief. If it is a philosopher, I try to become acquainted with the essence of his philosophy; if a scholastic theologian I busy myself in examining his theological reasoning; if a Sufi, I yearn to fathom the secret of his mysticism; if an ascetic, I investigate the basis of his ascetic practices; if one of the Zanadiqah or Mu`attilah (extremists), I look beneath the surface to discover the reasons for his bold adoption of such a creed.

To thirst after a comprehension of things as they really are was my habit and custom from a very early age. It was instinctive with me, a part of my God-given nature, a matter of temperament and not of my choice or contriving. Consequently as I drew near the age of adolescence the bonds of mere authority ceased to hold me and inherited beliefs lost their grip upon me, for I saw that Christian youths always grew up to be Christians, Jewish youths to be Jews and Muslim youths to be Muslims. I heard, too, the Tradition related of the Prophet of God according to which he said: "Everyone who is born is born with a sound nature; it is his parents who make him a Jew or a Christian or a Magian." My inmost being was moved to discover what this original nature really was and what the belief derived from the authority of parents and teachers really were. The attempt to distinguish between these authority-based opinions and their principles developed the mind, for in distinguishing the true in them from the false differences appeared.

(At this point Ghazali describes his period of skepticism.)

The classes of seekers

When God by His grace and abundant generosity cured me of this disease (skepticism), I came to regard the various seekers (sc. after truth) as comprising four groups:

(1) the Theologians (*mutakallimu*n), who claim that they are the exponents of thought and intellectual speculation;

(2) the *Batiniyah,* who consider that they, as the part of "authoritative instruction" (*ta'lim*), alone derive truth from the infallible imam;

(3) the Philosophers, who regard themselves as the exponents of logic and demonstration;

(4) the Sufis or Mystics, who claim that they alone enter into the "presence" (of God), and possess vision and intuitive understanding.

I said within myself: "The truth cannot lie outside these four classes. These are the people who tread the paths of the quest for truth. If the truth is not with them, no point remains in trying to apprehend the truth. There is certainly no point in trying to return to the level of naive and derivative belief (*taqlid*) once it has been left, since a condition of being at such a level is that one should not know one is there; when a man comes to know that, the glass of his naive beliefs is broken. This is a breakage which cannot be mended, a breakage not to be repaired by patching or assembling of fragments. The glass must be melted once again in the furnace for a new start, and out of it another fresh vessel formed."

I now hastened to follow out these four ways and investigate what the groups had achieved, commencing with the science of theology and then taking the way of philosophy, the "authoritative instruction of the Batiniyah, and the way of mysticism in that order.

(The science of theology: Its aims and achievements.)

I commenced, then, with the science of Theology, and obtained a thorough grasp of it. I read the books of sound theologians and myself wrote some books on the subject. But it was a science, I found, which, though attaining its own aim, did not attain mine. Its aim was merely to preserve the creed of orthodoxy and to defend it against the deviations of heretics.

Now God sent to His servants by the mouth of His messenger, in the Qur'an and Traditions, a creed which is the truth and whose contents are the basis of man's welfare in both religious and secular affairs. But Satan too sent, in the suggestions of heretics, things contrary to orthodoxy; men tended to accept his suggestions and almost corrupted the true creed for its adherents. So God brought into being the class of theologians, and moved them to support traditional orthodoxy with the weapon of systematic argument by laying bare the confused doctrines invented by the heretics at variance with traditional orthodoxy. This is the origin of theology and the theologians.

In due course a group of theologians performed the task to which God invited them; they successfully preserved orthodoxy, defended the creed received from the prophetic source and rectified heretical innovations. Nevertheless in so doing they based their arguments on the premises which they took from their opponents and which they were compelled to admit by naive belief, or the consensus of the community, or bare acceptance of the Qur'an and Traditions. For the most part their efforts were devoted to making explicit the contradictions of their opponents and criticizing them in respect to the logical consequences of what they admitted.

This was of little use in the case of one who admitted nothing at all save logically necessary truths. Theology was not adequate to my case and was unable to cure the malady of which I complained. It is true that, when theology appeared as a recognized discipline and much effort had been expended in it over a considerable period of time, the theologians, becoming very earnest in their endeavors to defend orthodoxy by the study of what things really are, embarked on a study of substances and accidents with their nature and properties. But, since that was not the aim of their science, they did not deal with the question thoroughly in their thinking and consequently did not arrive at results sufficient to dispel universally the darkness of confusion due to the different views of men. I do not exclude the possibility that for others than myself these results have been sufficient; indeed, I do not doubt that this has been so for quite a number. But these results were mingled with naive belief in certain matters which are not included among first principles.

My purpose here, however, is to describe my own case, not to disparage those who sought a remedy thereby, for the healing drugs vary with the disease. How often one sick man's medicine proves to be another's poison!

(Philosophy.)

After I had done with theology I started on philosophy. I was convinced that a man cannot grasp what is defective in any of the sciences unless he has so complete a grasp of the science in question that he equals its most learned exponents in the appreciation of its fundamental principles, and even goes beyond and surpasses them, probing into some of the tangles and profundities which the very professors of the science have neglected. Then and only then is it possible that what he has to assert about its defects is true.

So far as I could see none of the doctors of Islam had devoted thought and attention to philosophy. In their writings none of the theologians engaged in polemic against the philosophers, apart from obscure and scattered utterances so plainly erroneous and inconsistent that no person of ordinary intelligence would be likely to be deceived, far less one versed in the sciences.

I realized that to refute a system before understanding it and becoming acquainted with its depths is to act blindly. I therefore set out in all earnestness to acquire a knowledge of philosophy from books, by private study without the help of an instructor. I made progress toward this aim during my hours of free time after teaching in the religious sciences and writing, for at this period I was burdened with the teaching and instruction of three hundred students in Baghdad. By my solitary reading during the hours thus snatched God brought me in less than two years to a complete understanding of the sciences of the philosophers. Thereafter I continued to reflect assiduously for nearly a year on what I had assimilated, going over it in my mind again and again and probing its tangled depths, until I comprehended surely and certainly how far it was deceitful and confusing and how far true and a representation of reality.

Hear now an account of this discipline and of the achievement of the sciences it comprises. There are various schools of philosophers, I perceived, and their sciences are divided into various branches; but throughout their numerous schools they suffer from the defect of being infidels and irreligious men, even although of the different groups of philosophers—older and most ancient, earlier and more recent—some are much closer to the truth than others.

[Ghazali goes on to divide philosophers into Materialists, Naturalists, and Theists, and asserts that they are all affected by unbelief. The Materialists claim that the world has existed everlastingly without need of a Creator. Naturalists are led to believe in the Creator through their study of nature but, also because of this study, they deny the possibility of resurrection and the last day. The Theists include Socrates, Plato and Aristotle and their Muslim interpreters (largely Ibn Sina and Farabi); this group attacks the other two

groups but also argues against the truth of religion. Thus students of the philosophers all fall into heresy and unbelief by taking as the highest authorities those who deny or overlook religion.

Ghazali next attacks the Ta`limiyya (groups like the Shi`ites and Isha`ilites), who accept their imam, or religious leader, as an infallible instructor in charge of the Truth. Ghazali states that the proper response to the Ta`limiyya is to accept the need for an infallible instructor, but to insist that Muhammad and not some other imam was that instructor.]

(The ways of mysticism.)

When I had finished with these sciences, I next turned with set purpose to the method of mysticism (or Sufism). I knew that the complete mystic "way" includes both intellectual belief and practical activity; the latter consists in getting rid of the obstacles in the self and in stripping off its base characteristics and vicious morals, so that the heart may attain to freedom from what is not God and to constant recollection of Him.

The intellectual belief was easier to me than the practical activity. I began to acquaint myself with their belief by reading their books . . . and other discourses of their leading men. I thus comprehended their fundamental teachings on the intellectual side, and progressed, as far as is possible by study and oral instruction, in the knowledge of mysticism. It became clear to me, however, that what is most distinctive of mysticism is something which cannot be apprehended by study, but only by immediate experience (literally "tasting"), by ecstasy and by a moral change. What a difference there is between *knowing* the definition of health and satiety, together with their causes and presuppositions, and *being* healthy and satisfied! What a difference between being acquainted with the definition of drunkenness—namely, that it designates a state arising from the domination of the seat of the intellect by vapors arising from the stomach—and being drunk! Indeed, the drunken man while in that condition does not know the definition of drunkenness nor the scientific account of it; he has not the very least scientific knowledge of it. The sober man, on the other hand, knows the definition of drunkenness and its basis, yet he is not drunk in the very least. Again the doctor, when he is himself ill, knows the definition and causes of health and the remedies which restore it, and yet is lacking in health. Similarly there is a difference between knowing the true nature and cause and conditions of the ascetic life and actually leading such a life and forsaking the world.

I apprehended clearly that the mystics were men who had real experiences, not men of words, and that I had already progressed as far as was possible by way of intellectual apprehension. What remained for me was not to be attained by oral instruction and study but only by immediate experience and by walking in the mystic way.

Now from the sciences I had labored at and the paths I had traversed in my investigation of the revelational and rational sciences (theology and philosophy), there had come to me a sure faith in God most high, in prophethood (or revelation), and in the Last Day. These three creedal principles were firmly rooted in my being, not through any carefully argued proofs, but by reason of various causes, coincidences and experiences which are not capable of being stated in detail.

It had already become clear to me that I had no hope of the bliss of the world to come save through a God-fearing life and the withdrawal of myself from vain desire. It was clear to me too that the key to all this was to sever the attachment of the heart to worldly things by leaving the mansion of deception and returning to that of eternity, and to advance toward God most high with all earnestness. It was also clear that this was only to be

achieved by turning away from wealth and position and fleeing from all time-consuming entanglements.

Next I considered the circumstances of my life, and realized that I was caught in a veritable thicket of attachments. I also considered my activities, of which the best was my teaching and lecturing, and realized that in them I was dealing with sciences that were unimportant and contributed nothing to the attainment of eternal life.

After I examined my motive in my work of teaching, and realized that it was not a pure desire for the things of God, but that the impulse moving me was the desire for an influential position and public recognition. I saw for certain that I was on the brink of a crumbling bank of sand and in imminent danger of hell-fire unless I set about to mend my ways.

I reflected on this continuously for a time, while the choice still remained open to me. One day I would form the resolution to quit Baghdad and get rid of these adverse circumstances; the next day I would abandon my resolution. I put one foot forward and drew the other back. If in the morning I had a genuine longing to seek eternal life, by the evening the attack of a whole host of desires had reduced it to impotence. Worldly desires were striving to keep me by their chains just where I was, while the voice of faith was calling, "To the road! to the road! What is left of life is but little and the journey before you is long. All that keeps you busy, both intellectually and practically, is but hypocrisy and delusion. If you do not prepare *now* for eternal life, when will you prepare? If you do not now sever these attachments, when will you sever them?" On hearing that, the impulse would be stirred and the resolution made to take to flight.

Soon, however, Satan would return. "This is a passing mood," he would say; "do not yield to it, for it will quickly disappear; if you comply with it and leave this influential position,

these comfortable and dignified circumstances where you are free from troubles and
disturbances, this state of safety and security
where you are untouched by the contentions
of your adversaries, then you will probably
come to yourself again and will not find it
easy to return to all this."

For nearly six months beginning with
Rajab 488 A.H. (July 1095), I was continuously tossed about between the attractions of
worldly desires and the impulses toward eternal life. In that month the matter ceased to be
one of choice and became one of compulsion.
God caused my tongue to dry up so that I was
prevented from lecturing. One particular day
I would make an effort to lecture in order to
gratify the hearts of my following, but my
tongue would not utter a single word nor
could I accomplish anything at all.

This impediment in my speech produced
grief in my heart, and at the same time my
power to digest and assimilate food and drink
was impaired; I could hardly swallow or
digest a single mouthful of food. My powers
became so weakened that the doctors gave up
all hope of successful treatment. "This trouble
arises from the heart," they said, "and from
there it has spread through the constitution;
the only method of treatment is that the anxiety which has come over the heart should be
allayed."

Thereupon, perceiving my impotence and
having altogether lost my power of choice, I
sought refuge with God most high as one who
is driven to Him, because he is without further resources of his own. He answered me,
He who "answers him who is driven (to Him
by affliction) when he calls upon Him"
(Qur'an 27,63). He made it easy for my heart
to turn away from position and wealth, from
children and friends. I openly professed that I
had resolved to set out for Mecca, while pri-
vately I made arrangements to travel to
Syria. I took this precaution in case the
Caliph and all my friends should oppose my

resolve to make my residence in Syria. This
stratagem for my departure from Baghdad I
gracefully executed, and had it in mind never
to return there. There was much talk about
me among the religious leaders of `Iraq, since
none of them would allow that withdrawal
from such a state of life as I was in could have
a religious cause, for they looked upon that as
the culmination of a religious career; that was
the sum of their knowledge.

Much confusion now came into people's
minds as they tried to account for my conduct.
Those at a distance from `Iraq supposed that
it was due to some apprehension I had of
action by the government. On the other hand
those who were close to the governing circles
and had witnessed how eagerly and assiduously they sought me and how I withdrew
from them and showed no great regard for
what they said, would say, "This is a supernatural affair; it must be an evil influence
which has befallen the people of Islam and
especially the circle of the learned."

I left Baghdad, then. I distributed what
wealth I had, retaining only as much as would
suffice myself and provide sustenance for my
children. This I could easily manage, as the
wealth of `Iraq was available for good works,
since it constitutes a trust fund for the benefit of the Muslims. Nowhere in the world have
I seen better financial arrangements to assist
a scholar to provide for his children.

In due course I entered Damascus, and
there I remained for nearly two years with no
other occupation than the cultivation of
retirement and solitude, together with religious and ascetic exercises, as I busied myself
purifying my soul, improving my character
and cleansing my heart for the constant recollection of God most hight, as I had learnt from
my study of mysticism. I used to go into
retreat for a period in the mosque of
Damascus, going up the minaret of the
mosque for the whole day and shutting myself
in so as to be alone. At length I made my way

from Damascus to the Holy House (that is, Jerusalem). There I used to enter into the precinct of the Rock every day and shut myself in.

Next there arose in me a prompting to fulfill the duty of the Pilgrimage, gain the blessings of Mecca and Medina, and perform the visitation of the Messenger of God most high (peace be upon him), after first performing the visitation of al-Khalil, the Friend of God (God bless him). I therefore made the journey to the Hijaz. Before long, however, various concerns, together with the entreaties of my children, drew me back to my home; and so I came to it again, though at one time no one had seemed less likely than myself to return to it. Here, too, I sought retirement, still longing for solitude and the purification of the heart for the recollection (of God). The events of the interval, the anxieties about my family, and the necessities of my livelihood altered the aspect of my purpose and impaired the quality of my solitude, for I experienced pure ecstasy only occasionally, although I did not cease to hope for that; obstacles would hold me back, yet I always returned to it.

I continued at this stage for the space of ten years, and during these periods of solitude there were revealed to me things innumerable and unfathomable. This much I shall say about that in order that others may be helped: I learnt with certainty that it is above all the mystics who walk on the road of God; their life is the best life, their method the soundest method, their character the purest character; indeed, were the intellect of the intellectuals and the learning of the learned and the scholarship of the scholars, who are versed in the profundities of revealed truth, brought together in the attempt to improve the life and character of the mystics, they would find no way of doing so; for to the mystics all movement and all rest, whether external or internal, brings illumination from the light of the lamp of prophetic revelation; and behind the light of prophetic revelation there is no other light on the face of the earth from which illumination may be received.

In general, then, how is a mystic "way" described? The purity which is the first condition of it (sc. as bodily purity is the prior condition of formal Worship for Muslims) is the purification of the heart completely from what is other than God most high; the key to it, which corresponds to the opening act of adoration in prayer, is the sinking of the heart completely in the recollection of God; and the end of it is complete absorption in God. At least this is its end relatively to those first steps which almost come within the sphere of choice and personal responsibility; but in reality in the actual mystic "way" it is the first step, what comes before it being, as it were, the antechamber for those who are journeying toward it.

With this first stage of the "way" there begin the revelations and visions. The mystics in their waking state now behold angels and the spirits of the prophets; they hear these speaking to them and are instructed by them. Later, a higher state is reached; instead of beholding forms and figures, they come to stages in the "way" which it is hard to describe in language; if a man attempts to express these, his words inevitably contain what is clearly erroneous.

In general what they manage to achieve is nearness to God; some, however, would conceive of this as "inherence," some as "union" and some as "connection." All that is erroneous. In my book, *The Noblest Aim,* I have explained the nature of the error here. Yet he who has attained the mystic "state" need do no more than say:

Of the things I do not remember, what
  was, was;
Think it good; do not ask an account of
  it.

(Ibn al-Mu'tazz; mystic who died in 908 C.E.)

In general the man to whom He has granted no immediate experience at all, apprehends no more of what prophetic revelation really is than the name. The miraculous graces given to the saints are in truth the beginnings of the prophets; and that was the first "state" of the Messenger of God (peace be unto him) when he went out to Mount Hira', and was given up entirely to his Lord, and worshipped, so that the bedouin said, "Muhammad loves his Lord passionately."

Now this is a mystical "state" which is realized in immediate experience by those who walk in the way leading to it. Those to whom it is not granted to have immediate experience can become assured of it by trial (sc. contact with mystics or observation of them) and by hearsay, if they have sufficiently numerous opportunities of associating with mystics to understand that (sc. ecstasy) with certainty by means of what accompanies the "states." Whoever sits in their company derives from them this faith; and none who sits in their company is pained.

Those to whom it is not even granted to have contacts with mystics may know with certainty the possibility of ecstasy by the evidence of demonstration, as I have remarked in the section entitled *The Wonders of the Heart* of my *Revival of the Religious Sciences* (c. 1106).

Certainty reached by demonstration is *knowledge;* actual acquaintance with that "state" is *immediate experience;* the acceptance of it as probably from hearsay or trial (observation) is *faith.* These are three degrees. "God will raise those of you who have faith and those who have been given knowledge in degrees (Qur'an 58,12).

Behind the mystics, however, there is a crowd of ignorant people. They deny this fundamentally, they are astonished at this line of thought, they listen and mock. "Amazing," they say. "What nonsense they talk!" About such people God most high has said: "Some of them listen to you, until, upon going out from you, they say to those to whom knowledge has been given, 'What did he say just now?' These are the people on whose hearts God sets a seal and they follow their passions" (Qur'an 47,18). He makes them deaf, and blinds their sight.

Among the things that necessarily became clear to me from my practice of the mystic "way" was the true nature and special characteristics of the prophetic revelation. . . .

(At this point Ghazali explains his reasons for returning to teaching.)

In myself I know that, even if I went back to the work of disseminating knowledge, yet I did not go back. To go back is to return to the previous state of things. Previously, however, I had been disseminating knowledge by which worldly success is attained; by word and deed I had called men to it; and that had been my aim and intention. But now I am calling men to the knowledge whereby worldly success is given up and its low position in the scale of real worth is recognized. This is now my intention, my aim, my desire; God knows that this is so. It is my earnest longing that I may make myself and others better. I do not know whether I shall reach my goal or whether I shall be taken away while short of my object. I believe, however, both by certain faith and by intuition that there is no power and no might save with God, the high, the mighty, and that I do not move of myself but am moved by Him, I do not work of myself but am used by Him. I ask Him first of all to reform me and then to reform through me, to guide me and then to guide through me, to show me the truth of what is true and to grant of His bounty that I may follow it, and to show me the falsity of what is false and to grant of His bounty that I may turn away from it. . . .

(Reply to the philosophers who deny prophecy.)

The man who verbally professes belief in prophecy, but equates the prescriptions of the revealed scriptures with (philosophic) wisdom, really disbelieves in prophecy, and believes only in a certain judge (the philosopher) the ascendancy of whose star is such that it determines men to follow him. This is not prophecy at all. On the contrary, faith in prophecy is to acknowledge the existence of a sphere beyond reason; into this sphere an eye penetrates whereby man apprehends special objects-of-apprehension. For these reason is excluded in the same way as the hearing is excluded from apprehending colors and sight from apprehending sounds and all the sense from apprehending the objects-of-reason. . . .

Most of the philosophers' proofs in natural science and theology are constructed in this fashion. They conceive of things according to the measure of their observations and reasonings. What they are unfamiliar with they suppose impossible. If it were not that veridical vision in sleep is familiar, then, when someone claimed to gain knowledge of the unseen while his sense were at rest, men with such intellects would deny it. If you said to one, "Is it possible for there to be in the world a thing, the size of a grain, which, if placed in a town, will consume that town in its entirety and then consume itself, so that nothing is left of the town and what it contained nor of the thing itself?"; he would say, "This is absurd; it is an old wives' tale." Yet this is the case with fire, although, when he heard it, someone who had no acquaintance with fire would reject it. The rejection of the strange features of the world to come usually belong to this class. To the physicist we reply: "You are compelled to admit that in opium there is a property which leads to freezing, although this is not consonant with nature as rationally conceived; why then is it not possible that there should be in the positive precepts of the divine law properties leading to the healing and purifying of

hearts, which are not apprehended by intellectual wisdom but are perceived only by the eye of prophecy?". . .

If the philosopher denies the possibility of there being such properties in the number of rak'ahs (units of prayer consisting of three postures), the casting of stones (in the valley of Mina during the Pilgrimage), the number of elements of the Pilgrimage and the other ceremonies of worship of the sacred law, he will not find, in principle, any difference between these and the properties of drugs and stars. He may say, "I have some experience in medical and astronomical matters, and have found some points in the science true; as a result belief in it has become firmly settled in me and my heart has lost all inclination to shun it and look askance at it; prophecy, however, I have no experience of; how shall I know that it actually exists, even if I admit its possibility?"

I reply: "You do not confine yourself to believing what you have experience of, but, where you have received information about the experience of others, you have accepted them as authorities. Listen then to the words of the prophets, for they have had experience, they have had direct vision of the truth in respect of all that is dealt with in revelation. Walk in their way and you too will come to know something of that by direct vision."

Moreover I say: "Even if you have not experienced it, yet your mind judges it an absolute obligation to believe in it and follow it. Let us suppose that a man of full age and sound mind, who has never experienced illness, now falls ill; and let us suppose that he has a father who is a good man and a competent physician, of whose reputation in medicine he has been hearing as long as he can remember. His father compounds a drug for him, saying, `This will make you better from your illness and cure your symptoms.' What judgment does his intellect make here, even if the drug is bitter and disagreeable to the taste? Does he take it? Or does he disbelieve and say, 'I do not understand the connection of this drug with the achieving of a cure; I have had no experience of it.' You would certainly think him a fool if he did that! Similarly people of vision think you a fool when you hesitate and remain undecided." You may say: "How am I to know the good will of the Prophet (peace be upon him) and his knowledge of this medical art?" I reply: "How do you know the good will of your father, seeing this is not something perceived by the senses? The fact is that you have come to know it necessarily and indubitably by comparing his attitude at different times and observing his actions in various circumstances."

If one considers the saying of the Messenger of God (peace be upon him) and what is related in Tradition about his concern for showing to people the true way and about his graciousness in leading men by various acts of sympathy and kindness to improve their character and conduct and to better their mutual relations—leading them, in fine, to what is the indispensable basis of all betterment, religious and secular alike—if one considers this, one comes to the necessary knowledge that his good will toward his people is greater than that of a father toward his child.

Again, if one considers the marvelous acts manifested in his case and the wonderful mysteries declared by his mouth in the Qur'an and in the Traditions, and his predictions of events in the distant future, together with the fulfillment of these predictions, then one will know necessarily that he attained to the sphere which is beyond reason, where an eye opened in him by which the mysteries were laid bare which only the elect apprehend, the mysteries which are not apprehended by the intellect.

This is the method of reaching necessary knowledge that the Prophet (peace be upon him) is to believed. Make the experiment, reflect on the Qur'an, read the Traditions; then you will know that by seeing for yourself.

IBN RUSHD (AVERROES), *THE DECISIVE TREATISE* AND *UNVEILING OF THE PROGRAMS OF PROOF, INCOHERENCE OF THE INCOHERENCE*

The thinker who came to the defense of philosophy against the attacks of Ghazali was the great Spanish Muslim philosopher Ibn Rushd (1126–1198 C.E.), known in the West as Averroes. He was a product of the brilliant Spanish Muslim culture which was superior to the Christian West in its intellectual institutions, knowledge of ancient philosophy, astronomy, medicine, and mathematics. Like his contemporary, the great Spanish Jewish thinker, Moses Maimonides, Ibn Rushd was a universal genius who combined a life of study with active involvement in public life. He studied theology, jurisprudence, medicine, mathematics and philosophy; and he also held judicial posts at both Seville and Cordoba, and became physician to the caliph in 1182 C.E. Eventually he fell into disfavor with the caliph al-Mansun and was banished from court. He later left Spain for Morocco where he died in 1198.

Ibn Rushd believed that Aristotle was the final culmination of the human intellect, and he devoted much of his scholarly career to writing commentaries on the works of Aristotle. In the Christian West he became known simply as "the Commentator." In his *Decisive Treatise* Ibn Rushd defends the study of philosophy, in its Aristotelian form, against its religious opponents on the basis of texts from the Qur'an itself. He begins with a definition of philosophy as "the study of existing beings and the reflection on them as indication of the Artisan (or Creator)." Given this definition, he can conclude that if beings are the products of the divine Artisan, then knowledge of the art in them gives us a more perfect knowledge of the Artisan. He then notes that the Law (of the Qur'an) summons Muslims to reflection on creation in the saying of God: "Reflect, you have vision" (Qur'an 59:2). Another text specifically urges the study of the totality of beings: "Have you not studied the kingdom of the heavens and the earth, and whatever things God has created?" (Qur'an 8:185). Ibn Rushd then goes on to argue that the reflection commanded by the Qur'an is the type of reasoning found in Aristotelian philosophy which works by "drawing out the unknown from the known" and by logical demonstration. Ibn Rushd concludes that, before one can gain a "demonstrative knowledge of God the Exalted and all the beings of His creation," it is necessary to learn the principles of Aristotelian logic: "the kinds of demonstrations and their conditions (of validity)," the ways in which "demonstrative reasoning differs from dialectical, rhetorical and fallacious reasoning," the types of demonstrations, "their premises and their kinds." Against the conservative objection that this type of reasoning did not exist among the first believers and is therefore heretical, Ibn Rushd points out that "the study of legal reasoning and its kinds is also something which has been discovered since the (time of) the first believers, yet it is not considered a heretical innovation."

Ibn Rushd recognizes that some may be led into error by the study of philosophy, but this is not due to the nature of philosophy itself. Rather, this is caused by something "accidental" like the "deficiency" in a person's natural capacity or "being dominated by passions, or not finding the right teacher." He concludes that to forbid the study of philosophy for those who are intellectually and morally qualified "is the extreme of ignorance and estrangement from God the Exalted" because it blocks "people from the door by which the Law summons them to knowledge of God, the door of theoretical study which leads to the truest knowledge of Him." This last statement reflects the philosopher's belief that the "truest knowledge" is that arrived at through the study of philosophy. The impact of this position can be seen in the way that Ibn Rushd approaches the question of the types of truth found in the Qur'an and in philosophy.

Ibn Rushd, like Maimonides and Aquinas, believes that philosophy should not lead to conclusions conflicting with scripture (the Qur'an) because "truth does not oppose truth but accords with it and bears witness to it." If there is an apparent conflict between philosophy and scripture, then "there is a need for allegorical interpretation" of scripture. By "allegorical interpretation" Ibn Rushd means "the extension of the significance of an expression from real to metaphorical significance, . . . such as calling a thing by the name of something resembling it or a cause or a consequence or accompaniment of it, or other such things as are enumerated in accounts of the kinds of metaphorical speech." Because the various schools of Islamic interpretation rarely agree unanimously on which passages are to be interpreted in their "apparent (literal) meaning" and which are to be understood metaphorically, there is considerable latitude for the philosopher to use allegory in the interpretation of the Qur'an. Ibn Rushd also believes that only the philosophers "who are firmly rooted in knowledge" are capable of reaching a "belief" based on philosophical demonstration and only they are able to use "the science of allegorical interpretation." The "unlearned believers'" faith "is not based on demonstration," and they are only capable of understanding the literal level of the Qur'an.

A good illustration of these differences in interpretation of the Qur'an is the way various Muslims understand the afterlife. As Ibn Rushd notes "All religions agree on the fact that souls experience states of happiness or misery after death, but they disagree in the manner of symbolizing these states and explaining their existence to men." He distinguishes "three sects with regard to the understanding of the symbolization which is used in our religion referring to the states of the future life." One group, the majority of unlearned believers, "holds that existence is identical with this existence here with respect to bliss and pleasure, i.e., they hold that it is the same sort and that the two existences differ only in respect to permanence and limit of duration." The other two groups hold "that there is a difference in the kind of existence." One believes "that the existence symbolized by these sensible images is spiritual;" the other "that it is corporeal, but think that the corporeality of the life beyond differs from the corporeality of this life in that the latter is perishable while the former is immortal."

Ibn Rushd apparently agrees with this last group, and he does so on rational grounds which can be discussed and understood only by "the elite." In this way he differs from Ghazali who believed that the souls of the just were reunited with the same bodies they had on earth. First of all, Ibn Rushd believes that "the soul is immortal." Secondly, he thinks "that the return of the soul (after death) to other bodies does not involve the same absurdity as its return to these same (earthly) bodies." The reason for this is that "the material of bodies that exist here is successively transferred from one body to another." Because they share the same matter, these bodies could not all exist at the same time. Ibn Rushd then concludes "that what arises from the dead are simulacra of these earthly bodies, not these bodies themselves, for that which has perished does not return individually and a thing can only return as an image of that which has perished, not as a being identical with what has perished."

The translations of *The Decisive Treatise* and the *Unveiling of the Programs of Proof* are by G.F. Hourani in *Averroes on the Harmony of Religion and Philosophy* (London: Luzac & Company, 1961) 44–46, 48–49, 76–77. The translation of the *Incoherence of the Incoherence* is by Simon van den Bergh (London: Luzac & Company, 1954) 350–362.

THE DECISIVE TREATISE

(The law commands the study of philosophy.)

Praise be to God with all due praise, and a prayer for Muhammad, His chosen servant and Messenger. The purpose of this treatise is to examine, from the standpoint of the study of the (Islamic) Law, whether the study of phi-

losophy and logic is allowed by the Law, or prohibited, or commanded, either by way of recommendation or as obligatory.

We say: If the activity of philosophy is no more than the study of existing beings and the reflection on them as indications of the Artisan (or Creator), that is, inasmuch as they are products of art, for beings also indicate the Artisan through our knowledge of the art in them, and the more perfect this knowledge is, the more perfect the knowledge of the Artisan becomes, and if the Law has encouraged and urged reflection on beings, then it is clear that what this name (of philosophy) signifies is either obligatory or recommended by the Law.

That the Law summons us to reflection on beings, and the pursuit of knowledge about them by the intellect is clear from the several verses of the Book of God, blessed be He and exalted, such as the saying of the Exalted, "Reflect, you have vision" (Qur'an 59:2); this is textual authority for the obligation to use intellectual reasoning, or a combination of intellectual and legal reasoning. Another example is His saying, "Have you not studied the kingdom of the heavens and the earth, and whatever things God has created?" (Qur'an 8:185); this is a text urging the study of the totality of beings. Again, God the Exalted has taught that one of those whom He singularly honored by this knowledge was Abraham, peace be upon him, for the Exalted said, "So we made Abraham see the kingdom of the heavens and the earth, that he might be ..." etc. (Qur'an 2:5–6). The Exalted also said, "Do they not observe the camels, how they have been created, and the sky, how it has been raised up?" (Qur'an 2:6–7); and He said, "and they gave thought to the creation of the heavens and the earth" (Qur'an 2:7), and so in countless other verses.

Since it has now been established that the Law has rendered obligatory the study of beings by the intellect, and reflection on them, and since reflection is nothing more than inference and drawing out of the unknown from the known, and since this is reasoning or at any rate done by reasoning, therefore we are under an obligation to carry on our study of beings by intellectual reasoning. It is further evident that this manner of study, to which the Law summons and urges, is the most perfect kind of study using the most perfect kind of reasoning; and this is the kind called "demonstration."

The Law, then, has urged us to have demonstrative knowledge of God the Exalted and all the beings of His creation. But it is preferable and even necessary for anyone who wants to understand God the Exalted and the other beings demonstratively to have first understood the kinds of demonstration and their conditions (of validity), and in what respects demonstrative reasoning differs from dialectical, rhetorical and fallacious reasoning. But this is not possible unless he has previously learned what reasoning as such is, and how many kinds it has, and which of them are valid and which invalid. This in turn is not possible unless he has previously learned the parts of reasoning, of which it is composed, that is, the premises and their kinds. Therefore he who believes in the Law and obeys its commands to study beings, ought prior to his study to gain a knowledge of things, which have the same place in theoretical studies as instruments have in practical activities.

(Reply to objection that intellectual reasoning did not exist among the early believers.)

It cannot be objected: "This kind of study of intellectual reasoning is a heretical innovation since it did not exist among the first believers." For the study of legal reasoning and its kinds is also something which has been discovered since the (time of) the first believers, yet it is not considered a heretical innovation. So the objector should believe the same about the study of intellectual reasoning. For this there is a reason, which is not the place to answer here. But most (masters) of this religion (that is, Islam) support intellectual reasoning, except a small group of gross literalists, who can be refuted by (sacred) texts.

(Study of philosophy should be allowed for those who are intellectually and morally qualified.)

From (all) this it is evident that the study of the books of the ancients is obligatory by (Islamic) Law, since their aim and purpose in their books is just the purpose to which the Law has urged us, and that whoever forbids the study of them to anyone who is fit to study them, that is, anyone who unites the two qualities of natural intelligence and religious integrity and moral virtue is blocking people from the door by which the Law summons them to knowledge of God, the door of theoretical study which leads to the truest knowledge of Him; and such an act is the extreme of ignorance and estrangement from God the Exalted.

And if someone errs or stumbles in the study of these books owing to a deficiency in his natural capacity, or bad organization of his study of them, or being dominated by his passions, or not finding a teacher to guide him to an understanding of their contents, or a combination of all or more than one of these causes, it does not follow that one should forbid them to anyone who is qualified to study them. For this manner of harm which arises owing to them is attached to them by accident, not by essence; and when a thing is beneficial by its nature and essence, it ought not to be shunned because of something harmful contained in it by accident. This was the thought of the Prophet, peace be upon him, on the occasion when he ordered a man to give his brother honey to drink for his diarrhea, and the diarrhea increased after he had given him the honey; when the man complained to him about it, he said, "God spoke the truth; it was your brother's stomach that lied." We can even say that a man who prevents a qualified person from studying books of philosophy, because some of the most vicious people may be thought to have gone astray through their study of them, is like a man who prevents a

thirsty person from drinking cool, fresh water until he dies from thirst because some people have choked to death on it. For death from water by choking is an accidental matter, but death by thirst is essential and elementary.

(There is one truth and allegorical interpretation resolves the apparent contradiction between the Qur'an and reason.)

Now since this religion is true and summons to the study which leads to the knowledge of the Truth, we the Muslim community know definitively that demonstrative study (that is, philosophy) does not lead to (conclusions) conflicting with what Scripture has given us; for truth does not oppose truth but accords with it and bears witness to it.

This being so, whenever demonstrative study leads to any manner of knowledge about any being, that being is inevitably either unmentioned or mentioned in Scripture. If it is unmentioned, there is no contradiction, and it is the same case as an act whose category is unmentioned so that the (Muslim) lawyer has to infer it by reasoning from Scripture. If Scripture does speak about it, the apparent meaning of the words inevitably either accords or conflicts with the conclusions of (philosophical) demonstration about it. If this apparent meaning accords, there is no conflict. If it conflicts, there is a call for allegorical interpretation. The meaning of "allegorical interpretation" is: the extension of the significance from real to metaphorical significance, without forsaking therein the standard metaphorical practices of Arabic, such as calling a thing by the name of something resembling it or a cause or consequence or accompaniment of it, or other such things as are enumerated in accounts of the kinds of metaphorical speech. . . .

Muslims are unanimous in holding that it is not obligatory either to take all the expressions of Scripture in their apparent (or external) meaning or to extend them all from the apparent meaning by means of allegorical interpretation. They disagree (only) over which of them should and which should not be so interpreted: the Ash'arites (that is, certain dialectical theologians) for instance give an allegorical interpretation to the verse about God's directing Himself (Qur'an 2:29) and the Prophetic tradition about His descent (into this world), while the Hanbalites (that is, fundamentalist lawyers and traditionists) take them in their apparent meaning. . . .

It may be objected: There are some things in Scripture which the Muslims have unanimously agreed to take in their apparent meaning, others (which they have agreed) to interpret allegorically, and others about which they have disagreed; is it permissible, then, that demonstration should lead to interpreting allegorically what they (that is, the Muslims) have agreed to take in its apparent meaning, or to taking in its apparent meaning what they have agreed to interpret allegorically? We reply: If unanimous agreement is established by a method which is certain, such (a result) is not sound; but if (the existence of) agreement on those things is a matter of opinion, then it may be sound. This is why Abu Hamid (al-Ghazali) and Abu'l-Ma'ali (al-Juwayni) and other leaders of thought said that no one should be definitely called an unbeliever for violating unanimity on a point of interpretation in matters like these.

(The lack of unanimity gives great latitude to the exegete.)

That unanimity on theoretical matters is never determined with certainty, as it can be on practical (or behavioral) matters, may be shown to you by the fact that it is not possible for unanimity to be determined on any question at any period unless that period is strictly limited by us, and all the scholars existing in that period are known to us, that is, known as individuals and in their total number, and the doctrine of each of them on the question

has been handed down to us on assailable authority. And in addition to all this, unless we are sure that the scholars existing at the time were in agreement that there is not both an apparent and an inner meaning in scripture, that knowledge of any question ought not to be kept secret from anyone, and there is only one way for people to understand Scripture. But it is recorded in tradition that many of the first believers used to hold that Scripture had both an apparent and an inner meaning, and that the inner meaning ought not to be learned by anyone who is not a man of learning in this field and who is incapable of understanding it. . . . So how can it possibly be conceived that a unanimous agreement can be handed down to us about a single theoretical question, when we know definitely that not a single period has been without scholars who held that there are things in Scripture whose true meaning should not be learned by all people? . . .

(Two types of believers.)

It is evident from what we have said that a unanimous agreement cannot be established in (theoretical) questions of this kind, because of the reports that many of the believers of the first generation (of Muslims), as well as others, have said that there are allegorical interpretations which ought not to be expressed except to those who are qualified to receive allegories. These are those who "are firmly rooted in knowledge." For we prefer to place a stop after God's words "and those who are firmly rooted in knowledge" (and not before it, because if the scholars did not understand allegorical interpretation but only God), there would be no superiority in their assent which would oblige them to a belief in Him not found among the unlearned. God has described them as those who believe in Him, and this can only refer to a belief which is based on (scientific or philosophical) demonstration; and this belief only occurs together with the science of allegorical interpretation. For the unlearned believers are those whose belief in Him is not based on demonstration; and if this belief which God has attributed to the scholars (in Qur'an 3:7) is peculiar to them, it must come through demonstration, and if it comes through demonstration, it only occurs together with the science of allegorical interpretation. For God the Exalted has informed us that those (verses) have an allegorical interpretation which is the truth, and demonstration can only be of the truth. That being the case, it is not possible for general unanimity to be established about allegorical interpretations, which God has made peculiar to scholars. This is self-evident to any fair-minded person.

UNVEILING OF THE PROGRAMS OF PROOF

(The afterlife.)

All religions agree on the fact that souls experience states of happiness or misery after death, but they disagree in the manner of symbolizing these states and explaining their existence to men. And it seems that the kind of symbolization that is found in this religion of ours is the most perfect means of explanation to the majority of men and provides the greatest stimulus to their souls to the life beyond; and the primary concern of religions is with the majority. . . . It seems that corporeal symbolization provides a stronger stimulus to the life beyond that the spiritual kind; the spiritual (kind) is more acceptable to the class of debating theologians, but they are the minority.

For this reason we find the people of Islam divided into three sects with regard to the understanding of the symbolization which is used in (the texts of) our religion referring to the states of the future life. One sect holds that existence is identical with this existence here with respect to bliss and pleasure, i.e., they hold that it is the same sort and that the

two existences differ only in respect to permanence and limit of duration, i.e., the former is permanent and the latter is of limited duration. Another group holds that there is a difference in the kind of existence. This group has two subdivisions. One subgroup holds that existence symbolized by these sensible images is spiritual, and it has been symbolized thus (that is, in sensible material images) only for the purpose of exposition; these people are supported by many well-known arguments from Scripture, but there would be no point in enumerating them. Another subgroup thinks that it is corporeal, but think that the corporeality of the life beyond differs from the corporeality of this life in that the latter is perishable while the former is immortal. They too are supported by arguments from Scripture.

It seems that this opinion is more suitable to the elite, for the admissibility of this opinion is founded on facts which are not discussed in front of everyone. One is that the soul is immortal. The other is that the return of the soul (after death) to other bodies does not involve the same absurdity as its return to these same (earthly) bodies. This is because it is apparent that the material of the bodies that exist here is successively transferred from one body to another. . . . Bodies like these cannot possibly all exist actually (at the same time), because their material is one. A man dies, for instance, his body is transformed into dust, that dust is transformed into a plant, another man feeds on that plant; then semen proceeds from him, from which another man is born. But if other bodies are supposed, this state of affairs does not follow as a consequence.

INCOHERENCE OF THE INCOHERENCE

(The afterlife.)

The truth in this question is that every man's duty is (to believe) whatever his study of it leads him to (conclude), provided that it is not such a study as would cause him to reject the principle altogether, by denying the existence (of the future life) altogether; for this manner of belief obliges us to call its holder an unbeliever, because the existence of this (future state) for man is made known to people through their Scriptures and their intellects.

The whole of this (argument) is founded on the immortality of the soul. If it is asked "Does Scripture contain an indication of the immortality of the soul or (at least) a hint of it?" we reply: This is found in the precious Book in the words of the Exalted, "God receives the souls at the time of their death, and those which have not died He receives in their sleep," [and so on to the end of] the verse. The significant aspect of this verse is that in it He has equated sleep and death with respect to the annihilation of the soul's activity. Thus if the cessation of the soul's activity in death were due to the soul's dissolution, not to a change in the soul's organ, the cessation of its activity in sleep [too] would have to be due to the dissolution of its essential being; but if that were the case, it would not return on waking to its normal condition. So since it does return to it, we know that this cessation does not happen to it through anything which attaches to it in its substantial nature, but is only something which attaches to it owing to a cessation of its organ; and [we know] that it does not follow that if the organ ceases the soul must cease. Death is a cessation; it must therefore be of the organ, as is the case in sleep. As the Philosopher says, "If the old man were to find an eye like the young man's eye, he would see as the young man sees."

This is as much as we see fit to affirm in our investigation of the beliefs of this religion of ours, the religion of Islam.

(Problem of the soul's independent existence apart from the body.)

As for Ghazali's objection, that a man knows of his soul that it is in his body although he cannot specify in which part—this indeed is true, for the ancients had different opinions about its seat, but our knowledge that the soul is in the body does not mean that we know that it receives its existence through being in the body; this is not self-evident, and is a question about which the philosophers ancient as well as modern differ, for if the body serves as an instrument for the soul, the soul does not receive its existence through the body; but if the body is like a substratum for its accident, then the soul can only exist through the body. . . .

(Some famous philosophers argue for the individuality of the soul.)

In the intellect there is no individuality whatever; the soul, however, although it is free from the matters through which the individuals receive their plurality, is said by the most famous philosophers not to abandon the nature of the individual, although it is an apprehending entity. This is a point which has to be considered. . . .

The philosophers, however, can answer (the charge that souls will perish with bodies) that it is by no means necessary that, when there exists between two things a relation of attachment and love, for instance, the relation between the lover and the beloved and the relation between iron and the magnet, the destruction of one should cause the destruction of the other. . . .

He who claims the survival and the numerical plurality of souls should say that they are in a subtle matter, namely the animal warmth which emanates from the heavenly bodies, and this is a warmth which is not fire, and in which there is not a principle of fire; in this warmth there are the souls which create the sublunary bodies and those which inhere in these bodies. . . .

What Ghazali says against them [the heretics and those who believe that the end of human beings only consists in sensual enjoyment] is right, and in refuting them it must be admitted that the soul is immortal, as is proved by rational and religious proofs, and it must be assumed that what arise from the dead are simulacra of those earthly bodies, not those bodies themselves, for that which has perished does not return individually and a thing can only return as an image of that which has perished, not as a being identical

with what has perished, as Ghazali declares. Therefore the doctrine of resurrection of those theologians who believe that the soul is an accident and that the bodies which arise are identical with those that perished cannot be true. For what perished and became anew can only be specifically, not numerically, one . . . Ghazali accused the philosophers of heresy on three points. One concerns this question [the immortality of the individual soul] and we have already shown what opinion the philosophers hold about this, and that according to them it is a speculative problem. . . .

IBN AL-`ARABI, *THE BEZELS OF WISDOM*

Muslim Spain also produced the greatest of the medieval Sufi writers, Ibn al-`Arabi (1165–1240 C.E.). The son of a high ranking state official, al-`Arabi studied the Qur'an, the Traditions of the prophet, Arabic grammar and Islamic law. From an early age he was also exposed to Sufism and was initiated as a Sufi at the age of twenty. As a teenager Ibn al-`Arabi met Ibn Rushd, and his account of the meeting reflects both the supreme self-confidence of the young mystic and the differences between the philosopher's approach to God and the way of mysticism.

I spent a good day in Cordoba at the house of Abu al-Walid Ibn Rushd [Averroes]. He had expressed a desire to meet with me in person, since he had heard of certain revelations I had received while in retreat, and had shown considerable astonishment concerning them. In consequence, my father, who was one of his close friends, took me with him on the pretext of business, in order to give Ibn Rushd the opportunity of making my acquaintance. I was at the time a beardless youth. As I entered the house the philosopher rose to greet me with all the signs of friendliness and affection, and embraced me. Then he said to me, "Yes!" and showed pleasure on seeing that I had understood him. I, on the other hand, being aware of the motive for his pleasure, replied, "No!" Upon this, Ibn Rushd drew back from me, his color changed and he seemed to doubt what he had thought of me. He then put to me the following question, "What solution have you found as a result of mystical illumination and divine inspiration? Does it agree with what is arrived at by speculative thought?" I replied, "Yes and No. Between the Yea and the Nay the spirits take their flight beyond matter, and the necks detach themselves from their bodies." At this Ibn Rushd became pale, and I saw him tremble as he muttered the formula, "There is no power save from God." This was because he had understood my allusion. (Translated by R.W.J. Austin in *Ibn Al-`Arabi: The Bezels of Wisdom* [Paulist Press, 1980] 2–3.

Arabi's early adult life was spent in Spain and North Africa, but in 1200 he went to

Egypt and then on pilgrimage to Mecca. After extensive travel in the Near East, in 1223 he settled in Damascus where he remained until his death in 1240.

Ibn al-ʿArabi was a prolific writer who produced over two hundred books, the greatest of which are *The Bezels of Divine Wisdom,* a kind of summary of his thought, and his monumental *Meccan Revelations* which still exists in an autographed copy of 37 volumes. Because of his wide travels in both the western and eastern Muslim worlds, ʿArabi had a lasting influence on Sufi thought in both areas. His thought may also have influenced Christian medieval mysticism and Dante's *Commedia.* He himself incorporates elements of Neoplatonic philosophy, Christian and Kabbalistic mysticism, and possibly even Hindu and Buddhist mysticism.

Our selections are taken from *The Bezels of Wisdom* which according to Ibn al-ʿArabi's preface was composed in the year 627 (1230 C.E.) after he had settled in Damascus. According to the preface ʿArabi had a vision in which Muhammad appeared to him holding a book in his hand and saying: "This is the book of the bezels of Wisdom; take it and bring it to men that they might benefit from it." ʿArabi goes on to say, "I carried out the wish, made pure my intention, and devoted my purpose to the publishing of this book, just as the Apostle had laid down, without any addition or subtraction." The book takes the form of presenting individual aspects of divine wisdom as they are manifested in the lives of twenty-seven prophets revered in the Muslim tradition. These prophets include many figures from the Hebrew Scriptures (Adam, Seth, Noah, Enoch, Abraham, Isaac, Ishmael, Jacob, Joseph, Lot, Ezra, Solomon, David, Jonah, Job, Elias, Aaron, and Moses); from the Christian tradition (Jesus, John, Zakariah); and from the Arab tradition (Hud, Salih, Shuʿaib, Luqman, Khalid, and Muhammad). Although the work begins with Adam and ends with Muhammad, the chapters are neither arranged chronologically nor systematically. Sometimes the material is related to the life of the prophet as recorded in the Qur'an, but at other times the material seems to be completely unrelated to the prophet's life. I have chosen to include small selections from two chapters: "The Wisdom of Divinity in the Word of Adam," and "The Wisdom of Prophecy in the Word of Jesus."

For Ibn al-ʿArabi God as infinite being, beauty and wisdom is driven toward self-manifestation. In the selection from the opening chapter of *The Bezels of Wisdom,* ʿArabi is paraphrasing a divine utterance that was well-known in Sufi thought: "I was a hidden treasure who longed to be known; therefore I created the world." In ʿArabi's paraphrase, "The Reality wanted to see the essences of His Most Beautiful Names . . . to see His own Essence, in an all-inclusive object encompassing the whole [divine] Command, which, qualified by existence, would reveal to Him His own mystery." Before creation Reality or Being is one. It is polarized into God and Cosmos only after and because of Reality's desire to experience itself in another. Creation then is the mirror in which Reality contemplates His own beauty and wisdom. Each creature is the word of the absolute addressed to Himself; in each word a particular aspect of Reality's infinite beauty and wisdom is objectified and expressed.

Without the creation of Adam, the archetype of humanity, the world was without soul and the mirror of creation was "unpolished." Each human has the capacity to become a "microcosm" of the cosmos by reflecting and mediating the divine unity that underlies the whole of creation. In this sense, Adam is higher than the angels who "were only certain faculties of that form which was the form of the Cosmos, called in the terminology of the Folk, the Great Man." The angels are "the psychic and physical faculties in the human formation." They are isolated from one another and have nothing of the human capacity to synthesize and reflect the fullness of the divine self-manifestation.

Al-`Arabi uses a whole series of metaphors to express the mystery of Adam as both the created mirror of God and the divine self-consciousness in creation. According to the Qur'anic and biblical accounts of creation, man is the image or vice-regent (*khalifa*) of God. The name for man in Arabic is *insan* which is also the word for "pupil" of the eye. Therefore Adam is to God "as the pupil is for the eye" (*insan al-`ayn*), and "it is by him that the Reality looks on His creation and bestows the Mercy [of existence] on them." Adam is the paradoxical union of the eternal and the created.

> He is Man, the transient [in his form], the eternal [in his essence]; he is the perpetual, the everlasting, the [at once] discriminating and unifying Word.

Another favorite image of humanity is that from which the book draws its title: Adam is the bezel-stone or "seal" of the signet ring on which is inscribed the sign "with which the King seals his treasure." The bezel was the setting in which a gem engraved with a name was set to make a signet ring. Adam then is the receptive being who can receive the divine imprint with which God "seals his treasure." He is God's "Vice-Regent" because he bears God's seal and safeguards the "treasure" of creation. Al-`Arabi's thought has analogues in both the Augustinian-Franciscan tradition of Bonaventure who uses the mirror imagery and speaks of the footprints of God in creation, and in the monistic thought of Meister Eckhart who finds the divine within the creature.

Ibn al-`Arabi's chapter on "The Wisdom of Prophecy in the Word of Jesus," takes the form of a reflection on the Qur'anic traditions about Jesus, especially Gabriel's annunciation to Mary and Jesus' ability to raise the dead. `Arabi accepts the virginal conception of Jesus and insists that he is a unique manifestation of the divine in human history. Jesus is at once "the Word of God, the Spirit of God, and the slave of God, and such a [triple] manifestation in sensible form belongs to no other." All creatures are words of God and therefore potential manifestations of the divine, but Jesus, because of his unique conception, was able to communicate the divine Spirit in both notional (word) form and in actual (life-giving) form. Jesus is what every human potentially is: the life-giving Spirit of God. The precise relation between the divine and the human in Jesus, and by extension in all humans, is something that al-`Arabi never succeeds in expressing adequately because of the limitations of language.

The translation is by R.W.J. Austin, *Ibn Al-`Arabi: The Bezels of Wisdom* (New York, Ramsey, Toronto: Paulist Press, 1980) 50–51, 175–178.

THE BEZELS OF WISDOM

"The Wisdom of Divinity in the Word of Adam"

The Reality wants to see the essences of His Most Beautiful Names or, to put it another way, to see His own Essence, in an all-inclusive object encompassing the whole [divine] Command, which, qualified by existence, would reveal to Him His own mystery. For the seeing of a thing, itself by itself, is not the same as its seeing itself in another, as it were in a mirror; for it appears to itself in a form that is invested by the location of the vision by that which would only appear to it given the existence of the location and its (the location's) self-disclosure to it.

The Reality gave existence to the whole Cosmos [at first] as an undifferentiated thing without anything of the spirit in it, so that it was like an unpolished mirror. It is in the nature of the divine determination that He does not set out a location except to receive a divine spirit, which is also called [in the Qur'an] "the breathing into him" (Qur'an, XXI:91). The latter is nothing other than the coming into operation of the undifferentiated form's [innate] disposition to receive the inexhaustible overflowing of self-revelation, which has always been and will ever be. There is only that which is receptive and the receptive had been only from the most Holy Superabundance [of the Reality], for all power to act [all initiative] is from Him in the beginning and at the end. All command derives from Him, even as it begins with Him.

Thus the [divine] Command required [by its very nature] the reflective characteristic of the mirror of the Cosmos, and Adam was the very principle of reflection for that mirror and the spirit of that form, while the angels were only certain faculties of that form which was the form of the Cosmos, called in the terminology of the Folk, the Great Man. In relation to it the angels are as the psychic and physical faculties in the human formation. Each of these [cosmic] faculties or powers is veiled [from knowing the whole] by its own self [being limited by its relative individuality], so that it cannot know anything that excels it. It also claims that it has the qualification for a very high position and exalted abode with God by virtue of its participation in the divine Synthesis, deriving both the Sphere of Divinity and the Reality of Realities and, finally, with respect to the formation assuming these characteristics, from the exigencies of the Universal Nature, which contains and comprises all the receptivities of the Cosmos, higher and lower.

This [knowledge] cannot be arrived at by the intellect by means of any rational thought process, for this kind of perception comes only by a divine disclosure from which is ascertained the origin of the forms of the Cosmos receiving the spirits. The [above-mentioned] formation is called Man and Vice-Regent [of God]. As for the first term, it stems from the universality of his formation and the fact that he embraces all the realities. For the Reality, he is as the pupil is for the eye through which the act of seeing takes place. Thus he is called *insan* [meaning both man and pupil], for it is by him that Reality looks on His creation and bestows the Mercy [of existence] on them. He is Man, the transient [in his form], the eternal [in his essence]; he is the perpetual, the everlasting, the [at once] discriminating and unifying Word. It is by his existence that the Cosmos subsists and he is, in relation to the Cosmos, as the seal is to the ring, the seal being that place whereon is engraved the token with which the King seals his treasure. So he is called the Vice-regent, for by him God preserves His creation, as the seal preserves the king's treasure. So long as the king's seal is on it no one dares to open it except by his permission, the seal being [as it were] a regent in charge of the kingdom. Even so is the Cosmos preserved so long as the Perfect Man remains in it.

"The Wisdom of Prophecy in the Word of Jesus"

When the trusty spirit, which was Gabriel, presented itself to Mary as a perfectly formed human, she imagined that he was some ordinary man who desired to lie with her. Accordingly, she sought refuge from him in God, totally, so that He might rid her of his attentions, knowing that to be forbidden (Qur'an XIX:17–21). Thus she attained to perfect presence with God, which is the [pervasion of] the unseen spirit. Had he blown [his spirit] into her at that moment, Jesus would have turned out too surly for any to bear, because of his mother's state. When he said to her, "I am only a messenger of your Lord, come to give you a pure boy" (Qur'an XIX:19), her anxiety subsided and she relaxed. It was at that moment that he blew Jesus into her.

Gabriel was, in fact, transmitting God's word to Mary, just as an apostle transmits His word to his community. God says, "He is His word deposited with Mary, and a spirit from Himself" (Qur'an IV:171).

Thus did desire pervade Mary. The body of Jesus was created from the actual water of Mary and the notional water [seed] of Gabriel inherent in the moisture of that blowing, since breath from the vital body is moist owing to the element of water in it. In this way the body of Jesus was brought into being from a notional and an actual water, appearing in mortal form because of his mother's [being human] and the appearance of Gabriel in human form, since all creation in this human species occurs in the usual way.

Jesus came forth raising the dead because he was a divine spirit. In this the quickening was of God, while the blowing itself came from Jesus, just as the blowing was from Gabriel, while the Word was of God. As regards what was made apparent by his blowing, Jesus' raising of the dead was an actual bringing to life, just as he himself became manifest from the form of his mother. His

raising of the dead, however, was also notional, as coming from him, since, in truth it came from God. Thus he combined both [the notional and the actual] by the reality according to which he was created, seeing, as we have said, that he was created of notional and actual water. . . .

The humility of Jesus was such that his community was commanded "that they should pay the poll-tax completely, humbling themselves" (Qur'an IX:29), that if any one of them were struck on one cheek, he should offer also the other, and that he should not hit back or seek retribution. This aspect [of his teaching] derives from his mother, since woman is lowly and humble, being under the man, both theoretically and physically. His powers of revival, on the other hand, derive from the blowing of Gabriel in human form, since Jesus revived the dead in human form. Had Gabriel not come in human form, but in some other, whether animal, plant or mineral, Jesus would have been able to quicken the dead only by taking that form to himself and appearing in it. Similarly, had Gabriel appeared in a luminous, incorporeal form, not going beyond his nature, Jesus would not have been able to revive the dead without first appearing in that luminous natural form, and not in the elemental human form deriving from his mother.

It used to be said of him, when he revived the dead, "It is he and yet not he." Both the sight of the observer and the mind of the intelligent man were confused at seeing a mortal man bring the dead to life, rationally as well as physically, which is a divine prerogative. The spectator would be utterly bewildered to see a mortal man performing divine acts.

This matter has led certain people to speak of incarnation and to say that, in reviving the dead, he is God. Therefore, they are called unbelievers [concealers], being a form of concealment, since they conceal God, Who in reality revives the dead, in the human form of Jesus. He has said, "They are concealers [unbelievers] who say that God is the Messiah, son of Mary." The real error and unbelief in the full sense of the word is not in their saying "He is God" nor "the son of Mary," but in their having turned aside from God by including [God in human form] in the matter of reviving the dead, in favor of a merely mortal form in their saying [He is] "the son of Mary," albeit that he is the son of Mary without doubt. . . .

Considered in his [particular] mortal form, one might say that he is the son of Mary. Considered in his form of humanity, one might say that he is of Gabriel, while considered with respect to the revival of the dead, one might say that he is of God as Spirit. Thus one might call him the Spirit of God, which is to say that life is manifest into whomsoever he blows. Sometimes it might be imagined, using the passive participle, that God is in him, sometimes that an angel is in him, and at other times mortality and humanity. He is indeed according to that aspect [of his reality] which predominates in the one who considers him.

Thus he is [at once] the Word of God, the Spirit of God, and the salve of God, and such a [triple] manifestation in sensible form belongs to no other. Every other man is attributed to his formal father, not to the one who blows His Spirit into human form. God, when He perfected the human body, as He says, "When I perfected him" (Qur'an XV:29), blew into him of His spirit, attributing all spirit in man's being and essence to Himself. The case of Jesus is otherwise, since the perfecting of his body and human form was included in the blowing of the spirit [by Gabriel into Mary], which is not so of other men. All creatures are indeed words of God, which are inexhaustible, stemming as they do from [the command] "Be," which is the Word of God (Qur'an II:117). Now, can the Word be attributed to God as He is in Himself, so that its nature may never be known, or can God descend to the form of him who says "Be," so that the word "Be" may be said to the reality of the form to which He descends and in which He is manifest? Some gnostics support the former, some the latter, while others are confused and do not know what is the truth of the matter.

7

CHRISTIAN THEOLOGY AND MYSTICISM IN THE HIGH MIDDLE AGES

ANSELM

In the eleventh century Christian Europe began to recover from a second "Dark Age" when invasions by the Vikings, Muslims, and Magyars in the ninth and tenth centuries almost destroyed the achievements of the Carolingian Renaissance. Feudalism, which had increased in the wake of the collapse of the Carolingian Empire, gradually helped ambitious lords establish some type of centralized political authority in Germany, France and England. The resulting peace enabled trade and commerce to revive, and cities reemerged as economic centers for markets.

The church also began to recover from the horrors of a time when both the papacy and local churches were dominated by the worldly concerns of local nobility and such abuses as simony, clerical concubinage, and lay investiture of bishops and abbots. As may be expected, the monasteries were the source of both spiritual and intellectual revival. The Cluniac reform movement attempted to free the church from the feudal abuses of lay investiture and put a limit on the brutality of endemic feudal warfare. Eventually reform reached the papacy itself when Hildebrand, who became Pope Gregory VII, and like-minded reformers asserted the papacy's spiritual independence from control by the Holy Roman Empire. By 1095, a reinvigorated papacy was in a position to lead the First Crusade against the Seljuk Turks for the recovery of the shrines in the Holy Land. Europe was on the verge of what scholars have called "The Twelfth Century Renaissance."

The sources for intellectual and theological revival were the monasteries and the schools connected with the cathedrals. The first great theologian of the High Middle Ages was Anselm of Canterbury (1033–1109) who was born in Aosta in northern Italy, but at the age of thirty entered the Norman abbey of Bec because of the intellectual renown of its abbot, Lanfranc. Anselm spent most of his life as a monk in the monastery of Bec in Normandy, where he became abbot fifteen years later. At the age of sixty he was forced against his will by the English King William Rufus to become Archbishop of Canterbury. As archbishop he found himself fighting against William Rufus and Henry I over the evils of lay investiture. In fact, he twice went into voluntary exile in protest over the king's exploitation of the church.

Anselm is often called "the Father of Scholasticism" because he introduced a way of doing theology which eventually became traditional in the medieval schools. Anselm went beyond his immediate theological predecessors who simply quoted and organized various authorities on theological topics. He began to use reason in a meditative way in order to understand the truths of the Christian faith. Such a positive attitude toward the use of reason in theology was by no means universal. Peter Damian (1007–1072), a zealous Italian reformer and cardinal, attacked the use of reason/philosophy in a manner reminiscent of Tertullian. According to him, "had philosophy been necessary to save mankind, God would have sent philosophers to convert it, not fishermen."

Anselm took a middle position between extreme rationalism and naive fideism. Against the rationalists, he insisted that theology begins with faith. Against the fideists, he asserted the need for reason to understand, as far as humanly possible, the truths of faith. At the beginning of his proof for the existence of God in his *Proslogion,* he expresses this balanced position with perfect clarity.

> I am not trying, O Lord, to penetrate thy loftiness, for I cannot begin to match my understanding with it, but I desire in some measure to understand thy truth, which my heart believes and loves. For I do not seek to understand in order to believe, but I believe in order to understand. For this too I believe, that "unless I believe, I shall not understand" (Isa 7:9).

Anselm's two most famous works are his *Proslogion,* an attempt to prove the existence of God simply from the idea of God as the most perfect being, and *Cur Deus Homo* ("Why God Became Man"), a proof for the necessity of the incarnation. In both works Anselm uses reason in a kind of meditative way to argue to truths that he and his readers, primarily Christian monks, already accepted by faith. On the other hand, the arguments do not simply rely upon the authority of truths revealed in the scriptures or the church's dogmatic teachings. Rather, they attempt to proceed almost completely by the use of reason.

In an earlier work entitled *Monologion,* Anselm had attempted to establish the existence of God solely from a consideration of truth and goodness as intellectual notions. The argument proved to be long and complicated and failed to satisfy Anselm's desire for a more esthetically simple argument. In his *Proslogion* he presents a much simpler proof based on the idea of God as the perfect being. It has come to be known in the history of philosophy and theology as the "ontological argument."

In the *Proslogion* Anselm tries to discover why Psalm 14 claims that it is the fool who denies the existence of God—that is to say, why that denial is folly. The starting point for Anselm's proof is not some observable fact in the external world, but simply the idea of God as "a being than which none greater can be thought." According to Anselm, even the fool must admit that he has in his intellect the idea of something than which no greater can be conceived. But in order to be the greatest conceivable being, this being cannot exist simply in the mind. To actually exist in reality would be greater. Therefore, to assert that a "being than which none greater can be thought" exists only in the mind is a contradiction, because if it does not exist in reality, it is not the greatest being that can be thought. To avoid such a contradiction the fool must admit that such a being also exists in reality.

Even in his own lifetime, Anselm's argument did not win universal approval. Shortly after its publication, Gaunilo, a monk of Marmoutiers, wrote a *Defense of the Fool* in which he objected to two of Anselm's assumptions. First of all, he argued that the fool who is an atheist does not really have in his mind the idea of a "being above which nothing greater can be conceived." The fool may understand the meaning of the words which come together to form this idea, but he does not, nor does anyone, fully understand the idea of God which is beyond human comprehension. Therefore, one cannot draw conclusions from the rather hazy idea that may be in the fool's mind. Secondly, Gaunilo argued that the existence of something cannot be implied from its conception as an idea, even if that idea may be of a perfect being. For example, one may conceive of a perfect island, but this does not imply that such an island exists in reality.

Anselm replied to Gaunilo's objections in his *Defense Against Gaunilo*. He does not really adequately respond to Gaunilo's first objection, but rather argues that a perfect being can be conceived as is evidenced by Gaunilo's own faith in such a being. This does not meet Gaunilo's objection that the fool can understand which ideas come together to form the idea of a supreme being but he does not believe that they can properly be joined in one. To the second objection Anselm argues that Gaunilo's argument about the perfect island is true about contingent or possible beings. The idea of a perfect being within some species of contingent beings does not imply its existence. But according to Anselm, God as the perfect being does not belong to any genus. Perfection itself cannot be thought of as nonexistent, because it would then be an imperfect perfection which is a contradiction.

Later in the thirteenth century theologians like Bonaventure, who are in the Augustinian and Platonic tradition, will defend the argument because they accept the presuppositions that existence is a perfection, that it can be conceived, and that the structures of reality correspond to the structures of thought. Other thinkers, like Thomas Aquinas who accept the newly discovered Aristotelian philosophy of knowledge and science, will reject Anselm's argument as making an invalid leap from an idea in the mind to its existence in reality. For Aquinas, as an Aristotelian, any proof of the existence of God must begin with observable sense data in the physical world.

In his second great work, *Cur Deus Homo* ("Why God Became Man"), Anselm proposes a new argument for the necessity of the incarnation. Since the time of Origen, theologians had explained the death of Christ as a ransom of human beings from the power of the devil. Anselm proposes to argue for the necessity of the incarnation and the death of Christ through a theology of atonement, which is understood as the satisfaction due to the outraged majesty of God. He begins with the Christian dogmas of the fall, incarnation and Trinity and then reasons to the necessity of the union of the divine and human natures in the one person of the Son in the Trinity.

Anselm's conception of God in this work is heavily influenced by the feudal society in which he lived. God is thought of as a liege lord to whom perfect honor is due. Sin is an infinite offense against that honor for which no human can make adequate atonement. Only God could satisfy this infinite offense, but man is the one who has made the offense. The only way to satisfy both the justice and mercy of God is for the divine Son to take on full humanity and make restitution to God in man's stead.

The translations are by Eugene R. Fairweather in *A Scholastic Miscellany: Anselm to Ockham,* volume X in *The Library of Christian Classics,* 73–75, 117–129, 122–23, 136–37, 138–39, 148, 150–51, 181–82.

PROSLOGION

Chapter I: The awakening of the mind to the contemplation of God

I acknowledge, O Lord, with thanksgiving, that thou hast created this thy image in me, so that, remembering thee, I may think of thee, may love thee. But this image is so effaced and worn away by my faults, it is so obscured by the smoke of my sins, that I cannot do what it was made to do, unless thou renew and reform it. I am not trying, O Lord, to penetrate thy loftiness, for I cannot begin to match my understanding with it, but I desire in some measure to understand thy truth, which my heart believes and loves. For I do not seek to understand in order to believe, but I believe in order to understand. For this too I believe, that "unless I believe, I shall not understand" (Isa 7:9).

Chapter II: God Truly Is

And so, O Lord, since thou givest understanding to faith, give me to understand—as far as thou knowest it to be good for me—that thou dost exist, as we believe, and that thou art what we believe thee to be. Now we believe that thou art a being than which none greater can be thought. Or can it be that there is no such being, since "the fool hath said in his heart, 'There is no God'" (Ps 14:1; 53:1)? But when this same fool hears what I am saying—"A being than which none greater can be thought"—he understands what he hears, and what he understands is in his understanding, even if he does not understand that it exists.

For it is one thing for an object to be in the understanding, and another thing to understand that it exists. When a painter considers beforehand what he is going to paint, he has it in his understanding, but he does not suppose that what he has not yet painted already exists. But when he has painted it, he both has it in his understanding and understands that what he has now produced exists. Even the fool, then, must be convinced that a being than which none greater can be thought exists at least in his understanding, since when he hears this he understands it, and whatever is understood is in the understanding. But clearly that than which a greater cannot be thought cannot exist in the understanding alone. For if it is actually in the understanding alone, it can be thought of as existing also in reality, and this is greater. Therefore, if that than which a greater cannot be thought is in the understanding alone, this same thing than which a greater cannot be thought is that than which a greater can be thought. But obviously this is impossible. Without doubt, therefore, there exists, both in the understanding and in reality, something than which a greater cannot be thought.

CUR DEUS HOMO

BK 1,11
THE MEANING OF SIN, AND OF
SATISFACTION FOR SIN

Anselm. We are to ask, then, on what ground God forgives men their sins. In order to do this more clearly, let us first see what it means to sin and to make satisfaction for sin. *Bosco.* It is for you to explain, and for me to listen.

A. If an angel or a man always rendered to God what is due to him, he would never sin.

B. I cannot contradict you.

A. Thus to sin is the same thing as not to render his due to God.

B. What is the debt which we owe to God?

A. Every inclination of the rational creature ought to be subject to the will of God.

B. Nothing could be truer.

A. This is the debt which angels and men owe to God. No one who pays it sins; everyone who does not pay it sins. This is the justice or rectitude of the will which makes men just or upright in heart, that is in will. This is the sole and entire honor which we owe to God, and God requires from us. For only such a will does works pleasing to God, when it is able to act; and when it cannot act, it pleases by itself alone, since apart from it no work is pleasing. One who does not render this honor to God takes away from God what belongs to him, and dishonors God, and to do this is to sin. Moreover, as long as he does not repay what he has stolen, he remains at fault. And it is not enough merely to return what was taken away; in view of the insult committed, he must give back more than he took away. For it is not enough for someone who has injured another's health to restore his health without making some recompense for the pain and injury suffered, and, similarly, it is not enough for someone who violates another's honor to restore the honor, unless he makes

some kind of restitution that will please him who was dishonored, according to the extent of the injury and dishonor. We should also note that, when someone pays back what he unjustly took away, he ought to give something that could not be required of him if he had not stolen another's property. So, then, everyone who sins must repay to God the honor that he has taken away, and this is the satisfaction that every sinner ought to make to God.

B. Although you frighten me a little, I have nothing to say against any of these statements, since we promised to follow reason.

BK 1,12
WHETHER IT WOULD BE FITTING FOR GOD TO
FORGIVE SINS BY MERCY ALONE, WITHOUT
ANY PAYMENT OF MAN'S DEBT

A. Let us go back and see whether it is fitting for God to remit sins by mercy alone, without any payment for the honor taken away from him.

B. I do not see why it is not fitting.

A. To remit sin in this way is the same thing as not to punish it. And since to deal rightly with sin without satisfaction is the same thing as to punish it, if it is not punished it is remitted irregularly.

BK 1,13
NOTHING IS LESS TOLERABLE IN THE ORDER
OF THINGS THAN FOR THE CREATURE TO
TAKE AWAY THE HONOR DUE TO THE CRE-
ATOR AND NOT REPAY WHAT HE TAKES AWAY

A. Again, if nothing is greater or better than God, then the highest justice, which is none other than God himself, maintains nothing more justly than his honor, in the ordering of things.

B. Nothing can be plainer than this.

A. Then God maintains nothing more justly than the honor of his dignity.

B. I must grant this.

A. Does it seem to you that he preserves it wholly if he permits it to be taken away from him, and neither receives recompense nor punishes him who took it away?

B. I dare not say so.

A. Therefore, either the honor that was taken away must be repaid or punishment must follow. Otherwise, God will be either unjust to himself or powerless to accomplish either; but it is impious even to imagine this.

BK 1,14
HOW GOD IS HONORED IN THE PUNISHMENT OF THE SINNER

B. . . . But I want to hear from you whether the punishment of the sinner brings honor to God, and what sort of honor this is. For when the sinner does not repay what he took away, but is punished, if the punishment of the sinner is not to the honor of God, then God loses his honor and does not regain it. . . .

A. It is impossible for God to lose his honor. For if a sinner does not freely pay what he owes, God takes it from him against his will.

BK 1,20
THERE MUST BE SATISFACTION ACCORDING TO THE MEASURE OF SIN AND MAN CANNOT MAKE IT BY HIMSELF

A. Tell me, then, what will you pay to God for your sin?

B. Repentance, a contrite and humble heart, fastings and all sorts of bodily labors, mercy in giving and forgiving, and obedience.

A. In all this what do you give to God?

B. Do I not honor God . . . ?

A. When you pay what you owe to God, even if you have not sinned, you must not count this as part of the debt you owe for sin. . . . As for obedience, what do you give God that you do not owe him, to whose command you owe all that you are and have and can do?

B. I do not dare now to say that in all these things I give God anything that I do not owe.

A. What, then, will you pay to God for your sin?

B. If I owe him myself and all that I can do, even when I do not sin, lest I should sin, I have nothing to repay him for sin.

BK 1,21
WHAT A GREAT WEIGHT SIN IS

A. You have not yet considered what a heavy weight sin is.

B. Show me now.

A. Picture yourself in God's presence. Someone says to you, "Look this way," but God, on the contrary, says, "I wish you on no account to look." Now ask yourself, in your own heart, what there is among all the things that exist for whose sake you ought to cast that glance in opposition to God's will. . . .

A. . . . But consider also what you could pay for this sin, if you did happen to cast that glance against God's will. . . .

A. We sin thus gravely, every time we knowingly do even the slightest thing against God's will, because we are always in his sight, and he is always commanding us not to sin. . . .

A. It is clear that God requires satisfaction according to the greatness of the sin.

B. I cannot deny it.

A. Therefore, you do not make satisfaction unless you repay something greater than that for the sake of which you were obliged not to commit the sin.

B. I see that reason requires this, and at the same time it is quite impossible.

BK 2,4
GOD WILL COMPLETE WHAT HE BEGAN WITH HUMAN NATURE

A. Then it is necessary for him to complete what he began with human nature. But, as we have said, this can be done only by means of a complete satisfaction for sin, which no sinner can make.

BK 2,6
ONLY A GOD-MAN CAN MAKE THE SATISFACTION BY WHICH MAN IS SAVED

A. But this cannot be done unless there is someone to pay to God for human sin something greater than everything that exists, except God.

B. So it is agreed.

A. If he is to give something of his own to God, which surpasses everything that is beneath God, it is also necessary for him to be greater than everything that is not God.

B. I cannot deny it.

A. But there is nothing above everything that is not God, save God himself.

B. That is true.

A. Then no one but God can make this satisfaction.

B. That follows.

A. But no one ought to make it except man; otherwise man does not make satisfaction.

B. Nothing seems more just.

A. If then, as is certain, that celestial city must be completed from among men, and this cannot happen unless the aforesaid satisfaction is made, while no one save God can make it and no one save man ought to make it, it is necessary for a God-Man to make it.

BK 2, 20
HOW GREAT AND HOW JUST GOD'S MERCY IS!

A. When we were considering God's justice and man's sin, God's mercy seemed to you to vanish. But we have found how great it really is, and how it is in such harmony with his justice that it cannot be conceived to be greater or more just. For, indeed, what greater mercy could be imagined, than for God the Father to say to the sinner, condemned to eternal torments, and without any power of redeeming himself from them, "Receive my only-begotten Son, and give him for yourself," and for the Son himself to say, "Take me, and redeem yourself"? For they as much as say this when they call us and draw us to the Christian faith. And what could be more just, than for Him to whom the price more valuable than every debt is paid to forgive every debt (if the price is given with the right disposition)?

PETER ABELARD

The leading philosopher and theologian of the first half of the twelfth century was Peter Abelard (1079–1142 C.E.). His tumultuous life, partially recounted in his own short autobiography (*History of My Calamities*) is a brilliant illustration of the new movements that were sweeping twelfth-century Europe: the literature of romantic love, the growth of towns and universities, new rational methods in philosophy and theology, and heated controversy over dogmatic issues in the church.

Abelard is remembered today, as he has been in every generation since his own, for his famous love affair with Heloise. As a brilliant young scholar at the Cathedral of Notre Dame in Paris, Abelard was commissioned by Canon Fulbert to tutor Heloise, his attractive and intelligent young niece. Because of Abelard's reputation for continence, Fulbert naively allowed Abelard to conduct their lessons in private. In his *History* Abelard frankly admits that he was "wholly inflamed with love for the girl," and their lessons soon were given over to passionate love making.

So, under the pretext of discipline, we abandoned ourselves utterly to love, and those secret retreats which love demands, the study of our texts afforded us. And so, our books lying open before us, more words of love rose to our lips than of literature, kisses were more frequent than speech. Oftener went our hands to each other's bosom than to the pages; love turned our eyes more frequently to itself than it directed them to the study of texts.

In due course Heloise became pregnant and bore their son Astrolabe. Against Heloise's wishes, they were married secretly. She considered the marriage a detriment to Abelard's academic career because in the Middle Ages the life of scholarship was reserved almost completely to celibate clergy who studied at cathedral or monastic schools. Although Fulbert attended the wedding and promised to keep the marriage secret, eventually he began to divulge it. When Heloise publicly denied her uncle's story, he became angry and began to badger her to make the marriage public. At this point, Abelard arranged for Heloise to enter an abbey of nuns near Paris called Argenteuil, the place where she was educated as a child. Thinking that Abelard was trying to rid himself of Heloise, Fulbert had a band of thugs set upon Abelard in his bed and castrate him. As Abelard laconically notes in the *History,*

On a certain night while I slumbered and slept in an inner room of my lodging, . . . they punished me with a most cruel and shameful vengeance, . . . amputating . . . those parts of my body wherewith I had committed that of which they complained.

Eventually, Heloise was forced to leave the convent at Argenteuil and settle at the Paraclete, a small house of prayer and study Abelard had established outside Paris. There Heloise, still deeply in love with Abelard, lived as the abbess of a convent of nuns until her death. In the meantime, Abelard's "calamities" continued as he moved from monastery to monastery, harried on the one hand by small-minded and often irregular monks, and on the other by jealous theologians and bishops who sought to have his theological works condemned as heretical. Within their own life-times the story of their love was immortalized in Abelard's own songs, and even today one cannot hear about their ill-fated lives and read their letters without being moved. As Heloise implies in her greeting to Abelard in one of her letters, their relationship passed through every conceivable stage of affection and trust.

To her master, nay father, to her husband, nay brother; his handmaid, nay daughter, his spouse, nay sister to Abelard, Heloise.

Abelard's career and method of doing philosophy and theology make an interesting contrast to his older contemporary, Anselm of Canterbury (1033–1109 C.E.). Anselm had gone to the Benedictine monastery to find both intellectual and spiritual sustenance. Like so many monks before him, he lived a vow of stability and would have gladly spent all of his days as a monk and abbot at the Abbey of Bec if he had not been forced to become the Archbishop of Canterbury. Abelard, on the other hand, was an itinerant scholar who early in his career moved from school to school in search of knowledge and intellectual combat, or dialectic. As he tells us in his *History of My Calamities*:

> I finally relinquished the court of Mars [the life of a knight] that I might be educated in the lap of Minerva [the goddess of Wisdom]. And in as much as I preferred the equipment of dialectic to all the teachings of philosophy, I exchanged those weapons for these and to the trophies of war preferred the conflicts of discussion. Thereafter, perambulating divers provinces in search of discussion, wherever I heard the study of this art to flourish, I became an emulator of the Peripatetics.

Abelard was on the crest of the wave of the future, for the various cathedral schools of France were in the process of becoming the universities which would dominate intellectual life in the thirteenth century. Because of his combative personality and considerable intelligence, Abelard found himself embroiled in intellectual conflicts throughout his life. On the important philosophical question of the status of universals, concepts like "man" which apply to many individuals within a species, Abelard presumed to differ with two of his philosophical mentors. William of Champeaux (1070–1121 C.E.), who taught at Paris and later became bishop of Chalons, was what scholars call an "exaggerated realist." He argued that universals are real and that they exist before particular things and are totally present in each of them. Roscelin (1050–1125 C.E.), on the other hand, was a nominalist who said that only individual things exist. Universals are not real; they are simply "names" or "the emission—or wind—of the voice." Logic is merely a discussion about words and has no connection to the things in reality. Abelard took an intermediate position between his two teachers and thereby earned the wrath of both. His position has been called "moderate realism" or "conceptualism." He disagrees with William of Champeaux in according independent status to the universals, but he does not go as far as Roscelin in reducing the universals to mere names. For Abelard the universals are names, but meaningful names. They are not independent "things"—that is, they do subsist in themselves. But they are real in that they exist in things, as form exists in matter. One can abstract the form from the matter, but the form is never actually given without matter. Similarly, universals can be abstracted from individuals—and one must do so in order to think—but they are never given apart from concrete particular things. Abelard's position on the universals did not win universal acceptance, but it was followed by those scholars who were heavily influenced by the philosophy of Aristotle in the universities of the thirteenth century, especially Thomas Aquinas.

Abelard's contributions to theological method were no less original, and here too he found himself in conflict with one of his teachers, Anselm of Laon. Abelard's immediate predecessors tended to do theology by simply quoting revered authorities, like scripture or Augustine, on a particular theological topic. Even Anselm, for all his daring use of reason, began by accepting the truths of the Christian faith and tried to further understand them as being rationally necessary. Abelard went in a completely new methodological direction. In an early work entitled *Sic et No*n (Yes and No) Abelard confronted his students with contradictory opinions from the authorities ("the Fathers") on one hundred and fifty-six theological questions. Abelard did not presume to tell his students "what" they were to think on these important questions; rather he gave them a method of "how" to think about the questions raised by his collection.

He introduced them to the problems of textual criticism: determining authorship, textual corruption, and the possibility of errors by copyists. By pointing to Augustine's *Retractiones,* Abelard alerted his students to the fact that thinkers change their minds on issues in the course of their careers. He also noted it was important to distinguish between an author's own opinion and that of a source he may be quoting.

In the interpretation of matters of canon law, Abelard explained that it is important to discover "the underlying purpose of the opinion, whether it is meant to grant an indulgence or exhort to some perfection." Distinctions must be made between definitive judgments which have "general application" and those which only apply "to a particular case." The "when" and the "why" of a law must be considered because "what is allowed at one time is often forbidden at another, and what is often laid down as the strict letter of the law may be sometimes moderated by a dispensation."

In reading texts, students must be aware of the problem of the deceptive character of sense appearances which may lead "the Fathers" to state some matters as "opinion" rather than truth. If they learn to distinguish the "different senses" in which a particular word is used by different authors, many apparent contradictions may also be alleviated. After all of these ways of reconciling contradictions have been used, then the rival authorities must be compared and the view that has the heaviest backing be adopted.

Abelard's purpose in collecting these divergent opinions is quite different from Anselm's motto of "faith seeking understanding." Rather than beginning with faith, Abelard seeks to create doubt and thereby stimulate intellectual investigation.

> . . . I hope to provoke young readers to push themselves to the limit in the search for truth, so that their wits may be sharpened by their investigation. It is by doubting that we come to investigate, and by investigating that we recognize the truth.

Abelard's goal of reconciling conflicting authorities will become central to the so-called scholastic method of reasoning and argumentation in the great "schools" or universities of the High Middle Ages.

In his ethical treatise entitled *Know Thyself,* Abelard also breaks new ground by making the intention with which an act is performed the determinative factor in assigning guilt or merit. Abelard does not deny that there are good and evil actions, but he wants to insist that it is intention that determines guilt or merit. In this he claims to be following Augustine who "reduces every sin or command to terms of charity and covetousness, and not to works," and Paul, who asserts: "All the law is contained in one word: thou shalt love they neighbor as thyself" (Rom 13:8,10), and again, "Love is the fulfilling of the law."

As an illustration of his theory Abelard considers the intentions with which God the

Father, the Lord Jesus Christ, and Judas do "the self-same action," the handing over of Jesus to death. For God the Father and the Son the delivering up of the Son was an act of love by which God redeemed the world. This will become more evident in our discussion of Abelard's theology of redemption or atonement. But for Judas the same act was sinful because he intended to betray his master.

In considering the sinfulness of an action, Abelard carefully distinguishes four things: (1) "imperfection of soul" which we inherit from Adam and which makes us liable to sin; (2) "sin itself, which . . . is consent to evil or contempt of God"; (3) "the will or desire of evil"; and (4) "the evil deed." By using the example of the devil's temptation of Eve, he argues that sin proceeds through three stages: suggestion, delight and consent.

> The devil's persuasion comes *first* promising from the taste of the forbidden fruit immortality. Delight follows. When the woman sees the beautiful tree, and perceives that the fruit is good, her appetite is whetted by the anticipated pleasure of tasting. This desire she ought to have repressed, so as to obey God's command. But in consenting to it, she was drawn *secondly* into sin. By penitence she should have put right this fault, and obtained pardon. Instead, she *thirdly* consummated the sin by the deed. Eve thus passed through the three stages to the commission of sin.

Notice that Abelard, on the one hand, does not make "delight" a part of the sin. He later argues that things like "carnal suggestion" arise naturally and are not sinful. Only willful consent makes a sin. Also, Abelard separates the consent to evil from the act of sin. Once consent has occurred, sin has been committed and penitence is called for. The actual doing of the deed is simply the consummation of the sin.

This distinction is evident in Heloise's evaluation of her own relationship with Abelard. In a letter to him which she wrote after reading his *History of My Calamities*, Heloise describes her actions in their love affair in the following manner.

> And, though exceeding guilty, I am, as thou knowest, exceeding innocent. For it is not the *deed* but the *intention* that makes the crime. It is not what is done but the spirit in which it is done that equity considers. And in what state of mind I have ever been towards thee, only thou, who hast knowledge of it, canst judge.

(Translated by C.K. Scott Moncrieff, *The Letters of Abelard and Heloise* [New York: Cooper Square Publishers Inc., 1974] 59. She goes on to question Abelard's motives in the same affair because his subsequent neglect of her in not writing or visiting seems to imply that he only acted out of lust, and now that he has lost the capacity to physically express his love, it has disappeared.

> Tell me one thing only, if thou canst, why, after our conversion, which thou alone didst decree, I am fallen into such neglect and oblivion with thee that I am neither refreshed by thy speech and presence nor comforted by a letter in thine absence. Tell me, one thing only,

if thou canst, or let me tell thee what I feel, nay what all suspect. Concupiscence joined thee to me rather than affection, the ardour of desire rather than love. When therefore what thou desiredst ceased, all that thou hadst exhibited at the same time failed. . . . (*The Letters of Abelard and Heloise,* 59)

Abelard's teaching on the redemptive work of Christ also makes an interesting contrast to Anselm's and might demonstrate that he was more moved by his experience of Heloise's love than she suspects in the above letter. He rejects both the traditional theory that Christ came to pay a debt to the devil and Anselm's view in *Cur Deus Homo* that Christ came to atone for the offended honor of God. Abelard points out that both theories attribute inferior, not to say sadistic, motives to God. He notes that Christ forgave sins long before his passion, as in the cases of Mary Magdalene and the paralytic to whom he said, "Son, thy sins are forgiven thee." There was no necessity that the Son of God should endure intolerable anguish, when God's compassion could forgive sins simply by the word of the Son. It is both cruel and unjust to demand the blood of the innocent Jesus in some kind of bargain with the devil or to satisfy God's own sense of justice. Besides the very remedy, the cruel death of the Son is clearly a much more heinous sin than the original sin of tasting a single apple. What will expiate the death of Christ at the hands of sinful men?

Rather than approaching the redemptive act of Christ through a kind of feudal theology of offended honor, Abelard considers it from the perspective of God's love for fallen humanity and the goal of rekindling love within his fallen creatures.

Now it seems to us that we have been justified by the blood of Christ and reconciled to God in this way: through this unique act of grace manifested to us—in that his Son has taken upon himself our nature and persevered therein in teaching us by word and example even unto death—he has more fully bound us to himself by love; with the result that our hearts should be enkindled by such a gift of divine grace, and true charity should not shrink from enduring anything for him (*Commentary on Romans*).

This same theology of redemption is evident in the selection from the hymn for the nuns of the Paraclete where Heloise was abbess. In his hymn for Good Friday Abelard prays: "Let our hearts suffer for thy passion, Lord,/ That very suffering may thy mercy win." And later, he petitions: "So may our hearts share in Thine anguish, Lord, / That they may sharers of thy glory be." The purpose of Jesus' suffering is to enkindle in our hearts compassion for him and thereby to win his mercy.

Our final selection is from a letter from Abelard to Heloise in which he is responding to her request to write a rule for her nuns. In it Abelard shows a very modern sensitivity to the heroic role of the women in the gospel story, in contrast to the cowardly portrait of the male disciples. The twelfth century is often cited as a time when a new awareness of feminine virtues entered European Christian thought. The usual examples cited are the widespread devotion to Mary, found for example in the sermons of St. Bernard and in the many cathedrals built in honor of Notre Dame (Our Lady), but this is nowhere more evident than in Abelard's discussion of the role of women in the gospel.

In his treatment of the stories of Jesus' anointing by women (see Lk 7:36–50; Matt 26:6–13; Mk 14:3–9; Jn 12:1–8), Abelard notes in connection with the sinful woman's anointing of Jesus in Luke 7:36–50 that her dignity is superior to that of bishops who, "dressed in splendid and golden vestments" take "glory" in their power to anoint "earthly kings" and "mortal priests."

> The humble woman, with no change of garment, with no prepared rite, with the Apostles themselves even enangered, performs these sacraments before Christ, not by the office of prelation but by the zeal of devotion. He also elaborates on Mary Magdalene's and the other women's fidelity to Jesus in his passion and death. For these (the women), when the Prince of the Apostles himself denied Him, and when the Apostle beloved of the Lord fled, and the rest were scattered, stayed fearless, nor could any fear or any desperation part them from Christ, either in His Passion or in His Death.

Finally, as Abelard notes, this fidelity was rewarded by giving the women the privilege of being the first witnesses of Jesus' resurrection and giving them the task of being the apostles to the apostles.

> The Lord Himself also, appearing first to Mary Magdalene, says to her: "Go to my brethren, and say unto them, I ascend unto my father." From which we gather that these holy women were constituted as it were female Apostles over the Apostles. Since sent to the Apostles either by the Lord or by angels they announced that great joy of the Resurrection, for which all were waiting, that by them the Apostles might first learn what presently they were to preach to the whole world.

The translation of *The Exposition of the Epistle to the Romans* is by Gerald E. Moffatt (Volume X: The Library of Christian Classics) 282–284. The translation of the "Hymn for Good Friday: the Third Nocturn" is by Helen Waddell in *Mediaeval Latin Lyrics* (New York: Norton, 1977) 167. The translation for "Touching the Origin of Nuns" is by C.K. Scott Moncrieff in *The Letters of Abelard and Heloise* (New York: Cooper Square Publishers, 1974) 131–139.

THE EXPOSITION OF THE EPISTLE TO THE ROMANS

So what compulsion, or reason, or need was there—seeing that by its very appearing alone the divine pity could deliver man from Satan—what need was there, I say, that the Son of God, for our redemption, should take upon him our flesh and endure such numer-ous fastings, insults, scourgings and spittings, and finally that most bitter and disgraceful death upon the cross, enduring even the cross of punishment with the wicked? In what way does the apostle declare that we are justified or reconciled to God through the death of his Son (Rom 5:10), when God ought to have been the more angered against man, inasmuch as men acted more criminally by crucifying his Son than they ever did by transgressing his first command in paradise through the tasting of a single apple? For the more men's sins were multiplied, the more just it would have been for God to be angry with men. And if that sin of Adam was so great it could be expiated only by the death of Christ, what expiation will avail for that act of murder committed against Christ, and for the many great crimes committed against him or his followers? How did the death of his innocent Son so please God the Father that through it he should be reconciled to us—to us who by our sinful acts have done the very things for which our innocent Lord was put to death? Had not this very great sin been committed, could he not have pardoned the former much lighter sin? Had not evil deeds been multiplied, could he not have done such a good thing for man?

In what manner have we been made more righteous through the death of the Son of God than we were before, so that we ought to be delivered from punishment? And to whom was the price of blood paid for our redemption but to him in whose power we were—that is, to God himself, who (as we have said) handed us over to his torturer? For it is not the torturers by the masters of those who are held captive who arrange or receive such ransoms. Again, how did he release these captives for a price if he himself exacted or settled the price for release of the same? Indeed, how cruel and wicked it seems that anyone should demand the blood of an innocent person as the price for anything, or that it should in any way please him that an innocent man should be slain—still less that God should consider the death of his Son so agreeable that by it he should be reconciled to the whole world!

These, and like queries, appear to us to pose a considerable problem concerning our redemption or justification through the death of our Lord Jesus Christ.

Now it seems to us that we have been justified by the blood of Christ and reconciled to God in this way; through this unique act of grace manifest to us—in that his Son has taken upon himself our nature and preserved therein in teaching us by word and example even unto death—he has more fully bound us to himself by love; with the result that our hearts should be enkindled by such a gift of divine grace, and true charity should not now shrink from enduring anything for him.

And we do not doubt that the ancient Fathers, waiting in faith for this same gift, were aroused to very great love of God in the same way as men of this dispensation of grace, since it is written: "And they that went before and they that followed cried, saying: 'Hosanna to the Son of David,'" (Mk 11:9), etc. Yet everyone becomes more righteous—by which we mean a greater lover of the Lord—after the Passion of Christ than before, since a realized gift inspires greater love than one which is only hoped for. Where, our redemption through Christ's suffering is that deeper affection (*dilectio*) in us which not only frees us from slavery to sin, but also wins for us the true liberty of sons of God (Rom 8:21), so that we do all things out of love rather than fear—love to him who has shown us such grace that no greater can be found, as he himself asserts, saying, "Greater love than this no man hath, that a man lay down his life for his friends" (Jn 15:13). Of this love the Lord says elsewhere, "I am come to cast fire on the earth, and what will I, but that it blaze forth?" So does he bear witness that he came for the express purpose of spreading this true liberty of love amongst men.

GOOD FRIDAY: THE THIRD NOCTURN

Alone to sacrifice Thou goest, Lord,
Giving Thyself to death whom Thou wilt slay.
For us Thy wretched folk is any word,

Whose sins have brought Thee to this agony?
For they are ours, Lord, our deeds, our deeds.
Why must Thou suffer torture for our sin?
Let our hearts suffer for Thy passion, Lord,
That very suffering may Thy mercy win.
This is that night of tears, the three days'
    space,
    Sorrow abiding of the eventide,
Until the day break with the risen Christ,
    And hearts that sorrowed shall be
      satisfied.
So may our hearts share in Thine anguish,
    Lord,
    That they may sharers of Thy glory be:
Heavy with weeping may the three days pass,
    To win the laughter of Thine Easter Day.

TOUCHING THE ORIGIN OF NUNS

And so Christ, the end of justice, and the consummation of all good, coming in the fullness of time that He might make perfect the good things that had been begun, or reveal things hidden; as He had come to call either sex and to redeem them, so thought fit to unite both sexes in the true monkhood of His congregation, that thereafter authority for this profession might be given both to men and to women, and the perfect way of life might be laid before all, which they should imitate. For there with His Apostles and the rest of the disciples we read of an assembly of holy women with His Mother: who renouncing the world and abandoning all possessions, that they might possess only Christ, as it is written: "The Lord is the portion of mine inheritance," devoutly performed that office whereby all, according to the rule given by the Lord, converted from the world are initiated into the community of this life: "Whosoever he be of you that forsaketh not all that he hath, he cannot be my disciple."

And how devoutly these most holy women and true nuns followed Christ, and what thanks and honour both Christ Himself and afterwards the Apostles paid to their devotion the Sacred Scriptures diligently record. We read in the Gospel that a Pharisee murmured who had taken the Lord into his house, and was rebuked by Him, and that the service of the woman which was a sinner was set far above his hospitality. We read also that when Lazarus, after he was restored to life, sat down with the rest, his sister Martha alone served the tables, and Mary poured a pound of precious ointment over the Lord's feet, and wiped them with her hair, and that the house was filled with the odor of this precious ointment, and by the price thereof, because it seemed to be so vainly consumed, Judas was led to concupiscence, and the disciples were indignant. And so Martha being busy with food, Mary dispensed the ointment; and Him whom the one inwardly restored the other in His weariness refreshed outwardly. Nor does the text of the Gospel record that any but women ministered to the Lord; which moreover had dedicated their own possessions to His daily nourishment, and chiefly procured for Him the necessities of this life. He Himself to the disciples at table, He Himself in the washing of feet showed Himself a most humble servant. But from none of the disciples, nor indeed from any man do we learn that He accepted this service; but that women alone, as we have said, performed the ministry of these or the other services of humanity. And as in one thing Martha, so we know that in the other Mary rendered service. Who indeed in the exhibition of this was much more devout as she had been aforetime more sinful. The Lord with water poured into a basin performed the office of ablution. But she exhibited it to Him with the intimate tears of compunction, not with water from without. The feet of the disciples, when they were washed, the Lord dried with a linen towel. She, in place of linen, used her hair. The application of ointment she added over and above, which we nowhere read that the Lord employed.

And who does not know that a woman so far presumed upon His favor that she anointed His head also with ointment? Which ointment indeed was not poured forth from the alabaster box but is said to have been spilled when the alabaster was broken, that the vehement desire of extreme devotion might be expressed, which considered that this vessel should be kept for no further use which she had employed in such a service. Wherein also she displays by her very deed that effect of unction which aforetime Daniel had prophesied that it should come to pass, to wit after the Most Holy had been anointed. For behold, a woman anoints the Most Holy, and by her deed proclaims Him at once to be Him in Whom she believes, and Whom the Prophet had foretold in words. What, I ask, is this bounty of the Lord, or what the dignity of women, that He should allow both His head and His feet to be anointed by women only? What, I demand, is this prerogative of the weaker sex that the supreme Christ, anointed from His very conception with all the unguents of the Holy Spirit, a woman also should anoint and, as though with bodily sacraments consecrating Him to be King and priest, make Him in body the Christ, that is to say the anointed? . . .

We know that first of all a stone was anointed by the Patriarch Jacob as a type of the Lord. And afterwards it was permitted to men only to celebrate the anointing of priest or kings, or whatsoever sacraments of unction. Albeit at times women may presume to baptize. Aforetime the Patriarch sanctified a stone for the temple, now also the pontiff sanctifies the altar with oil. And so men imprint the sacraments by figures. But the woman wrought in very truth, as the Word Himself attesteth, saying: "She hath wrought a good work on men." Christ Himself by a woman, Christians by men are anointed. To wit, the Head by a woman, the members by men. And the woman is recorded to have well poured forth the ointment, not dropped it on his head. According to what the bride sings of Him in the Canticles, saying: "Thy name is ointment poured forth." The abundance also of that ointment, by the fact that it ran down from the head to the hem of the garment, the Psalmist mystically prefigures, saying: "It is like the precious ointment upon the head, that ran down upon the beard, even Aaron's beard; that went down to the skirts of his garments." A threefold unction, as Saint Jerome also comments on the twenty-fifth Psalm, we read that David received, and so Christ or the Christians. For the feet of the Lord, or His head, received the unction of a woman. But after He was dead Joseph of Arimathea and Nicodemus, as John relates, buried Him with spices. Christians also are sanctified by a threefold unction: whereof one is given in baptism, one in confirmation, and the third is the anointing of the sick. Perpend therefore the dignity of woman, from whom when He was alive Christ, being twice anointed, to wit both on the head and on the feet, received the sacraments of Kingship and Priesthood. But the ointment of myrrh and aloes which is used to preserve the bodies of the dead, prefigured the future incorruptibility of the Lord's Body, which also the elect shall enjoy in the resurrection. But the former anointings by the woman show forth His special dignity both as King and as Priest. The anointing of the head the higher, that of the feet the lower dignity. And lo, he receives the sacrament of Kingship also from a woman, Who nevertheless rejected the Kingdom that was offered to Him by men, and fled from those who would have taken Him by force to make Him a King. Of the heavenly, not the earthly King the woman performs the sacrament; of Him, I say, who touching Himself, said afterwards: "My kingdom is not of this world."

Bishops glory when with the applause of

the populace they anoint earthly kings, when they consecrate mortal priests, adorned with splendid and golden vestments. And often they bless those whom the Lord curses. The humble woman, with no change of garment, with no prepared rite, with the Apostles themselves even endangered, performs these sacraments before Christ, not by the office of prelation but by the zeal of devotion. O great constancy of faith, O inestimable ardor of charity, which believeth all things, hopeth all things, endureth all things. The Pharisee murmurs when by the woman which was a sinner the feet of the Lord are anointed; the Apostles are openly indignant, because the woman has presumed also to touch His head. The faith of the woman remains on each occasion unmoved, trusting in the bounty of the Lord, nor does the advocacy of the Lord's commendation fail her on either. Whose ointment indeed, how acceptable, how pleasing the Lord found it He Himself professes when, demanding that it be kept for Him, He says to the indignant Judas: "Let her alone; against the day of my burial she has done this." As who should say: Turn not away this her service from the living, lest thou take from the dead the exhibition of her devotion in this matter. One thing certain is, that holy women prepared spices for the Lord's burial. Which this woman would then have been less concerned to do, had she before been put to shame by rejection. He, however, while the disciples were indignant at such presumption on the part of the woman, and, as Mark records, murmured against her, after He had turned away their wrath by soft answers, so greatly extolled this offering that He wished it to be inserted in the Gospel, that it might be preached with the Gospel wheresoever that should be preached for a memorial, to wit, and in praise of the woman who had done this thing, in doing which she was charged with no mean presumption. And nowhere do we read of the services of any other person whatsoev-

er, that such commendation was given by the Lord or such sanction. Who also, preferring the poor widow's charity to all the offerings of the Temple, diligently shows how acceptable to Him is the devotion of women. Peter indeed made bold to boast that he and his fellow Apostles had left all things for Christ. And Zacchaeus, having received the Lord at His coming for which he longed, gave the half of his goods to the poor, and if he had taken anything falsely restored it fourfold. And many others incurred greater expense in Christ, or for Christ, or brought things far more precious to sacrifice to God, or left them.

And yet they did not so win the praise of the Lord's commendation as did the women. Whose devotion, how great it had ever been towards Him the end of the Lord's life plainly shows. For these, when the Prince of the Apostles himself denied Him, and when the Apostle beloved of the Lord fled, and the rest scattered, stayed fearless, nor could any fear or any desperation part them from Christ, either in His Passion or in His death. So that to them specially that saying of the Apostle may seem to apply: "Who shall separate us from the love of Christ? Shall tribulation or distress?" Wherefore Matthew, when he had related of himself and of the rest: "Then all the disciples forsook him, and fled," added thereto the perseverance of the women, who remained by the Crucified as long as it was permitted them. "And many women," he says, "were there beholding afar off, which followed Jesus from Galilee, ministering unto him." Whom moreover remaining unmoved by His sepulcher the same Evangelist diligently describes, saying: "And there was Mary Magdalene, and the other Mary, sitting over against the sepulcher." Which women Saint Mark also commemorating, says: "There were also women looking on afar off: among whom was Mary Magdalene, and Mary the mother of James the less and of Joses, and Salome (who also, when he was in Galilee, followed him, and ministered unto him;) and many other women which came up with him into Jerusalem." John relates that he himself stood by the Cross, and remained with the Crucified, who before had fled; but he sets first the perseverance of the women, as though by their example he had been animated and called back: "Now there stood by the cross of Jesus his mother, and his mother's sister, Mary the wife of Cleophas, and Mary Magdalene. When Jesus therefore saw his mother, and the disciple standing by," and so forth. . . .

And by that same solicitude which they had felt over His Passion and Death, they first were rejoiced by His Resurrection into life. For when, according to John, Joseph of Arimathea and Nicodemus, winding the Lord's Body in linen clothes, with spices, buried Him, Mark relates, touching the zeal of these women, that Mary Magdalene, and Mary the mother of Joses beheld where he was laid. Of them also Luke makes record, saying: "And the women also which came with him from Galilee, followed after, and behold the sepulcher, and how his body was laid. And they returned, and prepared spices and ointments." Evidently regarding the spices of Nicodemus as insufficient, unless they added their own. And on the Sabbath day indeed they rested, according to the commandment. But (says Mark) when the Sabbath was past, Mary Magdalene, and Mary the mother of James, and Salome, very early in the morning, on the day of the Resurrection itself, came unto the sepulcher at the rising of the sun. Now, as we have shown their devotion, let us proceed to show what honour they merited. First of all by an angelic vision they were comforted concerning the Lord's Resurrection, now accomplished, then the Lord Himself they first saw and touched. And first indeed Mary Magdalene, who was more fervent than the rest. Afterwards she, and with her the others, of whom it is written that after the angelic vision, "they departed from the sepulcher, and did run to bring his disciples word. And behold, Jesus met them, saying, 'All hail'! And they came and held him by the feet, and worshipped him. Then said Jesus unto them, 'Go tell my brethren that they go into Galilee, and there shall they see me.'" Whereof Luke also treating says: "It was Mary Magdalene, and Joanna, and Mary the mother of James, and other women that were with them, which told these things unto the apostles."

That these also were first sent by the angel to tell the news to His disciples Mark hides not, where it is written that the angel speaking to the women said: "He is risen; he is not here. But go your way, tell his disciples and Peter that he goeth before you into Galilee." The Lord Himself also, appearing first to Mary Magdalene, says to her: "Go to my brethren, and say unto them, I ascend unto my father." From which we gather that these holy women were constituted as it were female Apostles over the Apostles. Since sent to the Apostles either by the Lord or by angels they announced that great joy of the Resurrection, for which all were waiting, that by them the Apostles might first learn what presently they were to preach to the whole world. Whom also after the Resurrection, the Lord meeting them, the Evangelist records to have been greeted by Him, that both by His meeting and by His greeting them He might show how solicitous and how grateful He was to them. For we do not read of His having saluted others with that special form of words, to wit, "All hail;" nay, we read rather that He had already forbidden the Apostles that salutation, when He said to them: "Salute no man by the way." As though He would reserve the privilege thenceforward for devout women, which in His Own Person He showed to them when He had already acquired the glory of immortality.

BERNARD OF CLAIRVAUX

The figure who is usually contrasted with Abelard is Bernard of Clairvaux (1091–1154 C.E.), the great Cistercian mystic who so dominated the first half of the twelfth century that it is sometimes called "the Age of Bernard." Although Bernard was only an abbot in the strict new Cistercian Order, he exercised an unprecedented spirituality in the church of his age solely by the power of his personality. His powerful influence extended to the papacy itself. In the disputed papal election of 1130, for example, Bernard literally toured the courts and towns of Europe to insure the accession of the legitimate pope, Innocent II, over his rival Anacletus II. And, when one of his former monks was elected Pope Eugenius III in 1145, Bernard wrote the tract *De Consideratione,* as a meditative guide for the pope in his conduct of this high office. In a manner reminiscent of Gregory I's *Pastoral Rule,* Bernard insisted that a life of prayer and contemplation is the core of the pastor's life, and he warned Eugenius about the dangers of abusing papal power and becoming too concerned with the business of a rapidly growing Roman Curia that was hearing appealed cases from all over Europe.

> What is this your power? An estate to be exploited? Nay: a burden to be taken up. Be not proud of Peter's throne; it is but an observation post, a high place from which, like a sentry you may cast your glance over the world beneath. You are not the owner of that world; you are not more than a trustee. The world belongs to Christ. . . to rule well is to rule with love. You are the servant of Christ's flock; it is not your slave. . . . There is no iron or poison that I fear so much for you as I fear the pride of power. (*De Consideratione,* Book II, Ch. VI)

When Eugenius III ordered the Second Crusade to recover lands lost to Muslim armies in the Holy Land, he called upon Bernard to preach the crusade among the French and Bavarian nobility. Bernard undertook his task with the spiritual fervor that marked all his undertakings. In his letters and sermons he envisioned the crusade as a spiritual enterprise which could rid Europe of senseless feudal warfare and offer the knights an opportunity for mercy and pardon for their past sins of violence.

> But now, O brave knight, now, O warlike hero, here is a battle you may fight without danger, where it is glory to conquer and gain to die. . . . Take the sign of the cross, and you shall gain pardon for every sin that you confess with a contrite heart. (*Life and Works of Saint Bernard* II, 910)

Bernard was also careful to warn the knights not to attack the Jews who were so often the targets of their crusading zeal.

> The Jews must not be persecuted, slaughtered nor even driven out. Inquire of the pages of Holy Writ. I know what is written in the Psalms as prophecy about the Jews. "God hath commanded me," says the Church, 'Slay them not, lest my people forget.'"

When the crusade failed due to feuding among the participants, Bernard was greatly disappointed, but surmised that the disaster was due to the crusaders' loss of God's favor because of their sins.

In many ways Bernard might appear to be a reactionary who opposed the new cultural forces that were stirring Europe during the twelfth century. He entered the new Cistercian Order which was founded in 1098 in an effort to return to the rigor of the original *Rule of Benedict*. Because of the growth of towns and the development of trade with markets in the East opened by contacts with the crusading armies, Europe was experiencing a growing affluence and an improvement in the general standard of living. Bernard, however, was critical of these developments, especially as they affected life in the monasteries. The Cistercian Order was founded to reform abuses in the Cluniac monastic system which had come to dominate Europe. Although the Cluniac monasteries were in the Benedictine tradition, they had developed several practices which contradicted the spirit of the original *Rule of Benedict*. Their monasteries had become extremely wealthy, and the monks themselves no longer did the manual labor mandated in the Rule. This was done by serfs so that the monks could supposedly be free for their liturgical duties and scholarship. In his *Apology to William of St.-Thierry,* Bernard brilliantly satirizes the affluence of the Cluniac monks.

> I marvel how monks could grow accustomed to such intemperance in eating and drinking, clothing and bedding, riding abroad and building, that, wheresoever these things are wrought most busily and with most pleasure and expense, there Religion is thought to be best kept. For behold! spare living is taken for covetousness, sobriety for austerity, silence for melancholy; while, on the other hand, men rebaptize laxity as "discretion," waste as "liberality," garrulousness as "affability," giggling as "jollity," effeminacy in clothing and bedding as "neatness" . . .

Bernard's criticism of Cluny extended to the architectural styles for their monastic churches. Europe was entering the age of the great Gothic cathedrals which would blanket France with towering monuments in stone and glass to the Christian faith in the mysteries of human redemption through Christ. But Bernard saw these wonderful edifices as monuments to human pride which distracted from the life of prayer.

> I will not speak of the immense height of their churches, nor their immoderate length, nor superfluous breadth. Is not this avarice rather than piety? By the sight of wonderful and costly vanities men are prompted to give rather than pray. . . . If we cannot spare sacred figures, can we not spare at least beautiful colors? Is the object of such things to promote penitence of the contrite or the admiration of the beholder? . . . They show, indeed, far more admiration of what is beautiful than veneration for what is sacred. . . . On the walls of the cloisters where brethren read, what place have these absurd monsters, these odd and beautiful deformities, so striking and varied that the brethren are attracted to gaze at them rather than read their books. The statues of stone are splendidly adorned but the poor are left naked and bare. (*Apology to William of St.-Thierry*).

Bernard was also an ardent opponent of the new rationalism in theology represented by Abelard. Like his contemporaries Judah HaLevi and Ghazali in the Jewish and Muslim traditions, Bernard was a mystic who based his religious belief on a personal experience of God's mercy and love. He was, therefore, as they were, suspicious of any attempt by human reason to dissect or rationalize the truths of the faith.

> The human intelligence usurps all for itself, leaving nothing to faith; it wishes to go too high in researches that are beyond its strength; what is well closed and sealed, it does not open but breaks; what it does not find easy of access, it thinks to be nothing and disdains to believe. . . . What do the holy apostles teach us? Not to read Plato or to turn and return the subtleties of Aristotle, not to be always learning and never reaching the knowledge of truth. They have taught me to live. Do you think that to know how to live is a small thing? It is great, and even the greatest. (From *Sermon on the Feast of Peter and Paul*)

This hostility to rationalism is not obscurantism; rather, it is derived from the same conviction that Judah HaLevi and Ghazali had. The truths of faith can be grasped only by living them, not by processes of logic. Mystics are existentialists.

Given his opposition to dialectic in theology, Bernard could never understand the new methods of Abelard. It is therefore not surprising that, when he was asked to enter the controversies caused by Abelard's teaching, Bernard condemned his rationalism and several of the propositions of his theology including the following:

1. That Christ did not take the flesh in order to free us from the devil.
2. That free will of itself suffices to do some good.
3. That we have not received the guilt of Adam, but only the penalty.
4. That those who crucified Christ did not sin, for they did not know what they were doing, and that there is no guilt in that which is done out of ignorance.

Despite his seemingly reactionary opposition to dialectical theology, Bernard's mysticism was potentially more revolutionary than the philosophers he attacked, for he spoke and wrote of religion, not as a system of dogmas, but as a personal experience of sin, mercy and love which involved deep emotion. The essence of religion for Bernard was not obedience to or thought about God, but love of God, and in this he and Abelard, for all their differences in methodology, were in agreement. For Bernard, the core of religion is mystical unity with God. In mystical ecstasy the soul is swallowed up in divinity, like a drop of water lost in wine, or an incandescent coal absorbed by fire, or air becoming transparent when the sun's rays pass through it.

Bernard understood his mystical experience as a validation of Christian dogma about Adam's fall and human redemption through Christ. The soul is first separated from God by original sin. It can find salvation only by learning to love God which Christ not only teaches, but instills, through mercy. In the love of God, the soul regains the freedom and integrity which had been lost by the sin of Adam, thus realizing its true nature.

Bernard's love for God was expressed in personal terms, not simply in the repetition of established dogmatic formulae. Like the troubadours who at the nearby court of Marie de Champagne were praising romantic love in their ballads and romances, Bernard spoke of the love of God as the highest and most ennobling of human affections. In contrast to the romances, however, where the relationship was often an adulterous one between a married lady and an unmarried knight, the love of God that Bernard describes is like that between a chaste bride and her faithful bridegroom.

This is most evident in his famous sermons on the Song of Songs. In our first selection from his *Sermon 7 on the Song of Songs,* Bernard is commenting on the verse: "Let him kiss me with the kiss of his mouth" (Sg 1:1). Like many before him, Bernard understands the whole work as an allegory about the human soul in relation to God. Bernard then proceeds to contrast the bride/soul's desire for love with other inferior forms of affection: the fear the slave has for his master, the desire for reward that motivates a servant, the pupil's expectation of instruction, the son's dutiful honoring of his father. In contrast, the bride and bridegroom share all: inheritance, home, table, bed, and flesh. Unlike the inferior forms of affection, the bride does not want freedom or reward, inheritance or instruction, only the kiss of affection.

The potentially revolutionary nature of Bernard's mystical theology is evident in our second selection from Bernard's earliest published work, *On the Steps of Humility and Pride.* In the course of discussing pride and humility, Bernard speaks about the purpose of the incarnation. His understanding is much closer to Abelard's than he realized, and he also anticipates Luther's doctrine of justification by faith. In fact, Luther read, quoted and praised the works of Bernard. Like Abelard, Bernard sees the purpose of the incarnation as instilling love and mercy in the hearts of humans. And, as Luther will argue later, Bernard believes that the process of salvation begins with humans becoming aware of their own wretched state as a consequence of sin.

According to Bernard, in the incarnation God the Creator acted out of mercy and came seeking humans who were lost in wretchedness because of the sins of pride and curiosity on the part of our first parents. God wanted to experience for himself the wretchedness humans were suffering because they had gone against his will. God became man, not out of curiosity, but out of charity. He wanted to "free those who were wretched as one made merciful." At this point, Bernard distinguishes between two types of mercy. The one is the divine mercy which makes God act to save humanity in the first place. The second is what might be called the human mercy which Christ "discovered as a mediator who was one of us." The goal of the incarnation is to make us merciful as the human Christ was merciful.

For Bernard, the first step in achieving that goal is for humans to become "meek" by realizing their sinfulness. A key text for Bernard in this regard is Paul's advice to the Galatians.

Brothers, even if a person is caught in some transgression, you who are spiritual should correct that one in a gentle spirit, looking to yourself, so that you also may not be tempted. Bear one another's burdens, and so you will fulfill the law of Christ. For if anyone thinks he is something when he is nothing, he is deluding himself. (Gal 6:1–3)

In his comments, Bernard paraphrases Paul by saying, "Think of yourself . . . how easily you are tempted, how prone you are to sin, how easily you let yourself off, and so hasten to help others in a spirit of gentleness." Bernard is arguing that if Christ submitted himself to human misery not only to know it but also to draw us out of it, we must begin by becoming aware of our own wretchedness and so learn to be merciful.

Two of Jesus' teachings in the gospels are crucial for Bernard in this regard. The first is Jesus' warning in the Sermon on the Mount: "Hypocrite, first cast out the beam from your own eye, and then you will see clearly to cast out the mote from your brother's eye" (Mt 7:5). The first step in coming to salvation is to "remove the beam of pride" and confess in truth and humility that one is sinful. The second step is to come to the awareness that all are sinners or, in the words of Psalm 115:11: that "Every man is a liar," that is, that "Every man is weak, powerless, unable to save himself or others."

The second teaching of Jesus which is important for Bernard in connection with humans' coming to an awareness of their own sinfulness is the parable of the Pharisee and the Publican (Lk 18:9–14). The Pharisee in the parable makes the crucial mistake of judging all others as sinners but exempting himself. Bernard says of him: "The Pharisee deceives only himself in making an exception of himself while he condemns others. . . . He had not yet cast out his beam and he was counting the motes in his brothers' eyes" (Mt 7:5).

At this point Bernard describes the human plight of consciousness of sin and human helplessness in language very similar to that Luther will use:

When they are distressed to see what they are, they long to be what they are not, and fear that they will never be by their own efforts. They grieve deeply over themselves, and the only consolation they can find is to judge themselves severely. They hunger and thirst after righteousness (Mt 5:6) and despise themselves utterly out of love for the truth. They demand full satisfaction for themselves, and a better life. But since they see that they cannot do it by themselves—for when they have done all that they were commanded they call themselves unprofitable servants (Lk 17:10)— they fly from justice to mercy. Truth advises them to do so. "Blessed are the merciful for they shall obtain mercy" (Mt 5:7). This is the second step of truth, to look beyond one's own needs to the needs of one's neighbors, and to know how to suffer with them in their troubles. (Heb 4:15)

Our final selection is from Bernard's sermons on the annunciation scene in which Mary receives the news that she is to be the mother of the savior. These sermons in which Bernard shows a knightly dedication to Mary are a good example of the new Marian devotion that swept Europe in the twelfth century. Many of the new cathedrals were dedicated to Notre Dame, and the annunciation was a favorite subject in medieval and Renaissance art. Bernard's own Cistercian Order was especially devoted to Mary, and in his sermons Bernard is both honoring Mary for her privileged place in the plan of salvation as the virgin mother of God, but he is also holding her up as a model for the monks of important Christian virtues, especially humility and chastity. Finally, like a courtly lady who can ask for favors from the king, Mary, under her title as Star of the Sea, is an advocate for the Christian or monk who may be living in a stormy and turbulent world.

The translation of Bernard's *Sermon 7 on the Song of Songs* and *On the Steps of Humility and Pride* is by G.R. Evans, *Bernard of Clairvaux: Selected Works* in the Classics of Western Spirituality Series (New York/Mahwah: Paulist Press, 1987) 110–115, 231–233. The translations of the *Sermons on the Virgin Mary* is by S.J. Eales, from Dom J. Mabillon (ed.), *The Life and Works of St. Bernard of Clairvaux* (London, 1896), vol III, 293–299, 315–316.

SERMON 7 ON
THE SONG OF SONGS

I.2. . . . "Let him kiss me," she says, "with the kiss of his mouth" (Sg 1:1). Who is speaking? The Bride. But why "Bride"? She is the soul which thirsts for God. I set out the different affections so as to make it clearer which properly belongs to the Bride. If someone is a slave, he fears his master's face. If he is a hireling, he hopes for payment from his master's hand. If he is a pupil, he bends his ear to his master. If he is a son, he honors his father. But she who asks for a kiss feels love. This affection of love excels among the gifts of nature, especially when it returns to its source, which is God. For no names can be found as sweet as those in which the Word and the soul exchange affections, as Bridegroom and Bride, for to such everything is common, nothing is the property of one and not the other, nothing is held separately. They share one inheritance, one table, one house, one bed, one flesh. For this she leaves her father and her mother and clings to her husband and they two are one flesh (Gen 2:24). She is also commanded to forget her people and her father's house so that he may desire her beauty (Ps 44:1).

So then love especially and chiefly belongs to those who are married and it is not inappropriate to call the loving soul a Bride. For she who asks a kiss feels love. She does not ask for freedom or payment or an inheritance or learning, but for a kiss, in the manner of a most chaste bride, who signs for holy love; and she cannot disguise the flame which is so evident.

It is a great thing which she will ask of the Great One, but she does not flirt with him as others do, and she does not beat about the bush. She tells him clearly what she desires. She uses no preliminaries. She does not try to win him round. But with an open face she bursts out suddenly from a full heart (Mt 12:34), "Let him kiss me," she says, "with the kiss of his mouth." Surely it seems to you as though she said, "Who have I in heaven but you and who but you do I want upon earth?" (Ps 72:25).

III.3. She loves most chastely who seeks him whom she loves and not some other thing which belongs to him. She loves in a holy way, because she does not love in fleshly desire but in purity of spirit. She loves ardently, because she is drunk with love so that she cannot see his majesty. What? He it is "who looks on the earth and causes it to tremble" (Ps 103:32). And she asks him for a kiss? Is she drunk? Indeed she is! And perhaps then when she burst forth thus she had come out of the wine-cellar (Sg 1:3; 2:4). She said afterward that she had been there, glorying in it. For David, too, said to God concerning such, "They shall be intoxicated with the plenty of your house, and you will give them the torrents of your pleasure to drink" (Ps 35:9). Oh, what force of love! What great confidence of spirit! What freedom! What is more evident than that perfect love casts out fear? (1 Jn 4:18).

ON HUMILITY AND PRIDE

III.12. You see, then, that Christ has two natures in one Person, one which always was and another which began to be. And according to that nature which was eternally his he always knew everything. But according to that which began in time (Rom 1:3), he experienced many things in time. In this way he began to know the miseries of the flesh, by that mode of cognition which the weakness of the flesh instructs.

Our first parents were wiser and happier when they did not know that which they came to know only foolishly and in wretchedness. But God their Creator, seeking what was lost, came down in mercy in pursuit of his wretched creatures, to where they had miserably fallen (Ez 34:16). He wanted to experience for himself what they were (rightly) suffering because they had gone against his will. He came not out of a curiosity like theirs, but out of a wonderful charity. He did not intend to remain wretched among them, but to free those who were wretched as one made merciful. "Made merciful" (Heb 2:17), I say, not with that mercy which he who remained happy had had from eternity (Ps 102:17), but with that mercy which he discovered as a mediator who was one of us. The work of his holiness, which began at the prompting of the first mercy, was completed in the second; not because the first mercy was not enough, but because only the second kind could fully satisfy us. Both were needed, but the second kind fitted our condition better. Oh, supreme delicacy of thoughtfulness! Should we have been able to imagine that wonderful mercy if we

had not seen it come to us in wretchedness? Should we have been able even to conceive of that unknown compassion toward us if the impassability which is everlasting had not come to us in the Passion?

Yet if he who did not know wretchedness had not first had mercy, he would not have come to that which is the mother of wretchedness. If he had not come, he would not have drawn us to himself. If he had not drawn us, he would not have drawn us out.

From what did he draw us out? From the slough of misery and the mire of sin (Ps 39:3). He did not lose anything of his everlasting mercy. But he added this to it. He did not change it but he multiplied it, as it is written, "You will save man and beast, Lord. How you have multiplied your mercy, O God!" (Ps 35:7–8).

IV.13. But let us return to our subject. If he submitted himself to human misery so that he might not simply know it, but also experience it, how much more ought you, not perhaps to make yourself what you are not, but to be aware of what you are, that you are truly wretched; and so learn to be merciful, for you can learn it in no other way.

If you see your neighbor's failing and not your own you will be moved not to mercy but to indignation, not to help him but to judge him, not to instruct him in a spirit of gentleness but to destroy him in a spirit of anger. "You are spiritual," says the Apostle, "teach in a spirit of gentleness" (Gal 6:1). His advice, or rather his precept, is to be gentle, that is to help your brother as if he were sick—as you would wish to be helped yourself in sickness. And so that you may know how gentle you may be toward a wrongdoer, "Consider yourself," he says, "lest you too are tempted" (Gal 6:1).

IV.14. Notice how well Truth's pupil follows the sequence of his master's thoughts. In the beatitudes which I mentioned above, just as the merciful came before the pure in heart, so the meek are placed before the merciful (Mt 5:4–8). When the Apostle tells the spiritual man to teach the carnal-minded, he adds, "In a spirit of gentleness." The teaching of brothers belongs to the merciful, and the spirit of gentleness to the meek. It is as though he said that he who is not meek in himself cannot be counted among the merciful. See how the Apostle clearly shows what I promised above that I would show, that truth is first to be sought in yourself and then in your neighbor. "Think of yourself," he says, that is, how easily you are tempted, how prone you are to sin, how easily you let yourself off, and so hasten to help others in a spirit of gentleness (Gal 6:1).

If you do not listen to the disciple's warning, fear that of the Master, "Hypocrite, first cast out the beam from your own eye, and then you will see clearly to cast out the mote from your brother's eye" (Mt 7:5). Pride in the mind is a great beam which is bloated rather than heavy, swollen rather than solid, and it blocks the mind's eye and blots out the light of truth, so that if your mind is full of it you cannot see yourself as you really are.

Nor can you see what you might be. You see what you would like to be and think yourself to be, or hope that you will be. For what else is pride but, as one of the saints defines it, love of one's own excellence? That is why we can say the opposite, that humility is contempt of one's own worth. . . .

IV.15. He who wants to know the whole truth about himself must, when he has removed the beam of pride (Mt 7:5) which is cutting off his eye from the light, cut steps in his heart (Ps 83:6) by which he can find himself in himself, and thus he will come after the twelve steps of humility to the first step of pride. For when he has discovered the truth about himself, or better, when he has seen himself in truth, he can say, "I have believed, and therefore I have spoken. I have been profoundly humbled" (Ps 115:10).

Such a man has come to the depths of his heart (Ps 63:7), and truth is exalted. When he arrives at the second step he will say, in ecstasy, "Every man is a liar" (Ps 115:11). Do you think that David was not here? Do you think this prophet did not feel what the Lord, the Apostle, and we ourselves feel after them and through them? "I have believed," he says, speaking to the Truth. "He who follows me will not walk in darkness" (Jn 8:12).

"I have believed," he continues, "and therefore I have spoken," in faith. In what faith? Believing the truth I have known. Afterward we have, "I have believed," to righteousness, and "I have spoken," for salvation, and "I have been profoundly," that is completely, "humbled" (Jas 2:23).

It is as though he said, "Because I have not been ashamed to confess the truth against myself which I have come to know in myself, I have progressed to utter humility. . . ." We can interpret him as saying, "I, when I was still in ignorance of the truth, thought myself something when I was nothing (Gal 6:3). But after I had come to believe in Christ, that is, to imitate his humility, I learned the truth and that truth is raised up in me by my confession. But 'I am profoundly humbled,' that is, I have been greatly lowered in my own estimation" (Ps 115:10).

V.16 The prophet has been humbled then in this first step of humility, as he says in another Psalm, "And in your truth you have humbled me" (Ps 118:75). He has been thinking about himself. Now he looks from his own wretchedness to that of others, and so passes to the second step, saying in his ecstasy (*excessus*), "Every man is a liar" (Ps 115:11). . . .

What does it mean to say that "Every man is a liar"? Every man is weak, powerless, unable to save himself or others. . . . He cannot hope for salvation from himself, nor can anyone else hope for salvation from him. Rather, he who places his hope in man is cursed (Jer 17:5). And so the humble prophet makes progress, led along by truth. What he grieved at in himself, he now grieves at in others. What he sees he grieves at (Eccl 1:18), and he cries, speaking generally but truly, "Every man is a liar" (Ps 115:11).

V.17. This is very different from what the proud Pharisee feels about himself. What does he say in his "ecstasy"? "My God, I thank you that I am not like other men" (Lk 18:11). While he exults in himself alone he arrogantly insults others. David is different. He says, "Every man is a liar." He made no exceptions, in case anyone should deceive himself, for he knew that "all have sinned and everyone needs the glory of God" (Rom 3:23). The Pharisee deceives only himself in making an exception of himself while he condemns others. The prophet does not except himself from the general wretchedness, lest he be left out of the mercy, too. The Pharisee waved mercy away when he denied his wretchedness. The prophet said of everyone, including himself, "Every man is a liar" (Ps 115:11). The Pharisee asserted it of everyone but himself. "I am not," he says, "like other men." He gave thanks not because he was good, but because he was unique. He was not so concerned with his own good as with the wickedness he saw in others. He had not yet cast out his beam and he was counting the motes in his brothers' eyes (Mt 7:5). For he added, "Unjust, robbers" (Lk 18:11). . . .

V.18. Now let us come back to our subject. Those whom truth brings to know themselves it also causes to think little of themselves. It follows inevitably that all that they used to love will now become bitter to them. Brought face to face with themselves, they are forced to see things which fill them with shame. When they are distressed to see what they are, they long to be what they are not, and fear that they will never be by their own efforts. They grieve deeply over themselves, and the only consolation they can find is to judge themselves severely. They hunger and thirst after righteousness (Mt 5:6) and despise themselves utterly out of love for the truth. They demand full satisfaction for themselves, and a better life. But since they see that they cannot do it by themselves—for when they have done all that they were commanded they call themselves unprofitable servants (Lk 17:10)—they fly from justice to mercy. Truth advises them to do so. "Blessed are the merciful for they shall obtain mercy" (Mt 5:7). This is the second step of truth, to look beyond one's own needs to the needs of one's neighbors, and to know how to suffer with them in their troubles (Heb 4:15).

HOMILY I ON THE ANNUNCIATION

5. To that city then was sent the Angel Gabriel by God; but to whom was he sent? "To a Virgin, espoused to a man whose name was Joseph." Who is this virgin so worthy of reverence as to be saluted by an Angel: yet so humble, as to be betrothed to a carpenter? A beautiful combination is that of virginity with humility. But of how great respect must she not be thought worthy, in whom maternity consecrates virginity, and the splendor of a Birth exalts humility? You hear her, a virgin, and humble: if you are not able to imitate the virginity of that humble soul, imitate at least her humility; Virginity is a praiseworthy virtue; but humility is more necessary. . .

6. What say you to this O Virgin who art proud? Mary forgets her virginity and dwells only upon her humility: And you think only of flattering yourself about your virginity, while neglecting humility. "The Lord," said she, "has had regard to the humility of His handmaid." Who was she who speaks this? A virgin holy, prudent and pious. Would you claim to be more chaste, more pious than she? Or do you think that your modesty is more acceptable than the purity of Mary, since you think that you are able by it to please God without humility, whilst she was not able? The more

honorable you are by the singular gift of chastity, the greater is the injury you do to yourself; by staining it with an admixture of pride. It were better for you not to be a virgin, than to grow haughty about virginity. It is not granted to all to live in virginity; but to much fewer to do so with humility. . . .

7. There is something still more admirable in Mary: namely, her maternity joined with virginity. For from the beginning was never such a thing heard, as that one should be at the same time Mother and Virgin. If you consider also of whom she is Mother, to what degree will not your admiration of such a marvelous advancement soar? Will you not feel that you can hardly admire it enough? Will not your judgment or rather that of Truth, be, that she whose Son is God is exalted even above the choirs of Angels? Is it not Mary who says boldly to God, the Lord of Angels, "Son, why hast thou thus dealt with us?" Who of the Angels would dare to speak thus? It is sufficient for them, and they count it for a great thing, that they are spirits by nature, that they were made and called Angels by His grace, as David testifies: "Who makes his Angels Spirits?" (Ps 104:4). But Mary, knowing herself to be Mother, with confidence names Him Son, whom they obey with reverence. Nor does God disdain to be called by the name which He has deigned to assume. For a little after the Evangelist adds: "And He was subject unto them" (Lk 2:51). Who, and to whom? God, to human beings; God, I say, to whom the Angels are subject, whom Principalities and Powers obey, was subject unto Mary; and to Joseph also for her sake. Admire then both the benign condescension of the Son and the most excellent dignity of the Mother; and choose whether of the two is more admirable. Each is a wonder, each a miracle. God is obedient to a woman, an unexampled humility! a woman is in the place of ancestor to God, a distinction without a sharer! When the praises of virgins are sung, it is

said, that they follow the Lamb whithersoever he goeth (Apoc 14:4), of what praise shall she be thought worthy, who even goes before Him?

8. Learn, O man, to obey; learn, O dust and ashes, to abase thyself and submit. The Evangelist, speaking of thy Creator, says: "He was obedient to them," that is, to Mary and Joseph. Blush then, O ashes, that dares to be proud! God humbles Himself, and dost thou raise thyself up? God submits Himself unto men, and dost thou lord it over thy fellow creatures, and prefer thyself to thy Creator? Would that God, if ever I should nourish such an inclination, would deign to reply to me as He once reproached His Apostle: "Get thee behind Me, Satan, for thou savor not the things which be of God (Matt 16:23). . . .

17. The verse of the Evangelist ends thus: "And the Virgin's name was Mary." Let us say a few words upon this name also. The word Mary means "Star of the Sea," which seems to have a wonderful fitness to the Virgin Mother. For she is fitly compared to a star; for just as a star sends forth its ray without injury to itself, so the Virgin, remaining a virgin, brought forth her Son. The ray does not diminish the clearness of the star, nor the Son of the Virgin her Virginity. She is even that noble star risen out of Jacob, whose ray enlightens the whole world, whose splendor both shines in the Heavens and penetrates into Hell: and as it traverses the lands, it causes minds to glow with virtues more than bodies with heart, while vices it burns up and consumes. She, I say, is that beautiful and admirable star, raised of necessity above this great and spacious sea of life, shining with virtues and affording an illustrious example. Whosoever thou art who knowest thyself to be tossed about among the storms and tempests of this troubled world rather than to be walking peacefully upon the shore, turn not thine eyes away from the shining of this star, if thou wouldst not be overwhelmed with the tem-

pest. If the winds of temptation arise, if you are driving upon the rocks of tribulation, look to the star, invoke Mary. If you are tossed upon the waves of pride, of ambition, of envy, or rivalry, look to the star, invoke Mary. If wrath, avarice, temptations of the flesh assail the frail skiff of your mind, look to Mary. If you are troubled by the greatness of your crimes, confessed by the foulness of your conscience, and desperate with the horror of judgment, you feel yourself drawn into the depth of sorrow and into the abyss of despair; in dangers, in difficulties, in perplexities: invoke and think of Mary. Let not the name depart from heart and from lips; and that you may obtain a part in the petitions of her prayer, do not desert the example of her life. If you think of and follow her you will not go wrong, nor despair if you beg of her. With her help you will not fall or be fatigued; if she is favorable you will be sure to arrive; and thus you will learn by your own experience how rightly it is said: "The Virgin's name was Mary." . . .

HILDEGARD OF BINGEN

The twelfth century also produced one of the greatest women mystics of the Middle Ages: the abbess Hildegard of Bingen (1098–1179 C.E.). In an era when very few women had the ability, or even the opportunity, to write, Hildegard's achievements are remarkable. Not only was she an active and forceful abbess of her own convent, but she has left a literary legacy in Latin which fills an entire volume of the *Patrologia Latina*. She was deeply involved in the religious and political disputes of her day, as is evident from her letters to important figures like St. Bernard, Pope Eugenius III, and Emperor Frederick I Barbarosa. She also produced accounts of her visions, prophecies, liturgical songs, a morality play, explications of the gospels and the *Rule of Benedict,* and even several scientific works, including a handbook on medicine. She supervised the production of thirty-five miniature illustrations for her greatest mystical work entitled *Scivias* ("Know the ways [of the Lord]").

Like most of the women mystics of the Middle Ages, Hildegard had to be forced to write down her personal religious experiences. Although she had been having visions since she was a girl of fifteen, Hildegard had shared them with but a few religious confidants. Only in mid-life did she begin to write them down and make them public. As she tells us in the Preface to her *Scivias,* she had to be commanded by God himself to do this. Her account of the commissioning seems to be modeled on that of John the Elder in the Book of Revelation (see Rev 1).

> Behold in the forty-third year of my age, while with a trembling effort and in great fear I fixed my gaze upon a celestial vision, I saw a very great splendor, from which a voice from Heaven came to me saying: "O fragile man, ashes of ashes and dust of dust, say and write what you see and hear."

Hildegard goes on to give us a very interesting account of the nature of her mystical experiences. First of all, she tells us that they did not give some new esoteric revelation, but rather they clarified for her the meaning of the revelation found in scripture. She also insists that this new understanding was not from scholarly insight, as might be gained in the monastic and cathedral schools, but from a revelation of the spiritual meaning of the scriptures.

> And suddenly I knew and understood the explanation of the Psalter, the Gospels and other Catholic books of the Old and the New Testaments, but not the interpretation of the text of the words, nor the division of the syllables, nor did I understand the cases and the tenses.

This emphasis on the spiritual sense of the scripture, as opposed to the learned and often acrimonious debates about theological issues in the male dominated schools, is characteristic of the women mystics of the medieval period.

A second noteworthy feature of Hildegard's experiences is that they were not the result of some paranormal ecstatic or dream state, but rather an intense inner vision.

> But I saw these visions not in dreams, nor sleeping, nor in frenzy, nor with the eyes of my body, neither did I hear them with my exterior ears, nor in hidden places did I perceive them, but watching them, and looking carefully in an innocent mind, with the eyes and ears of the interior man, in open places, did I perceive them according to the Will of God.

Finally, Hildegard insists that because of her mystical encounters she knew God had chosen her to be a special vessel of revelation.

> But when my girlhood was passed, when I had arrived at the aforesaid age of perfect strength, I heard a voice from Heaven saying: "I am the living and obscure Light, illuminating one whom I desired, and whom I sought out according to what pleased me in her wonderful gifts, beyond those of the ancients who saw many secrets in Me, but I humbled her to the dust lest she should be elated.

Hildegard follows this account of her call with an interesting speech by God in which she is spoken of in the third person. The emphasis is on the humility that God instilled in her to protect her from pride.

> The world had no joy nor pleasure in her, nor recreation in the things that pertained to her, and I delivered her, fearing and trembling in her labors, from obstinate presumption. For in the marrow of her bones and in the veins of her flesh, she was aching, having her mind and judgment bound, so that no security dwelt in her and she judged herself culpable in all things. . . .

God's speech goes on to recount how Hildegard asked "a faithful man" whom she loved (the monk Volmar) to assist her in recording her visions. In the concluding paragraphs of the Preface, Hildegard returns to the first person and speaks of how she still refused the duty of writing for a long time, and did not finally begin until she fell ill and "was compelled to write by my many infirmities." At this point a noble woman, the nun Richarda, and the monk, Volmar, assisted her in recording her visions.

Scivias includes twenty-six visions on such theological topics as the relationship between God and the cosmos, the human person, and other major theological themes. I have included her vision "Of the Blessed Trinity," which is Vision II from Book II. It is what scholars call a "doctrinal vision," which responds to a dilemma that the visionary and/or her audience may have about a dogma of the Christian faith. In this case the problem is the human mind's inability to conceive of how there can be one God in three Persons. Toward the end of her explication of the vision, Hildegard says:

> Thus understand, O man, One God in three Persons. But thou in the foolishness of thy mind thinkest God to be so impotent, that it is not possible to Him to subsist truly in three Persons, but to be able only to consist of One. . . .

Hildegard begins with a vivid account of her vision and then proceeds to explicate it by a close allegorical reading of the elements. She also provided beautiful miniature illustrations of her visions to enable the reader to visualize what she saw. In the vision "Of the Blessed Trinity" Hildegard describes an experience of "a most splendid light . . . which burnt in a most beautiful, shining fire" and within this light "was the figure of a man of a sapphire color." She stresses that each element of the vision was present in the whole. The emphasis is mine.

> Then I saw a most splendid light, and in that light, *the whole* of which burnt in a most beautiful, shining fire, was the figure of a man of sapphire color, and that most splendid light poured over *the whole* of that shining fire, and the shining fire over *all* that splendid light, and that most splendid light and shining fire over *the whole* figure of the man, appearing *one* light in *one* virtue and power.

The living Light then speaks to Hildegard and tells her the import of her vision.

> This is the meaning of the mysteries of God, that it may be discerned and understood discreetly what that fullness may be, which is without beginning and to which nothing is wanting, who by the most powerful strength planted all the rivers of the strong [places].

The living Light then goes on to explicate the vision for Hildegard. The splendid Light, "which is without beginning and to Whom nothing can be wanting," is the Father. The "man of sapphire color, without any spot of the imperfection of envy and iniquity," is the Son. The "beautiful, shining fire" is the Holy Spirit, "by Whom the same only-begotten Son of God was conceived according to the flesh, and born in time of the Virgin, and poured forth the light of true brightness upon the world." Then the Light stresses the inseparability of the three. Each is fully present within the other "because the Trinity is not able to be divided, but remains always inviolable without change, for the Father is declared through the Son, and the Son through the birth of creatures, and the Holy Spirit through the same Son, Incarnate."

The purpose of Hildegard's vision is not simply to clarify the meaning of the Trinity in an intellectual sense. Rather, it is meant to inspire those who see it to the love of God. The voice tells Hildegard:

> . . . never let man forget to invoke Me as One God in three Persons, because these things are shown to man, that he may burn more ardently in My love, when for love of him I sent My own Son into the world, as My beloved John testified, saying: "In this appeared the Love of God to us, because He sent His only begotten Son into the world that we might live through Him. In this is love, not as if we had loved God, but because He first loved us, and sent His Son as a propitiation for our sins" (1 Jn 4).

At this point Hildegard presents her view of the purpose of the incarnation. In contrast to Anselm who understood the incarnation as necessary to rectify God's offended sense of justice, Hildegard's vision approaches the question from the perspective of God's love for creation and humans who were lost in darkness and unable "to return to the holiness which they had lost." The Father out of "paternal love" sent the Word to educate and heal. He taught humans "how to live in repentance" and humility which are the antidotes to the pride by which the crafty serpent deceived man. The Creator out of love sent the Son as savior "who washed and dried our wounds."

In the remainder of her account Hildegard does an allegorical reading of the elements of the vision as revealing the mystery of the Trinity, "three Persons living inseparably in the unity of the Divinity." She finds three "virtues" in each of the major elements of the experience: the sapphire stone, the flame and the word that was spoken to her. In this section we can see Hildegard's scientific interests as well. For example, in the stone she sees the virtues of moisture, palpability, and fire; each symbolizes a person of the Trinity. Moisture signifies the Father whose power "is never dried up nor finished." Palpability points to the Son who was "born of the Virgin" and "is able to be touched and comprehended." "The fiery power signifies the Holy Spirit Who is the kindler and the illuminator of the hearts of faithful men."

Our second brief selection is from Hildegard's *The Book of Divine Works*. It illustrates her view of the cosmos as a living organism in which God is the fiery power which is the source of life and order. Humanity is both the divine image and likeness of God and the microcosm which unites the higher and lower creatures. The beautiful and radiant human form at the center of the cosmos in this vision is the symbol of God's love for humans who have been placed in the position of splendor and honor once meant for the fallen angels.

Hildegard's worldview is reminiscent of the thought of the ancient Greek philosopher, Heraclitus, and his Stoic successors who understood the universe as a living organism guided by a divine fire. Her positive and optimistic view of the material world and humanity's place in it stands in sharp contrast to the negative view of the physical world found in the various forms of Manicheism which began to revive in Europe in the late twelfth century. Hildegard's thought anticipates the love of nature as God's gift that will be affirmed by Francis of Assisi and Franciscan thinkers in the thirteenth century.

The translation of *Scivias* is by Francesca Maria Steele, *The Life and Visions of St. Hildegarde* (London: Heath, Cranston and Ousely, 1914). The translation of *The Book of Divine Works* is by Matthew Fox in *Hildegard of Bingen's, The Book of Divine Works* (Santa Fe: Bear and Company Inc., 1987).

SCIVIAS

PREFACE

Behold in the forty-third year of my age, while with a trembling effort and in great fear I fixed my gaze upon a celestial vision, I saw a very great splendor, from which a voice from Heaven came to me saying: "O fragile man, ashes of ashes and dust of dust, say and write that thou seest and hearest.

"But because thou art timid in speaking, and simple in expounding, and unlearned in writing these things, say and write them not according to the speech of man, nor according to the human intellect and will, but according to that which thou seest and hearest in celestial matters from above, in the wonderful things of God.

"In declaring these things, act even as one who hears the words of his preceptor, and in receiving and publishing them, [he being willing] gives them out according to the purport of his speech.

"Thus, O man! do thou therefore speak what thou hearest and seest, and write these things not according to thyself, nor according to another man, but according to the desire of seeing, knowing, and setting down all things according to the secrets of their mysteries."

And again I heard a voice from Heaven, saying to me: "Tell these wonderful things and write them, taught in this manner, and way:

"'It happened in the year 1141 of the Incarnation of the Son of God, Jesus Christ, when I was forty-two years and seven months old, that a fiery light of the greatest brilliancy coming from the opened heavens, poured into all my brain, and kindled in my heart and my breast a flame, that warms but does not burn, as the sun heats anything over which he casts his rays.'"

And suddenly I knew and understood the explanation of the Psalter, the Gospels and other Catholic books of the Old and New Testaments, but not the interpretation of the text of the words, nor the division of the syllables, nor did I understand the cases and the tenses.

But from my girlhood, that is to say from the fifteenth year, I felt in myself in a wonderful way the power of the mysteries of secret and wonderful visions. Nevertheless I showed these things to no one except a few religious people, living in the same way as I was. In the meantime, till God wished His favors to be manifested, I repressed them in quiet silence. But I saw these visions not in dreams, nor sleeping, nor in frenzy, nor with the eyes of my body, neither did I hear them with my exterior ears, nor in hidden places did I perceive them, but watching them, and looking carefully in an innocent mind, with the eyes and ears of the interior man, in open places, did I perceive them according to the Will of God.

In what way this may be, it is difficult to explain to the carnal man. But when my girlhood was passed, when I had arrived at the aforesaid age of perfect strength, I heard a voice from Heaven saying: "I am the living and obscure Light, illuminating one whom I desired, and whom I sought out according to what pleased me in her wonderful gifts, beyond those of the ancient who saw many secrets in Me, but I humbled her to the dust lest she should be elated.

"The world had no joy nor pleasure in her, nor recreation in the things that pertained to her, and I delivered her, fearing and trembling in her labors, from obstinate presumption. For in the marrow of her bones and in the veins of her flesh, she was aching, having her mind and judgment bound, so that no security dwelt in her and she judged herself culpable in all things. For I guarded her heart from danger lest her mind should be elated by pride and vainglory, but rather that she should feel fear and grief than joy or wanton pleasure in all these things.

"Then she considered in her mind, where she could find some one in My love who would run in the way of salvation. And she found such an one [the monk Volmar] and loved him, recognizing what a faithful man he was, like to herself in that part of his work which concerned Me. And holding fast to him, she labored together with him in all these matters, in the high and earnest endeavor that My hidden miracles should be revealed.

"And this man did not exalt himself above her, but yielded to her with many sighs in the height of that humility which he obtained, and in the intention of a good will. Thou, therefore, oh man, who receives these things not in the inquietude of deception, but in the straightforward purity of simplicity, for the manifestation of hidden things, write what thou seest and hearest."

But I, although I had seen and heard these things, nevertheless because of the doubt and bad opinion and divers remarks of men, refused for a long time the duty of writing, not in obstinacy but in humility, until I fell on a bed of sickness, cast down by the scourge of God, until at length I was compelled to write by many infirmities.

By the evidence of a certain noble girl [the nun Richarda, daughter of the Margrave of Stada] of good morals, and of that man whom as beforesaid I had secretly sought and found, I applied my hand to write. While I did this, feeling the deep profundity of the explanation of the books as I said above, and the strength I received raising me from my sick-bed, at the end of ten years I had with difficulty finished this work. But in the days of Henry, Archbishop of Mainz, and Conrad, the Roman Emperor, and Kuno, Abbot of Mount St. Disibode, under Pope Eugenius III, these visions and words were completed. And I said and wrote them not according to the curious invention of my heart, nor of any man, but as I saw, heard, and perceived them in a heavenly way, through the secret mysteries of God. And again I heard a voice from Heaven saying to me, "Cry aloud therefore, and write thus."

VISION II (FROM BOOK II)
OF THE BLESSED TRINITY

Then I saw a most splendid light, and in that light, the whole of which burnt in a most beautiful, shining fire, was the figure of a man of sapphire color, and that most splendid light poured over the whole of that shining fire, and the shining fire over all that splendid light, and that most splendid light and shining fire over the whole figure of the man, appearing one light in one virtue and power. And again I heard that living Light saying to me: This is the meaning of the mysteries of God, that it may be discerned and understood discreetly what that fullness may be, which is without beginning and to which nothing is wanting, who by the most powerful strength planted all the rivers of the strong [places]. For if the Lord is wanting in His own strength, what then would His work be?

Certainly vain, and so in a perfect work is seen who was its maker. On which account thou seest this most splendid Light, which is without beginning and to Whom nothing can be wanting: this means the Father, and in that figure of a man of sapphire color, without any spot of the imperfection of envy and iniquity, is declared the Son, born of the Father, according to the Divinity before all time, but afterwards incarnate according to the humanity, in the world, in time. The whole of which burns in a most beautiful, shining fire, which fire without a touch of any dark mortality shows the Holy Spirit, by Whom the same only-begotten Son of God was conceived according to the flesh, and born in time of the Virgin, and poured forth the light of true brightness upon the world.

But that splendid Light pours forth all that shining fire, and that shining fire all that splendid Light, and the splendid shining light of the fire, the whole of the figure of the man, making one Light existing in one strength and power: this is because the Father, Who is the highest equity, but not without the Son or the Holy Spirit, and the Holy Spirit who is the kindler of the hearts of the faithful, but not without the Father and the Son, and the Son who is the fullness of virtue, but not without the Father and the Holy Spirit, are inseparable in the majesty of the Divinity; because the Father is not without the Son, neither the Son without the Father, nor the Father and the Son without the Holy Spirit, neither the Holy Spirit without them, and these three Persons exist one God in one whole divinity of majesty: and the unity of the Divinity lives inseparable in the three Persons, because the Trinity is not able to be divided, but remains always inviolable without any change, for the Father is declared through the Son, and the Son through the birth of creatures, and the Holy Spirit through the same Son, Incarnate.

How? It is the Father Who before all ages begat the Son, the Son, through Whom all things were made in the beginning of creatures, by the Father, and the Holy Spirit Who appeared in the form of a dove, in the baptism of the Son of God in the end of the ages.

Whence never let man forget to invoke Me

as One God in three Persons, because these things are shown to man, that he may burn more ardently in My love, when for love of him I sent My own Son into the world, as My beloved John testified, saying: "In this appeared the Love of God to us, because He sent His only begotten Son into the world that we might live through Him. In this is love, not as if we had loved God, but because He first loved us, and sent His Son as a propitiation for our sins" (1 Jn 4).

Why so? Because in this way God loved us; another salvation has sprung up, than that which we had in the creation, when we were heir of innocence and of sanctity, because the Father above showed His love, when we in our peril were placed in punishment, sending His Word, Who alone among the sons of men was perfect in holiness, into the darkness of this world, where that same Word, doing all good works, led them back to life though His meekness, who were cast out by the malice of transgression, nor were they able to return to that holiness which they had lost.

Why so? Because through that fountain of life came the paternal love of the embrace of God, which educated us to life, and in our dangers was our help, and is the most deep and beautiful light teaching us repentance.

In what way? God mercifully remembered His great work and His most precious pearl, man, I say, whom He formed from the dust of the earth, and into whom He breathed the breath of life. In what manner? He taught [us] how to live in repentance which brings forth humility, which the devil neither knew nor made, because he was ignorant of how to rise to a just life.

Thence this salvation of love did not spring from us, because we did not know, neither were we able to love God unto salvation, but because He the Creator and Lord of all so loved the world, that He sent His Son for its salvation, the prince and Savior of the faithful, Who washed and dried our wounds, and from

Him also came that most sweet medicine, from which all the good things of salvation flow.

Wherefore, O man, do thou understand that no shadow (*instabilitas*) of change touches God. For the Father is the Father, the Son is the Son, and the Holy Spirit is the Holy Spirit, three Persons living inseparably in the unity of the Divinity.

In what manner? There are three virtues in a stone, three in a flame and three in a word. How? In the stone is the virtue of moisture, the virtue of palpability, and the power of fire, for it has the virtue of moisture lest it should be dissolved and broken in pieces, but it shows its palpable comprehension when used as a habitation and a defense, and it has the virtue of fire so that it may be heated and consolidated to its hardness. And this virtue of moisture signifies the Father, Whose power is never dried up nor finished; and the palpable comprehension means the Son, Who being born of the Virgin is able to be touched and comprehended, and the fiery power signifies the Holy Spirit Who is the kindler and illuminator of the hearts of faithful men.

How is this? As man frequently attracts into his body the damp power of the stone, and falling ill is weakened, so man who through the instability of his thoughts will fear to look up to the Father, loses his faith: and in the palpable comprehension of the stone is shown that men make a habitation with it for themselves, as a defense against enemies, thus the Son of God, Who is the true Corner-stone, is the habitation of the faithful, protecting them from evil spirits.

But as the shining fire illuminates darkness, burning those things upon which it had been lying, thus the Holy Spirit drives away infidelity, taking away all the foulness of iniquity. And in the same way that these three powers are in one stone, so the true Trinity is in one Deity.

Again, as the flame in one fire has three powers, so the One God is in Three Persons. In what manner? For in the flame abides splendid light, innate vigor, and fiery heat, but it has splendid light that it may shine, innate vigor that it may flourish, and fiery heat that it may burn. Thence consider in the splendid light, the Father Who in His paternal love sheds His light upon the faithful, and in that innate vigor of the splendid flame in which that same flame shows its power, understand the Son, Who took flesh from the Virgin, in which the Divinity declared His wonders, and in the fiery heat, behold the Holy Spirit, Who gently kindles the hearts and minds of the faithful.

But where there is neither a splendid light, nor innate vigor, nor fiery heat, there no flame is discerned: thus where neither the Father, nor the Son, nor the Holy Spirit is worshipped, there neither is He worthily venerated.

Therefore as in one flame these three powers are discerned; thus in the unity of the Divinity, three Persons are to be understood.

So also as three powers are to be noted in a word, thus the Trinity in the Unity of the Divinity is to be considered. In what way? In a word there is sound, power and breath. For it has sound that it may be heard, power that it may be understood, breath that it may be perfected.

In the sound, note the Father, Who with unerring power makes manifest all things. In the power, not the Son, Who is wonderfully begotten of the Father; and in the breath, not the Holy Spirit, Who breathes where He will and all things are accomplished.

But where no sound is heard, there neither power works, nor breath is raised, thence neither there is the Word to be understood; so also the Father, the Son, and the Holy Spirit are not to be divided from themselves, but their work is performed unanimously. . . .

Thus understand, O man, One God in three Persons. But thou in the foolishness of thy mind thinkest God to be so impotent, that it is not possible to Him to subsist truly in three Persons, but to be able only to consist of

One, when neither dost thou see a voice to consist without three. Why so? God is certainly in three Persons, one true God first and last. . . .

THE BOOK OF DIVINE WORKS

FIRST VISION: ON THE ORIGIN OF LIFE
VISION ONE: 1

And I saw within the mystery of God, in the midst of the southern breezes, a wondrously beautiful image. It had a human form, and its countenance was of such beauty and radiance that I could have more easily gazed at the sun than at that face. A broad golden ring circled its head. . . . The figure was wrapped in a garment that shone like the sun. . . .[This "spirit of the macrocosm" then spoke to her:]

I, the highest and fiery power, have kindled every spark of life, and I emit nothing that is deadly. I decide on all reality. With my lofty wings I fly above the globe: With wisdom I have rightly put the universe in order. I, the fiery life of divine essence, am aflame beyond the beauty of the meadows, I gleam in the waters, and I burn in the sun, moon, and stars. With every breeze, as with invisible life that contains everything, I awaken everything to life. The air lives by turning green and being in bloom. The waters flow as if they were alive. The sun lives in its light, and the moon is enkindled, after its disappearance, once again by the light of the sun so that the moon is again revived. The stars, too give a clear light with their beaming. I have established pillars that bear the entire globe as

well as the power of the winds which, once again, have subordinate wings—so to speak, weaker winds—which through their gentle power resist the mighty winds so that they do not become dangerous. In the same way, too, the body envelops the soul and maintains it so that the soul does not blow away. For just as the breath of the soul strengthens and fortifies the body so that it does not disappear, the more powerful winds, too, revive the surrounding winds so that they can provide their appropriate service.

And thus I remain hidden in every kind of reality as a fiery power. Everything burns because of me in such a way as our breath constantly moves us, like the wind-tossed flame in a fire. All of this lives in its essence, and there is no death in it. For I am life. I am also Reason, which bears within itself the breath of the resounding Word, through which the whole of creation is made. I breathe life into everything so that nothing is mortal in respect to its species. For I am life. . . .

VISION ONE: 3

And again I heard a voice from heaven saying to me: God, who created everything, has formed humanity according to the divine image and likeness, and marked in human beings both the higher and lower creatures. God loved humanity so much that God designated for it the place from which the fallen angel was ejected, intending for human beings all the splendor and honor which that angel lost along with his bliss. The countenance you are gazing at is an indication of this fact.

FRANCIS OF ASSISI

At the end of the twelfth and the beginning of the thirteenth century C.E., Europe was ready for an authentic and creative rediscovery of the spirit of the Christian gospel which was originally meant to be lived within society. This spirit is best exemplified by Franciscans and the Dominicans, the two new mendicant orders of friars which were founded in the early thirteenth century. In contrast to the monks who continued to follow the Benedictine rule by withdrawing from society and taking vows of stability to pursue lives of prayer and work at a monastery in the rural countryside, these friars (brothers) found their apostolate as wandering preachers and teachers in the vibrant cities and new universities. Their lives were to be shaped by the ideals Jesus had given to his disciples in sending them on mission in the gospel, especially his emphasis on poverty.

> "As you go, make this your proclamation: 'the kingdom of heaven is at hand. . . .' Without cost you have received; without cost you are to give. Do not take gold or silver or copper for your belts; no sack for the journey, or a second tunic, or sandals, or walking stick. The laborer deserves his keep. Whatever town or village you enter, look for a worthy person in it, and stay there until you leave. As you enter a house, wish it peace. If the house is worthy, let your peace come upon it; if not, let your peace return to you. Whoever will not receive you or listen to your words—go outside that house or town and shake the dust from your feet" (Mt 10:7–14).

By the end of the twelfth century, some members of the emerging merchant and working classes living in the bustling towns of Europe, especially in southern France and northern Italy, were inspired by a desire for preaching in their vernacular tongues and a return to the spirit of apostolic living described in the New Testament, particularly its primitive simplicity and poverty. This way of life stood in sharp contrast to high ranking churchmen who enjoyed power and prestige while living in luxury like feudal lords.

One of the earliest of these movements was the Waldensians, or Poor Men of Lyons. They were founded by Peter Waldo (c. 1170 C.E.) a merchant of Lyons, who adopted a life of austere poverty and apostolic preaching after hearing the story of the rich young man in the gospel who was challenged by Jesus with the words, "If you will be perfect go and sell all that you have and give to the poor . . ." (Matt 19:21). Although we know of their teachings and practices primarily from their enemies, even these sources express admiration for their way of life. Stephen of Bourbon describes the Waldensians in the following way:

> They know the Apostles' Creed excellently in the vulgar tongue and learn by heart the gospels of the New Testament in the vulgar tongue, and repeat them aloud to each other. . . . I have seen a young cowherd who had lived for only one year in the house of a Waldensian heretic, yet had attended so diligently and repeated so carefully all he had heard there, that he had learnt by heart 40 Sunday Gospels, not counting those for feast days—all learnt word for word in his native tongue. (From Stephen of Bourbon on Waldenses translated by Walter Wakefield and A.P. Evans in *Heresies of the High Middle Ages*, [New York: Columbia University Press, 1991] 211)

Despite this begrudging admiration for their life and piety, Peter and his followers were condemned as heretics for a whole series of practices and teachings which anticipate disputes which will arise in the Reformation of the sixteenth century. Like the Anabaptists in the sixteenth century, the Waldensians attempted to follow literally Jesus' teachings in the Sermon on the Mount by refusing to take oaths and rejecting capital punishment. Like Luther and many other reformers, they rejected the special sacramental powers of the ordained priests and claimed for themselves the right to hear confessions and grant absolution. Like Luther, they also rejected as useless the teaching of indulgences, the doctrine of purgatory, and prayers for the dead. Their criticism of the prelates of the church was condemned as a revival of the old heresy of Donatism. Finally, they were condemned for asserting that they as laity could preach and expound the sacred scriptures.

If the Waldensians began as an attempt at reform within the church, the Albigensians (named for the town of Albi in southwestern France) were heretics from the beginning. They revived the teachings of the Manicheans of Augustine's time by insisting that there was not one Creator but two eternal powers, one good, and one evil. The visible world, according to the Albigensians, was the creation of the evil power, while the spiritual world was created by the good God. There were two classes of followers within the Albigensians: the "believers" who were allowed to marry and act outwardly as Catholics and "the perfect" who were continent and refused to eat meat or any products of reproduction. These practices were based on the belief that the material world was evil, and they explain the Albigensians name for themselves, *Cathari,* "The Pure," from the Greek word for clean. Unlike the Waldensians, the Albigensians also developed a system of spiritual sacraments and rites including a spiritual baptism known as the *consolamentum* and a fast called the *endura* which often led to death by starvation.

Francis of Assisi (1186–1226) belonged to this time of religious rebirth in Europe. He shared with the Waldensians the desire to return to the simplicity of Jesus' gospel teachings, but he did so in a way that humbly remained within the Catholic Church. Like Peter Waldo, Francis had a conversion experience in which he turned from a worldly and pampered life as the son of a wealthy cloth merchant to embrace the poverty of the gospel. According to Francis' own testimony in his *Testament,* written in the last year of his life, the key event in this process was the Lord's enabling him to overcome his revulsion for lepers.

> The Lord granted me, Brother Francis, to begin to do penance in this way: While I was in sin, it seemed very bitter to me to see lepers. And the Lord Himself led me among them and I had mercy upon them. And when I left them that which seemed bitter to me was changed into sweetness of soul and body; and afterward I lingered a little and left the world.

In contrast to Peter Waldo, Francis' conversion did not lead to an attack on the hierarchical church. In fact, he tells us that from the beginning of his new life he had great reverence for both church buildings and priests, even if priests were leading lives of sin.

> And the Lord gave me such faith in churches that I would simply pray and speak in this way: "We adore You, Lord Jesus Christ, in all Your churches throughout the world, and we bless You, for through Your holy cross You have redeemed the world."

Afterward the Lord gave me and still gives me such faith in priests who live according to the manner of the holy Roman Church because of their order, that if they were to persecute me, I would still have recourse to them. . . . And I do not consider sin in them because I discern the Son of God in them and they are my masters. And I act in this way since I see nothing corporally of the Most High Son of God in this world except His Most holy Body and Blood which they receive and which they alone administer to others. . . (*Testament*).

This respect for priests as ministers of the eucharist reflects the spirituality of Francis' age. During his lifetime, Innocent III (r. 1198–1216), the most powerful of the medieval popes, called the Fourth Lateran Council (1215) at which the doctrine of transubstantiation was officially defined. According to this doctrine, when the priest pronounces the words of consecration at the eucharist, the bread and wine are substantially changed into the body and blood of Christ.

Like Peter Waldo, Francis simply wanted to live the way of life taught by Jesus in the gospel, especially its poverty. In the early days of his new life he spent his time repairing rundown and abandoned churches. This work and his simple way of life quickly attracted a band of followers. As he says in his *Testament,*

And after the Lord gave me brothers, no one showed me what I should do, but the Most High revealed to me that I should live according to the form of the Holy Gospel.

Given his humble submission to the church, it is not surprising that in 1210 Francis went to Pope Innocent III for approval of his way of life.

And I had this [the gospel way of life] written down simply and in a few words and the Lord Pope confirmed it for me. And those who came to receive life gave to the poor everything which they were capable of possessing and they were content with one tunic, patched inside and out, with a cord and short trousers. And we had no desire for anything more. We [who were] clerics used to say the Office as other clerics did; the lay brothers said the Our Father; and we quite willingly stayed in churches. And we were simple and subject to all.

At first Innocent III tried to get Francis to adopt one of the existing rules like Benedict's or Augustine's, but Francis apparently convinced the pope to allow him and his followers to live this gospel way of life. It would hardly be appropriate for the pope to declare that living the gospel was impossible. The original simple rule of 1210 is no longer extant, but it is no doubt imbedded in the more formal language of the Rule of 1221. Even in this so-called "Earlier Rule" the difference between the Franciscan way of life and that of Benedict's monastic life is evident.

Whereas Benedict's Rule stressed the vows of amendment of life, obedience to the abbot, and stability in order to correct the problems of wandering and undisciplined monks in the early Middle Ages, Francis' Rule places the greatest emphasis on the life of gospel poverty. Francis was born into the rapidly expanding bourgeois society of the northern and central Italian city states. He had first-hand experience of the evils of avarice. His father, Pietro Bernadone was, according to all the early biographies of Francis, a wealthy cloth merchant who was consumed by greed. Francis himself had, as a young man, participated in the endemic warfare between competing city states brought on by emerging capitalism. This is not to say that Francis embraced a life of poverty out of a concern for economic justice and a redistribution of property. Nor was he idealizing the lives of the abject poor. Rather, Francis' dedication to poverty was a direct response to the gospel imperative of Jesus, "Do not take gold or silver or copper for your belts; no sack for the journey . . ." (Mt 10:9ff). In embracing poverty, Francis simply wanted to follow Jesus.

The spirit of poverty runs throughout the Rule. It quotes directly from Jesus' words to the rich young man: "If you wish to be perfect, go and sell everything you have and give it to the poor, and you will have treasure in heaven; and come follow me" (Mt 19:21). In describing the entrance of the brothers, the Rule makes particular mention of selling all one's possessions and giving them to the poor. The dress of the brothers is to mark them as *Fratres Minores,* "Lesser Brothers." They are to wear "poor clothes, and they can patch them with sackcloth and other pieces with the blessing of God." Although they are to work and pursue trades, the Friars Minor are to receive no money, only the necessities for their life. If they do not receive adequate compensation, they are not to be ashamed to beg. This is why both the Franciscans and Dominicans were called mendicant, or begging, orders.

The biographies and early legends about Francis are filled with examples of his knightly dedication to his bride "Lady Poverty." In his *Salutation of the Virtues,* Francis, like a troubadour, praises Poverty along with the other virtues as one might praise ladies in a feudal court. He also links them together in pairs that reflect his own unique vision in which the following of Christ is combined with chivalric idealism.

> Hail, Queen Wisdom, may the Lord protect you
>   with your sister, holy pure Simplicity.
> Lady, holy Poverty, may the Lord protect you
>   with your sister, holy Humility.
> Lady, holy Charity, may the Lord protect you
>   with your sister, holy Obedience.
> O most holy Virtues, may the Lord protect all of you,
>   from Whom you come and proceed.
> There is surely no one in the entire world
>   who can possess any of you
>   unless he dies first.
> Whoever possesses one [of you]
>   and does not offend the others,
>   possesses all.
> And whoever offends one [of you]

does not possess any
and offends all.
And each one destroys vices and sins.
Holy Wisdom destroys
    Satan and all his subtlety.
Pure holy Simplicity destroys
    all the wisdom of this world
    and the wisdom of the body.
Holy Poverty destroys
    the desire of riches
    and avarice
    and the care of this world.
Holy Humility destroys
    pride
    and all the people who are in the world
    and all things that belong to the world.
Holy Charity destroys
    every temptation of the devil and of the flesh
    and every carnal fear.
Holy Obedience destroys
    every wish of the body and of the flesh
    and binds its mortified body
to obedience of the Spirit
and to obedience of one's brother
and [the person who possesses her] is subject and submissive
    to all persons in the world
    and not to man only
    but even to all beasts and wild animals
    so that they may do whatever they want with him
    inasmuch as it has been given to them from above
    by the Lord.

(Translated by Regis Armstrong, O.F.M. Cap. and Ignatius Brady in *Francis and Clare: the Complete Works* [Paulist Press, 1982] 151–152.)

Within the community of the Lesser Brothers a spirit of poverty and humility is to mark their relationship with one another. None of the brethren is to have power or dominion over the others; even the head of the Order or of the various provinces is to be called "Minister" or Servant. No one is to be called "prior," and the basis for this is Jesus' teaching that "The princes of the Gentiles exercise dominion over them, and they that are great exercise authority over them, but it shall not be so among you" (Matt 20:25–27; Lk 22:26). The model for the friars' life together is the Jesus who washed his disciples' feet at the Last Supper (Jn 13:1–14).

In contrast to the Benedictine monks who withdrew from society to the rural countryside for lives of prayer and work, Francis, in imitation of Jesus, sent his lesser brothers into the world to preach the gospel. In this work also they were to be guided by Jesus' instructions to his apostles in the gospel. As itinerant preachers, they were to carry nothing with them, "neither a knapsack, nor a purse, nor bread, nor money, nor a staff" (Lk 9:3). Into whatever house they entered, they were to first say, "Peace to this house" (Lk 10:5), and if they were not received hospitably, they "should not offer resistance to evil." Rather, they were to follow literally Jesus' teachings in the Sermon on the Mount: "If someone should strike them on one cheek, let them offer him the other as well" (Mt 5:39; Lk 6:29).

Francis' poverty and asceticism had a positive quality. He did not spend his life bemoaning his sins and punishing his body because of the wickedness of carnal desire. Rather, he welcomed the suffering and deprivation that came in the course of trying to live the gospel. These were seen as a means to higher spiritual qualities, and hence they were to be received with joy. As he says in his *Salutation* to the virtues, "Holy Poverty destroys the desire of riches and avarice and the cares of this world."

The sense of freedom derived from Francis' life of poverty is closely associated with his new attitude toward nature. This might be the most important aspect of the spiritual revolution explicit in Francis' teaching. For centuries Christian saints, while recognizing that nature was originally God's creation, had regarded it as too corrupted by human sinfulness and too full of carnal temptations to be worthy of human enjoyment. The sense of natural beauty which had been expressed in the parables and sayings of Jesus had been all but lost. In fact, the Albigensians of Francis' own day saw nature as the product of Satan or an evil god, and therefore their elite "perfect" attempted to live as if they had no bodies. In contrast to the Albigensian aversion to nature, Francis saw all natural things as full of joy and a source of wonder. The reason for this was quite simple. He took the doctrine of creation by God seriously, though less intellectually as the theologian Thomas Aquinas would do later in the century, but in a deeply spiritual sense. Belief in God's act of creation was a reason to affirm the beauty and goodness of all God's creatures. Creation was God's bounty granted to his children and inspiring them to know and worship him, teaching them gentleness, consideration, reverence and love for the whole family of creation.

The biographies and early legends are filled with anecdotes illustrating Francis' love for and fellowship with all creatures, but perhaps the best illustration of this new attitude is his incomparable *Canticle of Brother Sun*. It is a song of praise to God as "Most High, all-powerful, good Lord" and to his gift of creation which is invited to be a part of Francis' praise. He speaks of God's creatures as his brothers and sisters who reveal the masculine and feminine characteristics of God. The sun, wind, weather, and fire are Francis' brothers who speak of God's beauty, radiance, splendor, sustaining power, playfulness, robustness and strength. The moon, stars, water, and earth are Francis' sisters who speak of God's precious clarity, beauty, cleanliness, humility, pure love, and fecundity. The later verses of the *Canticle* were added in the last days of Francis' life, and they integrate humans into this family of creation. Humans who are willing, according to

Jesus' teaching in the gospel, to "give pardon for [God's] love" are joined to Francis' song of praise. Finally in the last verse, Francis praises his Lord "through our Sister Bodily Death." By the time he composed this verse Francis was blind and weakened from the wounds of the stigmata which he had received while at prayer on Mt. Alverna in 1224. For Francis, "Sister Bodily Death" is part of the natural order and is not to be feared except by those "who die in mortal sin."

In a militant crusading age, Francis' attitude toward Muslims and nonbelievers is striking for its tolerance and Christ-like character. Although as a young man Francis attempted to go on crusade as a knight, after his conversion he repeatedly attempted to go as a missionary to the Muslims and finally succeeded in 1219, during the Fifth Crusade, in preaching to the Sultan of Egypt, Malik-al-Kamil. Jacques de Vitry (1180–1240), the bishop of Acre who was involved in the Fifth Crusade, tells the simple story of Francis' travelling unharmed into the Sultan's camp at Damietta where he preached the gospel and then was escorted back to the Christian camp by the Muslim forces. In his Rule Francis insists that any brother who is inspired by God "to go among the Saracens and nonbelievers should go with the permission of his minister and servant." When they go among the Saracens, the brothers are "to live spiritually among (them) in two ways." One is to simply live as Christians without engaging "in arguments or disputes." The other is "to proclaim the word of God when they see it pleases the Lord. . . ." In neither case are they to physically or spiritually attack the Saracen or nonbeliever.

Francis' personal charisma attracted enormous numbers to the Franciscan movement. His male Order of Friars grew exponentially in his own lifetime, and it is estimated that by the fourteenth century the Friars Minor numbered 28,000. Francis also founded two other orders: an order of cloistered nuns called the Poor Clares, named for Clare, an aristocratic woman of Assisi, who was inspired by Francis to embrace a life of gospel poverty, and a Third Order of laity who continued to live in the world while following the ideals of Francis.

In the last years of Francis' life he seems to have been increasingly disillusioned with the direction the order was taking, particularly in its approach to poverty. When he returned from Egypt in 1220, he discovered that the brothers had built a house, and he personally attempted to tear it down. At a general chapter in 1220, he himself resigned leadership of the order and pledged his obedience to his successor, Brother Elias. He also reluctantly consented to the writing of more formal versions of the Rule in 1221 and 1223 in which the friars' life was detailed in language more acceptable to the institutional church.

After Francis' death in 1226, the Franciscan movement was marked by stormy disagreements over the important question of poverty. This was closely linked with the question of whether the order would become a clerical order, dominated by priests, or an order primarily of lay brothers who would preach the gospel while living lives as simple laborers. Francis himself remained a deacon all of his life and never became an ordained priest. He was always fearful of the order becoming clerical with its concomitant needs for books, libraries, and houses of study. However, almost immediately after his death, this is the direction the Franciscans took. One party of friars wanted to modify Francis' teachings to allow the owning of property in order to further the order's increasingly clerical duties of study and preaching. By 1230, Pope Gregory IX had declared that Francis' *Testament,* which enjoined a strict life of poverty and forbade alterations to the Rule, was not legally binding. In 1245, the Franciscans began to have the use of property, although the Holy See reserved technical title to it.

These modifications were not achieved without protest. A second party, called the Spirituals, advocated a strict adherence to Francis' teachings on poverty. They even temporarily gained great influence in the order while John of Parma was Minister General (1247–1257). However, they became increasingly enamored of the apocalyptic teachings of Joachim of Fiore (c.1132–1202), who had predicted an age of the Holy Spirit to be inaugurated in 1260. This last age would see the rise of new "spiritual" religious orders which would convert the world. In the midst of this situation, John of Parma was succeeded by John of Fidanza, known as Bonaventure, who has been called "the second founder" of the Franciscans because he suppressed the spirituals by forcibly imprisoning them in convents, and guided the Franciscans in the direction of becoming a clerical order with houses at the universities like the Dominicans. The rigorist spirituals were forced more and more to the fringes of the order and the church. In the fourteenth century, they were called "the Fraticelli" and were eventually condemned by the worldly Avignon Pope John XXII in 1323 when he declared that belief in the absolute poverty of Christ and the apostles was heretical.

The translations are from Regis J. Armstrong, O.F.M. Cap. and Ignatius Brady, O.F.M. *Francis and Clare: The Complete Works* (Mahwah: Paulist Press, 1982) 109–112, 115–117, 120–122, 151–152, 154–156.

THE EARLIER RULE

Chapter I
The Brothers Must Live Without Anything of Their Own and in Chastity and in Obedience

1. The rule and life of these brothers is this: to live in obedience, in chastity, and without anything of their own, and to follow the teaching and the footprints of our Lord Jesus Christ, Who says: 2. "If you wish to be perfect, go (Mt 19:21) and sell everything (cf. Lk 18:22) you have and give it to the poor, and you will have treasure in heaven; and come, follow me" (Mt 19:21). 3. And, "If anyone wishes to come after me, let him deny himself and take up his cross and follow me" (Mt 16:24). 4. Again: "If anyone wishes to come to me and does not hate father and mother and wife and children and brothers and sisters, and even his own life, he cannot be my disciple" (Lk 14:26). 5. And: "Everyone who has left father or mother, brothers or sisters, wife or children, houses or lands because of me, shall receive a hundredfold and shall possess eternal life" (cf. Mt 19:29; Mk 10:29, Lk 18:30).

Chapter II
The Reception and the Clothing of the Brothers

1. If anyone, desiring by divine inspiration to accept this life, should come to our brothers, let him be received by them with kindness. . . . 4. When this has been done, . . . [he]

should sell all his possessions and strive to give them all to the poor. . . . 14. And all the brothers should wear poor clothes, and they can patch them with sackcloth and other pieces with the blessing of God; for the Lord says in the Gospel: "Those who wear costly clothes and live in luxury (Lk 7:25) and "who dress in soft garments are in the houses of kings" (Mt 11:8).

Chapter IV
The Ministers and The Other Brothers: How They Are Related

1. In the name of the Lord. 2. All the brothers who have been established as ministers and servants of the other brothers should assign their brothers to the provinces and to the places where they are to be, and they should visit them frequently and spiritually admonish and encourage them. 3. And all my other blessed brothers should diligently obey them in those matters which concern the well-being of their soul and [which] are not contrary to our life. And among themselves let them behave according to what the Lord says: "Whatever you wish that men should do to you, do that to them (Matt 7:12); 5. and, "That which you do not wish to be done to you, do not do to another" (Tb 4:16). 6. And let the ministers and servants remember what the Lord says: "I have not come to be served, but to serve" (Matt 20:28); and because the care of the souls of the brothers has been entrusted to them, if anyone of them should be lost because of their fault or bad example, [these ministers and servants] will have to "render an account' before the Lord Jesus Christ "on the day of judgment" (cf. Matt 12:36).

Chapter VI
The Recourse of the Brothers to the Minister; No Brother Should Be Called Prior

1. If the brothers, in whatever places they are, cannot observe our life, they should have recourse as quickly as possible to their minis-

ter and report this to him. 2. The minister, on his part, should be eager to provide for them as he would wish to be done for him were he in a similar position (cf. Matt 7:12). 3. And no one should be called Prior, but all generally should be called Friars Minor. And the one should wash the feet of the others (cf. Jn 13:14).

Chapter VII
The Manner of Serving And Working

1. None of the brothers should be administrators or managers in whatever places they are staying among others to serve or to work, nor should they be supervisors in the houses in which they serve; nor should they accept any office which might generate scandal or be harmful to their souls (cf. Mk 8:36); 2. Instead, they should be the lesser ones and subject to all who are in the same house.

3. And the brothers who know how to work should do so and should exercise that trade which they [already] know, if it is not against the good of the soul and can be performed honestly. For the prophet says: "You shall eat the fruits of your labors; you are blessed and it will be well for you" (Ps 127:2). 5. And the Apostles [says]: "Whoever does not wish to work shall not eat" (cf. 2 Thes 3:10); 6. and, "Everyone should remain" in that skill and office "in which he has been called" (1 Cor 7:24). 7. And they may receive for their work everything necessary except money. 8. And when it should be necessary, let them seek also like other poor people. 9. And they may have the tools and instruments suitable for their trades.

Chapter IX
Begging Alms

1. All the brothers should strive to follow the humility and the poverty of our Lord Jesus Christ and remember that we should have nothing else in the whole world except, as the Apostle says, "having something to eat and something to wear, we be content with

these" (cf. 1 Tim 6:8). And they must rejoice when they live among people [who are considered to be] of little worth and who are looked down upon, among the poor and the powerless, the sick and the lepers, and the beggars by the wayside.

Chapter XIV
The Manner Of The Brothers' Conduct In The World

1. When the brothers go about through the world, they should carry "nothing" for the journey, "neither a knapsack, nor a purse, nor bread, nor money, nor a staff" (Lk 9:3; cf. Lk 10:4; Matt 10:10). And "into whatever house they enter, let them first say: Peace to this house" (cf. Lk 10:5). And, remaining in that house, they may eat and drink "whatever [their hosts] have offered" (cf. Lk 10:7). 4. They should "not offer resistance to evil" (Matt 5:39), but if someone should strike them on one cheek, let them "offer him the other as well" (cf. Matt 5:39; Lk 6:29). 5. And if someone "should take away their clothes," they should not deny him also their tunic (cf. Lk 6:29). They should give "to all who ask; and if anyone takes what is theirs," they should not demand that it be returned (cf. Lk 6:30).

Chapter XV
The Brothers Are Not to Ride Horses

1. I enjoin upon all my brothers both cleric and lay that, when they go through the world or stay in places, they should in no way have any animal either with themselves or in the care of another or in any other way. 2. Nor may they ride horses unless they are compelled by sickness or great necessity.

Chapter XVI
Those Who Are Going Among The Saracens and Other Nonbelievers

1. The Lord says: "Behold, I am sending you as lambs in the midst of wolves. 2. Therefore, be "prudent as serpents and simple

as doves" (Matt 10:16). 3. Therefore, any brother who, by divine inspiration, desires to go among the Saracens and other nonbelievers should go with the permission of his minister and servant. . . . 5. As for the brothers who go, they can live spiritually among [the Saracens and nonbelievers] in two ways. 6. One way is not to engage in arguments or disputes, but to be subject "to every human creature for God's sake" (1 Pet 2:13) and to acknowledge that they are Christians. Another way is to proclaim the word of God when they see that it pleases the Lord, so that they believe in the all-powerful God—Father, and Son, and Holy Spirit—the Creator of all, in the Son Who is the Redeemer and Savior, and that they be baptized and become Christians; because "whoever has not been born again of water and the Holy Spirit cannot enter into the kingdom of God" (cf. Jn 3:5).

THE TESTAMENT

1. The Lord granted me, Brother Francis, to begin to do penance in this way: While I was in sin, it seemed very bitter to me to see lepers. 2. And the Lord Himself led me among them and I had mercy upon them. 3. And when I left them that which seemed bitter to me was changed into sweetness of soul and body; and afterward I lingered a little and left the world.

4. And the Lord gave me such faith in churches that I would simply pray and speak in this way: "We adore You, Lord Jesus Christ, in all Your churches throughout the world, and we bless You, for through Your holy cross You have redeemed the world."

6. Afterward the Lord gave me and still gives me such faith in priests who live according to the manner of the holy Roman Church because of their order, that if they were to persecute me, I would [still] have recourse to them. 7. And if I possessed as much wisdom as Solomon had and I came upon pitiful priests of

this world, I would not preach contrary to their will in the parishes in which they live. 8. And I desire to fear, love, and honor them and all others as my masters. 9. And I do not wish to consider sin in them because I discern the Son of God in them and they are my masters. 10. And I act in this way since I see nothing corporally of the Most High Son of God in this world except His Most holy Body and Blood which they receive and which they alone administer to others. 11. And these most holy mysteries I wish to have honored above all things and to be reverenced and to have them reserved in precious places. 12. Wherever I come upon His most holy written words in unbecoming places, I desire to gather them up and I ask that they be collected and placed in a suitable place. 13. And we should honor and respect all theologians and those who minister the most holy divine words as those who minister spirit and life to us (cf. Jn 6:64).

14. And after the Lord gave me brothers, no one showed me what I should do, but the Most High Himself revealed to me that I should live according to the form of the Holy Gospel. 15. And I had this written down simply and in a few words and the Lord Pope confirmed it for me. 16. And those who came to receive life gave to the poor everything which they were capable of possessing and they were content with one tunic, patched inside and out, with a cord and short trousers. 17. And we have no desire for anything more. 18. We [who were] clerics used to say the Office as other clerics did; the lay brothers said the Our Father; and we quite willingly stayed in churches. 19. And we were simple and subject to all.

20. And I used to work with my hands, and I [still] desire to work; and I firmly wish that all my brothers give themselves to honest work. 21. Let those who do not know how [to work] learn, not from desire of receiving wages for their work but as an example and in order to avoid idleness. 22. And when we are not paid for our work, let us have recourse to the table

of the Lord, seeking alms from door to door. 23. The Lord revealed to me a greeting, as we used to say: "May the Lord give you peace."

24. Let the brothers beware that they by no means receive churches or poor dwellings or anything which is built for them, unless it is in harmony with [that] holy poverty which we have promised in the Rule, [and] let them always be guests there as pilgrims and strangers (1 Pet 2:11). 25. And I firmly command all of the brothers through obedience that, wherever they are, they should not be so bold as to seek any letter from the Roman Curia either personally or through an intermediary, neither for a church or for some other place or under the guise of preaching or even for the persecution of their bodies; 26. But where they have not been received, let them flee into another country to do penance with the blessing of God.

27. And I firmly wish to obey the minister general of this fraternity and another guardian whom it might please him to give me. 28. And I wish to be so captive in his hands that I cannot go [anywhere] or do [anything] beyond obedience and his will, for he is my master.

29. And although I may be simple and infirm, I wish nonetheless always to have a cleric who will celebrate the Office for me as it is contained in the Rule. 30. And all the other brothers are bound to obey their guardians and to celebrate the Office according to the Rule. 31. And [if] any are found who do not celebrate the Office according to the Rule and [who] wish to alter it in any way or [who] are not Catholics, let all the brothers be obliged through obedience that wherever they come upon [such a brother] they must bring him to the custodian [who is] nearest to that place where they have found him. 32. And the custodian is strictly bound through obedience to guard him strongly as a prisoner day and night, so that he cannot be snatched from his hands until he can personally deliver him into the hands of his minister. 33. And the minister

is strictly bound through obedience to send him with brothers who shall guard him as a prisoner day and night until they deliver him before the Lord of Ostia who is the master, protector, and corrector of the entire fraternity.

34. And let the brother not say: This is another Rule; because this is a remembrance, an admonition, an exhortation, and my testament, which I, little Brother Francis, prepare for all of you, my blessed brothers, so that we may observe in a more Catholic manner the Rule which we have promised to the Lord.

35. And the minister general and all other ministers and custodians are bound through obedience not to add to or subtract from these words. 36. And let them always have this writing with them alone with the Rule. 37. And in all the chapters which they hold, when they read the Rule, let them also read these words. 38. And I through obedience strictly command all my brothers, cleric and lay, not to place glosses on the Rule or on these words, saying: They are to be understood in this way. 39. But as the Lord has granted me to speak and to write the Rule and these words simply and purely, so shall you understand them simply and without gloss, and observe them with [their] holy manner of working until the end.

40. And whoever shall have observed these [things], may he be filled in heaven with the blessing of the most high Father and on earth with the blessing of His beloved Son and the most Holy Spirit the Paraclete and with all the powers of heaven and all the saints. 41. And I, little brother Francis, your servant, inasmuch as I can, confirm for you this most holy blessing both within and without.

THE CANTICLE OF BROTHER SUN

1. Most High, all-powerful, good Lord,
   Yours are the praises, the glory, the honor, and all blessing.
2. To You alone, Most High, do they belong,
   and no man is worthy to mention Your name.
3. Praised be You, my Lord, with all your creatures,
   especially Sir Brother Sun,
   Who is the day and through whom You give us light.
4. And he is beautiful and radiant with great splendor;
   and bears a likeness of You, Most High One.
5. Praised be You, my Lord, through Sister Moon and the stars,
   in heaven You formed them clear and precious and beautiful.
6. Praised be You, my Lord, through Brother Wind,
   and through the air, cloudy and serene, and every kind of weather
   through which You give sustenance to Your creatures.
7. Praised be You, my Lord, through Sister Water,
   which is very useful and humble and precious and chaste.
8. Praised be You, my Lord, through Brother Fire,
   through whom You light the night and he is beautiful and playful and robust and strong.
9. Praised be You, my Lord, through our Sister Mother Earth,
   who sustains and governs us, and who produces varied fruits with colored flowers and herbs.
10. Praised be You, my Lord, through those who give pardon for Your love
    and bear infirmity and tribulation.
11. Blessed are those who endure in peace for by You, Most High, they shall be crowned.
12. Praised be You, my Lord, through our Sister Bodily Death,
    from whom no living man can escape.
13. Woe to those who die in mortal sin.

Blessed are those whom death will find
in Your most holy will,
for the second death shall do them no
harm.

14. Praise and bless my Lord and give Him
thanks
and serve Him with great humility.

BONAVENTURE

The greatest Franciscan theologian of the thirteenth century was Giovanni di Fidanza, better known as St. Bonaventure (1217–1274). Bonaventure is a representative of the so-called Augustinian school of Franciscan theologians who continued the tradition we have seen in Augustine, Pseudo-Dionysius, Anselm and Bernard. Like his predecessors, Bonaventure begins with faith in the truths of revelation and uses reason to explicate them. He also places a priority on will over reason and love over truth. In order to know real wisdom (*sapientia*), according to Bonaventure, one must do God's will and one must live the gospel life. Bonaventure seems to have been attracted first to the life of scholarship and then through his pursuit of wisdom to the Franciscan Order. He was born in Bagnoregio, Italy, in 1217, and according to tradition was cured as a young teenager by the intercession of St. Francis. In 1234 he went to the University of Paris where he eventually studied theology and philosophy under the famous English scholar, Alexander of Hales, who became a Franciscan in 1236. In 1243, Bonaventure followed his master's footsteps and entered the Franciscans; by 1253, he was a master in theology and the head of the Franciscan school at Paris. In 1257 Bonaventure was elected Minister General of the Franciscans and did much to settle internal dissension in the order over how to interpret the vow of poverty. He was made a cardinal in 1273 and died while attending the Council of Lyons in 1274.

As a theologian Bonaventure attempted to unite the Christ-centered gospel simplicity of Francis with the sophisticated scholasticism of Paris. For Bonaventure the link that held the two together was his understanding of God as a Trinity of three Persons united in love. Basing himself on the Christian Platonism found in the Greek fathers and Augustine, Bonaventure treated the Trinity as the mystery of the self-diffusion of God. The Father is the fountain source of divine fecundity in whom divinity is dynamic, self-expressive. The Father generates the Son out of his fullness, thereby expressing himself in his perfect image, his eternal Word. This divine fecundity issues further in the procession of the Holy Spirit from the Father and the Son as their mutual love and gift in whom all good gifts are given.

Bonaventure's theology bears certain similarities to the thought of contemporary mystics in the Muslim and Jewish traditions. Like Ibn al-'Arabi (d. 1240), the great Spanish Muslim mystic, and Moses de Leon (d. 1305), the Spanish Jewish kabbalist, Bonaventure understood the created world as an overflow and expression of divine fecundity. For Bonaventure, each object in creation reflects the power, wisdom and goodness of the triune God. Creation can be a "ladder" leading the soul to God. It will bear the "vestige," the footprint or the trace, of God its Creator. Creatures are "mirrors" in which the divine love is reflected for those who have eyes of faith and can read "the book" of creation. In a similar manner, Ibn al-'Arabi in the *Bezels of Wisdom* understood creatures as so many "bezels" or settings for mirroring the goodness of God. Likewise, Moses de Leon's *Zohar* speaks of the way God's divine attributes, the *sefirot,* are manifested through creation.

A major difference between Bonaventure and the Muslim and Jewish traditions is his Christocentric thought. In Bonaventure's trinitarian theology, as the Father generates the Son, he produces in the Son the archetypes of all he can create. When the Father does create through the divine Word, the world reflects these archetypes. The Son is the link between God and creation. All created reality is an expression of the Son and refers back to him, by way of exemplarism, i.e., being grounded in him as the divine exemplar. For Bonaventure, as for all Christian theologians of the era, in its present state the created order is "bent" by sin. The way back to God is through the incarnate Son who, because of sin, came as the crucified one.

In the debates at the University of Paris over the role of the newly discovered works of Aristotle, Bonaventure took a more conservative stance than the Dominican theologian, Thomas Aquinas, who was willing to rethink the whole of theology using Aristotelian categories. Bonaventure, as has been mentioned, continued the theological tradition associated with Augustine, Neoplatonism and the mysticism of Pseudo-Dionysius. Like Augustine, Bonaventure believed that all knowledge depends upon divine illumination, whereas Thomas insisted that some truths are attainable by the natural light of reason alone. In the process of coming to true knowledge Bonaventure emphasized the importance of the right disposition of the human will and the need for God's grace. As an Aristotelian, Thomas will argue that natural knowledge depends upon the senses and the abstracting powers of the human intellect. For Bonaventure, creatures are important only insofar as they provide traces of God. Thomas, by contrast, will consider creatures in themselves, not simply as reflections of God.

In our selections from *The Soul's Journey into God* the Franciscan, Augustinian and mystical elements of Bonaventure's theology are all quite prominent. The occasion for this work was Bonaventure's reflections on Francis' vision of a six-winged seraph in the form of the crucified Christ on Mount Alverna when he received the stigmata. Bonaventure himself had come to Mount Alverna seeking peace in the midst of his duties as the seventh Minister General of the Order which was embroiled in disputes over the observance of Francis' teaching on poverty. His meditation leads Bonaventure to explore the road by which the soul can come to the contemplation of and union with God as Francis had experienced it in his reception of the stigmata.

The title of the work is significant. In the Latin original it reads *Itinerarium mentis ad Deum.* Like Augustine and most medieval thinkers, Bonaventure understands life as a "journey" (*Itinerarium*); we are all pilgrims who are really citizens of the heavenly Jerusalem, the place of ultimate peace. The term translated as "soul" in the title is *mentis* in Latin and is often translated as "mind." For Bonaventure however, *mens* means more than the mental faculty; it includes the human capacity to love. The goal of the journey is not simply knowledge of God, but union with God in love, and therefore the preposition *ad* should be translated as "into" rather than "to."

In the Prologue the influence of Augustine, Pseudo-Dionysius, Anselm, and Francis is evident. Like Augustine, Bonaventure believes that, in order to know and see the world truly, the mind must be illumined by God and faith. This explains the prayer for enlightenment and grace at the beginning and throughout the work.

> I call upon the Eternal Father through his Son, our Lord Jesus Christ, that through the intercession of the most holy Virgin Mary, the mother of the same God and Lord Jesus Christ, and through the intercession of blessed Francis, our leader and father, he may enlighten the eyes of our soul to guide our feet in the way of peace which surpasses all understanding.

Bonaventure understands the six wings of the seraph in the vision of Francis as symbols for the six levels of illumination by which the soul can come to an ecstatic experience of God. This is not, then, a purely intellectual journey. It is ultimately a mystical journey of love and, for Bonaventure, the only way to God is through the crucified Christ. His models are Paul and Francis. Paul's mystical experience of God came through "the burning love of the Crucified, as is seen in his words: 'With Christ I am nailed to the cross. I live, now not I, but Christ lives in me'" (Gal 2:20). Likewise, the love of the crucified so absorbed Francis that for the last two years of his life he carried in his body the sacred stigmata. Therefore, as Bonaventure begins his reflections he invites the reader to pray through the crucified Christ for divine wisdom, not simply intellectual insight.

In the body of the work Bonaventure systematically examines the six stages by which the soul can pass into God by contemplation. These are: 1) contemplating God through his vestiges in the universe, 2) contemplating God through his vestiges in the sense world, 3) contemplating God through his image stamped upon humans' natural powers, 4) contemplating God in his image reformed by the gift of grace, 5) contemplating the divine unity through its primary name which is being, and 6) contemplating the Trinity in its name which is good. In the final chapter Bonaventure explores spiritual and mystical ecstasy when our affection passes over entirely into God. Our selections are taken from chapters one and seven.

Bonaventure begins chapter one like a medieval sermon with a quotation from scripture which will set the terms for his reflection. "Blessed is the man whose help is from you;/ in his heart he has prepared to ascend by steps in the valley of tears,/ in the place which he has set" (Ps 83:6–7). Following Augustine, Bonaventure notes that "the highest good" is above human powers and can be reached only by an ascent "of the heart" which requires divine aid. He then, like Dionysius, turns to prayer as "the mother and source of the ascent." Prayer will enable the soul to receive the light to discern the steps of ascent into God.

At this point Bonaventure gives us his understanding of the universe as a "ladder by which we can ascend to God." He divides reality into three divisions, or what is often called the three books, where the soul can read the signs of God: the material world which is outside humans and contains the vestiges of God, the interior spiritual world of the human soul which contains the image of God, and the eternal and most spiritual world which tells of God as the First Principle. Using allegorical interpretations, Bonaventure goes on to see these ways as foreshadowed in various places in scripture. He also sees them as corresponding to the orientations of the mind toward the material world, toward itself, and above itself.

When he actually begins to consider the material world as a mirror that reveals the supreme "Craftsman," Bonaventure looks at created things as revealing the power, wisdom and benevolence of the Creator. In this section he consistently finds groups of threes in the created world which reflect the triune character of God: the Father's power, the Son's wisdom, and the Spirit's benevolence. For example, in contemplating or considering things in themselves the mind sees in them "weight, number and measure"; also "mode, species and order"; and finally "substance, power and operation." Bonaventure concludes by noting, "From these, as from a vestige, we can rise to knowledge of the immense power, wisdom and goodness of the Creator."

In the last sections of chapter one, Bonaventure considers what he calls the sevenfold properties of creatures: origin, magnitude, multitude, beauty, fullness, activity and order. All of these are explored in a kind of hymn to God's power, wisdom and goodness. This section is a theologian's version of Francis' *Canticle of Brother Sun*. Bonaventure concludes by inviting his readers to open their eyes to see the signs of God in the splendor of created things.

Whoever, therefore, is not enlightened by such splendor of created things is blind;
whoever is not awakened by such outcries is deaf;
whoever does not praise God because of all these effects is dumb;
Whoever does not discover the First Principle from such clear signs is a fool.
Therefore, open your eyes, alert the ears of your spirit, open your lips and apply your heart so that in all creatures you may see, hear, praise, love and worship, glorify and honor your God. . . .

In the final chapter Bonaventure exhorts the reader to "pass over" or "transcend" the material world and his own mind in mystical ecstasy. The way of full return to God for the fallen creature is through the crucified Christ, "the way and the door," and in faith, hope, and love. In the earlier chapters, reason and philosophy offer partial help by the knowledge they give of the sensible world and of the nature of the human mind itself, its powers and activities as the image of its Creator. But in this final chapter, Bonaventure, like Bernard, invites the reader to union with God in the fire of the love of the crucified.

But if you wish to know how these things [ecstasy] come about, ask grace not instruction, desire not understanding, the groaning of prayer not diligent reading, the Spouse not the teacher, God not man, darkness not clarity, not light but the fire that totally inflames and carries us into God by ecstatic unctions and burning affections. This fire is God, and his furnace is in Jerusalem; and Christ enkindles it in the heart of his burning passion. . . .

The translation and notes are by Ewert Cousins in *Bonaventure: The Soul's Journey into God, The Tree of Life, The Life of St. Francis* (Mahwah, NJ: Paulist Press, 1978) 53–68, 110–116.

THE SOUL'S JOURNEY INTO GOD

Prologue

1. In the beginning I call upon the First Beginning (Gen 1:1; Jn 1:1), from whom all illuminations descend as from the "Father of Lights," from whom comes "every good and every perfect gift" (James 1:17). I call upon the Eternal Father through his Son, our Lord Jesus Christ, that through the intercession of the most holy Virgin Mary, the mother of the same God and Lord Jesus Christ, and through the intercession of blessed Francis, our leader and father, he "may enlighten the eyes of our soul to guide our feet in the way of that peace which surpasses all understanding" (cf. Eph 1:18; Lk 1:79; Phil 4:7). This is the peace proclaimed and given to us by our Lord Jesus Christ and preached again and again by our father Francis. At the beginning and end of every sermon he announced peace; in every greeting he wished for peace; in every contemplation he sighed for ecstatic peace—like a citizen of that Jerusalem of which that Man of Peace says, who "was peaceable with those who hated peace: Pray for the peace of Jerusalem" (Ps 119:7; 121:6). For he knew that the throne of Solomon would not stand except in peace, since it is written, "In peace is his place and his abode in Sion" (Ps 75:3).

2. Following the example of our most blessed father Francis, I was seeking this peace with panting spirit—I a sinner and utterly unworthy who after our blessed father's death had become the seventh Minister General of the Friars. It happened that about the time of the thirty-third anniversary of the Saint's death, under divine impulse, I withdrew to Mount La Verna, seeking a place of quiet and desiring to find there peace of spirit. While I was there reflecting on various ways by which the soul ascends into God, there came to mind, among other things the miracle which had occurred to blessed Francis in this very place; the vision of a winged Seraph in the form of the Crucified. While reflecting on this, I saw at once that this vision represented our father's rapture in contemplation and the road by which this rapture is reached.

3. The six wings of the seraph can rightly be taken to symbolize the six levels of illumination by which, as if by steps or stages, the soul can pass over to peace through ecstatic elevation of Christian wisdom. There is no other path through the burning love of the Crucified, a love which so transformed Paul into Christ when he "was carried up to the third heaven" (2 Cor 12:2) that he could say: "With Christ I am nailed to the cross. I live, now not I, but Christ lives in me" (Gal 2:20). This love also so absorbed the soul of Francis that his spirit shone through his flesh when for two years before his death he carried in his body the sacred stigmata of the passion. The six wings of the Seraph, therefore, symbolize the six steps of illumination that begin from creatures and lead up to God, whom no one rightly enters except through the Crucified. For "he who enters not through the door, but climbs up another way is a thief and a robber." But "if anyone enter" through this door, "he will go in and out and will find pastures" (Jn 10:1,9). Therefore John says in the Apocalypse: "Blessed are they who wash their

robes in the blood of the Lamb that they may
have a right to the tree of life and may enter
the city through the gates" (Apoc 22:14). It is
as if John were saying that no one can enter
the heavenly Jerusalem by contemplation
unless he enter though the blood of the Lamb
as through a door. For no one is in any way
disposed for divine contemplation that leads
to mystical ecstasy unless like Daniel he is "a
man of desires" (Dan 9:23). Such desires are
enkindled in us in two ways: by an outcry of
prayer that makes us "call aloud in the groaning of our heart" (Ps 37:9) and by the flash of
insight by which the mind turns most directly and intently toward the rays of light.

4. First, therefore, I invite the reader to the
groans of prayer through Christ crucified,
through whose blood we are cleansed from the
filth of vice—so that he not believe that reading is sufficient without unction, speculation
without devotion, investigation without wonder, observation without joy, work without
piety, knowledge without love, understanding
without humility, endeavor without divine
grace, reflection as a mirror without divinely
inspired wisdom. To those, therefore, predis-
posed by divine grace, the humble and the
pious, the contrite and the devout, those
anointed with "the oil of gladness" (Ps 44:8),
the lovers of divine wisdom, and those
inflamed with a desire for it, to those wishing
to give themselves to glorifying, wondering at
and even savoring God, I propose the following considerations, suggesting that the mirror
presented by the external world is of little or
no value unless the mirror of our soul has
been cleaned and polished. Therefore, man of
God, first exercise yourself in remorse of conscience before you raise your eyes to the rays
of Wisdom reflected in its mirrors, lest perhaps from gazing upon these rays you fall into
a deeper pit of darkness.

5. It seemed good to divide this work into
seven chapters, giving each a title for a better
understanding of the contents. I ask you,
then, to weigh the writer's intention rather
than his work, the meaning of his words
rather than his uncultivated style, truth
rather than beauty, the exercise of affection
rather than erudition of intellect. To do this,
you should not run rapidly over the development of these considerations, but should mull
them over slowly with the greatest care.

HERE ENDS THE PROLOGUE
HERE BEGINS THE REFLECTION OF THE POOR
MAN IN THE DESERT

*Chapter One: On the Stages of the Ascent
into God and on Contemplating Him through
His Vestiges in the Universe*

1. "Blessed is the man whose help is from
you; in his heart he has prepared to ascend by
steps in the valley of tears, in the place which
he has set" (Ps 83:6–7). Since happiness is
nothing other than the enjoyment of the highest good and since the highest good is above,
no one can be made happy unless he rise
above himself, not by an ascent of the body,
but of the heart. But we cannot rise above
ourselves unless a higher power lift us up. No
matter how much our interior progress is
ordered, nothing will come of it unless accompanied by divine aid. Divine aid is available to
those who seek it from their hearts, humbly
and devoutly; and this means to sigh for it in
this "valley of tears," through fervent prayer.
Prayer, then, is the mother and source of the
ascent. Dionysius, therefore, in his book
Mystical Theology, wishing to instruct us in
mystical ecstasy, places a prayer at the outset. Let us pray, therefore, and say to the Lord
our God: "Lead me, Lord, in your path, and I
will enter in your truth. Let my heart rejoice
that it may fear your name" (Ps 85:11).

2. By praying in this way, we receive light
to discern the steps of the ascent into God. In
relation to our position in creation, the universe itself is a ladder by which we can ascend
into God. Some created things are vestiges,

others images; some are material, others spiritual; some are temporal, others everlasting; some are outside us, others within us. In order to contemplate the First Principle, who is most spiritual, eternal and above us, we must pass through his vestiges, which are material, temporal and outside us. This means "to be led in the path of God." We must also enter into our soul, which is God's image, everlasting, spiritual and within us. This means "to enter in the truth of God." We must go beyond to what is eternal, most spiritual and above us, by gazing upon the First Principle. This means to "rejoice in the knowledge of God and in reverent fear of his majesty" (cf. Ps 85:11).

3. This threefold division, then, corresponds to the three days' journey into the wilderness (Exod 3:18), and to the threefold intensity of light during a single day: The first is like evening, the second like morning, the third like noon. This division reflects also the threefold substance in Christ, who is our Ladder: bodily, spiritual and divine.

4. Corresponding to this threefold movement, our mind has three principal perceptual orientations. The first is toward exterior material objects and is the basis of its being designated as animal or sensual. The second orientation is within itself and into itself and is the basis for its being designated as spirit. The third is above itself and is the basis for its being designated as mind. By all of these we should dispose ourselves to ascend into God so as to love him "with our whole mind, with our whole heart and with our whole soul" (Mk 12:30; Matt 22:37; Luke 10:27). In this consists both perfect observance of the Law and Christian wisdom.

5. Any one of these ways can be doubled, according to whether we consider God as "the Alpha and the Omega" (Apoc 1:8). Or in each of these ways we can see him through a mirror or in a mirror. Or we can consider each way independently or as joined to another.

Therefore it is necessary that these three principal stages be multiplied to a total of six. Just as God completed the whole world in six days and rested on the seventh, so the smaller world of man is led in a most orderly fashion by six successive stages of illumination to the quiet of contemplation. This is symbolized by the following: Six steps led up to the throne of Solomon (1 Chr 10:19); the Seraphim which Isaiah saw had six wings (Isa 6:2); after six days the Lord called Moses "from the midst of the cloud" (Exod 24:16); and "after six days," as is said in Matthew, Christ "led his disciples up a mountain and was transfigured before them" (Matt 17:1–2).

6. Just as there are six stages in the ascent into God, there are six stages in the powers of the soul, through which we ascend from the lowest to the highest, from the exterior to the interior, from the temporal to the eternal. These are the senses, imagination, reason, understanding, intelligence, and the summit of the mind or the spark of conscience. We have these stages implanted in us by nature, deformed by sin and reformed by grace. They must be cleansed by justice, exercised by knowledge and perfected by wisdom.

7. In the initial state of creation, man was made fit for the quiet of contemplation, and therefore "God placed him in a paradise of delights" (Gen 2:15). But turning from the true light to changeable good, man was bent over by his own fault, and the entire human race by original sin, which infected human nature in two ways: the mind with ignorance and the flesh with concupiscence. As a result, man, blinded and bent over, sits in darkness and does not see the light of heaven unless grace with justice come to his aid against concupiscence and unless knowledge with wisdom come to his aid against ignorance. All this is done through Jesus Christ, "whom God made for us wisdom, justice, sanctification and redemption" (1 Cor 1:30). Since he is "the power of God and the wisdom of God" (1 Cor

1:24), the incarnate Word "full of grace and truth" (Jn 1:14), he made "grace" and "truth." That is, he pours out the grace of charity, which, since it flows "from a pure heart and a good conscience and faith unfeigned" (1 Tim 1:5), rectifies the entire soul in the threefold orientation mentioned above. He has taught the knowledge of truth according to the threefold mode of theology: symbolic, literal and mystical, so that through the symbolic we may rightly use sensible things, through the literal we may rightly use intelligible things and through the mystical we may be lifted above to ecstasy.

8. Whoever wishes to ascend to God must first avoid sin, which deforms our nature, then exercise his natural powers mentioned above: by praying, to receive restoring grace; by a good life, to receive purifying justice; by meditating, to receive illuminating knowledge; and by contemplating, to receive perfecting wisdom. Just as no one comes to wisdom except through grace, justice and knowledge, so no one comes to contemplation except by penetrating meditation, a holy life and devout prayer. Since grace is the foundation of the rectitude of the will and of the penetrating light of reason, we must first pray, then live holy lives and thirdly concentrate our attention upon the reflections of truth. By concentrating there, we must ascend step by step until we reach the height of the mountain "where the God of gods is seen in Sion" (Ps 83:8).

9. Since we must ascend Jacob's ladder before we descend it, let us place our first step in the ascent at the bottom, presenting to ourselves the whole material world as a mirror though which we may pass over to God, the supreme Craftsman. Thus we shall be true Hebrews passing over from Egypt to the land promised to their fathers (Exod 13:3ff); we shall also be Christians passing over with Christ "from this world to the Father" (Jn 13:1); we shall be lovers of wisdom, which

calls to us and says: "Pass over to me all who long for me and be filled with my fruits" (Eccles 24:26). "For from the greatness and beauty of created things, their Creator can be seen and known" (Wis 13:5).

10. The Creator's supreme power, wisdom and benevolence shine forth in created things, as the bodily senses convey this to the interior senses in three ways. For the bodily senses assist the intellect when it investigates rationally, believes faithfully or contemplates intellectually. In contemplating, it considers the actual existence of things; in believing, the habitual course of things; and in reasoning, the potential excellence of things.

11. In the first way, that of contemplation, we consider things in themselves and see in them weight, number and measure: weight, by which they tend to their position; number, by which they are distinguished; and measure, by which they are limited. Thus we see in them mode, species and order as well as substance, power and operation. From these, as from a vestige, we can rise to knowledge of the immense power, wisdom and goodness of the Creator.

12. In the second way, that of faith, we consider this world, in its origin, process and end. For "by faith" we believe that "the world was fashioned by the Word of life" (Heb 11:3). By faith we believe that the periods of the three laws—of nature, Scripture and grace—succeeded each other and progressed in a most orderly way. By faith we believe that the world must come to an end with final judgment. In the first, we consider the power of the supreme Principle; in the second, his providence; and in the third, his justice.

13. In the third way, that of investigating by reason, one sees that some things merely exist, others exist and live, and other exist, live and discern. He sees that the first are less perfect; the second, intermediate; and the third, more perfect. Likewise he sees that some things are material, others partly mate-

rial and partly spiritual. From this he realizes that others are purely spiritual and are better and more noble than the two previous classes. He sees, finally, that some things are changeable and corruptible, as are earthly bodies; others are changeable and incorruptible, as are heavenly bodies. From this he realizes that other things are unchangeable and incorruptible, as are supercelestial realities.

From these visible things, therefore, one rises to consider the power, wisdom and goodness of God as existing, living, intelligent, purely spiritual, incorruptible and unchangeable.

14. This reflection can be extended according to the sevenfold properties of creatures—which is a sevenfold testimony to the divine power, wisdom and goodness—if we consider the origin, magnitude, multitude, beauty, fullness, activity and order of all things.

The *origin* of things, according to their creation, distinction and embellishment, as the work of the six days, proclaims the divine power that produces all things from nothing, the divine wisdom that clearly distinguishes all things, and the divine goodness that lavishly adorns all things.

The *magnitude* of things, in the mass of their length, width and depth; in their great power extending in length, width and depth as appears in the diffusion of light; in the efficiency of their operations which are internal, continuous and diffused as appears in the operation of fire—all this clearly manifests the immensity of the power, wisdom and goodness of the triune God, who by his power, presence and essence exists uncircumscribed in all things.

The *multitude* of things in their generic, specific and individual diversity in substance, form or figure, and efficiency—beyond all human calculation—clearly suggests and shows the immensity of the three previously mentioned attributes in God.

The *beauty* of things, in the variety of light,

shape and color in simple, mixed and even organic bodies—such as heavenly bodies, and minerals (like stones and metals), and plants and animals—clearly proclaims the three previously mentioned attributes.

The *fullness* of things by which matter is full of forms because of seminal principles, form is full of power because of its active potency, power is full of effects because of its efficiency, clearly declares the same attributes.

The *activity*, multiple inasmuch as it is natural, artificial and moral, by its manifold variety shows the immensity of that power, art and goodness which is "the cause of being, the basis of understanding and the order of living."

The *order* in duration, position and influence, that is, before and after, higher and lower, nobler and less noble, in the book of creation clearly indicates the primacy, sublimity and dignity of the First Principle and thus the infinity of his power. The order of the divine law, precepts and judgments in the book of Scripture shows the immensity of his wisdom. And the order of the divine sacraments, benefits and recompense in the body of the Church shows the immensity of his goodness. In this way order itself leads us most clearly into the first and highest, the most powerful the wisest and the best.

15. Whoever, therefore, is not enlightened by such splendor of created things is blind; whoever is not awakened by such outcries is deaf; whoever does not praise God because of all these effects is dumb; whoever does not discover the First Principle from such clear signs is a fool. Therefore, open your eyes, alert the ears of your spirit, open your lips and "apply your heart" (Prov 22:17) so that in all creatures you may see, hear, praise, love and worship, glorify and honor your God lest the whole world rise against you. For because of this "the whole world will fight against the foolish" (Wis 5:20). On the contrary, it will be

a matter of glory for the wise, who can say with the Prophet: "You have gladdened me, Lord, by your deeds and in the works of your hands I will rejoice. How great are your works, Lord! You have made all things in wisdom; the earth is filled with your creatures" (Ps 91:5–6; 103:24).

Chapter Seven: On Spiritual and Mystical Ecstasy in which Rest is Given to our Intellect when through Ecstasy our Affection Passes over entirely into God

1. We have, therefore, passed through these six considerations. They are like the six steps of the true Solomon's throne, by which we arrive at peace, where the true man of peace rests in a peaceful mind as in the interior Jerusalem. They are also like the six wings of the Seraph by which the mind of the true contemplative can be borne aloft, filled with the illumination of heavenly wisdom. They are also like the first six days, in which the mind has been trained so that it may reach the sabbath of rest. After our mind has beheld God outside itself through his vestiges and in his vestiges, within itself through his image and in his image, and above itself through the similitude of the divine Light shining above us and in the Light itself, insofar as this is possible in our state as wayfarers and through the exercise of our mind, when finally in the sixth stage our mind reaches that point where it contemplates in the First and Supreme Principle and in the *mediator of God and men* (1 Tim 2:5), Jesus Christ, those things whose likenesses can in no way be found in creatures and which surpass all penetration by the human intellect, it now remains for your mind, by contemplating these things, to transcend and pass over not only this sense world but even itself. In this passing over, Christ is the "way and the door" (Jn 14:6; 10:7); Christ is the ladder and the vehicle, like the Mercy Seat placed above the ark of God and the "mystery hidden from eternity" (Eph 3:9).

2. Whoever turns his face fully to the Mercy Seat and with faith, hope and love, devotion admiration, exultation, appreciation, praise and joy beholds him hanging upon the cross, such a one makes the pasch, that is, the passover, with Christ. By the staff of the cross he passes over the Red Sea, going from Egypt into the desert, where he will taste the hidden manna; and with Christ he rests in the tomb, as if dead to the outer world, but experiencing, as far as is possible in this wayfarer's state, what was said on the cross to the thief who adhered to Christ; "Today you shall be with me in paradise" (Luke 23:43).

3. This was shown also to blessed Francis, when in ecstatic contemplation on the height of the mountain—where I thought out these things I have written—there appeared to him a six-winged Seraph fastened to a cross, as I and several others heard in that very place from his companion who was with him then. There he passed over into God in ecstatic contemplation and became an example of perfect contemplation as he had previously been of action, like another Jacob and Israel, so that through him, more by example than by word, God might invite all truly spiritual men to this kind of passing over and spiritual ecstasy.

4. In this passing over, if it is to be perfect, all intellectual activities must be left behind and the height of our affection must be totally transferred and transformed into God. This, however, is mystical and most secret, which "no one knows except him who receives it" (Apoc 2:17), no one receives except him who desires it, and no one desires except him who is inflamed in his very marrow by the fire of the Holy Spirit whom Christ sent into the world. And therefore the apostle says that this mystical wisdom is revealed by the Holy Spirit (1 Cor 2:10ff.).

5. Since, therefore, in this regard nature can do nothing and effort can do but little, lit-

tle importance should be given to inquiry, but much to unction; little importance should be given to the tongue, but much to inner joy; little importance should be given to words and to writing, but all to the gift of God, that is, the Holy Spirit; little or no importance should be given to creation, but all the creative essence, the Father, Son and Holy Spirit, saying with Dionysius to God the Trinity: "Trinity, superessential, superdivine and supereminent overseer of the divine wisdom of Christians, direct us into the superunknown, superluminous and most sublime summit of mystical communication. There new, absolute and unchangeable mysteries of theology are hidden in the superluminous darkness of a silence teaching secretly in the utmost obscurity which is supermanifest—a darkness which is superresplendent and in which everything shines forth and which fills to overflowing invisible intellects with the splendors of invisible goods that surpass all good" (Dionysius, *De mystica theologia,* I,1). This is said to God. But to the friend to whom these words were written, let us say with Dionysius: "But you, my friend, concerning mystical visions, with your journey more firmly determined, leave behind your sense and intellectual activities, sensible and invisible things, all nonbeing and being; and in this state of unknowing be restored, insofar as is possible, to unity with him who is above all essence and knowledge. For transcending yourself and all things, by the immeasurable and absolute ecstasy of a pure mind, leaving behind all things and freed from all things, you will ascend to the superessential ray of the divine darkness" (*De mystica theologia,* I,1).

6. But if you wish to know how these things come about, ask grace not instruction, desire not understanding, the groaning of prayer not diligent reading, the Spouse not the teacher, God not man, darkness not clarity, not light but the fire that totally inflames and carries us into God by ecstatic unctions and burning affections. This fire is God, and "his furnace is in Jerusalem" (Isa 31:9); and Christ enkindles it in the heat of his burning passion, which only he truly perceives who says: "My soul chooses hanging and my bones death" (Job 7:15). Whoever loves this death can see God because it is true beyond doubt that "man will not see me and live" (Exod 33:20). Let us, then, die and enter into the darkness; let us impose silence upon our cares, our desires and our imaginings. With Christ crucified let us pass "out of this world to the Father" (Jn 13:1) so that when the Father is shown to us, we may say with Philip: "It is enough for us" (Jn 14:8). Let us hear with Paul: "My grace is sufficient for you" (2 Cor 12:9). Let us rejoice with David saying: "My flesh and my heart have grown faint; You are the God of my heart, and the God that is my portion forever. Blessed be the Lord forever and all the people will say: Let it be; let it be. Amen" (Ps 72:26; 105:48).

HERE ENDS THE SOUL'S JOURNEY INTO GOD

THOMAS AQUINAS

The greatest Christian theologian of the High Middle Ages was the Dominican master, Thomas Aquinas (1225–1274). He received his early education at Monte Cassino and the University of Naples. At the age of eighteen he entered the Dominican order over the strenuous objections of his family. The Dominicans had been founded by St. Dominic de Guzman, a Spaniard, as an order devoted to preaching and study, hence their official title, the Order of Preachers. As early as 1203 Dominic, a canon of Osma, had been working to convert the Albigensians in Languedoc to Roman Catholicism. In order to facilitate this work, Dominic was convinced that preachers needed a solid grounding in the dogmatic theology of the church and had to be committed to the living of the Christian gospel, especially poverty. When the order was formally recognized in 1216, it adopted the Rule of Augustine and the practice of corporate poverty, like the Franciscans. A major difference between the two orders, however, was the Dominican emphasis on theological education. In contrast to Francis who was not a trained theologian and was always suspicious of his order becoming involved in houses of study, Dominic from the beginning sent his friars to the universities to become trained theologians.

This way of life suited Thomas, who from 1245–1251 studied at Paris and Cologne under Albert the Great, the other renowned Dominican philosopher and theologian of the age. Thomas himself taught at Paris (during two different periods), Rome, Bologna, and Naples. Although actively engaged in the affairs of the church and the Dominican Order, Thomas steadfastly refused to accept an appointment as a cardinal. His lasting contribution to Western theology was through his monumental works of theology, especially his *Summa Theologica*. By an unusual coincidence, Thomas, like his friend and colleague Bonaventure, died in 1274, while journeying to the Council of Lyon.

The first selection is taken from Thomas' *Summa Theologica* which is designed as a complete, reasoned summary of the whole of Christian theology. Like the magnificent Gothic cathedrals and Dante's *Divine Comedy*, Thomas' *Summa* brilliantly illustrates the spirit of the High Middle Ages: a golden age of Christian faith which sought to use reason to comprehend all reality as an ordered whole under God's rule. The *Summa* is a brilliant attempt at the harmonization of faith and reason, of traditional Christian theology based on the scriptures and the church fathers (especially Augustine) and the recently translated philosophical works of Aristotle.

Reflecting the traditional Augustinian scheme of the coming forth of creation from God and the return of humans to God in Christ, the *Summa* is divided into three parts. Part one considers God in himself, in the unity of his nature and in the Trinity of the divine persons, and the coming forth of creatures from God. In part two Thomas treats the return of the rational creature to God by analyzing the true end of humans and the nature of human acts as the means of return to God. In this long section Thomas creatively uses Aristotle's philosophy to systematically probe human acts. He considers both human acts in general, by considering the acts themselves and their causes both intrinsic (powers and habits) and extrinsic (law and grace), and in particular by treating the theological and cardinal virtues, special graces and vocations. Finally, part three presents Christ, who inasmuch as he is the God-man, is the way by which we return to God. In this unfinished section, Thomas treats first Christ himself, the mystery of the incarnation, Christ's deeds, and sufferings. Then he discusses the sacraments which have their efficacy through the incarnate Word. Last of all, Thomas presents immortal life by considering the resurrection and the last things.

The first article of the first question of the *Summa* on "the nature and extent of sacred doctrine" is presented in full to illustrate the scholastic method of organizing material into a series of questions and dividing each question into a series of separate articles, each treating a particular issue raised by the question. For each article Thomas lists objections to his position; then expresses his own point of view, citing authorities to support it; and finally he replies to each objection in sequence. Each question is treated in this careful and precise manner so that the *Summa* is a massive, yet detailed and structured work.

The remainder of the selections are taken from Thomas' *Compendium of Theology*, a treatise on faith, hope and charity which illustrates his major theological positions. Thomas, like Peter Abelard and unlike Augustine and Bonaventure, had a great respect for the unaided powers of human reason and the autonomy of philosophy, especially the "new" Aristotelean philosophy which had come to the University of Paris through the Muslim and Jewish philosophers. His position on the relationship between reason and faith, or philosophy and theology stands in sharp contrast to that of Bonaventure who believed that pagan philosophy had a very limited authority and value as an aid in penetrating the mysteries of the faith. According to Thomas, natural reason can know the external world without divine illumination and can discern the structure of created things through its sciences. Reason has a legitimate domain in analyzing the human person, ethics and politics. Thomas even extends reason's competence to certain "spiritual" truths; for example, he, like Maimonides, believes that reason can prove the existence of God. In the *Summa* he offers five proofs from reason for God's existence; each of them uses principles of Aristotelean philosophy and begins with the observation of a fact in the external world. This approach is quite different from Anselm's more Augustinian and Platonic method of arguing for the existence of God on the basis of the idea of God in one's mind. The selection from the *Compendium of Theology* includes Thomas' argument from motion which reasons back to God as the immobile principle of all motion. Thomas also argues that human reason can arrive at a "negative" knowledge of God's attributes (e.g. simplicity, infinity, unchangeability, etc.) and can prove truths about the human person, such as the immortality of the human soul.

Despite his tremendous respect for the powers of reason, Thomas nevertheless insists that there are supernatural truths which transcend beyond reason that humans would not know if God had not revealed them through the sacred scriptures and the church's teaching. These "revealed" truths include: the Trinity, Christ's divinity, the need for grace, the sacraments, and the final things (heaven and hell). However, even in these matters, reason has the capacity to clarify, but not exhaust or fully comprehend, these truths and to order them in a coherent way. In his discussion of the Trinity in the *Compendium of Theology* for example, Thomas uses the human processes of knowledge and love to probe the mystery of the unity of Father, Son and Holy Spirit in the Trinity.

For Thomas, philosophy and theology differ in their starting points and methods. Whereas philosophy begins with human reason and moves toward the truth by a rigorous intellectual enquiry, theology starts with revealed truths and uses reason to clarify, order, and even draw out the implications of revelation.

Philosophy and theology may consider the same matter, for example, the nature of God, but they do so by using their respective methods.

> The diversification of the sciences is brought about by the diversity of aspects under which things can be known. Both an astronomer and a physical scientist may demonstrate the same conclusion, for instance that the earth is spherical. . . . Accordingly there is nothing to stop the same things from being treated by the philosophical sciences when they can be looked at in the light of natural reason and by another science when they are looked at in the light of divine revelation. (S. Th., I q. 1, art. 1)

Because the human mind is weak and only a few would be able to arrive at some truths about God after a long time, Thomas argued that it was necessary for God to reveal the truths which are necessary for salvation.

> Hence it was necessary for the salvation of man that certain truths which exceed human reason should be made known to him by divine revelation. Even as regards those truths about God which human reason could have discovered, it was necessary that man should be taught by divine revelation; because the truth about God such as reason could discover, would only be known by a few, and that after a long time and with the admixture of many errors. Whereas man's whole salvation, which is in God, depends upon the knowledge of this truth. (S. Th. I, q. 1, art. 1)

This is essentially the same position that Averroes and Maimonides held on the necessity for revelation within their own traditions.

Despite his great respect for the powers of human reason, Thomas did not think that reason could define or grasp God's essence as it is in itself. Like Aristotle, Thomas insisted that all knowledge begins in the senses, but we cannot directly observe God through our senses. Our knowledge of God through reason is drawn from creatures who manifest multiple perfections because they come from God who is absolutely simple and unites all perfections in unity. Therefore, following the mystical tradition of Pseudo-Dionysius, Thomas believes our knowledge of God is largely a "negative" knowledge.

> We cannot know what God is, but only what He is not; we must therefore consider the ways in which God does not exist rather than the ways in which He does. (S. Th. q. 1. art. 3)

In his treatment of human language about God, Aquinas steers a careful middle path between a naive optimism and a pessimistic agnosticism. On the one hand, Thomas does not think that we can predicate terms of God in an univocal or equivalent sense; that is, words like "wisdom" and "goodness," whose meaning we learn from observing God's creatures, do not mean the same thing when we apply them to the infinite and perfect being of God.

Nevertheless, Thomas insists that our language about God is not pure equivocation. Because creatures do bear some resemblance to their Creator, Thomas uses the term "analogy" to indicate that terms are predicated of creatures and of God, the origin of perfection in creatures, in some proportion.

> Therefore such terms are not predicated altogether equivocally about God and about other things, as happens in fortuitous equivocation. Consequently they are predicated according to analogy, that is, according to their proportion to one thing. For, from the fact that we compare other things with God as their first origin, we attribute to God such names as signify perfections in other things. This clearly brings out the truth, that as regards the assigning of the names, such names are primarily predicated of creatures, inasmuch as the intellect that assigns the names ascends from creatures to God. But as regards the thing signified by the name, they are primarily predicated of God, from whom the perfections descend to other beings (Com. Th. ch. 27).

In his treatment of the nature and end of the human person, Thomas also has a respect for the natural dignity and capacities of human nature, even apart from God's grace. Following Aristotle and against Plato and Augustine, Thomas thinks the human person is not simply a soul using a body, but rather a composite of both soul and body, so that neither by itself is human. Thomas also agrees with Aristotle that every being is directed toward a certain end or goal and that the end of the human person is happiness or beatitude which is found through habitual virtuous behavior. For Aristotle the virtues were temperance, courage, justice and wisdom which correspond to the various functions of the human soul. The highest and distinctive function of the human soul is its capacity for knowledge which will not be satisfied until it knows God, the highest good.

As a Christian theologian Thomas, of course, believed in original sin and the subsequent disordering and weakening of human nature which can only be restored by the incarnation and Christ's redeeming death and resurrection. Ultimate happiness, which is the beatific vision of God, is now beyond the natural powers of the human person. The beatific vision will only be attained fully in the future life through God's supernatural aid or grace in Christ.

> Man's happiness . . . is twofold. One is proportional to human nature, a happiness which man can obtain by means of the principles of his nature. The other is a happiness surpassing man's nature, and which man can obtain by the power of God alone, by a kind of participation in the Godhead, and thus it is written (2 Pet 2:14) that by Christ we are made partakers of the divine nature. (S. Th. II 1–2, 621)

Grace for Thomas is a "power of God" without which humans cannot achieve their ultimate end. Because of his respect for the innate powers of human nature, Thomas can also speak of "growth" in grace and human cooperation with God's grace. God infuses "certain supernatural forms or qualities," whereby the person may be moved sweetly and promptly to acquire eternal good. Grace perfects nature according to Thomas. The theological virtues of faith, hope and charity which come from the original gift of sanctifying grace (a share in God's life) perfect the natural capacities of the human person for knowledge, courage and love.

Thomas always considers Christ in the context of humanity's return to God, and therefore he does not speculate about Christ in isolation from the way in which he actually came, that is, as redeemer for a fallen humanity. Like Anselm, Thomas argued that the justice of God demanded that only Christ as the God-man could make reparation for fallen humanity, but Thomas also recognized other reasons for the incarnation: to restore humans to the spiritual life, to display the dignity of human nature, to show the immensity of God's love for humans and to stir them to love of God, to offer the ideal of a created intellect joined to the uncreated Spirit, and to complete the circular movement whereby humans as the last creatures to be created return to God, the very principle of all things.

Thomas' Christology is based on the gospels and the teachings of the early church councils which defined the nature of Christ as one person who is fully human and divine. Thomas' term for this is the hypostatic union, i.e., the union of the divine and human nature in the one person of the Word of God. By virtue of that union Thomas can say that in Christ the divine Word was born of a virgin, suffered, died, and rose. Because human destiny is union with God, it is fitting that Christ who is both true God and true man is the instrument of grace by which this union is effected.

The translation of the *Summa* is from *Summa Theologica,* English Dominican trans., I, 1. The translation of the *Compendium* is by Cyril Vollert in *Compendium of Theology* (St. Louis: B. Herder Book Co., 1947)

SUMMA THEOLOGICA

FIRST PART
QUESTION 1

The Nature and Extent of Sacred Doctrine
(In Ten Articles)

To place our purpose within proper limits, we first endeavor to investigate the nature and extent of this sacred doctrine. Concerning this there are ten points of inquiry:—

(1) Whether it is necessary? (2) Whether it is a science? (3) Whether it is one or many? (4) Whether it is speculative or practical? (5) How it is compared with other sciences? (6) Whether it is the same as wisdom? (7) Whether God is its subject-matter? (8) Whether it is a matter of argument? (9) Whether it rightly employs metaphors and similes? (10) Whether the

Sacred Scripture of this doctrine may be expounded in different sense?

FIRST ARTICLE

Whether, besides Philosophy, Any Further Doctrine Is Required?

We proceed thus to the First Article:—

Objection 1. It seems that, besides philosophical science, we have no need of any further knowledge. For man should not seek to know what is above reason: *Seek not the things that are too high for thee* (Ecclus. iii. 22). But whatever is not above reason is fully treated of in philosophical science. Therefore any other knowledge besides philosophical science is superfluous.

Obj. 2. Further, knowledge can be concerned only with being, for nothing can be known, save what is true; and all that is, is true. But everything that is, is treated of in philosophical science—even God Himself; so that there is a part of philosophy called theology, or the divine science, as Aristotle has proved (*Metaph.* vi). Therefore, besides philosophical science, there is no need of any further knowledge.

On the contrary, It is written (2 Tim. iii. 16): *All Scripture inspired of God is profitable to teach, to reprove, to correct, to instruct in justice.* Now Scripture, inspired of God, is no part of philosophical science, which has been built up by human reason. Therefore it is useful that besides philosophical science there should be other knowledge—i.e., inspired of God.

I answer that, it was necessary for man's salvation that there should be a knowledge revealed by God, besides philosophical science built up by human reason. Firstly, indeed, because man is directed to God, as to an end that surpasses the grasp of his reason: *The eye hath not seen, O God, besides Thee, what things Thou hast prepared for them that wait for Thee* (Isa. lxvi. 4). But the end must first be known by men who are to direct their thoughts and actions to the end. Hence it was necessary for the salvation of man that certain truths which exceed human reason should be made known to him by divine revelation. Even as regards those truths about God which human reason could have discovered, it was necessary that man should be taught by a divine revelation; because the truth about God such as reason could discover, would only be known by a few, and that after a long time, and with the admixture of many errors. Whereas man's whole salvation, which is in God, depends upon the knowledge of this truth. Therefore, in order that the salvation of men might be brought about more fitly and more surely, it was necessary that they should be taught divine truths by divine revelation. It was therefore necessary that, besides philosophical science built up by rea-

son there should be a sacred science learned through revelation.

Reply Obj. 1 Although those things which are beyond man's knowledge may not be sought for by man through his reason, nevertheless, once they are revealed by God they must be accepted by faith. Hence the sacred text continues, *For many things are shown to thee above the understanding of man* (Eccles. iii. 25). And in this the sacred science consists.

Reply Obj. 2. Sciences are differentiated according to the various means through which knowledge is obtained. For the astronomer and the physicist both may prove the same conclusion—that the earth, for instance, is round: the astronomer by means of mathematics (i.e., abstracting from matter), but the physicist by means of matter itself. Hence there is no reason why those things which may be learned from philosophical science, so far as they can be known by natural reason, may not also be taught us by another science so far as they fall within revelation. Hence theology included in sacred doctrine differs in kind from that theology which is part of philosophy.

COMPENDIUM OF THEOLOGY

CHAPTER I
SCOPE OF THE PRESENT WORK

To restore man, who had been laid low by sin, to the heights of divine glory, the Word of the eternal Father, though containing all things within His immensity, willed to become small. This He did, not by putting aside His greatness, but by taking to Himself our littleness. No one can say that he is unable to grasp the teaching of heavenly wisdom; what the Word taught at great length, although clearly, throughout the various volumes of Sacred Scripture for those who have leisure to study, He has reduced to brief compass for the sake of those whose time is taken up with the cares of daily life. Man's salvation consists in knowing the truth, so that the human mind may not be confused by divers errors; in making for the right goal, so that man may not fall away from true happiness by pursuing wrong ends; and in carrying out the law of justice, so that he may not besmirch himself with a multitude of vices.

Knowledge of the truth necessary for man's salvation is comprised within a few brief articles of faith. The Apostle says in Romans 9:28: "short word shall the Lord make upon the earth"; and later he adds: "This the word of faith, which we preach" (Rom 10:8). In a short prayer Christ clearly marked out man's right course; and in teaching us to say this prayer, he shows us the goal of our striving and our hope. In a single precept of charity He summed up that human justice which consists in observing the law: "Love therefore is the fulfilling of the law" (Rom 13:10). Hence the Apostle, in 1 Corinthians 13:13, taught that the whole perfection of this present life consists in faith, hope, and charity, as in certain brief headings outlining our salvation: "Now there remain faith, hope, and charity." These are the three virtues, as St. Augustine says, by which God is worshiped.

Wherefore, my dearest son Reginald, receive from my hands this compendious treatise on Christian teaching to keep continually before your eyes. My whole endeavor in the present work is taken up with these three virtues. I shall treat first of faith, then of hope, and lastly of charity. This is the Apostle's arrangement which, for that matter, right reason imposes. Love cannot be rightly ordered unless the proper goal of our hope is established; nor can there be any hope if knowledge of the truth is lacking. Therefore the first thing necessary is faith, by which you may come to a knowledge of the truth. Secondly, hope is necessary, that your intention may be fixed on the right end. Thirdly,

love is necessary, that your affections may be perfectly put in order.

CHAPTER 3
THE EXISTENCE OF GOD

Regarding the unity of the divine essence, we must first believe that God exists. This is a truth clearly known by reason. We observe that all things that move are moved by other things, the lower by the higher. The elements are moved by heavenly bodies; and among the elements themselves, the strong moves the weaker; and even among the heavenly bodies, the lower are set in motion by the higher. This process cannot be traced back into infinity. For everything that is moved by another is a sort of instrument of the first mover. Therefore, if a first mover is lacking, all things that move will be instruments. But if the series of movers and things moved is infinite, there can be no first mover. In such a case, these infinitely many movers and things moved will all be instruments. But even the unlearned perceive how ridiculous it is to suppose that instruments are moved, unless they are set in motion by some principal agent. This would be like fancying that, when a chest or a bed is being built, the saw or the hatchet performs its functions without the carpenter. Accordingly there must be a first mover that is above all the rest; and this being we call God.

CHAPTER 4
THE IMMOBILITY OF GOD

We clearly infer from this that God, who moves all things, must Himself be immovable. If He, being the first mover, were Himself moved, He would have to be moved either by Himself or by another. He cannot be moved by another, for then there would have to be some mover prior to Him, which is against the very idea of a first mover. If He is moved by Himself, this can be conceived in two ways:

either that He is mover and moved according to the same respect, or that He is a mover according to one aspect of Him and is moved according to another aspect. The first of these alternatives is ruled out. For everything that is moved is, to that extent, in potency, and whatever moves is in act. Therefore if God is both mover and moved according to the same respect, He has to be in potency and in act according to the same respect, which is impossible. The second alternative is likewise out of the question. If one part were moving and another were moved, there would be no first mover Himself as such, but only by reason of that part of Him which moves. But what is per se is prior to that which is not per se. Hence there cannot be a first mover at all, if this perfection is attributed to a being by reason of a part of that being. Accordingly the first mover must be altogether immovable.

Among things that are moved and that also move, the following may also be considered. All motion is observed to proceed from something immobile, that is, from something that is not moved according to the particular species of motion in question. Thus we see that alterations and generations and corruptions occurring in lower bodies are reduced, as to their first mover, to a heavenly body that is not moved according to this species of motion, since it is incapable of being generated, and is incorruptible and unalterable. Therefore the first principle of all motion must be absolutely immobile.

CHAPTER 22
UNITY OF ALL PERFECTIONS IN GOD

If we gather together the various points established thus far, we perceive that all perfections in God are in reality one. We have shown above that God is simple. But where there is simplicity, there can be no distinction among the perfections that are present. Hence, if the perfections of all things are in

God, they cannot be distinct in Him. Accordingly they are all one in Him.

This will become evident to anyone who reflects on our cognitive powers. A higher faculty has a unified knowledge of all that is known through the lower faculties according to diverse aspects. All that the sight, the hearing, and the other senses perceive, the intellect judges with the one, simple power that belongs to it. Something similar appears in the sciences. The lower sciences are multiplied in accord with the various classes of beings that constitute their objects. Yet one science which holds the primacy among them is interested in all classes of beings. This is known as first philosophy. The same situation is observed in civil power; in the royal power, which is but one, are included all the powers that are distributed through various offices within the jurisdiction of the kingdom. In the same way perfections which in lower things are multiplied according to the diversity of these things, must be united in the pinnacle of being, that is, in God.

CHAPTER 24
GOD'S SIMPLICITY NOT CONTRADICTED BY THE MULTIPLICITY OF NAMES APPLIED TO HIM

This enables us to perceive the reason for the many names that are applied to God, even though in Himself He is absolutely simple. Since our intellect is unable to grasp His essence as it is in itself, we rise to a knowledge of that essence from the things that surround us. Various perfections are discerned in these things, the root and origin of them all being one in God, as has been shown. Since we cannot name an object except as we understand it (for names are signs of things understood), we cannot give names to God except in terms of perfection perceived in other things that have their origin on Him. And since these perfections are multiple in such things, we must assign many names to God. If we saw His essence as it is in itself, a multiplicity of names would not be required; our idea of it would be simple, just as His essence is simple. This vision we hope for in the day of our glory; for, according to Zacharias 14:9, "In that day there shall be one Lord, and His name shall be one."

CHAPTER 25
THE NAMES OF GOD NOT SYNONYMOUS

In this connection three observations are in order. The first is that the various names applied to God are not synonymous, even though they signify what is in reality the same thing in God. In order to be synonymous, names must signify the same thing, and besides must stand for the same intellectual conception. But when the same object is signified according to diverse aspects, that is, notions which the mind forms of that object, the names are not synonymous. For then the meaning is not quite the same, since names directly signify intellectual conceptions, which are likeness of things. Therefore, since the various names predicated of God signify the various conceptions our mind forms of Him, they are not synonymous, even though they signify absolutely the same thing.

CHAPTER 26

A second point is this: since our intellect does not adequately grasp the divine essence in any of the conceptions which the names applied to God signify, the definitions of these terms cannot define what is in God. That is, any definition we might formulate of the divine wisdom would not be a definition of the divine power, and so on regarding other attributes.

The same is clear for another reason. A definition is made up of genus and specific differences, for what is properly defined is the species. But we have shown that the divine essence is not included under any genus or species. Therefore it cannot be defined.

CHAPTER 27
ANALOGY OF TERMS PREDICATED OF GOD AND OF OTHER BEINGS

The third point is that names applied to God and to other beings are not predicated either quite univocally or quite equivocally. They cannot be predicated univocally, because the definition of what is said of a creature is not a definition of what is said of God. Things predicated univocally must have the same definition.

Nor are these names predicated in all respects equivocally. In the case of fortuitous equivocation, a name is attached to an object that has no relation to another object bearing the same name. Hence the reasoning in which we engage about one cannot be transferred to the other. But the names predicated of God and of other things are attributed to God according to some relation He has to those things; and in their case the mind ponders what the names signify. This is why we can transfer our reasoning about other things to God.

Therefore such terms are not predicated altogether equivocally about God and about other things, as happens in fortuitous equivocation. Consequently they are predicated according to analogy, that is, according to their proportion to one thing. For, from the fact that we compare other things with God as their first origin, we attribute to God such names as signify perfections in other things. This clearly brings out the truth that, as regards the assigning of the names, such names are primarily predicated of creatures, inasmuch as the intellect that assigns the names ascends from the creatures to God. But as regards the thing signified by the name, they are primarily predicated of God, from whom the perfections descend to other beings.

CHAPTER 35
THE FOREGOING TRUTHS EMBRACED IN ONE ARTICLE OF FAITH

From all the details thus far discussed, we can gather that God is one, simple, perfect, and infinite, and that He understands and wills. All these truths are assembled in a brief article of our Creed, wherein we profess to believe "in one God, almighty." For, since this name "God" (*Deus*), is apparently derived from the Greek name, *Theos,* which comes from *theasthai,* meaning to see or to consider, the very name of God makes it clear that He is intelligent and consequently that He wills. In proclaiming that He is one, we exclude a plurality of gods, and also all composition; for a thing is not simply one unless it is simple. The assertion that He is almighty is evidence of our belief that He possesses infinite power, from which nothing can be taken away. And this includes the further truth that He is infinite and perfect; for the power of a thing follows the perfection of its essence.

CHAPTER 36
PHILOSOPHICAL CHARACTER OF THIS DOCTRINE

The truths about God thus far proposed have been subtly discussed by a number of pagan philosophers, although some of them erred concerning these matters. And those who propounded true doctrine in this respect were scarcely able to arrive at such truths even after long and painstaking investigation. But there are other truths about God revealed to us in the teaching of the Christian religion, which were beyond the reach of the philosophers. These are truths about which we are instructed, in accord with the norm of Christian faith, in a way that transcends human perception. The teaching is this: although God is one and simple, as has been explained, God is Father, God is Son, and God is Holy Ghost. And these three are not three gods, but are one God. We now turn to a consideration of this truth, so far as it is possible to us.

CHAPTER 37
THE WORD IN GOD

We take from the doctrine previously laid down that God understands and loves Himself; likewise, that understanding and willing in Him are not something distinct from His essence. Since God understands Himself, and since all that is understood is in the person who understands, God must be in Himself as the object understood is in the person understanding. But the object understood, so far as it is, in the one who understands, is a certain word of the intellect; we signify by an exterior word what we comprehend interiorly in our intellect. For words, according to the Philosopher, are signs of intellectual concepts. Hence we must acknowledge in God the existence of His Word.

CHAPTER 38
THE WORD AS CONCEPTION

What is contained in the intellect, as an interior word, is by common usage said to be a conception of the intellect. A being is said to be conceived in a corporeal way if it is formed in the womb of a living animal by a life-giving energy, in virtue of the active function of the male and the passive function of the female, in whom the conception takes place. The being thus conceived shares in the nature of both parents and resembles them in species.

In a similar manner, what the intellect comprehends is formed in the intellect, the intelligible object being, as it were, the active principle, and the intellect the passive principle. That which is thus comprehended by the intellect, existing as it does within the intellect, is conformed both to the moving intelligible object, of which it is a certain likeness, and to the quasi-passive intellect, which confers on it intelligible existence. Hence what is comprehended by the intellect is not unfittingly called the conception of the intellect.

CHAPTER 39
RELATION OR THE WORD TO THE FATHER

But here a point of difference must be noted. What is conceived in the intellect is a likeness of the thing understood and represents its species; and so it seems to be a sort of offspring of the intellect. Therefore, when the intellect understands something other than itself, the thing understood is, so to speak, the father of the word conceived in the intellect, and the intellect itself resembles rather a mother, whose function is such that conception takes place in her. But when the intellect understands itself, the word conceived is related to the understanding person as offspring to father.

Consequently, since we are using the term "Word" in the latter sense, that is, according as God understands Himself, the Word itself must be related to God, from whom the Word proceeds, as Son to Father.

CHAPTER 40
GENERATION IN GOD

Hence in the rule of Catholic faith we are taught to profess belief in the Father and Son in God by saying: "I believe in God the Father, and in His Son." And lest anyone, on hearing Father and Son mentioned, should have any notion of carnal generation, by which among us men father and son receive their designation, John the Evangelist, to whom were revealed heavenly mysteries, substitutes "Word" for "Son," (Jn 1:14) so that we may understand that the generation is intellectual.

CHAPTER 41
THE SON EQUAL TO THE FATHER IN EXISTENCE AND ESSENCE

Since natural existence and the action of understanding are distinct in us, we should note that a word conceived in our intellect, having only intellectual existence, differs in nature from our intellect, which has natural existence. In God, however, to be and to understand are identical. Therefore the divine Word that is in God, whose Word He is according to intellectual existence, has the same existence as God, whose Word He is. Consequently the Word must be of the same essence and nature as God Himself, and all attributes whatsoever that are predicated of God, must pertain also to the Word of God.

CHAPTER 42
THIS TEACHING IN CATHOLIC FAITH

Hence we are instructed in the rule of Catholic faith to profess that the Son is "consubstantial with the Father," a phrase that excludes two errors. First, the Father and the Son may not be thought of according to carnal generation, which is effected by a certain separation of the son's substance from the father. If this were so in God, the Son could not be consubstantial with the Father. Secondly, we are taught not to think of the Father and the Son according to intellectual generation in the way that a word is conceived in our mind. For such a word comes to our intellect by a sort of accidental accretion, and does not exist with the existence proper to the essence of the intellect.

CHAPTER 45
GOD IN HIMSELF AS BELOVED IN LOVER

As the object known is in the knower, to the extent that it is known, so the beloved must be in the lover, as loved. The lover is, in some way, moved by the beloved with a certain interior impulse. Therefore, since a mover is in contact with the object moved, the beloved must be intrinsic to the lover. But God, just as He understands Himself, must likewise love Himself; for good, as apprehended, is in itself lovable. Consequently God is in Himself as beloved in lover.

CHAPTER 46
LOVE IN GOD AS SPIRIT

Since the object known is in the knower and the beloved is in the lover, the different ways of existing in something must be considered in the two cases before us. The act of understanding takes place by a certain assimilation of the knower to the object known; and so the object known must be in the knower in the sense that a likeness of it is present in him. But the act of loving takes place through a sort of impulse engendered in the lover by the beloved: the beloved draws the lover to himself. Accordingly the act of loving reaches its perfection, not in a likeness of the beloved, in the way that the act of understanding reaches perfection in a likeness of the object understood, but in a drawing of the lover to the beloved person.

The transferring of the likeness of the original is effected by univocal generation whereby, among living beings, the begetter is called father, and the begotten is called son. Among such beings, moreover, the first motion occurs conformably to the species. Therefore, as within the Godhead the way whereby God is in God as the known in the knower, is expressed by what we call "Son," who is the Word of God, so the way by which God is in God as the beloved is in the lover is brought out by acknowledging in God a Spirit, who is the love of God. And so, according to the rule of Catholic faith, we are directed to believe in the Spirit.

CHAPTER 49
PROCESSION OF THE HOLY GHOST FROM THE FATHER AND THE SON

We should recall that the act of understanding proceeds from the intellectual power of the mind. When the intellect actually understands, the object it understands is in it. The presence of the object known in the knower results from the intellectual power of the mind, and is its word, as we said above. Likewise, what is loved is in the lover, when it is actually loved. The fact that an object is actually loved, results from the lover's power to love and from the lovable good as actually known. Accordingly, the presence of the beloved object in the lover is brought about by two factors: the appetitive principle and the intelligible object as apprehended, that is, the word conceived about the lovable object. Therefore, since the Word in God who knows and loves Himself is the Son, and since He to whom the Word belongs is the Father of the Word, as is clear from our exposition, the necessary consequence is that the Holy Spirit, who pertains to the love whereby God is in Himself as beloved in lover, proceeds from the Father and the Son. And so we say in the Creed: "Who proceeds from the Father and the Son."

CHAPTER 50
THE TRINITY OF DIVINE PERSONS AND THE UNITY OF THE DIVINE ESSENCE

We must conclude from all we have said that in the Godhead there is something threefold which is not opposed to the unity and simplicity of the divine essence. We must acknowledge that God is, as existing in His nature, and that He is known and loved by Himself.

But this occurs otherwise in God than in us. Man, to be sure, is a substance in his nature; but his actions of knowing and loving are not his substance. Considered in his nature, man is indeed a subsisting thing; as he exists in his mind, however, he is not a subsisting thing, but a certain representation of a subsisting thing; and similarly with regard to his existence in himself as beloved in lover. Thus man may be regarded under three aspects: that is, man existing in his nature, man existing in his intellect, and man existing in his love. Yet these three are not one, for man's knowing is not his existing, and the same is true of his loving. Only one of these three is a subsisting thing, namely, man existing in his nature.

In God, on the contrary, to be, to know, and to love are identical. Therefore God existing in His natural being and God existing in the divine intellect and God existing in the divine love are one thing. Yet each of them is subsistent. And as things subsisting in intellectual nature are usually called persons in Latin, or hypostases in Greek, the Latins say that there are three persons in God, and the Greeks say that there are three hypostases, namely, the Father, the Son, and the Holy Ghost.

CHAPTER 103
THE DIVINE GOODNESS AS THE END OF ALL ACTION AND MOVEMENT IN CREATURES

The divine goodness is not only the end of the creation of things; it must also be the end of every operation and movement of any creature whatever. The action of every being corresponds to its nature; for example, what is hot, causes heat. But every created thing has, in keeping with its form, some participated likeness to the divine goodness, as we have pointed out. Therefore, too, all actions and movements of every creature are directed to the divine goodness as their end.

Besides, all movements and operations of every being are seen to tend to what is perfect. Perfect signifies what is good, since the perfection of anything is its goodness. Hence every movement and action of anything whatever tend toward good. But all good is a certain imitation of the supreme Good, just as all being is an imitation of the first Being. Therefore the movement and action of all things tend toward assimilation with the divine goodness.

Moreover, if there are many agents arranged in order, the actions and movements of all the agents must be directed to the good of the first agent as to their ultimate end. For lower agents are moved by the higher agent, and every mover moves in the direction of his own end. Consequently the actions and movements of lower agents must tend toward the end of the first agent. Thus in an army the actions of all the subordinate units are directed, in the last instance, to victory, which is the end intended by the commander-in-chief. But we showed above that the first mover and agent is God, and that His end is nothing else than His goodness. Therefore all the actions and movements of all creatures exist on account of the divine goodness, not, of course, in the sense that they are to cause or increase it, but in the sense that they are to acquire it in their own way, by sharing to some extent in a likeness of it.

Created things attain to the divine likeness by their operations in different ways, as they also represent it in different ways comformably to their being. For each of them acts in a manner corresponding to its being. Therefore, as all creatures in common represent the divine goodness to the extent that they exist, so by their actions they all in common attain to the divine likeness in the conservation of their being and in the communication of their being to others. For every creature endeavors, by its activity, first of all to keep itself in perfect being, so far as this is possible. In such endeavor it tends, in its own way, to an imitation of the divine permanence. Secondly, every creature strives, by its activity, to communicate its own perfect being, in its own fashion, to another; and in this it tends toward an imitation of the divine causality.

The rational creature tends, by its activity, toward the divine likeness in a special way that exceeds the capacities of all other creatures, as it has a nobler existence as compared with other creatures. The existence of other creatures is finite, since it is hemmed in by matter, and so lacks infinity both in act and in potency. But every rational nature has infinity either in act or in potency, according to the way its intellect contains intelligibles. Thus our intellectual nature, considered in its first state, is in potency to its intelligibles; since these are infinite, they have a certain potential infinity. Hence the intellect is the species of species, because it has a species that is not determined to one thing alone, as is the case with a stone, but that has capacity for all species. But the intellectual nature of God is infinite in act, for prior to every consideration it has within itself the perfection of all being, as was shown above. Accordingly intellectual creatures occupy a middle position between potency and act. By its activity, therefore, the intellectual creature tends toward the divine likeness, not only in the sense that it preserves itself in existence, or that it multiplies its existence, in a way, by communicating it; it also has as its end the possession in act of what by nature it possesses in potency. Consequently the end of the intellectual creature, to be achieved by its activity, is the complete actuation of its intellect by all the intelligibles for which it has a potency. In this respect it will become most like to God.

CHAPTER 106
FRUITION OF NATURAL DESIRE IN THE BEATIFIC VISION

Once this end is reached natural desire must find its full fruition. The divine essence

thus united to the intellect of the one who sees God, is the adequate principle for knowing everything, and is the source of all good, so that nothing can remain to be desired. This, too, is the most perfect way of attaining likeness with God: to know God in the way He knows Himself, by His own essence.

Of course, we shall never comprehend Him as He comprehends Himself. This does not mean that we shall be unaware of some part of Him, for He has no parts. It means that we shall not know Him as perfectly as He can be known, since the capacity of our intellect for knowing cannot equal His truth, and so cannot exhaust His knowability. God's knowability or truth is infinite, whereas our intellect is finite. But His intellect is infinite, just as His truth is; and so He alone knows Himself to the full extent that He is knowable; just as a person comprehends a demonstrable conclusion if he knows it through demonstration, but not if he knows it only in an imperfect way, on merely probable grounds.

This ultimate end of man we call beatitude. For a man's happiness or beatitude consists in the vision whereby he sees God in His essence. Of course, man is far below God in the perfection of his beatitude. For God has this beatitude by His very nature, whereas man attains beatitude by being admitted to a share in the divine light, as we said in the previous chapter.

CHAPTER 199
THE REPARATION OF HUMAN NATURE BY CHRIST

Nevertheless in the plan of divine providence it was decreed that human nature, which had been ravaged in the manner described, should be restored. It could not be admitted to perfect beatitude unless it were freed of its defilement. Beatitude, being a perfect good, tolerates no defect, especially the defect of sin; for sin is, in its own way, opposed to virtue, which is the path leading to beatitude, as was established above. And so, since man was made for beatitude, seeing that beatitude is his ultimate end, one might conclude that God's work in creating so noble a being was doomed to frustration. But this the Psalmist holds to be inadmissible, for he says in Psalm 88:48: "Hast Thou made all the children of men in vain?" Accordingly it was fitting that human nature should be restored.

Furthermore, divine goodness exceeds the creature's capacity for good. As long as man leads a mortal life in this world, we know that his condition is such that he is neither immovably confirmed in good nor immovably obstinate in evil. Hence the very condition of human nature implies that it is capable of being cleansed from the contamination of sin. Surely the divine goodness would hardly allow this capacity to remain forever unrealized; but this would have been so had God not provided a remedy devised for man's restoration.

We indicated above that the reparation of human nature could not be effected either by Adam or by any other purely human being. For no individual man ever occupied a position of preeminence over the whole of nature; nor can any mere man be the cause of grace. The same reasoning shows that not even an angel could be the author of man's restoration. An angel cannot be the cause of grace, just as he cannot be man's recompense with regard to the ultimate perfection of beatitude, to which man was to be recalled. In this matter of beatitude angels and men are on a footing of equality. Nothing remains, therefore, but that such restoration could be effected by God alone.

But if God had decided to restore man solely by an act of His will and power, the order of divine justice would not have been observed. Justice demands satisfaction for sin. But God cannot render satisfaction, just as He cannot merit. Such a service pertains to one who is subject to another. Thus God was not in a position to satisfy for the sin of the whole of human nature; and a mere man was unable to do so, as we have just shown. Hence divine Wisdom judged it fitting that God should become man, so that thus one and the same person would be able both to restore man and to offer satisfaction. This is the reason for the divine incarnation assigned by the Apostle in 1 Timothy 1:15: "Christ Jesus came into this world to save sinners."

CHAPTER 201
OTHER REASONS FOR THE INCARNATION

There are also other reasons for the divine incarnation. Man had withdrawn from spiritual things and had delivered himself up wholly to material things, from which he was unable by his own efforts to make his way back to God. Therefore divine Wisdom, who had made man, took to Himself a bodily nature and visited man immersed in things of the body, so that by the mysteries of His bodily life He might recall man to spiritual life.

Furthermore, the human race had need that God should become man to show forth the dignity of human nature, so that man might not be subjugated either by devils or by things of the body.

At the same time, by willing to become man, God clearly displayed the immensity of His love for men, so that henceforth men might serve God no longer out of fear of death, which the first man had scorned, but out of the love of charity.

Moreover, the incarnation holds up to man an ideal of that blessed union whereby the created intellect is joined, in an act of understanding, to the uncreated Spirit. It is no longer incredible that a creature's intellect should be capable of union with God by beholding the divine essence, since the time when God became united to man by taking a human nature to Himself.

Lastly, the incarnation puts the finishing touch to the whole vast work envisaged by God. For man, who was the last to be created, returns by a sort of circulatory movement to his first beginning, being united by the work of the incarnation to the very principle of all things.

CHAPTER 213
PERFECTION OF GRACE AND
WISDOM IN CHRIST

As was mentioned in the preceding chapter, the humanity of Christ is related to His divinity as a sort of organ belonging to it. The disposition and quality of organs are gauged chiefly by the purpose, though also by the dignity, of the person using them. Consequently we are to esteem the quality of the human nature assumed by the Word of God in accord with these norms. The purpose the Word of God had in assuming human nature was the salvation and reparation of human nature. Therefore Christ had to be of such excellence in His human nature that He could fittingly be the author of man's salvation. But the salvation of man consists in the enjoyment of God, whereby man is beatified; and so Christ must have had in His human nature a perfect enjoyment of God. For the principle in any genus must be perfect. But fruition of God has a twofold aspect: it requires the satisfaction of the will and of the intellect. The will must adhere unreservedly to God by love, the intellect must know God perfectly.

Perfect attachment of the will to God is brought about by love and by grace, whereby man is justified, according to Romans 3:24: "Being justified freely by his grace." For man is made just by union with God through love. Perfect knowledge of God is effected by the light of wisdom, which is the knowledge of divine truth. Therefore the incarnate Word of God had to be perfect in grace and in the wisdom of truth. Hence we read in John 1:14: "The Word was made flesh, and dwelt among us; and we saw His glory, the glory as it were of the only begotten of the Father, full of grace and truth."

8

LATE MEDIEVAL MYSTICISM
AND RENAISSANCE HUMANISM

MEISTER ECKHART

The fourteenth century was a time of turmoil for Western Europe. The vigorous expansion into bordering areas which had marked European history since the eleventh century came to an end. In Eastern Europe Christian forces had to fight the expansion of the Ottoman Turks, and in the West the Black Death, famine and recurrent war between England and France decimated populations and ended former prosperity.

The church was wracked by the twin tragedies of the so-called "Babylonian Captivity" of the papacy and the Great Western Schism. From 1308 through 1378 the popes lived in Avignon in what is today southern France, rather than in Rome. During this period they largely represented French political interests and therefore retained little respect from other European peoples. Worse conditions followed in 1377, when an attempt to restore the papacy to Rome only resulted in a schism with rival popes at Rome and Avignon. Normalcy was not restored until 1417, when the Council of Constance succeeded in winning general recognition for a single pope, Martin V, with his headquarters at Rome.

In this time of low prestige for the institutional church, powerful mystical and heretical movements and new critical currents in Scholasticism challenged the confident synthetic spirit of Thomas Aquinas' great *Summa Theologica*. In the Rhineland, Dominican preachers began a mystical movement which was rooted in the Neoplatonic aspects of Aquinas' thought and emphasized spiritual fulfillment for the individual. The greatest of these Dominican mystics was Johannes Eckhart (c. 1260–1328), who is better known as Meister Eckhart from the title given him as a Master of Theology at the University of Paris.

Eckhart was actively involved in all aspects of the Dominican life in the late thirteenth and early fourteenth centuries. He studied and taught theology at the University of Paris, served in various academic and administrative posts for the order, and was especially active as a gifted preacher. Although Eckhart wrote theological commentaries, he was not a system builder and did not write a *Summa* of theology like his great Dominican predecessor, Thomas Aquinas. Rather, Eckhart's special contribution was as a preacher who developed a mystical piety that met the needs of laity living in the turbulent years of the early fourteenth century. Our selections, accordingly, will be taken from three representative sermons of Eckhart: *On Solitude and the Attainment of God, Blessed are the Poor,* and *The Birth of the Son in the Soul.*

Eckhart stands in the Neoplatonic tradition of Christian thinkers who understand humans as creatures who have come from God and are to return to God through Christ. Before our creation we were one with God. We had no self-will and did not know a god of our own creation.

> Back in the Womb from which I came, I had not god and merely was, myself. I did not will or desire anything, for I was pure being, a knower of myself by divine truth. Then I wanted myself and nothing else. And what I wanted, I was, and what I was, I wanted, and thus, I existed untrammeled by god or anything else. (*Blessed are the Poor*)

Creation then is, as in Neoplatonic thought, and as William Blake in his "Songs of Innocence" and "Songs of Experience," was to say centuries later, a kind of fall which introduces duality. This idea is essentially the same as is found in the kabbalist mysticism of the *Zohar* by Moses de Leon (d. 1303).

> But when I parted from my free will and received my created being, then I had a god. For before there were creatures, God was not god, but, rather, he was what he was. When creatures came to be and took on creaturely being, then God was no longer God as he is in himself, but god as he is with creatures. (*Blessed are the Poor*)

For Eckhart, in our present created condition God is paradoxically both the transcendent One, but also the immanent One to be found within ourselves at the very ground or depth of our being. God and humans are one, not in the sense that we are now God, but in the sense that there is something uncreated and divine within the soul. This idea is rooted in the Genesis text that God created man in his image (Gen 1:26). Therefore, Eckhart can say metaphysically that "God's blood flows in our veins," or we have within us the "divine spark." In our selection from the sermon *On Solitude and the Attainment of God,* Eckhart insists that God is within the good person everywhere.

> But if a man does well, God is really in him, with him everywhere, on the streets and among people just as much as in church, or a desert place, or a cell.

True religion, for Eckhart, is poverty in the sense of a complete negation of self-will, detachment not only from worldly things, but also from self-assertive striving even for God. True religion is total surrender to the God who is within the soul as the principle of life; it returns us to our original state of being one with God.

> He is a poor man who wants nothing, knows nothing, and has nothing. . . . For if one wants to be truly poor, he must be as free from his creature will as when he had not yet been born.

For, by the everlasting truth, as long as you will do God's will and yearn for eternity and God, you are not really poor, for he is poor who wills nothing, knows nothing, and wants nothing.

Therefore, for Eckhart, the turmoils of the world or a corrupt church cannot disturb the person who has surrendered totally to God.

If he really has God, and only God, then nothing disturbs him. Why? Because he has *only* God and everything is nothing but God to him. He discloses God in every act, in every place. The whole business of his person adds up to God. His actions are due only to Him who is the author of them and not to himself, since he is merely the agent. (*On Solitude and the Attainment of God*)

This attitude of poverty or "God-consciousness" should be maintained at all times and in all places. In the sermon *On Solitude and the Attainment of God* Eckhart advises:

One ought to keep hold of God in everything and accustom his mind to retain God always among his feelings, thoughts, and loves. Take care how you think of God. As you think of him in church or closet, think of him everywhere. Take him with you among the crowds and turmoil of the alien world. . . . You should, however, maintain the same mind, the same trust, and the same earnestness toward God in all your doings. Believe me, if you keep this kind of evenness, nothing can separate you from God-consciousness.

While accepting the dogmas of the orthodox Christian faith, Eckhart interpreted them in bold new ways as allegories about the spiritual union between the individual soul and God. For example, the dogma of the incarnation, that the divine Word of God took human flesh, is for Eckhart also a truth about the constant rebirth of the divine spirit within the individual human soul.

The Father gives birth to his Son in eternity, equal to himself. "The Word was with God, and God was the Word" (Jn 1:1); it is the same in the same nature. Yet I say more: He has given birth to him in my soul. Not only is the soul with him and he equal with it, but he is in it, and the Father gives his Son birth in the soul in the same way as he gives him birth in eternity and not otherwise. He must do it whether he likes it or not. The Father gives birth to his Son without ceasing; and I say more: He gives birth not only to me, his Son, but he gives birth to me as himself and himself as me and to me as his being and nature. . . .

Eckhart's teachings were so novel that toward the end of his life he fell under suspicion of heresy. The issues revolved around the relationship between the individual soul and God. In speaking of the union between the soul and God, Eckhart seems to totally absorb the individual in God, and therefore he was accused of pantheism. For him the ultimate core of the self is the divine in us. In his sermon on *The Birth of the Son in the Soul,* for example, he speaks of the individual soul as if it is identical with the divine Son.

In the innermost source, there I spring out in the Holy Spirit, where there is one life and one being and one work. Everything God performs is one; therefore he gives me, his Son, birth without any distinction. My fleshly father is not actually my father except in one little portion of his nature, and I am separated from him; he may be dead and I alive. Therefore, the heavenly Father is truly my Father, for I am his Son and have everything that I have from him, I am the same Son and not a different one.

In 1325 the Dominicans of Venice became disturbed with the rumors that Eckhart was saying things in his sermons to the common people that might easily lead them into error. Eckhart replied, "If the ignorant are not taught they will never learn, and none of them will ever know the art of living and dying. The ignorant are taught in the hope of changing them from ignorant to enlightened people" (quoted in *Meister Eckhart: The Man from Whom God Hid Nothing* by Ursula Fleming, 15). But in 1327 Eckhart had to appear before the Franciscan archbishop of Cologne to face charges of heresy. His famous answer was: "I may err but I may not be a heretic—for the first has to do with the mind and the second with the will." When the charges against him were not dropped, Eckhart appealed his case to the papal court and began the journey to Avignon. He died before his case was heard, but after his death twenty-eight propositions ascribed to him were condemned as heretical. The issue of Eckhart's orthodoxy continues to be the source of scholarly debate to this day.

Despite the questions about his orthodoxy, Eckhart's mysticism became a vital force in various parts of the Rhineland. Under his influence a group of lay and clerical mystics formed the *Gottesfreunde* ("friends of God"). They stressed the transforming personal union of their souls with God, and although they remained within the church, they were deeply aware of the corruption of many of the clergy during the time of the Avignon papacy. Some of the best known writers within the Friends of God were Johannes Tauler, Henry Suso, and Blessed Margaret Hebner—all of them Dominicans who were disciples of Eckhart.

The translations of *On Solitude and the Attainment of God* and *Blessed are the Poor* are by Raymond Blakney in *Meister Eckhart: A Modern Translation* (New York and London: Harper & Brothers, 1941) 7–10, 227–232. The translation of *The Birth of the Son in the Soul* is from *Meister Eckhart—The Essential Sermons, Commentaries, Treatises, and Defense,* trans. and edited by Edmund Colledge, O.S.A. and Bernard McGinn (Mahwah, N.J.: Paulist Press, 1981) 186–189.

ON SOLITUDE AND THE ATTAINMENT OF GOD

I was asked this question: "Some people withdraw from society and prefer to be alone; their peace of mind depends on it; wouldn't it be better for them to be in the church?" I replied, No! and you shall see why.

Those who do well do well wherever they are, and in whatever company, and those who do badly do badly wherever they are, and in whatever company. But if a man does well, God is really in him, and with him everywhere, on the street and among people just as much as in church, or a desert place, or a cell.

If he really has God, and only God, then nothing disturbs him. Why?

Because he has only God and thinks only God and everything is nothing but God to him. He discloses God in every act, in every place. The whole business of his person adds up to God. His actions are due only to Him who is the author of them and not to himself, since he is merely the agent. If we mean God and only God, then it is He who does what we do and nothing can disturb him—neither company nor place. Thus, neither can any person disturb him, for he thinks nothing, is looking for nothing, and relishes nothing but God, who is one with him by perfect devotion. Furthermore, since God cannot be distracted by the numbers of things, neither can the person, for he is one in One, in which all divided things are gathered up to unity and there undifferentiated.

One ought to keep hold of God in everything and accustom his mind to retain God always among his feelings, thoughts, and loves. Take care how you think of God. As you think of him in church or closet, think of him everywhere. Take him with you among the crowds and turmoil of the alien world. As I have said so often, speaking of uniformity, we do not mean that one should regard all deeds, places, and people as interchangeable. That would be a great mistake; for it is better to pray than to spin and the church ranks above the street. You should, however, maintain the same mind, the same trust, and the same earnestness toward God in all your doings. Believe me, if you keep this kind of evenness, nothing can separate you from God-consciousness.

On the other hand, the person who is not conscious of God's presence, but who must always be going out to get him from this and that, who has to seek him by special methods, as by means of some activity, person, or place—such people have not attained God. It can easily happen that they are disturbed, for they have not God and they do not seek, think,

and love only him, and therefore, not only will evil company be to them a stumbling block, but good company as well—not only the street, but the church; not only bad deeds and words, but good ones as well. The difficulty lies within the man, for whom God has not yet become everything. If God were everything, the man would get along well where he went and among whatever people, for he would possess God and no one could rob him or disturb his work.

Of what does this true possession of God consist, when one really has him? It depends on the heart and an inner, intellectual return to God and not on steady contemplation by a given method. It is impossible to keep such a method in mind, or at least difficult, and even then it is not best. We ought not to have or let ourselves be satisfied with the god we have thought of, for when the thought slips the mind, that god slips with it. What we want is rather the reality of God, exalted far above any human thought or creature. Then God will not vanish unless one turns away from him of his own accord.

When one takes God as he is divine, having the reality of God within him, God sheds light on everything. Everything will taste like God and reflect him. God will shine in him all the time. He will have the disinterest, renunciation, and spiritual vision of his beloved, ever-present Lord. He will be like one athirst with a real thirst; he cannot help drinking even though he thinks of other things. Wherever he is, with whomsoever he may be, whatever his purpose or thoughts or occupation—the idea of the Drink will not depart as long as the thirst endures; and the greater the thirst the move lively, deep-seated, present, and steady the idea of the Drink will be. Or suppose one loves something with all that is in him, so that nothing else can move him or give pleasure, and he cares for that alone, looking for nothing more; then where he is or with whomsoever he may be, whatever he tries or does, that Something he loves will not be extin-

guished from his mind. He will see it everywhere, and the stronger his love grows for it
the more vivid it will be. A person like this
never thinks of resting because he is never
tired.

The more he regards everything as
divine—more divine than it is of itself—the
more God will be pleased with him. To be
sure, this requires effort and love, a careful
cultivation of the spiritual life, and a watchful, honest, active oversight of all one's mental attitudes toward things and people. It is
not learned by world-flight, running away
from things, turning solitary and going apart
from the world. Rather, one must learn an
inner solitude, wherever or with whomsoever
he may be. He must learn to penetrate things
and find God there, to get a strong impression
of God firmly fixed in his mind.

It is like learning to write. To acquire this
art, one must practice much, however dis-
agreeable or difficult it may be, however
impossible it may seem. Practicing earnestly
and often, one learns to write, acquires the
art. To be sure, each letter must first be considered separately and accurately, reproduced
over and over again; but once having acquired
skill, one need not pay any attention to the
reproduction [of the letters] or even think of
them. He will write fluently and freely
whether it be penmanship or some bold work,
in which his art appears. It is sufficient for
the writer to know that he is using his skill
and since he does not always have to think of
it, he does his work by means of it.

So a man should shine with the divine
Presence without having to work at it. He
should get the essence out of things and let
the things themselves alone. That requires at
first attentiveness and exact impressions, as
with the student and his art. So one must be
permeated with divine Presence, informed
with the forms of beloved God who is within
him, so that he may radiate that Presence
without working at it.

BLESSED ARE THE POOR

Now, there are two kinds of poverty. One is
external poverty, and it is good and much to
be praised in people who take it upon themselves willingly, for the love of our Lord Jesus
Christ, for he himself practiced it in the
earthly realm. Of this poverty I shall say
nothing more, for there is another kind of
poverty, an inward poverty. . . . He is a poor
man who wants nothing, knows nothing, and
has nothing. . . . For if one wants to be truly
poor, he must be as free from his creature will
as when he had not yet been born. For, by the
everlasting truth, as long as you will do God's
will and yearn for eternity and God, you are
not really poor, for he is poor who wills nothing, knows nothing, and wants nothing.

Back in the Womb from which I came, I had
no god and merely was, myself. I did not will
or desire anything, for I was pure being, a
knower of myself by divine truth. Then I wanted myself and nothing else. And what I want,
I was, and what I was, I wanted, and thus, I
existed untrammeled by god or anything else.
But when I parted from my free will and
received my created being, then I had a god.
For before there were creatures, God was not
god, but, rather, he was what he was. When
creatures came to be and took on creaturely
being, then God was no longer God as he is in
himself, but god as he is with creatures.

Now we say that God, insofar as he is only
god, is not the highest goal of creation, nor is
his fullness of being as great as that of the
least creatures, themselves in God. . . .
Therefore, we pray that we may be rid of god,
and taking the truth, break into eternity,
where the highest angels and souls, too, are
like what I was in my primal existence, when
I wanted what I was and was what I wanted.
Accordingly, a person ought to be poor in will,
willing as little and wanting as little as when
he did not exist. This is how a person is poor,
who wills nothing. . . . More: he shall be quit
and empty of his own knowledge, as he was

when he did not exist, and let God achieve what he will and be as untrammeled by humanness as he was when he came from God. Now the question is raised: In what does happiness consist most of all? Certain authorities have said that it consists in loving. Others say that it consists in knowing and loving, and this is a better statement. But we say that it consists neither in knowledge nor in love, but in that there is something in the soul, from which both knowledge and love flow and which, like agents of the soul, neither knows nor loves. To know this is to know what blessedness depends on. This something has no "before" or "after," and it waits for nothing that is yet to come, for it has nothing to gain or lose. Thus, when God acts in it, it is deprived of knowing that he has done so. What is more, it is the same kind of thing that, like God, can enjoy itself. . . .

If it is the case that a man is emptied of things, creatures, himself, and god, and if still god could find a place in him to act, then we say: as long as that [place] exists, this man is not poor with the most intimate poverty. For God does not intend that man shall have a place reserved for him to work in, since true poverty of spirit requires that man shall be emptied of god and all his works, so that if God wants to act in the soul, he himself must be the place in which he acts—and that he would like to do. . . .

Thus we say that a man should be so poor that he is not and has not a place for God to act in. To reserve a place would be to maintain distinctions. Therefore I pray God that he may quit me of god, for [his] unconditioned being is above god and all distinctions. It was here [in unconditioned being] that I was myself, wanted myself, and knew myself to be this person [here before you], and therefore, I am my own first cause, both of my eternal being and of my temporal being. To this end I was born, and by virtue of my birth being eternal, I shall never die. It is of the nature of this eternal birth that I *have been* eternally, that I am now, and *shall be* forever. What I am as a temporal creature is to die and come to nothingness, for it came with time, and so with time it will pass away. In my eternal birth, however, everything was begotten. I was my own first cause as well as the first cause of everything else. If I had willed it, neither I nor the world would have come to be! If I had not been, there would have been no god. There is, however, no need to understand this.

A great authority says: "His bursting forth is nobler than his efflux." When I flowed forth from God, creatures said: "He is a god!" This, however, did not make me blessed, for it indicates that I, too, am a creature. In bursting forth, however, when I shall be free within God's will and free, therefore, of the will of god and all his works, and even of god himself, then I shall rise above all creature kind, and I shall be neither god nor creature, but I shall be what I was once, now, and forevermore. I shall thus receive an impulse which shall raise me above the angels. With this impulse, I receive wealth so great that I could never again be satisfied with a god, or anything that is a god's, nor with any divine activities, for in bursting forth I discover that God and I are One. Now I am what I was and I neither add to nor subtract from anything, for I am the unmoved Mover, that moves all things. Here, then, a god may find no "place" in man, for by his poverty the man achieves the being that was always his and shall remain his eternally. Here, too, God is identical with the spirit and that is the most intimate poverty discoverable. . . .

THE BIRTH OF THE SON IN THE SOUL

The Father gives birth to his Son in eternity, equal to himself. "The Word was with God, and God was the Word" (Jn 1:1); it was the same in the same nature. Yet I say more: He has given birth to him in my soul. Not only is the soul with him and he equal with it, but he is in it, and the Father gives his Son birth in the soul in the same way he gives him birth in eternity and not otherwise. He must do it whether he likes it or not. The Father gives birth to his Son without ceasing; and I say more: He gives birth not only to me, his Son, but he gives birth to me as himself and himself as me and to me as his being and nature. . . . In the innermost source, there I spring out in the Holy Spirit, where there is one life and one being and one work. Everything God performs is one; therefore he gives me, his Son, birth without any distinction. My fleshly father is not actually my father except in one little portion of his nature, and I am separated from him; he may be dead and I alive. Therefore, the heavenly Father is truly my Father, for I am his Son and have everything that I have from him, and I am the same Son and not a different one. Because the Father performs one work, therefore his work is me, his Only-Begotten Son without any difference. "We shall all be completely transformed and changed into God" (2 Cor 3:18). See a comparison. In the same way, when in the sacrament bread is changed into the Body of the Lord, however many pieces of bread there were, they still become one Body. Just so, if all the pieces of bread were changed into my finger, there would still not be more than one finger. But if my finger were changed into the bread, there would be as many of one as the other. What is changed into something else becomes one with it. I am so changed into him that he produces his being in me as one, not just similar. By the living God, this is true! There is no distinction.

The Father gives his Son birth without ceasing. Once the Son has been born he receives nothing from the Father because he has it all, but what he receives from the Father is his being born. In this we ought not to ask for something from God as if he were a stranger. . . . One should not accept or esteem God as being outside oneself, but as one's own and as what is within one; one should not serve or labor for any recompense, not for God or for his honor or for anything that is outside oneself, but only for that which one's own being and one's own life is within one. . . God and I, we are one. I accept God into me in knowing; I go into God in loving. There are some who say that blessedness consists not in knowing but in willing. They are wrong; for if it consisted only in the will, it would not be one. . . .

JULIAN OF NORWICH, *SHOWINGS*

Throughout the medieval period Christian women, who were not allowed to receive a traditional university education in theology and philosophy, gave profound and unique expression to their religious sensibilities in mystical writings. During the chaos of the fourteenth and fifteenth centuries women mystics were particularly active and influential. Catherine of Siena (1347–1380), who was simply a member of the Third Order of the Dominicans, was a visionary mystic who during the last years of her short life campaigned tirelessly to have the papacy return from Avignon to Rome. She went from city to city in Italy in an attempt to end the endemic warfare which made it unsafe for the pope to return. She also wrote humble but firm letters to Pope Gregory XI (1370–1378) in which she complained of God's being offended by the papacy's long stay in Avignon. Although it is not possible to determine how influential Catherine's advice was, on January 17, 1377, Gregory XI returned the papacy to Rome amid great rejoicing.

In late fourteenth-century England at the same time Chaucer was writing his *Canterbury Tales* and John Wyclif was criticizing the evils of the institutional church, a solitary woman mystic, traditionally known as Julian of Norwich (1342–1424), produced an extraordinary book of mystical writings in English entitled *Showings*. This work is extant in two texts: a short text which scholars believe was written shortly after Julian's original experiences in 1373 and a longer text which records both an account of her visionary experiences and a reflective analysis of them that took place over a twenty-year period.

We know very little of Julian's life beyond the incidental information she gives us in the text; in fact, even her traditional name probably comes from the parish church of St. Julian in Conisford at Norwich where she had her hermitage. Surprisingly, her writings also make no direct mention of the disturbing events of her age: the Black Death, the Avignon papacy and schism, the Hundred Years War, and the Peasant Revolt in England in 1381. Although there is no specific reference to these tragedies, in her mystical experiences Julian struggles with the problems of sin and evil raised by these events.

In many ways the circumstances of Julian's visionary experience are typical of women mystics in the medieval period. In the first chapter of the short text of her *Showings,* Julian tells us that as a young woman, she identified with Mary Magdalen and the other women "who were Christ's lovers" at the cross. Devotion to the humanity of Jesus, especially as it was manifested in his sufferings and passion, was very popular in the Middle Ages. It reached fever pitch in the fourteenth and fifteenth centuries in the wake of the Black Death. Groups known as flagellants put on sackcloth and ashes, confessed their sins, and beat their bodies in ritual penance until they bled in the apparent hope of avoiding God's wrath. Julian tells us she wanted to see Christ's sufferings and suffer with him, and therefore she prayed for three graces from God: to have recollection of Christ's passion, to have a bodily sickness, and to have God's gift of three wounds: contrition, compassion and longing for God. She mentions explicitly that her devotion to the passion of Christ was enkindled by the church's teachings and "paintings of the Crucifixion."

In chapter two of the short text, Julian tells us that her prayer was answered when she became gravely ill at the age of thirty. A near death experience from which the visionary remarkably recovers is typical of many women mystics like Hildegard of Bingen, Catherine of Siena, and Teresa of Avila. They intepret it as a mystical death and resurrection. Julian's description is extremely detailed.

> And when I was thirty and a half years old, God sent me a bodily sickness in which I lay for three days and three nights; and on the fourth night I received all the rites of Holy Church . . . but . . . I suffered on for two days and two nights . . . and on the third night . . . my reasoning and my suffering told me that I should die; . . . so I lasted until day, and by then my body was dead from the middle downwards. . . . After this my sight began to fail, and it was dark all around me in my room, dark as night. . . . After that I felt as if the upper part of my body were beginning to die. My hands fell down on either side, and I was so weak that my

head lolled to one side. The greatest pain that I felt was my shortness of breath and the ebbing of my life. Then truly I believed that I was at the point of death. And suddenly in that moment all my pain left me, and I was as sound, particularly in the upper part of my body, as ever I was before or have been since. (*Showings* [Short text] ch. 2)

In writing about their visionary experiences, women mystics often speak of a humble reluctance to publish them, but also of an awareness that they are commanded by God to make their visions known. In chapter six of the short text of *Showings,* Julian says,

I write as the representative of my fellow Christians—and the more I love in this way whilst I am here, the more I am like the joy that I shall have in heaven without end, that joy which is the God who out of his endless love willed to become our brother and suffer for us. And I am sure that anyone who sees it so will be taught the truth and be greatly comforted, if he have need of comfort. But God forbid that you should say or assume that I am a teacher, for that is not and never was my intention; for I am a woman, ignorant, weak, and frail. But I know very well what I am saying I have received at the revelation of him who is the sovereign teacher. . . . But because I am a woman, ought I therefore to believe that I should not tell of the Goodness of God, when I saw at the same time that it is his will that it be known?

Like Hildegard of Bingen, Julian reflected on her initial visions over a long period of time and gradually came to understand them in an allegorical way as having several layers of meaning. Just as biblical and literary texts, like Dante's *Divine Comedy,* can be read on literal, allegorical (typological), tropological (moral), and anagogical (mystical) levels, so too can these visions.

In her meditation on the vision of the "hazelnut" in the long text, Julian learns the same spiritual truth that Augustine states in the opening book of his *Confessions:* "Our hearts find no peace until they rest in you." Her reflection on the small hazelnut reveals to Julian both the love of God and the frailty and nothingness of creation. As she looked at the small hazelnut, Julian says, "I was amazed that it could last." The answer that she receives upon reflection is: "It lasts and always will, because God loves it; and thus everything has being through the love of God." This emphasis on the love of God and his continuous preservation of creation through his will that it continue to exist is characteristic of the voluntarism of the English Franciscan theologians of the fourteenth century, especially John Duns Scotus.

From her reflections on the fact that God made, loves and preserves the little hazelnut, Julian also concludes that because "God is the Creator and the protector and the lover," she "can never have perfect rest or true happiness" until she is attached to God. No created thing can satisfy the human heart. At this point she appears to be very close to Eckhart's idea of true poverty.

God wishes to be known, and it pleases him that we should rest in him; for everything which is beneath him is not sufficient for us. And this is the reason why no soul is at rest until it has despised as nothing all things which are created. When it by its will has become nothing for love, to have him who is everything, then is it able to receive spiritual rest.

In the section entitled "I shall make all things well" Julian is struggling with the problem of evil which, no doubt, was raised by the horrors of her age. She frames the question by asking why God in his wisdom allowed sin to occur. Would not the state of humans be better if sin had never occurred? She learns in the revelation that sin is necessary, but that "all will be well."

Julian's optimism is rooted in a long reflection on the nature of sin, the purpose of Christ's atonement in the passion, and the very nature of the Trinity. Like Augustine, Julian comes to understand sin as having "no kind of substance." It is the absence of good, and the pain caused by sin is both its own punishment and the beginning of its remedy.

But I did not see sin, for I believe that it has no kind of substance, no share in being, nor can it be recognized except by the pain caused by it. And it seems to me that this pain is something for a time, for it purges and makes us know ourselves and ask for mercy; for the Passion of our Lord is comfort to us against all this, and that is his blessed will.

Christ's atonement for humans is rooted in his "compassion on us because of sin." The "Holy Church" can expect to "be shaken in sorrow and anguish and tribulation in this world" because of sin, but Christ is with his servants in their tribulations leading them in pity and compassion to turn from "the pomps and the pride and vainglory of this wretched life" so that he can gather them "meek and mild, pure and holy" in union with him.

This is what Julian calls the "open portion" of understanding which she received to her question about evil. The "hidden and closed" portion is known only to God, but a reflection on the nature of the Trinity can give the soul a basis for hope and trust in the triumph of God's love over evil. Julian says that "our good Lord answered to all the questions and doubts which I could raise . . . I may make all things well, and I can make all things well, and I shall make all things well, and I will make all things well; and you will see yourself that every kind of thing will be well." She goes on to say that she understands the "I may" to apply to the Father, the "I can" to the Son, the "I will" to the Holy Spirit, the "I shall" to the unity of the blessed Trinity, and the "You shall see yourself" as "the union of all men who shall be saved in the blessed Trinity."

The words of Jesus which reveal to Julian this understanding of the Trinity are his words from the cross in John's gospel: "I thirst" (Jn 19:28). For Julian, Christ as the second person of the Trinity has had this thirst and longing from all eternity; he had it on the cross; he continues to have it in Julian's own time; and he will continue to have it until "the last soul which will be saved has come up into his bliss." Christ's thirst will continue until Judgment Day which, for Julian, will come at "the best time."

All this was seen to reveal his compassion, for on Judgment Day that will cease. So he has pity and compassion for us, and he has longing to possess us, but his wisdom and his love do not allow the end to come until the best time.

"The Parable of the Lord and the Servant" is also for Julian a double allegory for the mystery of salvation. She meditated on this parable for twenty years by taking heed "to all the attributes, divine and human, which were revealed in the example." The lord in the parable is God who "sits in state, in rest and peace" and who throughout looks on the servant "very lovingly and sweetly and mildly." The figure of the servant functions in two ways. On one level he is Adam, and therefore all humans, fallen in sin. He is sent by the Lord to a certain place to do his will, but he hastily dashes off and soon falls into a dell and is greatly injured. He cannot rise or help himself, and his greatest hurt is his lack of consolation because he cannot "turn his face to look on his loving Lord, who was very close to him." On a second level, Julian comes to understand the servant as a figure for Christ who was united to Adam (humanity) even in heaven.

> When Adam fell, God's Son fell; because of the true union which was made in heaven, God's Son could not be separated from Adam, for by Adam I understand all mankind.

Christ is from all eternity the suffering servant who fell "into the valley of the womb of the maiden who was the fairest daughter of Adam" and "brought him out of hell." On this level the parable is about the sufferings endured by Christ in interceding for humanity.

Julian is so overwhelmed with Christ's identification with humanity that she seems to say that God must eventually save the whole of mankind.

> For all mankind, which will be saved by the sweet Incarnation and the Passion of Christ, all is Christ's humanity, for he is the head, and we are his members, to which members the day and the time are unknown when every passing woe and sorrow will have an end, and everlasting joy and bliss will be fulfilled, which day and time all the company of heaven longs and desires to see.

The technical Greek term for this idea is *apocatatasis;* it is found in the teachings of Origen, but was condemned at the Council of Constantinople in 543.

Our final selection is on "The Motherhood of God and of Christ." Julian was not the first writer in the Middle Ages to apply the concept of Mother to God; Anselm and others also have it, but she uses it most extensively. She finds it particularly appropriate to describe the role of Christ in the plan of salvation. Her approach here is not rigidly logical, but rather suggestive and fluid. She speaks in the traditional medieval ways of Mary, as mother, and of the church as the spouse and wife of Christ. But then she goes on to say that "our savior is our true Mother, in whom we are endlessly born and out of whom we shall never come." Motherhood is a way of speaking of the fecundity of Christ's life-giving and protective action in creation and salvation.

As she contemplates the Trinity, Julian sees three properties: fatherhood, mother-hood, and lordship. She associates fatherhood with the Father who is our protection and bliss, as regards our natural substance which is ours by creation; motherhood with the Son "in whom in knowledge and wisdom we have our perfection as regards our sensual-ity, our restoration and our salvation, for he is our Mother, brother, and savior"; and lord-ship with the Holy Spirit in whom "we have our reward and our gift for our living and our labor." Motherhood is particularly associated with wisdom and love in Christ.

> As truly as God is our Father, so truly is God our Mother, and he revealed that in everything, and especially in these sweet words where he says: . . . I am he, the wisdom and the loving-ness of motherhood.

The motherhood of God is evident in three works of Christ: creation, the incarnation, the work of salvation.

> Our Mother in nature, our Mother in grace, because he wanted altogether to become our Mother in all things, made the foundation of his work most humbly and most mildly in the maiden's womb . . . arrayed and prepared himself in this humble place, all ready in our poor flesh, himself to do the service and office of motherhood in everything. The mother's service is nearest, readiest and surest: nearest because it is most natural, readiest because it is most loving and surest because it is truest.

Julian even goes so far as to compare the sustenance that Christ gives through the eucharist and the way Christ reveals the love of the Godhead to the action of the mother providing suck for her infant.

> The mother can give her child to suck of her milk, but our precious Mother Jesus can feed us with himself, and does, most courteously and most tenderly, with the blessed sacrament, which is the precious food of true life. . . .
> The mother can lay her child tenderly to her breast, but our tender Mother Jesus can lead us easily into his blessed breast through his open side, and show us there a part of the Godhead and of the joys of heaven, with inner certainty of endless bliss. . . .

The translation is by Edmund Colledge, O.S.A. and James Walsh, S.J., *Julian of Norwich: Showings* (Mahwah, N.J.: Paulist Press, 1978) 183–184, 224–231, 267–276, 292–298.

SHOWINGS

The Fifth Chapter: "No bigger than a hazel-nut."

At the same time as I saw this sight of the head bleeding, our good Lord showed a spiri-tual sight of his familiar love. I saw that he is to us everything which is good and comforting for our help. He is our clothing, who wraps and enfolds us for love, embraces us and shel-ters us, surrounds us for his love, which is so tender that he may never desert us. And so in this sight I saw that he is everything which is good, as I understood.

And in this he showed me something small, no bigger than a hazelnut, lying in the palm of my hand, as it seemed to me, and it was round like a ball. I looked at it with the eye of my understanding and thought: What can this be? I was amazed that it could last, for I thought that because of its littleness it would suddenly have fallen into nothing. And I was answered in my understanding: It lasts and always will, because God loves it; and thus everything has being through the love of God.

In this little thing I saw three properties. The first is that God made it, the second is that God loves it, the third is that God preserves it. But what did I see in it? It is that God is the Creator and the protector and the lover. For until I am substantially united to him, I can never have perfect rest or true happiness,—until, that is, I am so attached to him that there can be no created thing between my God and me.

This little thing which is created seemed to me as if it could have fallen into nothing because of its littleness. We need to have knowledge of this, so that we may delight in despising as nothing everything created, so as to love and have uncreated God. For this is the reason why our hearts and souls are not in perfect ease, because here we seek rest in this thing which is so little, in which there is no rest, and we do not know God who is almighty, all wise and all good, for he is true rest. God wishes to be known, and it pleases him that we should rest in him; for everything which is beneath him is not sufficient for us. And this is the reason why no soul is at rest until it has despised as nothing all things which are created. When it by its will has become nothing for love, to have him who is everything, then is it able to receive spiritual rest.

And also our good Lord revealed that it is very greatly pleasing to him that a simple soul should come naked, openly, and familiarly. For this is the loving yearning of the soul through the touch of the Holy Spirit, from the understanding which I have in this revelation: God, of your goodness give me yourself, for you are enough for me, and I can ask for nothing which is less which can pay our full worship. And if I ask anything which is less, always I am in want; but only in you do I have everything.

The Twenty-Seventh Chapter: "I shall make all things well."

And after this our Lord brought to my mind the longing that I had for him before, and I saw that nothing hindered me but sin, and I saw that this is true of us all in general, and it seemed to me that if there had been no sin, we should all have been pure and as like our Lord as he created us. And so in my folly before this time I often wondered why, through the great prescient wisdom of God, the beginning of sin was not prevented. For then it seemed to me that all would have been well.

The impulse to think this was greatly to be shunned; and nevertheless I mourned and sorrowed on this account, unreasonably, lacking discretion. But Jesus, who in this vision informed me about everything needful to me, answered with these words and said: Sin is necessary, but all will be well, and all will be well, and every kind of thing will be well. In this naked word "sin," our Lord brought generally to my mind all which is not good, and the shameful contempt and the direst tribulation which he endured for us in this life, and his death and all his pains, and the passions, spiritual and bodily, of all his creatures. For we are all in part troubled, and we shall be troubled, following our master Jesus until we are fully purged of our mortal flesh and all our inward affections which are not very good.

And with the beholding of this, with all the pains that ever were or ever will be, I understood Christ's Passion for the greatest and surpassing pain. And yet this was shown to me in an instant, and it quickly turned into consolation. For our good Lord would not have the soul frightened by this ugly sight. But I did not see sin, for I believe that it has no kind of substance, no share in being, nor can it be recognized except by the pain caused by it. And it seems to me that this pain is something for a time, for it purges and makes us know ourselves and ask for mercy; for the Passion of our Lord is comfort to us against all this, and that is his blessed will. And because of the tender love which our good Lord has for all who will be saved, he comforts readily and sweetly, meaning this: It is true that sin is the cause of all this pain, but all will be well, and every kind of thing will be well.

These words were revealed most tenderly, showing no kind of blame to me or to anyone who will be saved. So it would be most unkind of me to blame God or marvel at him on account of my sins, since he does not blame me for sin.

And in these same words I saw hidden in God an exalted and wonderful mystery, which he will make plain and we shall know in heaven. In this knowledge we shall truly see the cause why he allowed sin to come, and in this sight we shall rejoice forever.

The Twenty-Eighth Chapter.

So I saw how Christ has compassion on us because of sin; and just as I was before filled full of pain and compassion on account of Christ's Passion, so I was now in part filled with compassion for all my fellow Christians, because he loves very dearly the people who will be saved, that is to say God's servants. Holy Church will be shaken in sorrow and anguish and tribulation in this world as men shake a cloth in the wind; and in this matter our Lord answered, revealing in this way: Ah, I shall turn this into a great thing, of endless honor and everlasting joy, in heaven. Yes, I

even saw that our Lord rejoices with pity and compassion over the tribulations of his servants; and he imposes on every person whom he loves, to bring him to his bliss, something that is no defect in his sight, through which souls are humiliated and despised in this world, scorned and mocked and rejected. And he does this to prevent the harm which they might have from the pomps and the pride and the vainglory of this wretched life, and to prepare their way to come to heaven, into endless, everlasting bliss. For he says: I shall completely break down in you your empty affections and your vicious pride, and then I shall gather you and make you meek and mild, pure and holy through union with me.

And then I saw that every natural compassion which one has for one's fellow Christians in love is Christ in us, and that every kind of self-humiliation which he manifested in his Passion was manifested again in this compassion, in which there were two different understandings of our Lord's intention. One was the bliss that we are brought to, in which he wants us to rejoice. The other is for consolation in our pain, for he wants us to know that it will all be turned to our honor and profit by the power of his Passion, and to know that we suffered in no way alone, but together with him, and to see in him our foundation. And he wants us to see that his pains and his tribulation exceed all that we may suffer so far that it cannot be comprehended in full. And if we well contemplate his will in this, it keeps us from lamenting and despairing as we experience our pains; and if we see truly that your sins deserve them, still his love excuses us. And of his great courtesy he puts away all our blame, and regards us with pity and compassion as innocent and guiltless children.

The Twenty-Ninth Chapter.

But in this I stood, contemplating it generally, darkly and mournfully, saying in intention to our Lord with very great fear: Ah, good

Lord, how could all things be well, because of the great harm which has come through sin to your creatures? And here I wished, so far as I dared, for some plainer explanation through which I might be at ease about this matter. And to this our blessed Lord answered, very meekly and with a most loving manner, and he showed that Adam's sin was the greatest harm ever done or ever to be done until the end of the world. And he also showed me that this is plainly known to all Holy Church upon earth.

Furthermore, he taught that I should contemplate the glorious atonement, for this atoning is more pleasing to the blessed divinity and more honorable for man's salvation, without comparison, than ever Adam's sin was harmful. So we should pay heed to this: For since I have set right the greatest of harms, then it is my will that you should know through this that I shall set right everything which is less.

The Thirtieth Chapter.

He gave understanding of two portions. One portion is our savior and our salvation. This blessed portion is open, clear, fair and bright and plentiful for all men who are of good will are comprehended in this portion. We are bound to this by God, and drawn and counselled and taught, inwardly by the Holy Spirit, and outwardly through the same grace by Holy Church. Our Lord wants us to be occupied in this, rejoicing in him, for he rejoices in us. And the more plentifully we accept this with reverence and humility, the more do we deserve thanks from him, and the more profit do we win for ourselves. And so we may see and rejoice that our portion is our Lord.

The other portion is hidden from us and closed, that is to say all which is additional to our salvation; for this is our Lord's privy counsel, and it is fitting to God's royal dominion to keep his privy counsel in peace, and it is fitting to his servants out of obedience and respect not to wish to know his counsel.

Our Lord has pity and compassion on us because some creatures occupy themselves so much in this; and I am sure that if we knew how greatly we should please him and solace ourselves by leaving it alone, we should do so. The saints in heaven, they wish to know nothing but what our Lord wishes them to know, and furthermore their love and their desire are governed according to our Lord's will; and we should do this, so that our will resembles theirs. Then we shall not wish or desire anything but the will of our Lord as they do, for we are all one in God's intention.

And in this I was taught that we shall rejoice only in our blessed savior Jesus, and trust in him for everything.

The Thirty-First Chapter.

And so our good Lord answered to all the questions and doubts which I could raise, saying most comfortably: I may make all things well, and I can make all things well, and I shall make all things well, and I will make all things well; and you will see yourself that every kind of thing will be well. When he says "I may," I understand this to apply to the Father; and when he says "I can," I understand it for the Son; and when he says "I will," I understand it for the Holy Spirit; and when he says "I shall," I understand it for the unity of the blessed Trinity, three persons and one truth, and when he says, "You will see yourself," I understand it for the union of all men who will be saved in the blessed Trinity.

And in these five words God wishes us to be enclosed in rest and in peace. And so Christ's spiritual thirst will have an end. For this is Christ's spiritual thirst, his longing in love, which persists and always will until we see him on the day of judgment, for we who shall be saved and shall be Christ's joy and bliss are still here, and some are yet to come, and so will some be until that day. Therefore this is his thirst and his longing in love for us, to gather us all here into him, to our endless joy, as I see it. For we are not now so wholly in him as we then shall be.

For we know in our faith, and it was also revealed in all this, that Christ Jesus is both God and man; and in his divinity he is himself supreme bliss, and was from without beginning, and he will be without end, which true everlasting bliss cannot of its nature be increased or diminished. And this was plentifully seen in every revelation, and especially in the twelfth, where he says: I am he who is highest. And with respect to Christ's humanity, it is known in our faith and it was also revealed that with all the power of his divinity, for love, to bring us to his bliss, he suffered pains and Passion and he died. And these are the deeds of Christ's humanity, in which he rejoices; and that he revealed in the ninth revelation, where he says: It is a joy, a bliss, and endless delight to me that ever I suffered my Passion for you. And this is the bliss of Christ's deeds, and this is what he means when he says in the same revelation: We are his bliss, we are his reward, we are his honor, we are his crown. For insofar as Christ is our head, he is glorious and impassible; but with respect to his body, to which all his members are joined, he is not yet fully glorified or wholly impassible. For he still has that same thirst and longing which he had upon the Cross, which desire, longing and thirst, as I see it, were in him from without beginning; and he will have this until the time that the last soul which will be saved has come up into his bliss.

For as truly as there is in God a quality of pity and compassion, so truly is there in God a quality of thirst and longing; and the power of this longing in Christ enables us to respond to his longing, and without this no soul comes to heaven. And this quality of longing and thirst comes from God's everlasting goodness, just as the quality of pity comes from his everlasting goodness. And though he may have both longing and pity, they are different qualities, as I see them; and this is the characteristic of spiritual thirst, which will persist in him so long as we are in need, and will draw us up into his bliss.

And all this was seen to reveal his compassion, for on Judgment Day that will cease. So he has pity and compassion for us, and he has longing to possess us, but his wisdom and his love do not allow the end to come until the best time.

The Fifty-First Chapter.
"The Parable of the Lord and the Servant."

And then our courteous Lord answered very mysteriously by revealing a wonderful example of a lord who has a servant and gave me sight for the understanding of them both. . . . The lord sits in state, in rest and in peace. The servant stands before his lord, respectfully, ready to do his lord's will. The lord looks on the servant very lovingly and sweetly and mildly. He sends him to a certain place to do his will. Not only does the servant go, but he dashes off and runs at great speed, loving to do his lord's will. And soon he falls into a dell and is greatly injured; and then he groans and moans and tosses about and writhes, but he cannot rise or help himself in any way. And in all this, the greatest hurt which I saw him in was lack of consolation, for he could not turn his face to look on his loving lord, who was very close to him, in whom is all consolation; but like a man who was for the time extremely feeble and foolish, he paid heed to his feelings and his continued distress, in which distress he suffered seven great pains. . . .

I was amazed that this servant could so meekly suffer all this woe; and I looked carefully to know if I could detect any fault in him or if the lord would impute to him any kind of blame; and truly none was seen, for the only cause of his falling was his good will and his great desire. And in spirit, he was as prompt and as good as he was when he stood before his lord, ready to do his will. . . .

For twenty years after the time of the revelation except for three months, I received an inward instruction, and it was this: You ought to take heed to all the attributes, divine and human, which were revealed in the example, though this may seem to you mysterious and ambiguous. . . . I understood that the lord who sat in state, in rest and peace, is God. I understood that the servant who stood before him was shown for Adam, that is to say, one man was shown at that time and his fall, so as to make it understood how God regards all men and their falling. For in the sight of God, all men are one man, and one man is all men. This man was injured in his powers and made most feeble, and in his understanding he was amazed, because he was diverted from looking on his lord, but his will was preserved in God's sight. I saw the lord commend and approve him for his will, but he himself was blinded and hindered from knowing this will. And this is a great sorrow and a cruel suffering to him, for he neither sees clearly his loving lord, who is so meek and mild to him nor does he truly see what he himself is in the sight of his loving lord. And I know well that when these two things are wisely and truly seen, we shall gain rest and peace, here in part and the fullness in the bliss of heaven, by God's plentiful grace.

And this was a beginning of the teaching which I saw at the same time, whereby I might come to know in what manner he looks on us in our sin. And then I saw that only pain blames and punishes, and our courteous Lord comforts and succors, and always he is kindly disposed to the soul, loving and longing to bring us to his bliss. . . . And the loving regard which he kept constantly on his servant, and especially when he fell, it seemed to me that it could melt our hearts for love and break them in two for joy. . . .

In the servant is comprehended the second Person of the Trinity, and in the servant is comprehended Adam, that is to say all men. And therefore when I say "the Son," that means the divinity which is equal to the Father, and when I say "the servant," that means Christ's humanity, which is the true Adam. The lord is God the Father, the servant is the Son, Jesus Christ, the Holy Spirit is the equal love which is in them both. When Adam fell, God's Son fell; because of the true union which was made in heaven, God's Son could not be separated from Adam, for by Adam I understand all mankind. Adam fell from life to death into the valley of this wretched world and after that into hell. God's Son fell with Adam into the valley of the womb of the maiden who was the fairest daughter of Adam, and that was to excuse Adam from blame to heaven and on earth; and powerfully he brought him out of hell. By the wisdom and the goodness which were in the servant is understood God's Son by the poor laborer's clothing and standing close by on the left is understood Adam's humanity with all the harm and weakness which follow. For in all this our good Lord showed his own Son and Adam as only one man. The strength and the goodness that we have is from Jesus Christ; the weakness and blindness that we have is from Adam, which two were shown in the servant.

And so has our good Lord Jesus taken upon him all our blame; and therefore our Father may not, does not wish to, assign more blame to us than to his own beloved Son Jesus Christ. So he has the servant before he came to earth, standing ready in purpose before the Father until the time when he would send him to do the glorious deed by which mankind was brought back to heaven. That is to say, even though he is God, equal with the Father as regards his divinity, but with his prescient purpose that he would become man to save mankind in fulfillment of the will of his Father, so he stood before his Father as a servant, willingly taking upon him all our charge. And then he rushed off very readily at the Father's bidding, and soon he fell very low into the maiden's womb, having no regard for himself or for his cruel pains.

The white tunic is his flesh, the scantiness signifies that there was nothing at all separating the divinity from the humanity. The tight fit is poverty, the age is Adam's wearing, the wornness is the sweat of Adam's labor, the shortness shows the servant-laborer.

And so I saw the Son stand, saying in intention: See, my dear Father, I stand before you in Adam's tunic, all ready to hasten and run. I wish to be on earth to your glory, when it is your will to send me. How long shall I desire it? Very truly, the Son knew when was the Father's will, and how long he would desire it, that is to say as regards his divinity, for he is the wisdom of the Father. Therefore, this meaning was shown for understanding of Christ's humanity. For all mankind, which will be saved by the sweet Incarnation and the Passion of Christ, all is Christ's humanity, for he is the head and we are his members, to which members the day and the time are unknown when every passing woe and sorrow will have an end, and everlasting joy and bliss will be fulfilled, which day and time all the company of heaven longs and desires to see. And all who are under heaven will come there; their way is by longing and desire, which desiring and longing was shown in the servant standing before the lord, or, otherwise, in the Son standing before the Father in Adam's tunic. For the longing and desire of all mankind which will be saved appeared in Jesus, for Jesus is in all who will be saved, and all who will be saved are in Jesus; all is of the love of God, with obedience, meekness and patience, and the virtues which befit us.

Also in this marvelous example I have teaching within me, as it were, the beginning of an ABC, whereby I may have some understanding of our Lord's meaning, for the mysteries of the revelation are hidden in it, even though all the showings are full of mysteries.

The Fifty-Seventh Chapter.
"The Motherhood of God and of Christ."

So our Lady is our mother, in whom we are all enclosed and born of her in Christ, for she who is mother of our savior is mother of all who are saved in our savior; and our savior is our true Mother, in whom we are endlessly born and out of whom we shall never come.

Plenteously, fully and sweetly was this shown; and it is spoken in the first revelation, where it says that we are all enclosed in him, and he is enclosed in us. And it is spoken of in the 16th revelation, where he says that he sits in our soul, for it is his delight to reign blessedly in our understanding, and sit restfully in our soul, and to dwell endlessly in our soul, working us all into him. . . .

And so in our making, God almighty is our loving Father, and God all wisdom is our loving Mother, with the love and the goodness of the Holy Spirit, which is all one God, one Lord. And in the joining and the union he is our very true spouse and we his beloved wife and his fair maiden, and which wife he was never displeased; for he says: I love you and you love me, and our love will never divide in two.

I contemplated the work of all the blessed Trinity, in which contemplation I saw and understood these three properties: the property of the fatherhood, and the property of the motherhood, and the property of the lordship in one God. In our almighty Father we have our protection and our bliss, as regards our natural substance, which is ours by our creation from without beginning; and in the second person, in knowledge and wisdom we have our perfection, as regards our sensuality, our restoration, and our salvation, for he is our Mother, brother, and savior; and in our good Lord the Holy Spirit we have our reward and our gift for our living and our labor, endlessly surpassing all that we desire in this marvelous courtesy, out of his great plentiful grace. For all our life consists of three: In the first we have our being, and in the second we have our increasing, and in the third we have our fulfillment. The first is nature, the second is mercy, the third is grace.

As to the first, I saw and understood that the high might of the Trinity is our Father, and the deep wisdom of the Trinity is our Mother, and the great love of the Trinity is our lord; and all these we have in nature and in our substantial creation. And furthermore, I saw that the second person, who is our Mother, substantially the same beloved person, has now become our mother sensually, because we are double by God's creating, that is to say substantial and sensual. . . .

And our substance is in our Father, God almighty, and our substance is in our Mother, God all wisdom, and our substance is in our Lord God, the Holy Spirit, all goodness, for our substance is whole in each person of the Trinity, who is one God. And our sensuality is only in the second person, Christ Jesus, in whom is the Father and the Holy Spirit; and in him and by him we are powerfully taken out of hell and out of the wretchedness on earth, and gloriously brought up into heaven, and blessedly united to our substance, increased in riches and nobility by all the power of Christ and by the grace and operation of the Holy Spirit. . . .

So Jesus Christ, who opposes good to evil, is our true Mother. We have our being from him, where the foundation of motherhood begins, with all the sweet protection of love which endlessly follows.

As truly as God is our Father, so truly is God our Mother, and he revealed that in everything, and especially in these sweet words where he says: I am he; that is to say: I am her, the power and goodness of fatherhood; I am he, the wisdom and the lovingness of motherhood; I am he, the light and the grace which is all blessed love; I am he, the Trinity; I am he, the unity. . . .

Our great Father, almighty God, who is being, knows us and loved us before time began. Out of this knowledge, in his most wonderful deep love, by the prescient eternal counsel of all the blessed Trinity, he wanted the second person to become our Mother, our brother, and our savior. From this it follows that as truly as God is our Father, so truly is God our Mother. Our Father wills, our Mother works, our good Lord the Holy spirit confirms. . . .

And so Jesus is our true Mother by nature by our first creation, and he is our true Mother in grace by his taking our created nature. All the lovely works and all the sweet loving offices of beloved motherhood are appropriated to the second person, for in him we have this godly will, whole and safe forever, both in nature and in grace, from his own goodness proper to him. I understand three ways of contemplating motherhood in God. The first is the foundation of our nature's creation; the second is his taking of our nature, where the motherhood of grace begins; and the third is the motherhood at work. And in that, by the same grace, everything is penetrated, in length and in breadth, in height and in depth without end; and it is all one love. . . .

Our Mother in nature, our Mother in grace, because he wanted altogether to become our Mother in all things, made the foundation of his work most humbly and most mildly in the maiden's womb. . . arrayed and prepared himself in this humble place, all ready in our poor flesh, himself to do the service and the office of motherhood in everything. The mother's service is nearest, readiest and surest: Nearest because it is most natural, readiest because it is most loving, and surest because it is truest. No one ever might or could perform this office fully, except only him. We know that all our mothers bear us for pain and for death. . . .

The mother can give her child to suck of her milk, but our precious Mother Jesus can feed us with himself, and does, most courteously and most tenderly, with the blessed sacrament, which is the precious food of true life; and with all the sweet sacraments he sustains us most mercifully and graciously. . . . The mother can lay her child tenderly to her breast, but our tender Mother Jesus can lead us easily into this blessed breast through his open side, and show us there a part of the Godhead and of the joys of heaven, with inner certainty of endless bliss.

THOMAS À KEMPIS, *THE IMITATION OF CHRIST*

From the Rhine Valley mysticism spread to the Low Countries. Here the leading figure was Gerard Groote of Deventer (1340–1384) the founder of a group called the Brethren of the Common Life, a loose association of secular priests and lay persons who attempted to live a higher level of Christian life while staying within the world. They took no vows, but continued to pursue their ordinary vocations. Many of them opened free schools in which they provided fine educations for youth. Both Erasmus and Luther were educated by the Brethren of the Common Life.

The piety that characterized this group is called the *Devotio Moderna,* the "Modern Devotion." In contrast to the older monastic piety of the early Middle Ages, it was aimed at enabling one to live the full Christian life while working within the world. It emphasized the inner life of the individual and encouraged meditation on and imitation of the life of Christ. The classical expression of this individualistic piety is found in Thomas à Kempis' *Imitation of Christ,* which, after the Bible, is probably the most widely read work of Christian piety. In contrast to the abstract dogmatism of late medieval scholasticism, à Kempis stresses living according to the spirit of the Jesus of the gospels. "Let it then be our main concern to meditate on the life of Jesus Christ." Learned discourse on the Trinity without the humility taught by Jesus is actually displeasing to God. In fact, *The Imitation* seems to go so far as to make reason and affection, or learning and experience, enemies.

> Esoteric words neither make us holy nor righteous; only a virtuous life makes us beloved of God. I would rather experience repentance in my soul than know how to define it.

Although many of the Brethren of the Common Life were engaged in humanistic studies, the *Imitation* rejects the pursuit of worldly honor and riches as vanity. The world and the flesh are enemies of the world to come and the spirit.

> It is vanity to seek riches that are sure to perish and to put your hope in them.
> It is vanity to follow the desires of the flesh and crave those things which will eventually bring you heavy punishment.

Even Aristotle's description of humans as having a natural desire for knowledge is seen as a threat to true piety. "Everyone has a natural desire for knowledge but what good is knowledge without the fear of God?" The "humble peasant who serves God is better than the proud astronomer" who "lacks all knowledge of himself." This emphasis on self-knowledge is reminiscent of Socrates, but the *Imitation* gives it a distinctly Christian twist by emphasizing humility and charity.

> If I truly knew myself I would consider myself insignificant and would not enjoy hearing others praise me. If I knew everything in the world and were still without charity, what advantage would I have in the eyes of God who is to judge me according to my deeds?

Under the influence of late scholastic nominalism which separated the realms of reason and faith, the *Imitation* seems to juxtapose philosophy and the gospel message as enemies. Philosophy argues "about obscure and recondite matters" and is concerned with such words as "genera and species," but the eternal Word set us "free from a multitude of frivolous theories." The only truly "useful and necessary" knowledge is a humble knowledge of yourself because this leads to God. Although education and learning are not evil in themselves, one's chief concerns should be uprooting vice and living virtuously.

The way to this virtuous life is first of all through the spiritual study of the scriptures. They are not to be read in order "to debate and discuss" obscure passages, but in order to be edified by the Christian virtues of humility, simplicity, and faith. The process of acquiring virtue bears some resemblance to the teaching of the classical philosophers, especially the Stoics. It involves gaining control of one's inordinate affections, such as pride and avarice, by becoming poor and humble in spirit. By not being "slaves" to our passions we will find "true peace of heart." But virtue is not acquired simply by one's own powers. *The Imitation* warns: "Do not rely on yourself but place your trust in God. Do whatever lies in your power and God will assist your good intentions." This view of the cooperation between human free will and God's grace will be the position taken by Erasmus in his famous debate with Luther over the role of the will and grace in the process of salvation.

Some see the mystical movements of the late Middle Ages as a preparation for the Reformation, but it must be remembered that these movements all stayed within the institutional church and continued to encourage their members to receive the traditional sacraments. It might be better to say that these movements emphasized individualism: God and the individual soul, personal imitation of Jesus, self-knowledge and the personal pursuit of virtue. This emphasis on the individual was understandable at a time when the institution was often corrupt and when the threat of an early and unexpected death was ever present. In this way these movements do prepare for the Reformation and the Catholic Counter Reformation. Luther will come to his conversion experience through the tortured suffering of his individual conscience in the pursuit of virtue. And, in responding to the reformers, the Council of Trent will work out a careful tract on the process of justification for the individual.

The translation is by Joseph N. Tylenda, S.J., *The Imitation of Christ* (Wilmington, Del.: Glazier, 1984) 29–43.

THE IMITATION OF CHRIST

*Book I: Helpful Counsels for
the Spiritual Life*

1. THE IMITATION OF CHRIST
AND CONTEMPT FOR
THE VANITIES OF THE WORLD

He who follows Me will not walk in darkness, says the Lord. These are the words of Christ by which He directs us to imitate His life and His ways, if we truly desire to be spiritually enlightened and free of all blindness of heart. Let it then be our main concern to meditate on the life of Jesus Christ.

2. Christ's teaching surpasses that of all the saints, and whoever has His spirit will find in His teaching *hidden manna.* But it happens that many are little affected even after a frequent hearing of His Gospel; this is because they *do not have the spirit of Christ.* If you want to fully understand Christ's words and to relish them, you must strive to conform your entire life to His.

3. What good does it do you to be able to give a learned discourse on the Trinity while you are without humility and, thus, are actually displeasing to the Trinity? Esoteric Words neither make us holy nor righteous; only a virtuous life makes us beloved of God. I would rather experience repentance in my soul than know how to define it.

If you memorized the whole Bible and knew all the maxims of the philosophers, what good would it do you if you were, at the same time, without God's love and grace? *Vanity of vanities!* All is vanity, except our loving God and *serving only Him.* This is the highest wisdom: to despise the world and seek the kingdom of heaven.

4. It is vanity to seek riches that are sure to perish and to put your hope in them.

It is vanity to pursue honors and to set yourself up on a pedestal.

It is vanity *to follow the desires of the flesh,* and crave those things which will eventually bring you heavy punishment.

It is vanity to wish for a long life and to care little about leading a good life.

It is vanity to give thought only to this present life and not to the one that is to come.

It is vanity to love what is transitory and not to hasten to where everlasting joy abides.

5. Keep this proverb often in mind: *The eye is not satisfied with seeing, nor the ear filled with hearing.* Therefore, withdraw your heart from the love of things visible and turn yourself to things invisible. Those who yield to their sensual nature dishonor their conscience and lose God's grace.

2. HAVING A HUMBLE OPINION OF
ONE'S SELF

Everyone has a natural desire for knowledge but what good is knowledge without the fear of God? Surely a humble peasant who serves God is better than the proud astronomer who knows how to chart the heavens' stars but lacks all knowledge of himself.

If I truly knew myself I would consider myself insignificant and would not enjoy hearing others praise me. If I knew everything in the world and *were still without charity*, what advantage would I have in the eyes of God who is to judge me according to my deeds?

2. Curb all undue desire for knowledge for in it you will find many distractions and much delusion. Those who are learned strive to give the appearance of being wise and desire to be recognized as such; but there is much knowledge that is of little or no benefit to the soul.

Whoever sets his mind on anything other than what serves his salvation is a senseless fool. A barrage of words does not make the soul happy, but a good life gladdens the mind and a *pure conscience* generates confidence in God.

3. The more things you know and the better you know them, the stricter will God's judgment be, unless you have also lived a holier life. Do not boast about the learning and skills

that are yours; rather, be somewhat circum-
spect since you do possess such knowledge.

4. If it seems to you that you know many
things and thoroughly understand them all,
realize that there are countless other things
of which you are ignorant. *Be not haughty,* but
admit your ignorance. Why should you prefer
yourself to another, when there are many who
are more learned and better trained in God's
law than you are? If you are looking for a
knowledge and a learning that is useful to
you, then love to be unknown and be
esteemed as nothing.

5. This is the most important and most
salutary lesson: to know and to despise ourselves. It is great wisdom and perfection to
consider ourselves as nothing and always to
judge well and highly of others. If you should
see someone commit a sin or do some grievous
wrong, do not think of yourself as someone
better, for you know not how long you will
remain in your good state.

We are all frail; but think of yourself as one
who is more frail than others.

5. READING THE HOLY SCRIPTURE

In Holy Scripture we seek truth and not
eloquence. All Sacred Scripture should be
read in the spirit with which it was written.

We should search the Scriptures for what
is to our profit, rather than for niceties of language. You should read the simple and devout
books as eagerly as those that are lofty and
profound. The authority of the author,
whether he be of great or little learning,
ought not to influence you, but let the love of
pure truth draw you to read them. Do not
inquire about who is the one saying this, but
pay attention to what he is saying.

2. Men enter and pass out of this world but
the *faithfulness of the Lord endures forever.*
God speaks to all of us in a variety of ways and
is no respecter of persons. Our curiosity proves
a hindrance to us for while reading the
Scriptures we sometimes want to stop to
debate and discuss, when we should simply
read on.

If you wish to derive profit from your reading of Scripture, do it with humility, simplicity, and faith; at no time use it to gain a reputation for yourself as being one who is
learned. Eagerly ask yourself questions and
listen in silence to the words of the saints, and
do not let the riddle of the ancients baffle you
but, remember, they were written down for a
definite purpose.

CHRISTIAN HUMANISM AND ERASMUS

In the late fifteenth and early sixteenth centuries Renaissance humanism moved from
Italy to northern Europe where it was manifest in literary works by writers such as
François Rabelais in France, Thomas More in England, and Desiderius Erasmus of
Rotterdam, "the prince of the humanists." In contrast to the nearly pagan commitment
to artistic beauty and fame by some figures of the Italian Renaissance, the northern
Renaissance combined a study of classical Greek and Roman antiquity with a program
of church reform based on a return to the ideals and spirit of early Christianity as found
in the New Testament and the early Christian fathers. The northern humanists advocated an ethical, as opposed to dogmatic, reform of the church through an educational
program which united the classical ideals of humanity and civic virtue with the
Christian ideals of charity and an interior spirituality.

Erasmus is an excellent example of this Christian humanism because he combined an interior piety with a humanistic dedication to the restoration of the texts of early Christianity. Born the illegitimate son of a priest, Erasmus was educated by the Brethren of the Common Life in the piety of the *devotio moderna,* an anti-speculative spirituality which emphasized imitating the Jesus of the gospels. His early training had a lasting influence on Erasmus, as he steadfastly avoided what he considered the sterile scholasticism of the Roman Catholic universities. Although he entered an Augustinian monastery and became a priest, Erasmus spent most of his life as an itinerant humanist scholar; he travelled throughout Europe to Paris, England (several times), Louvain, Italy, Basel and Freiburg in pursuit of a community of scholars, manuscripts, and printing houses for the publication of his writings and critical editions of classical and early Christian sources. As a humanist, Erasmus believed that the disciplined study of the classics, the Bible, and the early Christian fathers was the best way to reform both society and the church. He summarized his beliefs in the phrase "the philosophy of Christ," by which he meant a simple ethical spirituality in imitation of the pacifist Jesus of the gospels. This ideal stands in sharp contrast to the dogmatic, ceremonial and often superstitious religiosity of the early sixteenth century.

To promote "the philosophy of Christ," Erasmus dedicated himself to the study and publication of primary sources from the classical age and early Christianity. His greatest achievement as a humanist scholar was the publication of a critical edition of the Greek New testament (1516) which became the basis for a new Latin translation (1519) that presumed to correct Jerome's revered Vulgate, the official Bible of the church.

Despite his criticism of abuses in the church, Erasmus never joined ranks with Luther and the other reformers. His complaint against the church was ethical, not dogmatic, and he consistently attempted to mediate by reason between the reformers and the papacy. Eventually, he wrote against Luther in his famous tract *On Free Will* (1524), in which he argues that, although salvation rests on faith and grace, the human person freely cooperates with God's grace in the process of salvation. Erasmus' humanistic respect for the dignity of the human person would not allow him to accept Luther's predestinationism. In the end, Erasmus' pleas for reform of church practice, not dogma, from within the church pleased neither the Roman church authorities nor the reformers. Rome resented his pointed attacks on the foibles of contemporary church life and his "improvements" on the revered Vulgate, and Luther condemned as Pelagian his views on the freedom of human will in the process of salvation.

Northern hunanists often combined their classical scholarship with learned satire against the evils of sixteenth-century society and church. Erasmus' most famous work is his Latin satire entitled *Moriae Encomium, The Praise of Folly,* which was written in 1509 after he had returned to England from a trip to Italy and was staying at the home of his dear friend and fellow humanist, Thomas More. The title contains a pun on More's name which Erasmus alludes to in the preface: "First, of course, your family name of More prompted me; which comes as near to the word for folly (*moria* in Greek) as you are from the meaning of it."

The Praise of Folly revives the classical genre of the paradoxical encomium, or "declamation." The tone is playfully serious. Folly, personified in a farcical way as a goddess, praises herself and her many worshippers by making a travesty of the whole of sixteenth-century European society: stuffy scholastics and the pompous Stoic and Platonic philosophers of the Renaissance, grammarians, dialecticians, rhetoricians, theologians and scholars, doctors and lawyers, cuckholded husbands, hunters, architects, alchemists, princes and nobility, builders and scientists, nations and cities, popes and cardinals, bishops and monks. No one is spared, not even Erasmus himself and his friend More.

Throughout her speech Folly is an eloquent and witty spokeswoman for Erasmus' humanistic program. At first, she presents herself as the vital force of nature which is absolutely necessary for life in contrast to the presumptuous picture of human nature which optimistically defines man as a "rational animal." Later, Folly attacks the folly of superstitious religious devotion to the saints and indulgences and lays bare the pretensions and hypocrisy of the various sixteenth-century churchmen. These satirical attacks earned Erasmus the reputation as forerunner of the Reformation, but they were designed to promote reform of practice rather than a radical reinterpretation of dogma. Finally, Folly praises Christian folly, man's highest "folly," as a Christian virtue based on the teachings of Christ and Paul and a kind of Platonic madness or ecstasy in which the person transcends self and this world's concerns in a divine love.

The translation is by Hoyt Hopewell Hudson, *The Praise of Folly* (Princeton University Press, Princeton Paperback, 1970) 7, 11–15, 37–40, 56–59, 78–81, 87–88, 97–101, 114–117, 118–125.

THE PRAISE OF FOLLY

(FOLLY SPEAKS:)

However mortal folk may commonly speak of me (for I am not ignorant how ill the name of Folly sounds, even to the greatest fools), I am she—the only she, I may say—whose divine influence makes gods and men rejoice. One great and sufficient proof of this is that the instant I stepped up to speak to this crowded assembly, all faces at once brightened with a fresh and unwonted cheerfulness, all of you suddenly unbent your brows, and with frolic and affectionate smiles you applauded; so that as I look upon all present about me, you seem flushed with nectar, like gods in Homer, not without some nepenthe, also; whereas a moment ago you were sitting moody and depressed, as if you had come out of the cave of Trophonius. Just as it commonly happens, when the sun first shows his splendid golden face to the earth or when, after a bitter winter, young spring breathes mild west winds, that a new face comes over everything, new color and a sort of youthfulness appear; so at the mere sight of me, you straightway take on another aspect. And thus what great orators elsewhere can hardly bring about in a long, carefully planned speech, I have done in a moment, with nothing but my looks.

FOLLY'S PROGENITOR

But since it is not known to very many from what stock I have sprung, I shall now attempt, with the Muses' kind help, to set this forth. Not Chaos, or Orcus, or Saturn, or Iapetus, or any other of that old-fashioned and musty set of gods, was my father at all. It was Plutus, who only, in spite of Hesiod, Homer, and Jove himself to boot, is "the father of gods and men." At a single nod of Plutus, as of old so nowadays, all things sacred and profane are turned topsy-turvy. At his pleasure, all war, peace, empires, plans, judgments, assemblies, marriages, treaties, pacts, laws, arts, sports, weighty matters (my breath is giving out)—in short, all public and private affairs of mortal men, are governed. Without his help all that population of deities of the poets' making—nay, I speak very boldly, even those top gods—either would not exist at all or would be "diners at home," keeping house very meagerly. To the person who rouses Plutus's anger Pallas herself cannot bring help enough; on the other hand, whoever possesses his favor can bid great Jove and his thunder go hang themselves. "I glory to have such a father." And he did not procreate me out of his head, as Jupiter did that austere and homely Pallas; but rather out of Youth, the loveliest nymph of all, and the jolliest as well. Nor did he do this confined in the irksome marriage-bond—the way that blacksmith was born lame!—but indeed he did it in a much pleasanter manner, "mingled in love," as our father Homer puts it. Yet, make no mistake, it was not the Plutus of Aristophanes, already decrepit and weak in the eyes, that engendered me, but the same god healthy and as yet heated by his youth; nor by youth only, but also by nectar, which he had chanced to drink rather copiously and rather straight at a banquet of the gods.

FOLLY'S BIRTHPLACE AND NURSES

If you are also wanting to know the place of my nativity (seeing that in these days it is accounted a prime point of nobility, in what place you uttered your first cries), I was not brought forth in floating Delos, or on the foaming sea, or "in hollow caverns," but right in the Fortunate Isles, where all things grow "without ploughing or planting." In those islands is no drudgery or old age, nor is there any sickness. In the fields one never sees a daffodil, mallow, leek, bean, or any of such kind of trash; but one's eyes and nose are enchanted at the same time by moly, panacea, nepenthes, sweet marjoram, ambrosia, lotus, rose, violet, hyacinth, and the gardens of Adonis. And being born among these delights, I did not enter upon life with weeping, but right off I laughed sweetly at my mother. Nor indeed do I envy great Jupiter his nurse, a she-goat, since two charming nymphs nourished me at their breasts—Drunkenness, offspring of Bacchus, and Ignorance, Pan's daughter.

FOLLY'S ENTOURAGE

These two you see here in the company of my other attendants and followers. If you wish to know all their names, you will not hear them from me, so help me, except in Greek. This one whom you observe here, with the eyebrows haughtily raised, is Philavtia (self-love). She with the smiling eyes, so to speak, whom you see clapping her hands, is named Kolakia (flattery). The one who is half asleep, and like a drowsy person, is called Lethe (forgetfulness). She that leans on her elbows, with her hands folded, is Misoponia (laziness). Hedone (pleasure) is the one wearing the rosy wreath and smelling of perfumes. The lady with the uncertain eyes rolling here and there is called Anoia (madness) and she with the glistening skin and body in good point is Tryphe (sensuality). You see also two male gods among the girls, one of whom they call Comus, (intemperance) the other Negretos Hypnos (sound sleep). These, I say, are my household servants, with whose faithful help I bring every sort of thing under my rule, maintaining my empire even over emperors.

FOLLY IS RESPONSIBLE FOR THE
GIFT OF LIFE

You have learned of my family, upbringing, and companions. Now, that it may not look as if I have usurped the name of goddess for myself without good grounds, please give closest attention while I tell how many advantages I bestow on both gods and men, and how broadly my power is displayed. For if, as some one has judiciously observed, this only is to be a god, to help men, and if deservedly they have been admitted to the rank of gods who have shown to mortals the use of wine, or grain, or any other such commodity, why am not I of right named and venerated as the *alpha* of all gods, who single-handed bestow all things on all men?

In the first place, what can be dearer or more precious than life? And the beginning and first principle of life is owed to whom else but me? Not the spear of "potent-fathered" Pallas, not the shield of "cloud-compelling" Jove, procreates the children of men or multiplies their race. Even he, the father of gods and king of men, who shakes all heaven by a nod, is obliged to lay aside his three-pronged thunder and that Titanic aspect by which, when he pleases, he scares all the gods, and assumes another character in the slavish manner of an actor, if he wishes to do what he never refrains from doing, that is to say, to beget children. Now the Stoics believe that they are next-door neighbors to gods. But give me a triple Stoic, or a quadruple one, or, if you will, a Stoic multiplied by six hundred; if for this purpose he will not put off his beard, the ensign of wisdom (though displayed also by goats), yet he will certainly lay by his gravity, smooth his brow, renounce his rock-bound principles, and for a few minutes toy and talk nonsense. In fine, the wise man must send for me, I repeat, if he ever wishes to become a father. And why not speak to you still more frankly, as is my fashion? I beg to inquire whether the head, whether the face, the breast, the hand, or the ear—all of them

accounted honorable members—generates gods and men? I judge not; nay, rather that foolish, even silly, part which cannot be named without laughter, is the propagator of the human race. This is at last that sacred spring from which all things derive existence, more truly than from the elemental tetrad of Pythagoras.

Now tell me, what man, by heaven, could wish to stick his head into the halter of marriage if, as your wise-acres have the habit of doing, he first weighed with himself the inconveniences of wedded life? Or what woman would ever admit her husband to her person, if she had heard or thought about the dangerous pains of childbirth and the irksomeness of bringing up a child? But since you owe your existence to the marriage-bed, and marriage is owing to Anoia, a servant of mine, you can see how vastly indebted you are to me! Then, too, would a woman who has gone through all this, wish to make a second venture, if the power and influence of my Lethe did not attend her? And in spite of what Lucretius claims, Venus herself would not deny that without the addition of my presence her strength would be enfeebled and ineffectual. So it is that from this brisk and silly little game of mine come forth the haughty philosophers (to whose places those who are vulgarly called monks have now succeeded), and kings in their scarlet, pious priests, and triply most holy popes; also, finally, that assembly of the gods of the poets, so numerous that Olympus, spacious as it is, can hardly accommodate the crowd.

In the Play of Life is it more prudent to be
wise and destroy the illusion or to be a fool
and go along with the comedy?

Now what else is the whole life of mortals but a sort of comedy, in which the various actors, disguised by various costumes and masks, walk on and play each one his part, until the manager waves them off the stage? Moreover, this manager frequently bids the same actor go back in a different costume, so that he who has but lately played the king in scarlet now acts the flunkey in patched clothes. Thus all things are presented by shadows; yet this play is put on in no other way.

But suppose, right here, some wise man who has dropped down from the sky should suddenly confront me and cry out that the person whom the world has accepted as a god and a master is not even a man, because he is driven sheeplike by his passions; that he is the lowest slave, because he willingly serves so many and such base masters. Or again, suppose the visitor should command some one mourning his fathers' death to laugh, because now his father has really begun to live—in a sense our earthly life is but a kind of death. Suppose him to address another who is glorying in his ancestry, and to call him low and base-born because he is so far from virtue, the only true fount of nobility. Suppose him to speak of others in like vein. I ask you, what would he get by it, except to be considered by everyone as insane and raving? As nothing is more foolish than wisdom out of place, so nothing is more imprudent than unseasonable prudence. And he is unseasonable who does not accommodate himself to things as they are, who is "unwilling to follow the market," who does not keep in mind at least that rule of conviviality, "Either drink or get out"; who demands, in short, that the play should no longer be a play. The part of a truly prudent man, on the contrary, is (since we are mortal) not to aspire to wisdom beyond his station, and either, along with the rest of the crowd, pretend not to notice anything, or affably and companionably be deceived. But that, they tell us, is folly. Indeed, I shall not deny it; only let them, on their side, allow that it is also to play out the comedy of life.

THE UNFEELING ARE INHUMAN

As for the next, O ye immortal gods! Shall I speak or be silent? But why should I be silent, when it is more true than truth? Yet haply for such an undertaking it might be well to send up to Helicon and fetch the Muses, whom the poets are wont to involve, quite often on most trivial occasions. Therefore, be present for a brief season, daughters of Jove, while I show to the world that one never attains to that renowned wisdom, which the wise themselves call the citadel of happiness, except by taking Folly as guide. And first, it is beyond dispute that all emotions belong to folly. Indeed, we distinguish a wise man from a fool by this, that reason governs the one, and passion the other. Thus the Stoics take away from the wise man all perturbations of the soul, as so many diseases. Yet these passions not only discharge the office of mentor and guide to such as are pressing toward the gate of wisdom, but they also assist in every exercise of virtue as spurs and goads—persuaders, as it were—to well doing. Although that double-strength Stoic, Seneca, stoutly denies this, subtracting from the wise man any and every emotion, yet in doing so he leaves him no man at all but rather a new kind of god, or demiurgos, who never existed and will never emerge. Nay, to speak more plainly, he creates a marble simulacrum of a man, a senseless block, completely alien to every human feeling.

Well, if they want it so, I give them joy of this wise man of theirs. They may love him with no fear of a rival, and may live with him in Plato's republic, or, if they prefer, in the world of ideas, or in the gardens of Tantalus. For who would not startle at such a man, as at an apparition or ghost, and shun him? He would be insensible to any natural sympathy, no more moved by feelings of love or pity than as if he were solid flint or Marpesian stone. Nothing gets by him; he never makes a mistake; as if another Lynceus, there is no thing he does not see; he measures everything with a standard rule; he forgives nothing; he alone is satisfied with himself alone, uniquely rich, uniquely sane, uniquely a king, uniquely a free man; in short, uniquely all things, but notably unique in his own judgment; he values no friend, himself the friend of none; he does not hesitate to bid the gods go hang themselves; he condemns as unwholesome whatever life may offer, and derides it. An animal of that description is your perfect wise man. I ask you, if it were a matter of votes, what city would choose such a one as magistrate? What army would want that kind of general? Nay, what woman would pick, or put up with, that kind of husband? What host would have such a guest? Who would not prefer just anyone from the middle ranks of human foolhood, who, being a fool, would be better prepared either to command fools or to obey them; who would please those like himself, that is, nearly everyone; who would be kind to his wife, welcome to his friends, a boon companion, an acceptable dinner-guest; and lastly, who would consider nothing human to be alone to him. But I grew bored with that wise man some time ago; let the speech betake itself to advantages not yet touched upon. . . .

FOOLISH DEVOTIONS

And the next to these come the folk who have arrived at the foolish but gratifying belief that if they gaze on a picture of Polyphemus-Christopher they will not die that day, or that whoever salutes in certain prescribed words an image of Barbara will come through a battle unharmed, or that by making application to Erasmus on certain days, using a certain kind of candles and certain prayers, one will shortly become rich. Indeed, they have discovered another Hercules, and even another Hippolytus, in George; whose horse, piously decked out with trappings and bosses, they all but worship, often commending themselves to him by some little gift; while to swear by St. George's brass helmet is an oath for a king. Then what shall

I say of the people who so happily fool themselves with forged pardons for sins, measuring out time to be spent in purgatory as if with an hour-glass, and figuring its centuries, years, months, days, and hours as if from a mathematical table, beyond possibility of error? Or I might speak of those who will promise themselves any and every thing, relying upon certain charms or prayers devised by some pious impostor either for his soul's sake or for money, to bring them wealth, reputation, pleasure, plenty, good health, long life, and a green old age, and at last a seat next to Christ's in heaven—but they do not wish to get it too soon. That is to say, when the pleasures of this life have finally failed them, willy-nilly, though they struggled tooth and nail to hold on to them, then it is time for the bliss of heaven to arrive.

I fancy that I see some merchant or soldier or judge laying down one small coin from his extensive booty and expecting that the whole cesspool of his life will be at once purified. He conceives that just so many perjuries, so many lustful acts, so many debauches, so many fights, murders, frauds, lies, and so many breaches of faith, are bought off as by contract; and so bought off that with a clean slate he may start from scratch upon a new round of sins. And who are more foolish, yet who more happy, than those who promise themselves something more than the highest felicity if they daily recite those seven verses of the Psalms? The seven, I mean, which some devil, a playful one, but blabbing rather than crafty, is believed to have pointed out to St. Bernard after he had been duped by the saint's trick. Things like that are so foolish, you know, that I am almost ashamed of them myself; yet they stand approved not only by the common people but even by teachers of religion. And is it not almost as bad when the several countries each lay claim to a particular saint of their own, and then assign particular powers respectively to the various saints and observe for each one his own peculiar rites of worship? One saint assists in time of toothache, another is propitious to women in travail, another recovers stolen goods, a fourth stands by with help in a shipwreck, and still another keeps the sheep in good repair; and so of the rest, though it would take too long to specify all of them. Some of them are good for a number of purposes, particularly the Virgin Mother, to whom the common people tend to attribute more than to the Son.

Yet what do men ask of these saints except things that pertain to folly? Think a bit: among all those consecrated gifts which you see covering the walls of some churches, and even hung on the ceiling, do you ever find one given in gratitude for an escape from folly, or because the giver has been made any whit wiser? One person has come safe to land. A second survived being run through in a duel. One no less fortunately than bravely got away from a battlefield, leaving the rest to fight. Another was brought near to the gallows, but by favor of some saint who is friendly to thieves he has decided that he should go on relieving those who are burdened with too much wealth. Another escaped in a jail-break. Another came through a fever, in spite of his doctor. The poisoned drink of another, by loosening his bowels, served to cure him instead of kill him, not at all to the joy of his wife, who lost both her labor and her expenses. Another's cart was turned over, but he drove both horses home safely. Another was dug out of the debris of a fallen house. Another, caught in the act by a husband, made good his escape. No one gives thanks for a recovery from being a fool. So sweet it is not to be wise that mortal men will pray to be delivered from anything sooner than from Folly.

But why should I launch out upon this ocean of superstition? "For if I had a hundred tongues, a hundred mouths, a voice of brass, I could not set forth all the shapes of fools or run over all the names of folly." Yet the whole life of Christian folk everywhere is full of fanaticisms of this kind. Our priests allow them, without regret, and even foster them, being aware of how much money is wont to accrue from this source. In this posture of affairs, suppose that some odious wise man were to step up and sing out this, which is true: "You will not die badly if you live well. You get quit of your sins if you add to the money payment a hatred of evil-doing, add tears, watchings, prayers, fastings; and if you alter the whole basis of your life. This or that saint will be gracious to you if you emulate his goodness." If the wise man, I say, were to start howling out things like that, just see from what contentment, and into what a turmoil, he would all of a sudden drive the souls of men!

THEOLOGICAL FOLLIES

But those are hackneyed. Here are questions worthy of the great and (as some call them) illuminated theologians, questions to make them prick up their ears—if ever they chance upon them. Whether divine generation took place at a particular time? Whether there are several sonships in Christ? Whether this is a possible proposition: God the Father hates the Son? Whether God could have taken upon Himself the likeness of a woman? Or of a devil? Of an ass? Of a gourd? Of a piece of flint? Then how would that gourd have preached, performed miracles, or been crucified? Also, what would Peter have consecrated if he had administered the sacrament while Christ's body hung upon the Cross? Also whether at that moment Christ could be said to be a man? And whether after the resurrection it will be forbidden to eat and drink? (Now, while there is time, they are providing against hunger and thirst!) These finespun trifles are numberless, with others even more subtle, having to do with instants of time, notions, relations, accidents, quiddities, entities, which no one can perceive with his eyes unless, like Lynceus, he can see in blackest darkness things that are not there.

We must put in also those hard sayings, contradictions indeed, compared to which the Stoic maxims which were called paradoxes seem the merest simplicity. For instance: it is less of a crime to cut the throats of a thousand men than to set a stitch on a poor man's shoe on the Lord's day; it is better to choose that the universe should perish, body, boots, and breeches (as the saying is), than that one should tell a single lie, however inconsequential. The methods our scholastics pursue only render more subtle these subtlest of subtleties; for you will escape from a labyrinth more quickly than from the tangles of Realists, Nominalists, Thomists, Albertists, Occamists, Scotists—I have not named all, but the chief ones only. But in all these sects there is so much learning and so much difficulty that I should think the apostles themselves must needs have the help of some other spirit if they were to try disputing on these topics with our new generation of theologies.

THE UNSUBTLE APOSTLES

Paul could exhibit faith; but when he said, "Faith is the substance of things hoped for, the evidence of things not seen," he did not define it doctorally. The same apostle, though he exemplified charity supremely well, divided and defined it with very little logical skill in his first epistle to the Corinthians, Chapter 13. And no doubt the apostles consecrated the Eucharist devoutly enough; but suppose you had questioned them about the *terminus a quo* and the *termius ad quem,* or about transubstantiation—how the body is in many places at once, the difference between the body of Christ when in heaven, when on the Cross, when in the sacrament of the Eucharist, about the point when transubstantiation occurs (seeing that the prayer effecting it is a discrete quantity having extension in time)—they would not have answered with the same

acuteness, I suggest, with which the sons of Scotus distinguish and define these matters. The apostles knew the mother of Jesus, but who among them has demonstrated philosophically just how she was kept clear from the sin of Adam, as our theologians have done? Peter received the keys, received them from One who did not commit them to an unworthy person, and yet I doubt that he ever understood—for Peter never did attain to subtlety—that a person who did not have knowledge could have the key to knowledge. They went about baptizing everywhere, and yet they never taught what is the formal, the material, the efficient, and the final cause of baptism, nor is mention made by them that it has both a delible character and an indelible one. They worshipped, to be sure, but in spirit, following no other teaching than that of the gospel, "God is a spirit, and they that worship Him must worship Him in spirit and in truth." It seems never to have been revealed to them that a picture drawn with charcoal on a wall ought to be worshipped with the same worship as Christ himself—at least if it is drawn with two fingers outstretched and the hair unshorn, and has three sets of rays in the nimbus fastened to the back of the head. For who would comprehend these things if he had not consumed all of thirty-six years upon the physics and metaphysics of Aristotle and the Scotists?

In similar wise, the apostles preach grace, and yet they never determined what the difference is between grace freely given and grace that makes some deserving. They urge us to good works, but do not separate work, work working, and work that has been worked. At all times they inculcate charity, but do not distinguish charity which is infused from that which is acquired, or explain whether charity is an accident or a substance, created or uncreated. They abhor sin, but may I be shot if they could define scientifically what it is we call sin, unless they had the luck to be instructed by the spirit of the Scotists.

GOOD WORKS OF MONKS

The greater number of them work so hard at their ceremonies and at maintaining the minutiae of tradition that they deem one heaven hardly a suitable reward for their labors; never recalling that the time will come when, with all these things held of no account, Christ will demand a reckoning of that which He has prescribed, namely, charity. One friar will then show a paunch which has been padded out with every kind of fish; another will spill out a hundred bushels of hymns. Another will count off so many myriads of fasts, and will lay the blame for his almost bursting belly upon his having always broken his fasts by a single dinner. Another will point to a pile of ceremonies so big that seven ships could scarcely carry it. Another will boast that for sixty years he never touched money, except when his fingers were protected by two pairs of gloves. Another will wear a cowl so dirty and greasy that no sailor would deign to put it on. Another will celebrate the fact that for more than fifty-five years he lived the life of a sponge, always fastened to one spot. Another will show a voice grown hoarse with assiduous chanting; another, a lethargy contracted by living alone; another, a tongue grown dumb under his vow of silence. But Christ, interrupting their boasts, which otherwise could go on endlessly, will say: "Whence comes this new race of Jews? I recognize one commandment which is truly mine, and of that I hear nothing. Of old in the sight of all men and using no device of parable I promised the inheritance of my Father, not to cowls, orisons, or fasts, but to works of charity. Nor do I acknowledge those who acknowledge too well their own good works; let those that wish to seem holier than myself dwell, if they like, in those six hundred heavens of Basilides, or let them command a new heaven to be built for themselves by the very ones whose petty traditions they have preferred above my commandments." When they shall hear these words and shall see common sailors and teamsters preferred above them, with what faces, think you, will they look wistfully on each other! Yet meanwhile, with some assistance from me, they are happy in their good hope.

BISHOPS

Our popes, cardinals, and bishops for some time now have earnestly copied the state and practice of princes, and come near to beating them at their own game. Let a bishop but consider what his alb, the white emblem of sincerity, should teach him, namely, a life in every way blameless; and what is signified on his part by the two-horned miter, the two peaks bound by the same knot—I suppose it is a perfect knowledge of the Old and New Testaments; what is meant by covering his hands with gloves, a clean administration of the sacrament and one unsullied by any taint of human concerns; what the crozier symbolizes, most watchful care of the flock put under his charge; what is indicated by the cross that is carried before him, to wit, a victory over all carnal affections. If he would contemplate these and other lessons of the sort, I say, would he not lead a sad and troubled life? But as it is, they do well enough by way of feeding themselves; as for the other, the care of the sheep, they delegate that to Christ himself, or else refer it to their suffragans, as they call them, or other deputies. Nor do they keep in mind the name they bear, or what the word "bishop" means—labor, vigilance, solicitude. Yet in raking in moneys they truly play the bishop, overseeing everything—and overlooking nothing.

CARDINALS

In a similar way the cardinals, if they considered the fact that they have succeeded to the places of the apostles, would see that the same works are required of them as were performed by their predecessors; that they are not lords, but stewards, of spiritual things, and that shortly they are to render an exact account of what they hold in trust. Yes, let them too philosophize a bit concerning their vestments, and question themselves in this fashion: "What does the whiteness of this upper garment mean? Is it not a notable and singular purity of heart? What the crimson lower garment? Is it not a burning love of God? What, again, that outer robe flowing down in broad folds and spreading over the mule of his Exalted Reverence, though it would suffice to cover a camel? Is it not charity ample enough to embrace all men in its helpfulness, by way of teaching, exhorting, chastising, admonishing, ending wars, resisting wicked princes, and freely spending blood—not money alone—for the flock of Christ? And wherefore all this money, anyway, for those who hold the places of the needy apostles?" If they would weigh these things, I repeat, they would not be so ambitious for the post, and would willingly give it up, or at least they would lead a toilsome and watchful life of the sort lived by those ancient apostles.

POPES

As to these Supreme Pontiffs who take the place of Christ, if they tried to emulate His life, I mean His poverty, labors, teaching, cross, and contempt for safety, if even they thought upon the title of Pope—that is, Father—or the addition "Most Holy," who on earth would be more afflicted? Who would purchase that seat at the price of every resource and effort? Or who defend it, when purchased, by the sword, by poison, or by anything else? Were wisdom to descend upon them, how it would inconvenience them! Wisdom, did I say? Nay, even a grain of salt would do it—a grain of that salt which is spoken of by Christ. It would lose them all that wealth and honor, all those possessions, tri-

umphal progresses, offices, dispensations, tributes, and indulgences; it would lose them so many horses, mules, and retainers; so many pleasures. (See how I have comprehended in a few words many marketsful, a great harvest, a wide ocean, of goods!) In place of these it would bring vigils, fasts, tears, prayers, sermons, studies, sighs, and a thousand troublesome tasks of the sort. Nor should we pass over the circumstance that all those copyists and notaries would be in want, as would all those advocates, promoters, secretaries, muleteers, grooms, bankers, and pimps—I was about to add something more tender, though rougher, I am afraid, on the ears. In short, that great host of men which burdens—I beg your pardon, I mean adorns—the Roman See would beg for their bread. This would be inhuman and downright abominable, and, what is more accursed, those very princes of the church and true lights of the world would themselves be reduced to a staff and a wallet.

As it is now, what labor turns up to be done they hand over to Peter and Paul, who have leisure for it. But the splendor and the pleasure they take care of personally. And so it comes about—by my doing, remember—that scarcely any kind of men live more softly or less oppressed with care; believing that they are amply acceptable to Christ if with a mystical and almost theatrical finery, with ceremonies, and with those titles of Beatitude and Reverence and Holiness, along with blessing and cursing, they perform the office of bishops. To work miracles is primitive and old-fashioned, hardly suited to our times; to instruct the people is irksome; to interpret the Holy Scriptures is pedantry; to pray is otiose; to shed tears is distressing and womanish; to live in poverty is sordid; to be beaten in war is dishonorable and less than worthy of one who will hardly admit kings, however great, to kiss his sacred foot; and finally, to die is unpleasant, to die on the cross a disgrace.

There remain only those weapons and sweet benedictions of which Paul speaks, and the popes are generous enough with these: interdictions, excommunications, re-excommunications, anathematizations, pictured damnations, and the terrific lightning-bolt of the bull, which by its mere flicker sinks the souls of men below the floor of hell. And these most holy fathers in Christ, and vicars of Christ, launch it against no one with more spirit than against those who, at the instigation of the devil, try to impair or to subtract from the patrimony of Peter. Although this saying of Peter's stands in the Gospel, "We have left all and followed Thee," yet they give the name of his patrimony to lands, towns, tribute, imposts, and moneys. On behalf of these things, inflamed by zeal for Christ, they fight with fire and sword, not without shedding of Christian blood; and then they believe they have defended the bride of Christ in apostolic fashion, having scattered what they are pleased to designate as "her enemies." As if the church had any enemies more pestilential than impious pontiffs who by their silence allow Christ to be forgotten, who enchain Him by mercenary rules, adulterate His teaching by forced interpretations, and crucify Him afresh by their scandalous life!

WAR IS SANCTIFIED

Now the Christian church was founded on blood, strengthened by blood, and augmented by blood; yet nowadays they carry on Christ's cause by the sword just as if He who defends His own by His own means had perished. And although war is so cruel a business that it befits beasts and not men, so frantic that poets feign it is sent with evil purpose by the Furies, so pestilential that it brings with it a general blight upon morals, so iniquitous that it is usually conducted by the worst bandits, so impious that it has no accord with Christ, yet our popes, neglecting all their other concerns, make it their only task. Here you will see feeble old men assuming the strength of youth, not shocked by the expense or tired out by the labor, not at all discouraged, if only they may upset laws, religion, peace, and all humane usages, and turn them heels over head. Learned sycophants will be found who will give to this manifest madness the names of zeal, piety, and fortitude, devising a way whereby it is possible for a man to whip out his sword, stick it into the guts of his brother, and nonetheless dwell in that supreme charity which, according to Christ's precept, a Christian owes to his neighbor. Here I am at a loss as to whether certain bishops of the Germans furnished the popes the model for all this or took it from them. These bishops personally acted as colonels, laying by their garb, forgetting about benedictions and other such formalities, as though they esteemed it cowardly and lacking in decorum for a bishop to return his soul to God from any place but a battlefield.

But I am foolish to pursue these points, which are so numberless that all of them could not be contained in the books of Chrysippus or Didymus. At least I wish you to keep this in mind, that since things like that are permitted to theological masters, it is but fair to allow the same indulgence also to me (who am obviously but a pinchbeck divine), if I shall not make every quotation and citation with absolute exactness. Now at last I get back to Paul. "Suffer fools gladly," he says, speaking of himself; and again, "Receive me as a fool"; also, "I do not speak according to God, but as if in foolishness." Again, he says in another place, "We are fools for Christ's sake." From so great a writer you hear such great commendations of folly! What he does, in fact, is publicly to teach and enjoin this folly as a thing specially necessary and good for the town: "Let him that seems to be wise among you become a fool, that he may be wise!" And in Luke, the two disciples with whom Jesus joined company on the highway

He called "fools." Nor do I know any reason why it should seem strange that Paul attributed a measure of folly even to God: "The foolishness of God," he said, "is wiser than men." To be sure, Origen in his interpretation objects that this foolishness can hardly be equivalent to the ordinary fancies of men; which last are indicated in that other passage: "The preaching of the Cross is to them that perish foolishness."

Yet why am I so needlessly careful in going about to support these matters by all these proofs and witnesses when in the mystical psalms Christ himself, speaking to the Father, says for all men to hear, "Thou knowest my foolishness"? Nor indeed is it without cause that fools are so vastly pleasing to God; the reason being, I suggest, that just as great princes look suspiciously on men who are too clever, and hate them—as Julius Caesar suspected and hated Brutus and Cassius while he did not fear drunken Antony at all, Nero was suspicious of Seneca, Dionysius of Plato—while on the other hand they take delight in duller and simpler souls.

FOOLS PLEASING TO GOD

. . . so Christ detests and condemns those wise men who rely on their own prudence. Paul witnesses to this very clearly when he says, "God has chosen the foolish things of the world," and when he says, "It has pleased God to save the world by foolishness," seeing that it could never be redeemed by wisdom. But God points this out clearly enough, when He cries through the mouth of the prophet, "I will destroy the wisdom of the wise, and I will reject the prudence of the prudent." And again, our Lord gave thanks that God had concealed the mystery of salvation from the wise, but had revealed it to babes, that is, to fools. For the Greek word for "babes" is νηΠι′οις, generally used as the opposite to σοφῶν, "the wise." It tends to the same effect when in the Gospels. He often attacks the scribes and

Pharisees and doctors of the law, whereas He faithfully defends the ignorant multitude. For what is "Woe unto you, scribes and Pharisees" except "Woe unto you that are wise?" But He seems to find most potent delight in little children, women, and fishermen. And even in the class of brute creatures, those which are farthest from a foxlike cunning were best pleasing to Christ. He preferred to ride upon a donkey, though had He chosen He could have mounted the back of a lion without danger. And the Holy Spirit descended in likeness of a dove, not of an eagle or a kite. Here and there in Holy Writ, furthermore, there is repeated mention of harts, fawns, and lambs. Add to this that Christ calls those who are destined to eternal life by the name "sheep"—and there is no other creature more foolish, as is witnessed by the proverbial phrase in Aristotle, "sheepish temperament," which he tells us was suggested by the stupidity of the animal and commonly used as a taunt against dullwitted and foolish men. And yet Christ avows himself as shepherd of this flock and even delights in the name of Lamb, as when John pointed Him out, "Behold the Lamb of God!" There is much use of this term also in the book of Revelation.

What do all these things cry out to us if not this, that mortal men, even the pious, are fools? And that Christ, in order to relieve the folly of mankind, though Himself "the wisdom of the Father," was willing in some manner to be made a fool when He took upon Himself the nature of a man and was found in fashion as a man? And likewise He was made "to be sin" that He might heal sinners. Nor did He wish to bring healing by any other means than by "the foolishness of the cross," and by weak and stupid apostles upon whom He carefully enjoined folly, dissuading them from wisdom, while He incited them by the examples of children, lilies, mustard-seed, and sparrows—witless things and deficient in sense, living their lives by the guidance of nature with no art or anxious care. Beyond this, He forbade them to be troubled about what they should say before magistrates and He charged that they should not inquire into times and seasons; in a word, they should not trust to their own wisdom but wholly depend upon Him. To the same effect we learn that God, architect of the world, charged upon pain of death that men should not eat of the tree of knowledge, exactly as if knowledge is the bane of happiness. Likewise Paul specifically disavows knowledge as that which puffs up and works harm. St. Bernard is following him, I suppose, when he interprets that mountain whereon Lucifer established his headquarters as "the Mount of Knowledge."

CHRISTIAN FOLLY

But I should not further pursue that which is infinite; let me speak compendiously. The Christian religion on the whole seems to have a kinship with some sort of folly, while it has no alliance whatever with wisdom. If you want proofs of this statement, observe first of all how children, old people, women, and fools find pleasure beyond other folk in holy and religious things, and to that end are ever nearest the altars, led no doubt solely by an impulse of nature. Then you will notice that the original founders of religion, admirably laying hold of pure simplicity, were the bitterest foes of literary learning. Lastly, no fools seem to act more foolishly than do the people whom zeal for Christian piety has got possession of; for they pour out their wealth, they overlook wrongs, allow themselves to be cheated, make no distinction between friends and enemies, shun pleasure, glut themselves with hunger, wakefulness, tears, toils, and reproaches; they disdain life and dearly prefer death; in short, they seem to have grown utterly numb to ordinary sensations, quite as if their souls lived elsewhere and not in their bodies. What is this, forsooth, but to be mad? Whereby we should find it less strange that

the apostles appeared to be drunk with new wine, and that Paul, in the eyes of his judge, Festus, looked as if he had gone mad.

Come, now that I have "put on the lion's skin," I shall show this also, that the happiness of Christians, which they pursue with so much travail, is nothing else but a kind of madness and folly. Let these words give no offense; instead, keep your mind on the point. To begin with, Christians come near to agreeing with Platonists in this, that the soul is sunk and shackled by corporeal bonds, being so clogged by the grossness of the body that but little can it contemplate and enjoy things as they truly are. Hence Plato defined philosophy as "a study of death," because it leads the mind away from visible and bodily things, and certainly death does the same. And thus as long as the soul uses the bodily organs aright, so long it is called sane, but when with its bonds broken it attempts to make good its liberty, planning, as it were, escape from its prison, then it is called mad. If perchance this condition arises from sickness or a defect of some organ, then by common consent it is unmistakable insanity. Yet we see men of this sort predict future events, we see them understand languages and discourse which they have not previously known, and in general manifest something partaking of the divine. No doubt this happens because as the soul is a little more free from the taint of the body, it begins to exert its own native powers. I conceive the same to be the cause that something very similar is wont to happen with those who are near death in their sufferings. As if inspired, they speak things far above a common strain. Yet if such a thing results from zeal for religion, perhaps it is not the same sort of madness but so near to it that the greater part of mankind will judge it to be mere insanity, especially in view of the fact that only a handful of unimportant people out of the whole society of mortals thus differ completely from the rest in their way of life.

And so it ordinarily fares with men as it fared in Plato's myth, I gather, between those who admired shadows, still bound in the cave, and that one who broke away and, returning to the doorway, proclaimed that he had seen realities and that they who believed nothing existed except shadows were greatly deceived. Just as this wise man pitied and deplored the madness of those who were gripped by such an error, they, on their side, derided him as if he were raving, and cast him out. In like fashion the great masses of people admire what things are most corporeal and deem that such come near to being the only things there are. The religious, on the contrary, pay less attention to anything the more nearly it concerns the body, and they are wholly rapt away in the contemplation of things unseen. For the majority assign the leading role to riches and the next to bodily comforts, while they leave the lowliest for the soul, which most of them, however, believe does not exist, because it is not seen by the eye. In quite different fashion the religious with one accord direct their first endeavors toward God himself, the purest of all existences; next to Him, toward that which yet comes as close as possible to Him, namely, the soul. They neglect the care of the body. They altogether disdain riches as mere nutshells, and turn their backs upon them. Or if they are forced to handle matters of the kind, they do so grudgingly and uneasily, having as if they did not have, possessing as if they did not possess.

THE PIOUS VS. THE WORLD

On particular points there are great degrees of difference between these two sorts of persons. In the first place, although all the senses have alliance with the body, certain of them are grosser, such as touch, hearing, sight, smell, taste, while certain ones are less closely tied up with the body, as the memory,

intellect, and will. To whichever one the soul applies itself, that one grows strong. Forasmuch as every energy of the devout soul strives toward objects which are at farthest remove from the grosser senses, these grown numb, as it were, and stupefy; whence it comes that we hear about saints who have chanced to drink oil in place of wine. Among the passions and impulses of the mind, again, some have more connection with the physical body, as lust, love of food and sleep, anger, pride, envy. With these the pious are irreconcilably at war, while the multitude, on the other hand, consider that without them life does not exist. Then there are some feelings of a middle sort, merely natural, so to speak, such as love of one's father, affection for one's children, relatives, and friends; to these feelings the multitude pays considerable respect, but the pious endeavor to pluck them, too, out of their minds, except so far as, rising to the highest spiritual plane, they love a parent not as parent—for what did he beget but the body, and even that is owed to God as Father—but rather as a good man, one in whom is manifest the impress of that Supreme Mind which they call the *summum bonum* and beyond which, they assert, nothing is to be loved or sought for.

By the same rule they also measure all others of life's duties, and in general they either scorn that which is visible or make much less of it than of things invisible. They say also that both body and spirit enter into the sacraments and into the very offices of piety; as in fasting, they do not account it of much worth if a person abstains from meats or from a meal, that which the vulgar esteem an absolute fast, unless at the same time he in some measure frees himself from passions, yielding less than he is wont to anger, less to pride; and then the spirit, weighed down less by the burden of the body, may climb upwards even to the partaking and enjoying of celestial bounties. In like manner, too, with the

Eucharist, although it is not to be slighted, they say, merely because it is administered with ceremonies, yet of itself it is either of little profit or indeed harmful except so far as that which is spiritual is added to it—in a word, that which is represented under the visible symbols. For the death of Christ is so represented, and this it behooves mortal men to translate into the taming, extinguishing, and, as it were, burying of their carnal affections; that they may arise to a newness of life and be made one with Him, and one also with each other. Thus a devout man does, and such is his contemplation. The crowd, on the other hand, believes that the sacrament is no more than coming to the altar, as close as may be, hearing the noise of words, and watching the whole pageant of ceremonial details. Nor in this alone, which I set forth merely as an example, but in all of his life the pious man sincerely forsakes whatever has alliance with the body and is drawn to eternal, invisible, and spiritual objects.

THE SUMMUM BONUM

Wherefore, since there is so great contrariety between the pious and the vulgar, it comes about that each appears to the other to be mad—though in my opinion, to be sure, the word is more correctly applied to the pious than to the others. This will become clearer if I briefly demonstrate, as I promised to do, that their *summum bonum* itself is no other than a kind of insanity. First, let us suppose that Plato was dreaming of something very like it when he wrote that "the madness of lovers is the happiest state of all." Now he who loves intensely no longer lives in himself but in whatever he loves, and the more he can depart from himself and enter into the other, the happier he is. And when a mind yearns toward travelling out of the body, and does not rightly use its own bodily organs, you doubtless, and with accuracy, call the state of it madness. Otherwise, what do they mean by

those common phrases, "he is not at home," and "to come to yourself," and "he is himself again"? Furthermore, so far as the love is more perfect the madness is greater and more delightful. Of what sort, then, is that future life with those who dwell on high, toward which pious hearts aspire with such fervor? First the spirit, as conqueror and the more vital, will overmaster and absorb the body, and this it will do the more easily in that now it is in its own realm, so to speak, and also because already, during life, it has cleansed and lightened the body in preparation for this change. Then the spirit itself will be absorbed in marvelous wise by that supreme spirit, more potent than its infinity of parts. Thus the whole man will be outside of himself, nor will he be happy for any other reason than that, so placed outside of himself, he shall have some ineffable portion in that *summum bonum* which draws all things unto itself. And although this happiness arrives at its perfection only when souls, joined to their former bodies, shall be clothed with immortality, yet because the earthly life of pious folk is nothing but a contemplation and a kind of shadowing of that other, they sometimes feel a foretaste and a glow of the reward to come. Although this is as but the least little drop in comparison with that flowing fountain of eternal happiness, yet it far surpasses any bodily pleasure, yes, even if all mortal delights were brought together into one. By so much does the spiritual excel over the corporeal, and the invisible over the visible. This surely is what the prophet has promised: "Eye hath not seen, nor ear heard, neither have entered into the heart of man the things which God hath prepared for them that love Him." And this truly is the portion of Folly, that "good part" which "shall not be taken away" by the transformation of life, but will be perfected.

Hence those who are permitted to have a foretaste of this—and it comes to but few—suffer something very like to madness. They say things that are not quite coherent, and this not in the ordinary way of men, but they make a sound without meaning, and suddenly they change the whole aspect of their faces; now cheerful, now downcast, they will weep, then laugh, and then sigh; in brief, they are truly outside themselves. When presently they return to themselves they say that they do not know where they have been, whether in the body or out of it, waking or sleeping; they do not remember what they have heard, seen, spoken, or done; and yet through a cloud, or as in a dream, they know one thing, that they were at their happiest while they were thus out of their wits. So they are sorry to come to themselves again and would prefer, of all good things, nothing but to be mad always with this madness. And this is a tiny little taste of that future happiness.

PERORATION

But indeed I have long since forgotten myself and run out of bounds. If anything I have said shall seem too saucy or too glib, stop and think: 'tis Folly, and a woman, that has spoken. But of course you will also remember that Greek proverb, "Even a foolish man will often speak a word in season," unless, perhaps, you assume that this does not extend to women. I see that you are expecting a peroration, but you are just too foolish if you suppose that after I have poured out a hodgepodge of words like this I can recall anything that I have said. There is an old saying, "I hate a pot-companion with a memory." Here is a new one: "I hate a hearer that remembers anything."

And so farewell. . . . Applaud . . . live . . . drink . . . O most distinguished initiates of Folly!

9

THE REFORMATION AND COUNTER-REFORMATION

MARTIN LUTHER AND THE GERMAN REFORMATION

The conciliar movement and the nationalistic reforms of Wyclif and Hus in the fourteenth and fifteenth centuries did not destroy the religious unity of Western Christendom. And, early in the sixteenth century, many dedicated humanistic churchmen hoped that scholars like Erasmus would lead a peaceful reformation of church practice along humanist lines. Instead, the Reformation was to come in a revolutionary form which rejected the very pillars of the medieval church: the office of the papacy, the efficacy and extent of the sacramental system, and the superiority of monasticism as a higher form of the Christian way of life.

The place where the break began was the little German town of Wittenberg in Saxony, part of the Holy Roman Empire. Lack of political unity in the empire had prevented resistance to papal taxation and jurisdiction there, as was the case in the stronger national monarchies of England, France and Spain. Despite criticism of papal abuses by humanists, a superstitious German peasantry was easy prey to abuses in connection with the cult of relics and the selling of indulgences. The individual who would set the revolution in motion by challenging these abuses was Martin Luther, an Augustinian monk and theologian from the new University of Wittenberg, which had been founded in 1502 by Frederick the Wise, elector of Saxony.

To understand the beginnings of the Reformation, it is necessary to appreciate Luther's personal religious crisis in connection with traditional medieval faith and practice. Luther's theology, like Augustine's, is inseparable from his own faith experience. Like Erasmus, Luther was educated by the Brethren of the Common Life in the individualistic piety of the *devotio moderna*. While a student of law at the University of Erfurt, Luther studied the voluntarist and nominalist philosophy of late scholasticism with its emphasis on the priority of the will in God and the inability of reason to probe the mysteries of the faith. In 1505 Luther suddenly decided, against the will of his father who wanted a law career for his son, to enter an Augustinian monastery. The occasion was a terrifying experience in a summer thunderstorm during which he prayed to St.

Ann for assistance and vowed to become a monk if he survived. Unlike Erasmus who never took to the rigors of monastic life, Luther gave himself scrupulously to the disciplines of the monastery. By 1512 he had been ordained a priest, earned a doctorate in theology, and become a lecturer in scripture at the University of Wittenberg.

However, by his own account, Luther was a tortured soul, who never found consolation from pursuing the "higher way" of monasticism. On the contrary, he feared God as a righteous judge and vainly attempted to appease him by living "as a monk without reproach." After years of spiritual turmoil and study of the scriptures, Luther found the answer to his anxiety in the writings of Paul, and particularly in Paul's concept of justification through faith in God's mercy which is manifest in Christ's death on the cross for the forgiveness of sin. Paul had originally developed this doctrine as an argument for the abrogation of the Mosaic Torah as a way of salvation so that Jews and Gentiles could be included in a single messianic community. For Paul, the communal problem of uniting Jews and Gentiles and the historical issue of the role of the Mosaic law were primary. Luther, however, understood Paul's theology as applying to himself as an individual and to his own tortured conscience in respect to the commandments of the Law and the demands of the gospel. In Paul, Luther discovered what he terms "the passive righteousness with which the merciful God justifies us by faith," even though we are sinners.

The following excerpt from *The Preface to the Complete Edition of Luther's Latin Writings* gives Luther's recollection in 1545 of the way Paul's theology answered his religious dilemma.

I had indeed been captivated with an extraordinary ardor for understanding Paul in the Epistle to the Romans. But up till then it was not the cold blood about the heart, but a single word in Chapter 1, "In it the righteousness of God is revealed," that had stood in my way. For I hated that word "righteousness of God," which, I had been taught to understand philosophically regarding the formal or active righteousness, as they called it, with which God is righteous and punishes the unrighteous sinner. Though I lived as a monk without reproach, I felt that I was a sinner before God with an extremely disturbed conscience. I could not believe that he was placated by my satisfaction. I did not love, yes, I hated the righteous God who punishes sinners, and secretly, if not blasphemously, certainly murmuring greatly, I was angry with God, and said, "As if, indeed, it is not enough, that miserable sinners, eternally lost through original sin, we are crushed by every kind of calamity by the law of the decalogue, without having God add pain to pain by the gospel and also by the gospel threatening us with his righteousness and wrath!" Thus I raged with a fierce and troubled conscience. Nevertheless, I beat importunately upon Paul at that place, most ardently desiring to know what St. Paul wanted. At last, by the mercy of God, meditating day and night, I gave heed to the context of the words, namely, "In it the righteousness of God is revealed, as it is written, 'He who through faith is righteous lives by a gift of God, namely by faith.'" And this is the meaning: the righteousness of God is revealed by the gospel, namely, the passive righteousness with which the merciful God justifies us by faith, as it is written, "He who through faith is righteous shall live." Here I felt that I was altogether born again and had entered paradise itself through open gates. *(Preface to the Complete Edition of Luther's Latin Writings* in *Luther's Works,* Vol 34, ed. by Lewis W. Spitz [Philadelphia: Muhlenberg Press, 1960] 336–337.

In his commentary on Paul's Letter to the Romans, from this same period of Luther's life (1515–1516), he developed his understanding of the believing Christian as *simul justus et peccator,* "simultaneously just and sinner." We are in reality sinners, but also just by virtue of our faith and hope in God's promise of forgiveness given in the death of Christ for our sins.

Luther's understanding of righteousness as a gift given by God to the individual through faith alone, as opposed to being a work achieved by human merit, conflicted with the crass way in which indulgences were being preached in Germany in the early sixteenth century. The practice of granting indulgences had begun in the eleventh century in connection with the Crusades. An indulgence was the remission by the church of the temporal penalty due to forgiven sin, through the merits of Christ and the saints. The theology of indulgences assumes that sin has a penalty which must be paid either in this life or in purgatory, even after the sin has been forgiven through the sacrament of penance and absolution. It also assumes the concept of the Communion of Saints and that Christ and the saints in heaven may aid by their merits those in purgatory and on earth. Originally plenary, or full, indulgences were granted to those who went on crusade, but by Luther's time, the whole system had been reduced to a scandalous system for raising money for the church. The immediate occasion for Luther's protest was the preaching of indulgences by the famous Dominican Johann Tetzel.

> Listen now, God and St. Peter call you. Consider the salvation of your souls and those of your loved ones departed . . . Consider all who are contrite and have confessed and made contribution will receive complete remission of all their sins. Listen to the voices of your dear dead relatives and friends, beseeching you and saying, "Pity us, pity us. We are in dire torment from which you can redeem us for a pittance." Do you not wish to? Open your ears. Hear the father saying to his son, the mother to her daughter, "We bore you, nourished you, brought you up, left you our fortunes, and you are so cruel and hard that now you are not willing for so little to set us free. Will you let us lie here in flames? Will you delay our promised glory?"
> Remember that you are able to release them, for
> As soon as the coin in the coffer rings,
> the soul from purgatory springs.
> Will you not then for a quarter of a florin receive these letters of indulgence through which you are able to lead a divine and immortal soul in the fatherland of paradise? (Translated in R. Bainton's *Here I Stand,* Abingdon Press, 1950, 78)

Luther did not know that behind this preaching was a scandalous arrangement between Archbishop Albrecht of Mainz, the Fugger banking house and Pope Leo X. They had arranged to split the profits from the sale of indulgences in the territories of the archbishop. Albrecht needed to pay off the debts incurred in becoming bishop in three dioceses while still not of canonical age, and Leo X was financing the rebuilding of St. Peter's in Rome.

When Luther heard about Tetzel's preaching in the neighboring territories of the archbishop, he urged the people of Wittenberg to ignore it and published, on October 31, 1517, his famous Ninety-Five Theses for "Disputation on the Power and Efficacy of Indulgences." (The translation used below is by Bertram Lee Woolf, *The Reformation Writings of Martin Luther*, vol 1, *The Basis of the Protestant Reformation* [London: Lutterworth Press, 1953] 32–42).

At this point, Luther was still a loyal son of the Roman Catholic Church; he simply objected to the way in which the indulgences were being preached in German territories. But, in contrast to Erasmus, who only criticized the superstition involved in indulgences, Luther also found them unsound on dogmatic grounds. The idea of earning an indulgence was at odds with the scriptures which proclaimed a gospel of salvation through faith in Christ's redeeming death. As the following theses indicate, Luther emphatically rejected the idea that salvation is for sale and asserted that it is a gift which depends upon the will of God and the faith of the believer.

> # 27. There is not divine authority for preaching that the soul flies out of purgatory immediately the money clinks in the bottom of the chest.
> # 28. It is certainly possible that when the money clinks in the bottom of the chest avarice and greed increase; but when the church offers intercession, all depends on the will of God.
> # 62. The true treasure of the Church is the Holy Gospel of the glory and grace of God.

Luther also rejected the implication that the pope has control over purgatory. At this stage of his development Luther believed that the pope, like all other Christians, could only offer intercessory prayer in behalf of the souls in purgatory.

> # 26. The pope does excellently when he grants remission to the souls in purgatory on account of intercessions made on their behalf, and not by the power of the keys (which he cannot exercise for them).

In thesis # 82 he even facetiously asked,

> Why does not the pope liberate everyone from purgatory for the sake of love (a most holy thing) and because of the supreme necessity of their souls? This would be morally the best of all reasons. Meanwhile he redeems innumerable souls for money, a most perishable thing, with which to build St. Peter's church, a very minor purpose.

According to Luther, indulgences encouraged the wrong attitude in Christians who should live in fear for their eternal salvation so that they despair of their own merits, repent of their sins, and turn to God's mercy in faith. Indulgences only serve to give a false sense of security about one's salvation.

30. No one is sure of the reality of his own contrition, much less of receiving plenary forgiveness.

32. All those who believe themselves certain of their own salvation by means of letters of indulgence, will be eternally damned, together with their teachers.

36. Any Christian whatsoever, who is truly repentant, enjoys plenary remission from penalty and guilt, and this is given him without letters of indulgence.

40. A truly contrite sinner seeks out, and loves to pay, the penalties of his sins; whereas the very multitude of indulgences dulls men's consciences, and tends to make them hate the penalties.

For Luther, true Christian piety consists in the acts of charity mandated in the gospels, and not in the purchasing of indulgences.

43. Christians should be taught that one who gives to the poor, or lends to the needy, does a better action than if he purchases indulgences.

Finally, as a patriotic German, Luther also resented the fact that the hard-earned money of German peasants was being used by the Roman popes for the building of St. Peter's.

50. Christians should be taught that, if the pope knew the exaction of the indulgence-preachers, he would rather the church of St. Peter were reduced to ashes than be built with the skin, flesh, and bones of his sheep.

51. Christians should be taught that the pope would be willing, as he ought if necessity should arise, to sell the Church of St. Peter, and give, too, his own money to many of those from whom the pardon-merchants conjure money.

80. Again: Since the pope's income today is larger than that of the wealthiest of wealthy men, why does he not build this one church of St. Peter with his own money, rather than with the money of indigent believers?

Luther did not anticipate the reaction to the Ninety-Five Theses. Although originally published in Latin, they were soon translated into German and widely circulated. They made Luther famous overnight; humanists like Erasmus received them favorably, but they also led to church proceedings against him. In the period from 1518 through 1519, Luther was involved in a series of hearings and debates with representatives of his own Augustinian Order and with theologians from the Dominican Order. In the course of these proceedings Luther's own combative personality and the revolutionary implications of his evangelical theology led him further and further from the teachings of Rome.

Throughout this period Luther, with the help of his prince, Frederick, refused to go to Rome and insisted on being tried on German soil. By July, 1519, in the famous Leipzig debate with the Dominican Johann Eck, Luther challenged the infallibility of the pope and the inerrancy of church councils and appealed to the sovereign authority of scripture alone within the church.

The year 1520 was a major turning point in the development of the Reformation. In June a papal commission with the approval of Pope Leo X, a worldly Renaissance pope from the Medici family, issued the papal bull *Exsurge Domine* which condemned forty-one articles drawn from Luther's teachings "as either heretical, scandalous, false, offensive to pious ears or seductive of simple minds, and against Catholic truth." The articles focused on Luther's disparagement of the human capacity for salvation even after baptism, the importance of belief in the sacrament of penance, his questioning of the pope's power to bind and loose penalties and sins, his denial of the power of pope and councils to declare doctrine, and the rejection of the primacy of the pope and the Roman church. Because of these errors, Luther's works were to be burned publicly, and he was given sixty days to recant from the time the bull reached him. The bull did not reach Luther until October 10, 1520, and on December 10, 1520, Luther responded by burning the bull, textbooks of scholastic theology, and copies of the church's canon law. No action could more dramatically symbolize his break with the papacy and the end of medieval Christendom.

In the meantime, Luther himself had published three pamphlets which signaled the new direction his reformation was to take: *The Freedom of the Christian,* the *Address to the Christian Nobility of the German Nation,* and *The Babylonian Captivity of the Church*. The first was written in a conciliatory tone to Pope Leo X. It expounds Luther's key doctrine of justification by "faith alone," as opposed to justification by "works." In the course of his argument Luther uses what is for him an important concept for the treating of scripture. All scripture is either commandment or promise, law or gospel. The commandments function to make us aware of our inability to do good and despair of our capacity to save ourselves. The promises offer us the grace of God through our faith in Christ.

> Should you ask how it happens that faith alone justifies and offers us such a treasure of great benefits without works in view of the fact that so many works, ceremonies, and laws are prescribed in the Scriptures, I answer: first of all, remember what has been said, namely that faith alone, without works, justifies, frees, and saves. . . . The entire Scripture of God is divided into two parts: commandments and promises. Although the commandments teach things that are good, the things taught are not done as soon as they are taught, for the commandments show us what we ought to do but do not give us the power to do it. They are intended to teach man to know himself, that through them he may recognize his inability to do good and may despair of his own ability. That is why they are called the Old Testament and constitute the Old Testament. For example, the commandment, "You shall not covet," is a command which proves us all to be sinners, for no one can avoid coveting no matter how much he may struggle against it. Therefore, in order not to covet and to fulfill the commandment, a man is compelled to despair of himself, to seek the help which he does not find in himself elsewhere and from someone else as stated in Hosea: "Destruction is your own, O Israel: your help is only in me." As we fare with respect to one commandment, so we fare with all, for it is equally impossible for us to keep any of them.
>
> Now when a man has learned through the commandments to recognize his helplessness . . . the second part of Scripture comes to our aid, namely, the promises of God which declare

the glory of God, saying, "If you wish to fulfill the law and not covet, as the law demands, come, believe in Christ in whom grace, righteousness, peace, liberty, and all things are promised you." (Taken from *Luther's Works,* vol 31, *Career of the Reformer: I,* ed. by Harold J. Grimm, Philadelphia: Muhlenberg Press, 1957) 333–77.

Our selection is Luther's *Address to the Christian Nobility of the German Nation* in which he urges the German princes to take the lead in reforming the church in Germany. Following earlier thinkers like Marsilius of Padua and William of Ockham, Luther urges the princes to force reforms on the Roman church and especially to curb its political and economic power in the German territories. In the course of this treatise, Luther, like Joshua before the walls of Jericho in the Old Testament, attacks the "three walls" the "Romanists" have used to insulate themselves from reform. In each case he opposes the "Romanist" position to what he finds in scripture and the practice of the early church. Luther's persistent appeal to scripture and the early sources of Christianity are part of his humanist training. But the fervent spirit with which he advocates reform reflects both his German patriotism and his own faith experience.

The first wall was the claim that the temporal power has no jurisdiction over them and that, indeed, the spiritual power is above the temporal. In attacking this "first wall," Luther argues that all Christians belong to the spiritual estate on the basis of the New Testament teachings about the body of Christ and "the priesthood of all believers."

> For all Christians whatsoever really and truly belong to the religious class, and there is no difference among them except in so far as they do different work. That is St. Paul's meaning in 1 Corinthians 12, when he says: "We are all one body, yet each member hath his own work for serving others." This applies to us all, because we have one baptism, one gospel, one faith, and are all equally Christian. For baptism, gospel, and faith alone make men religious, and create a Christian people. . . . The fact is that our baptism consecrates us all without exception, and makes us all priests. As St. Peter says, 1 Peter 2, "You are a royal priesthood and a realm of priests," and Revelation, "Thou made us priests by Thy blood."

The second wall was that, when the Scriptures were used to admonish the popes, the Romanists claimed that no one except the pope was competent to expound scripture. Here again, Luther appeals to the scriptures themselves in which both Paul and John speak of individual Christians being inspired by God.

> But lest we fight them with mere words, let us adduce Scripture. St. Paul says, "If something superior be revealed to any one sitting there and listening to another speaking God's word, the first speaker must be silent and give place" (1 Cor 14). What would be the virtue of this commandment if only the speaker, or the person in the highest position, were to be believed? Christ Himself says, "that all Christians shall be taught by God" (Jn 6). Then if the pope and his adherents were bad men, and not true Christians, i.e., not taught by God to have a true understanding; and if, on the other hand, a humble person should have the true understanding, why ever should we not follow him? Has not the pope made many errors? Who

could enlighten Christian people if the pope erred, unless someone else, who had the support of Scripture, were more to be believed than he?

The third wall was that when threatened with a council, the Romanists claim that no one but the pope can summon a council. In challenging the third wall, Luther appeals to both scripture and the practice of the early church.

Romanists have no Scriptural basis for their contention that the pope alone has the right to summon or sanction a council. . . . Accordingly, we read in Acts 15 that it was not St. Peter, but all the apostles and elders, who called the Apostolic Council. . . . Further, the bishop of Rome neither called nor sanctioned the council of Nicea, the most celebrated of all, but the emperor, Constantine. After him, many other emperors did the same, and these councils were the most Christian of all.

In October, 1520, the same month in which he received the papal bull of excommunication, Luther published *The Babylonian Captivity of the Church* in which he attacks the traditional sacramental system. When Erasmus read this tract, he concluded, "The breach is irreparable." For Luther, a sacrament must be explicitly instituted by Christ in scripture and must be exclusively Christian, that is, it cannot be a custom like marriage which is found in almost all cultures. On the basis of these criteria, he reduces the number of sacraments from the traditional seven to three: baptism, penance, and the Lord's Supper.

The first thing for me to do is to deny that there are seven sacraments, and, for the present, to propound three: baptism, penance, and the Lord's Supper. (Translated by Bertram Lee Woolf, *The Reformation Writings of Martin Luther,* Vol I, *The Basis of the Protestant Reformation,* London: Lutterworth Press, 1953) 208–329. All subsequent quotes are from this translation.

For Luther the sacraments do not operate in and of themselves. Without faith there is indeed something there, but the recipient takes to his hurt rather than to his healing. In connection with the Lord's Supper, which for Luther is the most important sacrament, he, like John Hus, insisted that the laity should be given the cup on the basis of the New Testament accounts of the Lord's last supper.

Thus there remain two records which deal, and that very clearly, with this subject, viz.: the gospel passages on the Lord's Supper, and St. Paul in 1 Corinthians 11. Let us consider them. For, as Matthew, Mark, and Luke all agree, Christ gave all his disciples both kinds. And that Paul gave both kinds is so certain that no one has had the effrontery to say anything to the contrary.

Luther believed in the real physical presence of Christ in the bread and wine, but he rejected the term *transubstantiation* which had been used since the Fourth Lateran

Council (1215) to indicate the belief that at the words of consecration the bread and wine were changed substantially into the body and blood of Christ and only the accidents of bread and wine remained. Luther asked "Why could not Christ maintain His body within the substance of the bread as truly as within its accidents?" Using the image of a red-hot iron in which every part contains both fire and iron, he asked, "Why cannot the glorified body of Christ be similarly found in every part of the substance of the bread?" For Luther, the term *transubstantiation* smacked too much of Aristotelian philosophy and removed the mystery of faith in connection with Christ's presence in the bread and wine.

> Does it not seem that Christ used plain words in anticipation of these curious ideas? He did not say of the wine, "This substance is my blood," but "This is my blood." It is still clearer when He introduced the word "cup" and said, "This is the cup of the New Testament in my blood." Does He not seem to have wished us to continue in simple faith, and believe only that His blood was in the cup? When I fail to understand how bread can be the body of Christ, I for one, will take my understanding prisoner and bring it into obedience to Christ; and, holding fast with a simple mind to His words, I will firmly believe, not only that the body of Christ is in the bread, but that the bread is the body of Christ. My warrant is in the words which say, "He took bread and gave thanks and brake it, and said, 'Take and eat, this' (i.e., this bread which He had taken and broken) 'is my body.'" Paul says: "The bread which we break, is it not participation in the body of Christ?" . . . What if the philosophers do not grasp it? The Holy Spirit is greater than Aristotle. How can the Romanists maintain that their fine doctrine of transubstantiation is comprised in any system of philosophy at all, when they themselves confess that here all philosophy falls short?

Luther's understanding of the eucharist is consistent with the rest of his theology. First of all, he does not like the Catholic term "mass," but prefers the more Biblical term "the Lord's Supper," which he understands as "a promise made by God for the remission of our sins; a promise which was confirmed by the death of the Son of God." This promise seals the New Testament which brings forgiveness of sin for those who receive the promise in faith.

> Therefore the mass, in essence, is solely and simply the words of Christ . . . "Take and eat," etc.; as if He had said, "Lo! thou sinful and lost soul, out of pure and free love with which I love thee, and in accordance with the will of the Father of mercies, I promise thee with these words, and apart from any deserts or undertakings of thine, to forgive all thy sins, and give thee eternal life. In order that thou mayest be most assured that this promise is irrevocable, I will give my body and shed my blood to confirm it by my very death, and make both body and blood a sign and memorial of this promise. As often as thou partakest of them, remember me; praise and laud my love and bounty, and be thankful."
>
> From all of which you will see that nothing else than faith is needed for a worthy observance of the mass, and the mass is truly founded on this promise.

Because the Lord's Supper is a reception of a divine promise offered by God, Luther rejects the traditional Roman concept of the mass as a sacrifice in which humans offer Christ to the Father.

> But there is another misconception to be done away with which is much more serious and more specious, viz., the common belief that the mass is a sacrifice offered to God. This belief seems to be expressed in the words of the canon which speak of "these gifts, these offerings, these holy sacrifices;" and later, "this oblation." Moreover, the request is very definite that the sacrifice will be accepted as was Abel's sacrifice, etc. Then too Christ is said to be the victim on the altar. . . .
>
> We must resolutely oppose them all with the words and example of Christ, in spite of the fact that they are so strongly entrenched. For if we do not hold firmly that the mass is the promise, or testament, of Christ, as His words plainly show, we shall lose the whole gospel, and all its comfort.

For this reason, when Luther revised the liturgy in Wittenberg, he removed all references to the mass as a sacrifice. The priest does not offer up God upon the altar. Calvary is not reenacted. In the Lord's Supper, God gives and we receive and are thankful. The Lord's Supper is a thanksgiving or eucharist.

In April, 1521, Luther was summoned to the Imperial Diet at Worms which was presided over by the newly crowned emperor, young Charles V, a Hapsburg who as Charles I, was also the king of Spain. When he was asked to repudiate his books and the errors they contain, Luther gave the following answer:

> Unless I am convinced by the testimony of the Scriptures or by clear reason (for I do not trust either in the Pope or in councils alone, since it is well known that they have often erred and contradicted themselves), I am bound by the Scriptures I have quoted and my conscience is captive to the Word of God. I cannot and I will not recant anything, since it is neither safe nor right to go against conscience. . . . May God help me. Amen. (*Luther's Works,* Philadelphia: Muhlenberg Press, 1958) vol 32, 112–13.

Luther was placed under imperial ban and became an "outlaw" to secular and religious authorities. For the next year, from April, 1521 to March 1522, he lived in seclusion at Wartburg Castle in the protective custody of his prince, Frederick. Although he was frequently tormented by fits of depression, he completed his translation of the New Testament into German. The translation of the Old Testament would be completed in 1534.

Luther returned to Wittenberg in 1522 to restore order to a community divided between the more humanistic reforms of Philip Melancthon and the radical teachings of self-styled prophets from the neighboring town of Zwickau. Luther worked with secular authorities in implementing his reform measures, in a manner consistent with his views in the *Address to the Christian Nobility of the German Nation.* He abolished various Catholic practices: private masses, confession, and fasts. By 1524 he finally discarded the monk's habit, and in 1525 he married a former nun, Katherina Bora, with whom he had a large family. The Luthers' household was by all accounts a lively and love-filled home. To facilitate the spread and order of the Reformation in Germany, Luther composed two catechisms, powerful hymns, sermons for the church year and a new order of worship.

One of the saddest incidents in these years was Luther's role in the revolt of the German peasants. Initially, Luther appeared to be an ally to the peasants in promoting Christian freedom and criticizing greedy landowners, and when the Peasants' Revolt broke out in 1524, he at first attempted to mediate between the peasants and the landowners. However, when the peasants turned to violence, Luther proved to be a political conservative on the side of the nobles. He condemned the peasants and urged the princes to put down the revolt. For Luther, Christian freedom meant an inner freedom from guilt over sin given by the grace of God, and not the political freedom to restructure society.

During these years Luther also parted ways with Erasmus who had originally supported his attack on the preaching of indulgences. As a humanist peacemaker, Erasmus did not want to divide Christendom and feared the chaos and war which could result. He consistently attempted to mediate between Luther and the papacy, but was eventually prevailed upon to write against the reformer.

Erasmus chose to challenge Luther's predestinationism and the related question of free will in the process of salvation. As a humanist, Erasmus had a more optimistic view of the human person, even when wounded by sin, and therefore he insisted that although the initiative for salvation comes from God's free, unmerited grace, the human person responds to that grace freely.

> The mercy of God offers everyone favorable opportunities for repentance. One needs only to attach one's will to God's help, which merely invites to, but does not compel to betterment. . . . No one perishes except through his own fault. (*On Free Will*)

Luther responded with the treatise entitled *The Enslaved Will* in which he first praises Erasmus for having the wisdom to focus on the crucial issue of free will and then proceeds to attack his position. For Luther, we have freedom of choice in earthly matters, but not in the matter of salvation. When it comes to salvation our will is, according to Luther, "a beast of burden," to be ridden either by Satan or God. It is "necessary and wholesome for Christians to know" God's predestining will. This "thunderbolt" throws our free will flat "and utterly dashes it to pieces." In fact, Luther insists that were God to offer him free will, he would reject it because then he would be forced to labor for his salvation with no guarantee of success, with no certainty of salvation. This had been his own experience and is, Luther insists, "the experience of all who seek righteousness by works." Luther is supremely grateful that God's predestining will "has put my salvation out of the control of my own will and put it under the control of His and has promised to save me, not according to my effort or running, but . . . according to His own grace and mercy." Luther says that the doctrine of justification by faith gives him the assurance that he pleases God, "not by the merit of my works, but by reason of His (God's) merciful favor promised to me." Therefore, he insists that if he works "too little or badly," God does not impute it, but, "like a father, pardons me and makes me better."

The spread of the Reformation was facilitated because Emperor Charles V was distracted from affairs in the Holy Roman Empire by wars with the French Valois and the Turks. The Diet of Speyer in 1526 established the temporary right of princes to organize churches within their realms. At the Marburg Colloquy in 1529, Philip of Hesse attempted to forge a military alliance between the German and Swiss reformers, led by Ulrich Zwingli, to form a united front against the Catholic emperor. However, the theologians insisted upon agreement in religion before an alliance could be signed. Although Luther and Zwingli found that they were in agreement on many matters, they could not agree on the crucial issue of the nature of Christ's presence in the eucharist. Luther, although rejecting the term transubstantiation, insisted upon the real physical presence; Zwingli believed only in a spiritual presence of Christ in the bread and the wine.

When the Imperial Diet met again at Speyer in 1529, it was controlled by the Catholic majority. They attempted to demand the enforcement of the Edict of Worms (1521) in which Luther had been declared an outlaw to be handed over to civil authorities for punishment, and they also recommended that the Roman mass be allowed in all territories of the empire, and that Lutheranism not be tolerated in Catholic territories. Six princes and fourteen Lutheran cities made a formal "protest" against this arrangement, and from this time onward the reformers became known as Protestants. Despite the protest, the Catholic princes signed the agreement and added a promise not to attack one another "because of faith."

By 1530 Charles V himself was in a position to hold a meeting of the Imperial Diet at Augsburg in an attempt to restore the Lutheran princes to the Catholic faith. Luther, still under imperial ban, was not allowed to attend, but he approved the comparatively conciliatory Augsburg Confession which had been prepared by Philip Melancthon from previous confessional statements drawn up by Luther himself. It was signed by seven imperial princes and representatives of two free imperial cities. Our second selection is from this document which subsequently became the Lutheran confession of faith. It is divided into two parts. The first summarizes key Lutheran doctrines in twenty-one articles. The second lists in several articles the abuses of the Roman church which required correction: communion under one species, clerical celibacy, private masses, compulsory confession, monastic vows, and authority of bishops. Our selection summarizes the main points of the first half.

Melancthon worded the Augsburg Confession in the most conciliatory way possible. It includes traditional statements on the Trinity and the two natures in Christ which are drawn from the early dogmatic councils of the church. In more problematic areas, Melancthon is careful to avoid phrases and terms which would automatically be rejected by the Roman Catholic theologians. For example, although he frequently supports the Lutheran positions by reference to scripture and the practices of the early church, he omits any reference to Luther's phrase *sola scriptura* as the basis for authority in the church. In the section on Orders, the priesthood of all believers is not mentioned, and in the treatment of the Lord's Supper, belief in the real presence is affirmed without mentioning the problematic term transubstantiation.

In the statement of the key Lutheran position on justification by faith, as opposed to works, Melancthon repeatedly stresses that this doctrine is meant "to relieve terrified consciences" and is a rejection of the Pelagian heresy which argues that "we can love God above all things by the strength of our nature alone, without the Holy Spirit; and that we can perform the commands of God in respect of the *substance* of our actions." Although human will has some liberty "in the accomplishment of civil righteousness," it has "no power of accomplishing the righteousness of God" which comes "into being in our hearts when the Holy Spirit is conceived through the Word." Melancthon insists, moreover, that Lutherans do not reject the necessity of "good works." What is rejected is the idea that "good works" can "reconcile us to God or merit remission of sins and grace and justification." These gifts are the results of Christ's redeeming action which is received in faith. Good works flow from the Holy Spirit which is received through faith. As Ambrose taught: "Faith is the mother of good will and righteous action." Melancthon insists that the Lutheran position simply "shows how we can do good works."

After the public reading of the Augsburg Confession, discussion reduced the disagreement to five points: communion under both kinds for the laity, permission for priests to marry, abolition of monastic vows, the return of confiscated church property to its owners, and the sacrificial character of the mass. The emperor, hoping for the political support of the Lutheran princes, requested that the Catholics yield on all these points, but the pope's delegate refused. The disciplinary matters of communion under both species and a married clergy could be granted, but the other positions were nonnegotiable. The meeting ended with the emperor's demand that the Lutheran princes accept the confutation or prepare for war. The princes refused, but Charles V was not able to make good on his threat because of a renewed Turkish threat, and in the meantime the Lutherans formed the military alliance called the Schmalkaldic League which took the Augsburg Confession as its statement of faith.

The emperor's hope for reunion eventually came to rest on a twofold solution: a council to settle the religious differences and victory over the Protestant princes on the battlefield. Although the long-awaited council was finally called in 1545 at Trent in the territories of the empire, the Protestants were invited, but not given a deliberative vote. Although Charles was able to win a victory over the Schmalkaldic League in 1547, he was powerless to restore religious unity. Finally, in September, 1555, he reluctantly approved the Peace of Augsburg which followed the principle of *cuius regio, eius religio,* the prince of the territory determines the religion of that territory. The Peace of Augsburg recognized only two religions: the old Roman Catholic faith and those professing the Augsburg Confession. Nothing was said about Zwinglianism, Calvinism, or the Anabaptists. The emperor had failed in his lifelong commitment to maintain the Catholic unity of the empire, and, no doubt exhausted by war and political affairs, he abdicated in favor of Ferdinand I of Bavaria, a relative, and retired to spend his last days in a monastery in Spain.

The translation of the *Address to the Christian Nobility of the German Nation Respecting the Reformation of the Christian Estate,* is from *Luther's Primary Works,* ed. Henry Wace and C.A. Buchheim (London: Hodder and Stoughton, 1896) 161–180. The translation of *The Confessions of Augsburg, 1530 Corpus Reformatorum* is from B.J. Kidd, *Documents illustrative of the Continental Reformation* (Oxford, 1911), No. 116.

ADDRESS TO THE CHRISTIAN NOBILITY OF THE GERMAN NATION

To His Most Serene and Mighty Imperial Majesty and to the Christian Nobility of the German Nation.

DR. MARTINUS LUTHER

The grace and might of God be with you, Most Serene Majesty, most gracious, well-beloved gentlemen!

It is not out of mere arrogance and perversity that I, an individual poor man, have taken upon me to address your lordships. The distress and misery that oppress all the Christian estates, more especially in Germany, have led not only myself, but every one else, to cry aloud and to ask for help, and have now forced me too to cry out and to ask if God would give His Spirit to any one to reach a hand to His wretched people. Councils have often put forward some remedy, but it has adroitly been frustrated, and the evils have become worse, through the cunning of certain men. Their malice and wickedness I will now, by the help of God, expose, so that, being known, they may henceforth cease to be so obstructive and injurious. God has given us a young and noble sovereign, and by this has roused great hopes in many hearts; now it is right that we too should do what we can, and make good use of time and grace.

The first thing that we must do is to consider the matter with great earnestness, and, whatever we attempt, not to trust in our own strength and wisdom alone, even if the power of all the world were ours; for God will not endure that a good work should be begun trusting to our own strength and wisdom. He destroys it; it is all useless, as we read in Psalm xxxiii., "There is no king saved by the multitude of a host; a mighty man is not delivered by much strength." And I fear it is for that reason that those beloved princes the Emperors Frederick, the First and the Second, and many other German emperors were, in former times, so piteously spurned and oppressed by the popes, though they were feared by all the world. Perchance they trusted rather in their own strength than in God; therefore they could not but fall; and how would the sanguinary tyrant Julius II have risen so high in our own days but that, I fear, France, Germany, and Venice trusted to themselves? The children of Benjamin slew forty-two thousand Israelites, for this reason: that these trusted to their own strength (Judges xx., etc.).

That such a thing may not happen to us and our noble Emperor Charles, we must remember that in this matter we wrestle not against flesh and blood, but against the rulers of the darkness of this world (Eph. vi. 12), who may fill the world with war and bloodshed, but cannot themselves be overcome thereby. We must renounce all confidence in our natural strength, and take the matter in hand with humble trust in God; we must seek God's help with earnest prayer, and have nothing before our eyes but the misery and wretchedness of Christendom, irrespective of what punishment the wicked may deserve, if we do not act thus, we may begin the game with great pomp; but when we are well in it, the spirit of evil will make such confusion that the whole world will be immersed in blood, and yet nothing be done. Therefore let us act in the fear of God and prudently. The greater the might of the foe, the greater is the misfortune, if we do not act in the fear of God and with humility. If popes and Romanists have hitherto, with the devil's help, thrown kings into confusion, they may still do so, if we attempt things with our own strength and skill, without God's help.

THE THREE WALLS OF THE ROMANISTS

The Romanists have, with great adroitness, drawn three walls round themselves, with which they have hitherto protected themselves, so that no one could reform them, whereby all Christendom has fallen terribly.

Firstly, if pressed by the temporal power, they have affirmed and maintained that the temporal power has no jurisdiction over them, but, on the contrary, that the spiritual power is above the temporal.

Secondly, if it were proposed to admonish them with the Scriptures, they objected that no one may interpret the Scriptures but the Pope.

Thirdly, if they are threatened with a council, they pretend that no one may call a council but the Pope.

Thus they have secretly stolen our three rods, so that they may be unpunished, and intrenched themselves behind these three walls, to act with all the wickedness and malice, which we now witness. And whenever they have been compelled to call a council, they have made it of no avail by binding the princes beforehand with an oath to leave them as they were, and to give moreover to the Pope full power over the procedure of the council, so that it is all one whether we have many councils or no councils, in addition to which they deceive us with false pretenses

and tricks. So grievously do they tremble for their skin before a true, free council; and thus they have overawed kings and princes, that these believe they would be offending God, if they were not to obey them in all such knavish, deceitful artifices.

Now may God help us, and give us one of those trumpets that overthrew the walls of Jericho, so that we may blow down these walls of straw and paper, and that we may set free our Christian rods for the chastisement of sin, and expose the craft and deceit of the devil, so that we may amend ourselves by punishment and again obtain God's favour.

THE FIRST WALL

That the Temporal Power Has No Jurisdiction over the Spiritual

Let us, in the first place, attack the first wall.

It has been devised that the Pope, bishops, priests, and monks are called the *spiritual estate,* princes, lords, artificers, and peasants are the *temporal estate.* This is an artful lie and hypocritical device, but let no one be made afraid by it, and that for this reason: that all Christians are truly of the spiritual estate, and there is no difference among them, save of office alone. As St. Paul says (1 Cor xii), we are all one body, though each member does its own work, to serve the others. This is because we have one baptism, one Gospel, one faith and are all Christians alike; for baptism, Gospel, and faith, these alone make spiritual and Christian people.

As for the unction by a pope or a bishop, tonsure, ordination, consecration, and clothes differing from those of laymen—all this may make a hypocrite or an anointed puppet, but never a Christian or a spiritual man. Thus we are all consecrated as priests by baptism, as St. Peter says: "Ye are a royal priesthood, a holy nation" (1 Peter ii. 9); and in the book of Revelations: "and hast made us unto our god (by Thy blood) kings and priests" (Rev v. 10).

For, if we had not a higher consecration in us than pope or bishop can give, no priest could ever be made by the consecration of pope or bishop, nor could he say the mass, or preach, or absolve. Therefore the bishop's consecration is just as if in the name of the whole congregation he took one person out of the community, each member of which has equal power, and commanded him to exercise this power for the rest; in the same way as if ten brothers, co-heirs as king's sons, were to choose one from among them to rule over their inheritance, they would all of them still remain kings and have equal power, although one is ordered to govern.

And to put the matter even more plainly, if a little company of pious Christian laymen were taken prisoners and carried away to a desert, and had not among them a priest consecrated by a bishop, and were there to agree to elect one of them, born in wedlock or not, and were to order him to baptise, to celebrate the mass, to absolve, and to preach, this man would as truly be a priest, as if all the bishops and all the popes had consecrated him. That is why in cases of necessity every man can baptise and absolve, which would not be possible if we were not all priests. This great grace and virtue of baptism and of the Christian estate they have quite destroyed and made us forget by their ecclesiastical law. In this way the Christians used to choose their bishops and priests out of the community; these being afterwards confirmed by other bishops, without the pomp that now prevails. So was it that St. Augustine, Ambrose, Cyprian, were bishops.

Since, then, the temporal power is baptised as we are, and has the same faith and Gospel, we must allow it to be priest and bishop, and account its office an office that is proper and useful to the Christian community. For whatever issues from baptism may boast that it has been consecrated priest, bishop, and pope, although it does not beseem every one to exercise these offices. For, since we are all priests alike, no man may put himself forward or take upon himself, without our consent and election, to do that which we have all alike power to do. For, if a thing is common to all, no man may take it to himself without the wish and command of the community. And if it should happen that a man were appointed to one of these offices and deposed for abuses, he would be just what he was before. Therefore a priest should be nothing in Christendom but a functionary; as long as he holds his office, he has precedence of others; if he is deprived of it, he is a peasant or a citizen like the rest. Therefore a priest is verily no longer a priest after deposition. But now they have invented *charactères indélébiles,* and pretend that a priest after deprivation still differs from a simple layman. They even imagine that a priest can never be anything but a priest—that is, that he can never become a layman. All this is nothing but mere talk and ordinance of human invention.

It follows, then, that between laymen and priests, princes and bishops, or, as they call it, between spiritual and temporal persons, the only real difference is one of office and function, and not of estate; for they are all of the same spiritual estate, true priests, bishops, and popes, though their functions are not the same—just as among priests and monks every man has not the same functions. And this, as I said above, St. Paul says (Rom xii.; 1 Cor xii.), and St. Peter (1 Peter ii.): "We, being many, are one body in Christ, and severally members one of another." Christ's body is not double or twofold, one temporal, the other spiritual. He is one Head, and He has one body.

We see, then, that just as those that we call spiritual, or priests, bishops, or popes, do not differ from the Christians in any other or higher degree but in that they are to be concerned with the word of God and the sacraments—that being their work and office—in the same way the temporal authorities hold the sword and the rod in their hands to punish the wicked and to protect the good. A cobbler, a smith, a peasant, every man, has the office and function of his calling, and yet all alike are consecrated priests and bishops, and every man should by his office or function be useful and beneficial to the rest, so that various kinds of work may all be united for the furtherance of body and soul, just as the members of the body all serve one another.

Now see what a Christian doctrine is this: that the temporal authority is not above the clergy, and may not punish it. This is as if one were to say the hand may not help, though the eye is in grievous suffering. Is it not unnatural, not to say unchristian, that one member may not help another, or guard it against harm? Nay, the nobler the member, the more the rest are bound to help it. Therefore I say, forasmuch as the temporal power has been ordained by God for the punishment of the bad and the protection of the good, therefore we must let it do its duty throughout the whole Christian body, without respect of persons, whether it strike popes, bishops, priests, monks, nuns, or whoever it may be. If it were sufficient reason for fettering the temporal power that it is inferior among the offices of Christianity to the offices of priest or confessor, or to the spiritual estate—if this were so, then we ought to restrain tailors, cobblers, masons, carpenters, cooks, cellarmen, peasants, and all secular workmen, from providing the Pope or bishops, priests and monks, with shoes, clothes, houses, or victuals, or from paying them tithes. But if these laymen are allowed to do their work without restraint, what do the Romanist scribes mean by their laws? They mean that they withdraw themselves from the operation of temporal Christian power, simply in order that they may be free to do evil, and thus fulfill what St. Peter said: "There shall be false teachers among you, . . . and in covetousness

shall they with feigned words make merchandise of you" (2 Peter ii. 1, etc.).

Therefore the temporal Christian power must exercise its office without let or hindrance, without considering whom it may strike, whether pope, or bishop, or priest: whoever is guilty, let him suffer for it.

Whatever the ecclesiastical law has said in opposition to this is merely the invention of Romanist arrogance. For this is what St. Paul says to all Christians: "Let every soul" (I presume including the peoples) "be subject unto the higher powers; for they bear not the sword in vain: they serve the Lord therewith, for vengeance on evil-doers and for praise to them that do well" (Rom xiii. 1–4). Also St. Peter: "Submit yourselves to every ordinance of man for the Lord's sake, . . . for so is the will of God" (1 Peter ii. 13, 15). He has also foretold that men would come who should despise government (2 Peter ii), as has come to pass through ecclesiastical law.

Now, I imagine, the first paper wall is overthrown, inasmuch as the temporal power has become a member of the Christian body; although its work relates to the body, yet does it belong to the spiritual estate. Therefore it must do its duty without let or hindrance upon all members of the whole body, to punish or urge, as guilt may deserve, or need may require, without respect of pope, bishops, or priests, let them threaten or excommunicate as they will. That is why a guilty priest is deprived of his priesthood before being given over to the secular arm; whereas this would not be right, if the secular sword had not authority over him already by Divine ordinance.

It is, indeed, past bearing that the spiritual law should esteem so highly the liberty, life, and property of the clergy, as if laymen were not as good spiritual Christians, or not equally members of the Church. Why should your body, life, goods, and honour be free, and not mine, seeing that we are equal as Christians, and have received alike baptism, faith, spirit, and all things? If a priest is killed, the country is laid under an interdict: why not also if a peasant is killed? Whence comes this great difference among equal Christians? Simply from human laws and inventions.

It can have been no good spirit, either, that devised these evasions and made sin to go unpunished. For if, as Christ and the Apostles bid us, it is our duty to oppose the evil one and all his works and words, and to drive him away as well as may be, how then should we remain quiet and be silent when the Pope and his followers are guilty of devilish works and words? Are we for the sake of men to allow the commandments and the truth of God to be defeated, which at our baptism we vowed to support with body and soul? Truly we should have to answer for all souls that would thus be abandoned and led astray.

Therefore it must have been the arch-devil himself who said, as we read in the ecclesiastical law, if the Pope were so perniciously wicked, as to be dragging souls in crowds to the devil, yet he could not be deposed. This is the accursed and devilish foundation on which they build at Rome, and think that the whole world is to be allowed to go to the devil rather than they should be opposed in their knavery. If a man were to escape punishment simply because he is above the rest, then no Christian might punish another, since Christ has commanded each of us to esteem himself the lowest and the humblest (Matt xviii. 4; Luke ix. 48).

Where there is sin, there remains no avoiding the punishment, as St. Gregory says, We are all equal, but guilt makes one subject to another. Now let us see how they deal with Christendom. They arrogate to themselves immunities without any warrant from the Scriptures, out of their own wickedness, whereas God and the Apostles made them subject to the secular sword; so that we must fear that it is the work of antichrist, or a sign of his near approach.

That No One May Interpret the Scriptures but the Pope

The second wall is even more tottering and weak: that they alone pretend to be considered masters of the Scriptures; although they learn nothing of them all their life. They assume authority, and juggle before us with impudent words, saying that the Pope cannot err in matters of faith, whether he be evil or good, albeit they cannot prove it by a single letter. That is why the canon law contains so many heretical and unchristian, nay unnatural, laws; but of these we need not speak now. For whereas they imagine the Holy Ghost never leaves them, however unlearned and wicked they may be, they grow bold enough to decree whatever they like. But were this true, where were the need and use of the Holy Scriptures? Let us burn them, and content ourselves with the unlearned gentlemen at Rome, in whom the Holy Ghost dwells, who, however, can dwell in pious souls only. If I had not read it, I could never have believed that the devil should have put forth such follies at Rome and find a following.

But not to fight them with our own words, we will quote the Scriptures. St. Paul says, "If anything be revealed to another that sitteth by, let the first hold his peace" (1 Cor xiv. 30). What would be the use of this commandment, if we were to believe him alone that teaches or has the highest seat? Christ Himself says, "And they shall be all taught of God" (St. John v. 45). Thus it may come to pass that the Pope and his followers are wicked and not true Christians, and not being taught by God, have true understanding, whereas a common man may have true understanding. Why should we then not follow him? Has not the Pope often erred? Who could help Christianity, in case the Pope errs, if we do not rather believe another who has the Scriptures for him?

Therefore it is a wickedly devised fable —and they cannot quote a single letter to confirm it—that it is for the Pope alone to interpret the Scriptures or to confirm the interpretation of them. They have assumed the authority of their own selves. And though they say that this authority was given to St. Peter when the keys were given to him, it is plain enough that the keys were not given to St. Peter alone, but to the whole community. Besides, the keys were not ordained for doctrine or authority, but for sin, to bind or loose; and what they claim besides this from the keys is mere invention. But what Christ said to St. Peter: "I have prayed for thee that thy faith fail not" (St. Luke xxii. 32), cannot relate to the Pope, inasmuch as the greater part of the Popes have been without faith, as they are themselves forced to acknowledge; nor did Christ pray for Peter alone, but for all the Apostles and all Christians, as He says, "Neither pray I for these alone, but for them also which shall believe on Me through their word" (St. John xvii.). Is not this plain enough?

Only consider the matter. They must needs acknowledge that there are pious Christians among us that have the true faith, spirit, understanding, word, and mind of Christ: why then should we reject their word and understanding, and follow a Pope who has neither understanding nor spirit? Surely this were to deny our whole faith and the Christian Church. Moreover, if the article of our faith is right, "I believe in the holy Christian Church," the Pope cannot alone be right; else we must say, "I believe in the Pope of Rome," and reduce the Christian Church to one man, which is a devilish and damnable heresy. Besides that, we are all priests, as I have said, and have all one faith. What becomes of St. Paul's words, "But he that is spiritual judgeth all things, yet he himself is judged of no man" (1 Cor ii. 15), and also, "we having the same spirit of faith"? (2 Cor iv. 13). Why then should we not perceive as well as an unbelieving Pope what agrees or disagrees with our faith?

By these and many other texts we should gain courage and freedom, and should not let the spirit of liberty (as St. Paul has it) be frightened away by the inventions of the popes; we should boldly judge what they do and what they leave undone according to our own believing understanding of the Scriptures, and force them to follow the better understanding, and not their own. Did not Abraham in old days have to obey his Sarah, who was in stricter bondage to him than we are to any one on earth? Thus, too, Balaam's ass was wiser than the prophet. If God spoke by an ass against a prophet, why should He not speak by a pious man against the Pope? Besides, St. Paul withstood St. Peter as being in error (Gal ii.). Therefore it behooves every Christian to aid the faith by understanding and defending it and by condemning all errors.

THE THIRD WALL

That No One May Call a Council but the Pope

The third wall falls of itself, as soon as the first two have fallen; for if the Pope acts contrary to the Scriptures, we are bound to stand by the Scriptures, to punish and to constrain him, according to Christ's commandment, "Moreover, if thy brother shall trespass against thee, go and tell him his fault between thee and him alone; if he shall hear thee, thou hast gained thy brother. But if he will not hear thee, then take with thee one or two more, that in the mouth of two or three witnesses every word may be established. And if he shall neglect to hear them, tell it unto the Church; but if he neglect to hear the Church, let him be unto thee as a heathen man and a publican" (Matt xviii. 15–17). Here each member is commanded to take care for the other; much more then should we do this, if it is a ruling member of the community that does evil, which by its evil-doing causes great harm and offence to the others. If then I am to accuse him before the Church, I must collect the Church together. Moreover, they can show nothing in the Scriptures giving the Pope sole power to call and confirm councils; they have nothing but their own laws; but these hold good only so long as they are not injurious to Christianity and the laws of God. Therefore, if the Pope deserves punishment, these laws cease to bind us, since Christendom would suffer, if he were not punished by a council. Thus we read (Acts xv.) that the council of the Apostles was not called by St. Peter, but by all the Apostles and the elders. But if the right to call it had lain with St. Peter alone, it would not have been a Christian council, but a heretical *concilabulum*. Moreover, the most celebrated council of all—that of Nicaea—was neither called nor confirmed by the Bishop of Rome, but by the Emperor Constantine; and after him many other emperors have done the same, and yet the councils called by them were accounted most Christian. But if the Pope alone had the power, they must all have been heretical. Moreover, if I consider the councils that the Pope has called, I do not find that they produced any notable results.

Therefore when need requires, and the Pope is a cause of offence to Christendom, in these cases whoever can best do so, as a faithful member of the whole body, must do what he can to procure a true free council. This no one can do so well as the temporal authorities, especially since they are fellow-Christians, fellow-priests, sharing one spirit and one power in all things, and since they should exercise the office that they have received from God without hindrance, whenever it is necessary and useful that it should be exercised. Would it not be most unnatural, if a fire were to break out in a city, and every one were to keep still and let it burn on and on, whatever might be burnt, simply because they had not the mayor's authority, or because the fire perchance broke out at the mayor's house? Is not every citizen bound in this case to rouse and call in the rest? How much more should

this be done in the spiritual city of Christ, if a fire of offence breaks out, either at the Pope's government or wherever it may! The like happens if an enemy attacks a town. The first to rouse up the rest earns glory and thanks. Why then should not he earn glory that describes the coming of our enemies from hell and rouses and summons all Christians.

But as for their boasts of their authority, that no one must oppose it, this is idle talk. No one in Christendom has any authority to do harm, or to forbid others to prevent harm being done. There is no authority in the Church but for reformation. Therefore if the Pope wished to use his power to prevent the calling of a free council, so as to prevent the reformation of the Church, we must not respect him or his power; and if he should begin to excommunicate and fulminate, we must despise this as the doings of a madman, and, trusting in God, excommunicate and repel him as best we may. For this his usurped power is nothing; he does not possess it, and he is at once overthrown by a text from the Scriptures. For St. Paul says to the Corinthians "that God has given us authority for edification, and not for destruction" (2 Cor x. 8). Who will set this text as nought? It is the power of the devil and of antichrist that prevents what would serve for the reformation of Christendom. Therefore we must not follow it, but oppose it with our body, our goods, and all that we have. And even if a miracle were to happen in favour of the Pope against the temporal power, or if some were to be stricken by a plague, as they sometimes boast has happened, all this is to be held as having been done by the devil in order to injure our faith in God, as was foretold by Christ: "There shall arise false Christs and false prophets, and shall show great signs and wonders, insomuch that, if it were possible, they shall deceive the very elect" (Matt xxiv. 23); and St. Paul tells the Thessalonians that the coming of antichrist shall be "after the working of Satan with all power and signs and lying wonders" (2 Thess ii. 9).

Therefore let us hold fast to this: that Christian power can do nothing against Christ, as St. Paul says, "For we can do nothing against Christ, but for Christ" (2 Cor xiii. 8). But, if it does anything against Christ, it is the power of antichrist and the devil, even if it rained and hailed wonders and plagues. Wonders and plagues prove nothing, especially in these latter evil days, of which false wonders are foretold in all the Scriptures. Therefore we must hold fast to the words of God and with an assured faith; then the devil will soon cease his wonders.

And now I hope the false, lying spectre will be laid with which the Romanists have long terrified and stupefied our consciences. And it will be seen that, like all the rest of us, they are subject to the temporal sword; that they have no authority to interpret the Scriptures by force without skill; and that they have no power to prevent a council, or to pledge it in accordance with their pleasure, or to bind it beforehand, and deprive it of its freedom; and that if they do this, they are verily of the following of antichrist and the devil, and have nothing of Christ but the name.

THE CONFESSIONS OF AUGSBURG, 1530 CORPUS REFORMATORUM

OF ORIGINAL SIN

They teach that after the fall of Adam all men, born according to nature, are born with sin, that is, without the fear of God, without confidence towards God and with concupiscence, and that this original disease or flaw is truly a sin, bringing condemnation and also eternal death to those who are not reborn through baptism and the Holy Spirit.

They condemn Pelagians and others who say that the original flaw is not a sin and who argue that man can be justified in God's sight by his own strength of reason, so as to lessen the glory of the merit and the benefits of Christ.

OF JUSTIFICATION

They teach that the one Holy Church will remain for ever. Now this Church is the congregation of the saints, in which the gospel is rightly taught and the sacraments rightly administered.

And for the true unity of the Church it is enough to have unity of belief concerning the teaching of the Gospel and the administration of the sacraments. It is not necessary that there should everywhere be the same traditions of men, or the same rites and ceremonies devised by men. . . .

OF THE LORD'S SUPPER

They teach that the body and blood of Christ are truly present and are distributed to those who partake in the Lord's Supper; and they reject those that teach otherwise.

OF CONFESSION

They teach that private absolution is to be retained in the churches although it is not necessary to enumerate all sins in confession, because it is impossible, as the psalmist says "Who understands his offences?"

OF ORDERS

They teach that no one ought to teach publicly in churches or to administer the sacraments, unless duly called.

OF THE RITES OF THE CHURCH

They teach that those rites are to be preserved which can be preserved without sin and which are of service for tranquility and good order in the Church, as fixed holy days, feast-days and such like.

But men are warned not to burden their consciences in such matters, as if such observance were necessary to salvation.

They are also warned that traditions devised by man to propitiate God and to acquire grace and make satisfaction for sins are opposed to the Gospel and the teaching of faith. Wherefore vows and traditions concerning foods and days, etc., devised for the production of grace and satisfaction for sins, are useless and contrary to the Gospel.

OF FREE CHOICE

They teach that human will has some liberty in the accomplishment of civil righteousness and in the choice of things which are subject to reason. But without the Holy Spirit it has no power of accomplishing the righteousness of God, or spiritual righteousness "because animal man does not perceive the things which belong to the spirit of God": but these came into being in our hearts when the Holy Spirit is conceived through the Word. . . .

They condemn Pelagians and others who teach that we can love God above all things by the strength of our nature alone, without the Holy Spirit; and that we can perform the commands of God in respect of the *substance* of the actions. For although nature may in some way be able to accomplish the external works (for it can restrain the hands from thefts or from murder), nevertheless it cannot gain the interior motions—fear of God, confidence towards God, chastity, patience, etc.

OF THE CAUSE OF SIN

They teach that although God is the creator and preserver of nature, yet the cause of sin is the will of evil persons, namely of the devil and impious men, which, without God's help, turns itself away from God. . . .

OF FAITH AND GOOD WORKS

Our people are falsely accused of forbidding good works. For their writings on the Ten Commandments and other matters of similar import bear witness that they give useful teaching concerning all kinds of life and the various duties—what kinds of life and what works in each creation are pleasing to God. The popular preachers [*concionatores*] in former times taught too little on these subjects; for they only stressed certain childish and unnecessary works—fixed holidays and fasts, fraternities, pilgrimages, worship of saints, rosaries, monasticism and such-like.

OF FAITH

. . . Our works cannot reconcile us to God or merit remission of sins and grace and justification. This we obtain only by faith, when we believe that we are received into grace on account of Christ. . . .

. . . Men are warned that the word *faith* does not signify merely the knowledge of an event (the devils and impious men have that), but it signifies a faith which believes not in an event merely, but also in the effect of an event, namely this article, the remission of sins, i.e. that we have, through Christ, grace, righteousness, and remission of sins. . . .

OF GOOD WORKS

Moreover our people teach that it is necessary to do good works, not in order to trust to merit grace thereby, but because of the will of God. . . . Because the Holy Spirit is received through faith, and hearts are renewed and put on new affections so that they can accomplish good works. For Ambrose says: "Faith is the mother of good will and righteous action. . . . "

Hence it is readily seen that this doctrine is not to be accused of preventing good works, but much rather to be praised because it shows how we can do good works. . . .

THE SWISS REFORMATION AND HULDRYICH ZWINGLI

While Luther's teachings were spreading through Germany, Switzerland was experiencing its own reformation under the leadership of Huldryich Zwingli (1484–1531), a priest in Zurich and humanist scholar in the tradition of Erasmus. Switzerland in the sixteenth century was a loose federation of thirteen autonomous cantons that were joined together in independence from the Holy Roman Empire. A desire for church reform had persisted there since the time of the councils of Constance (1414–1417) and Basel (1431–1449). Zwingli first began his reform preaching over the moral abuses associated with the Swiss service as mercenary troops in the papal army. As chaplain to the Swiss troops, he had seen both the senseless loss of life and the moral corruption that resulted from mercenary service.

Eventually Zwingli, apparently quite independently from Luther, became convinced of the need for thorough church reform. But whereas Luther came to his reformed doctrines through a tortured search for a gracious God, Zwingli arrived at his convictions from a calm, humanistic study of the scriptures. He learned classical and *koine* Greek, and with the help of Erasmus' Greek text of the New Testament, began to preach from it book by book, rather than from the traditional lectionary.

Through his study of the New Testament, Zwingli formulated a reformation platform that aimed at the restoration of primitive Christianity. Whatever lacked literal support in scripture was neither to be believed nor practiced. On this basis, he affirmed many of the same doctrines as Luther: the gospel is the highest authority within the church, rather than human traditions; we are saved by faith and damned by unbelief; the mass is not a sacrifice, but only a remembrance of the one sacrifice of Christ; because Christ is the sole mediator, the intercession of the saints is not necessary; all Christians belong to the spiritual estate and have the same power as the pope; and there is no scriptural basis for the doctrine of purgatory. He also rejected many of the practices of medieval Christianity: the laws for fasting and abstinence; priestly celibacy; papal power of excommunication; and the use of images, relics, candles, and music in the church's liturgy. In fact, in his puritanical purging of all medieval practices, Zwingli went further than Luther because he insisted that whatever was not present in the New Testament was to be rejected. Luther only insisted that practices not be contrary to the spirit of the New Testament.

Outward reform in Zurich began in 1522 with Zwingli's vigorous preaching against Lenten fasts and rules as non-biblical. When the Bishop of Constance objected, Zwingli cited scholars and the New Testament and pressed the matter with the Zurich city council. They agreed that the New Testament did not impose fasts, but decided they should be observed for the sake of good order. Not satisfied, Zwingli and his followers continued to press the matter and by August had the decision overturned. Eventually in a series of three disputations, the council rejected the authority of the Bishop of Constance and approved Zwingli's reform platform that was drawn up in Sixty-Seven Articles that were all biblically based.

Although Luther and Zwingli shared many of the same beliefs, their reform movements were never united. In 1529 Philip of Hesse, who had embraced reformation tradition in 1526, attempted to unite the two branches of the Reformation in order to form a united military front against the Catholic emperor, Charles V. The theologians, including Luther and Zwingli, met at Marburg, and although they reached a remarkable degree of agreement on most subjects, they remained divided on their understanding of the eucharist. Ironically, the sacrament of Christian unity proved divisive. Although Luther rejected transubstantiation, he insisted on a belief in a real, as opposed to spiritual, presence of Christ in the bread and wine. Zwingli understood the eucharist simply as a memorial of the Last Supper in which the Christian may spiritually commune with Christ.

Zwingli's greatest theological work is a treatise entitled *Commentary on True and False Religion* which was published in 1525. For Zwingli, true religion is the biblical gospel recovered by the reformers, and false religion is medieval Catholic doctrine which is based on human traditions and the greed of the papacy. In his treatment of the eucharist, Zwingli's humanistic scholarship is evident. He bases his arguments for a symbolic and spiritual understanding of Christ's presence on a careful reading of the biblical text and on philosophical reasoning. First of all, he establishes that both the Old and New Testaments use metaphorical and symbolic language in which the verb "is" is best understood as meaning "signifies." Then he argues on the basis of the phrase—"The flesh profiteth nothing" (Jn 6:63)—that to limit the language of the Bible to a mere literal or fleshly sense is to miss the higher spiritual meaning of many of its most important passages. It is this spiritual meaning that is accessible to the person of faith. In arguing this way, Zwingli shows his debt to Erasmus and the Florentine Neoplatonists who have a characteristic contrast between flesh and spirit in their understanding of both biblical texts and the eucharist.

In the Epilogue Zwingli summarizes the argument of the whole treatise. Here both his similarities and differences from Erasmus and Luther are evident. He begins satirically in the spirit of Erasmus by insisting that the reason for having to give a rather lengthy explication of true religion is because the papacy's greed has turned Christianity into "an article of merchandise rather than holiness of life." This criticism is also very much in the spirit of Luther's Ninety-Five theses. True religion, for Zwingli, is actually very simple; it is the knowledge of God which separates humans from beasts. Zwingli then reviews the whole history of God's action in the Hebrew scriptures as a history of God's solicitude for fallen humanity and for Israel. He has a more positive understanding of the history of the Old Testament than Luther, who tends to reduce the whole of scripture to either law or gospel. For Zwingli, God's grace is evident at each stage of salvation history: in his calling out to Adam; in the sending of the fire of Sodom and the waters of flood "to keep man to his duty by fear also"; in his promises to the patriarchs; in the Exodus from Pharaoh's tyranny; in the gifts of manna, quail, and water in the wilderness; in the giving of the law. Although these actions were for Israel, Zwingli, as a good humanist, also understands them as consistent with God's universal purpose for all peoples.

> In this manner He showed Himself a most loving Father to one race; yet He was nowhere lacking to others, that the whole world might recognize that He is the one and the only one who can do all things, by whom all things exist, by whom all things are governed, that miserable man may not go over to the beasts; for he marked them off from the beasts by bringing their passions into line through laws.

For Zwingli, in contrast to Luther, law and faith are not antithetical, but work together in God's plan. Only those with faith in their hearts can accept the revelation of God's law which has the positive function of controlling human sinfulness and thereby raising humans above the beasts.

> Therefore, it is evident that, whenever God manifested Himself to the world, He also so entered the heart that what was heard or seen was recognized as being divine. For the flesh receiveth not what is opposed to it; and whatever the heavenly spirit does is opposed to the flesh. Therefore man cannot receive God, cannot listen to the law, unless God Himself draw the heart to Himself [cf. Jn 6:44], so that it shall recognize that He is its God, and shall receive the law as good.

Faith must precede obedience, and, for Zwingli the Erasmian humanist, this is also true of God's revelation to the Gentiles through philosophy and natural law.

> He hedges the human race about with laws, therefore, that it may begin nothing without regard to law; for He not only compassed the people of Israel about with laws, but also inscribed upon the hearts of the Gentiles the so-called laws of nature; for one of their prophets says: "Know thyself came down from heaven."

Zwingli has a much more positive view of philosophy and natural religion than do either Luther or Calvin. In this he is like other Renaissance humanists, and even Thomas Aquinas. For Zwingli, the fulfillment of the law rests on the Greek ideal of knowledge of self, for the whole law can be summarized in the golden rule: "What you wish done to yourself, do to another" and "What you do not wish done to yourself, do not to another."

Zwingli's definition of the Christian life is an interesting blend of the theologies of Luther and Erasmus. Like Erasmus, and Augustine and Paul, Zwingli understands the Christian life as a battle between flesh and spirit, or, as the struggle between body and soul. In this struggle laws, like the prohibition of coveting, have the positive role of giving humans a hint that true happiness does not consist in covetousness and greed. Like Luther, Zwingli believes that the struggle between flesh and spirit reduces humans "to the uttermost depth of despair by this ungovernableness of the flesh." And he understands Christ as God's answer to our despair. But, following Erasmus, Zwingli also understands Christ's coming as furnishing an example for the way we are to live.

He (Christ) was sent, then, for this purpose, that He might altogether take away this despair of the soul that springs from the ungovernableness of the flesh, as has been said, and that He might also furnish an example of life. For Christ everywhere emphasizes these two things, namely, redemption through Himself, and the obligation of those redeemed through Him to live according to His example.

The Christian life, then, becomes for Zwingli a matter of both trust in God's mercy through Christ and action in imitation of Christ, or a life of "faith and blamelessness." Although alone one could never win the "battle" of Christian life, loyalty to Christ insures "a lasting victory."

A Christian, therefore, is a man who trusts in the one true and only God; who relies upon His mercy through His Son Christ, God of God; who models himself upon His example; who dies daily [cf. 1 Cor 15:31]; who daily renounces self; who is intent upon this one thing, not to do anything that can offend God.

Through aggressive missionary activity, Zwingli's reform spread from Zurich to the northern Swiss towns of Bern, Basel, Schaffhausen, Constance, and St. Gall, but the southern, forest cantons remained Catholic. There were two major battles between the Catholic and Protestant Swiss cantons at Kappel in 1529 and 1531. In the first the Protestants were victorious and won recognition of the rights of Swiss Protestants, but when they assumed they also had the right to proselytize in Catholic areas, they antagonized the Catholic cantons who defeated them in a surprise attack in 1531. Zwingli, armed with helmet and sword, died in battle. He was treated as a traitor and heretic by the Catholics. His body was quartered and his ashes sown to the wind. The treaty ending the second Kappel War, however, gave each canton the right to determine its own religion. Heinreich Bullinger (1504–1575) succeeded Zwingli as the leader of the German Swiss Reformation. Tiny Switzerland was a foretaste of Europe. The old medieval ideal of one land, one God, one faith was gone forever.

THE ANABAPTISTS

For some in Zurich, Zwingli's attempts to restore primitive Christianity were neither rapid nor thorough enough. They did not accept the gradual removal of traditional practices as approved by the city government and formed a small group of about fifteen for Bible study. On the basis of the adult baptism of conversion in the New Testament, they refused to have their children baptized, and in 1525 George Blaurock, an ex-priest, made a profession of faith and had himself baptized by Conrad Grebel; Blaurock then proceeded to baptize the rest of the group. Soon Blaurock and Grebel were travelling round the country baptizing adults in streams and lakes and holding simplified services in houses and fields.

This group of "Swiss Brethren" was not the only one committed to adult believer baptism in the early stages of the Reformation. A wide variety of such groups shared a general desire for a thorough implementation of primitive Christianity and a literal following of the teachings of Christ in the gospels, especially the Sermon on the Mount (Matt 5–7) which commands love of enemies and prohibits retaliation against injury and the taking of oaths. In some ways they were a reaction against the dangers of a simplistic and libertine interpretation of the doctrine of salvation by faith alone which could lead to a life of lasciviousness and self-indulgence. The Anabaptists wanted to insist that true faith leads to a life of repentance in which one crucifies the flesh with its passions and lusts. Opponents gave these groups the name Ana-baptists which means those who "re-baptize" adults who were baptized as infants. This term was used to invoke old laws prohibiting re-baptism that were originally formulated against the Donatists in Augustine's time. The Anabaptists were perceived as a threat to civil order by all other parties in the Reformation because they insisted on separating the Christian community of committed believers from the state and refused to hold the office of magistrate or to bear arms. They modeled themselves on the early church before the time of Constantine, when Christianity was persecuted by the pagan Roman Empire. In a dualistic way the state was identified with the evil world and the flesh. Any compromise with the state only led to a dilution of the true Christian way of life.

The dualism and extreme biblicism of Anabaptism readily led to apocalyptic movements, and these often contributed to the general suspicion against the Anabaptists. Thomas Münzer, a German Anabaptist preacher from Zwickau, broke with Luther over infant baptism and linked himself with the peasants in the Peasants' Revolt. He placed himself at the head of the rebels, but was captured and executed in 1525. In 1534–1535 a radical, apocalyptic group of Anabaptists gained control of the town of Munster in Westphalia where they expelled all non-believers and set up a kind of Old Testament theocracy, complete with polygamy, as they awaited the apocalypse. Eventually in June 1535, some sane men opened the gates of the city, and the bishop's army entered and crushed the rebellion. The corpses of the Anabaptists' leaders were hung in cages which are still hanging on the tower of St. Lambert's Church.

On the more positive side, the true spirit of the Anabaptist movement was preserved by groups like the Hutterite brethren in Moravia and the Mennonites of the Netherlands and northern Germany. Following the example of Jacob Hutter who died as a martyr in 1536, the Hutterites emphasized the ideal life of the early Jerusalem community as described in Acts, particularly its community of goods. The Mennonites, led by Menno Simons (1496–1561), were known for their pacifism. Simons was fond of saying, "The regenerated do not go to war, nor engage in strife. They are the children of peace who have beaten their swords into plowshares and their spears into pruning hooks, and know of no war. . . ." Because most regions of Europe still maintained a unity of state and religion and only recognized the larger branches of Protestantism, the Anabaptist groups were forced to live on the fringes of European society in Poland and Russia; in fact, many also migrated to the New World.

To illustrate the beliefs of the Anabaptists I have chosen *The Schleitheim Confession of Faith* which is named after a small town on the Swiss-German border where South German and Swiss Anabaptists met in 1527 to draw up a confessional statement of their beliefs. The translation is by John C. Wegner, "The Schleitheim Confession of Faith," *Mennonite Quarterly Review*, 19 (1945), 243 ff.

THE SCHLEITHEIM CONFESSION OF FAITH

Dear brethren and sisters, we who have been assembled in the Lord at Schleitheim on the Border, make known in points and articles to all who love God that as concerns us we are of one mind to abide in the Lord as God's obedient children, His sons and daughters, we who have been and shall be separated from the world in everything, and completely at peace. To God alone be praise and glory without the contradiction of any brethren. In this we have perceived the oneness of the Spirit of our Father and of our common Christ with us. For the Lord is the Lord of peace and not quarreling, as Paul points out. That you may understand in what articles this has been formulated you should observe and note the following.

A very great offense has been introduced by certain false brethren among us, so that some have turned aside from the faith, in the way they intend to practice and observe the freedom of the Spirit and of Christ. But such have missed the truth and to their condemnation are given over to the lasciviousness and self-indulgence of the flesh. They think faith and love may do and permit everything, and nothing will harm them nor condemn them, since they are believers.

Observe, you who are God's members in Christ Jesus, that faith in the heavenly Father through Jesus Christ does not take such form. It does not produce and result in such things as these false brethren and sisters do and teach. Guard yourselves and be warned of such people, for they do not serve our Father, but their father, the devil.

But you are not that way. For they that are Christ's have crucified the flesh with its passions and lusts. You understand me well and know the brethren whom we mean. Separate yourselves from them for they are perverted. Petition the Lord that they may have the knowledge which leads to repentance, and pray for us that we may have constancy to persevere in the way which we have espoused, for the honor of God and of Christ, His Son, Amen.

The articles which we discussed and on which we were of one mind are these (1) Baptism; (2) The Ban [Excommunication]; (3) Breaking of Bread; (4) Separation from the Abomination; (5) Pastors in the Church; (6) The Sword; and (7) The Oath.

First. Observe concerning baptism: Baptism shall be given to all those who have learned repentance and amendment of life, and who believe truly that their sins are taken away by Christ, and to all those who walk in the resurrection of Jesus Christ, and wish to be buried with Him in death, so that they may be resurrected with Him, and to all those who with this significance request baptism of us and demand it for themselves. This excludes all infant baptism, the highest and chief abomination of the pope. In this you have the foundation and testimony of the apostles (Matt 28, Mark 16, Acts 2, 8, 16, 19). This we wish to hold simply yet firmly and with assurance.

Second. We are agreed as follows on the ban: The ban shall be employed with all those who have given themselves to the Lord, to walk in His commandments, and with all those who are baptized into the one body of Christ and who are called brethren or sisters, and yet who slip sometimes and fall into error and sin, being inadvertently overtaken. The same shall be admonished twice in secret and the third time openly disciplined or banned according to the command of Christ (Matt 18). But this shall be done according to the regulation of the Spirit (Matt 5) before the breaking of bread, so that we may break and eat one bread, with one mind and in one love, and may drink of one cup.

Third. In the breaking of bread we are of one mind and are agreed as follows: All those who wish to break one bread in remembrance of the broken body of Christ, and all who wish to drink of one drink as a remembrance of the shed blood of Christ, shall be united beforehand by baptism in one body of Christ which is the church of God and whose head is Christ. For as Paul points out we cannot at the same time be partakers of the Lord's table and the table of devils; we cannot at the same time drink the cup of the Lord and the cup of the devil. That is, all those who have fellowship with the dead works of darkness have no part in the light. Therefore all who follow the devil and the world have no part with those who are called unto God out of the world. All who lie in evil have no part in the good.

Therefore it is and must be thus: whoever has not been called by one God to one faith, to one baptism, to one Spirit, to one body, and with all the children of God's church, cannot be made [into] one bread with them, as indeed must be done if one is truly to break bread according to the command of Christ.

Fourth. We are agreed as follows on separation: A separation shall be made from the evil and from the wickedness which the devil planted in the world; in this manner, simply that we shall not have fellowship with them, the wicked, and not run with them in the multitude of their abominations. This is the way it is: Since all who do not walk in obedience of faith, and have not united themselves with God so that they wish to do His will, are a great abomination before God, it is not possi-

ble for anything to grow or issue from them except abominable things. For truly all creatures are in but two classes, good and bad, believing and unbelieving, darkness and light, the world and those who have come out of the world, God's temple and idols, Christ and Belial; and none can have part with the other.

To us then the command of the Lord is clear when he calls upon us to be separate from the evil and thus He will be our God and we shall be His sons and daughters.

He further admonishes us to withdraw from Babylon and the earthly Egypt that we may not be partakers of the pain and suffering which the Lord will bring upon them.

From all this we should learn that everything which is not united with our God and Christ cannot be other than an abomination which we should shun and flee from. By this is meant all popish and anti-popish works and church services, meetings and church attendance, drinking houses, civic affairs, the commitments made in unbelief and other things of that kind, which are highly regarded by the world and yet are carried on in flat contradiction to the command of God, in accordance with all the unrighteousness which is in the world. From all these things we shall be separated and have no part with them for they are nothing but an abomination, and they are the cause of our being hated before our Christ Jesus, who has set us free from the slavery of the flesh and fitted us for the service of God through the Spirit whom He has given us.

Therefore there will also unquestionably fall from us the un-Christian, devilish weapons of force—such as sword, armor and the like, and all their use either for friends or against one's enemies—by virtue of the word of Christ, Resist not him that is evil.

Fifth. We are agreed as follows on pastors in the church of God: The pastor in the church of God shall, as Paul has prescribed, be one who out-and-out has a good report of those who are outside the faith. This office shall be to read, to admonish and teach, to warn, to discipline, to ban in the church, to lead out in prayer for the advancement of all the brethren and sisters, to lift up the bread when it is to be broken, and in all things to see to the care of the body of Christ, in order that it may be built up and developed, and the mouth of the slanderer be stopped.

This one moreover shall be supported of the church which has chosen him, wherein he may be in need, so that he who serves the gospel may live of the gospel as the Lord has ordained. But if a pastor should do something requiring discipline, he shall not be dealt with except on the testimony of two or three witnesses. And when they sin they shall be disciplined before all in order that the others may fear.

But should it happen that through the cross this pastor should be banished or led to the Lord through martyrdom another shall be ordained in his place in the same hour so that God's little flock and people may not be destroyed.

Sixth. We are agreed as follows concerning the sword: The sword is ordained of God outside the perfection of Christ. It punishes and puts to death the wicked, and guards and protects the good. In the law the sword was ordained for the punishment of the wicked and for their death, and the same sword is now ordained to be used by the worldly magistrates.

In the perfection of Christ, however, only the ban is used for a warning and for the excommunication of the one who has sinned, without putting the flesh to death—simply the warning and the command to sin no more.

Now it will be asked by many who do not recognize this as the will of Christ for us, whether a Christian may or should employ the sword against the wicked for the defense and protection of the good, or for the sake of love.

Our reply is unanimously as follows: Christ teaches and commands us to learn of Him, for He is meek and lowly in heart and so shall we find rest to our souls. Also Christ says to the heathenish woman who was taken in adultery, not that one should stone her according to the law of His Father (and yet He says, As the Father has commanded me, thus I do), but in mercy and forgiveness and warning, to sin no more. Such an attitude we also ought to take completely according to the rule of the ban.

Secondly, it will be asked concerning the sword, whether a Christian shall pass sentence in worldly dispute and strife such as unbelievers have with one another. This is our united answer: Christ did not wish to decide or pass judgment between brother and brother in the case of the inheritance, but refused to do so. Therefore we should do likewise.

Thirdly, it will be asked concerning the sword, Shall one be a magistrate if one should be chosen as such? The answer is as follows: They wished to make Christ king, but He fled and did not view it as the arrangement of His Father. Thus shall we do as He did, and follow Him, and so shall we not walk in darkness. For He Himself says, He who wishes to come after me, let him deny himself and take up his cross and follow me. Also, He Himself forbids the employment of the force of the sword saying, "The worldly princes lord it over them, etc., but not so shall it be with you." Further, Paul says, Whom God did foreknow He also did predestinate to be conformed to the image of His Son, etc. Also Peter says, Christ has suffered (not ruled) and left us an example, that ye should follow His steps.

Finally it will be observed that it is not appropriate for a Christian to serve as a magistrate because of these points: The government magistracy is according to the flesh, but the Christians' is according to the Spirit; their houses and dwelling remain in this world, but the Christians' are in heaven; their citizenship is in this world, but the Christians' citizenship is in heaven; the weapons of their conflict and war are carnal and against the flesh only, but the Christians' weapons are spiritual, against the fortification of the devil. The worldlings are armed with steel and iron, but the Christians are armed with the armor of God, with truth, righteousness, peace, faith, salvation and the word of God. In brief, as is the mind of Christ toward us, so shall the mind of the members of the body of Christ be through Him in all things, that there may be no schism in the body through which it would be destroyed. For every kingdom divided against itself will be destroyed. Now since Christ is as it is written of Him, His members must also be the same, that His body may remain complete and united to its own advancement and upbuilding.

Seventh. We are agreed as follows concerning the oath: The oath is a confirmation among those who are quarreling or making promises. In the law it is commanded to be performed in God's name, but only in truth, not falsely. Christ, who teaches the perfection of the law, prohibits all swearing to His followers, whether true or false—neither by heaven, nor by the earth, nor by Jerusalem, nor by our head—and that for the reason which He shortly thereafter gives, For you are not able to make one hair white or black. So you see it is for this reason that all swearing is forbidden: we cannot fulfill that which we promise when we swear, for we cannot change even the very least thing on us. . . .

Christ also taught us along the same line when He said, Let your communication be Yea, yea; Nay, nay; for whatsoever is more than these cometh of evil. He says, Your speech or word shall be yea and nay. (However) when one does not wish to understand, he remains closed to the meaning. Christ is simply Yea and Nay, and all those who seek Him simply will understand His word. Amen.

JOHN CALVIN: *THE INSTITUTES OF THE CHRISTIAN RELIGION*

After Martin Luther, John Calvin (1509–1564) is the most important Protestant reformer and theologian. Luther set the Reformation in motion in Germany in the 1520s, but the spread of Lutheranism was largely confined to Germany and the Scandinavian countries. Calvin, a Frenchman, spent most of his career as a reformer in Geneva. He gave Protestantism a coherent and systematic theology, a spirit of activism, and a viable organizational structure which enabled Calvinism to spread internationally to Switzerland, France, the Netherlands, Hungary, Scotland, England and North America.

Calvin was a second-generation reformer who became interested in Reformation doctrines in the course of his humanistic, theological and legal studies at Paris and Orléans. Unlike Luther, Calvin rarely spoke of his own religious experience, and his great theological work, *The Institutes of the Christian Religion,* has a detached lucidity which is more like Aquinas' *Summa* in style than the impassioned tracts of Luther. Calvin is not a daringly original theological thinker like Augustine or Luther; he is more of a systematizer. As will be evident from the selections chosen from the *The Institutes of the Christian Religion,* Calvin is a synthetic and clear thinker whose exposition of Reformation theology is comparable to the synthesis of medieval theology in Thomas' *Summa*.

The elements of Calvin's synthesis are many. He shares with Paul and Augustine a view of history as a divine plan of salvation for the elect as revealed in scripture. He is indebted to Luther for the doctrine of justification by faith, as opposed to works, and the reduction of the sacraments to baptism and eucharist. He shares with Zwingli certain humanistic interests in the philosophy and religion of the pagans; his first published work was a commentary on Seneca's *Two Books on Clemency,* and he also shares Zwingli's inclination toward simplicity in worship.

Despite these dependencies, Calvin's synthesis has its own unique characteristics. First of all, there is his consistent emphasis on the majesty and glory of God and the utter depravity of humans apart from God's mercy. If, for Luther, the goal of faith was to find a gracious God and hear the words, "Your sins are forgiven," for Calvin the goal is to know God, to give him glory in this life and the next and to enjoy him forever. Therefore, he begins the *Institutes,* as Aquinas does his *Summa,* with a discussion of the knowledge of God the Creator. But unlike Aquinas, who has a positive view of the natural powers of the human person even apart from grace, Calvin begins by contrasting human depravity to divine goodness.

> Thus a sense of our ignorance, vanity, poverty, infirmity, depravity, and corruption leads us to perceive and acknowledge that in the Lord alone are to be found true wisdom, solid strength, perfect goodness, and unspotted righteousness; and so by our imperfections we are excited to a consideration of the perfections of God. (I.1.1)

Although Calvin believes all humans have a kind of natural religious sense of the deity, he characteristically concludes, that "they must be condemned by their own testimony for not having worshiped him and consecrated their lives to his service." He shares with the medieval theologians the belief that God's existence should be evident from his wisdom displayed in the order and wonders of creation, but he then goes on, in the spirit of Paul in Romans 1, to blame humans for their ingratitude in not acknowledging God.

> Though the light which presents itself to all eyes, both in heaven and in earth, is more than sufficient to deprive the ingratitude of men of every excuse—since God, in order to involve all mankind in the same guilt, sets before them all without exception, an exhibition of his majesty delineated in the creatures . . . (I.6.1)

Calvin also agrees with Aquinas and others that it was necessary for human salvation that God reveal himself and his plan of salvation in scripture. But, in contrast to Thomas' synthesis of reason and faith and to the optimism of humanists like Erasmus, Calvin neither sees these modes of knowledge as affirming the natural goodness of human reason nor the continuity of God's plan. Scriptural revelation is contrasted to the error and feebleness of human reason in its naturally sinful state.

> For, seeing the minds of all men to be agitated with unstable dispositions, when he had chosen the Jews as his peculiar flock he enclosed them as in a fold, that they might not wander after the vanities of other nations (I.6.1).

Following Luther, Calvin insists that scripture is the sole religious authority which creates and stands above the church. It is in the hearing of the gospel and the belief in its saving message that the church of the elect is created. This position should be contrasted with the Roman Catholic view that the scriptures were created by the church and were chosen by the church in the process of forming a canonical list of sacred books.

> But since we are not favored with daily oracles from heaven, and since it is only in the Scriptures that the Lord hath pleased to preserve his truth in perpetual remembrance, it obtains the same complete credit and authority with believers, when they are satisfied of its divine origin, as if they heard the very words pronounced by God himself. . . . He (Paul) testifies that the church is "built upon the foundation of the apostles and prophets." If the doctrine of the prophets and apostles be the foundation of the Church, it must have been certain, antecedently, to the existence of the Church. (I.7.1)

Like Luther, Calvin rejects the idea that only the official hierarchy of the church authoritatively has the right to interpret the scriptures. For Calvin, the truth of the scriptures is self-authenticating to those inwardly taught by the Spirit.

> Let it be considered, then, as an undeniable truth that they who have been inwardly taught by the Spirit feel an entire acquiescence in the Scripture, and that it is well-authenticated, carrying with it its own evidence, and ought not to be made the subject of demonstration and arguments from reason; but it obtains the credit which it deserves with us by the testimony of the Spirit. (I.7.5)

In the scriptures, Calvin finds a view of human nature as, apart from God's mercy, totally depraved and incapacitated because of original sin. He is much more pessimistic about natural humanity than Thomas and the Renaissance humanists, and possibly even than Luther himself. Calvin seems to have been overwhelmed with the human proclivity to vice and disorderliness.

> I shall be content with citing a single passage, which however, will resemble a very lucid mirror, in which we may behold at full length the image of our nature. For the Apostle (Paul), when he wishes to demolish the arrogance of mankind, does it by these testimonies: "There is none righteous, no, not one; there is none that understandeth, there is none that seeketh after God. They are all gone out of the way, they are together become unprofitable; there is none that doeth good, no, not one. Their throat is an open sepulcher; with their tongues they have used deceit; the poison of asps is under their lips; whose mouth is full of cursing and bitterness; their feet are swift to shed blood; destruction and misery are in their ways; there is no fear of God before their eyes" (Rom 3:10–18). In this terrible manner he inveighs not against particular individuals, but against all the posterity of Adam. (II.3.2)

Calvin's understanding of the law is more positive than Luther's. Luther set the law and gospel in dialectical opposition. For him, the law reveals to us our sin and weakness, the inability of our works to please God, and our need for faith and God's grace. The gospel is the saving message that we are saved by Christ's death and resurrection apart from the law and works. Calvin sees more continuity between God's revelation in the law (the Old Testament) and in the New Testament. As a result he distinguishes three functions for the law. First of all, he agrees with Luther that the moral law shows us God's righteousness and leads us to confess our own "feebleness and impurity" and seek God's grace. Secondly, the law functions to restrain the wicked by fear of punishment; this too can be of benefit for those who will eventually convert to the grace of Christ. The third function of the law is for believers in whom the Spirit of God already reigns. In the law believers learn more thoroughly the nature of God's will to which they aspire, and they are continuously confirmed in their understanding of that will. There is room for progress here in Calvin's theology. Daily instruction in the law leads to a purer knowledge of God's will. The law also serves the role of exhortation for the believer. By frequent meditation on the law, the believer is aroused to obedience and diverted from the slippery path of transgression. "The law is to the flesh like a whip to an idle and balky ass, to arouse it to work."

But justification is not the result of obedience to the law. Calvin follows Luther in insisting that the elect are justified by faith, apart from the law and one's own works. When judged by the law, we are always sinners. Yet because of Christ "we can be considered righteous."

> Avoiding, therefore, all mention of the law, and dismissing all thought of our own works, in reference to justification, we must embrace the Divine mercy alone, and turning our eyes from ourselves, fix them solely on Christ. For the question is, not how we can be righteous, but how, though unrighteous and unworthy, we can be considered righteous. And the conscience that desires to attain any certainty respecting this must give no admission to the law. . . . It is the office of the law to remind men of their duty, and thereby to excite them to pursuit of holiness and integrity. But when their consciences are solicitous how God may be propitiated, what answer they shall make, and on what they shall rest their confidence, if called to his tribunal, there must be no consideration of the requisitions of the law, but Christ alone must be proposed for righteousness, who exceeds all the perfection of the law. (III.19.2)

In discussing the benefits and effects which follow from the grace of Christ, Calvin follows Augustine in understanding the Christian life as a pilgrimage through this world to the heavenly city. Christians may use the gifts of this world, but they are to use them as pilgrims who are passing on to a more lasting form of life. In life's pilgrimage, each Christian has a vocation or calling from God which is a guide for the restlessness that inflames the human heart. Like the Stoical philosophers whom he admired, Calvin sees a person's life calling as "a post assigned him by the Lord, that he might not wander about in uncertainty all his days." This leads to a conservatism in Calvin's social thinking. Rather than calling for revolutionary social change, Calvin's version of the Christian gospel can be understood as an affirmation of the status quo. The private man is not to lay his hands on the tyrant. One's place in life is "burden laid upon him by God." All "employment," no matter how "mean and sordid," is "deemed highly important in the sight of God." Although Calvin himself does not go on to draw out the implications of this thinking for people suffering from political and social oppression, one may sense the inherent dangers in it.

Calvin's treatment of predestination occurs in the context of discussing justification and the Christian life and comes just before his treatment of the church. This is significant, because Calvin's teaching on predestination is meant for believers as an assurance that their salvation rests in the hands of the merciful God. If Luther was overwhelmed with the miracle of God's forgiveness in Christ, Calvin stresses the assurance of the ultimate success of God's purpose or plan for the world. Having said this, it cannot be denied that Calvin believes in double predestination to both salvation and damnation.

> Predestination we call the eternal decree of God by which he has determined in himself what he would have to become of every individual of mankind. For they are not all created with a similar destiny, but eternal life is foreordained for some and eternal damnation for others. Every man, therefore, being created for one or the other of these ends, we say he is predestined either to life or to death. (III.21.5)

The basis for the doctrine is found in the biblical tradition of election found in the Old Testament and in Paul's theology, especially in Romans and Galatians. Calvin does not accept the idea that the doctrine depends on God's foreknowledge of the merit of the elect, but insists that salvation is the gratuitous gift of God's grace. He also recognizes, with Augustine, whom he follows closely in this section, that preaching predestination to non-believers in such a way as to confirm them in their unbelief is counterproductive and un-Christian. We should desire every person's salvation and leave the results to the mystery of God's eternal plan which is beyond human comprehension.

In Calvin's ecclesiology he distinguishes, like Augustine, between the elect and the visible church which may include "many hypocrites." The visible church, though, is necessary as a sign on earth of the invisible communion of the elect which includes the whole communion of saints. Although only God knows who the true elect are, Calvin was confident that God has given us certain presumptive signs which mark the elect. These include public confession of faith, an exemplary life, participation in the sacraments, and profession of the same God and Christ as he has delineated in the *Institutes*. He rejects the hierarchical model of the church based on apostolic succession and replaces it with an evangelical and communal one which stresses the preaching of the gospel and administration of the sacraments according to the New Testament tradition.

> For wherever we find the word of God purely preached and heard, and the sacraments administered according to the institution of Christ, there, it is not to be doubted, is a Church of God; for his promise can never deceive—"where two or three are gathered together in my name, there am I in the midst of them." (IV.1.9)

Calvin was more concerned with church order than Luther. This reflects his experience with the church in Geneva. In 1536, while he was passing through Geneva on his way to Strasbourg, Calvin was persuaded by William Farel to remain in Geneva to help organize the Reformation in that French-speaking city. Although he and Farel were temporarily exiled (1538–1540) for being too strict in their implementation of their plan for reform, Calvin eventually returned to Geneva and succeeded in establishing a strictly ordered community. Calvin's legal training and love of orderliness is evident in his *Ecclesiastical Ordinances,* a constitution which he wrote for the governing of the church in Geneva. He provided for four ministries or offices—pastors, teachers, elders and deacons—and for a consistory of elders and pastors to maintain strict discipline in the community. The consistory had the power to excommunicate, and its legislation inflicted severe punishments and fines for purely religious offenses. This consistory had to work with the city magistrates in the governing of the city. The most infamous example of Calvin's strict rule was the burning, in 1553, of Michael Servetus, a Spanish physician and anti-trinitarian, who passed through Geneva in flight from the Catholic Inquisition in France.

In his discussion of the officers of the church and their duties in the *Institutes,* Calvin goes back to Paul's description in 1 Corinthians and Ephesians. According to Calvin, the only two authentic offices that still remain in the church are pastors and teachers. Pastors are to preach the gospel and administer the sacraments; they are also to discipline the community by admonishing and exhorting it to an upright life. Teachers are only concerned with the interpretation of the scripture to insure pure and sound doctrine among believers. Calvin also revived the office of permanent deacon to administer alms and to care for the poor and sick. His lists of qualifications for the various offices, the mode of selection, and ordination by the imposition of hands are all drawn from the New Testament. To keep the multitude from falling into any improprieties, the choice of a pastor is reserved to other pastors.

Calvin has an extensive discussion of the sacraments in the *Institutes* because they were a frequent point of controversy among all sides during the Reformation. As we have noted, they are an essential mark of the true church for Calvin, and his treatment of them is consistent with the rest of his theology. His definition of a sacrament is clear and straightforward.

> Now I think it will be a simple and appropriate definition if we say that it is an outward sign by which the Lord seals in our consciences the promises of his good will toward us to support the weakness of our faith; and we on our part testify our piety toward him, in his presence and that of angels, as well as before men. (IV.14.1)

The understanding of a sacrament as "a visible sign of a sacred thing" had been traditional since Augustine. Calvin's unique emphasis is on the role of the sacrament in sealing "in our consciences the promises of (God's) good will toward us to support the weakness of our faith." Because of his stress on God's promises and faith, Calvin insisted that the sacraments be celebrated in the words of scripture and that they be accompanied by preaching. Without faith the sacrament is ineffective. He does not accept the scholastic dictum that the sacraments offer grace *ex opere operato,* by virtue of their being performed correctly.

Like Luther, Calvin reduced the number of sacraments to those he found actually instituted by Christ in the New Testament. Because sacraments attest to the promises of God, humans cannot institute them. On the basis of this scriptural test, Calvin sees evidence for only two sacraments: baptism and the Lord's Supper. Baptism is "a kind of entrance into the Church, and an initiatory profession of faith." Despite his emphasis on faith in the reception of the sacraments, Calvin kept the baptism of infants. They should be baptized because, Calvin argues, "As the Lord does not exclude them from the hope of mercy but rather assures them of it, why should we refuse them the sign?" (IV.16.22).

The Lord's Supper was an extremely important sacrament for Calvin. In fact, he advocated frequent communion and would have preferred to celebrate the Lord's Supper each time the community gathered. For Calvin, under the visible signs of bread and wine, the Christian community is invisibly and spiritually nourished by Christ's body and blood. Note the contrast. Although the signs are visible, the union is invisible and spiritual. This spiritual food sustains and preserves the community in the life which God has begotten in it by his word.

But, for Calvin, the Lord's Supper does not create or effect union with God. This is done by the Spirit of God. The signs of the bread and wine show the believer the nourishment of Christ's body and blood that is available through the Spirit of God. For Calvin the sacrament of the Lord's Supper provides "a true and substantial communication of the body and blood of the Lord." But the manner in which this is understood to take place is spiritual. He, like Luther, rejected the scholastic term transubstantiation. The body of Christ is not "enclosed" in the bread. Calvin took quite literally the account in Acts 1 that at the ascension Jesus' body went to heaven where he now reigns at God's right hand. At the sacrament the Holy Spirit mysteriously unites the souls of the believers with Christ in heaven. United with Christ, we are also united with fellow communicants so that we cannot fail to love and care for them.

Calvin also differed from Luther in his understanding of Christ's presence in the elements of the bread and wine. Based on his belief in the ubiquity of the risen and glorified Christ, Luther believed that the eucharistic elements were both bread and wine as well as the true body and blood of Christ, whereas Calvin insisted that the bodily Christ is glorified in heaven. Through the Lord's Supper the soul may have spiritual communion with the risen Christ, but Christ does not descend bodily upon the altar.

The *Institutes* was very much Calvin's life's work; he completed the first edition, a short handbook of six chapters, in 1535, when he was only twenty-six years of age, but it went through several revisions and editions in both Latin and French during his lifetime. The final edition was published in 1559 and was eighty chapters in length. The selections from The Institutes are taken from the seventh American edition of the English translation of John Allen (1813), published by the Presbyterian Board of Christian Education, Philadelphia.

THE INSTITUTES OF THE CHRISTIAN RELIGION

BOOK I: ON THE KNOWLEDGE OF GOD THE CREATOR

6.1. Necessity of a scripture revelation.

Though the light which presents itself to all eyes, both in heaven and in earth, is more than sufficient to deprive the ingratitude of men of every excuse—since God, in order to involve all mankind in the same guilt, sets before them all, without exception, an exhibition of his majesty delineated in the creatures—yet we need another and better assistance properly to direct us to the Creator of the world. Therefore he has not unnecessarily added the light of his word to make himself known unto salvation, and has honored with this privilege those whom he intended to unite in a more close and familiar connection with himself. For, seeing the minds of all men to be agitated with unstable dispositions, when he had chosen the Jews as his peculiar flock he enclosed them as in a fold, that they might not wander after the vanities of other nations. And it is not without cause that he preserves us in the pure knowledge of himself by the same means; for otherwise they who seem comparatively to stand firm would soon fall. For, as persons who are old or whose eyes are by any means become dim, if you show them the most beautiful book, though they perceive something written but can scarcely read two words together, yet, by the assistance of spectacles, will begin to read distinctly—so the Scripture, collecting in our minds the otherwise confused notions of deity, dispels the darkness and gives us a clear view of the true God. This, then, is a singular favor, that in the instruction of the Church God not only uses mute teachers, but even opens his own sacred mouth; not only proclaims that some god ought to be worshiped, but at the same time pronounces himself to be the being to whom this worship is due; and it not only teaches the elect to raise their view to a deity, but also exhibits himself as the object of their contemplation. This method he has observed toward his Church from the beginning, beside those common lessons of instruction, to afford them also his word; which furnishes a more correct and certain criterion to distinguish him from all fictitious deities.

7.1 The Scriptures are above the Church.

But since we are not favored with daily oracles from heaven, and since it is only in the Scriptures that the Lord hath been pleased to preserve his truth in perpetual remembrance, it obtains the same complete credit and authority with believers, when they are satisfied of its divine origin, as if they heard the very words pronounced by God himself. . . . He (Paul) testifies that the Church is "built upon the foundation of the apostles and prophets." If the doctrine of the prophets and apostles be the foundation of the Church, it must have been certain, antecedently, to the existence of the Church.

7.5. To those inwardly taught by the Spirit, the Scripture is self-authenticating.

Let it be considered, then, as an undeniable truth that they who have been inwardly taught by the Spirit feel an entire acquiescence in the Scripture, and that it is self-authenticated, carrying with it its own evidence, and ought not to be made the subject of demonstration and arguments from reason; but it obtains the credit which it deserves with us by the testimony of the Spirit. For though it conciliate our reverence by its internal majesty, it never seriously affects us till it is confirmed by the Spirit in our hearts. Therefore, being illuminated by him, we now believe the divine original of the Scripture not from our own judgment or that of others, but we esteem the certainty that we have received it from God's own mouth by the ministry of men to be superior to that of any human judgment and equal to that of an intuitive perception of God himself in it. We seek not arguments or probabilities to support our judgment, but submit our judgments and understandings as to a thing concerning which it is impossible for us to judge; and that not like some persons who are in the habit of hastily embracing what they do not understand, which displeases them as soon as they examine it, but because we feel the firmest conviction that we hold an invincible truth; nor like those unhappy men who surrender their minds to superstitions, but because we perceive in it the undoubted energies of the divine power, by which we are attracted and inflamed to an understanding and voluntary obedience but with a vigor and efficacy superior to the power of any human will or knowledge.

BOOK II: ON THE KNOWLEDGE OF GOD THE REDEEMER IN CHRIST WHICH WAS REVEALED FIRST TO THE FATHERS UNDER THE LAW AND SINCE TO US IN THE GOSPEL

3.2. The total depravity of man.

I shall be content with citing a single passage, which however, will resemble a very lucid mirror, in which we may behold at full length the image of our nature. For the apostle (Paul), when he wishes to demolish the arrogance of mankind, does it by these testimonies: "There is none righteous, no, not one; there is none that understandeth, there is none that seeketh after God. They are all gone out of the way, they are together become unprofitable; there is none that doeth good, no, not one. Their throat is an open sepulcher; with their tongues they have used deceit; the poison of asps is under their lips; whose mouth is full of cursing and bitterness; their feet are swift to shed blood; destruction and misery are in their ways; there is no fear of God before their eyes" (Rom 3:10–19). In this terrible manner he inveighs, not against particular individuals, but against all the posterity of Adam.

BOOK III: ON THE MANNER OF RECEIVING THE GRACE OF CHRIST, THE BENEFITS WHICH WE DERIVE FROM IT, AND THE EFFECTS WHICH FOLLOW IT

2.6. Faith as knowledge of his will for us.

This, then is the true knowledge of Christ: to receive him as he is offered by the Father, that is, invested with his gospel; for, as he is appointed to be the object of our faith, so we cannot advance in the right way to him without the guidance of the gospel. The gospel certainly opens to us those treasures of grace without which Christ would profit us little. Thus Paul connects faith as an inseparable concomitant with doctrine where he says, "Ye have not so learned Christ; if so be that ye have been taught by him, as the truth is in Jesus (Eph 4:20,21). Yet I do not so far restrict faith to the gospel but that I admit Moses and the prophets to have delivered what was sufficient for its establishment; but because the gospel exhibits a fuller manifestation of Christ, it is justly styled by Paul "the words of faith and of good doctrine" (1 Tim 4:6). For the same reason, in another place he represents the law as abolished by the coming of faith (Gal 3:23–25), comprehending under this term the new kind of teaching by which Christ, since his appearance as our Master, has given a brighter display of the mercy of the Father and a more explicit testimony concerning our salvation. The more easy and convenient method for us will be to descend regularly from the genus to the species. In the first place, we must be apprised that faith has a perpetual relation to the word, and can no more be separated from it than the rays from the sun whence they proceed. Therefore God proclaims by Isaiah, "Hear, and your souls shall live" (Isa 55:3). . . . Lastly, it is not without reason that in Isaiah God distinguishes the children of the Church from strangers by this character: that they shall all be his disciples and be taught by him (Isa 54:13); for if this were a benefit common to all, why should he address himself to a few? Correspondent with this is the general use of the words "believers" and "disciples" as synonymous, by the evangelists on all occasions, and by Luke in particular very frequently in the Acts of the Apostles, in the ninth chapter of which he extends the latter epithet even to a woman. Wherefore, if faith decline in the smallest degree from this object, toward which it ought to be directed, it no longer retains its own nature but becomes an uncertain credulity and an erroneous excursion of the mind. The same divine word is the foundation by which faith is sustained and supported, from which it cannot be moved without an immediate downfall. Take away the word, then, and there will be no faith left. We are not here disputing whether the ministry of men be necessary to disseminate the word of God, by which faith is produced, which we shall discuss in another place; but we assert that the word itself, however it may be conveyed to us, is like a mirror in which faith may behold God. Whether, therefore, God in this instance uses the agency of men, or whether he operates solely by his own power, he always discovers himself by his word to those whom he designs to draw to himself (Rom 1:5). Whence Paul defines faith as an obedience rendered to the gospel, and praises the service of faith (Phil 2:17). For the apprehension of faith is not confined to our knowing that there is a God, but chiefly consists in our understanding what is his disposition toward us. For it is not of so much importance to us to know what he is in himself as what he is willing to be to us. We find, therefore that faith is a knowledge of the will of God respecting us, received from his word. And the foundation of this is a previous persuasion of the divine veracity, any doubt of which being entertained in the mind, the authority of the word will be dubious and weak, or rather it will be of no authority at all. Nor is it sufficient to believe that the veracity of God is incapable of deception or falsehood, unless you also admit, as beyond all doubt, that whatever proceeds from him is sacred and inviolable truth.

2.28. Faith does not secure for us worldly comfort but assures us of God's fatherly love.

Now in the divine benevolence, which is affirmed to be the object of faith, we apprehend the possession of salvation and everlasting life to be obtained. For if no good can be wanting when God is propitious, we have a sufficient certainty of salvation when he himself assures us of his love. "O God, cause thy face to shine, and we shall be saved" (Ps 80:3), says the Psalmist. Hence the Scriptures represent this as the sum of our salvation: that he has "abolished" all "enmity" (Eph 2:14,15) and received us into his favor. In which they imply that, since God is reconciled to us, there remains no danger, but that all things will prosper with us. Wherefore faith, having apprehended the love of God, has promises for the present life and the life to come, and solid assurance of all blessings; but it is such an assurance as may be derived from the divine word. For faith certainly promises itself neither longevity nor honor nor wealth in the present state—since the Lord has not been pleased to appoint any of these things for us—but is contented with this assurance: that whatever we may want of the conveniences or necessaries of this life, yet God will never leave us. But its principal security consists in an expectation of the future life, which is placed beyond all doubt by the word of God. For whatever miseries and calamities may on earth await those who are the objects of the love of God, they cannot prevent the divine benevolence from being a source of complete felicity.

6.3. Christ our example.

As a further incitement to us, it shows that as God the Father has reconciled us to himself in Christ, so he has exhibited to us in him a pattern to which it is his will that we should be conformed. Now let those who are of the opinion that the philosophers have the only just and orderly systems of moral philosophy show me, in any of their works, a more excellent economy than that which I have stated. When they intend to exhort us to the sublimest virtue, they advance no argument but that we ought to live agreeably to nature; but the Scripture deduces its exhortation from the true source when it not only enjoins us to refer our life to God the author of it, to whom it belongs, but, after having taught us that we are degenerated from the original state in which we were created, adds that Christ, by whom we have been reconciled to God is proposed to us as an example, whose character we should exhibit in our lives.

10.6. The Christian in his vocation.

Lastly, it is to be remarked that the Lord commands every one of us, in all the actions of life, to regard his vocation. For he knows with what great inquietude the human mind is inflamed, with what desultory levity it is hurried hither and thither, and how insatiable is its ambition to grasp different things at once. Therefore, to prevent universal confusion being produced by our folly and temerity, he has appointed to all their particular duties in different spheres of life. And that no one might rashly transgress the limits prescribed, he has styled such spheres of life "vocations," or "callings." Every individual's line of life, therefore, is, as it were, a post assigned him by the Lord, that he may not wander about in uncertainty all his days. And so necessary is this distinction that in his sight all our actions are estimated according to it, and often very differently from the sentence of human reason and philosophy. There is no exploit esteemed more honorable, even among philosophers, than to deliver our country from tyranny; but the voice of the celestial Judge

openly condemns the private man who lays violent hands on a tyrant. . . . It is sufficient if we know that the principle and foundation of right conduct in every case is the vocation of the Lord, and that he who disregards it will never keep the right way in the duties of his station. He may sometimes, perhaps, achieve something apparently laudable; but however it may appear in the eyes of men, it will be rejected at the throne of God; besides which, there will be no consistency between the various parts of his life. Our life, therefore, will then be best regulated when it is directed to this mark, since no will will be impelled by his own temerity to attempt more than is compatible with his calling, because he will know that it is unlawful to transgress the bounds assigned him. He that is in obscurity will lead a private life without discontent so as not to desert the station in which God has placed him. It will also be no small alleviation of his cares, labors, troubles, and other burdens when a man knows that in all these things he has God for his guide. The magistrate will execute his office with greater pleasure, the father of a family will confine himself to his duty with more satisfaction, and all, in their respective spheres of life, will bear and surmount the inconveniencies, cares, disappointments, and anxieties which befall them, when they shall be persuaded that every individual has his burden laid upon him by God. Hence also will arise peculiar consolation, since there will be no employment so mean and sordid (provided we follow our vocation) as not to appear truly respectable and be deemed highly important in the sight of God.

11.21. Summary statement on justification.

Now let us examine the truth of what has been asserted in the definition—that the righteousness of faith is reconciliation with God which consists solely in remission of sins. We must always return to this axiom: that the divine wrath remains on all men as long as they continue to be sinners. This Isaiah has beautifully expressed in the following words: "The Lord's hand is not shortened, that it cannot save; neither is his ear heavy, that it cannot hear; but your iniquities have separated between you and your God, and your sins have hid his face from you, that he will not hear" (Isa 59:1,2). We are informed that sin makes a division between man and God and turns the divine countenance away from the sinner. Nor can it be otherwise, because it is incompatible with his righteousness to have any communion with sin. Hence the Apostle teaches that man is an enemy to God till he be reconciled to him through Christ (Rom 5:8–10). Whom, therefore, the Lord receives into fellowship, him he is said to justify, because he cannot receive anyone into fellowship with himself without making him from a sinner to be a righteous person. This, we add, is accomplished by the remission of sins. For if they whom the Lord has reconciled to himself be judged according to their works, they will still be found actually sinners, who, notwithstanding, must be absolved and free from sin. It appears, then, that those whom God receives are made righteous no otherwise than as they are purified by being cleansed from all their defilement by the remission of their sins, so that such a righteousness may, in one word, be denominated a remission of sins.

19.2. Christian liberty.

Christian liberty, according to my judgment, consists of three parts. The first part is, that the consciences of believers, when seeking an assurance of their justification before God, should raise themselves above the law, and forget all righteousness of the law. For since the law, as we have elsewhere demonstrated, leaves no man righteous, either we must be excluded from all hope of justification, or it is necessary for us to be delivered from it, and that so completely as not to have any dependence on works. For he who imagines,

that in order to obtain righteousness he must produce any works, however small, can fix no limit or boundary, but renders himself a debtor to the whole law. Avoiding, therefore all mention of the law, and dismissing all thought of our own works, in reference to justification, we must embrace the divine mercy alone, and turning our eyes from ourselves, fix them solely on Christ. For the question is, not how we can be righteous, but how, though unrighteous and unworthy, we can be considered as righteous. And the conscience that desires to attain any certainty respecting this, must give no admission to the law. Nor will this authorize any one to conclude, that the law is of no use to believers, whom it still continues to instruct and exhort, and to stimulate to duty, although it has no place in their consciences before the tribunal of God. For these two things, being very different, require to be properly and carefully distinguished by us. The whole life of Christians ought to be an exercise of piety, since they are called to sanctification. It is the office of the law to remind them of their duty, and thereby to excite them to the pursuit of holiness and integrity. But when their consciences are solicitous how God may be propitiated, what answer they shall make, and on what they shall rest their confidence, if called to his tribunal, there must then be no consideration of the requisitions of the law, but Christ alone must be proposed for righteousness, who exceeds all the perfection of the law.

21.5. The eternal decree of God.

Predestination, by which God adopts some to the hope of life and adjudges others to eternal death, no one, desirous of the credit of piety, dares absolutely to deny. But it is involved in many cavils, especially by those who make foreknowledge the cause of it. We maintain that both belong to God; but it is preposterous to represent one as dependent on the other. When we attribute foreknowledge to God, we mean that all things have ever been, and perpetually remain, before his eyes, so that to his knowledge nothing is future or past, but all things are present; and present in such a manner that he does not merely conceive of them from ideas formed in his mind, as things remembered by us appear present to our minds, but really beholds and sees them as if actually placed before him. And this foreknowledge extends to the whole world and to all the creatures. Predestination we call the eternal decree of God by which he has determined in himself what he would have to become of every individual of mankind. For they are not all created with a similar destiny, but eternal life is foreordained for some and eternal damnation for others. Every man, therefore, being created for one or the other of these ends, we say he is predestined either to life or to death. This God has not only testified in particular persons, but has given a specimen of it in the whole posterity of Abraham, which should evidently show the future condition of every nation to depend upon his decision. "When the Most High divided the nations, when he separated the sons of Adam, the Lord's portion was his people; Jacob was the lot of his inheritance" (Deut 32:8–9). The separation is before the eyes of all: in the person of Abraham, as in the dry trunk of a tree, one people is peculiarly chosen to the rejection of others; no reason for this appears, except that Moses, to deprive their posterity of all occasion of glorying, teaches them that their exaltation is wholly from God's gratuitous love. . . .

23.14. Man's will cannot resist God's. We desire every man's salvation and leave the result to God.

And yet, being peculiarly desirous of edification, that holy man regulates his mode of teaching the truth so that offense may as far as possible be prudently avoided. For he suggests that whatever is asserted with truth may also be delivered in a suitable manner. If

anyone address the people in such a way as this: "If you believe not, it is because you are by a divine decree already destined to destruction"—he not only cherishes slothfulness, but even encourages wickedness. If anyone extend the declaration to the future—that they who hear will never believe because they are reprobated—this would be rather imprecation than instruction. Such persons, therefore, as foolish teachers or inauspicious, ominous prophets Augustine charges to depart from the Church (*De dono perseverantiae* XXII). In another place, indeed, he justly maintains "that a man then profits by correction when he, who causes whom he pleases to profit even without correction, compassionates and assists. But why some in one way and some in another? Far be it from us to ascribed the choice to the clay instead of the potter" (*De correptione et gratia* V.8). . . . "It is beyond all doubt, therefore, that the will of God, who has done whatever he has pleased in heaven and in earth, and who has done even things that are yet future, cannot possibly be resisted by the will of man so as to prevent the execution of his purposes since he controls the wills of men according to his pleasure" (*De correptione et gratia* XIV.43). Again: "When he designs to bring men to himself, does he bind them by corporeal bonds? He acts inwardly; he inwardly seizes their hearts; he inwardly moves their hearts and draws them by their wills, which he has wrought in them." But he immediately subjoins, what must by no means be omitted, "That because we know not who belongs, or does not belong, to the number of the predestinated, it becomes us affectionately to desire the salvation of all. The consequence will be that whomsoever we meet we shall endeavor to make him a partaker of peace. But our peace shall rest upon the sons of peace. On our part, therefore, salutary and severe reproof, like a medicine, must be administered to all, that they may neither perish themselves nor destroy others; but it will be the province of God to render it useful to them who he had foreknown and predestinated" (*De correptione et gratia* XVI.49).

BOOK IV: ON THE EXTERNAL MEANS OR AIDS BY WHICH GOD CALLS US INTO COMMUNION WITH CHRIST AND RESTRAINS US IN IT

1.7. The Church and the elect.

Sometimes when they (the Scriptures) mention the Church, they intend that which is really such in the sight of God, into which none are received but those who by adoption and grace are the children of God, and by the sanctification of the Spirit are the true members of Christ. And then it comprehends not only the saints at any one time resident on earth, but all the elect who have lived from the beginning of the world. But the word Church is also used in the Scriptures to designate the whole multitude, dispersed all over the world, who profess to worship one God and Jesus Christ, who are initiated into his faith by baptism, who testify their unity in true doctrine and charity by a participation of the sacred supper, who consent to the word of the Lord, and preserve the ministry which Christ has instituted for the purpose of preaching it. In this Church are included many hypocrites. . . . On the other hand, as he (God) saw it to be in some measure requisite that we should know who ought to be considered as his children, he has in this respect accommodated himself to our capacity. . . . we ought to acknowledge as members of the Church all those who by a confession of faith, an exemplary life, and participation of the sacraments, profess the same God and Christ with ourselves. . . .

1.9. The visible Church is marked by preaching of word and sacraments.

Hence the visible Church rises conspicuous to our view. For wherever we find the word of

God purely preached and heard, and the sacraments administered according to the institution of Christ, there, it is not to be doubted, is a Church of God; for his promise can never deceive—"where two or three are gathered together in my name, there am I in the midst of them" (Matt 18:20).

3.4. The officers of the Church and their duties.

Those who preside over the government of the Church, according to the institution of Christ, are named by Paul, first, "apostles"; secondly, "prophets"; thirdly, "evangelists"; fourthly, "pastors"; lastly, "teachers" (Eph 4:11). Of these, only the two last sustain an ordinary office in the Church: the others were such as the Lord raised up at the commencement of his kingdom, and such as he still raises up on particular occasions, when required by the necessity of the times. . . . Though I do not deny, that, even since that period, God has sometimes raised up apostles or evangelists in their stead, as he has done in our own time. For there was a necessity for such persons to recover the Church from the defection of Antichrist. Nevertheless, I call this an extraordinary office, because it has no place in well-constituted Churches. Next follow "pastors" and "teachers," who are always indispensable to the Church. The difference between them I apprehend to be this—that teachers have no official concern with the discipline, or the administration of the sacraments, or with the admonitions and exhortations, but only with the interpretation of the Scripture, that pure and sound doctrine may be retained among believers; whereas the pastoral office includes all these things.

14.1. Definition of a sacrament.

Now I think it will be a simple and appropriate definition if we say that it (a sacrament) is an outward sign by which the Lord seals in our consciences the promises of his good will toward us to support the weakness of our faith; and we on our part testify our piety toward him, in his presence and that of angels, as well as before men. It may, however, be more briefly defined, in other words, by calling it a testimony of the grace of God toward us, confirmed by an outward sign, with a reciprocal attestation of our piety toward him. Whichever of these definitions be chosen, it conveys exactly the same meaning as that of Augustine, which states a sacrament to be "a visible sign of a sacred thing," or "a visible form of invisible grace"; but it expresses the thing itself with more clearness and precision, for as his conciseness leaves some obscurity, by which many inexperienced persons may be misled, I have endeavored to render the subject plainer by more words, that no room might be left for any doubt.

17.1. A visible sign of that by which our souls are fed.

After God has once received us into his family—and not only so as to admit us among his servants but to number us with his children—in order to fulfill the part of a most excellent father, solicitous for his offspring, he also undertakes to sustain and nourish us as long as we live; and not content with this, he has been pleased to give us a pledge as a further assurance of this never-ceasing liberality. For this purpose, therefore, by the hand of his only begotten Son, he has favored his Church with another sacrament, a spiritual banquet, in which Christ testifies himself to be the bread of life, to feed our souls for a true and blessed immortality. . . . In the first place, the signs are bread and wine, which represent to us the invisible nourishment which we receive from the body and blood of Christ. For as in baptism God regenerates us, incorporates us into the society of his Church, and makes us his children by adoption, so we have said that he acts toward us the part of a provident father of a family in constantly supplying us with food, to sustain and preserve us in that life to which he has begotten us by his word. Now the only food of our souls is Christ; and to him, therefore, our heavenly Father invites us, that, being refreshed by a participation of him, we may gain fresh vigor from day to day till we arrive at the heavenly immortality. And because this mystery of the secret union of Christ with believers is incomprehensible by nature, he exhibits a figure and image of it in visible signs peculiarly adapted to our feeble capacity; and, as it were, by giving tokens and pledges, renders it equally as certain to us as if we behold it with our eyes; for the dullest minds understand this very familiar similitude, that your souls are nourished by Christ just as the life of the body is supported by bread and wine. We see, then, for what end this mystical benediction is designed—namely, to assure us that the body of the Lord was once offered as a sacrifice for us, so that we may now feed upon it, and, feeding on it, may experience within us the efficacy of that one sacrifice; and that his blood was once shed for us, so that it is our perpetual drink. And this is the import of the words of the promise annexed to it: "Take, eat; this is my body, which is given for you." The body, therefore, which was once offered for our salvation, we are commanded to take and eat, that seeing ourselves made partakers of it, we may certainly conclude that the virtue of that life-giving death will be efficacious within us. Hence, also, he calls the cup "the new testament," or rather covenant, in his blood. For the covenant which he once ratified with his blood he in some measure renews, or rather continues, as far as related to the confirmation of our faith whenever he presents us that sacred blood to drink.

17.32. The manner of this is a mystery of faith.

If anyone inquire of me respecting the manner, I shall not be ashamed to acknowledge that it is a mystery too sublime for me to be able to express, or even to comprehend; and, to be still more explicit, I rather experience it than understand it. Here, therefore, without any controversy, I embrace the truth of God, on which I can safely rely. He pronounces his flesh to be the food and his blood the drink of my soul. I offer him my soul to be nourished with such aliment. In his sacred supper he commands me, under the symbols of bread and wine, to take and eat and drink his body and blood. I doubt not that he truly presents and that I receive them. Only I reject the absurdities which appear to be either degrading to his majesty or inconsistent with the reality of his human nature and are at the same time repugnant to the word of God, which informs us that Christ has been received into the glory of the celestial kingdom where he is exalted above every condition of the world, and which is equally careful to attribute to his human nature the properties of real humanity. Nor ought this to seem incredible or unreasonable, because, as the kingdom of Christ is wholly spiritual, so his communications with his Church are not at all to be regulated by the order of the present world; or, to use the words of Augustine, "This mystery, as well as others, is celebrated by man, but in a divine manner; it is administered on earth, but in a heavenly manner" (These words have not been found in Augustine). The presence of Christ's body, I say, is such as the nature of the sacrament requires, where we affirm that it appears with so much virtue and efficacy as not only to afford our minds an undoubted confidence of eternal life, but also to give us an assurance of the resurrection and immortality of our bodies. For they are vivified by his immortal flesh, and in some degree participate in his immortality. If any person be not yet satisfied, I would request him to consider that we are now treating of a sacrament, every part of which ought to be referred to faith. Now we

feed our faith by this participation of the body of Christ which we have mentioned as fully as they do who bring him down from heaven. At the same time, I candidly confess that I reject that mixture of the flesh of Christ with our souls, or that transfusion of it into us, which they teach, because it is sufficient for us that Christ inspires life into our souls from the substance of his flesh, and even infuses his own life into us, though his flesh never actually enters into us. . . .

18.19. The two sacraments are sufficient, and none are to be added.

The readers may now see, collected into a brief summary, almost everything that I have thought important to be known respecting these two sacraments, the use of which has been enjoined on the Christian Church from the commencement of the New Testament until the end of time—that is to say, baptism, to be a kind of entrance into the Church and an initiatory profession of faith, and the Lord's supper, to be a continual nourishment with which Christ spiritually feeds his family of believers. Wherefore, as there is but "one God, one Christ, one faith," one Church, the body of Christ, so there is only "one baptism" and that is never repeated; but the supper is frequently distributed, that those who have once been admitted into the Church may understand that they are continually nourished by Christ. Besides these two, as no other sacrament has been instituted by God, so no other ought to be acknowledged by the Church of believers. For it is not left to the will of man to institute new sacraments will be easily understood if we remember what has been already very plainly stated—that sacraments are appointed by God for the purpose of instructing us respecting some promise of his, and assuring us of his good will toward us— and if we also consider that no one has been the counselor of God, capable of affording us any certainty respecting his will or furnishing us any assurance of his disposition toward us, what he chooses to give or to deny us. Hence it follows that no one can institute a sign to be a testimony respecting any determination or promise of his; he alone can furnish us a testimony respecting himself by giving a sign. I will express myself in terms more concise, and perhaps more homely, but more explicit—that there can be no sacrament unaccompanied with a promise of salvation. All mankind, collected in one assembly, can promise us nothing respecting our salvation. Therefore they can never institute or establish a sacrament.

THE ENGLISH REFORMATION

The English Reformation was of a quite different character from the continental reform movements associated with Luther, Zwingli, and Calvin. Although there had been pressures for church reform and challenges to Catholic doctrine in England since the days of Wyclif (c. 1330–1384), the catalyst for the break with Rome was a political question, rather than some burning theological issue, like justification by faith. The English Reformation begins as a schism in which the king, Henry VIII (r. 1509–1547), rejects papal authority and declares himself the supreme head of the Church in England.

The cause was the so-called "king's affair." Henry VIII desired a papal annulment of his marriage with Catherine of Aragon which had failed to produce a male heir for the Tudor line. Despite several pregnancies, Catherine had only produced one child who had survived infancy, a daughter Mary. The Tudors had only recently succeeded to the throne of England after a bitter civil war, the so-called War of the Roses, and Henry was convinced that political stability demanded a male heir who would be able to maintain the dynastic line. He was apparently genuinely troubled about the validity of his marriage to Catherine; Pope Julius II had had to grant a special dispensation for the marriage because she had been previously married to his brother Arthur as part of a political alliance between Ferdinand and Isabella of Spain and his father Henry VII. Henry convinced himself that the failure of his marriage to produce a male heir was a sign of its being cursed by God. But Pope Clement VII refused to grant the annulment; he was loath to rule that a papal predecessor had acted invalidly, and he was under extreme pressure from Catherine's nephew, Emperor Charles V, whose troops had rioted in Rome in 1527.

Having failed to secure an annulment through the papacy, Henry, with the help of Thomas Cromwell and Thomas Cranmer, pushed through the so-called Reformation Parliament (1529–1536) a flood of legislation which gradually separated England from Rome, annulled the marriage between Catherine and Henry, disinherited Mary, made Anne Boleyn, whom Henry had wed in 1533, queen, and recognized their daughter Elizabeth as heiress to the throne. The legislation culminated with the Supremacy Act of 1534 which confirmed the king and his successors as "the only supreme head on earth of the Church of England, called *Anglicana Ecclesia*." In the summer of 1535 Bishop John Fisher of Rochester and Sir Thomas More, the great humanist scholar and former chancellor, were executed for failing to swear to the supremacy. Between 1536 and 1539 Henry also dissolved the wealthy monasteries and gave much of the proceeds to Tudor nobility and gentry, though some was used to found six new dioceses.

Despite his break with Rome and suppression of the monasteries, Henry remained traditionally Catholic in his religious belief, and Roman teaching and liturgical practice were maintained during his reign. He did allow English Bibles to be placed in the churches, but *The Ten Articles,* published in 1536, and *The Six Articles,* passed by Parliament in 1539 at Henry's bidding, limited the spread of Protestantism and maintained traditional Catholic doctrine and practices like transubstantiation, communion in one kind, enforced clerical celibacy, monastic vows, private masses and auricular confession.

During the brief reign of Edward VI (1547–1553), Henry's son by his third wife Jane Seymour, the way was open for reformers, especially Thomas Cranmer the scholarly archbishop of Canterbury, to move England in the direction of the continental Reformation. Edward was only nine years old when he began his reign, and during the early years he was under the direction of Protector Somerset, a friend of Cranmer and a supporter of Lutheran reform teachings. In 1547 Edward's *Injunctions* required regular sermons against the pope's authority and in favor of royal supremacy in the church. This was followed by the recognition of clerical marriages in 1548. The most significant reform during Edward's reign was the change of the liturgy into English through the Acts of Uniformity in 1549 and 1552 requiring the use of the First and then Second Book of Common Prayer. These were largely the work of Thomas Cranmer, and they represent the greatest achievement of the English Reformation. Although he was working with diverse elements from traditional medieval Catholic liturgy and the recent innovations of continental Protestant groups, Cranmer was able to transform them into an elegant, but austere, English which was destined to be revered by the Anglican Church.

The Book of Common Prayer contains the daily offices for morning and evening prayer, the forms for the administration of the sacraments, the psalter, and, in the second edition, the rites for consecrating bishops, priests, and deacons. The first edition was an attempt to compromise between Roman Catholic and Lutheran doctrines, and it pleased no one. The second was published under the Duke of Northumberland as Protector and reflects the influence of the Swiss reformers, Zwingli and Calvin. The differences can be seen most clearly in the sentence for receiving holy communion. Whereas the 1549 edition reads: "The Body of our Lord Jesus Christ which was given for thee, preserve thy body and soul unto everlasting life," the 1552 edition reads: "Take and eat this in remembrance that Christ died for thee, and feed on him in thy heart by faith, with thanksgiving."

The course of the Reformation in England illustrates the principle used to settle the Lutheran question in Germany at the Peace of Augsburg: that is, that the ruler determines the religion of the territory. Under Henry VIII, England was outwardly Catholic in belief and practice but in schism from the pope over "the king's affair." Under Edward VI at the direction of Cranmer, Somerset, and Northumberland, England moved in the direction of Protestantism. When Mary Tudor, the Catholic daughter of Henry and Catherine of Aragon, succeeded to the throne, England was temporarily brought back to Roman Catholicism.

Mary ascended the throne in 1553 and immediately began to restore England to the Catholic faith and the conditions that prevailed before 1529. Parliament repealed all the religious legislation of Edward's reign concerning the Book of Common Prayer, uniformity, and married clergy. Two thousand clergy were rejected because they were married. The Catholic Latin mass was brought back, and some of the monasteries were reestablished. In 1554 Mary sealed an alliance with Catholic Spain by marrying Philip II, the son of Charles V, who was eleven years younger. The marriage proved to be a poor match, and was never popular in England. At the end of the same year Cardinal Reginald Pole, a papal legate to the Council of Trent, returned to England as the pope's legate, formally absolved Parliament from schism, and presided over synods of the Convocations of the clergy.

At first Mary showed leniency to her Protestant subjects, though she forbade their religion. But after the formal return to union with Rome in 1555, the persecutions of the Protestant heretics began. In the next three and half years nearly three hundred Protestants were burned in the famous fires of Smithfield, earning Mary the Protestant epithet, "Bloody Mary." One of the saddest cases was that of Thomas Cranmer, the Archbishop of Canterbury for twenty years under Henry and Edward. In February, 1556, he submitted to the Catholic Church and the pope and denounced the doctrines of Luther and Zwingli. But on March 18 when he was to be burned, he revoked his recantations, saying he had signed them in the hope of saving his life, and he held his right hand, with which he had signed his recantations, in the flames.

The spectacle of martyrs like Cranmer helped to give strength to the Protestant cause. The martyrs of Mary's persecutions were not wild, fringe heretics. Cranmer was a scholarly man of principle who believed in the royal supremacy and was now dying only because England had a different government. Under Henry and Edward, with the suppression of the monasteries and the changes in liturgy, the Protestant cause had been identified with robbery, destruction of property, irreverence, and even religious anarchy. Now it was identified with virtue, honesty, English loyalty, and resistance to the interference of Rome in English affairs.

When Mary died in 1558, she was succeeded by her half-sister Elizabeth, the Protestant daughter of Henry and Ann Boleyn. Elizabeth (1558–1603) was a gifted ruler who was blessed with a long reign. She was a *politique* who was determined to settle the religious question and to spare England the religious war that was beginning to ravage the continent. By 1558, England was divided between those who were loyal to the old Catholic faith, convinced reformers of various Protestant persuasions, and those who were indifferent to the religious squabbles and simply wanted a settlement. Elizabeth chose to steer a "middle way" of compromise between Protestantism and Roman Catholicism.

This via media is best illustrated by the *Thirty-Nine Articles,* first published in 1563 and given their final form in 1571. They are not really a creed, but short summaries of dogmatic tenets concerning points of controversy during the Reformation. In general, they reflect a broadly defined Protestant doctrine, with a centralized episcopal system of church government, with the queen having chief "government of all estates," including ecclesiastical and civil. The ritual was to be in English in the form of a slightly revised version of the *Book of Common Prayer*. The goal was to "comprehend" as many as possible into the church by compromise. Points of universal agreement were stressed; points of disagreement left as vague as possible.

The Catholic or ecumenical elements of the *Articles* are evident in the beginning articles on the Trinity, the incarnation, descent into hell, resurrection, Holy Ghost (I–V), and the affirmation of the ancient creeds (VIII). All the major Christian groups share these beliefs, and today they form a basis for ecumenical dialogue.

On the question of religious authority, the *Articles* attempt to reconcile the positions of the reformers who insist upon scripture as the sole authority and Roman Catholicism which places the church above scripture. Like the reformers, Article VI insists "Holy Scripture containeth all things necessary to salvation" and follows the shorter list of canonical Old Testament books accepted by Luther and Calvin, with the so-called apocrypha recommended "for example of life and instruction of manners." But Article XX begins with a statement that seems to affirm the Catholic position: "The Church hath power to decree Rites or ceremonies, and authority in Controversies of Faith." In an attempt to balance these two, Article XX continues to say:

> And yet it is not lawful for the Church to ordain any thing that is contrary to God's Word written, neither may it so expound one place of Scripture, that it be repugnant to another. Wherefore, although the Church be a witness and a keeper of holy Writ, yet, as it ought not to decree any thing against the same, so besides the same ought it not to enforce any thing to be believed for necessity of Salvation.

The Article does not make it clear how disputed interpretations of passages are to be settled. It seems to assume that the church will recognize when a matter of controversy is contrary to scripture.

On the crucial question of justification, the *Thirty Nine Articles* follow Luther and the other reformers in insisting upon justification by faith, but they do have a more positive statement of the role of good works after justification. Articles IX and X reject Pelagianism and insist, with Augustine, that original sin has so wounded man "that he cannot turn and prepare himself, by his own natural strength and good works, to faith, and calling upon God." Therefore, "we are accounted righteous before God, only for the merit of our Lord and Saviour Jesus Christ by Faith, and not for our own works or deservings." Having said this, Article XII insists that "Good Works . . . are the fruits of Faith, and follow after Justification." Although they "cannot put away our sins," they are "pleasing and acceptable to God in Christ, and do spring out necessarily of a true and lively Faith." As corollaries to justification by faith and the authority of scripture, the *Articles* reject works of supererogation (XIV), purgatory, indulgences, relics, and invocation of the saints (XXII) as having no warrant in scripture and being "repugnant to the Word of God."

Calvin's doctrines of predestination and election are clearly evident in Article XVII, but they are softened by concentrating on the positive message for the elect and omitting any statement of predestination to damnation. In fact, predestination is to be preached only to "godly persons" who "feel in themselves the working of the Spirit of Christ. . . ." It is not meant "for curious and carnal persons, lacking the spirit of Christ." For them it would only be the occasion for the devil to thrust them into desperation or unclean living.

The treatment of the church and sacraments in the *Thirty-Nine Articles* is very close to that found in Calvin's *Institutes*. "The visible Church of Christ" is defined as "a congregation of faithful men, in which the pure Word of God is preached, and the Sacraments be duly ministered according to Christ's ordinance in all those things that of necessity are requisite to the same." There are only two sacraments ordained by Christ in the gospel: baptism and the Lord's Supper. The other five commonly called sacraments in the Roman church, confirmation, penance, orders, matrimony, and extreme unction are maintained as rites in the church but are understood as not having "any visible sign or ceremony ordained of God." The definition of the sacraments contains elements of both Reformed and Catholic doctrine. With Calvin they are understood as "certain sure witnesses" of "God's good will towards us," but, in conformity to Catholic doctrine, they are also called "effectual signs of grace." Their mode of action is understood in the Calvinist sense; they work "invisibly" to quicken, "strengthen and confirm our Faith in him (Christ)." Although the faith of the recipient is stressed, unworthy ministers do not hinder the effect of the sacraments because they are done in Christ's name (XXVI).

Article XXVII on the Lord's Supper affirms belief in the real presence of Christ: "The Bread which we break is a partaking of the Body of Christ; and likewise the cup of Blessing is a partaking of the Blood of Christ." But, with Luther, it rejects the term transubstantiation as unbiblical and insists, with Calvin, that "the Body of Christ is given, taken, and eaten, in the Supper, only after an heavenly and spiritual manner." The means by which it is received is "Faith." "The Wicked" who eat without faith do not partake of Christ, but to "their condemnation." As with all the Protestant groups, the cup is not to be denied to the lay people, and Roman Catholic traditions of reserving, carrying, lifting up, or worshipping the sacrament are rejected as not being in conformity with "Christ's ordinance." Finally, Article XXXI follows Luther in affirming that Christ made one sacrifice for redemption from sin, and that masses are not new "sacrifices."

Articles XXXVI–XXXIX contain the distinctively Anglican elements. The offices of archbishop, bishop, priest, and deacon are maintained with the consecration and ordination ceremonies from the time of Edward VI. The queen has chief power in both ecclesiastical and civil matters in England and her dominions, but she does not have the power to minister "either of God's Word, or of the Sacraments." To clarify that the break with Rome is definitive, Article XXXVII adds: "The Bishop of Rome hath no jurisdiction in this Realm of England." Articles XXXVIII and XXXIX reject Anabaptist practices of sharing goods in common and refusing to swear oaths.

ANGLICAN ARTICLES OF RELIGION

ARTICLES AGREED UPON BY THE ARCHBISHOPS AND BISHOPS OF BOTH PROVINCES AND THE WHOLE CLERGY IN THE CONVOCATION HOLDEN AT LONDON IN THE YEAR 1562 FOR THE AVOIDING OF DIVERSITIES OF OPINIONS AND FOR THE ESTABLISHING OF CONSENT TOUCHING TRUE RELIGION.

VI. OF THE SUFFICIENCY OF THE HOLY SCRIPTURES FOR SALVATION

Holy Scripture containeth all things necessary to salvation: so that whatsoever is not read therein, nor may be proved thereby, is not to be required of any man, that it should be believed as an article of the Faith, or be thought requisite or necessary to salvation. In the name of the holy Scripture we do understand those Canonical Books of the Old and New Testament, of whose authority was never any doubt in the Church.

IX. OF ORIGINAL OR BIRTH-SIN

Original Sin standeth not in the following of *Adam,* (as the *Pelagians* do vainly talk) but it is the fault and corruption of the Nature of every man, that naturally is ingendered of the offspring of *Adam;* whereby man is very far gone from original righteousness, and is of his own nature inclined to evil, so that the flesh lusteth always contrary to the spirit; and therefore in every person born into this world, it deserveth God's wrath and damnation. And this infection of nature doth remain, yea in them that are regenerated; whereby the lust of the flesh called in the Greek, Φρόνημα σαρκός, which some do expound the wisdom, some sensuality, some the affection, some the desire, of the flesh, is not subject to the law of God. And although there is no condemnation for them that believe and are baptized, yet the apostle doth confess, that concupiscence and lust hath of itself the nature of sin.

X. OF FREE WILL

The condition of Man after the fall of *Adam* is such, that he cannot turn and prepare himself, by his own natural strength and good works, to faith, and calling upon God: Wherefore we have no power to do good works pleasant and acceptable to God, without the grace of God by Christ preventing us, that we may have a good will, and working with us, when he have that good will.

XI. OF THE JUSTIFICATION OF MAN

We are accounted righteous before God, only for the merit of our Lord and Saviour Jesus Christ by Faith, and not for our own works or deservings: Wherefore, that we are justified by Faith only is a most wholesome doctrine, and very full of comfort, as more largely is expressed in the Homily of Justification.

XII. OF GOOD WORKS

Albeit that Good Works, which are the fruits of Faith, and follow after Justification, cannot put away our sins, and endure the severity of God's Judgment; yet are they pleasing and acceptable to God in Christ, and do spring out necessarily of a true and lively Faith; insomuch that by them a lively Faith may be as evidently known as a tree discerned by the fruit.

XIII. OF WORKS BEFORE JUSTIFICATION

Works done before the grace of Christ, and the Inspiration of his Spirit, are not pleasant to God, forasmuch as they spring not of faith in Jesus Christ, neither do they make men meet to receive grace, or (as the School-authors say) deserve grace of congruity: yea rather, for that they are not done as God hath willed and commanded them to be done, we doubt not but they have the nature of sin.

XIV. OF WORKS OF SUPEREROGATION

Voluntary Works besides, over, and above, God's Commandments, which they call Works of supererogation, cannot be taught without arrogancy and impiety: for by them men do declare, that they do not only render unto God as much as they are bound to do, but that they do more for his sake, than of bounden duty is required: whereas Christ saith plainly, When ye have done all that are commanded to you, say, We are unprofitable servants.

XVI. OF SIN AFTER BAPTISM

Not every deadly sin willingly committed after Baptism is sin against the Holy Ghost, and unpardonable. Wherefore the grant of repentance is not to be denied to such as fall into sin after Baptism. After we have received the Holy Ghost, we may depart from grace given, and fall into sin, and by the grace of God we may arise again, and amend our lives. And therefore they are to be condemned, which say, they can no more sin as long as they live here, or deny the place of forgiveness to such as truly repent.

XVII. OF PREDESTINATION AND ELECTION

Predestination to Life is the everlasting purpose of God, whereby (before the foundations of the world were laid) he hath constantly decreed by his counsel secret to us, to deliver from curse and damnation those whom he hath chosen in Christ out of mankind, and to bring them by Christ to everlasting salvation, as vessels made to honour.

Wherefore, they which he endued with so excellent a benefit of God be called according to God's purpose by his Spirit working in due season: they through Grace obey the calling: they be justified freely: they be made sons of God by adoption: they be made like the image of his only-begotten Son Jesus Christ: they walk religiously in good works, and at length, by God's mercy, they attain to everlasting felicity.

As the godly consideration of Predestination, and our election in Christ, is full of sweet, pleasant, and unspeakable comfort to godly persons, and such as feel in themselves the working of the Spirit of Christ, mortifying the works of the flesh, and their earthly members, and drawing up their mind to high and heavenly things, as well because it doth greatly establish and confirm their faith of eternal Salvation to be enjoyed through Christ, as because it doth fervently kindle their love towards God: So, for curious and carnal persons, lacking the spirit of Christ, to have continually before their eyes the sentence of god's Predestination, is a most dangerous downfall, whereby the Devil doth thrust them either into desperation, or into wretchlessness of most unclean living, no less perilous than desperation.

Furthermore, we must receive God's promises in such wise, as they be generally set forth to us in holy Scripture: and, in our doings, that Will of God is to be followed, which we have expressly declared unto us in the Word of God.

XVIII. OF OBTAINING ETERNAL SALVATION ONLY BY THE NAME OF CHRIST

They also are to be had accursed that presume to say, That every man shall be saved by the Law or Sect which he professeth, so that he be diligent to frame his life according to that Law, and the light of Nature. For holy

Scripture doth set out unto us only the Name of Jesus Christ, whereby men must be saved.

XIX. OF THE CHURCH

The visible Church of Christ is a congregation of faithful men, in the which the pure Word of God is preached, and the Sacraments be duly ministered according to Christ's ordinance in all those things that of necessity are requisite to the same.

As the Church of *Jerusalem, Alexandria,* and *Antioch,* have erred; so also the Church of Rome hath erred, not only in their living and manner of Ceremonies, but also in matters of Faith.

XX. OF THE AUTHORITY OF THE CHURCH

The Church hath power to decree Rites or Ceremonies, and authority in Controversies of Faith: And yet it is not lawful for the Church to ordain any thing that is contrary to God's Word written, neither may it so expound one place of Scripture, that it be repugnant to another. Wherefore, although the Church be a witness and a keeper of holy Writ, yet, as it ought not to decree any thing against the same, so besides the same ought it not to enforce any thing to be believed for necessity of Salvation.

XXI. OF THE AUTHORITY OF THE COUNCILS

General Councils may not be gathered together without the commandment and will of Princes. And when they be gathered together, (forasmuch as they be an assembly of men, whereof all be not governed with the Spirit and Word of God) they may err, and sometimes have erred, even in things, pertaining unto God. Wherefore things ordained by them as necessary to salvation have neither strength nor authority, unless it may be declared that they be taken out of holy Scripture.

XXII. OF PURGATORY

The romish doctrine concerning Purgatory, Pardons, Worshipping, and Adoration, as well of Images of Reliques, and also invocation of Saints, is a fond thing vainly invented, and grounded upon no warranty of Scripture, but rather repugnant to the Word of God.

XXIII. OF MINISTERING IN THE CONGREGATION

It is not lawful for any man to take upon him the office of publick preaching, or ministering the Sacraments in the Congregation, before he be lawfully called, and sent to execute the same. And those we ought to judge lawfully called and sent, which be chosen and called to this work by men who have publick authority given unto them in the congregation, to call and send Ministers into the Lord's vineyard.

XXIV. OF SPEAKING IN THE CONGREGATION IN SUCH A TONGUE AS THE PEOPLE UNDERSTANDETH

It is a thing plainly repugnant to the Word of God, and the custom of the Primitive Church, to have publick Prayer in the Church, or to minister the Sacraments in a tongue not understanded of the people.

XXV. OF THE SACRAMENTS

Sacraments ordained of Christ be not only badges or tokens of Christian men's profession, but rather they be certain sure witnesses, and effectual signs of grace, and God's good will towards us, by the which he doth work invisibly in us, and doth not only quicken, but also strengthen and confirm our Faith in him.

There are two Sacraments ordained of Christ our Lord in the gospel, that is to say, Baptism, and the Supper of the Lord.

Those five commonly called Sacraments, that is to say, confirmation, Penance, Orders, Matrimony, and extreme Unction, are not to be counted for Sacraments of the gospel, being such as have grown partly of the corrupt following of the Apostles, partly are states of life allowed in the Scriptures; but yet have not like nature of Sacraments with Baptism, and the Lord's Supper, for that they have not any visible sign or ceremony ordained of God.

The Sacraments were not ordained of Christ to be gazed upon, or to be carried about, but that we should duly use them. And in such only as worthily receive the same they have a wholesome effect or operation: but they that receive them unworthily purchase to themselves damnation, as *Saint Paul* saith.

XXVII. OF THE LORD'S SUPPER

The Supper of the Lord is not only a sign of the love that Christians ought to have among themselves one to another; but rather is a Sacrament of our Redemption by Christ's death: insomuch that to such as rightly, worthily, and with faith, receive the same, the Bread which we break is a partaking of the Body of Christ; and likewise the cup of Blessing is a partaking of the Blood of Christ.

Transubstantiation (or the change of the substance of Bread and Wine) in the Supper of the Lord, cannot be proved by Holy Writ; but is repugnant to the plain words of Scripture, overthroweth the nature of a Sacrament, and hath given occasion to many superstitions.

The Body of Christ is given, taken, and eaten, in the Supper, only after an heavenly and spiritual manner. And the mean whereby the body of Christ is received and eaten in the Supper is Faith.

The Sacrament of the Lord's Supper was

not by Christ's ordinance reserved, carried about, lifted up, or worshipped.

XXX. OF BOTH KINDS

The Cup of the Lord is not to be denied to the Lay-people: for both the parts of the Lord's Sacrament, by Christ's ordinance and commandment, ought to be ministered to all Christian men alike.

XXXI. OF THE ONE OBLATION OF CHRIST FINISHED UPON THE CROSS

The Offering of Christ once made is that perfect redemption, propitiation, and satisfaction, for all the sins of the whole world, both original and actual; and there is none other satisfaction for sin, but that alone. Wherefore the sacrifices of Masses, in the which it was commonly said, that the Priest did offer Christ for the quick and the dead, to have remission of pain or guilt, were blasphemous fables, and dangerous deceits.

XXXII. OF THE MARRIAGE OF PRIESTS

Bishops, Priests, and Deacons, are not commanded by God's Law, either to vow the estate of single life, or to abstain from marriage: therefore it is lawful for them, as for all other Christian men, to marry at their own discretion, as they shall judge the same to serve better godliness.

XXXIV. OF THE TRADITIONS OF THE CHURCH

It is not necessary that Traditions and Ceremonies be in all places one, and utterly like; for at all times they have been divers, and may be changed according to the diversities of countries, times, and men's manners, so that nothing be ordained against God's Word. Whosoever through his private judgment, willingly and purposely, doth openly break the Traditions and ceremonies of the

Church, which be not repugnant to the Word of God, and be ordained and approved by common authority, ought to be rebuked openly, (that others may fear to do the like), as he that offendeth against the common order of the Church, and hurteth the authority of the Magistrate, and woundeth the consciences of the weak brethren.

Every particular or national Church hath authority to ordain, change, and abolish, ceremonies or rites of the Church ordained only by man's authority, so that all things be done to edifying.

XXXVI. OF CONSECRATION OF BISHOPS AND MINISTERS

The Book of consecration of Archbishops and Bishops, and Ordering of Priests and Deacons, lately set forth in the time of Edward the Sixth, and confirmed at the same time by authority of Parliament, doth contain all things necessary to such consecration and Ordering: neither hath it any thing, that of itself is superstitious and ungodly. And therefore whosoever are consecrated or ordered according to the Rites of that Book, since the second year of the forenamed King *Edward* unto this time, or hereafter shall be consecrated or ordered according to the same Rites; we decree all such to be rightly, orderly, and lawfully consecrated and ordered.

XXXVII. OF THE CIVIL MAGISTRATES

The Queen's Majesty hath the chief power in this Realm of *England,* and other of her dominions, unto whom the chief Government of all Estates of this Realm, whether they be Ecclesiastical or Civil, in all causes doth appertain, and is not, nor ought to be, subject to any foreign Jurisdiction.

Where we attribute to the Queen's Majesty the chief government, by which Titles we understand the minds of some slanderous folks to be offended; we give not to our Princes the ministering either of God's Word, or of the Sacraments, the which thing the Injunctions also lately set forth by *Elizabeth* our Queen do most plainly testify; but that only prerogative, which we see to have been given always to all godly Princes in holy Scriptures by God himself; that is, that they should rule all estates and degrees committed to their charge by God, whether they be Ecclesiastical or Temporal, and restrain with the civil sword the stubborn and evildoers.

The Bishop of *Rome* hath no jurisdiction in this Realm of *England.*

The Laws of the Realm may punish Christian men with death, for heinous and grievous offences.

It is lawful for Christian men, at the commandment of the Magistrate, to wear weapons, and serve in the wars.

THE CATHOLIC REFORMATION

Traditionally, the Catholic response to the Reformation has been termed the Counter-Reformation. This designation implies that Catholicism simply reacted defensively to the issues raised by the reformers. Although there is some truth in that old designation, in the early sixteenth century there were reform movements already active within the Roman Catholic Church. Throughout Europe Catholic humanist scholars, like Erasmus, were advocating a return to the gospels and the early sources of Christianity in an attempt to rid the church of superstition and moral abuses. In England John Colet (1466?-1519), the dean of St. Paul's, lectured on the New Testament in Greek and attacked ecclesiastical abuses, and Thomas More (1478–1535), Henry VIII's lord chancellor, wrote the *Utopia* as a challenge to all of Europe to embrace an enlightened humanism in economic, military and religious matters. In France, the great biblical scholar Jacques Lefevre d'Etaples influenced reformers in both the Catholic and Protestant camps. In Italy, a group of reforming churchmen formed an association called the Oratory of Divine Love which was to produce Gasparo Contarini (1483–1542), a nobleman of Venice, who eventually became a cardinal and worked toward agreement with the Protestants on the key doctrine of justification by faith. In Spain during the last decades of the fifteenth century, Ferdinand and Isabella had used Catholicism and the Spanish Inquisition to unite the land and fiercely persecute Jews and Muslims. But shortly after the expulsion of the Jews in 1492, the Spanish church began to take a different turn under the leadership of Francisco Ximenez De Cisneros (1436–1517) who became confessor to Queen Isabella. In 1495 he was named archbishop of Toledo and primate of all Spain. Ximenez combined a commitment to orthodoxy with high moral standards and a dedication to humanist scholarship. He initiated a thorough reform of the Spanish clergy, both secular and religious, and founded, with his own money, a new university at Alcala to promote clerical education at the collegiate and theological levels. For religious education of the laity, he promoted the publication of popular religious books. With the help of several scholars, he also produced the *Complutensian Polygot,* the first edition of the Bible in the original languages with an accompanying translation.

IGNATIUS LOYOLA, *THE SPIRITUAL EXERCISES*

The group most responsible for Catholic reform and counterattack against Protestantism in the sixteenth and seventeenth centuries was the Society of Jesus, or the Jesuits. Their founder was Ignatius Loyola (1491–1556), a Spaniard and former soldier who was forced to give up his military career in 1521 when he suffered a severe leg wound while defending the city of Pamploma against the French. During his convalescence, Ignatius, realizing his military career was over, underwent a conversion experience while reading the lives of the saints and the life of Christ. After months of spiritual torture and severe fasting during which he agonized, like Luther, over whether his sins had been forgiven, Ignatius at last found spiritual peace through his decision to abandon a worldly life and become a "knight for Christ." This conversion experience and his former military training had a profound impact on Ignatius' *Spiritual Exercises* and the constitutions of his order; both emphasize military-like discipline and the virtue of obedience to the authority of the Roman church.

After his conversion and a pilgrimage to the Holy Land, Loyola prepared himself for service in the church by studying at Barcelona, Alcala, Salamanca, and Paris. He gathered a small group of fellow students who bound themselves by vows of poverty, chastity and obedience and engaged in various works of charity. Ignatius named his group with the military term Company of Jesus (later changed to Society of Jesus) and offered its services to the pope for whatever work he might choose. The Society gained formal recognition in 1540 and rapidly became the "shock troops of the papacy" educating Catholic youth and clergy and working in foreign missions in Africa, India, Japan, and the Americas, as well as in Protestant areas like Germany.

Ignatius' *Spiritual Exercises* is a handbook of meditations and rules designed to lead the soul to conquer passion and give itself totally to God. It is meant to be used as a guide for a retreat of approximately thirty days. In the first week, the retreatant considers the evil of sin with the purpose of purifying the soul from attachment to it; in the second, the life of Christ in order to come to a knowledge and love of him; in the third, the passion in order to decide to follow Christ; and finally in the fourth, Christ's triumphant resurrection and ascension in order to be freed from false attachment to creatures.

The Spiritual Exercises reflect the ideals of the Jesuits and the spirit of the Counter-Reformation and make a striking contrast to Luther's theology. Ignatius presupposes that meditation, contemplation, mental and vocal prayer, and daily particular and general examinations of one's conscience are all exercises, analogous to physical exercises for the body, which prepare "the soul to remove ill-ordered affections" and to seek and find "the will of God with respect to the ordering of one's own life and the salvation of one's soul." This type of regimen is precisely what Luther meant by "works" which he saw as incapable of bringing salvation.

With Calvin, Loyola believes that, "Man was created that he might praise and reverence the Lord his God." But Loyola, in typical Roman Catholic fashion, understands service to God as the means by which one contributes to the soul's salvation. Grace plays a crucial role in the *Exercises,* and the retreatant is to frequently petition for grace and place the mind and body under the guidance of the Holy Spirit. But the role of grace is to help the will in making a choice, a commitment to obey God and the church as the voice of Christ. Whereas Luther and Calvin stress the faith of the believer, Loyola emphasizes the choice of the believer to serve God by submitting to the teachings of the Roman church, the true spouse of Christ. The first rule to be observed in order to think with the orthodox church is: "Removing all judgment of one's own, one must always keep one's mind prepared and ready to obey the true spouse of Christ, our Holy Mother, which is the Orthodox, Catholic, and Hierarchical Church."

The radical differences between Ignatius and Luther, both deeply spiritual men, on the questions of grace and free will, faith and works, and the church and the individual point to the strong feelings and deep divisions which will cause Europe to erupt into an age of religious wars for the next century.

The translation is adapted from that of Charles Seager, *The Spiritual Exercises of St. Ignatius Loyola,* (London: Dolman, 1847) 1–4, 15–17, 25–26, 173–85.

THE SPIRITUAL EXERCISES

Annotations

The first annotation is that the term Spiritual Exercise means any method of examining one's own conscience—of meditating, contemplating, praying mentally and vocally, and, finally, of performing any other spiritual operation that will be described hereafter. Just as walking, traveling, and running are bodily exercises, preparing the soul to remove ill-ordered affections, and after their removal seeking and finding the will of God with respect to the ordering of one's own life and the salvation of one's soul, are Spiritual Exercises.

The third annotation is that, whereas in all of the following Spiritual Exercises we use acts of the intellect when we reason, but of the will when we are affected, we must notice that . . . while we converse vocally or mentally with the Lord God or His Saints a greater reverence is required of us than when we use the intellect to attain understanding.

The fourth annotation is that the following Exercises are divided into four weeks: in the first week the consideration may be of sins; in the second, concerning the life of our Lord Jesus Christ up to His entrance into Jerusalem on Palm Sunday; in the third, concerning His Passion; in the fourth, concerning His Resurrection and Ascension. Then the three methods of prayer are added. Yet these weeks are not to be understood as if each should contain seven or eight days. It happens that some are slower, others more ready in attaining what they seek (for instance, in the first week contrition, grief, and tears for their sins), and that some are more or less agitated and tried by various spirits. It is, therefore, sometimes expedient that any week should be cut down or extended according to the nature of the subject matter. The Exercises customarily take up the space of thirty days or thereabouts.

CERTAIN SPIRITUAL EXERCISES BY WHICH A MAN MAY BE ABLE TO CONQUER HIMSELF AND, WITH DECISIONS FREE FROM HARMFUL DESIRES, PLAN HIS LIFE

In the first place, in order that exercises of this kind benefit him who gives and him who receives, it must be presupposed that every pious Christian prefers to put a good interpretation on another's opinion or proposition than to condemn it. But if he can in no way defend it, let him inquire the speaker's meaning and, if he thinks erroneously, correct him kindly. If this does not suffice, all suitable means should be tried to render his meaning sound and safe from error.

Man was created that he might praise and reverence the Lord his God, and, serving Him, at length be saved. But the other things which are placed on the earth were created for man's sake, that they might assist him in pursuing the end of his creation; whence it follows that they are to be used or abstained from in proportion as they profit or hinder him in pursuing that end.

DAILY AND PARTICULAR EXAMINATION

The first time of examining is morning when a man ought, as soon as he rises from sleep, to decide to guard against some particular sin or fault which he desires to overcome.

The second is the afternoon in which he must ask of God the grace to be able to remember how often he has fallen into that particular sin or fault and to beware of it in the future. Then let him perform the first reexamination, asking account of his soul concerning the sin or fault already spoken of and, running through the parts of the day from the hour in which he rose down to the present, see how many times he has committed it.

The third will be the evening in which, after the hour of supper, another review will have to be made by running through in like manner the several hours which have elapsed from the former examination to the present and in the same way remembering and enumerating the times he has been in fault.

A METHOD OF GENERAL EXAMINATION IN FIVE POINTS

The first point is to thank the Lord our God for the benefits we have received.

The second, to entreat grace for the knowledge and expulsion of our sins.

The third, to ask account of our soul concerning the sins committed during the present day, searching through the several hours from the time when we rose. Thoughts should come first, then words and deeds, in the same order laid down in the particular examination.

The fourth, to ask pardon concerning our faults.

The fifth, to propose amendment with the grace of God—and after all the above to say the Lord's Prayer.

THE USE OF GENERAL CONFESSION AND OF COMMUNION

From a general confession voluntarily made many advantages are gained, especially these three:

The first, although he who confesses at least once every year is not obliged to make a general confession, yet the person who does so gains much more merit on account of the greater sorrow he experiences for his sins and for the wickedness of his past life.

The second: having seen by means of the Spiritual Exercises much more clearly than before the nature and wickedness of sin, he will gain greater advantage and merit.

The third: it is reasonable to expect that he who has thus rightly confessed and is thus rightly disposed will be much better prepared for the reception of the Eucharist, which aids in the highest degree both the expulsion of sin

and the preservation and increase of grace received.

This general confession will be best placed after the exercises of the first week.

SOME RULES TO BE OBSERVED IN ORDER THAT WE MAY THINK WITH THE ORTHODOX CHURCH

The first: removing all judgment of one's own, one must always keep one's mind prepared and ready to obey the true Spouse of Christ, our Holy Mother, which is the Orthodox, Catholic, and Hierarchical Church.

The second: it is proper to commend confession of sins to the priest and the receiving of the Eucharist at least once a year. It is more commendable to receive the same Sacrament every eighth day or at least once in each month.

The third: one should commend to Christ's faithful people the frequent and devout hearing of the holy rite or sacrifice of the Mass; also the saying of the Church hymns, the psalms, and long prayers, either within the Churches or outside; also to approve the hours marked out for the Divine Office, for prayers of whatever kind, and for the Canonical Hours.

The fourth: to praise vows . . . of chastity, poverty, and perpetual obedience, and other works of perfection and supererogation. Here it must be noted in passing that . . . a vow relates to those things which lead more closely to the perfection of Christian life. Concerning other things which lead away from perfection, for example . . . matrimony, a vow is never to be made.

The sixth: to praise relics, the veneration and invocation of Saints, also the stations and pious pilgrimages, indulgences, jubilees, the candles lighted in the Churches, and other such aids to our piety and devotion.

The seventh: to praise abstinence and fasts, such as Lent, Ember Days, Vigils,

Fridays, Saturdays, and others undertaken for the sake of devotion; also voluntary afflictions of one's self, which we call penances, not merely internal, but external.

The eighth: to praise the construction of Churches and their adornment; also images . . . to be venerated . . . for the sake of what they represent.

The ninth: to uphold all the precepts of the Church and not impugn them in any manner; but, on the contrary, to defend them promptly, with reasons drawn from all sources against those who do impugn them.

The tenth: we ought to be more ready to approve and praise the statutes, recommendations, and the lives of our superiors than to reprove them; because, although sometimes they may not be worthy of praise, to speak against them either in public preaching or in speaking before the common people would cause murmuring and scandals rather than good. Consequently, the people would be angry with their superiors, either spiritual, or temporal. Therefore, as it is mischievous to speak ill to the people concerning superiors who are absent, so it may be useful to speak concerning their evil lives to those persons who can remedy them.

The eleventh: to put the highest value on sacred teaching, both the positive and the Scholastic, as they are commonly called. For as it was the object of the ancient holy Doctors, Jerome, Augustine, Gregory, and the like, to stir up men's minds to embrace the love and worship of God, so it is characteristic of Blessed Thomas, Bonaventure, the Master of the Sentences, and other more modern Divines, to lay down and define more exactly the things necessary for salvation, and according to what was fitting for their own times and for posterity, helpful in the confutation of heresies. Moreover, the Doctors of this kind, being later in date, are not merely endowed with the understanding of the Sacred Scripture, and assisted by the writings of the old authors, but also with the influx of the Divine Light, and use, happily for the help of our salvation, the decisions of Councils, the decrees, and various constitutions of Holy Church.

The twelfth: we must avoid the comparison of men still living on the earth, however worthy of praise, with the Saints, saying this man is more learned than St. Augustine, that man is another St. Francis, he is equal to St. Paul in holiness, or in some virtue he is not inferior, and so on.

The thirteenth: finally, so as to be altogether of the same mind and in conformity with the Church herself, if she shall have defined anything to be black which to our eyes appears to be white, we ought in like manner to pronounce it to be black. For we must undoubtingly believe that the Spirit of our Lord Jesus Christ, and the Spirit of the Orthodox Church, His Spouse, by which Spirit we are governed and directed to salvation, is the same; and that the God who of old delivered the precepts of the Decalogue is the same who now instructs and governs the Hierarchical Church.

The fourteenth: it must also be borne in mind that although it be most true that no one is saved except he who is predestinated, we must speak with circumspection concerning this matter lest, perchance stretching too far the grace of predestination of God, we should seem to wish to shut out the force of free will and the merits of good works, or on the other hand, attributing to the latter more than belongs to them. . . .

The fifteenth: for the like reason we should not speak on the subject of predestination frequently, and if it occur occasionally, we ought so to temper what we say as to give the people no occasion of erroneously saying: If my salvation or damnation is already determined regardless of whether I do ill or well, it cannot happen differently. It happens, consequently, that many neglect good works and other helps of salvation.

The sixteenth: it also happens not infrequently that from immoderate preaching and praise of faith without distinction or explanation being added, the people . . . become indifferent to good works which precede faith or follow it.

The seventeenth: nor must we push to such a point the preaching and inculcating of the grace of God that there may creep into the minds of the hearers the deadly error of denying the faculty of our free will. Concerning grace itself, therefore, it is allowable, indeed, to speak fully, God inspiring us, but no more than redounds to His more abundant glory,

lest in our dangerous times both the use of free will and efficacy of good works be taken away.

The eighteenth: although it is in the highest degree praiseworthy and useful to serve God from pure love, yet the fear of the Divine Majesty is greatly to be commended. And not that fear only which we call filial, which is the most pious and holy, but also the other which is called servile, as being . . . very often necessary . . . because it helps much towards rising from mortal sin. After a person has emerged from this, he easily arrives at the filial fear which is altogether acceptable and agreeable to our Lord God because it is inseparably joined with Divine Love.

THE COUNCIL OF TRENT (1545–1563)

The spread of the Reformation and the need for moral and administrative reforms in the Roman Catholic Church produced widespread demands for a general council as early as the 1520s, but the papacy's fear of a revival of conciliarism and disputes with Emperor Charles V tragically delayed it. Pope Leo X (r. 1513–1521) was a Medici and more of a worldly Renaissance prince than a pope. He failed to understand the seriousness of Luther's protest, and his inaction only served to deepen the divisions between Luther and the Roman church. Pope Hadrian VI (r. 1522–1523) was a Dutchman and a tutor to Charles V for whom he virtually ruled Spain from 1516 to his death. He was reform minded, but his reign was too short to allow the successful convening of a council. Although a man of personal good character, Pope Clement VII (r. 1523–1534), a Medici cousin of Leo X, was an irresolute leader who became involved in the political intrigue between Charles V and Francis I of France and only succeeded in humiliating the church. Thinking that the papal states were threatened by the power and lands of the Emperor, Clement VII formed an alliance with Francis I. In retaliation Charles' armies attacked the pope, and in 1527, an unpaid and poorly disciplined imperial army sacked and pillaged the city of Rome. Clement was subsequently involved in the troublesome affair of Henry VIII's request for a divorce from Catherine of Aragon, the aunt of Emperor Charles. The pope procrastinated in the matter, which provoked Henry's decision to break with Rome and declare himself head of the English church.

Finally, in 1534 in the person of Paul III (r. 1534–1549), the papacy had a man committed to calling the much needed council. Although he himself had been a worldly churchman, Paul III elevated reform-minded humanist scholars to the rank of Cardinal and, in preparation for a council, appointed a commission to produce a memorandum on reform. The commission's report, presented to the pope in 1537, bluntly criticized the

many abuses in the Roman church which had led to the Reformation: simony, absen-
teeism, erroneous preaching of indulgences, clerical concubinage, and abuses of monastic vows and episcopal authority.

Any hope for reunion between Protestantism and Rome was probably lost early in
Paul III's reign at the Conference of Ratisbon in 1541. It was convened by Charles V and
was attended by three Catholic and three Protestant theologians. The main figures were
Philip Melancthon and Martin Bucer on the Protestant side and Gaspar Contarini, a layman and a liberal reform-minded humanist, on the Catholic side. Under Contarini's
leadership, the theologians were able to come to considerable agreement, even on a
statement on justification by faith, but in the end discussions broke down over transubstantiation and the growing suspicions of Luther on the one side and conservative
Roman Curia members like Cardinal Caraffa on the other. By 1542 Contarini was dead,
and Cardinal Caraffa, the future Pope Paul IV (1555–1557), had succeeded in establishing the Roman Inquisition. The Curia was now dominated by conservatives who were
committed to moral reform in the church, but also to the reiteration of Catholic doctrine
against the Protestant heretics. The window of opportunity for reconciliation had closed.

Finally, after repeated delays, in 1545 Paul III succeeded in convening a council at the
imperial city of Trent just south of the Alps. It was to meet for several session in three
periods: 1545–47, 1551–52, 1562–63, through the reigns of four popes. Although the
reformers were invited, voting was limited to bishops, as was traditional for Roman
church councils. Attendance varied at each of the sessions, but the Italians were always
in the majority, and the agenda was under the control of the pope's legates. This all but
guaranteed that the council would reaffirm traditional Roman Catholic teaching against
Protestant criticism and that substantive discussions with the reformers about key theological issues would not take place.

Initially, Charles V and Pope Paul III had different expectations for the council. The
emperor still hoped for reunion with the Protestants and wanted the agenda limited to
disciplinary matters. He wanted to reconcile with the Protestants by concessions like a
married clergy and communion with the cup. Paul III, by contrast, instructed his legates
that the council was to concern itself first with the doctrinal matters raised by the
Protestants. A compromise was reached when it was decided to treat both questions
simultaneously.

In doctrinal matters the fathers at Trent tended to reaffirm traditional Catholic
teaching and formulated their decrees in opposition to the positions taken by the reformers. Luther and Calvin had both insisted that the sole religious authority in the church
is scripture alone which is to be interpreted by the individual inspired by God's Spirit.
In contrast, Trent decreed that the truth of the gospel was first preached orally by the
prophets, Christ himself, and then the apostles. This gospel has been preserved in the
church through both scripture and "unwritten traditions" which were "received by the
Apostles from the lips of Christ." It is not clear from the final decree whether these traditions are understood as a separate body of truths concerning faith and morals or
whether they are simply a complementary handing down of the truth found in the scrip-

tures. By giving tradition a status equal to the scriptures, the fathers of Trent were insisting that the scriptures were not to be interpreted by one's "own judgment" but by "holy mother Church to whom it belongs to judge of their true sense and interpretation."

In deciding upon the canon for scripture, Trent reiterated that the old Latin Vulgate Bible of St. Jerome was to be the Bible for liturgy, public lectures, disputations, sermons and expositions. The list of canonical books included in the Old Testament canon books and traditions which were originally written in Greek and were not part of the Jewish canon: Tobit, Judith, 1 & 2 Maccabees, Wisdom, Ecclesiasticus, Baruch, and additions to Daniel and Esther. Both of these decisions stood against the various Protestant groups who advocated the use of vernacular Bibles and the shorter Jewish Canon for the books of the Old Testament.

The decrees treating justification were the centerpiece of the council's work; they are of such a high quality that the distinguished Protestant church historian Adolf Harnack said that, had they been taught in 1517, the Reformation would never have happened. They follow a careful path between the reformers' pessimism about human nature apart from grace and the naive optimism of Pelagianism. In the decree on "The Impotency of Nature and of the Law to Justify Man," Trent agrees with Luther and Calvin that, because of original sin, humans "are so far the servants of sin and under the power of the devil and death, that not only the Gentiles by the force of nature, but not even the Jews by the very letter of the law of Moses, were able to be liberated or to rise therefrom. . . ." But then it adds the important qualification that "free will" though "weakened . . . in its powers and downward bent, was by no means extinguished in them." This will enable the fathers at Trent to give a role for human cooperation with or rejection of grace in the process of salvation.

The decree on "The Necessity of Preparation for Justification in Adults . . ." stresses both the initiative of "the predisposing grace of God through Jesus Christ" and the cooperation of the human will in responding to or rejecting grace. Calvin's doctrine of the irresistible grace of God is thereby rejected.

> It is furthermore declared that in adults the beginning of the justification must proceed from the predisposing grace of God through Jesus Christ, that is, from His vocation, whereby, without any merits on their part, they are called; that they who by sin had been cut off from God, may be disposed through His quickening and helping grace to convert themselves to their own justification by freely assenting to and cooperating with that grace; so that, while God touches the heart of man through the illumination of the Holy Ghost, man himself neither does absolutely nothing while receiving that inspiration, since he can also reject it, nor yet is he able by his own free will and without the grace of God to move himself to justice in His sight. Hence, when it is said in the sacred writings: "Turn ye to me, and I will turn to you," we are reminded of our liberty; and when we reply: "Convert us, O Lord, to thee, and we shall be converted," we confess that we need the grace of God.

In contrast to Luther's emphasis on justification by "faith alone," Trent stresses the roles of the three theological virtues—faith, hope and love—even in the preparation for adult justification through the reception of baptism. Adults are disposed to God's justice by grace when they receive faith by hearing which moves them "freely toward God, believing to be true what has been divinely revealed and promised, especially that the sinner is justified by God. . . ." Hope turns the sinner from fear of divine punishment to trust that God will be merciful for Christ's sake. Finally, sinners are then moved to love God as the fountain of all justice and to reject sin.

In the actual description of justification and its causes, Trent insists that it involves "not only the remission of sins but also the sanctification and renewal of the inward man through the voluntary reception of the grace and gifts whereby an unjust man becomes just. . . ." The fathers of Trent therefore reject Luther's and Calvin's concept of the Christian as simultaneously both sinner and just. We are not only reputed to be just because of Christ, but "we are truly called and are just, receiving justice within us, each one according to his own measure. . . ."

Trent's treatment of the causes of justification makes an interesting comparison and contrast with Calvin's in the *Institutes* (III.14.17). Both essentially agree on the efficient and final causes: For Calvin, the efficient cause is the Father's mercy and gratuitous love; for Trent, it is "the merciful God who washes and sanctifies gratuitously." For Calvin, the final cause is a demonstration of divine righteousness and a praise of divine goodness; for Trent, it is "the glory of God and Christ and life everlasting." Both, of course, insist on the central importance of Christ's obedient death on the cross. Calvin calls it the material cause; Trent the meritorious cause. It is in the discussion of the formal or instrumental causes that the two differ, and the difference involves the respective understandings of the role of faith in the process. For Calvin the formal and instrumental cause is faith alone. Trent, with a characteristic Roman Catholic emphasis on the sacraments, says that the instrumental cause is "the sacrament of baptism, which is the sacrament of faith, without which no man was ever justified." But then Trent goes on to speak of "the single formal cause" as the justice of God "by which He makes us just." In this long section, Trent insists that this involves a renewal "in the spirit of our mind," the cooperation of free will, and the infusion of faith, hope, and charity. The last section of the decree insists "that faith without works is dead" and that true faith "worketh by charity."

Because of its emphasis on human freedom in responding to grace, the decrees of Trent can also speak of "the increase of the justification received" and the meriting of eternal life once one has received the gift of justification. Luther understood Christian righteousness to be the result of the divine verdict on the believer which is accepted in faith. For him the life of sanctification was the process of faith producing good works, but they are never understood as meritorious. Trent, like Luther, begins the process of justification with the gift of grace and faith, but then speaks of Christian righteousness as deepening, growing, and increasing; we can be justified "more and more." Though no one can merit justification, the justified person can perform meritorious acts which deserve an increase in righteousness and in the end merit eternal life. But the Christian's merits are achieved only in the strength of Christ which "precedes, accompanies and follows" his good works. Thus Trent tries to hold together both grace and merit; the decrees agree with the reformers that justification is God's gift, but they understand it as a gift which enables us to respond freely and therefore, in some sense, merit our own salvation.

Trent also rejects the notion that Christians sin even in doing good works; they may fall into venial sin, but only mortal sin can end the life of grace in the soul, and even mortal sin does not put an end to faith. Although Trent does not deny predestination, its decrees concentrate on warning against the dangers of the doctrine. Only by a rare special revelation can one know certainly of one's predestination, and therefore one should not presume upon it. Rather, one should devote himself to obeying the commandments and doing good works in fear and trembling.

Grace and justification are tied to the sacramental system in the decrees of Trent. Through the sacraments, "all true righteousness either begins (in Baptism) or being begun is increased (the Eucharist), or being lost is restored (Penance)." Trent reaffirmed the number of sacraments as seven, a teaching first defined at the Fourth Lateran Council in 1215, and insisted that they were all instituted by Christ. Today Catholic scholars recognize that only baptism, the eucharist, penance, and the priesthood are directly instituted by Christ in the gospels. The other three—confirmation, matrimony, and extreme unction—are understood as having developed in the course of the church's history. Three of the sacraments are said to give to the soul an indelible character: baptism, confirmation, and orders. These three depute the person to worship, service, and pastoral leadership in the church and cannot be repeated.

The fathers at Trent carefully distinguished the way in which the sacraments convey grace from various Protestant positions. The sacraments do not merely nourish faith; nor are they simply outward signs of grace already received through faith; nor are they mere tokens of a Christian profession of faith. Trent insists that the sacraments contain the grace they signify and confer it on those who put no obstacle in the way of grace's operation. God gives grace through the sacraments "always to all," rather than Luther's "where and when God pleases." To express the objective efficacy of the sacraments the phrase *ex opere operato* is used; that is, the sacraments convey grace by virtue of being duly performed. This phrase stands in contrast to Luther's *sola fides;* that is, through "faith alone" in God's promises, the sacraments offer grace. Trent's teaching on the operation of the sacraments is not magical or mechanical. The recipient must not be in conscious mortal sin, and the sacrament's effectiveness depends on the faith of the recipient. The phrase *ex opere operantis* is used to express the recipient's important role in the sacrament.

Of the sacraments the eucharist is the most important. It is the "source from which all other sacraments derive goodness and perfection." This is because the eucharist contains the Lord Jesus' presence in a special way. Trent reaffirms the so-called real presence of Christ in the eucharist in language which excludes Zwingli's mere symbolic presence, and possibly also, Calvin's spiritual presence. Trent uses the terms "true, real and substantial presence" to speak of Christ's presence under the forms of bread and wine after the words of consecration. The basis for this teaching is a literal, as opposed to

Zwingli's symbolic, interpretation of Jesus' words of institution at the last supper. Trent also insists on using the term "transubstantiation": that is, the substances of bread and wine are changed into the substances of the body and blood of Christ, with only the accidents of bread and wine remaining. This term is used to reject Luther's distinction between the glorified presence of Christ in heaven and his sacramental presence in the world in the bread and wine.

Trent also reiterates the sacrificial character of the mass; but it does not teach, as some Protestant theologians supposed, that the mass is a new sacrifice. In the mass the same Christ who once shed his blood on the cross is "immolated in a bloodless manner" so that God's anger against sin is turned away. The one who offers the sacrifice is not the priest, as some reformers charged, but Christ himself. Rather than being a new sacrifice, the mass is the rite through which the "fruits" of the one sacrifice on the cross are made available to the faithful in the course of time. It is a "representation" of the one sacrifice of Christ, and through it the benefits of the cross are made available to the faithful. The way in which the mass was celebrated in Latin according to the Roman rite was fixed at Trent, and it remained the same until the reforms of the Second Vatican Council in 1963–1966. This insured a unity in Roman Catholic liturgical practice throughout the world, but at the same time often had the effect of turning the laity into mere spectators of the ritual, rather than participants.

In response to Luther and Calvin's teaching on the priesthood of all believers, Trent reiterated the special sacramental character of the ordained priesthood. This emphasis is crucial for maintaining the hierarchical structure of the church in Roman Catholicism. In the Roman Catholic view, Christ commissioned his apostles to preach the gospel. Their successors are the bishops who have the fullness of priesthood through the sacrament of ordination. They share that priesthood with priests and deacons through the sacrament of ordination.

According to Trent, priests do not have simply a delegated, functional role in the church as Luther taught. They, rather, have a sacerdotal dignity in virtue of the sacrament of Orders after the image of Christ, the supreme and eternal high priest. Through ordination, they are consecrated by God 1) to preach the gospel, 2) shepherd the faithful, and 3) celebrate the divine worship. They share in the unique office of Christ the mediator, and in the eucharist they exercise in a supreme degree their sacred function.

> Sacrifice and priesthood are by the ordinance of God so united that both have existed in every law. Since therefore in the New Testament the Catholic Church has received from the institution of Christ the holy, visible sacrifice of the Eucharist, it must also be confessed that there is in that Church a new, visible and external priesthood, into which the old has been translated. That this was instituted by the same Lord our Savior, and that to the Apostles and their successors in the priesthood was given the power of consecrating, offering and administering His body and blood, as also of forgiving and retaining sins, is shown by the Sacred Scriptures and has always been taught by the tradition of the Catholic Church. (H.J. Schroeder, trans., *Canons and Decrees of the Council of Trent*, p. 160)

In the later sessions of the council, the fathers of Trent reaffirmed many of the specific Roman Catholic doctrines and traditions which most offended Protestants: purgatory, and intercessory prayers in behalf of the souls detained there, the intercession of the saints, honor due to relics, the lawful use of images, indulgences, and clerical celibacy. Given the polemical spirit of the period, this emphasis is understandable, but from an ecumenical perspective, it was unfortunate because it only served to exaggerate the differences between Roman Catholicism and Protestantism. Only in the aftermath of the Second Vatican Council (1963–1966) has there been a real effort by both Catholic and Protestant theologians to rethink and discuss the issues involved in the Reformation in a spirit of mutual respect and sincere theological inquiry.

In disciplinary matters the decrees of Trent were thorough and quite successful. Simony and the erroneous teaching of indulgences were again condemned. Bishops were mandated to live in their dioceses, to preach regularly, and conduct annual visitations of parishes. Parish clergy were to be active among their parishioners, better educated, strictly celibate, and neatly dressed. To improve the education of the secular clergy, the council called for the construction of a seminary in every diocese. The curriculum was to be scholastic theology, rather than the humanistic and scriptural studies emphasized in Protestant schools.

The difference in the character of the papacy in the later decades of the sixteenth century after Trent and that of a century earlier is striking. The popes immediately prior to Luther's protest in 1517 were worldly Renaissance princes who were more concerned with the political welfare of the papal states than the spiritual welfare of Christendom. During the council and the decades immediately following, the popes were, for the most part, men of personal piety, dedicated to reform of abuses in the church, and committed to the defense of the faith against Protestantism. Indeed, in the late sixteenth and early seventeenth century, Roman Catholicism entered a new age of spiritual vitality marked by Baroque art, new mystical movements, and vigorous missionary activity in the New World and the Far East.

Nevertheless, the immediate aftermath of the Reformation was exactly what Erasmus had feared: the devastation of Europe by a century of religious warfare. Civil wars of religion divided Germany, France, the Spanish Netherlands, and England. And, from 1618 through 1648, much of Europe was engulfed in the so-called Thirty Years' War.

In Germany the Lutheran princes and cities of the Schmalkaldic League fought the so-called Schmalkaldic War with Emperor Charles V to establish independence from both pope and emperor. Although Charles was victorious on the battlefield, in the Religious Peace of Augsburg (1555) he was forced to recognize the rights of the German princes to determine the religion (either Catholicism or Lutheranism) within their territories.

In France, throughout the second half of the sixteenth century, a weak monarchy was unable to control the bitter fighting between Catholics and French Calvinists (Huguenots). Finally in 1598, Henry of Navarre, a Huguenot, became king and converted to Catholicism. He put an end to religious strife in 1598 by issuing the Edict of Nantes which gave broad toleration to the Huguenots in France.

The Spanish Netherlands were ravaged by a protracted war with Catholic Spain from the 1560s through 1609 over the recognition of the Calvinist faith in that land. With the truce in 1609, the Netherlands was divided by religion. The seven United Provinces of the north were Calvinist and became a separate nation; the ten southern provinces were Catholic and remained loyal to Spain. Eventually, in 1830, they would become the country of Belgium.

During the Thirty Years' War (1618–1648) all the major states of Western Europe, including Denmark and Sweden, became engulfed in a series of wars which began over the recognition of the Calvinist faith in Bavaria, but ended as a dynastic war between the House of Bourbon (France) and the House of Hapsburg (Spain and Austria). When the Thirty Years' War was ended by the Peace of Westphalia in 1648, Calvinism was given the same rights as Lutheranism in the territories of the empire under the provisions of the Peace of Augsburg (1555).

Finally, England, which had avoided religious war during the long reign of Elizabeth (1558–1603), the last of the Tudors, was rent by civil wars in the so-called Great Rebellion or Puritan Revolution (1642–1660). The Puritans were extremist English Calvinists who were dissatisfied with the Elizabethan religious settlement and wanted a further purification of the Church of England from any remnants of Roman Catholicism. When they joined forces with Parliament in its struggle with the Stuarts, James I (1603–1625) and Charles I (1625–1649), under the military leadership of Oliver Cromwell, they were able to defeat Charles I and behead the king in 1649. Their victory only served to make evident the deep religious divisions within England between moderate Presbyterians, who wanted to replace bishops with regional and national presbyteries and synods, Independents who wanted local independence for each congregation, Baptists who believed in a purified church of baptized adults, and other fringe groups like the Diggers and Quakers who advocated religious individualism and freedom of choice in religious matters. After the interregum of Cromwell (1649–1658), Parliament was forced to end the chaos by restoring the monarchy in the person of Charles II, the son of Charles I.

By the second half of the seventeenth century the religious bloodletting was largely spent. Western Europe was now religiously divided. Half of the West had chosen to remain within the traditional Roman church. The other half had chosen the Bible as the sovereign word of God and the judge of the church. Geographically, the division ran roughly North and South. Southern Europe (southern Germany, Italy, Spain and Portugal) and Ireland remained Roman Catholic; northern Europe was largely Protestant. Northern Germany and the Scandinavian countries were Lutheran. Switzerland was mostly Reformed or Calvinist. France was divided between Roman Catholicism and a strong Huguenot minority. The Netherlands were also divided between a Reformed north and a Catholic south. And England was restored to its own unique brand of Protestantism with some allowance for religious dissent.

In the next period two radically different movements will affect the course of Christian theology; both of them in different ways try to move beyond the dogmatic issues which had given rise to the Reformation. On the one hand, under the influence of the achievements of modern science, Enlightenment thinkers will attempt to apply the scientific method to religious questions with the hope of reducing dogmatic differences between competing religious traditions. This will lead to problems for all religious traditions, which are still being debated to this day. On the other hand, various Pietist movements will emphasize the importance of devotion and morality over intellectual speculation.

The translation of the decrees and canons of Trent is by H.J. Schroeder *Canons and Decrees of the Council of Trent* (St. Louis: B. Herder Book Co., 1941).

DECREE CONCERNING THE CANONICAL SCRIPTURES

The holy, ecumenical and general Council of Trent, lawfully assembled in the Holy Ghost, the same three legates of the Apostolic See presiding, keeps this constantly in view, namely, that the purity of the Gospel may be preserved in the Church after the errors have been removed. This [Gospel], of old promised through the Prophets in the Holy Scriptures, our Lord Jesus Christ, the Son of God, promulgated first with His own mouth, and then commanded it to be preached by His Apostles to every creature as the source at once of all saving truth and rules of conduct. It also clearly perceives that these truths and rules are contained in the written books and in the unwritten traditions, which, received by the Apostles from the mouth of Christ Himself, or from the Apostles themselves, the Holy Ghost dictating, have come down to us, transmitted as it were from hand to hand. Following, then, the examples of the orthodox Fathers, it receives and venerates with a feeling of piety and reverence all the books both of the Old and New Testaments, since one God is the author of both; also the traditions, whether they relate to faith or to morals, as having been dictated either orally by Christ or by the Holy Ghost, and preserved in the Catholic Church in unbroken succession.

DECREE CONCERNING THE EDITION AND USE OF THE SACRED BOOKS

Moreover, the same holy council considering that not a little advantage will accrue to the Church of God if it be made known which of all the Latin editions of the sacred books now in circulation is to be regarded as authentic, ordains and declares that the old Latin Vulgate Edition, which, in use for so many hundred years, has been approved by the Church, be it in public lectures, disputations, sermons and expositions held as authentic, and that no one dare or presume under any pretext whatsoever to reject it.

Furthermore, to check unbridled spirits, it decrees that no one relying on his own judgment shall, in matters of faith and morals pertaining to the edification of Christian doctrine, distorting the Holy Scriptures in accordance with his own conceptions, presume to interpret them contrary to that sense which holy mother Church, to whom it belongs to judge of their true sense and interpretation, has held and holds, or even contrary to the unanimous teaching of the Fathers, even though such interpretations should never at any time be published. Those who act contrary to this shall be made known by the ordinaries and punished in accordance with the penalties prescribed by the law.

IMPOTENCY OF NATURE AND OF THE LAW TO JUSTIFY MAN

The holy council declares first, that for a correct and clear understanding of the doctrine of justification, it is necessary that each one recognize and confess that since all men had lost innocence in the prevarication of Adam, having become unclean, and, as the Apostle says, *by nature children of wrath,* as has been set forth in the decree on original sin, they were so far *the servants of sin* and under the power of the devil and death, that not only the Gentiles by the force of nature, but not even the Jews by the very letter of the law of Moses, were able to be liberated or to rise therefrom, though free will, weakened as it was in its powers and downward bent, was by no means extinguished in them.

A BRIEF DESCRIPTION OF THE JUSTIFICATION OF THE SINNER AND ITS MODE IN THE STATE OF GRACE

In which words is given a brief description of the justification of the sinner, as being a translation from that state in which man is born a child of the first Adam, to the state of grace and of the adoption of the sons of God through the second Adam, Jesus Christ, our Savior. This translation however cannot, since the promulgation of the Gospel, be effected except through the laver of regeneration or its desire, as it is written: *Unless a man be born again of water and the Holy Ghost, he cannot enter into the Kingdom of God.*

THE NECESSITY OF PREPARATION FOR JUSTIFICATION IN ADULTS, AND WHENCE IT PROCEEDS

It is furthermore declared that in adults the beginning of the justification must proceed from the predisposing grace of God through Jesus Christ, that is, from His vocation, whereby, without any merits on their part, they are called; that they who by sin had been cut off from God, may be disposed through His quickening and helping grace to convert themselves to their own justification by freely assenting to and cooperating with that grace; so that, while God touches the heart of man through the illumination of the Holy Ghost, man himself neither does absolutely nothing while receiving that inspiration, since he can also reject it, nor yet is he able by his own free will and without the grace of God to move himself to justice in His sight. Hence, when it is said in the sacred writings: *Turn ye to me, and I will turn to you,* we are reminded of our liberty; and when we reply: *Convert us, O Lord, to thee, and we shall be converted,* we confess that we need the grace of God.

THE MANNER OF PREPARATION

Now, they [the adults] are disposed to that justice when, aroused and aided by divine grace, receiving *faith by hearing,* they are moved freely toward God, believing to be true what has been divinely revealed and promised, especially that the sinner is justified by God, *by his grace, through the redemption that is in Christ Jesus;* and when, understanding themselves to be sinners, they, by turning themselves from the fear of divine justice, by which they are salutarily aroused, to consider the mercy of God, are raised to hope, trusting that God will be propitious to them for Christ's sake; and they begin to love Him as the fountain of all justice, and on that account are moved against sin by a certain hatred and detestation, that is, by that repentance that must be performed before baptism; finally, when they resolve to receive baptism, to begin a new life and to keep the commandments of God. Of this disposition it is written: *He that cometh to God, must believe that he is, and is a rewarder to them that seek him;* and, *Be of good faith, son, thy sins are forgiven thee; and, The fear of the Lord driveth out sin;* and, *Do penance, and be baptized every one of you in the name of Jesus Christ, for the remission of your sins, and you shall receive the gift of the Holy Ghost;* and, *Going, therefore, teach ye all nations, baptizing them in the name of the Father, and of the son, and of the Holy Ghost, teaching them to observe all things whatsoever I have commanded you;* finally, *Prepare your hearts unto the Lord.*

IN WHAT THE JUSTIFICATION OF THE SINNERS CONSISTS, AND WHAT ARE ITS CAUSES

This disposition or preparation is followed by justification itself, which is not only a remission of sins but also the sanctification and renewal of the inward man through the voluntary reception of the grace and gifts whereby an unjust man becomes just and from being an enemy becomes a friend, that he may be *an heir according to hope of life everlasting.* The causes of this justification are: the final cause is the glory of God and of Christ and life everlasting; the efficient cause is the merciful God who *washes and sanctifies* gratuitously, signing and anointing *with the holy Spirit of promise, who is the pledge of our inheritance;* the meritorious cause is His most beloved only begotten, our Lord Jesus Christ, who, *when we were enemies, for the exceeding charity wherewith he loved us,* merited for us justification by His most holy passion on the wood of the cross and made satisfaction for us to God the Father; the instrumental cause is the sacrament of baptism, which is the sacrament of faith, without which no man was ever justified; finally, the single formal cause is the justice of God, not that by which He Himself is just, but that by which He makes us just, that, namely, with which we being endowed by Him, are *renewed in the spirit of our mind,* and not only are we reputed but we are truly called and are just, receiving justice within us, each one according to his own measure, which the Holy Ghost distributes to everyone as He wills, and according to each one's disposition and cooperation. For though no one can be just except he to whom the merits of the passion of our Lord Jesus Christ are communicated, yet this takes place in that justification of the sinner, when by the merit of the most holy passion, *the charity of God is poured forth by the Holy Ghost in the hearts* of those who are justified and inheres in them; whence man through Jesus Christ, in whom he is ingrafted, receives in that justification, together with the remission of sins, all these infused at the same time, namely, faith, hope and charity. For faith, unless hope and charity be added to it, neither unites man perfectly with Christ nor makes him a living member of His body. For which reason it is most truly said that *faith without works is dead and of no profit, and in Christ Jesus neither circumcision availeth anything nor uncircumcision, but faith that worketh by charity.* The faith, conformably to Apostolic tradition, catechumens ask of the Church before the sacrament of baptism, when they ask for the faith that gives eternal life, which without hope and charity faith cannot give. Whence also they hear immediately the word of Christ: If thou wilt enter into life, keep the commandments. Wherefore, when receiving true and Christian justice, they are commanded, immediately on being born again, to preserve it pure and spotless, as *the first robe* given them through Christ Jesus in place of that which Adam by his disobedience lost for himself and for us, so that they may bear it before the tribunal of our Lord Jesus Christ and may have life eternal.

HOW THE GRATUITOUS JUSTIFICATION OF THE SINNER BY FAITH IS TO BE UNDERSTOOD

But when the Apostle says that man is justified by faith and freely, these words are to be understood in that sense in which the uninterrupted unanimity of the Catholic Church has held and expressed them, namely, that we are therefore said to be justified by faith, because faith is the beginning of human salvation, the foundation and root of all justification, *without which it is impossible to please God* and to come to the fellowship of His sons; and we are therefore said to be justified gratuitously, because none of those things that precede justification, whether faith or works, merit the grace of justification. For, *if by grace, it is not now by works, otherwise,* as the Apostle says, *grace is no more grace.*

THE INCREASE OF THE JUSTIFICATION RECEIVED

Having, therefore, been thus justified and made the friends and *domestics of God,* advancing *from virtue to virtue,* they are renewed, as the Apostle says, *day by day,* that is *mortifying the members* of their flesh, and presenting them as instruments of justice unto sanctification, they, through the observance of the commandments of God and of the Church, faith cooperating with good works, increase in that justice received through the grace of Christ and are further justified, as it is written: *He that is just, let him be justified still;* and, *Be not afraid to be justified even to death;* and again, *Do you see that by works a man is justified, and not by faith only?* This increase of justice holy Church asks for when she prays: "Give unto us, O Lord, an increase of faith, hope and charity."

THE OBSERVANCE OF THE COMMANDMENTS AND THE NECESSITY AND POSSIBILITY THEREOF

But no one, however much justified, should consider himself exempt from the observance of the commandments; no one should use that rash statement, once forbidden by the Fathers under anathema, that the observance of the commandments of God is impossible for one that is justified. For God does not command impossibilities, but by commanding admonishes thee to do what thou canst and to pray for what thou canst not, and aids thee that thou mayest be able. *His commandments are not heavy,* and *his yoke is sweet and burden light.* For they who are the sons of God love Christ, but they who love Him, keep His commandments, as He Himself testifies; which, indeed, with the divine help they can do. For though during this mortal life, men, however holy and just, fall at times into at least light and daily sins, which are also called venial, they do not on that account cease to be just, for that petition of the just, *forgive us our trespasses,* is both humble and true; for which reason the just ought to feel themselves the more obliged to walk in the way of justice, for *being now freed from sin and made servants of God, they are able, living soberly, justly and godly,* to proceed onward through Jesus Christ, by whom they have access unto this grace. For God does not forsake those who have been once justified by His grace, unless He be first forsaken by them. Wherefore, no one ought to flatter himself with faith alone, thinking that by faith alone he is made an heir and will obtain the inheritance, even though *he suffer* not *with Christ, that he may be also glorified with him.* For even Christ Himself, as the Apostle says, *whereas he was the Son of God, he learned obedience by the things which he suffered, and being consummated, he became to all who obey him the cause of eternal salvation.* For which reason the same Apostle admonishes those justified, saying: *Know you not that they who run in the race, all run indeed, but one receiveth the prize? So run that you may obtain. I therefore so run, not as at an uncertainty; I so fight, not as one beating the air, but I chastise my body and bring it into subjection; lest perhaps when I have preached to others, I myself should become a castaway.* So also the prince of the Apostles, Peter: *Labor *the more, that by good works you may make sure your calling and election. For doing these things, you shall not sin at any time.* From which it is clear that they are opposed to the orthodox teaching of religion who maintain that the just man sins, venially at least, in every good work; or, what is more intolerable, that he merits eternal punishment; and they also who assert that the just sin in all works, if, in order to arouse their sloth and to encourage themselves to run the race, they, in addition to this, that above all God may be glorified, have in view also the eternal reward, since it is written: *I have inclined my heart to do thy justifications on account of the reward;* and of Moses the Apostle says; that *he looked unto the reward.*

RASH PRESUMPTION OF PREDESTINATION IS TO BE AVOIDED

No one, moreover, so long as he lives this mortal life, ought in regard to the sacred mystery of divine predestination, so far presume as to state with absolute certainty that he is among the number of the pre-destined, as if it were true that the one justified either cannot sin any more, or, if he does sin, that he ought to promise himself an assured repentance. For except by special revelation, it cannot be known whom God has chosen to Himself.

THE GIFT OF PERSEVERANCE

Similarly with regard to the gift of perseverance, of which it is written: *He that shall persevere to the end, he shall be saved,* which cannot be obtained from anyone except from Him who is able to make him stand who stands, that he may stand perseveringly, and to raise him who falls, let no one promise himself herein something as certain with an absolute certainty, though all ought to place and repose the firmest hope in God's help. For God, unless men themselves fail in His grace, as *he has begun a good work, so will he perfect*

it, working to will and to accomplish. Nevertheless, let those who think themselves to stand, take heed lest they fall, and with fear and trembling work out their salvation, in labors, in watchings, in almsdeeds, in prayer, in fastings and chastity. For knowing that they are born again unto the hope of glory, and not as yet unto glory, they ought to fear for the combat that yet remains with the flesh, with the world and with the devil, in which they cannot be victorious unless they be with the grace of God obedient to the Apostle who says: *We are debtors, not to the flesh, to live according to the flesh; for if you live according to the flesh, you shall die, but if by the spirit you mortify the deeds of the flesh, you shall live.*

THE FALLEN AND THEIR RESTORATION

Those who through sin have forfeited the received grace of justification, can again be justified when, moved by God, they exert themselves to obtain through the sacrament of penance the recovery, by the merits of Christ, of the grace lost. For this manner of justification is restoration for those fallen, which the holy Fathers have aptly called a second plank after the shipwreck of grace lost. For on behalf of those who fall into sins after baptism, Christ Jesus instituted the sacrament of penance when He said: *Receive ye the Holy Ghost, whose sins you shall forgive, they are forgiven them, and whose sins you shall retain, they are retained.* Hence, it must be taught that the repentance of a Christian after his fall is very different from that at his baptism, and that it includes not only a determination to avoid sins and a hatred of them, or *a contrite and humble heart,* but also the sacramental confession of those sins, at least in desire, to be made in its season, and sacerdotal absolution, as well as satisfaction by fasts, alms, prayers and other devout exercises of the spiritual life, not indeed for the eternal punishment, which is, together with the guilt, remitted either by the sacrament or by the desire of the sacrament, but for the temporal punishment which, as the sacred writings teach, is not always wholly remitted, as is done in baptism, to those who, ungrateful to the grace of God which they have received, have grieved the Holy Ghost and have not feared to *violate the temple of God*. Of which repentance it is written: *Be mindful whence thou art fallen; do penance, and do the first works;* and again, *The sorrow that is according to God worketh penance, steadfast unto salvation;* and again, *Do penance, and bring forth fruits worthy of penance.*

BY EVERY MORTAL SIN GRACE IS LOST, BUT NOT FAITH

Against the subtle wits of some also, who *by pleasing speeches and good words seduce the hearts of the innocent,* it must be maintained that the grace of justification once received is lost not only by infidelity, whereby also faith itself is lost, but also by every other mortal sin, though in this case faith is not lost; thus defending the teaching of the divine law which excludes from the kingdom of God not only unbelievers, but also the faithful [who are] *fornicators, adulterers, effeminate, liers with mankind, thieves, covetous, drunkards, railers, extortioners,* and all others who commit deadly sins, from which with the help of divine grace they can refrain, and on account of which they are cut off from the grace of Christ.

THE FRUITS OF JUSTIFICATION, THAT IS, THE MERIT OF GOOD WORKS, AND THE NATURE OF THAT MERIT

Therefore, to men justified in this manner, whether they have preserved uninterruptedly the grace received or recovered it when lost, are to be pointed out the words of the Apostle: *Abound in every good work, knowing that your labor is not in vain in the Lord. For God is not unjust, that he should forget your work, and the love which you have shown in his name;* and, *Do not lose your confidence, which hath a great reward.* Hence, to those who work well *unto the end* and trust in God, eternal life is to be offered, both as grace mercifully promised to the sins of God through Christ Jesus, and as a reward promised by God himself, to be faithfully given to their good works and merits. For this is the crown of justice which after his fight and course the Apostle declared was laid up for him, to be rendered to him by the just judge, and not only to him, but also to all that love his coming. For since Christ Jesus Himself, as the head into the members and the vine into the branches, continually infuses strength into those justified, which strength always precedes, accompanies and follows their good works, and without which they could not in any manner be pleasing and meritorious before God, we must believe that nothing further is wanting to those justified to prevent them from being considered to have, by those very works which have been done in God, fully satisfied the divine law according to the state of this life and to have truly merited eternal life, to be obtained in its [due] time, provided they depart [this life] in grace, since Christ our Saviour says: *If anyone shall drink of the water that I will give him, he shall not thirst forever; but it shall become in him a fountain of water springing up unto life everlasting.* Thus, neither is our own justice established as our own from ourselves, nor is the justice of God ignored or repudiated, for that justice which is called ours, because we are justified by its inherence in us, that same is [the justice] of God, because it is infused into us by God through the merit of Christ. Nor must this be omitted, that although in the sacred writings so much is attributed to good works, that even *he that shall give a drink of cold water to one of his least ones,* Christ promises, *shall not lose his reward;* and the Apostle testifies that, *That which is*

*at present momentary and light of our tribu-
lation, worketh for us above measure exceedingly an eternal weight of glory;* nevertheless,
far be it that a Christian should either trust
or glory in himself and not in the Lord, whose
bounty toward all men is so great that He
wishes the things that are His gifts to be their
merits. And since *in many things we all
offend,* each one ought to have before his eyes
not only the mercy and goodness but also the
severity and judgment [of God]; neither ought
anyone to judge himself, even though he be
not conscious to himself of anything; because
the whole life of man is to be examined and
judged not by the judgment of man but of
God, *who will bring to light the hidden things
of darkness, and will make manifest the counsels of the hearts, and then shall every man
have praise from God,* who, as it is written,
*will render to every man according to his
works.*

After this Catholic doctrine on justification,
which whosoever does not faithfully and firmly accept cannot be justified, it seemed good to
the holy council to add these canons, that all
may know not only what they must hold and
follow, but also what to avoid and shun.

CANONS CONCERNING JUSTIFICATION

Canon 1. If anyone says that man can be
justified before God by his own works,
whether done by his own natural powers or
through the teaching of the law, without
divine grace through Jesus Christ, let him be
anathema.

Can. 2. If anyone says that divine grace
through Christ Jesus is given for this only,
that man may be able more easily to live justly and to merit eternal life, as if by free will
without grace he is able to do both, though
with hardship and difficulty, let him be anathema.

Can. 3. If anyone says that without the
predisposing inspiration of the Holy Ghost
and without His help, man can believe, hope,

love or be repentant as he ought, so that the
grace of justification may be bestowed upon
him, let him be anathema.

Can. 4. If anyone says that man's free will
moved and aroused by God, by assenting to
God's call and action, in no way cooperates
toward disposing and preparing itself to
obtain the grace of justification, that it cannot
refuse its assent if it wishes, but that, as something inanimate, it does nothing whatever and
is merely passive, let him be anathema.

Can. 5. If anyone says that after the sin of
Adam man's free will was lost and destroyed,
or that it is a thing only in name, indeed a
name without a reality, a fiction introduced
into the Church by Satan, let him be anathema.

Can. 6. If anyone says that it is not in
man's power to make his ways evil, but that
the works that are evil as well as those that
are good God produces, not permissively only
but also *proprie et per se,* so that the treason
of Judas is no less His own proper work than
the vocation of St. Paul, let him be anathema.

Can. 7. If anyone says that all works done
before justification, in whatever manner they
may be done, are truly sins, or merit the
hatred of God; that the more earnestly one
strives to dispose himself for grace, the more
grievously he sins, let him be anathema.

Can. 9. If anyone says that the sinner is
justified by faith alone, meaning that nothing
else is required to cooperate in order to obtain
the grace of justification, and that it is not in
any way necessary that he be prepared and
disposed by the action of his own will, let him
be anathema.

Can. 23. If anyone says that a man once
justified can sin no more, nor lose grace, and
that therefore he that falls and sins was never
truly justified; or on the contrary, that he can
during his whole life avoid all sins, even those
that are venial, except by a special privilege
from God, as the Church holds in regard to
the Blessed Virgin, let him be anathema.

Can. 24. If anyone says that the justice received is not preserved and also not increased before God through good works, but that those works are merely the fruits and signs of justification obtained, but not the cause of its increase, let him be anathema.

THE REAL PRESENCE OF OUR LORD JESUS CHRIST IN THE MOST HOLY SACRAMENT OF THE EUCHARIST

First of all, the holy council teaches and openly and plainly professes that after the consecration of bread and wine, our Lord Jesus Christ, true God and true man, is truly, really and substantially contained in the August sacrament of the Holy Eucharist under the appearance of those sensible things. For there is no repugnance in this that our Savior sits always at the right hand of the Father in heaven according to the natural mode of existing, and yet is in many other places sacramentally present to us in His own substance by a manner of existence which, though we can scarcely express in words, yet with our understanding illumined by faith, we can conceive and ought most firmly to believe is possible to God. For thus all our forefathers, as many as were in the true Church of Christ and who treated of this most holy sacrament, have most openly professed that our Redeemer instituted this wonderful sacrament at the last supper, when, after blessing the bread and wine, He testified in clear and definite words that He gives them His own body and His own blood. Since these words, recorded by the holy Evangelists and afterwards repeated by St. Paul, embody that proper and clearest meaning in which they were understood by the Fathers, it is a most contemptible action on the part of some contentious and wicked men to twist them into fictitious and imaginary troupes by which the truth of the flesh and blood of Christ is denied, contrary to the universal sense of the Church, which, as the *pillar and ground of truth,* recognizing with a mind ever grateful and unforgetting this most excellent favor of Christ, has detested as satanical these untruths devised by impious men.

THE REASON FOR THE INSTITUTION OF THIS MOST HOLY SACRAMENT

Therefore, our Savior, when about to depart from this world to the Father, instituted this sacrament, in which He poured forth, as it were, the riches of His divine love towards men, *making a remembrance of his wonderful works,* and commanded us in the participation of it to reverence His memory and *to show forth his death until he comes* to judge the world. But He wished that this sacrament should be received as the spiritual food of souls, whereby they may be nourished and strengthened, living by the life of Him who said: *He that eateth me, the same also shall live by me,* and as an antidote whereby we may be freed from daily faults and be preserved from mortal sins. He wished it furthermore to be a pledge of our future glory and everlasting happiness, and thus be a symbol of that one body of which He is the head and to which He wished us to be united as members by the close bond of faith, hope and charity, that we might *all speak the same thing and there might be no schisms among us.*

THE EXCELLENCE OF THE MOST HOLY SACRAMENT OVER THE OTHER SACRAMENTS

The most Holy Eucharist has indeed this in common with the other sacraments, that it is a symbol of a sacred thing and a visible form of an invisible grace; but there is found in it this excellent and peculiar characteristic, that the other sacraments then first have the power of sanctifying when one uses them, while in the Eucharist there is the Author Himself of sanctity before it is used. For the Apostles had not yet received the Eucharist from the hands of the Lord, when He Himself told them that what He was giving them is His own body. This has always been the belief of the Church of God, that immediately after the consecration the true body and the true blood of our Lord, together with His soul and divinity exist under the form of bread and wine, the body under the form of bread and the blood under the form of wine *ex vi verborum;* but the same body also under the form of wine and the same blood under the form of bread and the soul under both, in virtue of that natural connection and concomitance whereby the parts of Christ the Lord, *who hath now risen from the dead, to die no more,* are mutually united; also the divinity on account of its admirable hypostatic union with His body and soul. Wherefore, it is very true that as much is contained under either form as under both. For Christ is whole and entire under the form of bread and under any part of that form; likewise the whole Christ is present under the form of wine and under all its parts.

TRANSUBSTANTIATION

But since Christ our Redeemer declared that to be truly His own body which He offered under the form of bread, it has, therefore, always been a firm belief in the Church of God, and this holy council now declares it anew, that by the consecration of the bread and wine a change is brought about of the whole substance of the bread into the substance of the body of Christ our Lord, and of the whole substance of the wine into the substance of His blood. This change the holy Catholic Church properly and appropriately calls transubstantiation.

CANONS ON THE MOST HOLY SACRAMENT OF THE EUCHARIST

Canon 3. If anyone denies that in the venerable sacrament of the Eucharist the whole Christ is contained under each form and

under every part of each form when separated, let him be anathema.

Can. 9. If anyone denies that each and all of Christ's faithful of both sexes are bound, when they have reached the years of discretion, to communicate every year at least at Easter, in accordance with the precept of holy mother Church, let him be anathema.

THE INSTITUTION OF THE MOST HOLY SACRIFICE OF THE MASS

Since under the former Testament, according to the testimony of the Apostle Paul, there was no perfection because of the weakness of the Levitical priesthood, there was need, God the Father of mercies so ordaining, *that another priest should rise according to the order of Melchisedech,* our Lord Jesus Christ, who might perfect and lead to perfection as many as were to be sanctified. He, therefore, our God and Lord, though He was by His death about to offer Himself once upon the altar of the cross to God the Father that He might there accomplish an eternal redemption, nevertheless, that His priesthood might not come to an end with His death, at the last supper, on the night He was betrayed, that He might leave to His beloved spouse the Church a visible sacrifice, such as the nature of man requires, whereby that bloody sacrifice once to be accomplished on the cross might be represented, the memory thereof remain even to the end of the world, and in its salutary effects applied to the remission of those sins which we daily commit, declaring Himself constituted *a priest forever according to the order of Melchisedech,* offered up to God the Father His own body and blood under the form of bread and wine, and under the forms of those same things gave to the Apostles, whom he then made priests of the New Testament, that they might partake, commanding them and their successors in the priesthood by these words to do likewise: *Do this in commemoration of me,* as the Catholic Church has always understood and taught. For having celebrated the ancient Passover which the multitude of the children of Israel sacrificed in memory of their departure from Egypt, He instituted a new Passover, namely, Himself, to be immolated under visible signs by the Church through the priests in memory of His own passage from this world to the Father, when by the shedding of His blood He redeemed and *delivered us from the power of darkness and translated us into his kingdom.* And this is indeed that clean oblation which cannot be defiled by any unworthiness or malice on the part of those who offer it; which the Lord foretold by Malachias was to be great among the Gentiles, and which the Apostle Paul has clearly indicated when he says, that they who are defiled by partaking of the table of devils cannot be partakers of the table of the Lord, understanding by table in each case the altar. It is, finally, that [sacrifice] which was prefigured by various types of sacrifices during the period of nature and of the law, which, namely, comprises all the good things signified by them, as being the consummation and perfection of them all.

THE INSTITUTION OF THE PRIESTHOOD OF THE NEW LAW

Sacrifice and priesthood are by the ordinance of God so united that both have existed in every law. Since therefore in the New Testament the Catholic Church has received from the institution of Christ the holy, visible sacrifice of the Eucharist, it must also be confessed that there is in that Church a new, visible and eternal priesthood, into which the old has been translated. That this was constituted by the same Lord our Savior, and that to the Apostles and their successors in the priesthood was given the power of consecrating, offering and administering His body and blood, as also of forgiving and retaining sins,

is shown by the Sacred Scriptures and has always been taught by the tradition of the Catholic Church.

THE ORDER OF THE PRIESTHOOD IS TRULY A SACRAMENT

Since from the testimony of Scripture, Apostolic tradition and the agreement of the Fathers it is clear that grace is conferred by sacred ordination, which is performed by words and outward signs, no one ought to doubt that order is truly and properly one of the seven sacraments of holy Church. For the Apostle says: *I admonish that thou stir up the grace of God which is in thee by the imposition of my hands. For God has not given us the spirit of fear, but of power and of love and of sobriety.*

THE ECCLESIASTICAL HIERARCHY AND ORDINATION

But since the sacrament of order, as also in baptism and confirmation, a character is imprinted which can neither be effaced nor taken away, the holy council justly condemns the opinion of those who say that the priests of the New Testament have only a temporary power, and that those who have once been rightly ordained can again become laymen if they do not exercise the ministry of the word of God. And if anyone should assert that all Christians without distinction are priests of the New Testament, or that they are all *inter se* endowed with an equal spiritual power, he seems to do nothing else than derange the ecclesiastical hierarchy, which is *an army set in array;* as if, contrary to the teaching of St. Paul, all are apostles, all prophets, all evangelists, all pastors, all doctors. Wherefore, the holy council declares that, besides the other ecclesiastical grades, the bishops, who have succeeded the Apostles, principally belong to this hierarchical order, and have been placed, as the same Apostle says, by the Holy Ghost to rule the Church of God; that they are superior to priests, administer the sacrament of confirmation, ordain ministers of the Church, and can perform many other functions over which those of an inferior order have no power. The council teaches furthermore, that in the ordination of bishops, priests and the other orders, the consent, call or authority, whether of the people or of any civil power or magistrate is not required in such wise that without this the ordination is invalid; rather does it decree that all those who, called and instituted only by the people or by the civil power or magistrate, ascend to the exercise of these offices, and those who by their rashness assume them, are not ministers of the Church, but are to be regarded as thieves and robbers, who have not entered by the door. These are the things which in general it has seemed good to the holy council to teach to the faithful of Christ regarding the sacrament of order. The contrary, however, it has resolved to condemn in definite and appropriate canons in the following manner, in order that all, making use with the help of Christ of the rule of faith, may in the midst of the darkness of so many errors recognize more easily the Catholic truth and adhere to it.

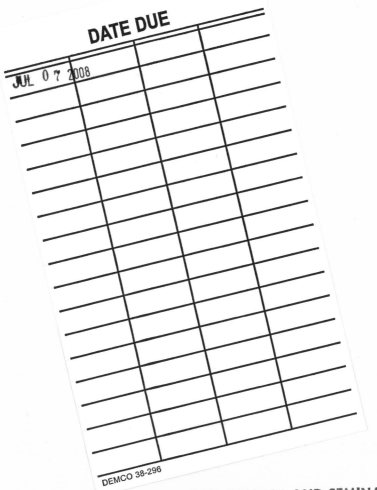